# Digital Media

## PRIMER

Digital Audio, Video, Imaging and Multimedia Programming

Second Edition

## Yue-Ling Wong

Boston   Columbus   Indianapolis   New York   San Francisco   Upper Saddle River
Amsterdam   Cape Town   Dubai   London   Madrid   Milan   Paris   Montreal   Toronto
Delhi   Mexico City   São Paulo   Sydney   Hong Kong   Seoul   Singapore   Taipei   Tokyo

Editorial Director: *Marcia Horton*
Executive Editor: *Tracy Dunkelberger*
Associate Editor: *Carole Snyder*
Director of Marketing: *Patrice Jones*
Marketing Manager: *Yez Alayan*
Marketing Coordinator: *Kathryn Ferranti*
Director of Production: *Vince O'Brien*
Managing Editor: *Jeff Holcomb*
Production Project Manager: *Kayla Smith-Tarbox*
Operations Supervisor: *Alan Fischer*

Manufacturing Buyer: *Lisa McDowell*
Art Director: *Anthony Gemmellaro*
Manager, Rights and Permissions: *Michael Joyce*
Text Permission Coordinator: *Dana Weightman*
Lead Media Project Manager: *Daniel Sandin*
Full-Service Project Management: *S4Carlisle Publishing Services*
Composition: *S4Carlisle Publishing Services*
Printer/Binder: *Edwards Brothers Malloy*
Cover Printer: *Lehigh-Phoenix Color/Hagerstown*
Text Font: *Times LT Std Roman*

Credits and acknowledgments borrowed from other sources and reproduced, with permission, in this textbook appear on page 515.

Microsoft® and Windows® are registered trademarks of the Microsoft Corporation in the U.S.A. and other countries. Screen shots and icons reprinted with permission from the Microsoft Corporation. This book is not sponsored or endorsed by or affiliated with the Microsoft Corporation.

Many of the designations by manufacturers and sellers to distinguish their products are claimed as trademarks. Where those designations appear in this book, and the publisher was aware of a trademark claim, the designations have been printed in initial caps or all caps.

**Library of Congress Cataloging-in-Publication Data is available upon request.**

10 9 8 7 6 5 4 3 2

ISBN 10:    0-13-289350-9
ISBN 13: 978-0-13-289350-3

# Brief Contents

# Table of Contents

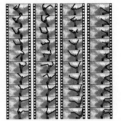

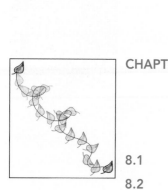

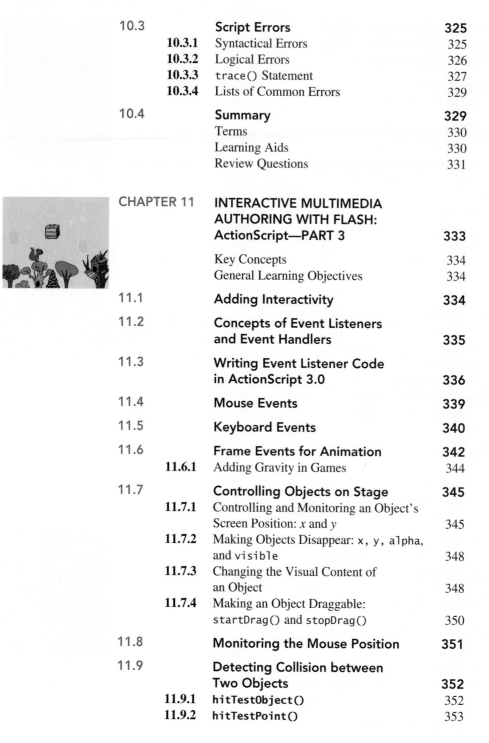

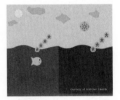

# Preface

Welcome to the second edition of *Digital Media Primer*. This book continues with the spirit of its first edition. It emphasizes both conceptual and production aspects of digital media. It adopts a conceptual approach and relates to digital media software applications. The coverage of software applications intends to show students a general picture of how the concepts are translated into the common commands found in software applications. Therefore, whenever possible, multiple software applications are used as examples. The intent is not about training of software application skills or providing a survey of these software applications. Digital media software applications of the same medium share common commands and features, which are based on the same technical concepts and principles. The differences may be that these concepts and principles are presented in the software applications using slightly different command names and user interfaces. It is the author's assumption that if the student understands the underlying concepts and principles and then sees examples of how they are actually translated into the commands or options found in application programs, the student can apply the knowledge to quickly pick up similar software applications and the ever-changing new versions of these software applications.

## What's New in This Edition?

The main motivation of the new edition is to update the materials with new technology and to expand the content to allow more different paths through this book for a wide range of digital media courses.

All of the chapters are revised, but the significant changes in this edition fall into three categories. One is the expansion of the multimedia authoring to a full introductory computer programming course in the context of game programming. Game programming is becoming one of the popular themes that many instructors have started considering for introductory computer programming courses. Chapters 8 through 11 cover about half a semester's worth of materials of a full introductory computer programming course. The new object-oriented programming (OOP) chapters provide the materials for the second half-semester of such courses. This revision allows the book to be used for a full introductory computer programming course in addition to digital media courses.

The second category of changes is the inclusion of a chapter on HTML5 video and audio. This is motivated by the fact that the Web is a common distribution method for digital media. In particular, HTML5 video and audio are emerging popular formats for sharing video and audio on the Web. In order to provide a foundation for learning HTML5, a chapter on HTML basics is also added.

The third category of changes is the revision of the video chapters to shift the focus from standard-definition video to high-definition video. At the time of writing the first edition, standard-definition video was the most available format and high-definition video cameras and editing software were limited. Now, with more video cameras and editing tools available for high-definition video, the video chapters are revised to put more focus on high-definition video.

Specifically, the new content and updates in this edition include:

- A new chapter introducing OOP in the context of game programming (Chapter 12)
- A new chapter on inheritance and polymorphism (Chapter 13)
- A new chapter on HTML basics (Chapter 14) to provide a foundation of HTML for the new HTML5 chapter to build upon
- A new chapter on HTML5 video and audio (Chapter 15) to cover structure, syntax, and semantics of HTML5, and to show how to share video and audio on the Web using HTML5
- Revised Chapter 6 (video concepts) to include more information on high-definition video
- Revised Chapter 7 (video production) to include updates on digital video cameras, examples of high-definition video editing tools, and examples of video effects
- Addition of a section on multitrack basics in the audio chapter (Chapter 5) to provide more information on working with multitrack sessions
- Replacement of the references to the Digital Art Module with the actual examples and explanations from the Digital Art Module
- New screenshots of the latest digital media software applications

## Coordinating Coursework with This Text

This book is written for introductory courses in digital media. It is for introductory students from all disciplines who are interested in learning the foundational scientific concepts and basic techniques in digital media production. There is no specific prerequisite to use this book. The courses in which this textbook will be useful include:

- Non-major introductory computer science courses that adopt a digital media theme, integrating both scientific concepts and hands-on production aspects of digital images, video, and audio, and giving students exposure to basic computer programming through animation and game programming
- Introductory computer programming courses that adopt the theme of game programming with Flash ActionScript
- Introductory digital art courses intended to help students harness the digital media tools by learning the underlying scientific concepts, thereby achieving intended artistic results and improving confidence to experiment with creative uses of such tools
- Introductory media production courses that introduce students to a solid technical foundation of digital video and audio

After completing this book, students will understand the underlying concepts of computer terms common to digital media and be able to connect these concepts with the tools and techniques of digital media application programs. The connection between scientific concepts and applications will help students make educated decisions, rather than relying on defaults or recipes, in using tools and techniques in application programs. In addition, the approach of this book intends to instill in students the ability and confidence to explore and teach themselves new application programs. After completing Chapters 1 through 7, students will be able to create and edit digital images, audio, and video. After completing Chapter 8, students will get an introduction on working with Flash and be able to create basic Flash animation. Building upon the knowledge of Flash, students will also learn basic computer programming concepts (procedural programming) with Flash ActionScript in the context of game programming (Chapters 9–11). Students may also continue on to the advanced topics of computer programming covered in Chapters 12 and 13—OOP, inheritance, and polymorphism. Chapter 14 covers HTML basics to prepare students with a sufficient foundation to build upon in learning how to add HTML5 video and audio to Web pages. In addition, students will learn the structure, syntax, and semantics of HTML5, as well as HTML5 video and audio, in Chapter 15. After completing Chapter 15, students will be able to construct a basic HTML5 document and embed video and audio on a Web page using the HTML5 video and audio tags.

Digital media classes may be taught from different disciplinary perspectives, and the background of students taking digital media classes are also diverse. There are many paths through this book for a digital media course. Thus, this book covers more than a semester's worth of materials. For some courses, this book may offer more technical background than the course's expectations. The role of the instructor is integral in deciding the best path through this book for the course. For example, not all the topics in Chapter 1 have to be the first week's lectures; they could be in the middle or end of the semester as the instructor sees fit. Listed in Table 1 are several suggested treatments employing this book and the three-book digital media series.

The first edition of this book serves as the primer of a three-book digital media series. The other two books in the series, which allow further specialization at the advanced, discipline-specific level, are:

- Digital Art Module: *Digital Art: Its Art and Science*[1]  ISBN: 0-13-175703-2
- Computer Science Module: *The Science of Digital Media*[2]  ISBN: 0-13-243580-2

All three books maintain the same number of parallel chapters—one on background, two on each of the image, audio, and video, and several on multimedia/Web authoring. The second edition of this book preserves the structure of the parallel chapters, allowing students to easily look up relevant information across perspectives.

The three-book series allows flexibility for different courses with respect to the breadth (the number of media) and depth (depth in the direction of art or computer science perspective) of the course content. You can pick and choose to add the computer science or digital art components, depending on the depth of the art or computer science components you want to incorporate into the course.

---

[1] Also by this author.
[2] By Jennifer J. Burg.

| TABLE I | Suggested Treatments Employing This Book and the Series |
|---|---|
| | **Suggested Chapter Coverage** |
| A course that covers the breadth of all three media: images, audio, and video | • Chapters 1–7 (this book)<br>• Chapters 14–15 (this book) |
| A course that covers only one medium | • Chapter 1 (this book)<br>• Two chapters of the medium (this book)<br>• Chapters 14–15 if the medium is video or audio<br>• Chapter 1 (either the Art or CS book)<br>• Two chapters of the medium (either the Art or CS book)<br><br>For example, for a course that focuses on digital images from the art perspective, you could cover Primer Chapters 1, 2, 3, and Art Module Chapters 1, 2, 3. |
| A course that covers multimedia authoring or basic programming through animation and games | • Chapters 1–3 (this book)<br>• Chapters 8–11 (this book) |
| An introduction to computer programming in the context of game programming | • Chapters 8–13 (this book)<br>• Chapters 1–3 (this book) if time allows |
| A course that focuses on concepts with minimal hands-on practice | Concept chapters:<br>• Chapters 1, 2, 4, 6 (this book)<br>• Chapters 1, 2, 4, 6 (either the Art or CS book) |
| A course that focuses on hands-on practice | • Chapters 1, 3, 5, 7, 14, 15 (this book)<br>• Chapters 1, 3, 5, 7 (either the Art or CS book)<br>• The concepts chapters (Chapters 2, 4, and 6) are highly recommended. If it is not possible to go over the concepts in class, refer students to self-study these concepts chapters. You may want to assign the end-of-chapter review questions to ensure they understand the concepts. |

## Text Organization

This book follows the organization of its first edition. The digital media curriculum is organized around a core concept of digital media: the digitization process—sampling and quantization (Figure 1). For example, the **sampling** process gives rise to the image resolution in digital images and the sampling rate in digital audio. The **quantization** process gives rise to the color depth in digital images and the bit depth in digital audio. Digital video also deals with frame size, which relates to image resolution. This way, students learn about image resolution, audio sampling rate, color depth, audio bit depth, and video frame size from the same central concepts applied in different contexts, rather than as separate bits and pieces of factual information for different media. The core concept of digitization also helps students understand the nature of digital media—their limitations and uses.

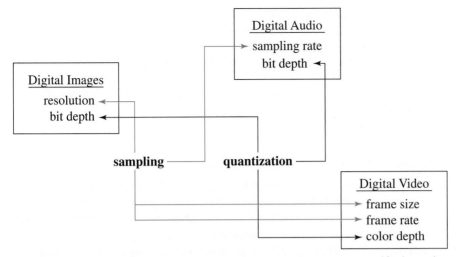

**Figure 1** Sampling and quantization serve as the central concepts to unify the topics for different media.

Each of the image, audio, and video topics consists of two chapters: one on **concepts** and the second one on **application** of the concepts and the **production** of the media.

Chapter 1: Background

Chapter 2: Digital Image (concepts)
Chapter 3: Digital Image (application and production)

Chapter 4: Digital Audio (concepts)
Chapter 5: Digital Audio (application and production)

Chapter 6: Digital Video (concepts)
Chapter 7: Digital Video (application and production)

Chapter 8: Multimedia Authoring and Animation

Chapters 9–13: Introduction to Computer Programming in the Context of Game Programming with Flash ActionScript

Chapter 14: HTML Basics
Chapter 15: HTML5 Video and Audio

The scientific concepts and technical information are discussed in the concepts chapters (Chapters 2, 4, 6). The applications of the concepts and the general techniques and tools of application programs are discussed in the production chapters (Chapters 3, 5, and 7). For example, Chapter 2 explains the concept of resolution of images. Correspondingly, Chapter 3 discusses how to estimate the scanning resolution and printing resolution. The determination of the scanning and printing resolution is an application of the concept of resolution.

For the multimedia authoring chapters, Chapter 8 introduces the basics of animation and working with Adobe Flash. Chapter 9 provides an overview on programming fundamentals that are common to most programming languages. Chapter 10 discusses some specific aspects in programming with Flash ActionScript. Chapter 11 introduces computer programming basics and explains how to add interactivity. Chapter 12 introduces object-oriented programming, and Chapter 13 discusses inheritance and polymorphism. The lab exercises are designed around programming computer games.

## Features in the Textbook

There are several pedagogic elements used in the book:

- **Key terms:** Key terms are boldfaced. When a key term appears at several places in the text, the term is usually boldfaced where its definition is given.
- **Learning aids:** There are several types of learning aids accompanying this text (see the subsequent subsection.) They are integral to the text and noted in the text in blue boxes. A title and a brief description are given for each learning aid. The learning aids can be found on the accompanying Web site of this text.
- **Boxed materials:** They intend to expand the discussion and explanation of the concept or terminology relevant to the current part of the text. The materials may be branched off from the main flow of the text. Thus, they are separated from the main text to avoid diversion from the flow of thoughts.
- **Margin notes:** They are generally used for a brief explanation of terminology, or for referring to the chapter that covers the basics that are needed for the current part of the text.
- **Self-test questions:** These questions are found in the text of some chapters. The answers are provided at the end of the question or the bottom of the page. These questions, unlike the end-of-chapter review questions, intend to provide the students an instant review of the topics. These topics are a little too involved to wait for the end-of-chapter review questions.
- **Summary:** Each chapter concludes with a summary of key concepts.
- **End-of-chapter review questions:** These are multiple-choice and short-answer questions to reinforce the retrieval of the learned foundational knowledge. They are to ensure that the student reaches the same level of competence of foundational knowledge.
- **Exploring the applications:** At the end of a production chapter, there is a list of suggested commonly used features and functionalities for the students to look up and explore in application programs. The goal is to help students to learn how to explore application programs in terms of tasks and then apply the basic concepts they have learned in the textbook. By taking this approach, the student is not tied to learning a particular software package or version.

## Student Learning Aids and Supplementary Materials

For access to the Learning Aids and Supplementary Materials, please go to http://www.pearsonhighered.com/digitalmedia.

There are several types of online learning aids accompanying this text. They appear in blue boxes with a small icon (⬈ or ✎) followed by a title and a brief description. The computer mouse icon indicates that the learning aid is interactive or has a hands-on component. These include interactive tutorials and demonstrations, labs, and worksheets. The filmstrip icon means that the learning aid is a movie (for example, the screen-captured movies that show how to use a tool in an application program), video files that demonstrate the effect of different compression settings, or supplementary reading materials.

- **Tutorials**

  The tutorials are used for various purposes:

  - Conceptual: To explain concepts, such as sampling and quantizing
  - Software tool how-to's: Short screen-captured movies showing how-to's of application programs
  - Example files: Files that you can download to open and see how they work
  - Visualization: To help visualize difficult concepts
  - Explanation of terminology
  - Step-by-step guide to solve a problem: such as Chapter 1's binary-decimal conversion

All of the tutorials can be used as outside class review by students. Some of the tutorials can be used by the instructor as interactive animated presentations during lecture—for example: Chapter 1's "Converting Analog to Digital—Sampling and Quantizing", Chapter 2's "Sampling and Quantizing in Digital Images", Chapter 3's "Understanding and Applying Histograms", and Chapter 4's "Sound as a Pressure Wave" and "Sampling and Quantizing in Digital Audio".

- **Demonstrations:** For example: audio files that let you hear how different sampling rates and bit depths affect the audio quality, or video files that let you see how different compression settings affect the visual quality.
- **Worksheets:** Worksheets are question-based PDF files that can be downloaded and printed out. They require more thinking than the end-of-chapter review questions. Some may require exploration or experimentation to discover answers. The syntax review worksheets in the programming chapters are intended to help students to summarize the syntax and practice writing code, which are important to success in an introductory programming course.

  My game programming class surveys showed that students unanimously found the syntax review worksheets very helpful and that they used their graded worksheets for studying. Some students even suggested having more review worksheets on topics that were not included in the worksheets. However, it was also a common response that the syntax review worksheets were boring. Therefore, if the syntax review worksheets were made optional, students very likely will not complete the worksheets that are beneficial to their learning. I found that it worked well to make the syntax review worksheets part of the homework assignments. I also advised students to keep the graded worksheets for use as syntax references in the lab and for studying for tests and the final exam. The intention of the syntax review worksheets is to help students create their own study aids and notes. Therefore, it would be best to help them to complete the worksheets correctly as much as possible.

  Some students may come to your office to ask questions on homework. However, many students may not be willing to do so. I have found that a short in-class Q&A section right before the students turn in the worksheets provides a good opportunity for offering such help. During the Q&A section, students are encouraged to ask questions that they have been stuck on and to discuss their thoughts on the answers. They are allowed to make corrections before they turn in the worksheets. Being able to make corrections before turning in the worksheets is an incentive for students to ask questions. It is also as if they are grading their own homework. This provides an opportunity for students to take a critical look at their code answers. While they are asking homework questions in class, they more likely also ask you to clarify some lecture materials, in which case you will get student feedback on the lecture materials and be able to clarify any misunderstandings that were usually the root of the homework problems.

- **Labs:** These are lab manuals, with instructions to edit or create digital media files. They are designed to provide hands-on opportunities to process and manipulate digital images, sound, and video. The labs for multimedia authoring include creating animation in Adobe Flash and programming games in ActionScript. In developing the labs, I tried to emphasize the tasks rather than giving command-by-command, recipe-type instructions. For the computer programming chapters (Chapters 8–13), labs are an important component. From my experience, for a 3-credit course (three 50-minute lectures per week) plus a lab section (1.5 hours per week), it worked well to turn one of the lecture periods into an extra lab period. A lab briefing that gives students a big picture of the steps and demonstrates how the final product should look and work is also important.

Worksheets and labs are different. Worksheets are question-based homework intended to help students review and summarize a topic at a time. Labs are hands-on instruction-based activities that create or modify media files. Labs provide opportunities for students to apply multiple learned concepts and techniques in practice.

## eText with Online Learning Aids

I encourage you to explore the eText with online learning aids and supplementary materials that are noted in the text. These materials can be accessed through the publisher's Companion Website for this text at http://www.pearsonhighered.com/digitalmedia. You will need to redeem the access code provided at the front of your new textbook. Some learning aids require Shockwave plug-in, some require Flash player, some require QuickTime player, and some require JavaScript enabled. For those who have trouble getting Shockwave plug-in installed on the lab computers, the Shockwave supplementary materials are now also available as standalone .exe (Windows) and .app (Mac OS) files. The file format and requirements of each of these learning aids are noted with its link on the Companion Website.

## Instructor Resources

Protected instructor resources are available on the Pearson Instructor Resource Center (IRC). Please contact your local Pearson sales representative to gain access to this site. Instructors will find the following support material on the IRC:

- Lecture PowerPoint slides
- Answers to the end-of-chapter questions
- Answers to the worksheets
- Completed lab files

## Software Tools for Practice and Labs

Although this book's approach of teaching media production application tools emphasizes identifying tasks and tries not to tie to any particular software, it is inevitable that you must select some representative application programs to demonstrate the tools and techniques in the text and in the practice exercises, such as labs and worksheets. Table 2 lists the different application programs used as examples in this book. The application programs that appear the most in the text, tutorials, labs, and worksheets are in bold.

| TABLE 2 | **Application Programs Used in This Text** |
|---|---|
| **Media Topic** | **Application Programs Used as Examples in the Text** (The main programs used the most in the text, tutorials, labs, and worksheets are boldfaced.) |
| Digital Image | **Adobe Photoshop**, Adobe Illustrator |
| Digital Audio | **Adobe Audition**, **Audacity**, **Apple Garage Band**, Sony Sound Forge, SONAR, Sony ACID Pro |
| Digital Video | **Adobe Premiere Pro**, Apple Final Cut Pro, Sony Vegas, Adobe Encore DVD, Sony DVD Architect |
| Multimedia Authoring and Introduction to Computer Programming in the Context of Game Programming | **Adobe Flash** |

## Acknowledgments

The materials have been class-tested and I would like to thank our students who provided us feedback to help us improve the text and its organization for the series. I would also like to thank the pre-revision reviewers of this book for their valuable comments and suggestions: Christopher T. Jennings of Metropolitan State College of Denver, J. Bryan Pittard of University of Central Florida, and Jonathan Ross of Asheville-Buncombe Technical Community College.

There would not have been a second edition without the first edition to serve as a basis. Thus, my thanks again go to the professors who participated in pilot-testing of the first edition of the three-book series: Julie Carrington of Rollins College, Kristian Damkjer of University of Florida, Ian Douglas of Florida State University, Edward A. Fox of Virginia Polytechnic Institute and State University, Martha Garrett of Bishop McGuinness High School (North Carolina), Kim Nelson of University of Windsor (Ontario, Canada), Naomi Spellman of The University of California San Diego and San Diego State University, Christopher Stein of Borough of Manhattan Community College, and Mark Watanabe of Keaau High School (Hawaii).

I would also like to thank my student assistants, who helped in developing and suggesting some of the learning aids, and my former students who let me include their class work as demonstrations and chapter openers in the book: Cory Bullock, Kevin Crace, Emma Edgar, Gretchen Edwards, Robert May, Lindsay Ryerse, Caldwell Tanner, and Daniel Verwholt.

## Support

The first edition of the three-book series is based on work supported by the National Science Foundation under Grant No. DUE-0127280 and DUE-0340969. Any opinions, findings, and conclusions or recommendations expressed in this material are those of the author(s) and do not necessarily reflect the views of the National Science Foundation. The PI and co-PI of the two grants are Yue-Ling Wong and Jennifer J. Burg, respectively. Professor Leah McCoy is the assessment expert in the second grant.

# 1

# Background

## TABLE OF CONTENTS

KEY CONCEPTS
- Analog information versus digital data
- Converting analog data to digital data: sampling and quantizing
- Bits and bytes
- Base-10 versus base-2
- File size calculation
- File compression

GENERAL LEARNING OBJECTIVES

In this chapter, you will learn

- The computer terms common to digital media fundamentals.
- The difference between analog information and digital data.
- What the binary system means.
- The basic steps of digitization: sampling and quantization.
- The general strategies for reducing digital media file sizes.
- The reasons for file compression and types of file compression.

## 1.1 INTRODUCTION

Digital media studies rely on both conceptual and creative knowledge. Although knowing how to use digital media application programs, such as Adobe Photoshop and Corel PaintShop Pro for digital imaging, Adobe Premiere Pro and Apple Final Cut for digital video, and Adobe Audition and Sony Sound Forge for digital audio, is required, understanding the underlying principles and concepts helps to realize a creative idea with predictable results. Simply learning a particular version of a particular program restricts your creativity to what that version of that program can do. If you generalize by associating the task you want to accomplish with the basic concept behind the tool, then when you have to switch to another program or a new version, you can easily look up the information associated with the task in the program's Help menu.

Many application programs provide default settings to create digital media products, allowing you to create a file without any knowledge of digital media fundamentals. For example, it is possible to apply a special effect with a filter without considering how its many settings affect the image. No error message will prevent you from applying the effect and saving the file, but achieving a desired effect often requires some trial-and-error experimenting. Understanding the concepts behind the tools helps you to make rational, educated decisions in using these tools to produce predictable and effective results.

## 1.1.1  Relevance of Binary Notation, Bits, and Bytes to Digital Media Studies

This chapter provides the foundational knowledge that is required to understand the digital media concepts introduced in the later chapters. Because computers handle data in the units of bits and bytes, it is inevitable that you will encounter these terms in studying digital media. This chapter will explain the meaning of bits and bytes. It also will explain the conversion between decimal and binary notations. The direct relevance of these concepts to digital media may not be obvious within this chapter alone, but these fundamentals will help you comprehend the terminology you will encounter in studying digital media. For example:

- *File size* and *prefixes*. Digital files—image, sound, and especially video files—can be very large. The file size is often an important consideration that affects your decisions in the creation and export steps. You often will need to monitor your file's size, which is reported in bits and bytes using prefixes (such as kilo, mega, and giga). In addition, later chapters have examples on file size calculations in bits, which then are converted to megabytes or gigabytes. Thus, you will need to know how to read a file's size and understand these units.
- *Binary notation*. By learning binary notation and decimal-to-binary conversion, you will see how information actually can be stored and handled on a computer as bits. Understanding the conversion of decimal to binary notations helps you understand why a number, representing a piece of information, requires a certain number of bits to store.
- *Bit depth*. You may have encountered the term *bit depth* or *color depth* (Chapters 2 and 3) if you have worked with digital images. Understanding binary systems helps you comprehend the connection between the bit depth or color depth of an image and the number of colors; for example, 8-bit refers to 256 colors and 24-bit refers to millions of colors.

     With an understanding of bits, you will understand why an image with more colors or higher bit depth has a larger file size.
- *Bit rate*. In working with digital video, you will often encounter the term *bit rate* (Chapters 6 and 7). The bit rate of a video affects the smoothness of its playback. Understanding bits helps you comprehend what bit rate is, its significance, and how you can calculate your video's average bit rate to predict its playback.
- In Web page creation, you use hexadecimal notation to designate a color for text color and background color. For example, #FF0000 represents red. The conversions from decimal to binary and decimal to hexadecimal notations are similar. What you learn in the conversion of decimal to binary notations also will help you learn how the hexadecimal notation of a color is obtained.

## 1.2  ANALOG VERSUS DIGITAL REPRESENTATIONS

It is often said that we live in a digital age. However, the natural world we live in is an analog world. For example, the sounds and music we hear are ***analog*** signals of sound waves. Computers store and transmit information using ***digital*** data. To connect our analog world with computers, analog and digital information must be converted from one form to the other and back again. Unfortunately, the conversion process may sacrifice the exactness of the original information. We will discuss the conversion process—sampling and quantization—in more detail later in this chapter. In order to understand the process, we must first understand the nature of analog and digital representations of information.

### 1.2.1 Analog Information

Most information that we perceive in the natural world is in analog form. To illustrate, let's try to measure the length of a pencil (Figure 1.1). The ruler shows that the pencil is between 7¼ and 7½ inches long, but the point is a little less than halfway between 7¼ and 7½ inches. Would you round it down to 7.25? You cannot reproduce the exact length of this pencil with 7.25 inches. But wait—the pencil tip is about midway between 7¼ and 7½. So should we say it is 7⅜ or 7.375? This measurement is a little closer to the pencil length than 7.25, but the pencil is shorter than 7⅜ inches. So, is it 7.374, 7.373, 7.3735, 7.37355, . . .? An infinite number of divisions exist between two points. How small should the divisions of a ruler be to allow us to make an exact measurement? Infinitely small, because there is always another value between two values!

(a) (b)

**Figure 1.1** (a) Measuring the length of a pencil with a ruler. (b) Close-up view of the pencil tip.

Examples of continuous information are time, weight, temperature, lines, waves (such as sound waves), and planes (such as photographs). Analog clocks, thermometers (Figure 1.2a), and weighing scales are examples of analog devices.

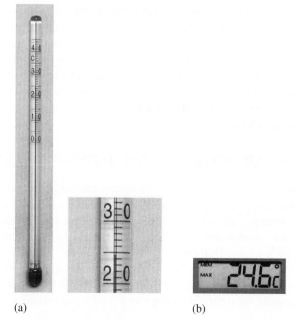

(a) (b)

**Figure 1.2** (a) Analog thermometer and its close-up view. (b) Digital thermometer.

## 1.2.2 Digital Data

Computers are built from electronic devices that have only two possible states because they are only stable at one of two voltages. Thus, they operate on a binary system, also called base-2. Regardless of the actual voltages of these two states, we might denote them as *off* and *on* or *false* and *true*. In computer science, we denote this pair of states numerically as 0 and 1, respectively.

Most people associate the binary system exclusively with computers. It is true that computers use it, whereas in our daily lives, we use many other numbers. For this reason, many people think it's difficult to understand the binary concept.

However, the binary system is not that difficult. For example, imagine using eye signals to communicate with your friends. Each eye has closed and open positions (Figure 1.3). When you want to signal your friend, you first will have to assign meaning to the various combinations of open and closed eyes—**encode** the message. Of course, your friend would have to know how to **decode** your signal—that is, interpret the meaning associated with each signal. For example, you may assign "yes" to "closed left eye, open right eye" and "no" to "both eyes closed." There are four open and closed combinations for two eyes. Therefore, you can send four different messages using eye signals. If we assign a numeric value to each of the open and closed eyes—say, open eye as 1 and closed eye as 0—then the four combinations can be represented as 00, 01, 10, and 11.

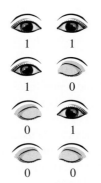

**Figure 1.3** The four combinations of open and closed eyes.

Suppose you want to use eye signals to send your friend a message about a color—one out of 16 different choices. You would need another friend to help because you would need four eyes—a 4-bit system, as in Figure 1.4. Using two eyes lets you signal your friend a color out of only four different choices.

Let's look at another example using hand signals. Suppose we consider only two possible positions for each finger: raised up or bent down. The number of different combinations with five fingers is $2^5 = 32$. How about with both hands using 10 fingers? $2^{10} = 1024$. Wow! This means that you can send your friend 1024 different messages using the hand signals with each finger either up or down. Of course, some combinations of the raised and bent fingers are quite challenging to make, if not impossible.

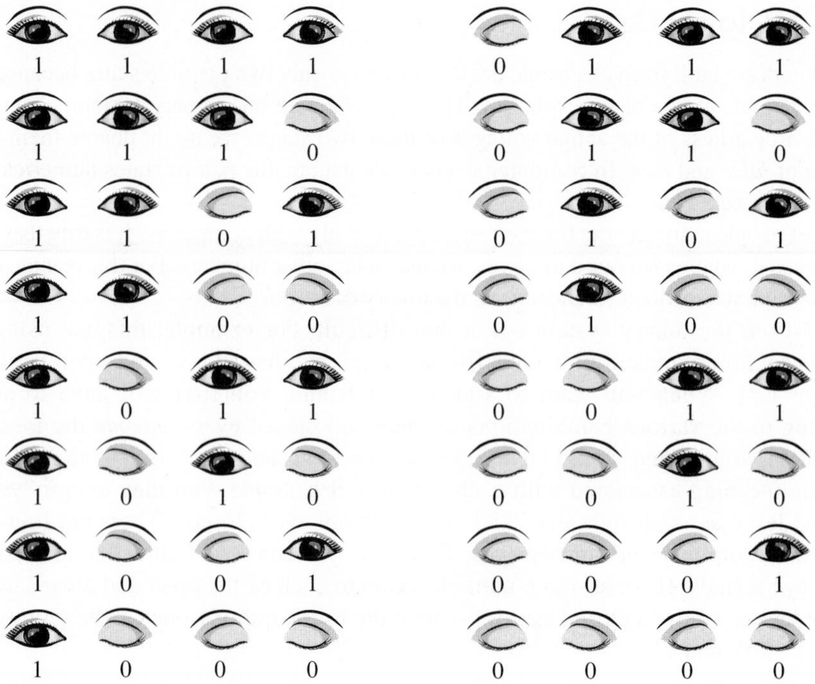

Figure 1.4 Sixteen different open and closed eye patterns created using four eyes.

## 1.3 BITS

In computer systems, data is stored and represented in *b*inary dig*its*, called **bits**. A bit has two possible values, 0 or 1. In the eye signal example, each eye can be considered a bit, as it can denote two possible states: open or closed. Although the two possible values of a bit are denoted numerically as 0 and 1, they can be used for much more than arithmetic.

One bit is not very useful in representing information, but a combination of bits forming larger sequences can represent content information, such as text characters, color information for digital images, and audio amplitudes.

In the eye signal analogy, each eye is like a bit—it has two states: closed and open, or 0 and 1. Using two eyes, we would call your system a 2-bit system. In the hand signal analogy, if you are using one hand, your system is 5-bit. As you see, the number of possible values corresponds to $2^{bit}$.

### 1.3.1 Prefixes

Computer file sizes are reported in bits and bytes. Eight bits make a **byte**. Digital files—image, sound, and especially video files—can be very large, and the file size is often an important consideration that affects your decisions in the file creation and export steps. You often will need to look up your files' sizes and monitor the available disk space on your computer's hard drive to make sure you have enough space for new files during the production process.

| TABLE 1.1 | The Relationship between Sizes and Prefixes under the Base-2 Definition | |
|---|---|---|
| **Prefix Name** | **Abbreviation** | **Size** |
| Kilo | K | $2^{10} = 1{,}024$ |
| Mega | M | $2^{20} = 1{,}048{,}576$ |
| Giga | G | $2^{30} = 1{,}073{,}741{,}824$ |
| Tera | T | $2^{40} = 1{,}099{,}511{,}627{,}776$ |
| Peta | P | $2^{50} = 1{,}125{,}899{,}906{,}842{,}624$ |
| Exa | E | $2^{60} = 1{,}152{,}921{,}504{,}606{,}846{,}976$ |
| Zetta | Z | $2^{70} = 1{,}180{,}591{,}620{,}717{,}411{,}303{,}424$ |
| Yotta | Y | $2^{80} = 1{,}208{,}925{,}819{,}614{,}629{,}174{,}706{,}176$ |

Because a file contains lots of bits and bytes, we use prefixes, such as *kilo (K)*, *mega (M)*, *giga (G)*, and *tera (T)*, to better conceive the size. In order for you to correctly interpret the size of your digital media file, you will need to have a clear idea of what these prefixes mean. Table 1.1 lists the prefixes, abbreviations, and sizes.

## DOES A KILO EQUAL 1,000 OR 1,024?

Most people know that 1 kilo equals exactly 1,000 (e.g., 1 kilogram equals 1,000 grams), and the other prefixes imply a number based on 10 to the power of an integer. Notice that under the base-2 definition, a kilobyte (KB) is 1,024 bytes, a megabyte (MB) is 1,048,576 bytes, and so forth (Table 1.1). This discrepancy has caused confusion among manufacturers of computer storage devices, telecommunication engineers, and the general public.

To avoid such confusion, in December 1998, the International Electrotechnical Commission (IEC) approved the prefixes for binary multiples for use in the fields of data processing and data transmission (Table 1.2).[*] However, at the time of this writing, these new standard names are not widely used by or known to the public.

| TABLE 1.2 | IEC Prefixes for Binary Multiples | | |
|---|---|---|---|
| **Original** | **Prefix Name** | **Symbol** | **Size** |
| Kilo | Kibi | Ki | $2^{10} = 1{,}024$ |
| Mega | Mebi | Mi | $2^{20} = 1{,}048{,}576$ |
| Giga | Gibi | Gi | $2^{30} = 1{,}073{,}741{,}824$ |
| Tera | Tebi | Ti | $2^{40} = 1{,}099{,}511{,}627{,}776$ |
| Peta | Pebi | Pi | $2^{50} = 1{,}125{,}899{,}906{,}842{,}624$ |
| Exa | Exbi | Ei | $2^{60} = 1{,}152{,}921{,}504{,}606{,}846{,}976$ |

[*] http://physics.nist.gov/cuu/Units/binary.html

With these new standard names and symbols, we have the following:

1 kilobyte = 1,000 bytes
1 kibibyte = $2^{10}$ bytes = 1,024 bytes
1 megabit = 1,000,000 bits
1 mebibit = $2^{20}$ bits = 1,048,576 bits

## YOUR COMPUTER HARD-DRIVE SPACE

The following exercise shows you how to look up your hard-drive space, both in bytes and gigabytes (GB).

- If you are using Windows, you can right-click on the C: drive in Computer and select Properties. Under the General tab, look up the Used Space and Free Space in bytes and GB. Verify that the numbers match the conversion, according to Tables 1.1 and 1.2.
- If you are using Mac OS, select the hard drive, and press Command-I.

For example, say that your computer lists 120,031,539,200 bytes for 111 GB. To convert 120,031,539,200 bytes into GB, you divide 120,031,539,200 by $2^{30}$ or 1,073,741,824:

$$\frac{120{,}031{,}539{,}200 \text{ bytes}}{1{,}073{,}741{,}824 \text{ bytes/GB}} = 111.8 \text{ GB}$$

The calculation shows you how the number of GB reported is obtained.

## 1.4 USING BITS TO REPRESENT NUMERIC VALUES

The mathematics we commonly use is based on the *decimal system*, a *base-10* notation. However, computer systems use *base-2* (the *binary system*), which relates to their basic storage units (bits and bytes) and measures file sizes. By learning what base-2 is and how it works, you will understand how binary notation is used to represent decimal numbers.

### 1.4.1 Base-10

The base-10 system uses 10 numerals: 0, 1, 2, 3, 4, 5, 6, 7, 8, and 9. The position of the digits in a number has significance. See the following interpretation of the decimal number 3,872.

$$3872$$
$$3 \times 10^3 + 8 \times 10^2 + 7 \times 10^1 + 2 \times 10^0$$
$$= 3 \times 1000 + 8 \times 100 + 7 \times 10 + 2 \times 1$$
$$= 3000 + 800 + 70 + 2$$
$$= 3872$$

The position of each digit represents a power of 10.

## 1.4.2 Base-2

In the binary system, there are only two possible numerals: 0 and 1. In binary notation, the position of each digit represents a power of 2. For example, the binary notation of 1011 can be interpreted as shown here.

$$1011$$
$$1 \times 2^3 + 0 \times 2^2 + 1 \times 2^1 + 1 \times 2^0$$
$$= 1 \times 8 + 0 \times 4 + 1 \times 2 + 1 \times 1$$
$$= 11 \text{ (in decimal notation)}$$

This example shows you how to convert binary notation to decimal notation by breaking it down into products of the power of 2.

### Decimal Notation to Binary Notation

Decimal notation can be converted to binary notation through two methods. Either one will give you the same binary representation. We will introduce one method here.

In this method, you repeatedly divide the decimal number by 2 until it becomes 0, noting the remainder of each division. The reverse order of the sequence of the remainders is the binary representation of the decimal number. For example, to convert 19 to binary notation:

> ⚓ **Base-10 and Base-2** An interactive tutorial explaining base-10 and base-2.

> ⚓ **Decimal to Binary Guided Practice** An interactive exercise guides you step by step to convert decimal to binary notation. You can practice with a decimal number of your choice or let the program randomly generate one for you.

| Division of Number | Remainder |
|---|---|
| 19/2 = 9 | 1 |
| 9/2 = 4 | 1 |
| 4/2 = 2 | 0 |
| 2/2 = 1 | 0 |
| 1/2 = 0 | 1 |

The sequence of the remainders you get in the repeated divisions is **11001.** The *reverse* order of this sequence, **10011,** is the binary notation of the decimal number 19.

## A "DIGITAL" CLOCK GADGET

A binary coded decimal (BCD) clock (Figure 1.5) is built with six columns of light-emitting diodes (LEDs). The first two read the hours, the middle two the minutes, and the last two the seconds. An off LED represents 0, and on represents 1.

**Figure 1.5** A binary coded decimal (BCD) clock.

The binary notation for the LED pattern shown in Figure 1.5 is

| | 0 | | 1 | | 0 |
|---|---|---|---|---|---|
| | 0 | 0 | 0 | 0 | 1 |
| 0 | 1 | 1 | 0 | 1 | 0 |
| 1 | 0 | 0 | 1 | 0 | 1 |
| h | h | m | m | s | s |

> 🖱 **Binary Coded Decimal (BCD) Clock**
> This shows a BCD clock in action. It could be
> fun to race to decode the time, as the LED
> patterns change by the second.

The bottom row represents $2^0$ (= 1), the next row up $2^1$ (= 2) then $2^2$ (= 4), and then $2^3$ (= 8).

Each decimal notation for the hour, minute, and second uses two digits. Let's see how the LED pattern representing the hour shown in Figure 1.5 represents 12.

- The leftmost digit of the hour: The bit pattern for the leftmost digit of the hour is 01. It is converted to 1 in the decimal system because

$$0 \times 2^1 + 1 \times 2^0 = 1$$

- The rightmost digit of the hour: The bit pattern for the rightmost digit of the hour is 0010. It is converted to 2 in the decimal system because

$$0 \times 2^3 + 0 \times 2^2 + 1 \times 2^1 + 0 \times 2^0 = 2$$

**Questions**

1. Verify that the time shown in Figure 1.5 is 12:29:25.
2. Explain the number of LEDs available in each column. That is, why are two LEDs sufficient for the first, four needed for the second, and so forth?

## 1.5 USING BITS TO REPRESENT NON-NUMERIC VALUES

Although computers use bits to deal with numbers, a sequence of bits can be used to represent almost anything. Recall that you can associate eye signals with "yes" and "no," colors, or even more complicated messages.

**TABLE 1.3    The Lower 128 ASCII Codes**

| 0 | NUL | 16 | DLE | 32 |   | 48 | 0 | 64 | @ | 80 | P | 96 | ` | 112 | p |
|---|-----|----|-----|----|---|----|---|----|---|----|---|-----|---|-----|---|
| 1 | SOH | 17 | DC1 | 33 | ! | 49 | 1 | 65 | A | 81 | Q | 97 | a | 113 | q |
| 2 | STX | 18 | DC2 | 34 | " | 50 | 2 | 66 | B | 82 | R | 98 | b | 114 | r |
| 3 | ETX | 19 | DC3 | 35 | # | 51 | 3 | 67 | C | 83 | S | 99 | c | 115 | s |
| 4 | EOT | 20 | DC4 | 36 | $ | 52 | 4 | 68 | D | 84 | T | 100 | d | 116 | t |
| 5 | ENQ | 21 | NAK | 37 | % | 53 | 5 | 69 | E | 85 | U | 101 | e | 117 | u |
| 6 | ACK | 22 | SYN | 38 | & | 54 | 6 | 70 | F | 86 | V | 102 | f | 118 | v |
| 7 | BEL | 23 | ETB | 39 | ' | 55 | 7 | 71 | G | 87 | W | 103 | g | 119 | w |
| 8 | BS | 24 | CAN | 40 | ( | 56 | 8 | 72 | H | 88 | X | 104 | h | 120 | x |
| 9 | TAB | 25 | EM | 41 | ) | 57 | 9 | 73 | I | 89 | Y | 105 | i | 121 | y |
| 10 | LF | 26 | SUB | 42 | * | 58 | : | 74 | J | 90 | Z | 106 | j | 122 | z |
| 11 | VT | 27 | ESC | 43 | + | 59 | ; | 75 | K | 91 | [ | 107 | k | 123 | { |
| 12 | FF | 28 | FS | 44 | , | 60 | < | 76 | L | 92 | \ | 108 | l | 124 | | |
| 13 | CR | 29 | GS | 45 | - | 61 | = | 77 | M | 93 | ] | 109 | m | 125 | } |
| 14 | SO | 30 | RS | 46 | . | 62 | > | 78 | N | 94 | ^ | 110 | n | 126 | ~ |
| 15 | SI | 31 | US | 47 | / | 63 | ? | 79 | O | 95 | _ | 111 | o | 127 | DEL |

The binary system can be used to represent non-numeric information. For example, each letter of the alphabet or other text characters can be represented by a different combination of bits. In the ASCII character set, each character is represented using 8 bits, which permits $2^8 = 256$ different characters. Table 1.3 shows the lower 128 ASCII codes. The upper 128 values can be used to handle special characters, such as accented characters in foreign languages.

# 1.6 THE FINITE AND DISCRETE NATURE OF COMPUTERS

Information in analog media is **continuous** and made up of an *infinite* number of data points. Computers can only handle data that are **discrete** and **finite**. This section will discuss the limitations and advantages of these two properties.

## 1.6.1 Limitations

**1.** As you can see from the eye-signal analogy, the more eyes you use, the more information the signal can represent. With a 2-bit system, we can represent four possible values. If we are representing shades of gray using a 2-bit system, we can only represent four different shades. We can represent 16 different shades with a 4-bit system. The more shades of gray we want to represent, the more bits we need.

To represent colors that change from one point to the next in a natural image would require an infinite number of points, because there are always more points between any two points in the analog world. However, computers have a limit on the number of bits that are

ASCII stands for American Standard Code for Information Interchange. It is an encoding standard for text characters, including the 26-letter English alphabet, and symbols in computer programs.

Another standard is called Unicode, which is not introduced in this chapter. It can represent a large repertoire of multilingual characters.

allowed for each piece of data. A sequence of bits in a computer cannot be infinite. Only a finite set of data can be represented digitally.

**2.** No matter what the bit limit, each value can only represent one discrete shade of gray. There are always shades of gray in between two consecutive gray values that cannot be captured in digital form.

Thus, the discrete and finite nature of computers restricts the exactness with which analog media—natural sights and sounds—can be captured and reproduced in digital form.

## 1.6.2 Advantages

Although digital representation sacrifices exactness in reproducing analog information, its discrete nature offers an advantage in precision, and its finite nature offers an advantage in compactness for media.

---

### INTEGERS AND DECIMAL NUMBERS

Integers are an example of a discrete number system. There is no other integer between any two consecutive integers. Computers can represent integers exactly, because they encode them in the discrete values of 0 and 1. Integers are inherently discrete but they are not inherently finite. A list of integers goes on forever. Although computers can only deal with a finite number of things, handling integers is not a problem, because they set a limit on the number of bits used to represent them.

Numbers with decimal points, such as 0.123, 1.30, and 1.7608, are an example of a continuous number system. Between any two numbers are other numbers. Although these numbers are inherently continuous, computers can handle them by limiting their precision by setting a limit on the number of bits used to represent them. Some such numbers cannot be represented exactly, but only approximately, on computers.

---

## 1.7 CONVERTING ANALOG TO DIGITAL

The conversion of analog information to digital is a two-step process: *sampling* and *quantizing*. Measuring the length of a pencil (Figure 1.1) illustrates a sampling and quantizing process. For this example, we only sample once; that is, we measure the length of the pencil once. In digital media, you often have to sample more than once, because color value changes over an image's 2-D plane and the amplitude of a sound wave changes over time, for example. In these cases, you must sample multiple times to collect enough information to represent the whole piece. The *sampling rate*—how frequently you take measurements—determines the level of detail at which the collected data can represent the original analog media.

To illustrate the sampling and quantizing steps, let's monitor a puppy's first year of growth by measuring its weight with an analog scale that uses a spring-loaded mechanism to sample the puppy's weight. The more the puppy weighs, the more compressed the spring will be. The spring responds to the extent of compression and rotates the pointer on the scale. This scale is an analog scale, because the spring can be compressed continuously. The reported weight, correspondingly, is analog information.

When you record the weight, you note a discrete number. You have to decide how to round the data, for example, to 0.1, 0.2, or 0.5. The process of rounding a value to one of the discrete values within a set of discrete values is called *quantizing*.

What number would you record for the puppy's weight (Figure 1.6)? You may choose to round off the reading to the nearest hash mark or estimate the reading between the hash marks. Either way, you may not be recording an exact weight. You sacrifice the accuracy of the measurement when you convert analog information into a discrete number but gain the advantage of reporting the puppy's weight as a precise value— although not necessarily an accurate one. Being distinct and unambiguous, discrete values easily can be processed mathematically, compared, or plotted on a chart. On the other hand, if you record the weight as "somewhere between 5 and 10 pounds," it is not distinct and precise, and you probably will be asked to round it off to a discrete number.

> **Converting Analog to Digital— Sampling and Quantizing** An interactive tutorial illustrating the process of sampling and quantizing using a task to monitor a puppy's first year of growth in weight.

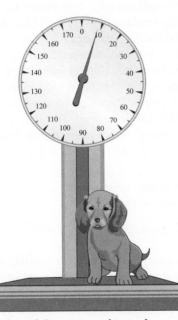

**Figure 1.6** Sampling a puppy's weight on an analog scale.

In recording a number, you must decide the number of decimal places to use. This will determine the precision of the measurement. Generally, increasing the number of decimal places increases the precision. However, recording the puppy's weight using more decimal places will require more paper and paperwork.

In digitizing analog media, the precision of the data is determined by the number of discrete values, or levels, to which the data can be assigned. Increasing the decimal places is one way to increase the number of levels. For example, allowing one decimal place gives you 10 discrete levels of precision between two consecutive integers; between 2 and 3, there are 2.0, 2.1, 2.2, 2.3, 2.4, 2.5, 2.6, 2.7, 2.8, and 2.9. In digital media, the number of possible levels is called ***bit depth***.

## BIT DEPTH DOES NOT MEAN NUMBER OF DECIMAL PLACES

The number of decimal places is used in the simple example of weighing the puppy to illustrate the concept of bit depth. However, increasing the bit depth does not necessarily mean increasing the number of decimal places.

Increasing bit depth means having more discrete levels to which the captured data can be assigned. For 10 discrete levels, you can have the 10 allowable values, as follows:

1. 2.0, 2.1, 2.2, 2.3, 2.4, 2.5, 2.6, 2.7, 2.8, 2.9
2. 0, 5, 10, 15, 20, 25, 30, 35, 40, 45

Using the first 10-level scale for recording the puppy's weight, you get a precision of one decimal place within 2 to 3 pounds. That means that if the puppy's weight is between 2 and 3 pounds, you can distinguish the difference to one decimal place. However, any weight lower than 2.0 will be recorded as 2.0, and any weight higher than 2.9 will be capped at 2.9. The weight obtained from Figure 1.6 would be recorded as 2.9. If this scale is used, it certainly would not be very useful for tracking the puppy's progress.

Using the second 10-level scale, a weight of 2 pounds would be rounded to 0 and a weight of 3 pounds to 5. The difference between 2 and 3 pounds is altered after they are mapped to the allowable value on this 10-level scale. The difference becomes 5 pounds, not 1 pound. However, because this scale has a wider range, a weight of, say, 45 pounds can be distinguished from 5 pounds. The weight obtained from Figure 1.6 would have been recorded as 10 pounds if this scale were used. This scale is a better choice than the first for weighing the puppy because a puppy's range of weight falls within the range of scale.

In summary, increasing the number of allowable levels—increasing the bit depth—in digital media can

- Increase the precision of the captured data
- Increase the overall range of the scale
- Increase the file size

Recall that in the eye signal analogy, you need more eyes to encode more choices. Similarly, increasing the number of allowable levels requires more bits to encode a level. Thus, increasing the number of allowable levels increases the file size.

To monitor the puppy's first-year growth by weight, you will have to decide how frequently you want to weigh it. This is the sampling rate. Do you want to weigh it annually, monthly, weekly, daily, or hourly? What factors do you take into consideration when you make this decision?

Based on how fast a puppy normally grows in the first year, weighing it monthly or weekly is reasonable. However, if you do not know how fast a puppy should normally grow, you probably feel a little lost when you are asked to choose how frequently to weigh it. If you sample too infrequently, you will miss critical details that show how the weight changes over time. In that case, how frequently do you sample so that you do not miss any information at all?

As mentioned earlier, when converting analog to digital data, no matter how high the sampling rate is, some analog information will be missed. If you sample too frequently, you will be busy weighing the puppy, and will need more paper to keep the records, more shelf space to store the records, and more time to read through the records later (besides annoying the puppy).

By analogy, if you increase the sampling rate, you increase the accuracy in digitally representing the original analog media. The computer has to sample faster, and the resulting file will have more samples or data. Files will be larger and require more time to process, which may cause noticeable delay in opening or editing the file.

What sampling rate should we use, then? There is no one strictly right or wrong sampling rate. The optimal sampling rate for your purpose will depend on the source content (for example, the rate of change of the original analog source), its intended use, and technical limitations (for example, limitations on the file size and your computer speed). In weighing the puppy, either monthly or weekly seems a reasonable sampling rate. Weekly data may represent the first few months' rapid growth rate more accurately but may yield redundant information in later months. In real life, you can choose to sample the first month's weight more frequently than that of the other months if you anticipate more dramatic changes. You can change the sampling rate in a task. However, in digital media, one sampling rate is normally set for a session.

How is this analogy related to digital media, such as images and sound? In general, the sampling rate for digital images is related to the image resolution (or amount of detail). Quantization is related to the image's bit depth or color depth, which affects the number of colors allowed in the image. For digital audio, quantization also is related to the bit depth, which determines how well the differences in sound amplitude can be represented, and the sampling rate relates to how frequently the amplitude is sampled.

*Detailed discussions of sampling and quantizing digital images and audio are covered in the chapters devoted to these media.*

### 1.7.1 Problems in Representing Analog Media on Computers

Sound and pictures are by nature continuous phenomena. Each piece of sound or picture is made up of an infinite amount of information. Due to the finite and discrete way that computers handle data, two inevitable problems arise when we want to represent sound and pictures on a computer:

1. Because computers operate on discrete values, the sampling step is required to choose some discrete samples of the information. In addition, computers have only finite capacity, so the sampling rate has to be finite.
2. A computer cannot represent numbers with infinite precision. Thus, the precision with which we represent colors or sounds is limited. Quantization maps the values of the samples to a discrete scale, that is, rounded to an allowable discrete value in the scale.

## 1.8 FILE SIZES

In a text document that uses ASCII code to represent text characters, each byte stores an ASCII code that corresponds to a character. The more characters in a text document, the more bytes are required to store the file.

### ACTIVITY/EXERCISE

**Using Windows 95, 98, 2000, XP, or 7:** Open a new text file in Notepad and type the sentence, "Eight bits make a byte." Save the file as file-size-exercise.txt. Then to look at its file size, right-click on the file-size-exercise.txt file and select Properties. You should find that the file size is 23 bytes because there are 23 characters in this sentence—1 byte for each character (including spaces, which are characters, too). What is the ASCII code for a space? Look it up in Table 1.3.

**Using Mac OS X:** Open a new text file in TextEdit and type the sentence, "Eight bits make a byte." Select `Format > Make Plain Text`. Then save the file as file-size-exercise.txt. In the Save dialog box, choose Western for the Plain Text Encoding. Verify that the file size is 23 bytes.

### Questions

In the file-size-exercise.txt file you created, add a blank line at the end of the sentence by hitting the Enter (Windows) or Return (Mac) key on your keyboard. Save the file. Then look at its file size again. What is the file size now? By how many byte(s) has it increased?

Creating a blank line in Notepad actually involves both a carriage return (CR) and a line feed (LF). Are they characters? Look them up in Table 1.3.

If you create a Microsoft Word document with the same sentence ("Eight bits make a byte."), will the file size also be 23 bytes? No. It is larger because other information (such as text formatting) is saved with the file.

Pixels and pixel dimensions will be discussed in more detail in the digital imaging chapters.

You will learn more about bit depth of digital images in the chapter on digital imaging.

A byte is not just for storing a character in a text document. A byte is 8 bits, with 256 possible values. It can be used for many purposes. If you use a byte to store the color information of each pixel in an image, then each pixel can be assigned with one of 256 colors that the image allows. Color images use more than one byte per pixel to represent color information if each pixel has more than 256 choices of color. The more bytes per pixel, the more bytes are needed to store the image, and the larger the file size. Thus, an image with more allowable colors has a larger file size. Whether one or more bytes are used for each pixel, the file size also increases with the number of pixels in an image. The more pixels an image has, the more bytes are needed to store the image, and the larger the file size.

Multimedia files—image, sound, and especially video files—can be very large and require tremendous amounts of storage space. In addition, the larger the file, the longer the transmission time to send it over the Internet and the longer the processing time. Longer processing time means that it may take longer for your audience to open your files and slow down your productivity when you are editing the file.

Generally, there are three strategies to reduce the size of a digital media file:

- Reduce the sampling rate
- Reduce the bit depth
- Apply file compression

When you reduce the sampling rate and bit depth, the resemblance between the resulting digital image and the original subject will be reduced, and digital audio quality may be noticeably degraded. In working with digital media files, you often have to weigh quality against file size.

## 1.9 COMPRESSION

*File compression* lets you reduce the total number of bits and bytes in a file. Reducing the file size allows a file to be transmitted faster over a network and take up less storage space. Nowadays, storage space is inexpensive, and many people have access to a high-speed network, but you still have to consider the playback performance of video files. Uncompressed videos require a very high data rate. Video playback will become jerky and skip frames if the computer cannot process the video data fast enough. If the data rate of a video on the Internet is too high for the network speed, video playback will also become choppy because it has to pause frequently to wait for enough data to be transmitted over the Internet. In addition to the waiting time for the Internet transfer, another factor you may want to consider is the cost of the data access. Many wireless carriers implement a limit on their data access plans. It costs the subscribers extra when they go beyond the data limit of their subscription plan.

In later chapters, you will learn some of the most common data compression methods applied to multimedia files. Some are not specific to multimedia files. Others are available only for a certain category of media files. For example, Sorenson is available for creating QuickTime movies but not for sound compression.

By learning the concepts behind these compression methods, you will understand the strengths and weaknesses of each. Some allow you to control certain parameters when saving a file in a multimedia application. Understanding what these parameters mean and how they affect the quality of your files will help you make decisions that are best for your multimedia work.

> ✎ Video Examples of Different Levels of Compression: Uncompressed, Low Compression, and High Compression  These sample videos are 60-frame computer animations, rendered frame by frame (720 × 480 pixels) as an image sequence, imported in Adobe Premiere Pro, and exported as QuickTime and MPEG-2 movies. Each exported movie uses a different compressor.
>
> - QuickTime, uncompressed (Note: This file takes longest to download and has the least smooth playback.)
> - QuickTime, using Animation Codec
> - QuickTime, using H.264 Codec
> - QuickTime, using Sorenson Video 3 Codec
> - MPEG-2
> - MPEG-4
>
>   Note the following properties of each movie:
>
> 1. Image quality for different codecs
> 2. File sizes
> 3. Smoothness of playback
>
> Why are the image quality, file size, and playback different with different compressors? You will understand them better when you learn more about digital video compression in the later chapters on digital video.

## 1.9.1 Lossy and Lossless Compression

Compression methods can be categorized as either lossy or lossless. With *lossy compression*, some information in the original file will be lost and cannot be recovered. JPEG, a popular image file format for Web images, is an example of lossy compression. MP3, a popular file format for digital audio, is another example of lossy compression. Many video codecs are also lossy, although a few use lossless algorithms. For files that you want to keep as the start file for further editing, you should avoid applying lossy compression. The exception is video files, which are normally applied with lossy compression.

*Side note (right margin, top):* You will learn more about different codecs (compression/decompression methods) and corresponding data rates in the digital video chapter.

*Side note (right margin, bottom):* For details on the compression algorithms, see the CS Module.

## 1.10 SUMMARY

The analog information we perceive through our senses is continuous and infinite. However, computers store and transmit information using discrete, finite data, which presents some limitations but also advantages in capturing and reproducing analog media.

Converting from analog to digital data involves a two-step process—sampling and quantizing. How frequently an analog medium is sampled during the sampling step is called the sample rate. For example, the sample rate in digital imaging determines the resolution of a digital image. In the quantization step, the number of discrete levels used to map the samples' values is called the bit depth. For example, the bit depth of a digital image specifies the number of colors available in the image. The discrete and finite nature of computers restricts the precision with which analog media—natural sights and sounds—can be reproduced in digital form. In converting from analog to digital, we sacrifice exactness.

Because of the current electronic technology that computer systems are built on, they operate on the binary system, which uses base-2 notation. Only two numerals are available in base-2, denoted as 0 and 1 in the language of computers. Base-10 can be converted to base-2 notation and vice versa. For example, the binary notation for the decimal number 19 is 10011.

Multimedia files—image, sound, and especially video files—can be very large. Such large file sizes can require tremendous amounts of storage space. In addition, the larger the file, the longer it takes to send the file over the Internet.

Generally, there are three strategies to reduce the size of a digital media file:

- Reduce the sampling rate
- Reduce the bit depth
- Apply file compression

Reducing the sampling rate or bit depth reduces the resemblance between your resulting digital media and the original analog media. When working with digital media files, you often have to weigh the quality against the file size. Compression methods can be categorized as either lossy or lossless. With lossy compressions, such as JPEG and MP3, some information in the original file will be lost and cannot be recovered. Whenever possible, you should avoid using this type of compression for any file that you want to keep as the start file for further editing.

## TERMS

| | | |
|---|---|---|
| analog  3 | decimal system  8 | kilo (K)  7 |
| base-10  8 | decode  5 | lossy compression  17 |
| base-2  8 | digital  3 | mega (M)  7 |
| binary system  8 | discrete  11 | quantizing  12 |
| bit depth  13 | encode  5 | sampling  12 |
| bits  6 | file compression  16 | sampling rate  12 |
| byte  6 | finite  11 | tera (T)  7 |
| continuous  11 | giga (G)  7 | |

## LEARNING AIDS

The following learning aids can be found at the book's companion Web site.

🖰 **Base-10 and Base-2**
An interactive tutorial explaining base-10 and base-2.

🖰 **Decimal to Binary Guided Practice**
An interactive exercise guides you step by step to convert decimal to binary notation. You can practice with a decimal number of your choice or let the program randomly generate one for you.

🖰 **Binary Coded Decimal (BCD) Clock**
This shows a BCD clock in action. It could be fun to race to decode the time, as the LED patterns change by the second.

🖰 **Converting Analog to Digital—Sampling and Quantizing**
An interactive tutorial illustrating the process of sampling and quantizing using a task to monitor a puppy's first year of growth in weight.

✇ **Video Examples of Different Levels of Compression: Uncompressed, Low Compression, and High Compression**
These sample videos are 60-frame computer animations, rendered frame by frame (720 × 480 pixels) as an image sequence, imported in Adobe Premiere Pro, and exported as QuickTime and MPEG-2 movies. Each exported movie uses a different compressor.

- QuickTime, uncompressed (*Note:* This file takes longest to download and has the least smooth playback.)
- QuickTime, using Animation Codec
- QuickTime, using H.264 Codec
- QuickTime, using Sorenson Video 3 Codec
- MPEG-2
- MPEG-4

Note the following properties of each movie:

1. Image quality for different codecs
2. File sizes
3. Smoothness of playback

Why are the image quality, file size, and playback different with different compressors? You will understand better when you learn more about digital video compression in the later chapters on digital video.

## REVIEW QUESTIONS

When applicable, please select all correct answers.

1. Digital data is _____ and analog information is _____.
   A. continuous; discrete
   B. discrete; continuous

2. Digitization means converting _____ into _____.

3. Converting from analog to digital involves a two-step process: _____ and _____.

**4.** When analog information is converted to digital data, we must consider two properties that affect the exactness of the digital representation, one from sampling and one from quantizing. Which of the following is from sampling?

A. Sampling rate
B. Bit depth

**5.** Which of the following refers to the number of allowable levels of digitized data?

A. Sampling rate
B. Bit depth

**6.** Which of the following can reduce the file size of digital media?

A. Decrease sampling rate
B. Increase sampling rate
C. Decrease bit depth
D. Increase bit depth

**7.** Our everyday decimal numbering system is base-_____. Computers use base-_____, which is also known as the _____ numbering system.

**8.** The smallest unit in a binary system is a _____,

A. bit
B. byte

which refers to a binary digit (i.e., a _____ or a _____). (Enter a digit or number.)

**9.** Fill in the blanks with "bit(s)" or "byte(s)": Eight _____ equals one _____.

**10.** The word *bit* comes from the shortening of the words _____ and _____.

**11.** If you want to use hand signals to communicate only two possibilities—yes or no— to your friend, what is the minimum number of fingers you need? _____ We may call this hand-signal system _____-bit.

**12.** A pixel that can have only one of two possible color values requires _____ bit(s) to store the color information.

**13.** If you use a byte to store the grayscale information of each pixel in a grayscale image, how many gray levels are possible for each pixel?

**14.** How many bits are in the binary notation 0011010? How many possible values can this many bits represent?

**15.** Which of the following sizes is the largest?

A. 24 GB
B. 24 MB
C. 240 MB
D. 2,400 KB

16. Fill in the names and abbreviations for the following:

| Name | Abbr. | Size in bytes |
|---|---|---|
| Kilobytes | KB | $2^{10} = 1,024$ |
| | | $2^{20} = 1,048,576$ |
| | | $2^{30} = 1,073,741,824$ |
| | | $2^{40} = 1,099,511,627,776$ |

17. How many bits is each of the following binary numbers? Also, convert each to a decimal number.

   i. 00000000
  ii. 0000
 iii. 01101000
 iv. 0110100
   v. 11
 vi. 111
vii. 0000000000000010

18. Convert the following decimal numbers into binary.

    i. 0
   ii. 1
  iii. 2
  iv. 3
   v. 12
  vi. 123
 vii. 11
viii. 111
  ix. 128
   x. 255

19. i. Name three general strategies to reduce the size of a digital media file.
   ii. Which of these strategies does not necessarily sacrifice the quality of the media file? Why?

20. You should avoid using lossy compression for any file that you want to keep as the start file for further editing because _____.

**(a)**

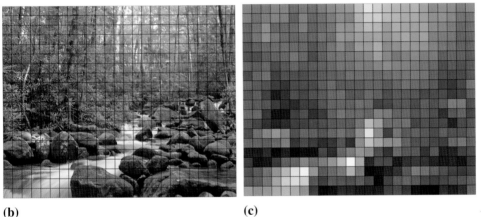

**(b)**                                      **(c)**

**(d)**                                      **(e)**

**Figure 2.1** (a) A natural image. (b) Imagine a grid of 25 $\times$ 20 cells is applied on the image. (c) The color of each of the 25 $\times$ 20 grid cells is averaged to a single value. (d) Imagine a grid of 100 $\times$ 80 cells is applied on the image. (e) The color of each of the 100 $\times$ 80 grid cells is averaged to a single value.

(a)       (b)

**Figure 2.2** The relative sizes of an image 25 pixels × 20 pixels (left) and 100 pixels × 80 pixels (right) captured from the same scene.

(a)       (b)

**Figure 2.3** (a) A 4-color palette. (b) An 8-color palette.

(a)                  (b)

**Figure 2.4** The sampled image is quantized into (a) four colors, and (b) eight colors.

(a)                  (b)

**Figure 2.5** (a) The colors in the original image (b) are quantized into four colors using the palette shown in Figure 2.3a. Some of the similar green colors, such as those in the outlined square box, are now mapped to a single color.

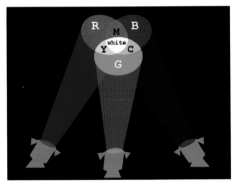

**(a)**          **(b)**

**Figure 2.6** (a) Using a different 8-color palette, (b) the sampled image is quantized.

| | | | | | | | | | 1 | 1 | 1 | 1 | 1 | 1 | 1 | 1 |
|---|---|---|---|---|---|---|---|---|---|---|---|---|---|---|---|---|
| | | | | | | | | | 1 | 1 | 1 | 1 | 1 | 1 | 1 | 1 |

| 1 | 1 | 1 | 1 | 1 | 1 | 1 | 1 |
|---|---|---|---|---|---|---|---|
| 1 | 1 | 1 | 1 | 1 | 1 | 1 | 1 |
| 1 | 1 | 1 | 1 | 1 | 1 | 0 | 1 |
| 1 | 1 | 1 | 1 | 1 | 0 | 1 | 1 |
| 1 | 1 | 1 | 1 | 0 | 1 | 1 | 1 |
| 1 | 1 | 1 | 0 | 1 | 1 | 1 | 1 |
| 1 | 1 | 0 | 1 | 1 | 1 | 1 | 1 |
| 1 | 1 | 1 | 1 | 1 | 1 | 1 | 1 |

**Figure 2.7** For each pixel in a 1-bit (i.e., 2-color) bitmap image, its color value can be represented by 0s and 1s.

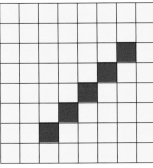

**Figure 2.12** RGB: An additive color system.

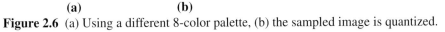

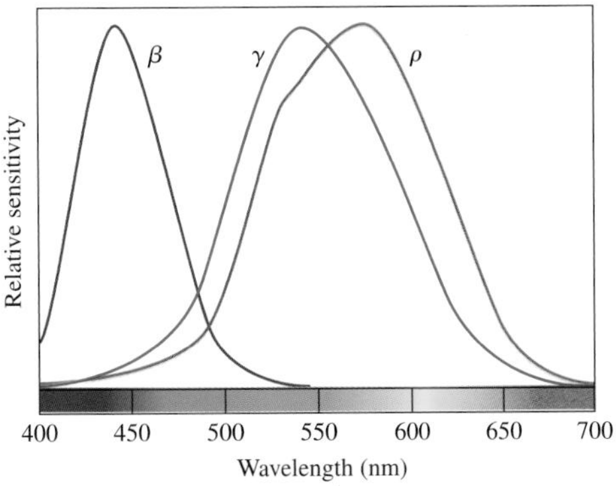

**Figure 2.13** Human spectral sensitivity to color.

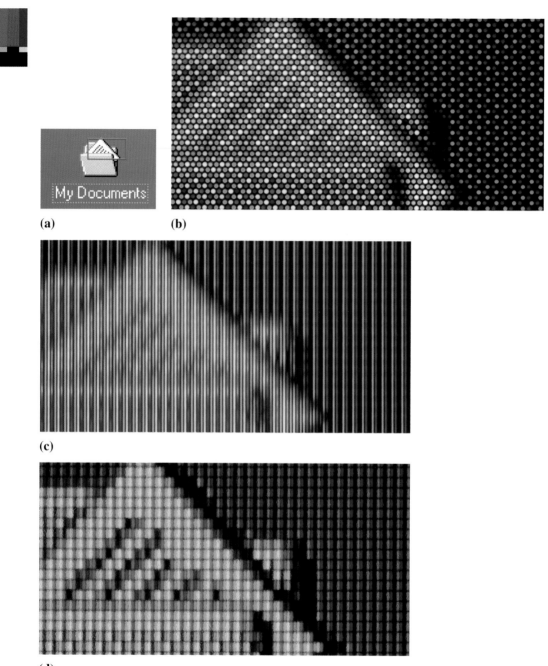

**(a)**

**(b)**

**(c)**

**(d)**

**Figure 2.14** Computer monitors: (a) An image displayed with an outlined square where the close-up photographs (b) through (d) were taken. (b) Close-up of a standard monitor screen. (c) Close-up view of a SONY Trinitron monitor screen. (d) Close-up view of an LCD display.

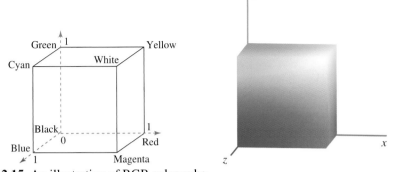

**Figure 2.15** An illustration of RGB color cube.

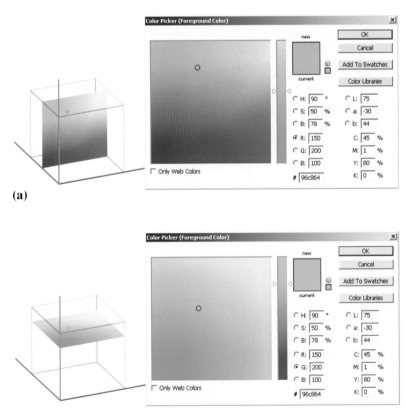

**(a)**

**(b)**

**Figure 2.16** Relationship between an RGB color cube and the color picker used in digital image applications. (*continued*)

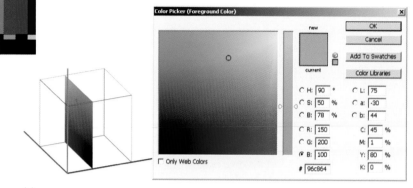

**(c)**

**(d)**

**Figure 2.16** (*continued*)

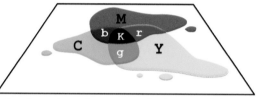

**Figure 2.17** CMYK: A subtractive color system. In theory, mixing cyan, magenta, and yellow gives black.

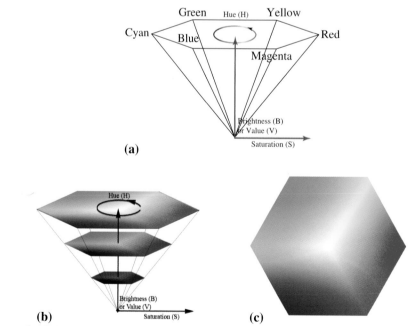

**Figure 2.18** (a) Hexacone of the HSB or HSV color model. (b) Hexacone with selected slices at different levels of brightness or value. (c) A slice of the color wheel from the HSB or HSV color model.

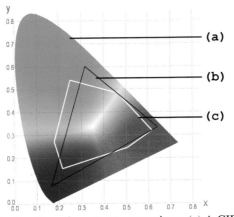

**Figure 2.20** An illustration for color gamut comparison: (a) A CIE chromaticity diagram. (b) RGB color gamut of typical CRT monitors. The exact shape of the device's color space depends on the monitor's red, green, and blue phosphors. Note that this does not include all the colors humans can see. (c) CMYK color gamut of typical inkjet printers. The exact shape of the color space depends on the colorants of the printer's ink.

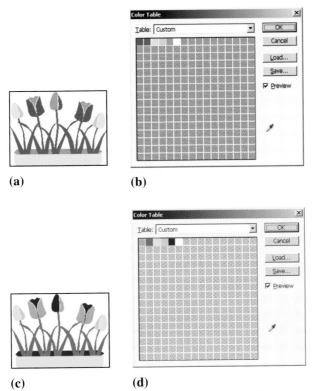

**Figure 2.21** (a) An image using indexed colors. (b) The color table or palette for the indexed colors. (c) The image with changes made to the indexed colors. (d) The color table that is used by the image in (c).

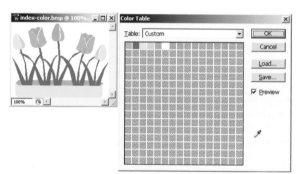

**Figure 2.22** An image is converted to indexed-color mode.

**Figure 2.23** The first color (index 0) on the color table is changed to a light blue.

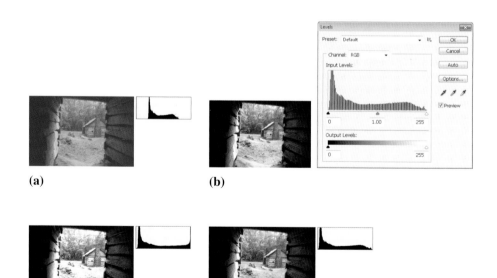

(a)　　　　　　　　　　　(b)

(c)　　　　　　　　　　　(d)

**Figure 3.1** Scanned images with their histograms: (a) Scanned using a narrow tonal range. (b) The tonal range of the scanned image (a) is adjusted by stretching the histogram. (c) Scanned with highlights cropped off. (d) Scanned with a maximized tonal range.

**(a)**

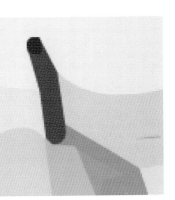

**(b)**

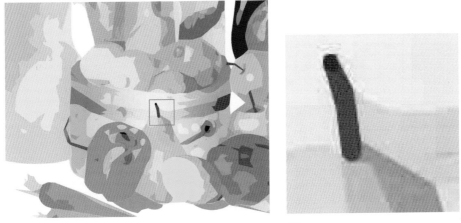

**(c)**                                    **(d)**

**Figure 3.27** (a) An uncompressed image. (b) A zoom-in view of the area outlined in the colored box in image (a). (c) A highly compressed JPEG image of (a). (d) A zoom-in view of the area outlined in color in the JPEG image (b) showing the JPEG artifact.

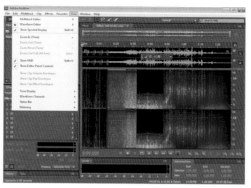

**(a)**

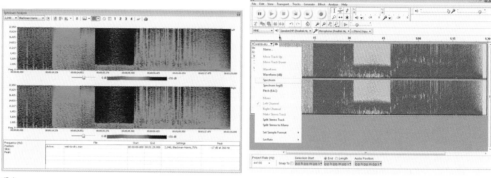

**(b)**                                                       **(c)**

**Figure 5.12** Spectral view of audio in Figure 5.10. (a) Adobe Audition CS5.5: `View > Show Spectral Display`. (b) Sony Sound Forge 10: `View > Spectrum Analysis` and click the Sonogram button. (c) Audacity 1.3 Beta: `Spectrum`.

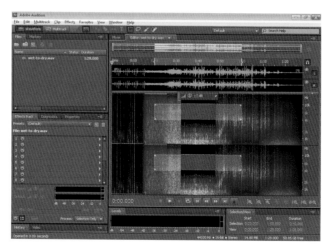

**Figure 5.13** The frequency range of about 4,000 to 10,000 Hz within the time frame between 20 second and 1 minute is selected (as indicated by the pale rectangle) in the spectral view.

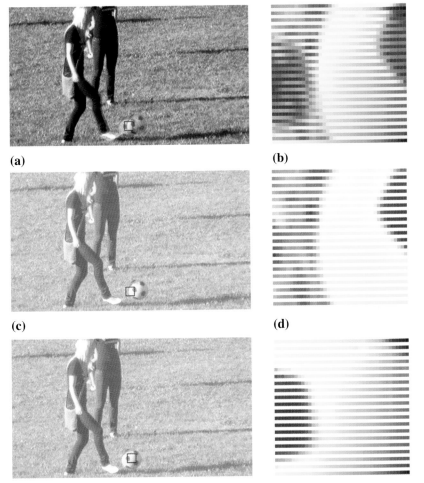

**(a)**  **(b)**

**(c)**  **(d)**

**(e)**  **(f)**

**Figure 6.1** (a) A digital video frame showing comb-like artifact caused by fast action and camera panning. (b) Close-up of the small outlined area in (a). (c) The upper field of the video frame. (d) Close-up of the small outlined area in (c). (e) The lower field of the video frame. (f) Close-up of the small outlined area in (e).

**(a)**  **(b)**

**Figure 6.2** (a) The video frame deinterlaced by eliminating the upper field and interpolating the lower field to fill in the gaps. (b) Close-up of the small outlined area.

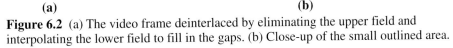

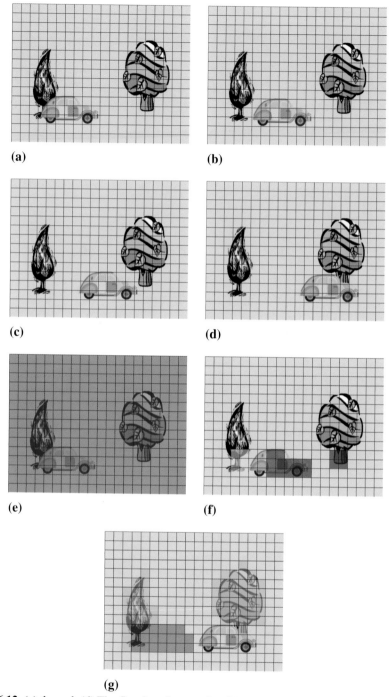

**Figure 6.12** (a) through (d) The first four frames of a video: (a) Frame 1, being the reference frame or the I-frame. (b) Frame 2, being a B-frame. (c) Frame 3, being a B-frame. (d) Frame 4, being a P-frame. (e) through (g) Areas highlighted in red are original pixel information and areas highlighted in blue are from the previous I-frame. Areas highlighted in cyan are from the previous I-frame at the same location, and those highlighted in yellow are from the next P-frame.

*Note:* Not all the blocks are labeled for their encoding method; only some are highlighted to illustrate the points.

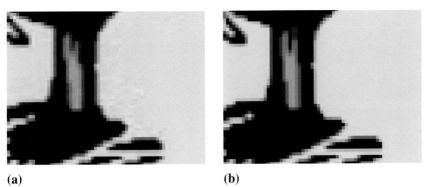

**Figure 6.14** (a) MPEG artifact, discernible at the intersect area of dark and light colors. (b) The original image before MPEG compression.

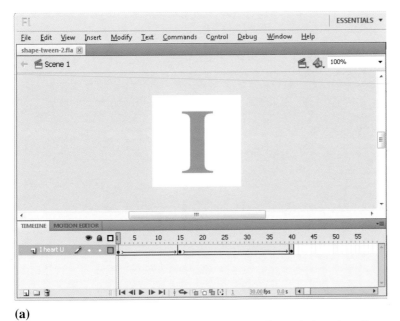

**(a)**

**Figure 8.19** A shape tweened animation. (a) Keyframe at frame 1. (*continued*)

**(b)**

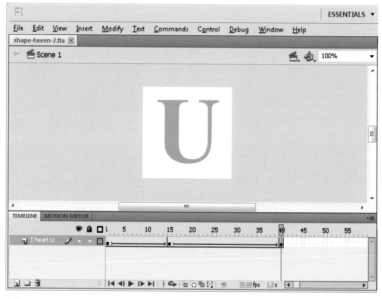

**(c)**

**Figure 8.19** (*continued*) (b) In the second keyframe (frame 15), the shape and color are altered. (c) In the last keyframe of this animation sequence (frame 40), the shape and color are further altered.

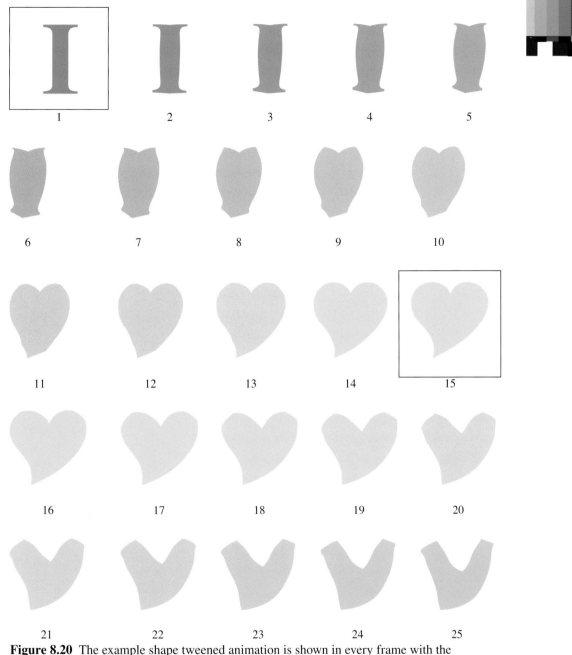

**Figure 8.20** The example shape tweened animation is shown in every frame with the corresponding frame number, where frames 1, 15, and 40 are the keyframes where the shapes are explicitly specified. (*continued*)

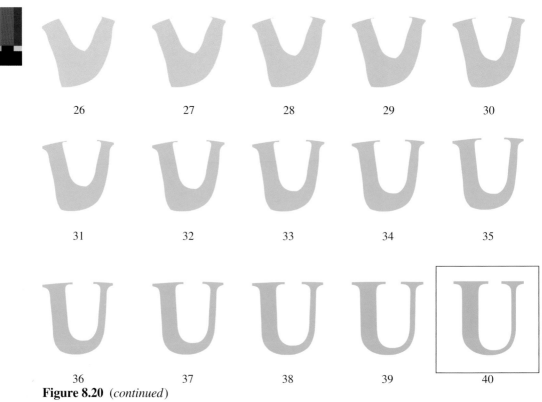

**Figure 8.20** (*continued*)

# 2

# Fundamentals of Digital Imaging

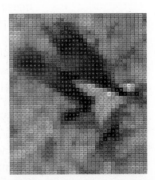

KEY CONCEPTS
- Sampling and quantizing in digitizing images
- Pixels and image resolution
- Image bit depth
- How pixels, image resolution, and bit depth are related to sampling and quantizing
- Color representation in digital images
- Bitmapped images versus vector graphics

GENERAL LEARNING OBJECTIVES

In this chapter, you will learn
- The common terms in digital imaging.
- The commonly used color models in digital imaging.
- The common file types for digital images.
- The basic steps of digitization: sampling and quantization in digital imaging.
- What resolution and color depth mean for digital images.
- The effects of resolution and color depth on image file size.
- The difference between bitmapped images and vector graphics.
- The color representation in digital imaging.
- The basic steps of digitization in digital imaging.
- The general strategies for reducing digital image file sizes.

## 2.1 INTRODUCTION

In Chapter 1, you learned that digitization of analog information involves a two-step process: sampling and quantizing. Digitization of any digital medium—images, sound, or videos—always involves these two steps. However, if you have worked with digital image processing programs, you may have noticed that you never encounter the terms "sampling" and "quantizing" explicitly in the program. On the other hand, you may have already heard about pixels, resolution, and bit depth. So, what do sampling and quantizing have to do with pixels, resolution, and bit depth? In this chapter, we are going to discuss the relationships among these fundamental concepts and their applications in digital imaging.

To understand pixels, resolution, and bit depth, we need to start with the concepts of sampling and quantizing. In fact, it is only by means of the two-step process of digitization that we ever arrive at pixels, resolution, and bit depth in digital imaging. Although you may not encounter the terms when you use digital imaging applications to work with pixels or manipulate the resolution or bit depth of digital images, you are applying the concepts of sampling and quantizing. Understanding these fundamental concepts and how they are applied to digital images will help you take full advantage of digital media tools and produce predictable results effectively in your creative process.

# 2.2 DIGITIZING IMAGES

Look up and let your eyes fall on the scene in front of you. Draw an imaginary rectangle around what you see. This is your "viewfinder." Imagine that you are going to capture this view on a pegboard. Why a pegboard, you may ask? A pegboard is a good analogy for a digitized image because each peg hole represents a *discrete sample*. In the following sections we will use the pegboard analogy to discuss sampling and quantization in detail.

> *Sampling and Quantizing in Digital Images* An interactive tutorial, complementary to the materials covered in Sections 2.2.1 and 2.2.2, explains sampling and quantizing in digitizing an image.

## 2.2.1 Step 1: Sampling

The natural scenes you see in the world around you are colored in continuous tones. There is no sharp division between one point of color and the next. Each point blends continuously into the next. In this respect, color is an analog phenomenon in human perception. In order to put it into a language that computers can understand, color must be digitized.

> *Pegboard and Resolution* An interactive tutorial using the pegboard as an analogy to explain resolution in capturing and displaying digital images.

The first step of the digitization process is ***sampling***, a process by which you record or sample the color in a natural image at discrete, evenly spaced points. Let's say that Figure 2.1a represents the natural image that you want to capture as a digital image with a digital camera.

Say this image is going to be sampled into a grid of 25 × 20 discrete samples (Figure 2.1b). Using the pegboard analogy, we could say that this image is going to be re-created on a pegboard with 25 × 20 peg holes. The color of each of these discrete samples is averaged to a single uniform value to represent the corresponding area in the image (Figure 2.1c). This 25 × 20 sampled image looks blocky. Details are lost because the grid is too coarse for this image.

In digital imaging, each of these discrete sample points is called a ***picture element***, or ***pixel*** for short. Each pixel stores the color information of the corresponding position on the image. The position is defined by its horizontal and vertical coordinates. ***Pixel dimensions*** refer to the image's width and height in pixels. The dimensions of your resulting digitized image in pixels will be 25 pixels × 20 pixels. In the pegboard analogy, the dimensions of your image in pegs would be 25 pegs × 20 pegs. Note that 25 pixels and 20 pixels are by no means realistic pixel dimensions in digital photography; they are only for illustration purposes here. Most digital cameras can capture images of over several thousand pixels in each dimension—for example, 3,000 pixels × 2,000 pixels.

Why discrete points? See discussion of analog versus digital in Chapter 1.

There are two methods of capturing digital images—scanning and digital photography. The concept of sampling and quantizing applies to both methods, not just digital photography. Topics in capturing digital images are discussed in the Chapter 3.

## MEGAPIXEL

Often, the word ***megapixel*** is associated with the features of a digital camera. One megapixel is equal to 1,000,000 pixels. The total number of pixels in a 3,000 × 2,000-pixel digital image is

$$3,000 \text{ pixels} \times 2,000 \text{ pixels} = 6,000,000 \text{ pixels}$$

This is sometimes referred to as 6 megapixels.

The implication of the megapixel is discussed and explored with a worksheet exercise in Chapter 3.

The relationship between pixel dimension and the image's physical dimension (in inches) is discussed in Chapter 3.

(a)

(b)

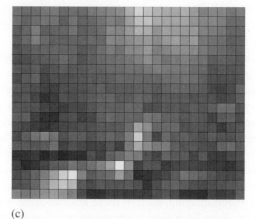

(c)

(d)

(e)

**Figure 2.1** (a) A natural image. (b) Imagine a grid of $25 \times 20$ cells is applied on the image. (c) The color of each of the $25 \times 20$ grid cells is averaged to a single value. (d) Imagine a grid of $100 \times 80$ cells is applied on the image. (e) The color of each of the $100 \times 80$ grid cells is averaged to a single value.  This image can be found on the insert.

How frequently you take a sample is defined by the sampling rate. The words "frequency" and "rate" are often associated with time. However, for an image, *frequency* refers to how close neighboring samples are in a 2-D image plane. If you sample the image with a finer grid than in the previous example, say $100 \times 80$ (Figures 2.1d and 2.1e), you are using a higher sampling rate because you are sampling more frequently within the same spatial distance. In digital imaging, increasing the sampling rate increases the image **resolution**. With higher resolution, you have more samples (pixels) to represent the same scene and thus you capture more details from the original scene (Figure 2.2). The pixel dimensions of the captured image are increased, and so is the file size of the digitized image.

(a)　　　　(b)

Figure 2.2 The relative sizes of an image 25 pixels $\times$ 20 pixels (left) and 100 pixels $\times$ 80 pixels (right) captured from the same scene. ▟ This image can be found on the insert.

## A PIXEL IS A PIXEL IS A POINT SAMPLE—NOT A LITTLE SQUARE BLOCK

When you zoom in on a digital image in an image editing program, you often see the pixels represented as little square blocks. However, keep in mind that a pixel is a sample at a single point; it is a point sample that does not really have a *physical* dimension associated with it.

## 2.2.2 Step 2: Quantizing

A natural image is colored in continuous tones, and thus it theoretically has an infinite number of colors. The discrete and finite language of the computer restricts the reproduction of an infinite number of colors and shades. The process of mapping an infinite number of possibilities—that is, an infinite number of colors and shades in the case of digital imaging—to a finite list of numbers—that is, a finite number of color codes in the case of digital imaging—is called *quantization*.

Before mapping the color of each pixel to a discrete and precise value, you need to consider how many possible colors you want to use in the image. To illustrate this process, let's revisit the example of the sampled image in Figure 2.1 and continue on to the quantization step.

Suppose the color of each sample in the 100-pixels × 80-pixels image (Figure 2.1e) is quantized into one of four discrete colors (Figure 2.3a) by mapping it to the closest color. Figure 2.4a shows the resulting quantized image. This 4-color palette obviously does not provide sufficient color levels for this scene.

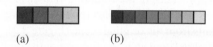

(a)                        (b)

**Figure 2.3** (a) A 4-color palette. (b) An 8-color palette. This image can be found on the insert.

(a)                                                    (b)

**Figure 2.4** The sampled image is quantized into (a) four colors, and (b) eight colors. This image can be found on the insert.

The image fidelity and details are lost because different colors from the original are now mapped to the same color on the palette. For example, the area in the outlined square in Figure 2.5b is made up of many different green colors. The same area in the 4-color image (Figure 2.5a) now has only one color. The details that rely on the subtle color differences are lost during quantization.

## YOU MAY ASK: WHY THE CHOICE OF THOSE FOUR OR EIGHT PARTICULAR COLORS?

The palette does not have to be restricted to those exact four or eight colors. The 4-color and 8-color palettes in this example all contain shades of green because the original scene is mainly green. However, you do not have to use only green colors for a scene like this. For any images, no matter what colors you choose, the bit depth for four colors is always 2 bits, and the bit depth for eight colors is always 3 bits. The actual colors included in the palette, however, may vary depending on the user's choice.

(a)                                                    (b)

**Figure 2.5**  (a) The colors in the original image (b) are quantized into four colors using the palette shown in Figure 2.3a. Some of the similar green colors, such as those in the outlined square box, are now mapped to a single color. ▄▄ This image can be found on the insert.

The number of colors used for quantization is related to the ***color depth*** or ***bit depth*** of the digital image. A bit depth of $n$ allows $2^n$ different colors. Therefore, a 2-bit digital image allows $2^2$ (i.e., 4) colors in the image.

## USING BINARY BITS TO REPRESENT COLORS ON COMPUTERS

Internally, a computer uses the binary system to represent colors. For example, for 2-bit color, the binary bits for the four colors are 00, 01, 10, and 11.

| Bit 2 | Bit 1 |
|:-----:|:-----:|
| 0 | 0 |
| 0 | 1 |
| 1 | 0 |
| 1 | 1 |

Then, will increasing the number of colors in the palette improve the image fidelity? The answer is: it depends, and in most cases, yes. The number of colors or the bit depth is not the only determining factor for image fidelity in quantizing an image; the choice of colors for the quantization also plays an important role in the reproduction of an image.

To illustrate the importance of the choice of colors in the palette, let's increase the bit depth to 3 ($2^3 = 8$ colors). An 8-color palette (Figure 2.6a) that is drastically different from the overall colors of the original natural image will be used. The resulting quantized image with this new palette is shown in Figure 2.6b.

The 8-color image (Figure 2.6b) that is quantized using a drastic 8-color palette does not look any closer to the original scene than the 4-color one (Figure 2.4a) that is quantized

**Figure 2.6** (a) Using a different 8-color palette, (b) the sampled image is quantized. This image can be found on the insert.

using a 4-color palette made up of green shades. Although the larger palette increases the image detail a little in certain areas—for example, in the sky and the water areas—by allowing more levels of color distinction, the colors are not faithful to the original image.

## 24-BIT, 32-BIT, AND 48-BIT COLOR DEPTH

A single 8-bit byte can be used to represent one of 256 different possible values. The values range from 0 to 255. An RGB (red, green, blue) color can be represented in three 8-bit bytes, one byte for each component of the R, G, and B. Thus, in this case, the color depth is *24 bits,* which means it allows $2^{24} = 16,777,216$ colors. Each of the R, G, and B components allows $2^8$ levels—that is, 256 levels (from 0 to 255).

Although 24-bit color is often sufficient for human vision to represent colors, as computer processors get faster and storage media get cheaper, higher color depth (such as 48-bit color) is increasingly supported by scanners and image editing programs. Forty-eight-bit RGB color is represented using 16 bits per component of R, G, and B.

### Questions[*]
1. How many possible colors can be represented with 48-bit color depth?
2. How many possible levels of red can be represented with 48-bit RGB color?
3. How many times would a file size increase by going from 24-bit to 48-bit color?

A *32-bit* image is basically 24-bit RGB with an additional 8-bit alpha channel. The alpha channel is used to specify the level of transparency. Unlike 24-bit images that are fully opaque, 32-bit images can be smoothly blended with other images.

### Question
4. How many levels of transparency does an 8-bit alpha channel allow?

---

[*] Answers to Questions: (1) $2^{48}$; (2) $2^{16}$; (3) double; (4) $2^8$, i.e., 256.

## 2.3 BITMAPPED IMAGES

Each pixel contains the color information using numeric values, which can be represented by a sequence of bits—1s and 0s. A 1-bit image allows two ($2^1$) colors, which can be represented by 1 and 0. The digit 1 can be used to designate a particular color and 0 another color. For example, a simple single-color diagonal line on a solid-color background can be represented in 1s and 0s, as shown in Figure 2.7.

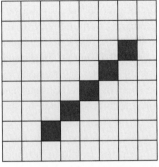

| | | | | | | | |
|---|---|---|---|---|---|---|---|
| 1 | 1 | 1 | 1 | 1 | 1 | 1 | 1 |
| 1 | 1 | 1 | 1 | 1 | 1 | 1 | 1 |
| 1 | 1 | 1 | 1 | 1 | 1 | 0 | 1 |
| 1 | 1 | 1 | 1 | 1 | 0 | 1 | 1 |
| 1 | 1 | 1 | 1 | 0 | 1 | 1 | 1 |
| 1 | 1 | 1 | 0 | 1 | 1 | 1 | 1 |
| 1 | 1 | 0 | 1 | 1 | 1 | 1 | 1 |
| 1 | 1 | 1 | 1 | 1 | 1 | 1 | 1 |

**Figure 2.7** For each pixel in a 1-bit (i.e., 2-color) bitmap image, its color value can be represented by 0s and 1s. ■ This image can be found on the insert.

Digital images described by pixel values such as the one shown in Figure 2.7 are called **bitmapped** images. The term *bitmapping* refers to how these bits representing the image are stored in computer memory. Bitmapped images also are called **raster graphics**. The term *rastering* refers to the way most video displays translate the images into a series of horizontal lines on the screen.

Bitmapped images commonly are used in image editing applications. Because they are composed of pixels, the image content can be edited pixel by pixel easily. However, their size and appearance depend on their output resolution to the device, for example, dots per inch for a monitor and pixels per inch for a printer. Bitmapped images can appear jagged when they're scaled up onscreen or printed at a low resolution.

## 2.4 VECTOR GRAPHICS

Besides using pixels to describe digital images, there is another way to create imagery—it is to describe the graphic mathematically. This type of digital image is called a **vector graphic**. For example, to describe a line like the one in Figure 2.8, you can use a simple equation. Using equations to represent graphics is more concise than bitmapping. Consider this analogy in the context of getting directions for a trip: Bitmapped images are like getting driving directions on a printed Google map. Vector graphics, on the other hand, are analogous to written directions. Instead of tracing out a route on a map, someone could give you written directions that say, for example, "Head southwest on N Main St toward W Dalton Rd. When you come to the stoplight, turn right. Go past the mall and turn at the first entrance to the restaurant." It may take you more time to translate the written directions into a mental image of where you're going, as compared to understanding a map that is already in visual form. An advantage of the written directions, however, is that they might actually be more concise and require less space than a full printed map.

In certain contexts, a bitmap refers to an image with 1 bit per pixel; that is, each pixel has a value of either 0 or 1. The term *pixmap* is used for the image that uses more than 1 bit for each pixel; that is, the image has more than two colors. In this book, the term *bitmap* or *bitmapped images* refers to all pixel-based images.

Similarly, vector graphics are generally more concise descriptions of digital images than bitmaps are. But the most distinct advantage of vector graphics is that they are resolution independent. Let's explain what resolution independence means and what characteristic of vector graphics makes them resolution independent.

In contrast to bitmapped images that already have the number of pixels or resolution specified when they are stored, vector graphics do not use pixels but equations. The images of vector graphics are produced for output or display by calculating the points, according to the equations that make up the graphics. The coordinate system for the equations is arbitrary. That is, its scale can be set to any level. Vector graphics are resolution independent because they can be scaled to any size and printed on any output device at any resolution, without losing detail or clarity in the picture. To illustrate resolution independence, let's return to the analogy of driving directions versus a map. You can produce a map from written directions at any size you want simply by following the description to draw on any size of paper. However, to scale a printed map into the size you want, you may need to rescale it on a photocopier. This will produce a fuzzy reproduction of the map, no matter whether you are blowing it up or shrinking it down.

Examples of vector graphic application programs are Adobe Illustrator, Adobe Flash, and CorelDRAW.

Consider a simple example of vector graphics, a line. A line can be described mathematically with an equation. In vector graphic programs, a line is defined by two end points (Figure 2.8a). A line can be stroked at a certain width, but it is still a vector graphic. When you zoom in on the line on a computer display, the line is still clear (Figure 2.8b). When the line is rasterized to a bitmapped image at a low resolution, as shown in Figure 2.8c, zooming in on the line will show that it is jagged. If the same vector graphic line is rasterized to a bitmapped image at a higher resolution setting (Figure 2.8d), the rasterized line appears smoother than the one from the lower resolution, although it still appears jagged.

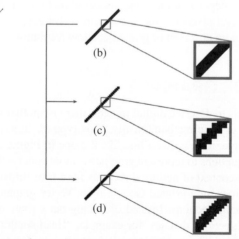

(a)

(b)

(c)

(d)

**Figure 2.8** Vector graphics and rasterized bitmapped images: (a) A line defined by two end points. (b) The line stroked at a certain width. (c) The line rasterized at a low resolution. (d) The line rasterized at a higher resolution.

## RASTERIZING VECTOR GRAPHICS

Most vector graphics programs let you *rasterize*, or convert, vector graphics into pixel-based bitmapped images. Because you are making a resolution-independent vector graphic into a resolution-dependent image, you need to specify a resolution for rasterizing, that is, how coarse or how fine the sampling.

The rasterized image will appear jagged. This jagged effect is a form of *aliasing* caused by undersampling or insufficient sampling rate. In addition, as you see in Figure 2.9b, the high contrast between black and white pixels makes the effect very noticeable. To soften the jaggedness, we can color the pixels with intermediary shades in the areas where the sharp color changes occur (Figure 2.9c). This technique is called *anti-aliasing*. With the same raster resolution setting, you can make the rasterized graphics appear smoother with anti-aliasing than without.

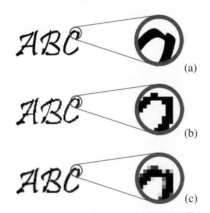

(a)

(b)

(c)

**Figure 2.9**  Vector graphics versus rasterized graphics: (a) Edges still appear smooth at higher magnification. (b) Rasterized vector graphic without anti-aliasing. (c) Rasterized vector graphic with anti-aliasing.

## 2.5 FILE TYPES OF DIGITAL IMAGES

The file types you will most commonly see and use are given in the Tables 2.1 and 2.2.

## 2.6 DIGITAL IMAGE FILE SIZE AND OPTIMIZATION

An image with a higher resolution or higher bit depth has a larger file size. Thus, to reduce the storage space requirement and allow faster download over the Internet, the file size of an image may be reduced by lowering its resolution or bit depth. However, if the image resolution and bit depth have to be maintained, the file size of an image can be reduced by applying compression.

**TABLE 2.1 Common File Types of Bitmapped or Pixel-Based Images**

| File Type | File Suffix | Standard Color Modes | Use | Compression |
|---|---|---|---|---|
| JPEG (Joint Photographic Experts Group) | .jpg or .jpeg | RGB, CMYK | • Best for continuous-tone images, such as photographs<br>• Can be used for Web images | Lossy compression method called JPEG compression that works well with photographs |
| GIF (Graphics Interchange Format) | .gif | Indexed color, grayscale | • Supports up to 8-bit color, best for illustration graphics or cartoon-like pictures with large areas of solid color and clear divisions between color areas<br>• A proprietary format of CompuServe<br>• Can be used for Web images<br>• Allows transparency of one designated color | Lossless compression method called LZW compression |
| PNG (Portable Network Graphics) | .png | RGB, indexed, grayscale, black and white | • Supports 8-bit and 24-bit color<br>• Can be used for Web images<br>• Allows variable transparency | Lossless compression |
| PICT (Macintosh Picture Format) | .pict | RGB, indexed, grayscale, black and white | Used on Mac OS | Allows JPEG compression |
| BMP (Bitmapped Picture) | .bmp | RGB, indexed, grayscale, black and white | Used on Windows | Allows run-length encoding compression (lossless) |
| TIFF (Tag Image File Format) | .tif or .tiff | RGB, CMYK, CIE-Lab, indexed, grayscale, black and white | • Supported on both Windows and Mac OS<br>• A common file format for digital imaging<br>• Supports alpha channel and layers | Allows uncompressed, LZW compression (lossless), ZIP (lossless), and JPEG (lossy) |
| PSD (Photoshop Digital Image) | .psd | RGB, CMYK, CIE-Lab, indexed, grayscale, black and white | • Proprietary format of Adobe Photoshop<br>• Good for any types of digital images that Photoshop supports<br>• Stores layers<br>• Supports alpha channel | Lossless compression |

**TABLE 2.2    Common File Types of Vector Graphics**

| File Type | File Suffix | Information and Use |
|---|---|---|
| Encapsulated PostScript | .eps | Standard file format for storing and exchanging files in professional printing |
| Adobe Illustrator file | .ai | |
| Adobe Flash file | .fla, .swf | |
| Windows Metafile format | .wmf | Many clip arts from Microsoft Office are in this format |
| Enhanced Metafile format | .emf | Developed by Microsoft as a successor to .wmf |

Let's look at the file size of a typical digital photograph without compression. A 6-megapixel digital camera can produce digital images of 3,000 × 2,000 pixels in 24-bit color depth. The uncompressed file size can be computed as follows:

Total pixels: 3,000 × 2,000 pixels = 6,000,000 pixels

File size in bits: 6,000,000 pixels × 24 bits/pixel = 144,000,000 bits

File size in bytes: 144,000,000 bits/(8 bits/byte) = 18,000,000 bytes

An uncompressed 6-megapixel image would require 144,000,000 bits, which is 18,000,000 bytes of disk space. There are three ways to reduce the file size of a digital image—reduce its pixel dimensions, lower its bit depth, and compress the file.

(1) **Reducing the pixel dimensions:**

This can be achieved by either of the following:

(a) Capture the image at a lower resolution in the first place.

- If you are capturing the image by scanning, use a lower scanning dpi. The scanned image will have smaller pixel dimensions.
- If you are capturing the image by digital photography and your camera has an option for the image size, you can set a smaller image size—lowering the pixel dimensions of the digital photo.

(b) Resample, or scale, the existing digital image to lower pixel dimensions.

As you see in the file size calculation, the file size is directly proportional to the number of pixels in an image. This means that reducing the number of pixels in half will lower the file size to half of the original.

**Exercise**[*]: The pixel dimensions of the image used in this example of file size calculation are 3,000 × 2,000 pixels. If you scale both the width and height of this image to half (i.e., 1,500 × 1,000 pixels), how much will the file size be reduced?

The destined pixel dimension you choose depends on the amount of detail you need in your image and your intended use of the image—that is, whether you intend to print out the picture or display it on a computer. Lowering the pixel dimension sacrifices the image detail, which affects the image quality. Therefore, in reducing the pixel dimension to reduce file size, you need to weigh the image detail against the file size.

---

[*] **Answer:** The number of pixels in the original image = 3,000 × 2,000 = 6,000,000. The number of pixels in the resized image = 1,500 × 1,000 = 1,500,000. Thus, the file size is reduced to one-fourth (not one-half) of the original.

(2) **Lowering the bit depth:**

The bit depth determines the number of distinct colors available in your image. The available options of bit depth given to you during capturing depend on your scanner or digital camera. At the time of writing this chapter, the most common bit depth for color digital images is 24 bits. The 48-bit option is also available.

As shown in the file size calculation for a 6-megapixel, 24-bit image, the bit depth is multiplied by the total number of pixels. This means that the file size is directly proportional to the bit depth. For example, reducing the bit depth from 24 bits to 8 bits will reduce the file size to one-third of the original. Depending on the content of your image, lowering the bit depth from 24 bits to 8 bits may produce a very noticeable degradation of the image's aesthetics. Lowering the bit depth from 48 bits to 24 bits will reduce the file size to half but the degradation of the image may not be as noticeable.

## WEIGHING BIT DEPTH AGAINST FILE SIZE

A color depth of 24 bits allows $2^{24}$ (i.e., 16,777,216) colors—about 16 million colors; 8 bits allows $2^8$ (i.e., 256) colors. In reducing 24-bit to 8-bit color depth, you can reduce the file size to one-third. However, you reduce the number of colors from 16,777,216 to 256. That is, you lose more than 16 million allowable colors in the image—this is about a factor of 65,000 decrease—to trade for a factor of 3 decrease in file size.

On the other hand, some images do not need more than 256 colors. You do not have to keep a higher bit depth than the image needs.

- Grayscale images, such as scanned images of black-and-white photos and hand-written notes in pen or pencil, can have a bit depth of 8 bits without much notice-able degradation in image quality.
- Some handwritten notes even may be reduced to 2-bit or 1-bit color depth.
- An illustration graphic, such as a poster or logo, that contains only a few colors as large areas of solid colors can benefit from a lower bit depth. If you capture these graphics, whether by scanning or digital photography, solid colors (such as in Figure 2.10) will become continuous tones. In this case, if you consolidate all these slightly different colors into the one single color it is supposed to be, you may be able to reduce the bit depth, thus reducing the file size. The additional advantage of doing so is that the resulting digital image actually will be more faithful to the large areas of solid colors in the original analog source.

**Figure 2.10** A 24-bit scanned image from a book cover has a supposedly solid blue background. The zoomed-in view would show that it is now made up of many slightly different colors although the differences may not show up well here in a printed copy.

## FILE SIZES OF DIGITAL IMAGES

In a 24-bit color image, you use 8 bits to store each of the red, green, and blue components. In principle, with the same pixel dimensions, the file size of a 24-bit image file is three times as large as that for a grayscale image (8-bit). The following exercises will help you confirm your answer.

### Activity/Exercise

If you have access to Adobe Photoshop, create a new file of 12 × 10 pixels. Convert the image to grayscale by selecting `Image > Mode > Grayscale`. Save the image as a RAW file format by selecting `File > Save As . . . .` In the Save dialog box, choose Photoshop Raw (`*.RAW`) for the file format, and name the file grayscale.raw. What do you think the file size of this grayscale.raw is?

> Check out the file size.
> (For Windows: Right-click on the file and choose Properties.)
> (For Mac: Select the file and hit Command-I.)
> **Answer:** The file size of grayscale.raw is 120 bytes (12 × 10 pixels, and each pixel uses 1 byte [8 bits] to hold its gray value).

> Now convert the original image to 24-bit color by selecting `Image > Mode > RGB Color`. Save the image as rgb.raw. What do you think the file size of this rgb.raw is?

> Check out the file size.
> **Answer:** The file size of rgb.raw is 360 bytes (12 × 10 pixels × 3 bytes per pixel; 1 byte for red color information, 1 for green, and 1 for blue.)

> In a raw file, 1 byte is used for each pixel in a grayscale picture, and 3 bytes are used for each pixel in a 24-bit image. What if you save the image as another format, such as .PSD, .BMP, or .TIF? The file size changes because the other file formats may embed additional image information in the file, such as dimensions. (Try opening in Adobe Photoshop the .raw file you have created. Notice that it prompts you for the pixel dimensions of the image and other information. But it does not prompt you for such information if you are opening a .PSD or a .BMP file.) In addition, some file formats are compressed using image compression algorithms. Therefore, unlike raw files, the file sizes for the image files in these different formats are difficult to predict by doing simple math. However, it is generally true that the following factors will increase the file size of a digital image:

> - Larger pixel dimensions of the image
> - Higher bit depth

(3) **Compressing the file:**

Compression is a method for reducing the size of a file by squeezing the same information into fewer bits. In a lossless compression algorithm, no information is lost. In a lossy compression algorithm, some information is lost. Lossy algorithms, however, are usually designed so that the information to be left out is the information that the human sensory system is not sensitive to anyway.

When you choose a format in which to save a digital image, you are implicitly choosing whether and how to compress the file. When you scan in a picture, you might be given the option of opening it with an image editing program or saving it as a

TIFF file, bitmapped picture, JPEG file, or GIF file. The file type is identified by a suffix on the file name: .tif or .tiff for a TIFF file, .bmp for a bitmapped picture, .jpg or .jpeg for a JPEG file, and .gif for a Graphics Interchange Format.

Generally, when working with digital images, it is best to keep the image in an uncompressed format. If you want to compress the image when you are still in the editing stage, you should use only a lossless compression method. For example, you can scan a color picture in as a TIFF file and open it in an image editing program to work on its tonal adjustment, contrast, color enhancement, refinements, and composition. After you have made the desired changes, you should save a copy of this final image either uncompressed or with lossless compression. When you are ready to save the image for distribution, you can choose a different file type with compression, even lossy, as is suitable for the intended use of the image. The file format depends on the type and use of the picture. For the Web, you can save the image as a JPEG, GIF, or PNG file. In the case of JPEG files, you also can choose the extent to which you want the file compressed, trading off image quality for a file size that is suitable for your needs.

## AN EXAMPLE OF LOSSLESS COMPRESSION

More extensive coverage of the RLE algorithm and other compression algorithms can be found in the CS Module of this book series.

Run-length encoding (RLE) is an example of a simple lossless compression algorithm. In this method, a sequence of the same repeated value is replaced by one instance of the value followed by the number of times it is repeated. For example, suppose that a blue color is represented in 8 bits as 00001010. If there is a section of sky in a digital image where blue is repeated for 100 pixels, then with no compression this section would take up 800 bits. With run-length encoding, this section could be encoded as one instance of blue—00001010—followed by the number 100 in binary (01100100). Instead of 800 bits, it now uses 16 bits.

This type of compression is used in .bmp files. For example, the file size of an uncompressed .bmp file of 100 × 100 pixels is 11,080 bytes. If the image contains only one single color, the file size can be reduced to 1,480 bytes with RLE compression. If the image contains two color blocks (Figure 2.11), the file size is 1,680 bytes with RLE compression.

Figure 2.11 A bitmapped image containing two color blocks.

## 2.7 COLOR REPRESENTATION

Color models are used to describe colors numerically, usually in terms of varying amounts of primary colors. Each model uses a different method and a set of primaries to describe colors. The most common color models are RGB, CMYK, HSB, and CIE and their variants.

### 2.7.1 RGB Color Model

In the *RGB color model*, the three primary colors are red, green, and blue. Red light added with green light gives yellow; green and blue gives cyan; blue and red gives magenta (Figure 2.12). Adding full intensity of all red, green, and blue light gives white. This model is appropriate to the physiology of the human eye, which has receptors for the three components.

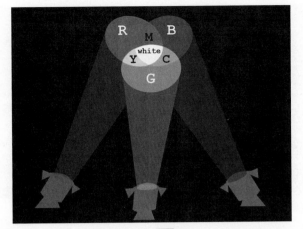

**Figure 2.12** RGB: An additive color system. 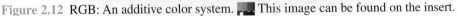 This image can be found on the insert.

## THE HUMAN EYE'S RESPONSE TO COLOR

The wavelengths of visible light range from about 380 to 700 nm (nanometers)—creating a continuous spectrum of rainbow color, from the violet end (380 nm) to the red end (700 nm). A particular wavelength in this spectrum corresponds to a particular color.

The retina of the human eye has two categories of light receptors: rods and cones. Rods are active in dim light but have no color sensitivity. Cones are active in bright light and have color sensitivity. There are three types of cones. Roughly speaking, one type is sensitive to red, one to green, and one to blue. They are designated by Greek letters *rho* ($\rho$), *gamma* ($\gamma$), and *beta* ($\beta$), respectively. The curves representing the relative sensitivity of these three receptors for the normal human eye are shown in Figure 2.13. The $\gamma$ and $\beta$ cone types correspond quite closely to green and blue regions.

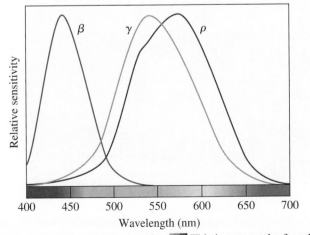

**Figure 2.13** Human spectral sensitivity to color. 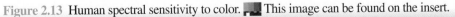 This image can be found on the insert.

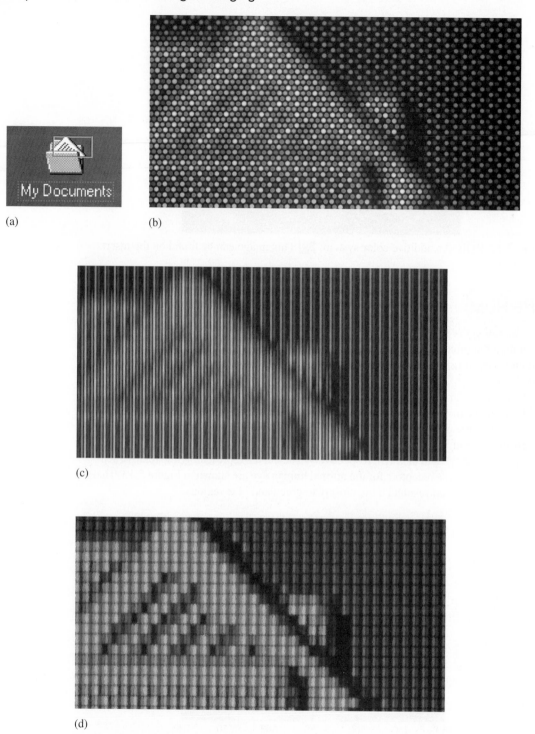

Figure 2.14 Computer monitors: (a) An image displayed with an outlined rectangle where the close-up photographs (b) through (d) were taken. (b) Close-up of a standard monitor screen. (c) Close-up view of a SONY Trinitron monitor screen. (d) Close-up view of an LCD display. ▄▄ This image can be found on the insert.

For computer monitors, colors are represented by points of light. They can be designed so that each pixel's color results from combined beams of red, green, and blue light. Computers are therefore based on an ***additive color system***, where the more colored light is blended in, the higher the overall light intensity. The close-up views of two CRT monitors and an LCD display shown in the color insert for Figure 2.14 show the dots and bands of red, green, and blue light. Despite the different shapes and patterns of the light spots used in the different displays, each pixel's color of the image is displayed by combined beams of red, green, and blue light of various intensity.

The RGB color model can be depicted graphically as a cube defined by three axes in 3-D space, as illustrated in Figure 2.15. The *x*-axis represents the red values, the *y*-axis the green values, and the *z*-axis the blue values. The origin (0, 0, 0) of the RGB color cube corresponds to black because all three colors have zero intensity. The corners of the cube correspond to red, green, blue, and their complementary colors— cyan, magenta, and yellow—respectively. The corresponding 24-bit RGB color mode in digital image editing programs allows values ranging from 0 to 255 for each of the three components, which also is referred to as a channel. Each channel uses 8 bits. In this case, white has an RGB value of (255, 255, 255). An RGB value of (255, 166, 38) is a light orange color.

> 🖰 **RGB Color Cube** An interactive tutorial lets you select a color and display its location in the 3-D space of the RGB color cube. You can drag to rotate the color cube to examine the color location.

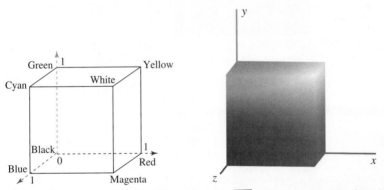

**Figure 2.15** An illustration of the RGB color cube. ▪▪ This image can be found on the insert.

## CORRELATING RGB COLOR CUBE WITH COLOR PICKERS

If you have worked with digital image editing programs such as Adobe Photoshop, you should have worked with color pickers like the one shown in Figure 2.16.

The color picker is often represented as a 2-D plane made up with gradients of colors. If you choose one of the R, G, or B components in the color picker, the vertical color slider displays the range of color for that component (0 is at the bottom of the slider and 255 is at the top). The 2-D plane next to the slider is a color field that displays all the colors that have the same R value but with varying values of other two color components, which are represented as the *x*- and *y*-axes. For example, if you click the red component (R), the color slider displays the range of color for red. A circle on the color field corresponds to the current selected color. This color has the red value equal to the selected

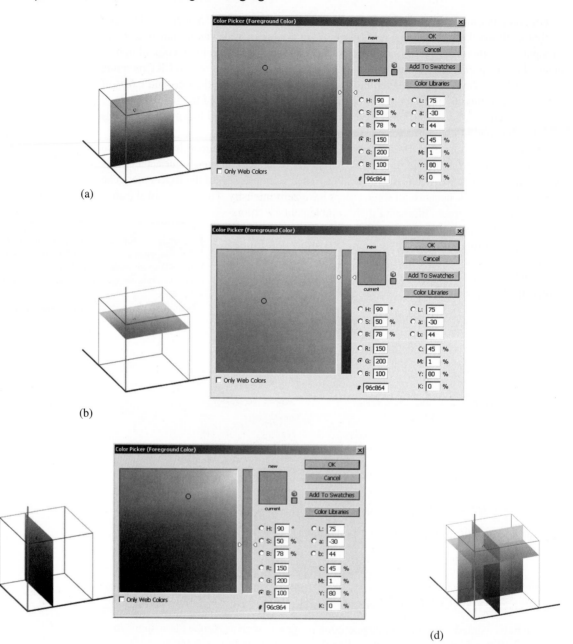

**Figure 2.16** Relationship between an RGB color cube and the color picker used in digital image applications. This image can be found on the insert.

value on the color slider. Its green and blue values correspond to the x and y coordinates of the circle on the color field.

The RGB value is a 3-D coordinate of that color within the 3-D space of the cube. The color field is only a rectangular slice from the RGB color cube. Let's take a color with an RGB value of (150, 200, 100) as an example. If you click on the R component, the color field is a 2-D slice from the RGB color cube at R = 150 (Figure 2.16a) with the green axis as the *y*-axis and the blue axis as the *x*-axis. All the colors on this color field has the red value of 150. This works analogously for the selection of the G and B components (Figures 2.16b and 2.16c).

As you see in Figure 2.16, the same color can be found on three different color fields or slices. You see one color field at a time in Photoshop's color picker. The choice of the color axis determines which color field is displayed in the color picker. If you imagine that all three slices are showing in the color cube, they intersect at a single point in space (Figure 2.16d). The 3-D coordinate of this intersection point is the RGB value of the selected color.

## 2.7.2 CMYK Color Model

At some point in your art education, you may have been told that you could create nearly any color by mixing red, yellow, and blue painting media—crayons, watercolor, oil paint, or acrylics. These three colors are the primary colors in a *subtractive color model*. The model is subtractive because the more color pigment you layer

> 🖰 Color Value Appraisal Be a "color value appraiser" and see how accurately you can estimate a color's "color value" in RGB.

on top or mix together, the more light you subtract out. Therefore, in theory, layering or mixing equal amounts of all three primaries should give you black.

In the *CMYK color model*, the three primaries are magenta, yellow, and cyan (Figure 2.17) instead of red, yellow, and blue. CMYK stands for cyan, magenta, yellow, and black. Mixing cyan with magenta gives blue; magenta with yellow gives red; and yellow with cyan gives green. In theory, mixing cyan, magenta, and yellow produces black. The CMY are the colors that are complementary to red, green, and blue, respectively. This means that mixing cyan with red gives black. This is the same for mixing magenta with green or yellow with blue.

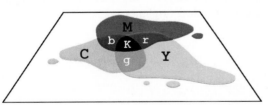

**Figure 2.17** CMYK: A subtractive color system. In theory, mixing cyan, magenta, and yellow gives black. ▄▆ This image can be found on the insert.

The printing process is essentially a subtractive process, and CMYK is a subtractive color model. When one ink is added on top of another, it can effectively cause its complementary color not to be reflected. In that sense, the color is being subtracted out. Each of these components is specified in percentages.

In theory, (100%, 100%, 100%) gives black. In practice, due to the imperfections in the inks, (100%, 100%, 100%) actually gives a rather muddy brownish kind of black, not a deep black. The last component, K (black), is added to overcome this problem. In addition, using black ink in place of equal amounts of the three color inks is also a cost-effective choice.

### 2.7.3 HSB Color Model

Although RGB corresponds well to the technology of computer displays and the physiology of the human eye, it is not necessarily the most natural way for us to think about color. When you have a color in mind, you would probably describe it in terms of its hue first, such as a color found in a rainbow. Then, you would describe its brightness. However, it is not intuitive to think in terms of how much of each of the red, green, and blue components makes up the color.

An alternative to RGB is to specify a color by its hue, saturation, and brightness:

- *Hue* is the basic color based on the colors in a rainbow.
- *Saturation* is the intensity or purity of the color—essentially how far away from the neutral gray of the same brightness. As a color's saturation value decreases, it looks more washed out until eventually it becomes the neutral gray of the corresponding brightness.
- *Brightness* defines the lightness or darkness of the color. The lower the brightness value of a color is, the more it moves toward black.

This model matches well with the way humans intuitively think about colors. The *HSB* (or HSV) *color model* is this type of model, as is the HSL (or HLS) model. There are some differences between the mathematical representations of HSL and HSB, but they are built upon the same concepts of hue, saturation, and brightness.

As shown in Figure 2.18a, the HSB or HSV model looks like an inverted pyramid or cone with six sides—a hexacone. Arranged on a color wheel (Figure 2.18c) is a spectrum of color from red, yellow, green, cyan, blue, to purple and back to red.

- The color or the hue (H) is expressed as a degree between 0° (starting from red) and 360° (back to red again) to indicate its location on a color wheel in the order of the colors in a rainbow.
- The saturation (S) is expressed in the percentage of distance from the center of the color wheel. The color at the center of the color wheel is a fully desaturated color—a gray color of the corresponding brightness.

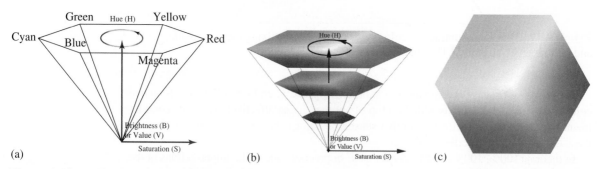

**Figure 2.18** (a) Hexacone of the HSB or HSV color model. (b) Hexacone with selected slices at different levels of brightness or value. (c) A slice of the color wheel from the HSB or HSV color model. ▄▄ This image can be found on the insert.

- The vertical axis is the brightness (B) or value (V). The higher the brightness or value is, the lighter the color. For example, at B = 0%, the color is black no matter what the values for saturation and hue are. At B = 100%, all colors are at their brightest. White is located at the center of the color wheel at B = 100%.

> ✎ **RGB Color Cube to HSV** A QuickTime movie illustrating the relationship between the RGB color cube and the HSV hexacone.

## HSB VERSUS HSL

HSL stands for hue, saturation, and luminance. The HSL color model is similar to the HSB model. In HSL, the most saturated colors can be found at L = 50%, which is compared to B = 100% in the HSB color model (Figure 2.19). At L = 0%, the color is black no matter what the hue and saturation are. Unlike the HSB color model, the color at L = 100% in HSL is white no matter what the hue and saturation are.

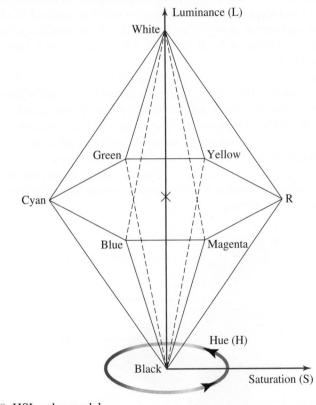

**Figure 2.19** HSL color model.

## 2.7.4 CIE XYZ

In 1931, the Commission Internationale d'Eclairage (CIE) worked out a color system to encompass all of the colors that are visible to average humans. It uses three "virtual primaries" designated as X, Y, and Z. These primaries are not any physical colors. With these primaries as the base, it is possible to graphically depict a color gamut to encompass all visible colors.

The CIE color model has evolved into new variants, but it is still the standard to which all other color models are compared, because its color space encompasses all of the colors humans can see.

## COLOR GAMUTS: VISIBLE COLORS, RGB, AND CMYK

A chromaticity diagram, as illustrated in Figure 2.20, often is used to define, compare, and explain *color gamuts* and *color spaces*. Color gamut refers to the range of colors that a specific system can produce or capture. Color space is defined by a color gamut and a color model that is used to describe the colors.

The given diagram is constructed based on the CIE XYZ color space. The colors encompassed in the horseshoe shape include all the colors visible to humans. The boundary line of this horseshoe shape follows the visible color spectrum. Because no printing device can output all of the visible colors, the colors you see in the color insert of this figure only give you a rough idea of the distribution of colors within this color space.

Figure 2.20 is used here to show you a comparison of RGB and CMYK color gamuts. As you see, the combination of the R, G, and B light sources cannot duplicate the full gamut of human vision.

CMYK printers normally have smaller gamuts (Figure 2.20c) than RGB monitors (Figure 2.20b). When printing a digital image, the colors that are out of the color gamut of the printer are mapped to other colors within the printer's color gamut. Note that the three corners of the RGB color gamut that contain the most saturated colors are outside of the CMYK gamut. This means that those highly saturated colors in your digital images may look bright and saturated on your computer but may appear a little duller when printed from an inkjet printer or an offset printer in a professional print shop. Printers with more than four colors (such as 6-color printers with additional light cyan and light magenta) can have larger gamuts.

Note that although the CMYK gamut is smaller than the RGB gamut, some CMYK colors are outside of the RGB gamut.

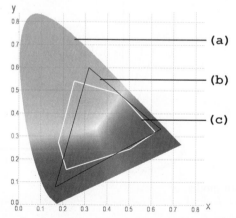

**Figure 2.20** An illustration for color gamut comparison: (a) A CIE chromaticity diagram. (b) RGB color gamut of typical CRT monitors. The exact shape of the device's color space depends on the monitor's red, green, and blue phosphors. Note that this does not include all the colors humans can see. (c) CMYK color gamut of typical inkjet printers. The exact shape of the color space depends on the colorants of the printer's ink. This image can be found on the insert.

## 2.7.5 Other Color Models

When working with digital images, you also may see a reference to the L*a*b*, YUV, or YIQ color models. These color models divide color into one luminance (brightness) component and two chrominance (color) components.

The YUV or YIQ models are not used in image editing, but you may read about them with regard to JPEG image compression, video standard, and television transmission. Originally, both the YUV and YIQ models were found to be useful in television transmission (when color TV was invented), because these models separate out the information needed for black-and-white transmission (all contained in the Y component) from that needed for color. The same signal could then be used for both types of television. YUV was originally the color model for video transmission in Europe under the PAL standard. YIQ is the model adopted by the National Television System Committee (NTSC) in the United States.

The advantages of the YIQ and YUV models in data compression have to do with the way the human eye perceives color. Human vision is more sensitive to differences in luminance than differences in chrominance. Thus, it is possible to reduce the amount of detail in the chrominance information by using a smaller data size for these components. This makes the image data more compact in size.

You may encounter the L*a*b* color model in your work with digital images. Like YUV and YIQ, this model has one luminance component (L*) and two chrominance components (a* ranging from green to red, and b* ranging from blue to yellow). Based on the original CIE model, L*a*b* has the advantage of allowing you to create device-independent colors. That is, with L*a*b* and proper calibration of the devices (displays and printers), you can ensure that the color you see on your computer will be faithfully reproduced on another computer display and printer—assuming that the colors are within the gamut for the device.

## 2.8  COLOR MODES

When you work in an image editing program, there are choices of color modes. For example, the color modes available in Photoshop include RGB color, CMYK color, Lab color, grayscale, bitmap, Duotone, indexed color, and Multichannel. You use one color mode at a time for your image file, but you can switch between different color modes during the image editing process.

Some color modes in digital image processing programs are based on the color models, but color modes differ from color models. Color modes specify which color model is used to display and print the image you're working on. They also determine the number of colors and the number of channels for the image you are working on.

For example, there are three channels in the RGB color mode—one for red, one for green, and one for blue. In most situations, each channel's default color depth is 8 bits, making the RGB mode 24 bits ($2^{24} = 16,777,216$ colors) in this case. In the grayscale color mode, there is only one channel. By default, the channel's color depth is 8 bits ($2^8 = 256$ colors).

The choice of color mode depends on the nature and intent of the digital image you are working on. Generally, you work and save your original images files in RGB mode. However, CMYK generally is used for images that are to be printed. If you are preparing a digital image for full-color offset printing, it is best to use the CMYK color mode. However, some inkjet printers recommend RGB color mode. If your image is intended for the Web, then you should stay in RGB mode.

You can switch between different color modes during the image editing process. However, switching from one color mode to another may cause loss of original color information, because each mode has different color gamuts. The out-of-gamut colors will be altered to fit within the new gamut.

## COLOR GAMUTS BETWEEN RGB AND CMYK COLOR MODES

### Activities/Exercises

The objectives of these activities are to demonstrate that: (1) the most saturated colors within the RGB color gamut are outside of the CMYK gamut (as illustrated in Figure 2.20) and (2) switching between color modes may result in loss of the original color information of the image.

### Activity 1: Switching from RGB Color Mode to CMYK Color Mode

1. Create a new Photoshop image in RGB color mode.
2. Create three solid blocks of most saturated red, green, and blue with RGB values of (255,0,0), (0,255,0), and (0,0,255), respectively.
3. Switch to CMYK color mode.

You will see these three colors become a little washed out.

If you switch back to RGB color mode, the colors will not be reverted to the original. If you check the color information of these colors using the eyedropper tool, you will see that the RGB values of these three colors are altered. They are not (255,0,0), (0,255,0), and (0,0,255) anymore.

### Activity 2: Switching from CMYK Color Mode to RGB Color Mode

1. Create a new Photoshop image in CMYK color mode.
2. Create three solid blocks of most saturated cyan, magenta, and yellow with CMYK values of (100%,0,0,0), (0,100%,0,0), and (0,0,100%,0), respectively.
3. Switch to RGB color mode, then switch back to CMYK color mode.

If you check the color information of these colors using the eyedropper tool, you will see that the CMYK values of these three colors are altered. Note that the cyan color has the most significant change. Recall that, as shown in Figure 2.20, the cyan area of the CMYK color gamut is outside of the RGB gamut.

## INDEXED COLOR

An additional color mode available in digital image processing programs is **indexed color**. It is a technique for limiting the number of representable colors to no more than 256 (8-bit) based on those actually used in the image. The colors used in the image are stored as a palette called a **color lookup table (CLUT)**. Each color in the table is assigned a number or an index. The index number starts with zero. The color information of each

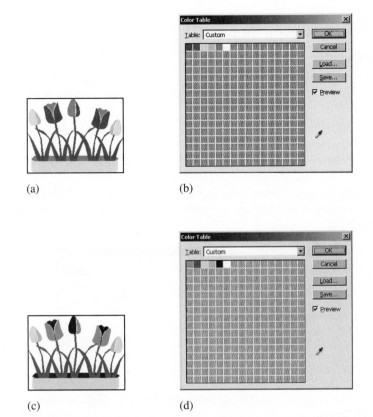

**Figure 2.21** (a) An image using indexed colors. (b) The color table or palette for the indexed colors. (c) The image with changes made to the indexed colors. (d) The color table that is used by the image in (c). ![] This image can be found on the insert.

pixel in the image is stored as a color number from the palette. This is analogous to paint-by-number art kits.

If the color of a particular index number in the palette is altered, all of the pixels in the image using the color of that index will be changed to the new color. The color is changed, but the index number remains the same. As you see in Figure 2.21, you can change the color in an indexed color image just by changing the color on the color table or applying a different color table to the same image.

The color table in Figure 2.21b consists of six colors (See the color insert). The color number 0, which is the first color on the table, is a red color. The index for the sixth color, which is white, is 5. In Figure 2.21c the red and orange tulips now become blue by altering the color 0 from a red to a light blue and color 4 from an orange to a dark blue. The base of the tulip changes from orange to the new dark blue, too, because the pixels in that area have the color index of 4. The color numbers assigned to the pixels in the image remain the same. The color table shown in Figure 2.21d shows the changes of color of indexes 0 and 4.

## ALTERING COLORS IN CLUT

### Activity/Exercise

The objectives of this activity are to demonstrate: (1) how to check out the CLUT of an indexed-color image in Photoshop, and (2) how changing the color in the CLUT can alter the color in the image.

1. Open a color image in Photoshop. An image with big blocks of distinct solid colors, such as the one shown in Figure 2.21, will work best for the purpose of this activity. You also can download the sample file (Figure 2.21a) from the Web site of this book or create a new file and add several blocks of colors.

2. Convert the image to indexed color mode: `Image > Mode > Indexed Color...` For the purpose of this activity, any settings for `Palette` and `Forced` should work (Figure 2.22).

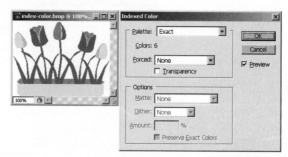

**Figure 2.22** An image is converted to indexed-color mode. 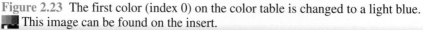 This image can be found on the insert.

If your image has more than 256 colors, you will see the option `Dither`. Make sure to set the `Dither` option to None. This will help you see the changes you are going to make in the next steps.

3. Check out the color table for this indexed-color image: `Image > Color Table...` You should see a color table similar to Figure 2.21b. Depending on your image, there may be different colors and different number of colors in your table.

4. Try to click on a color square in the color table and change it to a different color. You will see all the areas in the image that use this color change to the new color, as in Figure 2.23.

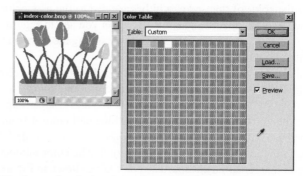

**Figure 2.23** The first color (index 0) on the color table is changed to a light blue. 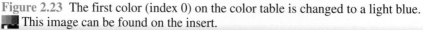 This image can be found on the insert.

# 2.9 DIFFICULTIES IN REPRODUCING COLORS IN DIGITAL IMAGES

There are at least two common problems in reproducing colors in digital images:

(1) **Digital devices cannot produce all of the colors visible to humans.**
Human vision has a larger gamut than the current existing digital devices can produce. The term *gamut* refers to the range of colors a specific system can produce or capture. The combination of R, G, and B phosphors of a computer display cannot create all the colors humans can see. Printers use the CMYK system, which has even smaller gamuts than the RGB system used for computer displays (Figure 2.20).

(2) **Difficulties exist in reproducing color across devices.**
The CMYK system used in printing is a subtractive color system, whereas the RGB system used in computer displays is an additive color system. The colors in digital images may not be reproduced exactly, whether from computer displays to printers or even from one computer display to another computer display. Although computer displays and other RGB devices use RGB color models, not all of them can produce the exact same range of colors. Different devices have different color gamuts and color spaces.

## COLOR SPACES

Color spaces differ from color models. A color model is a theoretical system that describes colors numerically in terms of primary colors or components. The primary components defined in a color model are used as the model's dimensional coordinates. For example, the RGB color model describes colors in terms of red, green, and blue values. A color space refers to a collection of colors that can be produced based on a color model.

When you work with colors of a digital image in an image editing program, you are adjusting numerical values in the file. These numerical values are not associated with absolute colors. For example, a red color with an RGB value of (255, 0, 0) may appear as different shades of red on different monitors and on prints from different printers. What specific color the numeric value means depends on the color space of the device that produces that color. The numeric value is interpreted by the color space of the device that is reproducing that color. The CIE XYZ color space usually is used as the reference color space for those colors, because it encompasses all of the colors visible to humans.

Example color spaces are Adobe RGB and sRGB. Both are based on the RGB model and have a triangular shape like the RGB one shown in Figure 2.20. Adobe RGB has a larger color space than sRGB. sRGB is recommended for Web images for onscreen viewing because sRGB defines the color space of the standard monitor.

## IDENTIFYING OUT-OF-GAMUT COLORS

Out-of-gamut colors are not reproduced correctly. In digital image editing programs such as Adobe Photoshop, you can tell whether a color is out of gamut based on your CMYK setting. In the Photoshop color picker and the color palette, you will see a warning symbol (Figure 2.24).

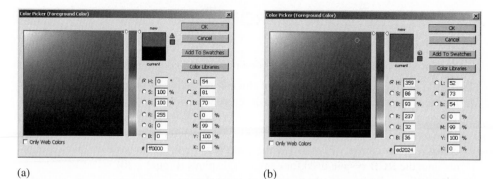

(a)                                         (b)

**Figure 2.24** Adobe Photoshop color picker showing an example of the out-of-gamut colors. (a) The red color has the saturation S = 100% and RGB = (255, 0, 0). Note the exclamation mark icon ⚠ next to the color chip. It is a warning of out of gamut for printing. Clicking on the icon ⚠ gives the closest color in gamut for printing. (b) Note the new RGB and HSB values of this new color.

> ✎ Concept of Color Management
> Supplementary reading on the difficulties in re-producing colors across devices and the concepts of color management.

A *color management system (CMS)* is a software solution intended to help reproduce colors across different devices—digital cameras, scanners, computer displays, and printers—in a predictable and reproducible way by reading and translating colors between the color gamuts of these different devices.

## 2.10 SUMMARY

Our vision of the world around us is inherently an analog phenomenon. Theoretically, an infinite number of color shades and tones is possible, and points of color in space are infinite because between every two points there is another. Because of the discrete and finite nature of computers, the analog information of natural images needs to be digitized in order to be stored on computers. Digitization involves a two-step process—sampling and quantizing.

The sampling step is to record discrete point samples on an image plane. The point sample is called a picture element, or pixel for short. Each pixel stores the color information of the corresponding position in the image. The position is defined by its horizontal and vertical coordinates in the image.

The sampling rate defines how frequently you take a sample. Imagine a two-dimensional grid is applied on the image and a single color sample is obtained from each tiny cell on the grid. The higher the sampling rate, the finer the grid and the more samples or pixels you will have in the digital image—that is, the higher the image resolution.

The quantizing step is to map an infinite number of colors and shades to a finite number of colors. The number of colors in this finite set is defined by the bit depth.

Increasing the sampling rate or bit depth increases the file size of the image. For an uncompressed file, doubling the sampling rate or the bit depth can double the file size.

Sampling and quantization errors are unavoidable results of the discrete, finite nature of digital media. It is not possible to create a digital version of a photograph or a real-world scene that has absolute fidelity to the original image. However, the human eye is not infinitely sensitive to differences in colors and color gradations across space, so it turns out that digital representations of pictures are often more than adequate for re-creations of what we see in the world.

Color models are used to describe colors numerically, usually in terms of varying amounts of primary colors. Each model uses a different method and a set of primaries to describe colors. The most common color models are RGB, CMYK, HSB, and CIE and their variants.

Color modes in digital image processing programs generally are based on the color models. Your choice of color mode in an image processing program depends on the nature and intent of a digital image. In general, you work on and save your original source files in RGB mode. If your digital image is for print, you can always convert the file to CMYK as needed. Keep in mind that CMYK has a smaller gamut, and thus switching from RGB to CMYK may cause some loss of colors. Some inkjet printers, though using CMYK inks, recommend that you keep the images in RGB mode. If your image is intended for the Web, then you should stay in RGB mode.

## TERMS

| | | |
|---|---|---|
| 24 bits  30 | color lookup table | pixel dimensions  25 |
| 32-bit  30 | (CLUT)  48 | quantization  27 |
| additive color system  41 | color management system | raster graphics  31 |
| aliasing  33 | (CMS)  52 | rasterize  33 |
| anti-aliasing  33 | color space  46 | resolution  27 |
| bit depth  29 | HSB color model  44 | RGB color model  38 |
| bitmapped  31 | hue  44 | sampling  25 |
| brightness  44 | indexed color  48 | saturation  44 |
| CMYK color model  43 | megapixel  25 | subtractive color |
| color depth  29 | picture element  25 | model  43 |
| color gamut  46 | pixel  25 | vector graphics  31 |

## LEARNING AIDS

The following learning aids can be found at the book's companion Web site.

### Sampling and Quantizing in Digital Images
An interactive tutorial, complementary to the materials covered in Sections 2.2.1 and 2.2.2, explaining sampling and quantizing in digitizing an image.

### Pegboard and Resolution
An interactive tutorial using the pegboard as an analogy to explain resolution in capturing and displaying digital images.

### RGB Color Cube
An interactive tutorial that lets you select a color and display its location in the 3-D space of the RGB color cube. You can drag to rotate the color cube to examine the color location.

### Color Value Appraisal
Be a "color value appraiser" and see how accurately you can estimate a color's "color value" in RGB.

✧ **RGB Color Cube to HSV**

A QuickTime movie illustrating the relationship between the RGB color cube and the HSV hexacone.

✧ **Concept of Color Management**

Supplementary reading on the concepts of color management and difficulties in reproducing colors across devices.

## REVIEW QUESTIONS

When applicable, please select all correct answers.

1. The process of converting from analog to digital information is a two-step process—sampling and quantizing. In converting an analog image to a digital image, the sampling rate affects _____.

   A. the bit depth of the resulting digital image
   B. the pixel dimensions of the resulting digital image

2. The process of converting from analog to digital information is a two-step process—sampling and quantizing. In the quantization step, to convert an analog image to a digital image, _____.

   A. a two-dimensional grid is applied on the image and each tiny cell on the grid is converted into a pixel
   B. a two-dimensional grid is applied on the image to apply dithering to the image
   C. an infinite number of color shades and tones in an analog image is mapped to a finite set of discrete color values
   D. the resulting digital image file is compressed to have a smaller file size

3. Which of the following factors will increase the file size of a digital image?

   A. Larger pixel dimensions of the image
   B. Higher color depth

4. A digital image captured at a higher resolution _____ than it would have if it had been captured at a lower resolution.

   A. captures more details
   B. has more different colors
   C. has a higher bit depth
   D. has a larger file size
   E. has larger pixel dimensions
   F. uses a higher sampling rate

5. A digital image captured at a higher bit depth _____ than it would have if it had been captured at a lower bit depth.

   A. captures more details
   B. has more different colors
   C. has a larger file size
   D. has larger pixel dimensions
   E. uses a higher sampling rate

6. The term *pixel* is contracted from the words _____ and _____.

7. **True/False**: A pixel is a point sample, not a little square.

8. **True/False**: An 1-bit color depth allows only black and white colors.

9. An 1-bit color depth allows _____ colors.

10. An 8-bit color depth allows _____ colors.

11. A 24-bit color depth allows _____ colors.

12. Bitmapped images are composed of _____.
    A. individual pixels, which represent spatial samples of the image or scene
    B. mathematical descriptions of image elements, which include points, lines, curves, and shapes

13. Vector graphics are composed of _____.
    A. individual pixels, which represent spatial samples of the image or scene
    B. mathematical descriptions of image elements, which include points, lines, curves, and shapes

14. The main advantage(s) of bitmapped images over vector graphics is (are) _____.
    A. scalability or resolution independence of images
    B. ease of editing the image content pixel by pixel
    C. more compact file size compared to vector graphics

15. The main advantage(s) of vector graphics over bitmapped images is (are) _____.
    A. scalability or resolution independence of images
    B. ease of editing the image content pixel by pixel
    C. more compact file size compared to bitmapped images

16. Sometimes when you magnify a picture on your computer screen, lines that should be straight lines appear to be jagged. This effect is called _____.
    A. anti-aliasing
    B. aliasing
    C. dithering
    D. indexing

17. Generally speaking, how does the file size change if the total number of pixels of an image is doubled?

18. Generally speaking, how does the file size change if the number of pixels of both the width and height of an image are doubled?

19. Generally speaking, how does the file size change if the bit depth of an image is increased from 8 bits to 16 bits?

20. Generally speaking, how does the file size change if the bit depth of an image is increased from 8 bits to 24 bits?

21. Give one example of the image file type that supports lossy compression and one that supports lossless compression.

22. Which of the following are file extensions of pixel-based files?

    BMP    DOC    JPEG    TXT    PNG    GIF

    JPG    PSD    TIFF    EPS    WMF

23. Which of the following are file extensions of vector graphic files?

BMP   DOC   JPEG   TXT   PNG   GIF   FLA

JPG   PSD   TIFF   EPS   WMF   SWF   AI

24. What are the primary colors in the RGB color model?

25. What are the primary colors in the CMY color model?

26. What are the primaries in the HSB color model?

27. Which of the following color models takes the form of a color cube?

A. RGB
B. CMY
C. HSB
D. CIE XYZ

28. Which of the following color models takes the form of a hexacone?

A. RGB
B. CMY
C. HSB
D. CIE XYZ

29. Which of the primaries in the HSB color model takes the form of a color wheel?

A. Hue
B. Saturation
C. Brightness

30. What is the color mixing method for the RGB color model?

A. Additive
B. Subtractive

31. What is the color mixing method for the CMY color model?

A. Additive
B. Subtractive

32. For the 24-bit color depth, what are the RGB values for (i) white, (ii) black, (iii) red, (iv) green, (v) blue, (vi) cyan, (vii) magenta, and (viii) yellow?

(You can use the color picker in your image editing program to confirm your answers.)

33. What are the theoretical CMY values for (i) white, (ii) black, (iii) red, (iv) green, (v) blue, (vi) cyan, (vii) magenta, and (viii) yellow?

34. What are the HSB values for (i) white, (ii) black, (iii) red, (iv) green, (v) blue, (vi) cyan, (vii) magenta, and (viii) yellow?

(You can use the color picker in your image editing program to confirm your answers.)

35. What is the primary use of the CMYK color model?

36. Why don't the colors in a printed image look exactly the same as those you see on the computer screen?

# Capturing and Editing Digital Images

# 3

## KEY CONCEPTS

- Working with scanners and scanning
- Digital photography
- Common tools in digital image editing programs—selection, layer, color and tonal adjustment, fine-tuning specific parts, sharpening
- Working with vector graphics programs
- Image ppi versus printer dpi
- Printing
- Images for the Web

## GENERAL LEARNING OBJECTIVES

In this chapter, you will learn

- What scanning and printing resolution mean and how to determine them.
- The common tools of image editing and vector graphics programs.
- The general image editing processes.
- How to prepare images for the Web.

## 3.1 INTRODUCTION

The two commonly used methods for capturing digital images are scanning and digital photography. In this chapter, we will discuss types of scanners, common scanning options, and how to determine the optimal scanning resolution. This knowledge will help you capture digital images with an optimal quality that suits your expectations.

We will also have a brief discussion of digital cameras. Later in this chapter, we will cover topics on general digital image editing tools, how to determine the resolution for images that are to be printed, and how to optimize images created for the Web.

## 3.2 SCANNERS

Generally, there are four common types of scanners classified in terms of their mechanisms:

- *Flatbed scanners:* This versatile scanner is the one most commonly used for digital media labs, offices, and personal use. A flatbed usually can scan documents of letter size (8.5 × 11 inches), legal size (8.5 × 14 inches), or even 11 × 14 inches on its flat glass plate. The motorized scan head, which consists of a light source and arrays of sensors, is underneath the glass. The scan head moves from one end to the other to capture the image.

  Here is a general procedure for scanning a document with a flatbed scanner:
  1. Put the document face down on the glass plate.
  2. Align the document to the corner indicated on the scanner.

3. Close the flap cover.
4. Start the scanner software and preview the scanning. The scanner will scan the whole scanning area.
5. Select the region that you want if your document is smaller than the available scanning area.
6. Choose the scanning options—if available—such as color mode, resolution, sharpening level, histogram, and brightness/contrast adjustments. We will discuss these options in detail later in this chapter.
7. Finalize the scanning and save the file. There may be many different file formats available.

Some flatbed scanners also can be used to scan negatives or slides using a negative or slide adaptor. Digital artists also use flatbed scanners to scan 3-D objects, such as fabrics, keys, dried plants, and hands. In these cases, the flatbed scanner is used like a focus-free camera. When an object is scanned without the flatbed cover, the background appears black, allowing easy extraction of the object to compose with others in a project.

- *Sheet-fed scanners:* Many smaller portable scanners are sheet-fed scanners in which the document moves through a fixed scan head. Because of the feeding mechanism, this type of scanner is not able to scan thick objects, such as a page in a book. Sheet-bed scanners are generally designed to scan no larger than letter-size paper.
- *Handheld scanners:* These scanners are also portable. The basic mechanism of handheld scanners is very similar to that of flatbeds, except that handhelds rely on the user to move the scan head. The scanning width of each pass is limited by the width of the device, which usually is less than the width of letter-size paper. For some models of handheld scanners, the image quality may rely on the user's steady hand movement. In general, handheld scanners do not provide very good image quality, but they offer the most convenient and fastest way of capturing documents. They are most useful for capturing text documents.
- *Drum scanners:* Drum scanners are capable of very high resolutions and can handle larger documents. They often are used in the publishing industry, where high-resolution images are required, or for scanning large documents, such as blueprints.

## TWAIN

TWAIN is a standard or specification for the interface between image software and image-capturing devices, such as scanners and digital cameras. Technically, TWAIN refers to an image-capture API (Application Programming Interface) for Microsoft Windows and Apple Mac OS. It is not a driver of any image-capturing devices.

The term TWAIN is not an acronym. The word was taken from the sentence "and never the twain shall meet" in Kipling's "The Ballad of East and West"—a fitting description of the challenges of connecting scanners to desktop computers in the early days of this technology. The whole word is capitalized to make it distinctive as a term. For more information, check out http://www.twain.org.

## 3.3 CAPTURING DIGITAL IMAGES BY SCANNING

One factor affecting the amount of detail in a scanned image is scanning resolution. Generally, the higher the resolution at which you scan the image, the more detail you can capture.

Advertisements for scanners often cite the high resolutions they offer. However, you should beware of these claims, as the term "resolution" can be used in two different ways with regard to scanners. In the scanner specification, you may find two numbers for resolution: one for the optical resolution and one for the enhanced or interpolated resolution.

The ***optical resolution*** is the hardware resolution, which is dependent on the number of sensors the scanner has to capture the image information. On the other hand, the ***enhanced resolution*** interpolates the image using software. The interpolation process increases the resolution by adding extra pixels to the ones that are actually captured by the sensors. Interpolated pixels are not truly or directly captured by the sensors. The color information of these extra pixels is based on the adjacent pixels. Many scanners now have unlimited software-enhanced resolution.

Scanner resolution is usually reported in ***dpi (dots per inch)***. To understand what dpi is and what the practical meaning of this number is, let's consider the general mechanism of a scanner. A flatbed scanner has a moving scan head that contains an array of light sensors. The scan head moves across the scanner bed during scanning. Its movement is controlled by a stepper motor.

So, how is a picture—analog information—captured with only a row of light sensors? To answer this question, we return to the concepts of sampling and sampling rate that are explained in Chapter 2. The number of sensors available in this single row corresponds to the sampling rate in the *x*-direction. The discrete stepwise movement of the scan head is related to the sampling rate in the *y*-direction. The sensor corresponds to the *dot* in the unit dpi. Each sample results in a pixel of the scanned image. For example, many flatbed scanners now have an optical resolution of at least 2,400 dpi in each direction. If you scan a 1-inch × 1-inch picture at this scanning resolution, you will get an image of 2,400 × 2,400 pixels. A detailed discussion of how to determine optimal scanning resolution is in the following section.

## 3.3.1 Scanning Resolution Determination

For best results, you should scan at a high enough resolution (in dpi) to generate an image with sufficient pixels in each dimension. The scanning resolution is determined by how the scanned image will be used:

- If it is intended for printing, then what are the physical dimensions of the print going to be and what are the requirements of the printing device?
- If the final image is for the Web, then what are the required pixel dimensions of the image?

If the scan resolution is not set high enough to produce the required pixel dimensions, you may have to scale up the image later. However, scaling up an image will only add pixels by interpolating the color information already in the image. Using interpolation, you do not get additional picture details. The more you scale up an image, the blurrier it will appear. If you scan at a higher resolution than you need, you will need to resize down the image later. When you shrink an image by reducing its pixel dimensions, some pixels are removed; that is, you lose information. The color information of the remaining pixels is altered to fit the new size. Thus, it is best to use a scan resolution such that resizing the scanned image is minimal.

### Intended for Web or Onscreen Display

If the final image is for Web or onscreen display, then its pixel dimensions are estimated relative to the screen resolution of the intended display device.

Suppose the screen resolution of your target audience is $1{,}280 \times 960$ pixels and you want your image to appear about half the width and height of the screen (i.e., the size of a quarter screen). This means that the resolution of your final image is about $640 \times 480$ pixels.

### Intended for Print

If you plan to print out the scan, you will need to know the resolution requirements of the printing device in addition to the print size (in inches). You should always think of the scan in terms of the pixel dimensions, not the ppi or the physical print size (inches). Just like any digital images, scanned images do not possess any inherent physical dimensions. The physical dimensions materialize when the image is printed out, defined by both the image's pixel dimensions and the printing ppi.

The inch in the pixel per inch (ppi) and dots per inch (dpi) is in linear inches, not square inches.

The following equation shows the relationships among pixel dimensions, print dimensions, and print resolution:

$$\text{Pixel Dimensions (in pixels)} = \text{Print Dimensions (in inches)} \\ \times \text{Print Resolution (in ppi)}$$

or,

$$\text{Print Dimensions (in inches)} = \frac{\text{Pixel Dimensions (in pixels)}}{\text{Print Resolution (in pixels per inch, ppi)}}$$

Let's see an example of determining the *print size* for a 2,400-pixel $\times$ 3,600-pixel image using the equations.

If this image is printed out on a printer at 600 ppi, then the print size will be $4 \times 6$.

$$\frac{2{,}400 \text{ pixels}}{600 \text{ ppi}} = 4 \text{ inches}$$

$$\frac{3{,}600 \text{ pixels}}{600 \text{ ppi}} = 6 \text{ inches}$$

If this same scan is printed out at 300 ppi, then the print will become $8 \times 12$.

$$\frac{2{,}400 \text{ pixels}}{300 \text{ ppi}} = 8 \text{ inches}$$

$$\frac{3{,}600 \text{ pixels}}{300 \text{ ppi}} = 12 \text{ inches}$$

If this same scan is printed out at 200 ppi, then the print will become $12 \times 18$.

$$\frac{2{,}400 \text{ pixels}}{200 \text{ ppi}} = 12 \text{ inches}$$

$$\frac{3{,}600 \text{ pixels}}{200 \text{ ppi}} = 18 \text{ inches}$$

These results, tabulated in Table 3.1, demonstrate that different sizes of prints can be made from the same scanned image by varying the print resolution.

In most situations when you scan a picture, you usually know the size you want for the final print of the scanned image. Now let's reverse the previous calculation process.

Suppose you want to scan a 1-inch $\times$ 1.5-inch area of a picture to make a 10-inch $\times$ 13-inch print (on the 11-inch $\times$ 14-inch paper) on an inkjet printer. To determine the scan resolution, you will first need to find out the pixel dimensions of the image you need. To find out the pixel dimensions, you need to know the print size and the print resolution.

| TABLE 3.1 | Various Physical Dimensions, or Print Sizes, from an Image of the Same Pixel Dimensions | | |
|---|---|---|---|
| | | Pixel Dimensions | |
| | | **2,400 pixels** | **3,600 pixels** |
| **Print Resolution** | 200 ppi | 12 inches | 18 inches |
| | 300 ppi | 8 inches | 12 inches |
| | 600 ppi | 4 inches | 6 inches |

Let's step through the math for determining the scan resolution.

**Step 1** **Determine the total pixels, or the pixel dimensions, of the final image**

Recall that:

$$\text{Pixel Dimensions (in pixels)} = \text{Print Dimensions (in inches)} \times \text{Print Resolution (in ppi)}$$

A print resolution of 150–300 ppi on an inkjet printer will give a good-quality print. Let's say you decide to print the image at 150 ppi. The pixel dimensions of a 10-inch $\times$ 13-inch image need to be 1,500 $\times$ 1,950 pixels.

$$10 \text{ inches} \times 150 \text{ ppi} = 1,500 \text{ pixels}$$
$$13 \text{ inches} \times 150 \text{ ppi} = 1,950 \text{ pixels}$$

**Step 2** **Calculate the scan resolution (dpi)**

To calculate the scan resolution, you use a similar equation:

$$\text{Scan Resolution (in dpi)} = \frac{\text{Pixel Dimensions (in pixels)}}{\text{Scan Source Dimensions (in inches)}}$$

The scan source in this example is 1 inch by 1.5 inches. Therefore, the scan resolution can be calculated as follows.

$$\frac{1,500 \text{ pixels}}{1 \text{ inch}} = 1,500 \text{ ppi, or dpi (because each dot translates to a pixel in scanning)}$$

$$\frac{1,950 \text{ pixels}}{1.5 \text{ inch}} = 1,300 \text{ ppi, or dpi}$$

Not all inkjet printers can print edge to edge or borderless. Depending on the printer, there are certain minimal margin requirements. In this example, although the image is intended to print on an 11-inch $\times$ 14-inch paper, we leave half an inch of margin on all four sides of the paper. Therefore, the dimensions of the image to be printed out are actually only 10 inches $\times$ 13 inches.

The discrepancy between the scan resolution calculations arises from the fact that the source picture and the target print have different width-to-height ratios, which is not an uncommon situation. But which calculated dpi should you use? In this example, no matter what resolution you choose, you will need to crop part of the image if you want the print to be exactly 10 inches $\times$ 13 inches.

If you are not sure whether you will crop the image to fit the exact size of 10 $\times$ 13, you should scan at the highest ppi calculated—in this case 1,500 dpi. Scanning at 1,500 dpi will give you an image of pixel dimensions of 2,250 $\times$ 1,500 pixels, which will be 10 inches $\times$ 15 inches if printed at 150 ppi. On the other hand, scanning at 1,300 dpi will give you an image of pixel dimensions of 1,300 $\times$ 1,950 pixels, which will give you an 8.7-inch $\times$ 13-inch print at 150 ppi print resolution.

**Exercise**[*]: Verify that an image of 1,300 × 1,950 pixels will give you an 8.7-inch × 13-inch print when it is printed at 150 ppi.

## 3.3.2 Tonal Adjustments

Although you can perform color correction and editing after the scanning process, it is best to optimize the tonal range and correct any significant color problems during the scanning process. It is because once you have scanned the picture, any image editing you make to the image will be based on the color information you got from the scan. Editing the image later in an image editing program is not going to create any extra true color information. If you do not get enough color information or sufficient tonal range for the image during the scanning process, you will be stuck with a limited amount of information with which to work.

> **Tonal Adjustments during Scanning** An interactive tutorial that explains and demonstrates why tonal optimization is necessary during scanning.

Figure 3.1 shows some examples of scanned images without optimizing the tonal range during the scan. Figure 3.1d shows a comparative scan of the same picture with the tonal range maximized *during* scanning.

The image scanned with a narrow tonal range (Figure 3.1a) looks dull and low in contrast. Although its tonal range may be adjusted later in an image editing program by stretching its histogram (Figure 3.1b), the result will not be as good as capturing the optimal tonal range during scanning.

A histogram is a graph showing the relative number of pixels at each color intensity level. Histogram-stretching concepts and techniques are discussed later in this chapter.

(a)                                    (b)

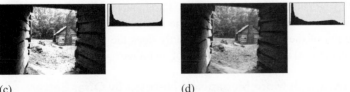

(c)                          (d)

**Figure 3.1** Scanned images with their histograms: (a) Scanned using a narrow tonal range. (b) The tonal range of the scanned image (a) is adjusted by stretching the histogram. (c) Scanned with highlights cropped off. (d) Scanned with a maximized tonal range. ▄▄ This image can be found on the insert.

---

[*]**Answer:** $\dfrac{1,300 \text{ pixels}}{150 \text{ ppi}} \approx 8.7 \text{ inches}$   $\dfrac{1,950 \text{ pixels}}{150 \text{ ppi}} = 13 \text{ inches}$

Figure 3.1c shows a scanned image with the highlights (i.e., the brightness) clipped off. The pixels whose highlight information is clipped off may contain subtle differences making up the details in the original image. However, they now all become white in the scanned image. Those highlights that have been cropped off during scanning cannot be recovered by *tonal adjustments* later in an image editing program.

## 3.4 CAPTURING DIGITAL IMAGES BY DIGITAL PHOTOGRAPHY

In traditional film photography, the image on a negative is made up of microscopic silver grains. The larger the negative, the more information about the scene is imprinted on the negative, and therefore the more information can be printed on paper. A larger negative takes less magnification to make a big print than a smaller one. This means that for prints of the same size, you get a sharper print from a larger negative than from a smaller one.

Some may consider the storage media used in the digital camera as the "digital film."

Digital cameras, on the other hand, use light sensors as the digital equivalent of film. The light hits the sensor and triggers electrical signals based on the light intensity. Such electrical signals are then converted into digital data and stored on the camera's storing device. Nowadays, the sensor that a digital camera uses is either a *CCD* (charge-coupled device) or a *CMOS* (complementary metal-oxide semiconductor). The size of the sensor and the number of light-sensing sites determine the maximum resolution of the digital camera.

Digital cameras are often advertised by the number of megapixels. Generally, the higher the number of megapixels, the more expensive the camera. But what is the practical meaning of the number of megapixels aside from being an indicator of the cost? If you are going to pay more for more megapixels, you should know what impact the number of megapixels has on the image quality of your creative photography work.

### 3.4.1 Megapixels

The total number of pixels in a digital image can be calculated by multiplying the pixel dimension of the width by the pixel dimension of the height. For example, an image of 1,600 $\times$ 1,200 pixels has a total number of pixels of:

$$1{,}600 \times 1{,}200 \text{ pixels} = 1{,}920{,}000 \text{ pixels}$$

One *megapixel* equals 1,000,000 pixels. In this example, the camera may be said to have 1.92 megapixels. The number tends to be rounded up in advertisements, so this camera would be advertised as offering 2 megapixels. The higher the total number of pixels, the higher the resolution of the image. But how exactly does the total number of pixels (reported in megapixels or not) affect any properties of an image?

With the same CCD size, having more megapixels means smaller sensor sites on the CCD. This in turn means that the sensor may be less sensitive to light and may have more noise in the image.

#### Does a Digital Camera with More Megapixels Necessarily Offer Better Image Quality?

As discussed in Chapter 2, the resolution of the captured image corresponds to the amount of detail. An image can capture more details from the original scene at a higher resolution. However, higher resolution alone does not necessarily mean higher image quality. For film cameras, with all other conditions being equal, the image quality depends on the quality of the lens optics, the size and quality of the film, and the film grain size. Similarly, the image quality for digital cameras depends on the optics, the size and quality of the CCD, and the camera electronics. It also depends on the camera's image processing software—how it processes the electronic data captured from the CCD into an RGB value for each pixel of the resulting image.

### Does a Digital Camera with a Higher Megapixel Rating Give Bigger Prints?

As discussed in Chapter 2, a pixel is a point sample; it does not possess any physical dimensions. The pixel dimensions of a digital image alone do not provide any information about physical dimensions. Recall the equation in the previous section on scanning:

$$\text{Print Dimensions (in inches)} = \frac{\text{Pixel Dimensions (in pixels)}}{\text{Print Resolution (in pixels per inch or ppi)}}$$

The print size of a digital image depends on both the total number of pixels and the print resolution in ppi. A higher megapixel rating only tells you that the image has larger pixel dimensions—only one of the two variables in the equation. *If* the ppi is kept the same, then, yes, the image with more pixels will be printed bigger in size.

## PRINT SIZE PER MEGAPIXEL

"Megapixel" is one of those loaded terms in digital imaging. The number of megapixels has been used to label a feature of a digital camera. However, what exactly are the implications of the term "megapixel"? Many consumers are concerned more about the actual print size of an image rather than the number of pixels. Is it possible to correlate the print size with megapixels?

The calculation of print size based on megapixels requires a deeper understanding of how the number of megapixels is calculated. There are many ways to approach the answer. So, let's spend some time analyzing the question and finding an answer.

As discussed previously, the physical size of the printed digital image depends on both its pixel dimensions and the ppi setting. However, given a ppi setting, it is possible to estimate the print size per megapixel.

Complicating the relationship between print size and megapixels is the fact that megapixels represent an *area*—that is, the product of the width (in pixels) by the height (in pixels). If you want to know the print size in width-by-height terms, you need to know the pixel dimensions of both the width and the height. Just the number of megapixels does not give you this information, because the same area size can be made up with many possible combinations of width and height. For 1 megapixel, the dimensions can be 1,000 × 1,000 pixels, 500 × 2,000 pixels, or approximately 1,155 × 866 pixels, and so on. Therefore, to correlate the print size to megapixels, you should think in area (square inches) first.

### Approach 1

You first make up a combination of width and height (in pixels) that will come to 1 megapixel—say, 1,000 × 1,000 pixels.

If printing at 150 ppi, then for both width and height you get:

$$\frac{1,000 \text{ pixels}}{150 \text{ ppi}} \approx 6.67 \text{ inches}$$

That means 6.67 inches × 6.67 inches, which is **approximately 45 square inches per megapixel**.

### Approach 2

Find an actual example of the image size of a digital camera. For example, a Canon EOS 5D Mark II can produce images of 5,616 × 3,744 pixels, that is, approximately 21 megapixels.

Printing at 150 ppi, you get:

$$37.44 \text{ inches} \times 24.96 \text{ inches} \approx 934 \text{ square inches per 21 megapixels}$$

that is still approximately 45 square inches per megapixel.

In the first approach, we assume the width and height are the same. However, in the second approach, we start from 5,616 × 3,744 pixels and still come to the same number of square inches per megapixel. As you see, no matter what combination of width and height you use—even if you use 500 × 2,000 pixels—you will still come up with **about 45 square inches per megapixel** *if the image is printed at the same 150 ppi*.

Most digital cameras produce digital images with the width-to-height ratio of 4:3, not 1:1. If you want to take the 45 square inches apart to get a sense of width and height in a print size of **4:3** instead of thinking in area, then you will get a print size of **about 7.6 inches × 5.7 inches**. (Well, roughly 8 inches × 6 inches if you round it up.)

If the image is in **3:2** ratio, then it will be **about 8.2 inches × 5.4 inches**. (Note that these numbers are based on printing at 150 ppi.)

Let's emphasize again that the number of megapixels is a *product* of the pixel dimensions of width and height. But the same number of megapixels can be made up of many possible combinations of width and height. As you see from the above examples, both 7.6 inches × 5.7 inches (4:3 ratio) and 8.2 inches × 5.4 inches (3:2 ratio) can be from a 1-megapixel image, depending on the image's width-to-height ratio. If you are looking for a digital camera that can produce images that can be printed 8.2 inches × 5.4 inches at 150 ppi, a 1-megapixel camera that shoots photos in 3:2 ratio will meet your requirement. However, a 1-megapixel camera that only can produce images in 4:3 ratio will not meet your requirement.

### ❓ Self-Test Exercises: Megapixels[*]

1. The calculations in the previous example are based on 150-ppi printing. What is the print size per megapixel if the image is printed at 300 ppi?

2. From the previous examples, we have about 7.6 inches × 5.7 inches of print size per megapixel for 150-ppi printing if the image is in a 4:3 ratio. What will the print size for 2 megapixels be with the same conditions? Does the calculation involve multiplying both the 7.6 inches and 5.7 inches by 2? Why or why not? If not, then how do you calculate the answer?

---

[*]Answers to Self-Test Exercises: Megapixels:

1. About 11.1 square inches per megapixels if printed at 300 ppi.
   *Explanation*: Repeat either of the approaches shown in the example for 150 ppi. Let's follow approach 1. 1,000 pixels/300 ppi = 3.33 inches for both width and height. Thus, the area = 3.33 inches × 3.33 inches = 11.1 square inches.

2. Not simply multiplying both dimensions by 2, but by the square root of 2.
   *Explanation*: For 150 ppi, we have 45 square inches per megapixel. Thus, for 2 megapixels, we have 90 square inches. 90 square inches translate to about 11 inches × 8.2 inches.

> ⏚ Worksheet: Making Sense out of Megapixels This worksheet guides you in looking up digital camera specifications and understanding how to calculate megapixels to suit your needs.

## 3.4.2 Digital Cameras

Like traditional film cameras, there are point-and-shoot, interchangeable-lens, and *digital single-lens reflex (D-SLR)* models for digital cameras. Mobile devices, such as cell phones, also have built-in cameras. Most of these digital cameras can shoot high definition videos in addition to still photos. Most D-SLR cameras support interchangeable lenses. There are also digital medium-format cameras, which use larger imaging sensor to deliver more pixels than those based on the 35 mm film frame. For example, at the time of writing, medium format D-SLR cameras, such as Hasselblad D-SLR cameras, shoot images in 40 to 60 megapixels. Nikon and Canon D-SLR cameras that are based on the 35 mm frame, shoot images in the range of 10 to 25 megapixels.

> ⏚ Photography: Understanding Shutter Speed, Aperture, and ISO This supplementary reading explains the meaning and determination of the shutter speed, aperture, and ISO.

## 3.5 DIGITAL IMAGE EDITING

In digital photography, the common traditional darkroom techniques have been translated into digital imaging tools by means of computer graphic algorithms. These tools often employ the language of photography and darkroom techniques, such as dodging, burning, filtering, cropping, and unsharp mask. If you have experience in darkroom techniques, you already may be familiar with the tasks for which these tools are intended. Digital image editing programs offer common tools (such as tonal adjustment, color correction, and sharpening) that allow you to perform image retouching. Many programs also support layers that allow you to composite and blend images in more creative ways beyond basic retouching. Creating a good digital image—aesthetics and craftmanship—however, still relies on traditional imaging basics, not just knowing the "how-to" of using the digital image editing program.

The general steps and tools for image retouching are explained as follows. Not all of the steps are necessary for all images. For example, dust and scratch clean-up is often needed for scanned photographs but is not necessary for digital photographs directly captured from a digital camera. Cropping and straightening often are not necessary for digital photographs. However, you still may want to straighten crooked pictures or selectively crop pictures to create a better composition.

Step 1 **Cropping and straightening the image.**

If you scan a picture, the picture may be placed tilted on the scanner glass. Even if the image is taken from a digital camera, the scene may appear tilted. Also, you may appear have included nonpicture areas in the scan. You can straighten and crop the scanned image in the image editing program. For example, in Photoshop, you can use the *Crop tool* on the tool palette to achieve the cropping and straightening in one step.

Step 2 **Repairing imperfections.**

Dirt and dust are common imperfections in images acquired by scanning. You will need to inspect for and remove dust, scratches, and blemishes resulting from the scanning process. One of the common tools for cleaning up these random small imperfections is a clone tool with which you can clone from one area of the image

Single-lens reflex (SLR): An SLR camera reflects the image optically onto the focusing screen or viewfinder by using the light coming through the lens. This means SLR cameras allow you to see the image area accurately from the viewfinder. However, many non-SLR digital cameras now have an LCD for previewing.

An interchangeable lens is a lens that can be detached from the camera body and replaced with a different one. Cameras with interchangeable lenses allow you to use a wide variety of lenses, from telephoto and wide-angle to close-up lenses.

to cover the blemish. This is a direct copying from one part of the image to the other. Therefore, the part that you are using as the source should have the same color and texture as the area of the blemish to cover. Adobe Photoshop also has a tool called the **Healing Brush** that can match the shading and texture of the source with the area to be repaired.

Step 3 **Adjusting the overall contrast or tonal range of the image.**

Many image editing programs let you control the tonal range of the image by adjusting the *highlights, midtones, and shadows* of the image's histogram. For example, in Photoshop, you can choose `Image` > `Adjustments` > `Levels`... and you can stretch the histogram in the Level dialog box (Figure 3.2). Figure 3.3a shows that the contrast of the resulting image is higher. As demonstrated in Figure 3.3b, the histogram now shows a full tonal range from white to black. But the relative differences in color values among these four colors are maintained after the adjustment.

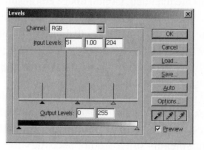

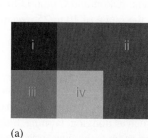

Figure 3.2 (a) An image of medium contrast consisting of four different colors. Three of the colors have the same number of pixels. The other has three times the number of pixels. No white or black color is in this image. Note: The numeric labels in cyan are not part of the image but are to show you the relationship between the color in the image and its corresponding "bar" in the histogram. (b) The histogram of this image. (c) Stretching the histogram by moving the highlight and shadow sliders to the edges.

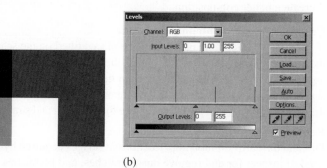

Figure 3.3 (a) The same 4-color image after stretching the histogram. (b) The histogram of this adjusted image.

Although there is a Brightness/Contrast command for image adjustments, stretching the histogram generally is the recommended tool over the simple brightness/contrast adjustment. This is because the relative color information of each pixel in the image remains the same when you stretch a histogram. However, the brightness/contrast adjustments will alter these relationships. (Compare Figure 3.4b to Figure 3.3b.)

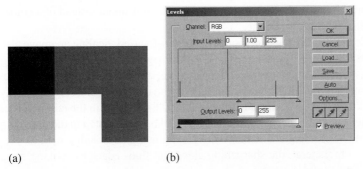

(a) (b)

**Figure 3.4** (a) The resulting 4-color image after adjustment using the Brightness/Contrast command. (b) The histogram of this adjusted image.

**Step 4** **Removing color casts.**

An image sometimes contains *color casts*—the image appears tinted. Color casts may be introduced during scanning or may have existed in the original source picture. Many digital cameras have a built-in color-correction function. However, sometimes it may not color-correct the way you want, or there still may be a slight unwanted color cast due to a mix of different lighting conditions in the scene.

One way to offset the color cast is to adjust the ***color balance***. To use this tool, you need to determine the imbalanced colors and then balance them by offsetting the color casts. In Photoshop, there are three sliders in the Color Balance dialog box (Figure 3.5), each labeled with a color at either end. The color pairs are complementary colors: cyan–red, magenta–green, and yellow–blue. For example, if your image has a red cast, you should drag the slider away from the red toward the cyan end to offset the red cast. The color correction can be selectively applied to the highlights, midtones, or shadows of the image. For example, darker areas often contain a blue cast while the brighter areas in the same image do not. In this case, you may want to target the shadow areas in removing the blue cast so that the color correction does not inadvertently add a yellow cast on the other areas of the image.

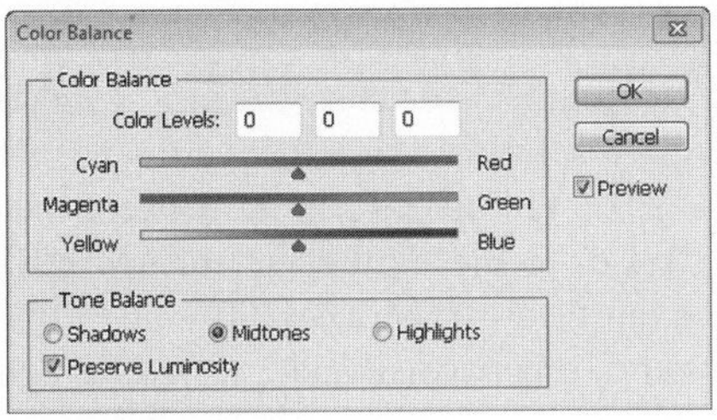

**Figure 3.5** A Color Balance dialog box

Step 5 **Fine-tuning specific parts of the image.**

Note that the previous editing steps are applied to the whole image. However, certain parts of the image may need specific enhancements. You can select those parts using selection tools before applying the adjustment. There are also other tools for fine-tuning specific parts of the image without having to make a selection first. Tools such as the dodge tool to bring out highlights, the burn tool to bring out shadows, and the sponge tool to saturate or desaturate colors work like a paint brush (except that you paint to apply the adjustment instead of a color).

Step 6 **Sharpening the image.**

Scanned images usually look a little soft-focused. Scaling an image also can make the image soft-focused. Even if your image is a straight digital photograph from a digital camera, it is a good idea to experiment with sharpening at the end of the image retouching to see if it improves the image's overall clarity. In any case, you should wait to do the sharpening until the final step in the editing process. To understand why the sharpening step should be the last step in the retouching process, you need to understand how sharpening in digital imaging works.

In general, the sharpening algorithm finds edges by looking for pixels with significant color differences from their neighboring pixels. Sharpening creates the illusion of sharpness by lightening the pixels on the lighter side of the edge and darkening on the other side. Thus, applying sharpening will alter the colors in the image. Because the edges are detected by the extent of color differences, all the color and tonal corrections or adjustments have to be made prior to the sharpening. Otherwise, the edge detection would have been based on the incorrect colors.

Sharpening should be the very last step of your image editing project. One exception is when you need to add elements with crisp, clean edges, such as a border, to the image; in this case you should do so after the sharpening. If you apply sharpening to a solid-color border, the edge of the border may not remain clean and sharp in the final image.

The sharpening tool in Photoshop is under `Filter` > `Sharpen`. There are four sharpening tools under Sharpen: `Sharpen, Sharpen Edges, Sharpen More`, and `Unsharp Mask....`

Generally, the *Unsharp Mask tool* is the recommended sharpening tool because it gives you more control on the sharpening settings. Using `Unsharp Mask...`, you can specify these options:

- `Amount`: the amount of the contrast increase around the edges
- `Radius`: the radius of the surrounding area where the color comparison and the sharpening take place
- `Threshold`: how much the pixels differ from surrounding pixels in order to be identified as "edges" to be sharpened

There are no magic numbers for these settings. It depends on the resolution of the image. For high-resolution images, experiment with an `Amount` setting between 100% and 200%, a `Radius` setting between 1 and 3, and a `Threshold` between 0 and 10. Lower these numbers for low-resolution images. For low-resolution images, an `Amount` between 50% and 100%, a `Radius` between 1 and 2, and a `Threshold` between 0 and 2 would be a good starting point for you to experiment with. Be careful not to oversharpen an image. If you notice increased graininess or unnatural halos around edges, you have probably oversharpened the image. Setting the `Amount` too high will exaggerate the intensity of the lighter and darker lines around edges, creating unnatural halos around edges. The halos will be spread out and become even more noticeable if the `Radius` setting is too high. If you notice increased graininess, you will need to increase the `Threshold` setting.

If you want to limit the sharpening to the more pronounced edges, raise the threshold value. The softer edges will be left unsharpened. The graininess resulting from sharpening is especially an undesired side effect for skin texture. Thus, raising the threshold can be an effective way in sharpening portraits—sharpen the image while leaving the soft skin texture soft. What would be the best threshold setting for portraits, then? It depends on your image—its content and resolution. But a threshold setting between 3 and 10 would be a good starting point for you to experiment with.

## THE ORDER OF THE IMAGE RETOUCHING STEPS

When retouching an image, try to keep the order of the image retouching steps listed in this section. Performing these steps out of order or jumping back and forth among steps may cause unwanted effects on the image. To understand why the order is important, let's think about the following questions.

### Questions†

1. What happens if you sharpen an image *before* stretching the histogram or performing color correction?
2. What happens if you stretch the histogram or perform color correction *before* cropping off the unwanted areas from an image?
3. What happens if you apply dodging and burning *before* removing the color casts?

 Image Retouching (Lab) Use the example image available from the book's Web site and practice the retouching steps discussed.

The word "unsharp" in the unsharp mask sounds counterintuitive to the sharpening function of the tool. However, the unsharp mask is a traditional film technique for sharpening an image by using a slightly out-of-focus (thus unsharp) duplicate negative as a mask. The original negative is sandwiched with this duplicate (an unsharp mask) during printing. This will make the lighter side of the edges lighter and the darker side of the edges darker, thereby making the image look sharper. Heightening the contrast between the lighter and darker lines around edges is basically the same technique of unsharp mask in digital imaging used to create a sharper look in an image.

---

† Answers to Questions:

1. The sharpening process involves detecting edges based on color differences of neighboring pixels. If sharpening is applied before the tonal and color corrections, the edge detection will be based on incorrect color information. In addition, sharpening increases the contrast of the edges. This contrast increase may exaggerate the problems (such as color casts) before they are fixed.
2. If you stretch the histogram or perform color correction before the cropping, you will be including a lot of unwanted color that should not be taken into consideration.
3. Color casts usually appear evenly in an image. However, the color cast at the dodged or burnt areas will be exaggerated or lessen. Either way, the color cast becomes uneven throughout the image. This will make it difficult to remove the color cast simply by applying one setting of color balance.

## 3.6 COLOR AND TONAL ADJUSTMENTS

There are a variety of color and tonal adjustment tools available in image editing programs. Depending on the program, the options available for the tools and the interface may vary. However, generally the tools work by mapping the existing color or tonal values of the pixels to new ones. The common tools include adjusting the histogram, color balance, color curves, and hue/saturation. Different tools use different graphical representations to map color or tonal values of the pixels in the image and thus offer different types of control. Adjusting the histogram (Section 3.6.1) lets you define and map the shadows, midtones, and highlights using sliders. The ***Color Balance tool*** lets you offset one color by moving the corresponding slider toward its complementary color. This is useful for removing color casts of images. This tool is discussed in the previous section on digital image retouching to remove color casts. The ***Curve tool*** (Section 3.6.3) lets you remap the color and tonal range by altering the shape of a curve. The horizontal axis of the graph used in the Curve tool represents the original color values of the pixels (input levels). Its vertical axis represents the new color values after adjustment (output levels). The ***Hue/Saturation tool*** has three basic controls—hue, saturation, and lightness.

### 3.6.1 Understanding and Reading Histograms

Parts of Sections 3.6.1 and 3.6.2 are available as a standalone online interactive tutorial at the book's Web site. You can read through the text while experimenting interactively in the tutorial. There are two practice exercise sections at the end of the tutorial to test your knowledge of applying histograms to image editing.

A ***histogram*** of an image is a bar chart that shows the relative number of pixels plotted against the color value. Figure 3.6 shows an example of a grayscale image and its histogram. In this example, the *x*-axis of the histogram is the gray level (with the darkest value on the left), and the *y*-axis is the relative number of pixels in the image that have the corresponding shade of gray. The histogram in Figure 3.6b does not look like the kind of bar chart you may have seen in business presentations. This is because this picture has a full range of 256 gray levels and the bars are packed next to each other, making the histogram look like a mountain range rather than a statistical bar chart.

(a)                                                    (b)

**Figure 3.6**  (a) A grayscale image. (b) The histogram of the image.

To learn how to read a histogram, let's first look at a very simple image that has only five different gray colors. The image shown in Figure 3.7a has five main different gray colors. Each gray takes up a different amount of space in the image. The background color is the lightest gray in this image. It is represented by the rightmost line (line [v]) in the histogram (Figure 3.7b). Notice that it is also the longest line in the histogram because this background color occupies the largest area in the image. In fact, the line is so long compared to other lines that it is truncated.

### ❓ Self-Test Exercises: Reading Histograms[‡]

1. Which gray has the least number of pixels; that is which solid gray area is the smallest?
2. For each of the bars, or lines, in the histogram in Figure 3.6, identify and label its corresponding gray color in the image, by comparing their relative gray levels.

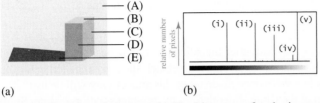

         (a)                         (b)

**Figure 3.7** (a) A simple grayscale image. (b) The histogram for the image.

## 3.6.2 Applying Histograms to Adjustment of Brightness and Contrast

Many image editing programs let you adjust image **brightness** and **contrast** with the image's histogram. For example, the histogram tool can be found in `Image > Adjustments > Levels...` in Adobe Photoshop. When you choose to adjust levels, a dialog box will appear showing the histogram of the image (Figure 3.8). There are three sliders on the *x*-axis of the histogram:

- A black slider on the left end marks the darkest color (shadow).
- A white slider on the right end marks the brightest color (highlight).
- A gray slider in the middle marks the 50% intensity of the color (midtone).

**Figure 3.8** A histogram showing three sliders: black (shadow), gray (midtone), and white (highlight)

You can move these triangles to modify the image's *brightness* and *contrast*. You can map the pixels to the darkest by repositioning the black slider. For example, if you drag the black slider to the peak that corresponds to the second darkest gray color (Figure 3.9b), you set this gray color as the darkest color (i.e., black) in the image. Any color that is originally darker than this gray will become black after this adjustment of the black slider. In the original image (Figure 3.7a), the front of the block and the block's shadow were in

---

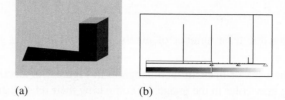

(a)                       (b)

**Figure 3.9** (a) The resulting grayscale image after moving the black slider toward the right. (b) The black slider is moved to where the bar for the second darkest color of the image is.

different tones of gray. But after the adjustment, they become black and indistinguishable (Figure 3.9a). As you see, if you move the black slider past the left end of the original histogram, details that were once made up of this area of gray will be lost.

The position of the white slider defines the brightness color—white. Similar to the black slider, if you move the white slider to the left, past the right end of the original histogram, the highlights that were once in this area of gray will be lost because they will all become white.

## HISTOGRAM

### Activity/Exercise

Experiment by dragging the sliders and observe how the position of the sliders affects the brightness and contrast in the image in the interactive tutorial or in Photoshop.

- Drag the white slider to the second peak on the right in the histogram. Note which colors in the image turn white.
- Drag the white slider to the rightmost peak and the black slider to the leftmost peak in the histogram. Note how the contrast of the image changes.

By defining the new positions of the black and the white sliders, you remap the whole spectrum of color values of the pixels. By repositioning the black slider to the leftmost peak and the white slider to the rightmost peak, you *stretch* the histogram (Figure 3.10a). That means you make the darkest color in the image to be black, and the brightest color in the

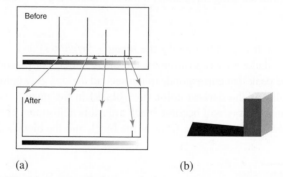

(a)                       (b)

**Figure 3.10** (a) The histograms before and after stretching. (b) The resulting image after stretching the histogram.

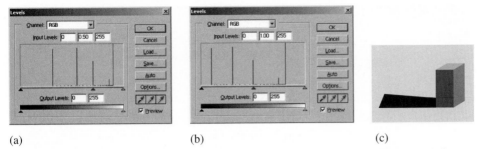

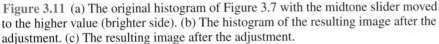

(a) (b) (c)

**Figure 3.11** (a) The original histogram of Figure 3.7 with the midtone slider moved to the higher value (brighter side). (b) The histogram of the resulting image after the adjustment. (c) The resulting image after the adjustment.

image to be white, as in Figure 3.10b. All other colors will be mapped in between relative to each other. By stretching the histogram, you maximize the use of the full spectrum of the gray tones. The overall contrast of the image is increased because the color value differences between colors are increased.

You also can move the gray slider in the middle to set the midtone. For example, if you move the gray slider to a new position, as shown in Figure 3.11a, you set the gray color that is originally a lighter gray as the midtone (value of 128 for an 8-bit color). If you click OK to accept the change and then look at the histogram again, you will see the bar that the gray slider was repositioned to is now in the middle (Figure 3.11b). That is, the color is changed to the middle gray. All other colors are remapped accordingly. As a result, any color darker than this is mapped to between 0 and 128. Any color brighter than this is mapped to between 128 and 255.

Because you shift the midtone to the lighter gray of the original image, the resulting image becomes darker overall.

However, if you shift the midtone to the gray color that is originally a darker gray (Figure 3.12a), the resulting image becomes lighter overall (Figure 3.12c). If you look at the histogram of the resulting image, you will see the bar that the gray slider was repositioned to is now in the middle (Figure 3.12b). That is, the color is changed to the middle gray. Again, all other colors are remapped accordingly.

In Figure 3.12, no color is darker than the midtone. Thus, all the bars in the histogram are positioned on the right half of the histogram. The image appears washed out.

In summary, a histogram is a bar chart showing the relative number of pixels versus color values. The color values of the *x*-axis are usually from 0 to 255. For a grayscale image (like the example shown here), the *x*-axis has 256 levels of possible gray tones, from 0 to 255—with 0 being black and 255 being white. The middle gray has a value of 128. For a color image, you can choose to adjust the levels for each of the red, green, and blue channels. You also can choose to adjust all three channels together.

To illustrate the concept of histograms, the examples here adjusted the levels by moving the three triangular sliders one at a time in the histogram. However, imaging editing programs, such as Adobe Photoshop, let you adjust the shadows, highlights, and midtones simultaneously by directly entering their values or moving the sliders.

It is not only in image editing programs that you encounter histograms; many digital cameras and scanners show you

> **Light Metering Emulation of Photography**
> This emulates photographing a still life and illustrates the relationship between spot-metering and the resulting image's midtone.

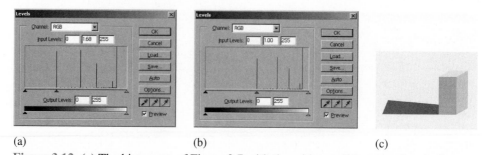

(a)  (b)  (c)

**Figure 3.12** (a) The histogram of Figure 3.7 with the midtone slider moved to the lower value (darker side). (b) The histogram of the resulting image after the adjustment. (c) The resulting image after the adjustment.

In Photoshop, you can add a new selection to the existing selection by holding down the Shift key while selecting. Hold down the ALT (Windows) or Option (Mac OS) key for subtracting.

the histogram of the captured image. This helps you see if you are getting the optimal tonal range of the captured image right away. Being able to see the histogram instantaneously helps you decide immediately if you need to take the photograph again while you are on location.

> ⚙ **Understanding and Applying Histograms** There are two parts of this learning aid: an interactive tutorial and practice exercises. The tutorial explains how to interpret an image's histogram and make tonal adjustments using histograms.
>
> To test your knowledge of histograms, check out the two interactive exercises in the tutorial:
>
> **Exercise I: Reading Histograms.** Practice relating the appearance of a histogram to the image characteristics.
>
> **Exercise II: Improving Image Contrast and Brightness.** Identify the problem of the image by examining the histogram, and then improve it.

### 3.6.3 Curves Adjustment Tool

Curve adjustment tool lets you remap the color and tonal range by using the shape of a 2-D curve.

In a 2-D plot, there are two axes: $x$-axis (horizontal) and the $y$-axis (vertical). The line or the curve shows the relationship between the $x$- and $y$-values. For adjustment curves, both the $x$- and $y$-axes represent the spectrum of the tonal values from darkest to brightest. Conceptually, each axis is similar to the horizontal axis in a histogram—except that now you have both the vertical and horizontal axes representing the tonal range shown as a gradient bar next to each axis.

So, how are the $x$- and $y$-axes different? In Photoshop, by default, the $x$-axis represents the input values and the $y$-axis the output values. Think of the input as "before" and the output as "after"—as in before and after applying the adjustment using the Curve tool.

#### Above or Below the Diagonal Line—Darker or Lighter

The default diagonal straight line shown in Figure 3.13 does not alter the tonal value of the image. For example, the color arrow in Figure 3.13 shows that a light gray on the $x$-axis (input) is mapped to the exact same light gray on the $y$-axis (output).

A curve that is shown in Figure 3.14 lowers the tonal value of the original image (i.e., the image becomes darker). For example, the color arrow in Figure 3.14 shows that a light gray on the $x$-axis (input) is mapped to a dark gray on the $y$-axis (output).

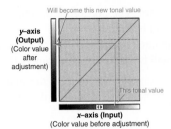
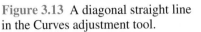

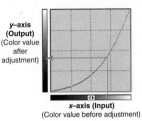

**Figure 3.13** A diagonal straight line in the Curves adjustment tool.

**Figure 3.14** This curve specifies lowering the original tonal value.

To help you see whether the resulting tonal value will be darker or brighter, you can imagine the presence of the default diagonal straight line—a straight line drawn from the upper-right corner to the lower-left corner—like the colored diagonal line shown in Figure 3.15.

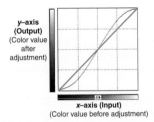

**Figure 3.15** Imagine a diagonal straight line, like the colored line shown here.

- If the portion of the curve is above the default straight line, then the resulting color will be brighter than that before the adjustment.
- If below, then the resulting color will be darker.

Because the direction of lightness on the axes can be reversed, be careful which direction you are using. No matter which direction is used it will give the same result if you adjust the curve correctly. Let's look at an example shown in Figure 3.16.

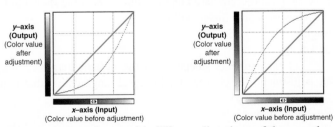

**Figure 3.16** The same curve shown with different directions of the *x*- and *y*-axis (a) Axes with default direction from black to white (b) Axes with a reversed direction from white to black.

- Figure 3.16a: The *y*-axis goes from dark to light upward. The portion of the curve is below the default straight line. The resulting color will be darker.
- Figure 3.16b: The *y*-axis goes from light to dark upward. The portion of the curve is above the default straight line. The resulting color will be darker, as in Figure 3.16a.

Either representation gives the same result—in this example, the tone of the image will become darker. The cyan-colored line is included to help you visualize the diagonal line.

### Curve Steepness and Image Contrast

The curvature of the curve controls the contrast. If a region of a curve is steeper than the default straight line, then the contrast of the tonal range within that region will be increased. In the example shown in Figure 3.16, the contrast of the highlight areas is increased, but the contrast of the shadow areas is lowered.

In summary, two properties of the Curves adjustment tool that determine the color adjustment are

- Being above or below the diagonal line determines the brighter or darker adjustment
- The steepness of the curve controls the contrast.

⌁ **Understanding and Applying Curves for Color Adjustments** An interactive tutorial and exercises help you understand the Curves tool for image adjustment.

❓ **Self-Test Exercises: Interpreting Curves**

I.

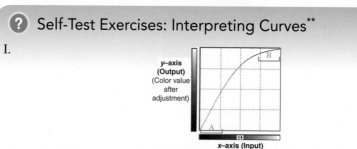

**Figure 3.17** An adjustment curve for Part I of the exercise.

The following questions are based on the adjustment curve shown in Figure 3.17.

1. After the adjustment, the image will be _____.
   A. brighter
   B. darker
2. _____ of the curve is steeper than the default diagonal line, and thus after the adjustment, the contrast for the tonal range within that region will be _____.

   A. Region A; higher
   B. Region A; lower
   C. Region B; higher
   D. Region B; lower

II. **The "S-curve"**

The "S-curve" often is used to boost the overall contrast of an image. Let's see why.

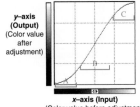

**y–axis (Output)** (Color value after adjustment)

**x–axis (Input)** (Color value before adjustment)

Figure 3.18  An adjustment curve for Part II of the exercise.

The following questions are based on the adjustment curve shown in Figure 3.18.
1. After the adjustment, the **highlights** (Region C) will become _____.
   A. brighter
   B. darker
2. After the adjustment, the **shadows** (Region A) will become _____.
   A. brighter
   B. darker
3. The curve in _____ is steeper than the default diagonal line, and thus after the adjustment, the contrast for the tonal range in that region will become _____.
   A. Region A; higher          D. Region B; lower
   B. Region A; lower            E. Region C; higher
   C. Region B; higher          F. Region C; lower

III.

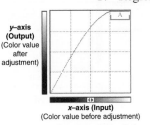

**y–axis (Output)** (Color value after adjustment)

**x–axis (Input)** (Color value before adjustment)

Figure 3.19  An adjustment curve for Part III of the exercise.

The following questions are based on the adjustment curve shown in Figure 3.19.
1. After the adjustment, the **highlights** (Region A) will become _____.
   A. all white
   B. all black
2. After the adjustment, the tonal values outside of Region A, will become _____.
   A. higher (brighter)
   B. lower (darker)
3. The curve other than in Region A is _____ than the diagonal line, and thus after the adjustment, the contrast for the tonal range outside of Region A will be

_____.

   A. steeper; higher
   B. steeper; lower
   C. less steep; higher
   D. less steep, lower

IV.

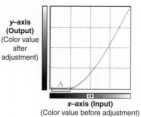

**Figure 3.20** An adjustment curve for Part IV of the exercise.

The following questions are based on the adjustment curve shown in Figure 3.20.
1. After the adjustment, the **shadows** (Region A) will become _____.
   A. all white
   B. all black
2. After the adjustment, the tonal values outside of Region A will become _____.
   A. higher (brighter)
   B. lower (darker)
3. The curve other than in Region A is _____ than the diagonal line, and thus after the adjustment, the contrast for the tonal range outside of Region A will be

_____.

    A. steeper; higher            C. less steep; higher
    B. steeper; lower             D. less steep; lower

V.

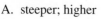
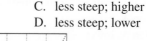
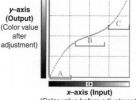

**Figure 3.21** An adjustment curve for Part V of the exercise.

The following questions are based on the adjustment curve shown in Figure 3.21.
1. After the adjustment, the **highlights** (Region C) will be _____.
   A. brighter
   B. darker
2. After the adjustment, the **shadows** (Region A) will be _____.
   A. brighter
   B. darker
3. The curve in _____ is **less steep** than the default diagonal line, and thus after the adjustment, the contrast for the tonal range in that region will be _____.
   A. Region A; higher
   B. Region A; lower
   C. Region B; higher
   D. Region B; lower
   E. Region C; higher
   F. Region C; lower

4. After the adjustment, the **contrast** of the **highlights** (Region C) will be _____.
   A. higher
   B. lower

5. After the adjustment, the **contrast** of the **midtones** (Region B) will be _____.
   A. higher
   B. lower

6. After the adjustment, the **contrast** of the **shadows** (Region **A**) will be _____.
   A. higher
   B. lower

# 3.7 SELECTION TOOLS IN IMAGE EDITING PROGRAMS

The ability to select a specific region of an image is crucial in image editing. Often, it is necessary to fine-tune specific parts of the image. If you apply any tonal or color changes on a selection, the changes are confined to the selected area; the rest of the image is protected from the alteration. Being able to make a specific selection is also important in compositing or collaging images together because once a selection is made, you can extract the selected parts of the image.

There are a variety of selection tools available in image editing programs. However, instead of trying to list and explain these tools one by one, we will categorize these tools in terms of their specialties or the way they are designed to work:

- **Predefined shapes:** The *Marquee tools* provide predefined shapes, such as rectangular and elliptical.
- **Lasso:** The *Lasso tool* and *Polygonal tool* let you create an irregularly shaped selection. The *Magnetic Lasso tool* makes a selection by tracing edges and thus is useful for selecting an area that has well-defined edges.
- **By color:** With the *Magic Wand tool*, you can specify the tolerance or the similarity of the color in the surrounding pixels to be included in the selection. You also can use the *Eyedropper tool* to pick out a color in the foreground color chip, and then choose `Select > Color Range....`
- **By painting with a brush to select or deselect a specific area:** Editing in *Quick Mask mode* allows you to use the paintbrush to paint in black to deselect, white to select, and grays to create semitransparent selections, as well as feathering and anti-aliasing.
- **By drawing an outline around the area to be selected:** The *Pen tool* lets you draw a vector shape outline around an area that you want to select.

----

[**] Answers to the self-test exercises:

   I. (1) **A**; (2) **A**
  II. (1) **A**; (2) **B**; (3) **C**
 III. (1) **A**; (2) **A**; (3) **A**
 IV. (1) **B**; (2) **B**; (3) **A**
  V. (1) **B**; (2) **A**; (3) **D**; (4) **A**; (5) **B**; (6) **A**

If you move the selection by using any of the selection tools instead of the Move tool, you will move the floating selection only. This may be useful if you want to use the shape of that selection for another area in the image.

To create a complex selection, you often need to use multiple selection tools to add, subtract, or intersect selections. After you have made a selection, you can manipulate the selected pixels. You can use the *Move tool* to move the pixels in the selected area. You can soften the hard edges of the selection by applying feathering (in Photoshop, choose `Select > Refine Edge...`). You also can save the selection (`Select > Save Selection...`) and load the selection (`Select > Load Selection...`) later. This is particularly useful if the selection you have made is time consuming and complex. It is a good idea to save the selection after each step in case you accidentally lose the selection, and, of course, save the final selection so you can load the selection at any time later.

> ✎ **Photoshop Basics: Selection** A screen-capture movie gives a quick demonstration of some of the selection tools in Photoshop. A worksheet exercise is also available.

> 🖱 **Image Alteration (Lab)** Use the example images (available from the book's Web site) to practice selectively altering areas.

## 3.8 LAYER BASICS AND ADVANCED LAYER TECHNIQUES

*Layers* in Photoshop are like a stack of transparencies; the content in a layer can block out those in the layers beneath it. However, layers are more than that, because you can also set the opacity and blending mode of each layer. You can rearrange the stacking order by dragging a layer in the *Layers panel* up or down the stack. Many image editing programs support layers. The following discussion is based on Adobe Photoshop but should be applicable to other image editing programs that support those features discussed here.

In Photoshop, there is a special layer called Background that is listed in italics in the Layers panel. This *Background layer* always stays at the bottom of the stack and cannot be rearranged. In addition, it is not a transparent layer. When you use the *Eraser tool* to erase the image content on this layer, you replace the content with the color that is set in the background color chip. However, erasing the image content on a regular layer will reveal transparency. The Background layer can be converted to a regular standard layer, for example, by double-clicking on it in the Layers palette.

> ✎ **Photoshop Basics: Using Layers** A screen-capture movie gives a quick demonstration of commonly used features of the Layers panel in Photoshop. A worksheet exercise is also available.

You can create new layers, delete layers, rename layers, control the visibility of each layer, and copy layers from one file to another. You also can apply a layer style (`Layer > Layer Style`), such as a drop shadow or bevel, to a layer. You can select multiple layers or link them together, so that you can move or scale them simultaneously.

Adjustment layers are used for applying image adjustments, such as levels and color balance, to a layer without altering the pixel content of that layer. An adjustment layer is a separate layer by itself. Think of it as a pair of sunglasses through which you see a world with reduced UV light intensity and glare but the sunglasses do not actually change the lighting condition of the world. Because the adjustment layer does not alter pixel content of other layers, the advantage of using an adjustment layer instead of directly applying the adjustment on an individual layer is that you can change the adjustment settings any time. In addition, to remove the adjustment any time, you can simply delete the adjustment layer. You can also hide the adjustment effect temporarily by turning off its layer visibility just like any other layers. An adjustment layer applies the adjustment to all the layers below it but you can apply the adjustment to specific layers by grouping them with the adjustment layer and changing the blending mode of the group from Pass Through to Normal.

A *layer mask* associated with a layer lets you *obscure*—just block, not delete—part of the image on that layer. This nondestructive method of editing offers the advantage of preserving the original image. Later, if you change your mind in how you want the image on that layer to show, you can edit the mask or remove the whole mask. See Figure 3.22 for an example of a layer mask. The black color of the mask hides the image while the white lets the content of the image show through. Figure 3.23a shows how the resulting image of the example shown in Figure 3.22 may look.

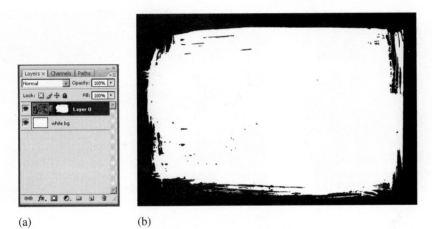

   (a)                      (b)

**Figure 3.22** (a) A layers panel showing a layer mask associated with the top layer. (b) The layer mask.

The *clipping mask* works very similarly to the layer mask (Figure 3.23). Whereas a layer mask is associated with one layer and only masks that one layer, the clipping mask works like a cookie cutter by cutting through multiple layers that are in the same group. In this example the clipping group is made up of two layers—the base layer (Figure 3.23c) that acts as a mask for the entire group, and a layer with the image (Figure 3.23d).

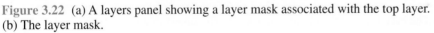

**Making Composites: Example 1—Replicating an Object in Its Environment** In this example, the final image (Figure 3.24b) contains an extra object—a humanoid chain sculpture—which is not in the original image (Figure 3.24a). This example demonstrates the following aspects of image editing:

- Application of selection
- Scaling with the perspective in mind
- Creation of shadows

(a)

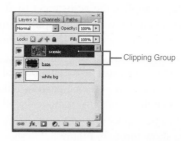

(b)

(c)

(d)

**Figure 3.23** (a) The resulting image using a clipping mask. (b) The layers panel of the image showing the arrangement of the layers. (c) The base layer of the clipping mask. (d) The image in the non-base layer of the clipping mask.

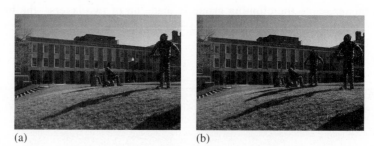

(a)                    (b)

**Figure 3.24** (a) The original digital photograph. (b) The final composite.

✎ **Making Composites: Example 2—Recreating a Sky Background** In this example, the final image (Figure 3.25c) contains an artificial sky and is created by compositing two digital images (Figures 3.25a and b). The tools used to make the composite include:

- Layer blending mode
- Layer mask
- Layer style
- Filters
- Stamp tool
- Dodge tool

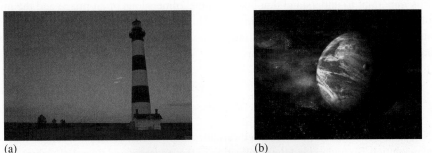

(a)                                        (b)

(c)

**Figure 3.25** (a) The original digital photograph. (b) An image that is used as an artificial sky background. (c) The final composite.

## 3.9 PRINTING THE FINAL IMAGE

In real-life situations, if you want to change the size of an object, you would think of scaling it up or down physically. However, the intuitive sense of size that you have learned from the physical world is not always applicable to the concept of size in digital images. The size of a digital image is described in terms of pixel dimensions. The physical print size (in inches) of an image depends on its pixel dimensions and the print resolution (in pixels per inch or ppi). The same image can be printed at different physical sizes using different ppi settings. Image editing programs let you resize or scale images by changing the pixel dimensions of the image. There are also options for changing the physical print size (in inches). The print size can be changed with or without changing the pixel dimensions.

To preserve the detail and quality of an image, it is best not to scale the original pixel dimensions of the image. The reason is as follows. As you have learned from the discussion of sampling and quantizing in digital images, the amount of detail in an image is related to its original pixel dimensions, which, in turn, are determined by the sampling rate. When you increase the pixel dimensions of an image by resizing, new pixels are added. But the color information of these new pixels is generated by interpolating the color information of the existing pixels. Therefore, although the pixel dimensions of the image increase, such resizing does not really add new detail to the image because it is only interpolating the existing pixel information. In fact, the resulting image often appears blurry. When you shrink an image by reducing its pixel dimensions, some pixels have to be removed; that is, you lose information. In addition, the color information of the remaining pixels is altered to fit the new size.

It is important to understand that both the pixel dimensions of an image and the image resolution (ppi) affect the image's print size. This relationship is discussed in the section on megapixels. It applies to all digital images, not only images that are obtained by digital photography. Let's revisit the equation.

$$\text{Print Dimension (in inches)} = \frac{\text{Pixel Dimension (in pixels)}}{\text{Print Resolution (in pixels per inch or ppi)}}$$

Note that this equation involves three variables: print dimensions, pixel dimensions, and print resolution. To understand the implication of this equation and the relationships among these variables, let's look at three different scenarios in each of which one variable is fixed at a known value.

Scenario 1 **Maintaining the Physical Print Dimensions**

If you want to print an image at higher print resolution (ppi) but maintain the print dimensions, you will need to increase the image's pixel dimensions. For example, an image of 600 × 600 pixels printed at 100 ppi will give a print of 6 inches × 6 inches. If you want to print at 200 ppi and still have a 6-inch × 6-inch print, then the pixel dimensions of the image need to be increased from 600 × 600 pixels to 1,200 × 1,200 pixels.

$$\text{Print Dimension (in inches)} = \frac{\text{Pixel Dimension (in pixels)}}{\text{Print Resolution (in pixels per inch or ppi)}}$$

$$\frac{600 \text{ pixels}}{100 \text{ ppi}} = \textbf{6 inches}$$

$$\frac{1,200 \text{ pixels}}{200 \text{ ppi}} = \textbf{6 inches}$$

$$\frac{1,800 \text{ pixels}}{300 \text{ ppi}} = \textbf{6 inches}$$

and so forth.

Scenario 2 **Maintaining the Pixel Dimensions**

If you want to print an image at higher physical print dimensions but do not want to scale up the image's pixel dimensions, you will need to lower print resolution (ppi). Using the previous example, an image of 600 × 600 pixels printed at 100 ppi will give a print of 6 inches × 6 inches.

$$\text{Print Dimension (in inches)} = \frac{\text{Pixel Dimension (in pixels)}}{\text{Print Resolution (in pixels per inch or ppi)}}$$

$$\frac{\textbf{600 pixels}}{100 \text{ ppi}} = 6 \text{ inches}$$

$$\frac{\textbf{600 pixels}}{200 \text{ ppi}} = 3 \text{ inches}$$

$$\frac{\textbf{600 pixels}}{300 \text{ ppi}} = 2 \text{ inches}$$

and so forth.

Scenario 3 **Maintaining the Print Resolution (ppi)**

Given a fixed ppi, an image with higher pixel dimensions will give a larger printout. Using the previous example, you see how the print size changes with the image's pixel dimension:

$$\text{Print Dimension (in inches)} = \frac{\text{Pixel Dimension (in pixels)}}{\text{Print Resolution (in pixels per inch or ppi)}}$$

$$\frac{600 \text{ pixels}}{\textbf{100 ppi}} = 6 \text{ inches}$$

$$\frac{1{,}200 \text{ pixels}}{\textbf{100 ppi}} = 12 \text{ inches}$$

$$\frac{1{,}800 \text{ pixels}}{\textbf{100 ppi}} = 18 \text{ inches}$$

and so forth.

So, how are these scenarios translated into the settings used in an image editing program? To adjust the output resolution or print size of an image, look in the image size setting. In Photoshop, for example, it can be found under `Image > Image Size...`.

The setting of the `Resample Image` option (Figure 3.26) separates Scenario 2 from the other two scenarios. For Scenario 2, in order to maintain the pixel dimensions of the image, you will need to uncheck the Resample Image option (Figure 3.26a). Then, when you alter the width and height in the Document Size section, the print resolution (ppi) will be updated automatically, and vice versa, if you change the print resolution.

If you check the Resample Image option (Figure 3.26b), then both Scenarios 1 and 3 apply. With the Resample Image option on, the pixel dimensions are allowed to vary. That is, the pixel dimensions can be varied with the print resolution (ppi) while maintaining the print size. They also can be varied with the print size while maintaining the print resolution (ppi).

Printer resolution is measured in dots per inch (dpi)—the number of ink dots per inch. Color inkjet printers produce a microscopic spray of ink that appears to be very tiny dots of ink. The number of color inks that a printer uses determines the number of colors of these ink dots. Although a printer uses only a limited number of color inks, these tiny ink dots are very close to each other and, by varying the relative number of different color dots on paper, can produce the many different colors by optical mixing. The color of a single pixel of an image is represented

Turning the Resample Image option on means that scaling of the image is allowed. Scaling the pixel dimensions of an image is referred to as resampling because the number of samples (pixels) is changed.

⌖ Optical Color Mixing in Pointillism, Dithering, and Inkjet Printing An interactive demonstration of optical color mixing.

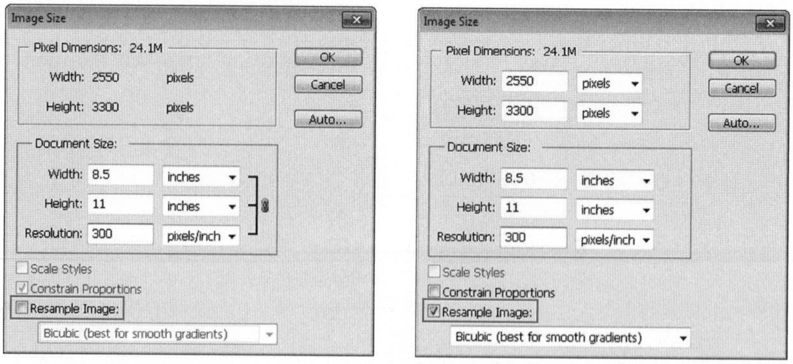

(a)                                      (b)

**Figure 3.26** Adobe Photoshop's Image Size dialog box. (a) Uncheck the Resample Image option to change the Document Size settings while maintaining the pixel dimensions (Scenario 2). (b) Check the Resample Image option to allow scaling of pixel dimensions to maintain the print dimensions (Scenario 1) or print resolution (Scenario 3).

---

> ⬆ **Worksheet: Image ppi versus Printer dpi** Learn the difference between the printer dpi and image ppi by:
>
> 1. Experimenting with how the image ppi affects the output dimensions of the image.
> 2. Experimenting with how the printer dpi affects the printing quality of the image.

by a group of these printer dots. Do not confuse the image print resolution (ppi) with the printer resolution (dpi). As you see in Scenario 2, the print resolution (ppi) affects the print size of an image. However, the printer resolution (dpi) does not affect the print size of the image; it affects the density of the ink dots on the print. Generally, the higher the dpi, the smoother the colors appear on the print. However, higher dpi uses more ink and requires a longer time to complete the print job.

## 3.10 OPTIMIZING THE FINAL IMAGE FOR THE WEB

The three image file formats currently supported by Web browsers are JPEG, GIF, and PNG. Each format has its characteristics that work best for different types of images. In addition, each employs different compression algorithms to compress the file size.

> ⬆ **Worksheet: JPEG Compression Artifact** Look at the impact of JPEG compression artifact on different digital images, and learn when and why an image may be or should not be saved in JPEG format.

The *JPEG* format works best with continuous-tone images with a broad color range and subtle color and brightness variations, such as photographs and images with gradients. JPEG supports 24-bit color (millions of colors). JPEG compression is a lossy compression method, which means it loses image data in order to make the file size smaller.

A highly compressed JPEG image tends to blur the image detail and shows a visible artifact around the high-contrast edges. For example, note the noises around the dark area in Figure 3.27d comparing to the same region of the uncompressed image shown in Figure 3.27b. Notice that the solid color areas in the original uncompressed image also no longer appear to be continuous solid color blocks in the JPEG images.

(a)

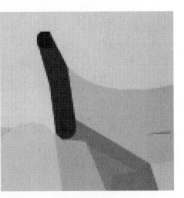

(b)

(c)

(d)

**Figure 3.27** (a) An uncompressed image. (b) A zoom-in view of the area outlined in color in image (a). (c) A highly compressed JPEG image of (a). (d) A zoom-in view of the area outlined in color in the JPEG image (b) showing the JPEG artifact.  This image can be found on the insert.

The *GIF* format uses a palette of up to 256 colors (8-bit color depth) to represent the image, and it also supports background transparency. The GIF format works well for images with solid colors such as illustrations, logos, and line art. GIF images also can be created as animated sequences and saved as animated GIF files.

GIF files use a lossless compression. However, if an original image has more than 256 colors, you will need to reduce the number of colors in order to save the image as a GIF file. Some colors in such images will be altered when they are saved in the GIF format. Figure 3.28a shows a a screenshot of Photoshop's Save For Web & Devices

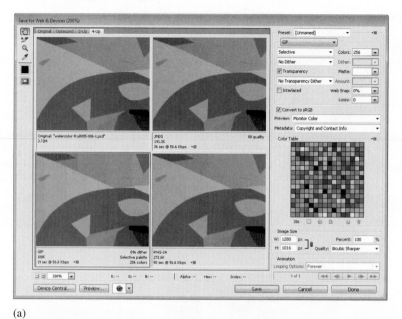

(a)

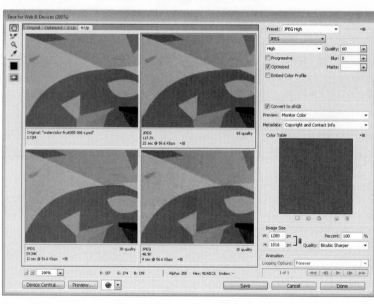

(b)

**Figure 3.28** Adobe Photoshop CS5's Save for Web & Devices dialog box, displaying four versions of the image side by side. (a) The original uncompressed image, JPEG, GIF, and PNG. (b) The original uncompressed image and three different JEPG settings. (*continued*)

dialog box, where you can adjust settings for saving an image in different Web formats. For GIF files, you can choose a preset palette or customize the colors to be included in the palette. The GIF version in the upper-right in Figure 3.28c shows bands of solid colors in the gradient. It is because the original image has more than 256 colors and the

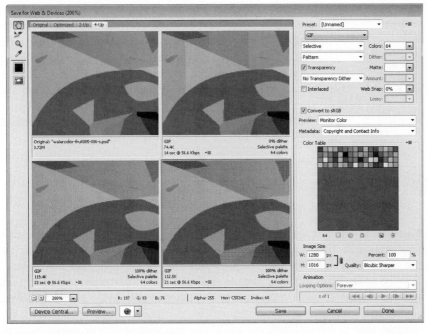

(c)

**Figure 3.28** (*continued*) (c) The original uncompressed image (upper left) and three different GIF settings.

colors in the gradient that are outside of the palette are mapped to the closest color on the palette. In gradient areas, neighboring pixels have similar colors. The colors that are similar are mapped to the same color. At some points in the gradient when the colors are changing more and more, the neighboring pixels eventually are mapped to a different color. This causes the banding effect. When the number of colors in an image is reduced, the undesirable banding is not limited to gradient-filled areas; it can be in any areas with gradual color changes. The banding can be remediated by applying dithering. **Dithering** is a technique to simulate colors that are outside of the palette by using a pattern of like-colored pixels. The two GIF versions in the second row in Figure 3.28c are applied with dithering—each with a different dithering pattern. The undesirable banding effect in the gradient is reduced. If a Web image needs to have more than 256 colors, choose the PNG-24 or JPEG format.

The PNG format has two options: PNG-8 and PNG-24. Like the GIF format, the *PNG-8* format uses up to 256 colors to represent the image. Like the JPEG format, the *PNG-24* format supports 24-bit color. However, unlike the JPEG format, the PNG format uses a lossless compression and support transparency. There is no undesirable compression artifacts in PNG images. However, an image saved in PNG-24 format often has a larger file size than if it is saved in JPEG format.

 Downloadable Figure 3.28 The effects of different Web image settings on the example image shown in Figures 3.28a–c may not show up very well on the printed page in the book. Figures 3.28a–c are available on the book's Web site for you to take a closer look.

🖰  Worksheet: JPEG versus GIF versus PNG

1. Learn to optimize files in JPEG, GIF, and PNG formats and to adjust the compression settings to achieve a balance between the file size and overall image quality.
2. Learn the type of images that each of these file formats is most effective at compressing.

Adobe Photoshop CS5's `Save For Web & Devices` dialog box (Figure 3.28) lets you preview different optimization settings before you save your images into a JPEG, GIF, or PNG. It also shows the estimated file size and download time for a specified network connection speed. Figure 3.28a shows a comparison of JPEG, GIF, and PNG. Figure 3.28b shows three sets of different JPEG settings with the original uncompressed image. Figure 3.28c shows three sets of different GIF settings.

## 3.11  WORKING WITH VECTOR GRAPHICS PROGRAMS

Vector graphics programs work differently from image editing or photographic editing programs because the basic units that they are dealing with are different. Images are represented with pixels. Image editing programs such as Adobe Photoshop are pixel based. An image can be edited pixel by pixel. The physical dimensions of the print size of an image depend on its pixel dimensions and its image resolution in ppi. On the other hand, a vector graphic is not made up of pixels but mathematical description of the graphic. Vector graphics programs, such as Adobe Illustrator and Flash, deal with objects or shapes made up of paths, points, strokes, and fills.

### 3.11.1  Paths and Points

A *path* is a mathematical description of an abstract line or curve. It is defined by a set of points, called *anchor points* (Figure 3.29). A path can be open (Figure 3.29a) or closed (Figure 3.29b). Each point has *direction handles or tangent handles*. The curviness and the tangent at each point are controlled by its handle's length and angle, respectively (Figure 3.30).

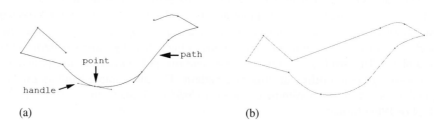

(a)                                                    (b)

**Figure 3.29**  (a) An open path, point, and handle. (b) A closed path.

There are two types of anchor points: corner points and smooth points. A *corner point* appears sharp and angular. Its handles have zero length. In vector graphics programs, a corner point does not have handles. Corner points (shown in color in Figure 3.31) are used for creating straight segments. A *smooth point* has direction handles to let you adjust the tangent and curviness at the point.

(a)                                   (b)                                   (c)

**Figure 3.30** (a) and (b) The length of the handle controls the curviness of the path. (c) The direction of the handle controls the tangent at the point.

**Figure 3.31** A path with corner points (colored).

In most vector graphics programs, one of the tools for creating paths is called the Pen tool. You use the Pen tool to define points for the path. In Adobe Illustrator and Flash, simply clicking with the Pen tool places a corner point. To create a new smooth point with the Pen tool, click-drag (i.e., drag while holding down the mouse button) and you can pull out the handles of the new point. A handle has two sides, each of which can be adjusted separately. For example, in Adobe Illustrator and Flash, you can ALT-drag (Windows) or Option-drag (Mac OS) using the Subselection tool on one of the handles to break their dependency, like the middle anchor point shown in Figure 3.32. In addition, corner points can be converted to smooth points at any time, and vice versa, by using the **Convert Anchor Point tool**.

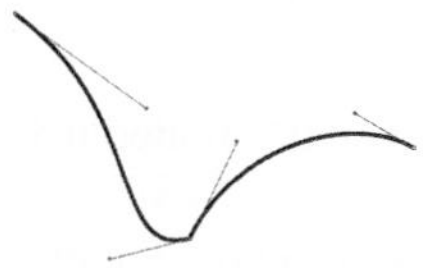

**Figure 3.32** The direction handles of the middle anchor point are broken out and can be adjusted independently.

## DRAWING PATHS WITH THE PEN TOOL

The shape of a path is defined by these aspects:

- The position of each point
- The length of the handles of each point
- The direction of the handles of each point

The Pen tool lets you click-drag to create and adjust the handles while you are creating new smooth points. Many people who are new to the Pen tool often find it difficult to draw a path this way because the shape of a path is made up of multiple points and, on top of this, each point has those three aspects you need to determine.

Don't forget that the Pen tool also lets you simply click (instead of click-drag) to create corner points. You can convert corner points to smooth points later and adjust their handles at any time. This means that you can break up the complex task into multiple, simple stepwise tasks.

The following instructions intend to help you get started with the Pen tool by dealing with one aspect of a smooth point at a time.

Before drawing a path on the computer, do some planning first:

1. Once you have the shape in mind, sketch it out on paper. Suppose you want to draw a path as in Figure 3.33.

**Figure 3.33** An example path that will be drawn.

2. Decide where to put the anchor points and figure out the minimum number of anchor points for the job. If the path is an open path, then each of the two ends of the path needs to have an anchor point.

   To decide where the anchor points are, look for the sharp change of direction. Keep in mind that a C-shaped segment can be created using only two smooth points (Figure 3.34).

**Figure 3.34** A C-shaped curve can be created using only two smooth points.

The path shown in Figure 3.33 is an open path. Thus, each of the two ends of the paths will have an anchor point. There is a sharp change of direction in the middle. Thus, we can add one more anchor point there, as in Figure 3.35. Note that the whole path is basically made up of two C-shaped segments.

**Figure 3.35** Decide the positions of the anchor points.

3. Eyeball the tangent of each anchor point on the curve and sketch it on paper. It will serve as a guide for you to adjust the direction of the anchor points' tangent handles.

   Returning to the example, the tangent for each point can be sketched out, as in Figure 3.36.

**Figure 3.36** Eyeball the tangent for each anchor point and sketch it out on paper.

Once you have a sketch, drawing it in your vector graphic application program will be easy.

**Activity/Exercise**

1. Use the Pen tool to create all corner points, as in Figure 3.37, based on your sketch. Only worry about the position of each anchor point for now. Do not worry about the curvature at each point.

**Figure 3.37** Create a path with corner points first.

2. After you have finished creating a path with all the corner points, convert those points that need to be smooth points using the Convert Anchor Point tool. Then, adjust each handle based on your sketch.

As you are getting more familiar with the Pen tool and using it more often, you may prefer the click-drag method because it saves the step of converting corner points to smooth points.

## 3.11.2 Strokes and Fills

A path does not have a physical appearance—line width or color—until the path is stroked with a specified line style, width, and color (Figures 3.38a and 3.38b). The vector graphics program may be set up to stroke the path by default. If so, whenever you create a path, it will be stroked with a line. If you set the *stroke* to none, the path will still be there, but you do not see it unless it is being selected and it will not be printed out.

A line style does not have to be a standard solid line. It can have an appearance of natural media, such as a dry paint brush like the one shown in Figure 3.38c. It can also be a custom defined style, such as the fish brush in Figure 3.38d.

A *fill* is a color, pattern, or gradient inside a shape defined by a path. Usually, fills also can be applied to open paths (Figure 3.39a) in addition to closed paths (Figure 3.39b).

## 3.11.3 Preset Shapes and Free-Form Drawing

There are tools to create common shapes such as ellipses, rectangles, polygon, stars, and spirals. Some programs also have a free-form drawing tool with which you can draw a

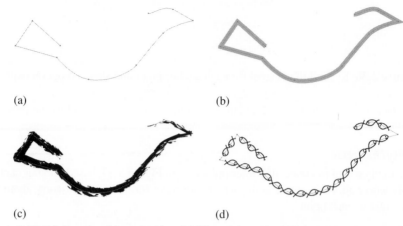

(a)                                              (b)

(c)                                              (d)

**Figure 3.38** (a) A path without stroke. (b) The path stroked with a solid line. (c) The path stroked with a line of charcoal brush style. (d) The path stroked with a line of custom brush style of a small fish.

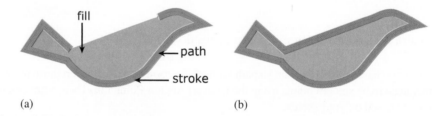

(a)                                              (b)

**Figure 3.39** Path, stroke, and fill. (a) An open path. (b) A closed path.

free-form path with a continuous stroke without manually defining the points. However, a free-form path is still made up of points; they are generated by the program.

### 3.11.4 Selection Tool

There are two basic selection tools in a vector graphics program: (1) the *Selection tool* in Adobe Illustrator and Flash, which lets you select the whole object; and (2) the *Subselection tool* in Flash or *Direct Selection tool* in Illustrator, which lets you select the points and their handles. Using the Selection tool, you can select the whole object and move, rotate, or scale it as a whole. With the Subselection or Direct Selection tool, you can alter the shape of an object by moving the points or their handles.

### 3.11.5 Layers, Effects, and Filters

Like many image editing programs, vector graphics programs also support layers that help you organize and manage the content. For example, you can toggle the visibility and the locking of a layer.

In addition, effects and filters, such as blur and drop shadow, that are available in image editing programs also are available in vector graphics programs. Some effects soften the edges of vector graphics to make them look more like bitmap images.

✏ **Example: Adding an Organic Feel to a Vector Graphic** This example demonstrates adding an organic feel to a vector graphic by using the following tools:

- Filters
- Gradient mesh
- Importing bitmapped images
- Clipping mask

## 3.11.6 Creating Complex Shapes Using Boolean Tools

Most vector graphic programs let you create complex shapes by performing *boolean operations* (such as union, subtract, and intersect) on overlapping simple shapes. For example, the *Pathfinder tool* (`Window > Pathfinder`) in Adobe Illustrator lets you merge, divide, trim, crop, outline, and minus overlapping shapes to create new shapes. To demonstrate the divide effect, in each of Figures 3.40a–c, one of the overlapping shapes is in thicker outline to show

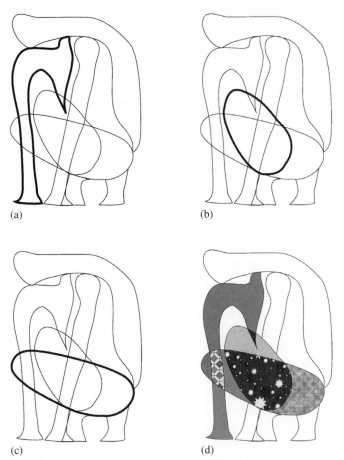

(a)

(b)

(c)

(d)

**Figure 3.40** (a)–(c) An overlapping simple shape is in thicker outline to show you its original shape before applying a Pathfinder operation. (d) After the divide operation, the three overlapping shapes are divided into individual shapes that can be filled with different colors and patterns. (*continued*)

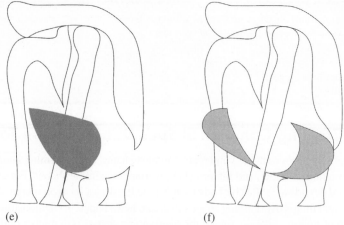

(e)                                    (f)

**Figure 3.40** (*continued*) (e) The result after applying the crop operation on the two overlapping oval shapes. (f) The result after applying the minus back operation on the two overlapping oval shapes.

you its original shape. These three overlapping shapes are then selected to apply with the divide operation using Pathfinder. The shapes are divided up into individual shapes, which now can be filled with different fills and strokes independently (Figure 3.40d). These individual shapes also can be repositioned, resized, or deleted independently. Figure 3.40e and Figure 3.40f show the result after applying the crop and minus back operations, respectively, on the two overlapping oval shapes.

## 3.12 SUMMARY

In general, there are two ways to acquire digital images: scanning a picture and digital photography.

To determine the scanning resolution (dpi), you need to first determine the final image's pixel dimensions. How you determine the final image's pixel dimensions depends on what the final image is intended for—the Web or print. If it is intended for print, then the pixel dimensions of the image can be calculated by multiplying the image's intended physical dimensions and its intended printing resolution (ppi). If the final image is for the Web, then its pixel dimensions are estimated relative to the screen resolution of the intended display device.

The equation used for estimating scanning resolution is:

$$\text{Scan Resolution (in dpi)} = \frac{\text{Pixel Dimension (in pixels)}}{\text{Scan Source Dimensions (in inches)}}$$

If you are scanning a picture, make sure the scan resolution and color mode are appropriate for the way you will use the image. Unless the scanned image is not going to be retouched or edited at all, you should turn off auto sharpening, which is often enabled by default in many scanner programs. If the scanning software lets you look at the histogram of the scan preview, make sure you are assigning the appropriate tonal range to the scan. It is best to optimize the tonal range and correct any significant color problems during the scanning process. This is because once you have scanned the picture, any image editing afterward will not be able to recover the color information that got clipped off during scanning.

There are several steps in image retouching in general. Although not all of the steps are necessary, the order of these steps is important:

1. Crop and straighten the image.
2. Remove dirt and dust.
3. Adjust the overall contrast or tonal range of the image.
4. Remove color cast.
5. Fine-tune specific parts of the image.
6. Sharpen the image.

The term *megapixel* is commonly used to describe the resolution capability of a digital camera. A megapixel refers to one million pixels. With the same printing resolution (ppi), an image with more megapixels can be printed at a larger size than the one with fewer megapixels. Digital cameras that support more megapixels do not necessarily offer a higher image quality. Other factors, such as the optics of the camera and how the image data from the sensor is processed, also determine the quality of digital photographs. This chapter shows you that for printing at 150 ppi, the print dimensions are about 45 square inches per megapixel. These numbers can be interpreted as follows:

- At 150 ppi, about 7.6 inches × 5.7 inches per megapixel for a print of 4:3 width:height ratio
- At 150 ppi, about 8.2 inches × 5.4 inches per megapixel for a print of 3:2 width:height ratio

The physical print size of an image depends on two factors: its pixel dimensions and the print resolution. The following equation shows the relationships among these three variables:

$$\text{Print Dimension (in inches)} = \frac{\text{Pixel Dimension (in pixels)}}{\text{Print Resolution (in pixels per inch or ppi)}}$$

You can adjust the print resolution (ppi) to suit the print dimensions. Be careful not to unknowingly resize the image's pixel dimensions. In Photoshop, the Resample Image option in the Image Size dialog box lets you specify if you want to alter the image's pixel dimensions in changing the image size settings. Unchecking the Resample Image option will preserve the pixel dimensions of the image when adjusting the physical print size and print resolution.

The two basic and essential tools in digital image editing are selection and layers. Selection tools allow you to limit the editing to the selected area. Various selection tools are available for different selection tasks. Layers allow you to organize components of an image. You can rearrange their stacking order, adjust opacity, and blend with other layers.

If the image is intended for the Web, then the image needs to be saved in the JPEG, GIF, or PNG format. The JPEG format works best with continuous-tone images with a broad color range and subtle color and brightness variations, such as photographs and images with gradients. JPEG images use a lossy compression. A highly compressed JPEG image often appears blurry and shows undesirable artifacts due to compression. GIF images work well for images with solid colors, such as illustrations, logos, and line art. GIF images also can be created as animated sequences and saved as animated GIF files. The PNG format has two options: (1) PNG-24 (24-bit color, like JPEG) works well with continuous-tone images, and (2) PNG-8 (8-bit color, like GIF) works well with solid colors. Unlike the JPEG format, the PNG format uses a lossless compression and support transparency. There is no undesirable compression artifacts in PNG images. However, an image saved in PNG-24 format often has a larger file size than if it is saved in JPEG format.

## TERMS

anchor points 92
Background layer 82
boolean operations 97
brightness 73
CCD (charge-coupled device) 64
clipping mask 83
CMOS (complementary metal-oxide semiconductor) 64
color balance 69
Color Balance tool 72
color casts 69
contrast 73
Convert Anchor Point tool 93
corner point 92
Crop tool 67
Curve tool 72
Direct Selection tool 96
direction handles or tangent handles 92

digital single-lens reflex (D-SLR) 67
dithering 91
dpi (dots per inch) 60
drum scanners 59
enhanced resolution 60
Eraser tool 82
Eyedropper tool 81
fill 95
flatbed scanners 58
GIF 89
handheld scanners 59
Healing Brush 68
highlights, midtones, and shadows 68
histogram 72
Hue/Saturation tool 72
JPEG 88
Lasso tool 81
layer mask 83
layers 82

Layers panel 82
Magic Wand tool 81
Magnetic Lasso tool 81
Marquee tools 81
megapixel 64
Move tool 82
optical resolution 60
path 92
Pathfinder tool 97
Pen tool 81
PNG-24 91
PNG-8 91
Polygonal tool 81
Quick Mask mode 81
Selection tool 96
sheet-fed scanners 59
smooth point 92
stroke 95
Subselection tool 96
tonal adjustments 64
Unsharp Mask tool 70

## LEARNING AIDS

The following learning aids can be found at the book's companion Web site.

### Tonal Adjustments during Scanning

An interactive tutorial that explains and demonstrates why tonal optimization is necessary during scanning.

### Worksheet: Making Sense out of Megapixels

This worksheet guides you in looking up digital camera specifications and understanding how to calculate megapixels to suit your needs.

### Photography: Understanding Shutter Speed, Aperture, and ISO

This supplementary reading explains the meaning and determination of the shutter speed, aperture, and ISO.

### Image Retouching (Lab)

Use the example image (available from the book's Web site) and practice the retouching steps discussed.

### Understanding and Applying Histograms

There are two parts of this learning aid: an interactive tutorial and practice exercises. The tutorial explains how to interpret an image's histogram and make tonal adjustments using histograms.

To test your knowledge of histograms, check out the two interactive exercises:

**Exercise I: Reading Histograms.** Practice relating the appearance of a histogram to the image characteristics.

**Exercise II: Improving Image Contrast and Brightness.** Identify the problem of the image by examining the histogram, and then improve it.

### Light Metering Emulation of Photography
This emulates photographing a still life and illustrates the relationship between spot-metering and the resulting image's midtone.

### Understanding and Applying Curves for Color Adjustments
An interactive tutorial and exercises help you undertand the Curves tool for the image ajdustment.

### Photoshop Basics: Selection
A screen-capture movie gives a quick demonstration of some of the selection tools in Photoshop. A worksheet exercise is also available.

### Image Alteration (Lab)
Use the example images (available from the book's Web site) to practice selectively altering areas.

### Photoshop Basics: Using Layers
A screen-capture movie gives a quick demonstration of commonly used features of the Layers panel in Photoshop. A worksheet exercise is also available.

### Making Composites: Example 1—Replicating an Object in Its Environment
In this example, the final image (Figure 3.24b) contains an extra object—a humanoid chain sculpture—which is not in the original image (Figure 3.24a). This example demonstrates the following aspects of image editing.

* Application of selection
* Scaling with the perspective in mind
* Creation of shadows

### Making Composites: Example 2—Recreating a Sky Background
In this example, the final image (Figure 3.25c) contains an artificial sky and is created by compositing two digital images (Figure 3.25a and b). The tools used to make the composite include:

* Layer blending mode
* Layer mask
* Layer style
* Filters
* Stamp tool
* Dodge tool

### Optical Color Mixing in Pointillism, Dithering, and Inkjet Printing
An interactive demonstration on optical color mixing.

### Downloadable Figure 3.28
The effects of different Web image settings on the example image shown in Figure 3.28 may not show up very well on the printed page in the book. Figures 3.28a–c are available on the book's Web site for you to take a closer look.

### Worksheet: Image ppi versus Printer dpi
Learn the difference between the printer dpi and image ppi by:

1. Experimenting with how the image ppi affects the output dimensions of the image.
2. Experimenting with how the printer dpi affects the printing quality of the image.

### Worksheet: JPEG Compression Artifact
Look at the impact of JPEG compression artifact on different digital images, and learn when and why an image may be or should not be saved in JPEG format.

**⊕ Worksheet: JPEG versus GIF versus PNG**

1. Learn to optimize files in JPEG, GIF, and PNG formats and to adjust the compression settings to achieve a balance between the file size and overall image quality.

2. Learn the type of images that each of these file formats is most effective at compressing.

**✎ Example: Adding an Organic Feel to a Vector Graphic**

This example demonstrates adding an organic feel to a vector graphic by using the following tools:

- Filters
- Gradient mesh
- Importing bitmapped images
- Clipping mask

## REVIEW QUESTIONS

When applicable, please select all correct answers.

1. What are the different types of scanners?

2. What is the method of acquiring digital images besides scanning?

3. Resampling an image is often referred to as _____.

    A. rotating
    B. scaling
    C. translating
    D. repositioning

4. Scaling an image usually deteriorates the image quality somewhat. In four sentences or less, explain why in terms of what happens to the pixels by scaling up and scaling down.

5. The Apple iPhone 4S camera can take digital photographs with pixel dimensions of 3264 $\times$ 2448 pixels.

    i. Show the math that the resolution capability of the camera is 8 megapixels.
    ii. Show the math that with these pixel dimensions, the physical dimensions of the printed image are about 10-inch $\times$ 8-inch if you print it at 300 ppi.

6. Suppose that you scan a 3-inch $\times$ 5-inch photograph in at a resolution of 300 dpi.

    i. What are the pixel dimensions of the scanned image? _____ $\times$ _____ pixels
    ii. What will the physical dimensions of the image be if you print it at 300 ppi, without altering the image's pixel dimensions? _____ inches $\times$ _____ inches
    iii. What will the physical dimensions of the image be if you print it at 600 ppi, without altering the image's pixel dimensions? _____ inches $\times$ _____ inches
    iv. What will the physical dimensions of the image be if you print it at 150 ppi, without altering the image's pixel dimensions? _____ inches $\times$ _____ inches
    v. **True/False**: You gain image detail if you print the image at 600 ppi as noted in (iii).
    vi. **True/False:** You lose image detail if you print the image at 150 ppi as noted in (iv).

7. **True/False:** When a digital image is printed, each image pixel is represented by one printer ink dot.

8. The "per inch" in the units dots per inch and pixels per inch is in _____.

    A. square inches
    B. linear inches

9. **True/False:** The optimization of tonal adjustment at the time of capturing images—scanning or digital photography—does not matter because you can always extend the tonal range of the image to any extent afterward in Photoshop to recover the missing color information.

10. Given here are the general steps of image retouching of a scanned image.

    i. Order the steps by labeling 1 through 6.

      _____ Adjust the overall contrast or tonal range of the image
      _____ Crop and straighten the image
      _____ Fine-tune specific parts of the image
      _____ Remove color casts
      _____ Remove dirt and dust
      _____ Sharpen the image

    ii. Explain your choice for the first step.

    iii. Explain your choice for the last step.

11. Suppose you want to scan part of a photograph to use in a digital collage. The part of the picture you want to scan is 2-inch × 2-inch on the photograph. You want this scanned piece to appear as 6-inch × 6-inch in the final collage that will be printed out at 300 ppi.

    If you scan the picture at a resolution insufficient to print it at a size of 6-inch × 6-inch at 300 ppi, you will have to scale up the scanned image, which will deteriorate the image quality and make it look pixelated.

    What is the minimal scanning resolution (dpi) you should use to scan this 2-inch × 2-inch area so that you do not have to resize the image to meet the printing requirement? Show your calculations.

    (*Tip*: First calculate the pixel dimensions of that piece of image needed in the final collage.)

12. What kind of images are GIF files most appropriate for?

    A. Images with big areas of solid colors      C. Images with lots of gradients
    B. Continuous-tone photographs

13. What kind of images are JPEG files most appropriate for?

    A. Images with big areas of solid colors      C. Images with lots of gradients
    B. Continuous-tone photographs

14. Shown in Figure 3.41 is a grayscale image and its histogram:

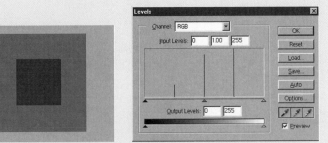

**Figure 3.41** (a) A grayscale image. (b) The image's histogram.

i. Match each of the bars in the histogram to the color it represents. (Draw arrows linking each bar and the color in the grayscale image in Figure 3.41.)

ii. To maximize the contrast and tonal range of this image, what changes of the sliders should be made? Show the new positions of the sliders in the histogram provided in Figure 3.41.

iii. Figure 3.42 shows four different adjustments of the sliders made in the grayscale image's histogram. For each of the four image outlines in Figure 3.42, label the areas with the resulting grays. Specify whether it is black, white, or gray. If it is gray, estimate an RGB value for that gray.

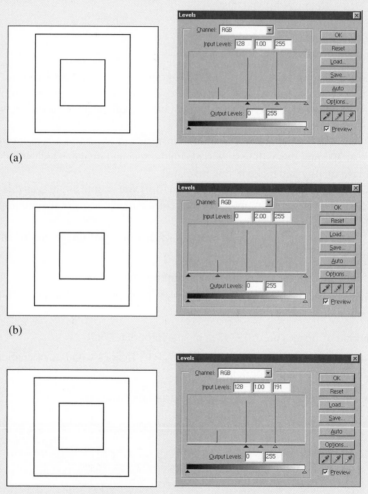

(a)

(b)

(c)

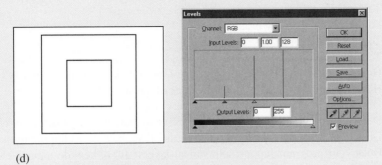

(d)

**Figure 3.42** Four pairs of histograms and outlines of images, the colors of which are to be predicted based on the adjustment made in their histograms.

## EXPLORING THE APPLICATIONS

1. Explore the selection tools of your image editing program. Use the Help menu or the user manual to find out the following how-to's. Write down the answers. Use your notes as a quick reference guide and refer to them as needed. (If your image editing program is Adobe Photoshop, there is a worksheet on selection tools of Photoshop available at the book's Web site.)

   - To select the whole image
   - To deselect
   - To inverse the selection
   - What are the different marquee tools available?
   - What are the different lasso tools available?
   - To add to a selection
   - To subtract from a selection
   - To select only an area intersected by other selections
   - To expand or contract a selection by a specific number of pixels
   - To feather the edge of a selection
   - To save a selection
   - To load a previously saved selection
   - How do you make selection by color?
   - Does your program have a Pen tool that allows you to draw paths to define the selection? If so, find out how it works.
   - Does your program let you make a selection by painting a "mask"? If so, find out how it works.

2. Explore the use of layers in your image editing program. Use the Help menu or the user manual to find out information for the following. Write down the answers. Use your notes as a quick reference guide and refer to them as needed. (If your image editing program is Adobe Photoshop, there is a worksheet on layers of Photoshop available at the book's Web site.)

   - To create a new layer
   - To delete a layer

- To duplicate a layer
- To toggle the visibility of a layer
- To rename a layer
- To adjust the opacity of a layer
- How do you move or scale the content of multiple layers simultaneously?
- How do you rearrange the stacking order of the layers?
- How does the stacking order of the layers affect the image?
- Does your program support layer masks? If so, how do layer masks work?
- Does your program support clipping mask? If so, how does clipping mask work?
- Does your program support adjustment layers? If so, how do adjustment layers work?

3. Explore your vector graphics program. Use the Help menu or the user manual to find out the information for the following. Write down the answers. Use your notes as a quick reference guide and refer to them as needed.
    - Find out the tools for creating paths
        - Pen tool
        - Free-form drawing tool
    - How do you add and delete points of a path?
    - How do you alter the curvature of a path?
    - How do you stroke a path?
    - How do you fill a shape?
    - Find out the selection tools for selecting whole objects and for selecting points and handles.
    - How do you create layers to organize the objects?
    - Find out the effects and filters available. Experiment with at least two.
    - Find out the tools that offer boolean operations on overlapping shapes to create new shapes.

4. Practice creating paths in a vector graphics program. If you are new to the vector graphics program, try to practice creating simple paths first, such as those shown in Figure 3.43, using corner points and smooth points. Use the same number of points as shown in the paths. The number of points on each of these paths is the minimum number of points for creating the path.

Figure 3.43 Some simple paths to start with when starting to learn the Pen tool.

Also, practice editing the paths by moving the points and their handles. If you are getting familiar with the program, try creating more complex vector shapes using minimum number of points.

# 4

# Fundamentals of Digital Audio

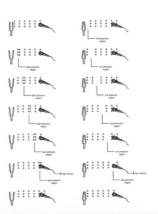

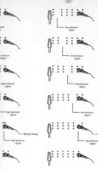

KEY CONCEPTS
- Sound wave
- Frequency and pitch
- Digitizing sound
- Sampling rate and bit depth of digital audio
- Nyquist's theorem
- Dynamic range
- Audio file size optimization
- MIDI

GENERAL LEARNING OBJECTIVES

In this chapter, you will learn

- The common terms in audio.
- The properties of sound waves.
- The basic steps of digitization—sampling and quantization—in digital audio.
- The effects of sampling rate and bit depth on digital audio quality.
- The meaning of *decibel*.
- The common file types for digital audio.
- The general strategies for reducing digital audio file sizes.
- The difference between digital audio recording and MIDI.

## 4.1 INTRODUCTION

Sound is an integral part of our everyday sensory experience. It is also an analog phenomenon. As is the case with most of our everyday sensory experiences, we seldom think of sound in its microscopic sense. However, in order to understand digital audio, you need to recognize the fundamental nature of sound as waves—the physics of sound. In this chapter we will explain and interpret the graphical depiction of sound as a *waveform*. A waveform serves as a means for us to "see" the information that we hear by providing quantitative properties of a sound, such as its amplitude and frequency.

## 4.2 THE NATURE OF SOUND WAVES

Sound is a wave that is generated by vibrating objects in a medium such as air. The vibrating objects can be the vocal cords of a person, a guitar string, or a tuning fork. Plucking a guitar string in the air causes the string to move back and forth. This creates a disturbance of the surrounding air molecules. When the string moves in one direction, it causes the air molecules to compress into a smaller space, raising the air pressure slightly in that region. The air molecules under higher pressure in that region then push the other air molecules surrounding them, and so forth. When the vibrating string moves in the reverse direction, it creates a gap between the string and the molecules. This lowers the air pressure in that region, causing the surrounding air molecules to move into that area. The displacement of air molecules propagates, radiating away from the string and causing periodic changes of air pressure—forming a sound wave. When this compression wave reaches your eardrums, it causes the eardrums to move back and forth. This sends a signal to your brain, which recognizes the changing air pressure as a sound. The harder you pluck the string, the greater the movement of the string, which causes greater displacement of the air molecules. This, in turn, causes higher pressure in the high-pressure region and lower pressure in the low-pressure region of the wave. When the string is plucked harder, the amplitude of the sound is higher and the sound is louder.

## SOUND AS A MECHANICAL WAVE

Because the propagation of a sound wave in a medium relies on the mechanism of particle interactions, a sound wave is characterized as a mechanical wave. The implication of this property is that a sound wave does not propagate in a vacuum.

The motion of a particle in a sound wave is parallel to the direction of the wave. This type of wave is characterized as a longitudinal wave. Notice that it is the *motion* of the particles that propagates, not the particles themselves.

If you place a microphone in the path of the sound wave, the periodic air-pressure change will be detected by the recorder and converted into varying electrical signals. The changes of pressure in the propagating sound wave reaching the recorder are thus captured as changes of electrical signals over time. The sound wave can be represented graphically with the changes in air pressure or electrical signals plotted over time—a waveform (Figure 4.1). The vertical axis of the waveform represents the relative air pressure or electrical signals caused by the sound wave. The horizontal axis represents time.

A vibrating guitar string in the air causes the string to move back and forth, causing periodic changes of air pressure. The changes of pressure in the propagating sound wave reaching the recorder are captured as changes of electrical signals over time. The sound wave can be represented graphically with the changes in air pressure or electrical

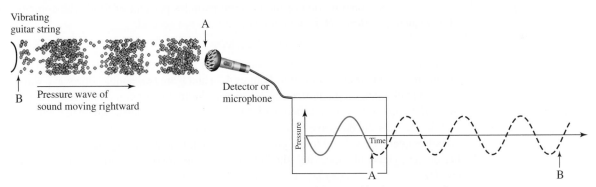

**Figure 4.1** A pressure sound wave from a guitar string and its graphical representation.

signals plotted over time—a waveform. Be careful *not* to interpret the waveform as a representation of the sound wave in *space*. The picture on the left in Figure 4.1 is a picture of the air molecules in space. On the right is a graph over *time*. The air-pressure information at point B is *not* where time is zero on the waveform graph. Instead, the pressure information of point B has not yet propagated to the microphone; it would have been after point A has been recorded—about three more cycles to the right of point A on the waveform.

A waveform is a graphical representation of the pressure–time (not pressure-space) fluctuations of a sound wave. A sound wave propagates in space. The waveform matches the pressure changes in time at a fixed location. The crests correspond to the high pressure (compression of air molecules), and troughs correspond to the low pressure (rarefaction). The horizontal axis is time. However, looking at an illustration of a longitudinal pressure wave of sound placed side by side with its waveform can mislead you to think of the horizontal axis of the waveform as distance if you are not careful. Remember that the horizontal axis of a waveform is time, not distance. Let's re-emphasize two key points about a waveform:

> **Sound as a Pressure Wave** An illustration of a sound wave as a longitudinal air-pressure wave.

1. Be careful *not* to interpret sound wave as a wave that has crests and troughs, as in a transverse wave. Sound wave is a longitudinal wave, in which the particles of the medium (such as air molecules) move back and forth, not up and down, in the direction of the wave propagation.

2. Be careful *not* to interpret the waveform as a representation of the sound wave in *space*. Instead, the waveform graph represents the pressure changes over *time*.

Besides visualization of the pressure oscillation of the sound wave over time, a waveform can also give us information about the pitch and loudness of the sound. The following sections discuss how these two properties are measured and derived from the waveform.

## 4.2.1 Frequency and Pitch

A sound wave is produced by a vibrating object in a medium, say air. No matter what the vibrating object is, it is vibrating or moving back and forth at a certain frequency. This causes the surrounding air molecules to vibrate at this same frequency, sending out the sound-pressure wave. The *frequency* of a wave refers to the number of complete back-and-forth cycles of vibrational motion of the medium particles per unit of time. The common unit for frequency is *Hertz (Hz)* where the unit of time is 1 second.

$$1 \text{ Hz} = 1 \text{ cycle/second}$$

The period of a wave is the time for a complete back-and-forth cycle of vibrational motion of the medium particles. Shown in Figures 4.2a and b are two simple sine wave waveforms. If the tick mark on the horizontal axis marks the first second, then the frequency of the wave in Figure 4.2a has a frequency of 2 Hz, because it completes two cycles within 1 second. In Figure 4.2b, the wave has a frequency of 4 Hz.

Sound frequency is related to the *pitch* of the sound. Higher frequencies correspond to higher pitches. Generally speaking, the human ear can hear sound ranging from 20 Hz to 20,000 Hz.

Two notes that are an octave apart correspond to sound waves whose frequencies are in a ratio of 2:1.

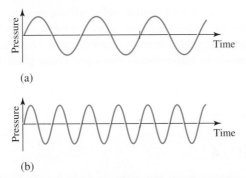

**Figure 4.2** Simple waveforms representing two different frequencies: (a) lower frequency, (b) higher frequency.

## 4.2.2 Sound Intensity and Loudness

*Sound intensity* is related to the perceived *loudness* of a sound, but the two are not exactly the same. Sound intensity is often measured in *decibels (dB)*. A decibel is based on a ratio of a louder sound to a softer one. By definition,

$$\text{Number of decibels} = 10 \times \log (I_1/I_{\text{ref}})$$

**(Equation 1)**

where $I_1$ and $I_{\text{ref}}$ are the two sound intensity values in comparison.

$$\text{Number of decibels} = 20 \times \log (V_1/V_{\text{ref}})$$

**(Equation 2)**

where $V_1$ and $V_{\text{ref}}$ are the magnitudes of two electrical voltages or currents in comparison.

Notice that the decibel is not an absolute unit. It is an expression of a ratio of two values. More precisely, it is a logarithm of the ratio of two values. The general implication of this is that doubling the sound intensity means an increase of about 3 decibels. Or, a louder sound that causes twice the magnitude of the electric voltages or currents as a softer sound is about 6 decibels higher than the softer one. Why 3 and 6? Let's plug some numbers into the previous equations.

Say that you have a sound whose pressure wave produces an electrical signal $V_1$, and this pressure is double the pressure of some reference sound ($V_{\text{ref}}$). This means

$$V_1 = 2 \times V_{\text{ref}}$$

Plugging this relationship into Equation 2, we get:

$$\begin{aligned}\text{Number of decibels} &= 20 \times \log (2 \times V_{\text{ref}}/V_{\text{ref}}) \\ &= 20 \times \log (2) \\ &\cong 20 \times 0.3 \\ &= 6\end{aligned}$$

Similarly, plugging numbers into Equation 1 for doubling the sound intensity gives you 3 decibels. It may seem that this explanation presents more mathematics than you really need to know in order to work with digital audio editing programs. However, in many audio editing programs, the audio amplitude is measured in decibels. In addition, 3 and 6 decibels are given as preset values in amplification filters. Understanding what decibels mean and their relationship to audio signals helps you create predictable results in audio editing.

## DECIBELS AND BELS

The unit called a *bel* was defined by scientists at Bell Labs to compare two power values. The unit was named after Alexander Graham Bell. By definition,

$$\text{Number of bels} = \log (P_1/P_0)$$

where $P_1$ and $P_0$ are the two power values in comparison. For sound, these can be considered the sound intensity.

A decibel (dB) is 1/10th of a bel (i.e., 1 bel equals 10 decibels.) So

$$\text{Number of decibels} = 10 \times \log (P_1/P_0)$$

Because power equals voltage times current, this relationship leads to the following (which we present without going into the mathematical derivation).

$$\text{Number of decibels} = 20 \times \log (V_1/V_0)$$

where $V_1$ and $V_0$ are the two voltage or amplitude values in comparison.

The threshold of hearing is the minimum sound-pressure level at which humans can hear a sound at a given frequency. It varies with frequency. Generally, 0 dB refers to the threshold of hearing at 1,000 Hz. Note that 0 dB does not mean zero sound intensity or the absence of a sound wave.

The threshold of pain is about 120 decibels, representing a sound intensity that is 1,000,000,000,000 (or $10^{12}$) times greater than that of 0 decibel.

## LOUDNESS VERSUS SOUND INTENSITY

The loudness of a sound is a subjective perception, but sound intensity is an objective measurement. Thus, loudness and sound intensity are not exactly the same properties.

To measure loudness, a 1,000-Hz tone is used as a reference tone. The volume of the reference tone is adjusted until it is perceived by listeners to be equally as loud as the sound being measured. Sound intensity, on the other hand, can be measured objectively by auditory devices independent of a listener.

The age of the listener is one of the factors that affect the subjective perception of a sound. The frequency of the sound is also a factor because of the human ear's sensitivity to different sound frequencies. The loudness of sound (as perceived by human ears) is only roughly proportional to the logarithm of sound intensity. However, in general, the higher the sound intensity, the louder the sound is perceived.

## 4.3 ADDING SOUND WAVES

A simple sine wave waveform represents a simple single tone—single frequency. When two or more sound waves meet, their amplitudes add up, resulting in a more complex waveform (Figure 4.3). The sound we perceive every day is seldom a single tone. The waveforms representing speech, music, and noise are complex waveforms that result from adding multiple waveforms of different frequencies. For example, Figure 4.4 shows a waveform of the spoken word "one."

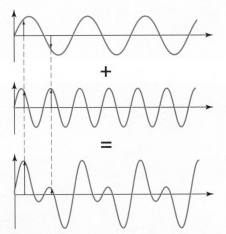

**Figure 4.3** Addition of two simple sine wave waveforms results in a more complex waveform.

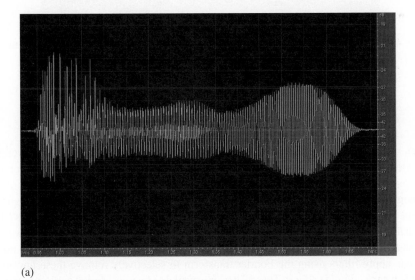

(a)

**Figure 4.4** (a) A waveform of the spoken word "one." *(continued)*

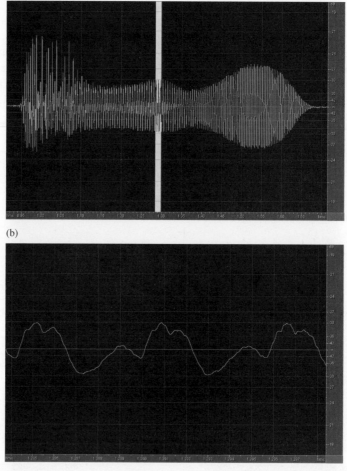

(b)

(c)

**Figure 4.4** *(continued)* (b) The highlighted segment to be magnified. (c) The zoomed-in view of the segment of the waveform.

The mathematical basis of the Fourier transform is discussed in the CS Module.

## DECOMPOSING SOUND

When we record a sound, such as the spoken word "one" in Figure 4.4, the waveform recorded is a complex one. Can a complex wave be decomposed into its simple component parts—the different sine waves that make up the complex wave? Yes! One of the mathematical methods to accomplish this decomposition is called the Fourier transform.

But why would you want to decompose a complex wave into simple sine waves? The frequency of a simple sine wave can be determined easily. When you want to remove certain sounds that can be characterized by a range of frequencies, such as low-pitched noise, you can apply filters using the Fourier transform to selectively remove these unwanted sounds from a complex sound. These filters are available in many digital audio-processing programs and are used for breaking down a sound to remove unwanted frequencies.

# 4.4 DIGITIZING SOUND

A sound wave is an analog phenomenon. In a sound wave, the amplitude changes continuously over time. Like the process of digitizing any analog information, the process of digitizing sound involves sampling and quantizing an analog sound wave.

## 4.4.1 Step 1: Sampling

In the *sampling* step, the sound wave is sampled at a specific rate into discrete samples of amplitude values. The higher the sampling rate, the higher the accuracy in capturing the sound. However, a higher sampling rate will generate more sample points, thus requiring more storage space and processing time. To give you a feel for the sampling rate for digital sound, the sampling rate for CD-quality audio is 44,100 Hz (i.e., 44,100 samples per second).

> 🖰 **Sampling and Quantizing in Digital Audio** An interactive tutorial illustrating the concepts of sampling and quantizing in digitizing a sound wave.

To keep the illustration simple and clear, our examples will use very low sampling rates. These rates are too low to be practical for digitizing sound in real life, but they are simple enough to demonstrate the point. Figure 4.5a represents a continuous sound wave signal. When we digitize the sound wave, we take discrete samples. Figure 4.5b shows a sampling rate of 10 Hz (that is, taking 10 samples of the pressure per second). Figure 4.5c shows a simple reconstruction of the wave by keeping the pressure value a constant between sample points. As you see, changes—crests and troughs—between any two sample points are missed.

The common reconstruction of an analog wave from the discrete sample points is not done by keeping the sample values constant between sample points, as shown in Figure 4.5c. Instead, it is usually done by interpolation of the sample points using mathematical algorithms to regenerate a smooth curve. However, no matter what technique is used to reproduce the sound wave, the number of sample points, and thus the sampling rate, is the limiting factor for the accuracy of the reconstruction.

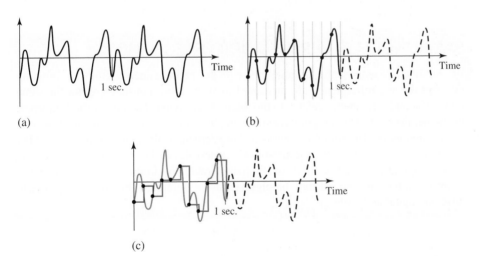

(a)                                        (b)

(c)

**Figure 4.5** (a) A theoretical continuous sound wave signal. (b) Ten samples of the pressure are taken per second—a sampling rate of 10 Hz. (c) A simple reconstruction by keeping the pressure value a constant between sample points.

What if we raise the sampling rate to 20 Hz? Figure 4.6a shows a sampling rate of 20 Hz, and Figure 4.6c shows a simple reconstruction of the wave. The reconstructed wave now looks closer to the original wave than the one sampled at 10 Hz does. As you see, a higher sampling rate can increase the accuracy of the reproduction of a sound wave.

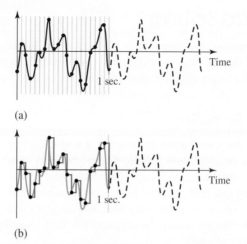

(a)

(b)

**Figure 4.6**  (a) A sampling rate of 20 Hz. (b) A simple reconstruction of the sound wave.

Because a higher sampling rate will produce more sample points, the file size of the resulting file will be larger. As in the 10-Hz example, changes—crests and troughs—between the sample points are still missed. This is an inherent limitation of the discreteness of digital data. No matter how high the sampling rate you adopt, there will always be missed points between those discrete sample points.

## SAMPLING RATE VERSUS AUDIO FREQUENCY

Be careful not to confuse the sampling rate with the audio frequency. Both the sampling rate and the audio frequency are measured in Hertz (Hz), but they are not the same thing. The audio frequency relates to the pitch of the sound. The higher the frequency, the higher the pitch. The sampling rate refers to the number of samples taken per second for a sound wave. The sampling rate is a characteristic of the digitization process, but the audio frequency describes the sensory characteristics of the sound we perceive. The same sampling rate may be used for digitizing sounds of different audio frequencies. Conversely, the same sound may be digitized using different sampling rates to create different digital audio files.

## 4.4.2 Step 2: Quantizing

In the *quantizing* step, each of the discrete samples of amplitude values obtained from the sampling step will be mapped and rounded to the nearest value on a scale of discrete levels. Therefore, the more levels available in the scale, the higher the accuracy in reproducing the sound. For digital audio, having more levels means higher *resolution*. However, higher resolution will require more storage space. The number of levels in the scale is expressed in *bit depth*—the power of 2. For example, an 8-bit audio allows $2^8 = 256$ possible levels in the scale. To give you a feel of the bit depth for digital sound, CD-quality audio is 16-bit (i.e., $2^{16} = 65,536$ possible levels in quantizing the samples of amplitude values).

For demonstration purposes, we use 3-bit as an example, which is a scale of eight discrete levels. Again, 3-bit is not a practical bit depth used in real-life applications. The sampled data are mapped to the nearest level on the scale (Figure 4.7). Some samples may deviate more from their original amplitudes. With a low bit depth, data with different original amplitudes may be quantized onto the same level—for example, note the quantized sample points of the last six sample points in Figure 4.7b.

> 🖱 **Audio Examples (a Short Musical Sound and a Sound Effect) with Various Combinations of Sampling Rate and Bit Depth** Audio examples of a short musical sound and an explosion sound effect with various sampling rates (44,100 Hz, 22,050 Hz, and 11,025 Hz) and bit depths (8 bit and 16 bit) are used to demonstrate the impact of sampling rate and bit depth on (i) the audio quality and (ii) the file size. Review questions on the impact of sampling rate and bit depth, the audio's waveforms, and frequency spectral views are also available.

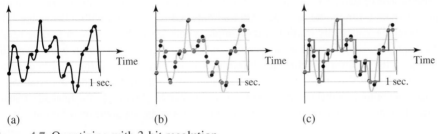

(a)          (b)          (c)

**Figure 4.7** Quantizing with 3-bit resolution.

## 4.5 DYNAMIC RANGE

In the quantization step, a scale of discrete levels of amplitude values is used to map the sample points. The range of the scale, from the lowest to highest possible quantization values in the scale, defines the ***dynamic range*** for digitizing audio. In the quantization example of the previous section, where a scale of eight levels (3-bit samples) is used, the lowest level of the scale is placed at about the lowest amplitude of the sound wave and the highest level at about the highest point of the sound wave. The remaining six levels are equally spaced in between these two levels. This scale is extended to include the highest- and lowest-amplitude values of the sound wave. That is, none of the sample points is outside of this range. The scale, shown in Figure 4.8, covers a full amplitude range of the sound wave.

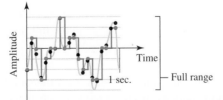

**Figure 4.8** Quantization using a scale range equal to the full amplitude range of the sound wave.

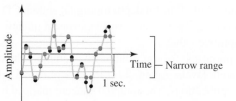

Figure 4.9 Quantization using a scale range narrower than the full amplitude range of the sound wave.

If the dynamic range is smaller than the full amplitude range of the sound wave (Figure 4.9), some data will be lost. The digitized sound wave will be "chopped" off at the limit of the range, causing clipping of the sound wave. Clipping is an undesirable effect because of loss of data. The clipped amplitude values are not recoverable. However, with a reduced dynamic range, the accuracy can be improved for the data within the range. This is an advantage, especially if most of the sample points are within a smaller middle region of the range. By sacrificing a small number of highest- and lowest-amplitude values, the accuracy of the majority of the sample points can be improved. In the simple example shown in Figure 4.9, you see that (with the same bit depth) reducing the dynamic range actually allows more subtle changes to be distinguishable (Figure 4.10). Instead of being quantized to the same value, some sample points can now be set apart on different levels.

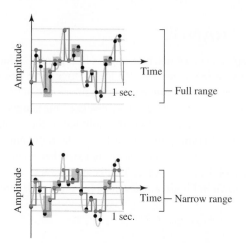

Figure 4.10 The quantized data (shaded in blue) in which subtle changes become more distinguishable in the reduced dynamic range than in the full range.

The dynamic range of a sound system refers to the range of the highest and lowest sound levels that the system can reproduce. In such context, a larger dynamic range is considered better because the sound system can then allow you to input audio components with wider ranges, and it can output the audio with minimal distortion.

What if you extend the dynamic range to more than the amplitude range of the sound wave? Then you will get the opposite result of reducing the dynamic range—the accuracy will be lost. As you see in Figure 4.11, the amplitude of the sound wave is now within only six levels of the range. So, although this extended dynamic range has eight quantization levels available, only six levels are utilized for this sound wave.

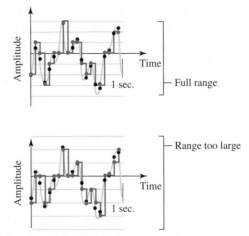

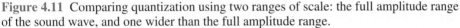

**Figure 4.11** Comparing quantization using two ranges of scale: the full amplitude range of the sound wave, and one wider than the full amplitude range.

## 4.6 FILE SIZE, FILE COMPRESSION, AND FILE TYPES OF DIGITAL AUDIO

Higher sampling rate and bit depth always deliver better fidelity of a digitized file—whether it is an image or audio. So the recurring question may come up again: If higher sampling rate and bit depth give better fidelity and less degradation, then why shouldn't we always choose the maximum possible values? Well, the answer to this question is always the file size. Large file sizes require more storage space, longer processing time, and longer transfer time. Especially if the digital media files are created for use on the Internet, the network transfer time of a file is often a more important consideration than the storage space, which is becoming less expensive. The larger the file size, the longer it will take to download to another person's computer.

In addition to the sampling rate and bit depth, do not forget that the duration of the audio also affects the file size. Audio is a time-based medium. Audio files (such as speech and music) often require long, continuous playback. Therefore, the file size increases very rapidly with a higher sampling rate and bit depth. Let's look at an example of a 1-minute CD-quality stereo audio. A stereo audio has two *channels*—a left channel and a right channel. The bit depth of CD-quality audio is 16 bits per channel—16 bits per sample for each channel. Its sampling rate is 44.1 kHz—that is, 44,100 samples per second. The number of bits rquired to store a 1-minute CD-quality stereo audio is calculated as follows:

$$1 \text{ minute} \times 60 \text{ seconds/minute} = 60 \text{ seconds}$$

$$60 \text{ seconds} \times 44,100 \text{ samples/second} = 2,646,000 \text{ samples}$$

$$2,646,000 \text{ samples} \times 16 \text{ bits/sample} = 42,336,000 \text{ bits}$$

Because stereo audio has two channels, the total bit size = 42,336,000 bits × 2 = 84,672,000 bits.

To convert the bit size into bytes,

$$84,672,000 \text{ bits}/(8 \text{ bits/byte}) = 10,584,000 \text{ bytes} \cong 10 \text{ MB}$$

As you see, it requires about 10 MB for each minute of CD-quality audio. An hour of such audio requires about 600 MB. At the time of writing, the average download speed of the 4G wireless connection is in the range of 2–6 mbps (megabits per second) for laptop modems and 1–2 mbps for smartphones.[1] The time it takes to download this 1-minute audio from the Web at 2 mbps would be

$$84{,}672{,}000 \text{ bits}/(2{,}000{,}000 \text{ bits/second}) \approx 42 \text{ seconds}$$

With 1 mbps on some smartphones, the time would be about 84 seconds, or almost 1.5 minutes. To reduce the download time, you may want to reduce the file size of the audio. As you may recall from Chapter 1, the three general strategies of reducing a digital media file size are reducing the sampling rate, reducing bit depth, and applying file compression. As you see in the example, the equation for the audio file size calculation can be expressed as follows:

File size = duration $\times$ sampling rate $\times$ bit depth $\times$ number of channels

The equation for calculating audio file size includes an additional factor—the number of channels. Therefore, by examining the equation of audio file size calculation, you see four general strategies of reducing a digital audio file's size:

- Reduce the sampling rate
- Reduce the bit depth
- Apply compression
- Reduce the number of channels

Note that duration of the audio is also a factor in the equation for file size calculation. We do not include reduction of audio duration in the listed strategies because in most situations you want to keep the duration of the audio. However, keep in mind that the duration of the audio has a direct effect on the file size. You may want to remove the unnecessary silent segments in an audio file where possible. For example, most voice-over or speech contains unnecessary silence or pauses that may be removed to reduce the audio duration and thus the file size.

- **Reducing the number of channels.**
  Stereo audio has two channels. If you reduce a stereo audio file to mono—which becomes one channel—then you reduce the file size in half. This may suit speech and short sound effects for online games. Your decision to reduce the audio from stereo to mono is very much dependent on the nature of your project. Reducing a channel causes a noticeable difference unless your final product is expected to be listened to with a mono-speaker.
- **Reducing the sampling rate.**
  Reducing the sampling rate and bit depth sacrifices the fidelity of the digitized audio, which means it will sound less like the original. However, when working with digital media files, you often have to weigh the quality against the file size. When you do so, you often need to take into consideration both human perception of the medium and how you're going to use the audio.

  First, let's consider that the human ear can hear sound ranging from approximately 20 Hz to 20,000 Hz. The range varies with individuals and their ages. Not all people can hear the two ends of the average range. The human ear is most sensitive in the range of about 2,000 to 5,000 Hz, not the two ends of the range.

  Second, according to a rule called *Nyquist's theorem*, we must sample at least two points in each sound wave cycle to be able to reconstruct the sound wave satisfactorily.

---

[1] Mark Sullivan. "4G Wireless Speed Tests: Which Is Really the Fastest? AT&T, Sprint, T-Mobile, and Verizon: PCWorld's exclusive performance tests reveal which 4G network delivers the fastest data speeds." *PCWorld*. March 13, 2011. URL: http://www.pcworld.com/printable/article/id,221931/printable.html

In other words, the sampling rate of the audio must be at least twice that of the audio frequency—called a ***Nyquist rate***. Therefore, a higher-pitch sound requires a higher sampling rate than a lower-pitch sound. In reality, the sound we hear, such as music and speech, is made up of multiple-frequency components. Then the sampling rate can be chosen as twice the highest-frequency component in the sound in order to reproduce the audio satisfactorily. Reducing the sampling rate sacrifices the sound quality of the higher frequencies.

The most common sampling rates you may encounter in a digital audio editing program are:

11,025 Hz: AM radio quality/speech
22,050 Hz: Near FM radio quality (common for multimedia projects)
44,100 Hz: CD quality
48,000 Hz: DAT (digital audio tape) quality
96,000 Hz: DVD audio quality
192,000 Hz: DVD audio quality

Based on the human hearing range and the Nyquist theorem, the sampling rate for CD-quality audio of 44.1 kHz is reasonable. But can we reduce the sampling rate, and if so, to what extent? Because the human ear is most sensitive in the range of about 2 to 5 kHz, then 11,025 Hz and 22,050 Hz seem to be reasonable sampling rates. 11,025 Hz causes more noticeable degradation to music than to speech because music has more higher-frequency components than speech. Because the human voice in speech normally does not exceed 5 kHz, the sampling rate setting of 11,025 Hz is reasonable for speech. Depending on the nature of your final product, a sampling rate setting of 11,025 Hz may also suit short sound effects (such as breaking glass and explosions), which may not require high fidelity.

So, how much can we lower the file size by reducing the sampling rate? From the file size equation, the file size can be reduced in the same proportion as the reduction of the sampling rate. In the example of 1 minute of CD-quality stereo audio, lowering the sampling rate from 44.1 kHz to 22.05 kHz will reduce the file size from about 10 MB to about 5 MB.

- **Reducing the bit depth.**
  The most common bit-depth settings you may encounter in a digital audio editing program are 8 bit and 16 bit. According to the file size equation, lowering the bit depth from 16 to 8 reduces the file size in half. In the example of a 1-minute CD-quality stereo audio, lowering the bit depth from 16 to 8 will reduce the file size from about 10 MB to about 5 MB. Suppose the sampling rate of the audio has been lowered from 44.1 kHz to 22.05 kHz, creating a 5-MB file. Lowering the bit depth of this file from 16 to 8 will reduce the file size further, from 5 MB to 2.5 MB.

  Eight-bit resolution is usually sufficient for speech. However, for music, 8-bit resolution is too low to accurately reproduce the sound satisfactorily. Our ears usually can notice the degradation in playback. Typically, 16-bit resolution is used for music.

- **Applying file compression.**
  An audio file can be compressed to reduce the audio file size. Compression can be lossless or lossy. Lossy compression gets rid of some data, but human perception is taken into consideration so that the data removed causes the least noticeable distortion. For example, the popular audio file format MP3 uses a lossy compression that gives a good compression rate while preserving the *perceptible* quality of the audio by selectively removing the least perceptible frequency components of the audio. Keep in mind that a file compressed with a lossy compression method should not be used as a source file for further editing. To achieve the best result in editing an audio file, you should always start with a source file that is uncompressed or compressed with lossless compression.

No matter which file size reduction strategies you want to apply to your audio file, you should always evaluate the acceptability of the audio quality of the reduced file based on the nature of your audio project and weigh the quality against the file size limitation. The intended use of your final audio dictates the acceptability of trade-offs.

Even working within a limitation of file size, you should record or digitize with at least CD or DAT quality and then apply file size reduction strategies later, instead of digitizing at a lower sampling rate and bit depth in the first place. One reason is that compression algorithms are often designed to selectively remove data that will cause minimal impact on the audio quality perceivable by the human ear. Another reason is that by keeping a higher sampling rate and bit depth, you will have a choice of optimizing the file size by a combination of the file optimization strategies. You can weigh the file size reduction against the quality at that point. However, if you do not digitize at a high enough sampling rate or bit depth, you will get stuck with an unsatisfactory audio.

Many digital audio editing programs let you choose the format in which you want to save your audio file. The common file types are listed in Table 4.1. Some file types already dictate the compression option to be used. Others allow you to choose whether you want to compress the file, and possibly the compression options.

Generally, the intended use of your audio file determines the file format. You should take into consideration the following factors:

The information in Section 6.10 on streaming video and progressive download also apply to audio.

HTML5 video and audio are covered in Chapter 15.

- **The file size limits.**
  If your audio is intended to be used on the Web, you may want to consider a file format that offers high compression or even a streaming audio file format to minimize the wait time to play your audio. Streaming audio means the audio will be played while it is being downloaded. The audio file does not have to be downloaded in its entirety before it can be played. However, it requires Internet connection during its playback.
- **The intended audience of your audio file.**
  How is your target audience going to listen to your audio? What equipment do they have? If they are listening on a computer, what is the operating system? If your audio will be played on multiple platforms, then the file should be a cross-platform format. If you want the audio to be played on a Web page without having to use external plug-ins, you may want to use HTML5 audio.
- **Keeping the file as a source file.**
  If you are keeping the file for future editing, then you should choose a file format that is uncompressed or uses lossless compression.

## CLOUD COMPUTING FOR VIDEO AND AUDIO DELIVERY

The term "cloud" refers to the Internet and cloud computing refers to the technologies that provide computing services (such as storage, software, database access) to users via the Internet. For online storage, you can download your files onto your devices whenever needed. The downloaded video and audio files can be played back *from your devices*. For video and audio files, cloud-based service providers often also support streaming the media—the media is played back *over the Internet*. For example, Amazon Cloud Drive offers online storage and supports downloading and streaming of music files that are saved on your Cloud Drive. Apple iCloud lets you stream the music files stored on your iCloud and download them on any of your devices.

## TABLE 4.1    Common Audio File Types

| File Type | Acronym For | Originally Created By | File Information and Type of Compression | Platforms and Additional Information |
|---|---|---|---|---|
| .aiff | Audio Interchange File Format | Apple, adopted later by Silicon Graphics | Usually not compressed, but has a compressed version | Primarily for Mac OS; also supported on Windows |
| .wav | | IBM and Microsoft | • Supports uncompressed and a number of different compression formats<br>• One of the HTML5 audio formats | • Primarily for Windows, but can be used on other systems<br>• Plays in Web browsers that support the .wav format of HTML5 audio; at the time of writing, the supported browsers are Firefox, Safari, Chrome, and Opera |
| .au and .snd | Also called μ-law or Sun μ-law format | Sun and NeXT | μ-law encoding compresses the file at a ratio of 2:1; slow decompression | Sun, Unix, or Linux operating system |
| .mp3 | MPEG audio layer 3 | Moving Pictures Experts Group | • Good compression rate with perceivably high-quality sound<br>• One of the HTML5 audio formats | • Cross-platform; many digital audio players can play it<br>• Plays in Web browsers that support the MP3 format of HTML5 audio; at the time of writing, it is supported by Safari, Internet Explorer (IE), and Chrome, but Chrome is dropping future support of MP3 |
| .m4a | MPEG-4 format without the video data | Moving Pictures Experts Group | • AAC compression; same compression as the MPEG-4 H.264 without the video data<br>• One of the HTML5 audio formats | Plays in Web browsers that support the AAC format of HTML5 audio; at the time of writing, it is supported by Safari, IE, and Chrome |
| .ogg or .oga | | Xiph.Org Foundation | • Usually referred to as Ogg Vorbis format<br>• Ogg is a container format<br>• The audio codec is Vorbis | Plays in Web browsers that support the Ogg Vorbis format of HTML5 audio; at the time of writing, it is supported by Firefox, Chrome, and Opera |
| .mov | QuickTime movie | Apple | • Not just for video<br>• Supports audio track and a MIDI track<br>• Supports a variety of sound compressors<br>• Files can be streamed with QuickTime Streaming Server<br>• "Fast Start" technology also allows users to listen to media as it is being downloaded | Cross-platform; requires QuickTime player |
| .wma | Windows Media Audio | Microsoft | | |
| .asf | Advanced streaming format | Microsoft | Proprietary compression algorithm | Primarily used with Windows Media Player |

## 4.7 MIDI

So far in this chapter, we have been describing the digital audio of captured analog audio that is produced by the vibration of objects in air. The continuous fluctuation of pressure in a propagating pressure wave is captured by a device or microphone, then digitized by sampling and quantization. The audio can be speech, music, noise, or a combination of these.

There is another method of storing music information—in ***MIDI*** format. MIDI (Musical Instrument Digital Interface) is a communications protocol, not a physical object. It defines the common interface for electronic digital musical instruments to communicate with computers or other instruments or devices containing microprocessors. It specifies the configurations of cables and cable plugs and the format of the data.

Many electronic keyboards have built-in synthesizers. A MIDI keyboard looks like a small piano, but upon receiving a signal such as a key being hit, its electronic device synthesizes sound using its own internal microprocessor (i.e., computer). Computers also can be attached directly to a MIDI keyboard to capture the musical notes being played. There are also software programs that let you enter the notes directly via the computer's mouse and keyboard. The composed music also can be played through a MIDI keyboard that has a synthesizer.

MIDI signals are not digitized audio sample points but contain note *information* played with a virtual instrument. Such information includes the instrument being played, the note being played, the duration of the note, and how loud to play the note. Unlike the digital audio we have been describing in the previous sections of this chapter, MIDI music creation does not involve capturing and digitizing analog sound waves or any analog information. Therefore, it does not involve sampling and quantization; that is, there is no sampling rate or bit-depth option in creating and editing a MIDI file.

Compared to the sampled audio files, the MIDI format has both advantages and disadvantages. Its file size can be much more compact. For example, the file size of a 1-minute MIDI file can be about 2 KB, but, as you have seen in the file size calculations, a 1-minute, stereo, 16-bit audio with a sampling rate of 44.1 kHz is about 10 MB. If you convert this MIDI file into a 44.1 kHz, 16-bit, stereo digital audio file, it will become about 10 MB. MIDI music can be easily edited like sheet music by changing the notation, timing, and instruments.

The composed music of a MIDI file requires a synthesizer to play. The quality of the sound depends on the quality of the synthesizer that plays back the composed music. This can be a disadvantage because the actual sound produced by different synthesizers may differ even for the same note of the same instrument. The composed music you hear from your MIDI keyboard may not sound the same on your friend's MIDI keyboard or computer synthesizer. For example, QuickTime has its own selection of high-quality MIDI instruments and thus can play MIDI without an external MIDI synthesizer. But it sounds different from a full-fledged synthesizer.

The analogy for MIDI music versus digitized audio may be a cake recipe versus the baked cake. It is much easier and lighter to send a cake recipe to your friends. But how exactly the cake tastes and looks may vary depending on the exact ingredients your friends use—even the same temperature setting varies from oven to oven. On the other hand, a baked cake is more bulky to mail to your friends. But it ensures the cake's taste and look that you intend the recipient to experience.

# 4.8 SUMMARY

Sound is a wave that is generated by vibrating objects in a medium such as air. The vibrating objects can be the vocal cords of a person, a guitar string, or a tuning fork. An object vibrating in air creates a disturbance of the surrounding air molecules, causing periodic changes of air pressure—forming a sound wave.

No matter what the vibrating object is, the object is vibrating or moving back and forth at a certain frequency. This causes the surrounding air molecules to vibrate at this same frequency. The common unit for frequency is Hertz (Hz); 1 Hz refers to 1 cycle per second. The sound frequency is related to the pitch of the sound. Higher frequencies correspond to higher pitches.

Sound intensity is related to, but not exactly the same as, the perceived loudness of a sound. The loudness of a sound is a subjective perception, but sound intensity is an objective measurement. Sound intensity is often measured in decibels (dB). A decibel is based on a ratio of a louder sound to a softer one; it is not an absolute measurement.

When two or more sound waves meet, their amplitudes add up, resulting in a more complex waveform. The waveforms of the sound we perceive every day (such as speech, music, and noise) are complex waveforms that result when multiple waveforms of different frequencies are added together.

Like the process of digitizing any analog information, the process of digitizing a sound wave involves sampling and quantizing an analog sound wave. In the sampling step, the sound wave is sampled at a specific rate into discrete samples of amplitude values. The higher the sampling rate, the higher the accuracy in capturing the sound. But a high sampling rate will generate more sample points, which will require more storage space and processing time. In the quantizing step, each of the discrete samples of amplitude values obtained from the sampling step will be mapped to the nearest value on a scale of discrete levels. Therefore, the more levels available in the scale, the higher the accuracy in reproducing the sound. For digital audio, having more levels means higher resolution. But higher resolution requires more storage space for the same reason that higher bit depth for any digital media will increase the file size.

Audio files, such as speech and music, usually require long, continuous playback. Therefore, the file size increases very rapidly with higher sampling rate and bit depth. To reduce the file size, there are four general file optimization approaches: reduce the sampling rate, reduce the bit depth, apply compression, and reduce the number of channels. No matter which file size reduction strategies you want to apply to your audio file, you should always evaluate the acceptability of the audio quality of the reduced file based on the nature of your audio project, and weigh the quality against the file size limitation. The intended use of your final audio dictates the consideration of the acceptable trade-offs.

Even working within a limitation of file size, you will get better results by recording or digitizing at a sampling rate and bit depth that produce good audio quality and then apply file size reduction strategies later.

Another method of storing music information is in MIDI format. MIDI stands for Musical Instrument Digital Interface. MIDI files do not contain digitized audio sample points. Instead, they contain information about musical notes to be played with a virtual instrument. Such information includes the instrument being played, the note being played, the duration of the note, and how loud to play the note. Unlike digitized audio, MIDI music creation does not involve digitizing analog sound waves or any analog information. Therefore, there are no sampling rate and bit depth settings. MIDI music has the advantage of very small file size. Another advantage is that the music content can be edited easily. The disadvantage is that the sound depends on the synthesizer that plays back the composed music. Thus, you do not know how your MIDI file sounds on your target audience's devices.

## TERMS

| | | |
|---|---|---|
| bit depth  116 | loudness  111 | resolution  116 |
| channels  119 | MIDI  124 | sampling  115 |
| decibels (dB)  111 | Nyquist rate  121 | sound intensity  111 |
| dynamic range  117 | Nyquist's theorem  120 | waveform  108 |
| frequency  110 | pitch  110 | |
| Hertz (Hz)  110 | quantizing  116 | |

## LEARNING AIDS

The following learning aids can be found at the book's companion Web site.

### Sound as a Pressure Wave
An illustration of a sound wave as a longitudinal air-pressure wave.

### Sampling and Quantizing in Digital Audio
An interactive tutorial illustrating the concepts of sampling and quantizing in digitizing a sound wave.

### Audio Examples (a Short Musical Sound and a Sound Effect) with Various Combinations of Sampling Rate and Bit Depth
Audio examples of a short musical sound and an explosion sound effect with various sampling rates (44,100 Hz, 22,050 Hz, and 11,025 Hz) and bit depths (8 bit and 16 bit) are used to demonstrate the impact of sampling rate and bit depth on (i) the audio quality and (ii) the file size. Review questions on the impact of sampling rate and bit depth, the audio's waveforms, and frequency spectral views are also available.

## REVIEW QUESTIONS

When applicable, please select all correct answers.

1. A sound with higher _____ is perceived to have a higher pitch.

   A. volume
   B. frequency
   C. fidelity
   D. sampling rate
   E. bit depth

2. The unit used for measuring _____ is Hertz (Hz).

   A. amplitude
   B. frequency
   C. sampling rate
   D. bit depth
   E. dynamic range

**3.** A waveform is a graphical representation of the _____ fluctuations of a sound wave.

    A. pressure–time
    B. space–time
    C. pressure–space

**4.** The horizontal axis of a waveform is _____.

    A. pressure
    B. distance
    C. time

**5.** The vertical axis of a waveform is _____.

    A. pressure
    B. distance
    C. time

**6. True/False:** Zero decibels is when there is absence of sound or no sound wave.

**7.** The _____ of a sound relates to the sound intensity or loudness.

    A. amplitude
    B. frequency
    C. sampling rate
    D. bit depth
    E. dynamic range

**8.** The _____ of a digitized sound affects the accuracy of the sampled amplitudes being stored.

    A. amplitude
    B. frequency
    C. sampling rate
    D. bit depth
    E. dynamic range

**9.** In digital audio, the number of sample points taken per second is called the _____.

    A. amplitude
    B. frequency
    C. sampling rate
    D. bit depth
    E. dynamic range

**10.** In digital audio, higher resolution means higher _____.

    A. amplitude
    B. frequency
    C. sampling rate
    D. bit depth
    E. dynamic range

**11.** How many levels of amplitude values does an 8-bit sound allow?

**12.** How many levels of amplitude values does a 16-bit sound allow?

**13.** Generally, the audio CD music sampling rate is _____ and bit depth is _____.

14. **True/False:** Eight-bit sound is generally considered to be more than adequate for recording music.

15. **True/False:** MP3 is a good file format to keep as a source file for further editing.

16. Which of the following are audio file formats?

    BMP     WAV     JPEG     AIFF     MP3     GIF

    JPG     PSD     TIFF     WMF

17. According to Nyquist's theorem, we must sample at least _____ points in each sound wave cycle to be able to reconstruct the sound wave satisfactorily. In other words, the sampling rate of the audio must be at least _____ of the audio frequency.

18. The reduction of a digital audio file size can be achieved by _____.

    A. reducing the sampling rate
    B. reducing the pitch of the audio
    C. reducing the bit depth
    D. reducing the amplitude of the audio
    E. applying file compression techniques

19. Higher _____ will result in larger file size.

    A. amplitude
    B. frequency
    C. sampling rate
    D. bit depth
    E. dynamic range

20. Reducing the sampling rate from 44.1 kHz to 22.05 kHz will _____.

    A. have no effect on the file size
    B. decrease the file size by half
    C. decrease the file size to about 1/22th
    D. decrease the file size to about 1/44th

21. Reducing the bit depth from 16 bit to 8 bit will _____.

    A. have no effect on the file size
    B. decrease the file size by half
    C. decrease the file size to 1/8th
    D. decrease the file size to 1/16th

22. Reducing the number of channels from two (stereo) to one (mono) will _____.

    A. have no effect on the file size
    B. decrease the file size by half
    C. decrease the file size to 1/5th
    D. decrease the file size to 1/10th

23. The MIDI standard specifies the _____.

    A. sampling rate for the synthesized sound
    B. bit depth for the synthesized sound
    C. configurations of cables and cable plugs
    D. format of the data

# Capturing and Editing Digital Audio

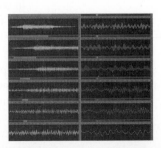

KEY CONCEPTS
- Methods of acquiring digital audio
- Techniques of digital audio touch-up and alteration
- Multitrack audio editing
- Loop music

GENERAL LEARNING OBJECTIVES
In this chapter, you will learn
- How to acquire sampled digital audio.
- The basic workspace of digital audio editing programs.
- The basic techniques of digital audio touch-up.
- The common techniques of digital audio alterations.
- The methods of creating music.
- How to embed audio on Web pages.

# 5.1 ACQUIRING DIGITAL AUDIO

Digital audio can be acquired by two methods: (1) recording sound directly into a digital format and (2) digitizing an existing analog audio media, such as analog audiotapes. In this section, we will discuss what hardware and software may be needed for each of these methods.

## 5.1.1 Recording

In order to record audio directly into digital format or to digitize analog audio, your computer needs to have a sound card. A *sound card* enables the playing and recording of sound on a computer. A sound card acts as an analog-to-digital converter that converts the electrical signals into digital format by sampling the signals based on the sampling rate and bit depth chosen. All new computers come with a sound card installed.

In order to record audio directly, you need a microphone. Most laptop computers have a built-in microphone. However, these built-in microphones (in general) do not produce sufficient sound quality for multimedia projects. Desktop computers usually do not have built-in microphones. Instead, an external microphone usually is needed for recording on a laptop or desktop computer.

Some microphones are designed to have a directional response to sound, unidirectional and omnidirectional, for example. Their sensitivity to sound varies with the angles of the sound approaching the microphone. A unidirectional microphone is most sensitive to the sound coming from the front. It has the advantage of isolating the sound source of interest from other noises coming from the rear. An omnidirectional microphone is equally sensitive to sounds coming from all directions. As a general rule for recording with a microphone, if you do not have access to the specifications of the microphone, place the sound source

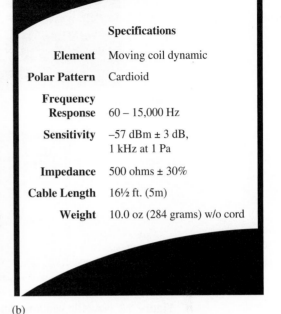

*Specifications*
Type: Dynamic microphone
Directivity: Uni-directional
Frequency response: 80 – 12,000 Hz
Output impedance: 600 ohms ± 30% at 1 kHz,
                  unbalanced
Effective output level: –56.8 ± 3 dBm (0 dBm =
                  1 mW/Pa, 1,000 Hz)
Dimensions: 54 mm (2⅛ inches) dia. × 211 mm
              (8⅜ inches) length
Mass (Microphone incl. cord): Approx. 255 g (9.0 oz.)
Operating temperature: 0°C – 40°C
Design and specifications are subject to change
without notice:

| | Specifications |
|---|---|
| **Element** | Moving coil dynamic |
| **Polar Pattern** | Cardioid |
| **Frequency Response** | 60 – 15,000 Hz |
| **Sensitivity** | –57 dBm ± 3 dB, 1 kHz at 1 Pa |
| **Impedance** | 500 ohms ± 30% |
| **Cable Length** | 16½ ft. (5m) |
| **Weight** | 10.0 oz (284 grams) w/o cord |

(a)  (b)

**Figure 5.1** Two examples of microphone specifications found on packaging: (a) A unidirectional microphone. (b) Cardioid polar pattern means unidirectional.

directly in front of the microphone. For example, if you are recording a voice-over, speak close to the front of the microphone; do not speak to the side of the microphone.

A microphone's frequency range and its directivity are useful information and can be looked up in the mircophone's specifications. This helps you get the most out of the microphone. For example, the microphone with the specifications shown in Figure 5.1a is unidirectional and has a frequency response range of 80 to 12,000 Hz. This covers human speech and musical instruments.

The microphone with the specifications shown in Figure 5.1b has a frequency response range of 60 to 15,000 Hz. This has a little wider range than the one in Figure 5.1a. There is no directivity listed, but the polar pattern describes the pattern of the sound sensitivity around the microphone. Its polar pattern is cardioid. The cardioid pattern is roughly a heart shape, hence the name "cardioid." It is most sensitive to the sound coming from the front but not from the rear. The cardioid polar pattern is also unidirectional.

The software component for audio recording is a digital audio recording program. Basically, all of the digital audio editing programs, such as Adobe Audition, Sony Sound Forge, and Audacity, let you record audio. At the time of writing, Adobe Audition is available for Windows and Mac OS X. Sony Sound Forge is a Windows application. Audacity is a free, open-source software available for Mac OS X, Microsoft Windows, GNU/Linux, and other operating systems. Audacity can be downloaded from the Web.

Before you start recording, you need to specify the sampling rate, bit depth, and the number of channels you want to use (Figure 5.2). The available sampling rate and bit depth for recording are determined by the capability of the hardware—the sound card. Most sound cards are capable of recording at least CD-quality sound—that is, a sampling rate of 44,100 Hz, a bit depth of 16, and two channels (stereo).

Cardioid shape: Imagine pinching the head of the microphone into a balloon. The shape of the pinched balloon approximates the cardioid shape. The volume of the balloon occupies the area where the microphone is most sensitive to where the sound is coming from.

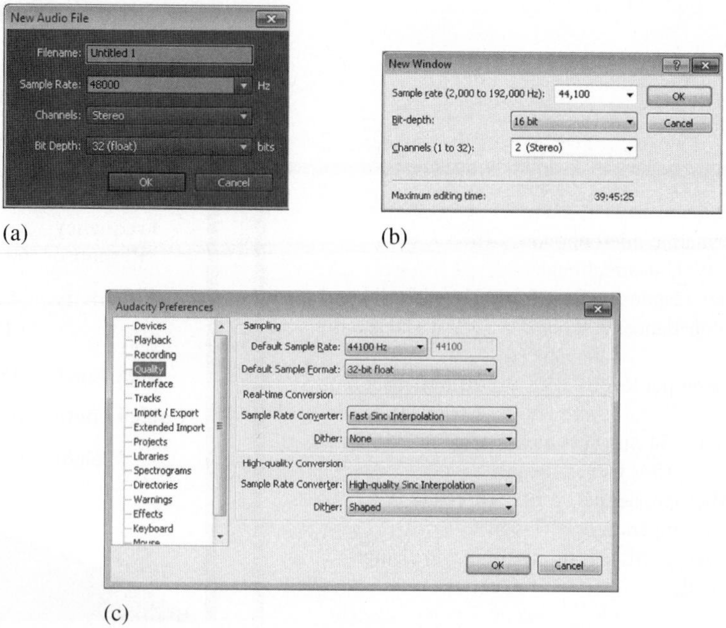

(a)

(b)

(c)

**Figure 5.2** New file window prompts to set the audio sampling rate, bit depth, and number of channels: (a) Adobe Audition. (b) Sony Sound Forge. (c) Audacity's Preference dialog box.

Audio software applications usually have an audio level meter that lets you monitor the sound input level during recording. By default, the level meter in Audition is located at the bottom of the window (Figure 5.3). In Sound Forge 10, the meter is vertical and is in a separate window (Figure 5.4). In Audacity, the meter is located at the top (Figure 5.5).

The input volume level can be adjusted so that the meter level stays below the red area (which is around 3 dB to 0 dB, as in Figure 5.3a). The loudest part of the audio may brush near the red area without going over it. Any data going over the limit of 0 dB will be given the value of zero. The areas of the waveform where this occurs will look chopped off and cause distortion of your recording (Figure 5.3b). This effect is called *clipping*. On the other hand, too low of a recording level produces a recording that is too soft (Figure 5.3c).

The optimal range depends on the nature of your audio. As a general guide, the signals between 12 and 3 dB should have sufficient strength. The meter gives you a technical depiction of the audio signal strength, but your ear should be the final judge of the audio. Occasional signals peaking over 0 dB will be fine if the overall audio and the most important part of the audio maintain a desired level and those clipped signals do not produce noticeable distortion.

Before the actual recording, rehearse your recording, if possible, and watch the meter. Adjust the audio input level and experiment with how close the sound source should be to your microphone so that the level for the majority of the audio is not too low or going over the red area.

- In Windows 7, you can adjust the recording volume by setting the sound properties from the Control Panel as follows.
    1. Click Sound in the Control Panel.

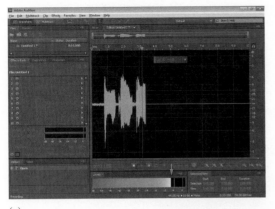
(a)

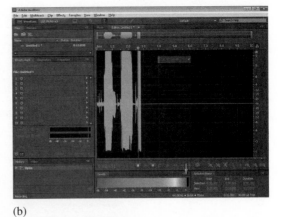
(b)

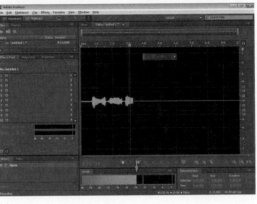
(c)

**Figure 5.3** The audio level meter in Adobe Audition CS5.5. The colored arrow shows where the meter is, and the thin line on the right side indicates the maximum level of the recording so far. (a) The optimal level. (b) The level is too high—going over the red area of the meter—causing undesirable clipping of the waveform. (c) The level is too low.

**Figure 5.4** The audio level meter in Sound Forge 10.

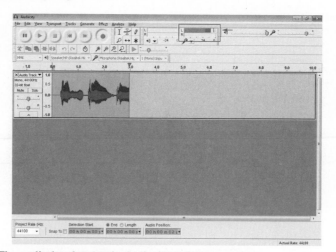

**Figure 5.5** The audio level meter in Audacity 1.3 Beta.

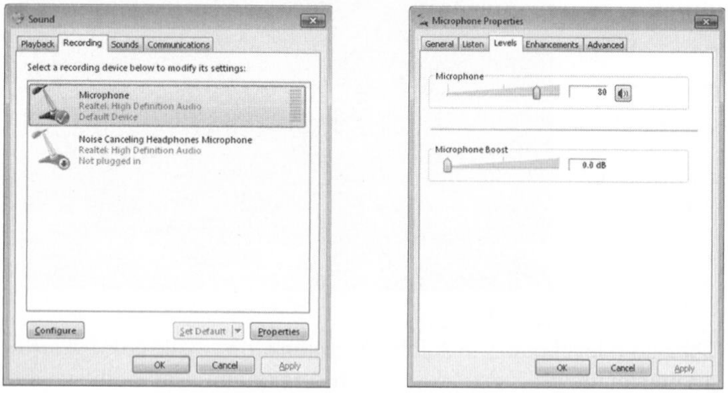

    (a)          (b)

**Figure 5.6** Setting microphone level in Windows 7: (a) Recording tab, and (b) Levels tab.

2. Select the Recording tab (Figure 5.6a), choose the microphone you want to use, and click the Properties button.
3. Select the Levels tab and adjust the microphone levels (Figure 5.6b).

- In Mac OS X,
  1. Look in the System preferences, and select Sound.
  2. Click on Input (Figure 5.7). You should see a list of devices for sound input, such as Internal microphone or External microphone.
  3. Select the microphone and drag the Input volume slider bar to adjust the volume. You can test the Input volume setting by speaking into a microphone and watching the response of the Input level meter.

> ✍ **Setting Recording Controls in Windows 7** Screen-capture movie that demonstrates how to set the recording device to microphone and adjust the volume in Windows.

> ✍ **Recording Audio in Adobe Audition** Screen-capture movie that demonstrates the basic steps of recording audio in Adobe Audition.

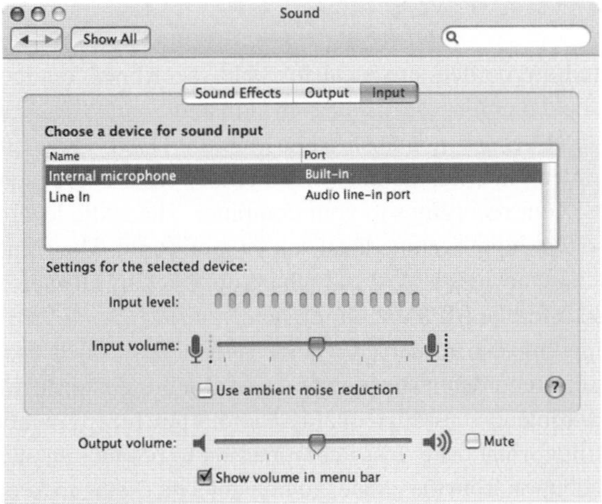

Figure 5.7 Mac OS X Sound preferences.

## SOUND CARD

Instead of being installed as a separate card on a computer, the sound subsystem is now commonly built into the motherboard of the computer. In this chapter, the term *sound card* is used synonymously with such a sound subsystem, regardless of its physical form.

*The role of sound card in the audio playback.* During recording, a sound card acts as an analog-to-digital converter that converts the electrical signals into digital format. During playback, a sound card acts as digital-to-analog converter. This means that it can convert the discrete samples in the digital format of the audio into analog signals by reconnecting the samples to reconstruct a waveform. It then sends the analog signals through the line-out port to your speakers.

*Working with a sound card.* A basic sound card has line-out, line-in, and microphone-in ports (Figure 5.8). Sound cards that are capable of surround sound have more ports. The line-out port is where the headphones or speakers are connected. The line-in and microphone ports are for recording. Laptop computers may not have a line-in port.

Figure 5.8 The back of a desktop computer showing the line-out (left, green), line-in (middle, blue), and the microphone (right, red) ports. Similar ports can be found on laptop computers that have a sound card.

## 5.1.2 Field Recording

Handheld digital audio recorders are ideal for field recordings, outdoor live events, and nature sound. Handheld recorders such as Zoom H4n and Sony PCM-D50 (Figure 5.9) also offer high quality stereo recording that surpasses standard DAT sound quality. The audio is recorded to the recorder's internal memory or a memory card. These recorders also support USB for transferring your recordings to your computer. The audio level meter is displayed on these recorder so that input volume level can be monitored. The common file format of the recording from these devices is WAV, which is supported by all audio-editing programs. Some recorders also offer the MP3 option for smaller files.

Voice recorder apps are also available for some cell phones, which also can be convenient handheld digital audio recorders. These apps generally are designed for recording audio memos, which are not intended for high quality audio. They record in mono and the recordings are saved in a file format using lossy compression to produce smaller files suitable for e-mail and Web distribution from the phone. To transfer a recording to a computer for editing, you can send the recording to yourself by e-mail and check your e-mails on the computer. You may also connect your phone to the computer. For example, after syncing your computer with your iPhone, the recordings will be listed in the Voice Memos under the Playlists section in iTunes on your computer. The sample rate, bit rate, and the location of a recording on your computer can be found by selecting the recording on the list and then File > Get Info. For Android phones, when it is connected to a computer, the phone will show up as a drive on the computer. You can copy the audio files from that drive onto the computer.

**Figure 5.9** A handheld digital audio recorder.

## 5.1.3 Digitizing Analog Media

The need to digitize analog audio media, such as cassette tapes, does not come up quite often nowadays. But when there is a need to do so, you will need to connect the line-out port of the cassette tape deck to the line-in port on your sound card using an audio cable.

Then start the sound recording on the computer before playing the cassette tape. The starting and stopping of the recording do not have to be synchronized with the starting and stopping of the cassette tape. You should always digitize a little more before and after the segment that you need. The extra audio can be edited out later.

## 5.2 BASIC WORKSPACE ELEMENTS IN DIGITAL AUDIO EDITING PROGRAMS

Examples of commercial digital audio editing application programs are Adobe Audition (Windows and Mac OS) and Sony Sound Forge (Windows). Audacity is a free digital audio program available for Mac OS X, Microsoft Windows, GNU/Linux, and other operating systems.

### 5.2.1 Basic Editing: Working with One Audio at a Time

The two very basic elements you will find in these digital audio editing programs are: (1) a waveform display window and (2) the transport controls where you find the play, record, rewind, and fast forward buttons. For example, Figure 5.10 shows screenshots of Adobe Audition, Sony Sound Forge, and Audacity, highlighting the areas of these two basic elements.

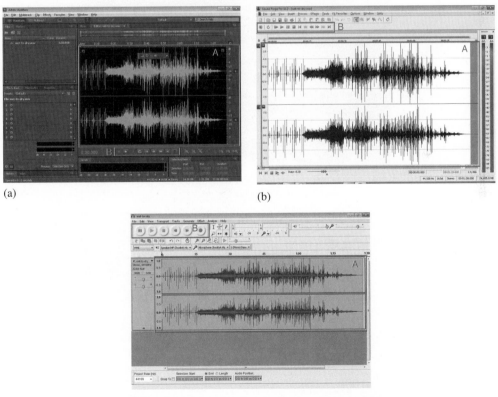

(a)                                                        (b)

(c)

**Figure 5.10** The area labeled **A** is the waveform display window. The area labeled **B** is the transport controls where you find the play, record, rewind, and fast forward buttons. (a) Adobe Audition CS5.5 workspace in the Edit view. (b) Sony Sound Forge 10 workspace. (c) Audacity 1.3 Beta.

In the waveform display, the $x$-axis represents the time and the $y$-axis represents the amplitude value. The example shown in Figure 5.10 depicts two waveforms in the window because the audio is stereo, which means the audio has two channels. Each channel has a waveform—the top waveform is for the left channel and the bottom one the right channel. If the audio is mono, there will be only one channel, and thus there will be only one waveform depicted in the window. You can click inside the waveform window to position the playhead at a particular time.

## 5.2.2 Audio Mixing: Working with Multiple Audio

In addition to the ability to edit a single waveform one at a time in the Waveform Editor, many programs also let you mix multiple audio. For example, Adobe Audition has the Multitrack Editor (Figure 5.11a). Using Audacity, you can add audio tracks (Figure 5.11b) by choosing `File > Import > Audio. . . .`

In a multi-track editor, each audio is placed on an audio track. Audios on different audio tracks can be placed at different times so that they start at different times. Mixing multiple

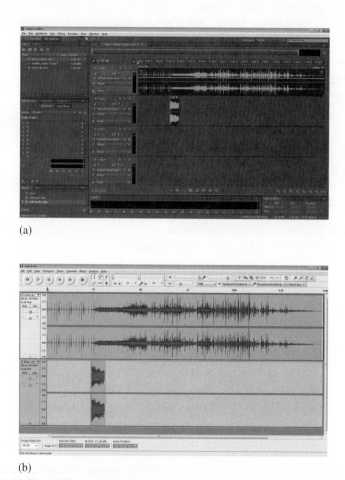

(a)

(b)

**Figure 5.11** (a) Two different audio are placed on two separate tracks in Adobe Audition CS5.5 Multitrack view. (b) Audacity 1.3 Beta with two audio tracks.

audio tracks is necessary and useful in situations such as when you want to mix a voice-over with background music, compose different musical clips, or mix multiple instrumental playbacks where each is recorded as a separate audio. When you are satisfied with the mixing results, you can export the audio as an audio mix-down. *Mixing down* means combining all of the tracks with effects. This is analogous to flattening an image in Photoshop. When you open a mixed-down audio piece, there are no separate tracks.

It is advantageous to create or record audio separately and mix them later. This way you can adjust the volume level and apply effects (such as fade-in and fade-out) to each audio independently. For example, if you record a voice-over with background music in one recording, it would require synchronization and control in matching the volume levels of voice-over with the background music all at once. What if later a change in your project requires an extra few seconds of pause within the voice-over and making the voice-over louder? You would have to record the whole audio again, because simply inserting a silence in the voice-over segment will also silence the background music. Simply making the voice-over segment louder will also make the background music louder altogether. However, if the voice-over and background music are recorded separately as different audio files, then all you need to do is to insert a few seconds of silence in the voice-over where it is needed. The volume of the voice-over can be adjusted independently. The background music will be unaffected and can be mixed with the edited voice-over as usual. The background music will still be playing during the newly added silence portion of the voice-over.

## 5.2.3 Spectral View

The waveform representation is the most frequently used view in digital audio editing. However, many audio editing programs also have a spectral view available. In the *spectral view* (Figure 5.12), the *x*-axis of the display is still time, as in the waveform display. However, the *y*-axis is the frequency of the audio, not the amplitude. The amplitude value is now represented using color. The spectral view can tell you the audio frequency information that you cannot get from the waveform view. For example, as you can tell from the spectral view shown in Figure 5.12, a middle section of the audio is missing sound that is higher than 3,000 Hz.

In general, the higher amplitude is represented by brighter colors. The brightest color of the section that is capped at 3,000 Hz occurs in the range of about 300 to 500 Hz. In the section after it, the brightest color occurs around 4,000 Hz but the 300- to 500-Hz range is very dark (low in amplitude). This means that a sound amplitude in the range of 300 to 500 Hz is very low. You would not be able to discern such frequency information from the waveform view of the same audio (Figure 5.10).

When working in the spectral view, you can still select audio data within a time range. Audition allows you to select the audio data in frequency in addition to time ranges (Figure 5.13). Thus, working in the spectral view also allows you to selectively edit a certain frequency range within a time frame. This is in contrast to selecting audio data in the waveform view, in which, when you make a selection, you select *all* the audio data within the selected time range, regardless of the frequency. Any change applied to the selection affects all frequencies within the selected time frame.

Spectral view is useful in analyzing the frequency range of the audio. It gives you an idea of the most important frequency range of the audio, so that when you need to reduce the audio file size by downsampling, you can estimate the lowest sampling rate without causing serious distortion. This is also useful in situations when it is necessary to isolate the frequency range responsible for an audio anomaly.

Lowest sampling rate without serious distortion: Recall the implication of the Nyquist theorem (Chapter 4)—the sampling rate of the audio must be at least twice the audio frequency. The audio with the highest amplitude usually is the most important part of the audio. If the frequency range that has the highest amplitude is around 4,000 Hz, then resampling your audio to at least 8,000 Hz.

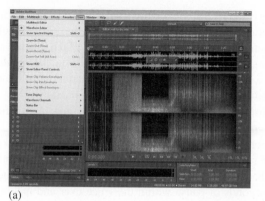

(a)

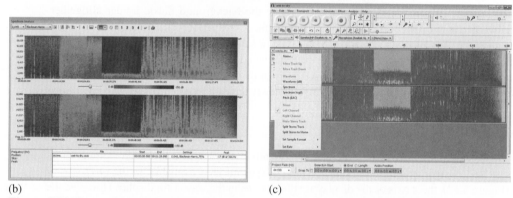

(b)                                                        (c)

**Figure 5.12** Spectral view of audio in Figure 5.10. (a) Adobe Audition CS5.5: View > Show Spectral Display. (b) Sony Sound Forge 10: View > Spectrum Analysis and click the Sonogram button. (c) Audacity 1.3 Beta: Spectrum. ▄▄ This image can be found on the insert.

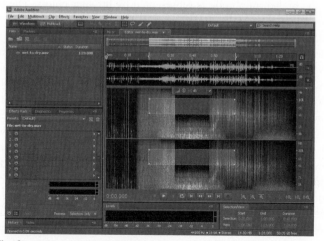

**Figure 5.13** The frequency range of about 4,000 to 10,000 Hz within the time frame between 20 second and 1 minute is selected (as indicated by the pale rectangle) in the spectral view. ▄▄ This image can be found on the insert.

# 5.3 BASIC DIGITAL AUDIO EDITING

In digital imaging, the scanned or digitally photographed image almost always needs retouching and editing, whether it is for cleaning up the image or artistic manipulation. This is also true for digital audio. Making connections across media with respect to the editing process will help you understand both the need for and the process of editing. So let's draw parallels from the common digital image editing processes.

You can edit an image by copying and pasting; adjusting the tonal value; cleaning up dirt, dust, and scratches; resizing the image; reducing its color depth; and applying filters, such as blurring or embossing. The basic ideas of these processes are transferable to digital audio editing (Table 5.1). In both digital image and audio editing, the changes will be applied to the selected area. If there is not a selection made, the changes will be applied to the whole image or audio. These basic audio editing operations are described in the following sections.

**TABLE 5.I    Parallels between Basic Digital Image and Digital Audio Editing**

| Basic Digital Image Editing | Basic Digital Audio Editing |
| --- | --- |
| Reassemble image content by cutting, copying, and pasting | Reassemble an audio waveform by cutting, copying, and pasting |
| Clean up dirt, dust, and scratches | Noise reduction |
| Adjust tonal value | Adjust volume |
| Resize the image | Resample the audio |
| Reduce the image's color depth | Reduce the audio's bit depth |
| Apply filters for special effects | Apply filters for special effects, such as reverb and pitch changes |
| If you want to save your file as JPEG for the Web, wait until the last step because JPEG uses lossy compression | If you want to save your file as MP3 for the Web, wait until the last step because MP3 uses lossy compression |

## 5.3.1 Reassembling a Waveform

The audio waveform can be selected and then applied with operations such as Cut, Copy, or Delete. To select a segment of a waveform, simply drag the cursor across the waveform and you can confirm the audio content of the selection by playing it.

Because the waveform is a visual representation of the audio amplitude in time, it is often possible to locate a sound segment in the waveform by looking for pauses or distinctive amplitude changes. You can edit out a specific word or pause from the audio by selecting it and then using the Cut or Delete operation. You can also click on a particular time on a waveform and paste a waveform segment that corresponds to a particular sound or speech segment. Figure 5.14a shows a waveform of the audio speech of the words one-two-three-four. The second word is cut and pasted before the first word (Figure 5.14c). The audio now becomes two-one-three-four.

Using the Cut or Delete operation, you can also trim unnecessary extra time off the beginning and end of the recording.

> ✐ **Reassembling Waveforms in Adobe Audition** Screen-capture movie demonstrating the selecting, cutting, and pasting of audio waveforms in Adobe Audition.

(a)

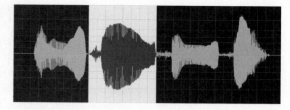

(b)

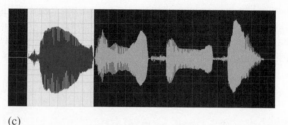

(c)

**Figure 5.14** Reassembling an audio waveform: (a) An original recording of speech saying "one-two-three-four." (b) The second word, "two," is selected. (c) The word "two" is cut and pasted before the first word.

## 5.3.2 Changing Volume

Adjusting the volume or amplitude of an audio is necessary when the recorded volume is too loud or too low for the intended use of the audio in a project. Another situation where volume adjustment is needed is when assembling multiple recordings into a single sound track. In this case, you often need to adjust the volume of each recording to give a consistent volume level across the recordings. There are two common menu items for simple volume adjustment: amplify and normalize. *Amplify* lets you specify amplification in dB (decibels) or percentage. *Normalize* lets you set a peak level for a file or selection, and it will amplify the entire file or selection so that the highest level is the peak level you specify. Use normalize instead of amplify to ensure the amplification does not result in clipping. For example, if you normalize an audio to 100%, you achieve the maximum amplitude that digital audio allows.

There are two extended applications of volume adjustment. The *fade-in* effect suppresses the volume at the beginning and gradually increases to 100% within the designated duration for the fade-in. Similarly, the *fade-out* effect lowers the volume level gradually to zero within the fade-out period.

The *Envelope* graph allows you to control the volume changes over time using a curve. The x-axis of the Envelope graph represents time and the y-axis represents amplification level. There are often presets available for Envelope graphs. You also can define your own curve. As you see in Figure 5.15, the fade-in and fade-out effects can be created by the Envelope graph.

## 5.3.3 Noise Reduction

Recordings often contain background noise, such as computer fan noise or hissing from the microphone. The two most useful features for noise reduction found in Adobe Audition are Hiss Reduction and Noise Reduction. *Hiss Reduction* can be used to reduce hiss from the source, such as microphone or audio cassette tape. Hissing noise is often characterized by a certain frequency range. The basic idea of how hiss reduction works is that a threshold

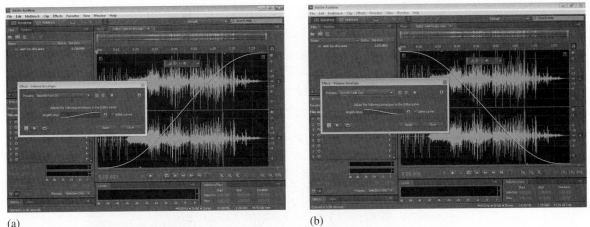

(a)                                                                          (b)

**Figure 5.15** Examples of Envelope graphs (Adobe Audition): (a) Fade-in. (b) Fade-out.

amplitude for a frequency range, called the *noise floor*, is defined—as preset or user-defined. If the audio amplitude within that frequency range falls below the threshold, the audio of that range will be greatly reduced. However, audio outside that frequency range and audio of any frequency that is louder than the threshold will remain unchanged.

*Noise Reduction* (Adobe Audition) or *Noise Removal* (Audacity) is another effect you can use to reduce noise that is constant throughout a waveform. This feature performs a statistical analysis of a pure noise segment that is selected by the user. Then it performs noise reduction on the whole audio based on this noise profile. Because it reduces noise based on a noise profile generated statistically, not a frequency range, the Noise Reduction can remove a wider range of noise. The downside of this effect compared to Hiss Reduction is that you need to have a sufficiently long segment (preferably more than 1 second) of pure noise for the statistical analysis to generate a representative profile for the noise. To get a pure noise segment, you can start the recording with a second or more of silence. That silence can be used as the Noise Reduction Profile for the final audio recording.

> **Applying Noise Reduction in Adobe Audition**  Screen-capture movie demonstrating the application of the Noise Reduction effects to an audio recording in Adobe Audition.

### 5.3.4  Special Effects

There are many special effects or filters you can apply to an audio. For example, many audio programs let you alter the pitch of a sound, alter the speed of its playback, and add echo or *reverb* (Figure 5.16). There are a wide variety of preset reverb effects, from auditorium to bathroom. You can also customize the reverb settings.

### 5.3.5  Downsampling and Reduction of Bit Depth

It is advantageous to record and work with audio at CD-quality levels (i.e., 44,100-Hz sampling rate, 16 bit, and stereo) or higher. However, depending on the project, you may need to downsample the audio to lower the file size before sharing your audio. In Adobe Audition, you can alter the sampling rate, bit depth, and channel number by choosing `Edit > Convert Sample Type. . . .` Save the altered audio file as a different name so that you can keep the original, higher quality audio file for any future editing.

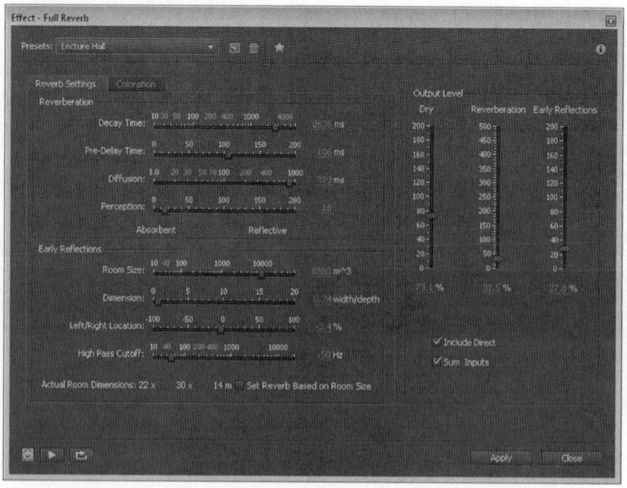

**Figure 5.16** Applying reverb to an audio in Adobe Audition CS5.5.

See Chapter 4 for a detailed discussion on optimization of audio files and effects of sampling rate, bit depth, and number of channels on the audio file size.

Another way of lowering file size is to save the audio file as a compressed file format, such as .mp3. MP3 files use a lossy but effective compression by applying human perception of sound. This means that some audio data are removed and the audio data are approximated, but the data removed are basically imperceptible to humans. Because MP3 uses a lossy compression, you should avoid using MP3 files as the master copy for further editing. The file that you plan to use for editing should be saved using a lossless compression method, if possible.

### 5.3.6 General Steps of Digital Audio Recording Touch-up

Even the most controlled studio recordings require touch-up before further manipulation of the audio. The general steps of touching up digital audio recordings are:

> ✏ **Audio Manipulation (Lab)** Practice recording your voice, removing background noise, reassembling the waveform, and applying audio effects.

1. **Noise reduction:** Remove background noise by applying the Noise Reduction effect.
2. **Trimming:** Remove extra time at the beginning or end of the audio recording. You also may remove unwanted long periods of silence within the audio.
3. Adjusting volume level to the desired level.

The audio should be touched up before applying any special effect, such as reverb. Otherwise, the background noise and the unwanted silence will be mixed with the effects and become harder, if not impossible, to remove.

### 5.4 MULTITRACK BASICS

The basic steps of working with a multitrack session are as follows.

Step 1  Place clips on tracks. You can always add and remove clips at any time during the process.

**Step 2** Apply effects; adjust volume and pan, if needed.

**Step 3** Export the final audio by mixing down the tracks.

Audition CS5.5 Multitrack view, Apple GarageBand '11, and Audacity 1.3 Beta are used as examples to demonstrate the basics in multitrack editing.

## 5.4.1 Placing Clips on a Track

To place a clip on a track:

- In Audition and GarageBand (Figure 5.17), you can drag a clip file onto a track.
- In Audacity, importing an audio file will add it to a new track.

To move a clip to another time on the track:

- **Audition:** Using the Move tool, click and drag the clip.
- **GarageBand:** Click and drag the clip.
- **Audacity:** Select the Time Shift tool (in the Tools toolbar, which is next to the Transport toolbar), then click and drag the clip.

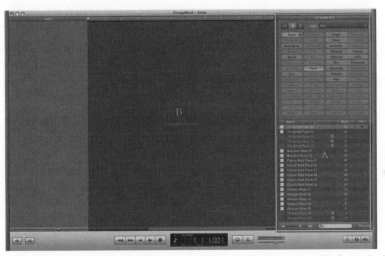

**Figure 5.17** To place a clip on a track in Apple GarageBand, drag a clip from the Loop Browser (A) onto the track window (B).

## 5.4.2 Applying Effects in Multitrack

### Audition

To apply an effect to a track, turn on the Effect (*fx*) button (Figure 5.18a). In the drop-down menu (Figure 5.18b), select the effect that you want to apply to the track. The effect will apply to the whole track (i.e., to all of the clips that are placed on that track). The effect can be toggled on and off by clicking the *fx* Power button (Figure 5.18c). This allows great flexibility for experimentation. In addition, the effect can be removed at any time.

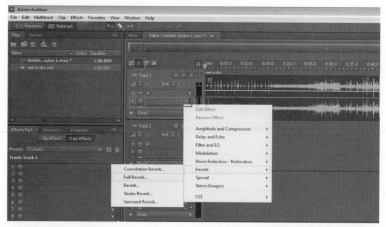

**Figure 5.18** Apply an effect to a track in Adobe Audition using (a) the Effect button, (b) a track's drop-down menu, and (c) the Effect Power button.

**Figure 5.19** GarageBand track effect settings found in the Effects section (A) in the Track Info pane. Clicking on the button (B) shows the effect settings in a popup window (Figure 5.20).

### GarageBand

The track effect settings can be found in the Track Info pane (Figure 5.19). To display the Track Info pane, choose `Track > Show Track Info`. To add an effect to a track, click on a slot under the Effects section. In the example shown in Figure 5.19, the first track is selected and a reverb effect is applied to this track. The settings of an applied effect can be adjusted in its popup window (Figure 5.20) that appears by clicking on the Effect button, such as the one labeled B in Figure 5.19.

### Audacity

Select the segment of the clip to which you want to apply an effect. If you want to apply the effect to the whole track, select the track by clicking on the left pane of the track. Then choose an effect from the `Effect` menu.

**Figure 5.20** Popup window of settings for a track effect in GarageBand.

# 5.5 MUSIC CREATION

Music scores can be created in MIDI format using sheet-music software. Creating an original music score requires musical composition skills. However, multimedia projects, such as games, product advertisements, and some digital art, often do not require a long musical score. Loop music software and libraries may be better solutions for non-music composers who are creating audio for such multimedia projects.

## 5.5.1 MIDI

MIDI and sampled digital audio are fundamentally different representations of digital sound. Therefore, the editing or creation of MIDI is also very different from that of sampled audio. MIDI is like sheet music in that it acts as an instruction for re-creating the music. You use musical notation and instrument assignment in a MIDI file.

See Chapter 4 for an introduction of MIDI. For a detailed description of MIDI messages, see Chapter 4 in the CS Module.

Examples of software application programs are Cakewalk SONAR, Steinberg Cubase, and MakeMusic! Finale. Figure 5.21 shows the different views available in Cakewalk SONAR for different creation and editing methods: *Staff view* for working with notation and staff; *Piano Roll view* for visualizing the notes as they would appear on a player-piano roll; and *Event List view* for working with a sequence of MIDI information or MIDI messages.

Figure 5.22 shows the assignment of harmonica to a MIDI track in Cakewalk SONAR. If a MIDI keyboard is connected to the computer, you can also play on the MIDI keyboard to record your performance into a MIDI file with most MIDI programs.

During the playback of a MIDI file, the sound card uses the synthesizer to re-create the sound of the notes using the specified instrument. Because not all synthesizers are the same, the MIDI file will sound differently depending on the sound card that plays it.

> ✏ **Creating and Editing MIDI in Cakewalk SONAR** Screen-capture movie that demonstrates creating and editing MIDI using Staff, Piano Roll, and Event List views in Cakewalk SONAR.

## 5.5.2 Loop Music

Composing in MIDI allows you to create your own original score. This requires expertise in musical composition to build a good score. Although you can always hire someone to compose a score for you, you have to first clearly identify the role of the music for your

(a)

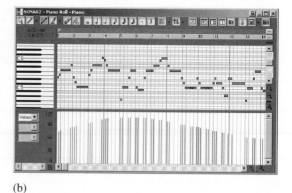

(b)

(c)

**Figure 5.21** Screen shots of workspace windows in Cakewalk SONAR: (a) Staff view of a MIDI track. (b) Piano Roll view of a MIDI track. The bottom pane shows the notes' velocity; the velocity corresponds to how hard the key is hit, and thus the note's loudness. (c) Event List view of a MIDI track.

**Figure 5.22** Assignment of harmonica to the instrument for a MIDI track in Cakewalk SONAR.

project. If the music is used for a film production, you will probably need an original score that matches the mood and theme of
your film. However, many multimedia projects, such as games and
product advertisements, do not require an original score but often
will require loop music.

*Loop music* is music that is created from short music clips that
are repeated. These music clips usually are designed to loop seamlessly (i.e., without noticeable discontinuity between repetitions).
There are many commercially available libraries of short sound
effects and music clips designed to loop seamlessly. There are also
fully orchestrated music pieces available for situations in which
loops are not desirable.

Loop music application programs, such as Sony ACID Pro (for Windows) in Figure 5.23
and Apple GarageBand (for Mac OS) in Figure 5.24, are designed to make the job of
sequencing and mixing loop music easier. These programs often also support MIDI and let
you import MIDI music.

Here is the basic idea of how these programs work. Loop music programs have multiple
audio tracks. You can import an audio clip to place on a track. The audio clip is represented by
a block. You create repetitions of the clip by dragging the right edge of the block to extend it.

Even programs that are not applications specific for loop music, such as Adobe Audition and Audacity, let you create loop music. In Audition, you can set the loop option for a
clip in *Multitrack view*, so that when you extend the duration of the clip, it will automatically repeat the clip without you having to manually copy and paste the clip multiple times
(Figure 5.25). In Audacity, an effect called Repeat lets you repeat a selection of the audio
for a specified number of times.

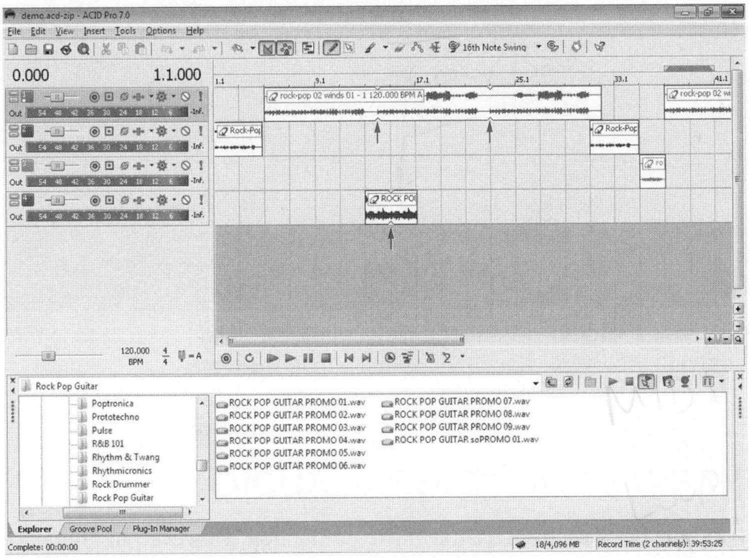

> ⬦ **Working with Loops in Sony ACID
> Pro** Screen-capture movie that demonstrates
> creating loop music in Sony ACID Pro.

> ⬦ **Working with Loops in Adobe
> Audition** Screen-capture movie that demon-
> strates creating loop music in Adobe Audition.

**Figure 5.23** Sony ACID Pro. The sound in track 1 is set to loop three times and the
sound in track 4 is set to loop twice simply by dragging the right edge of the sound clip
to the right. The colored arrows (not part of the user interface) mark the end of a cycle
of the loop.

**Figure 5.24** GarageBand. The colored arrows (not part of the user interface) mark the end of a cycle of the loop; for example, the clip in the fourth track has about 2.5 repetitions.

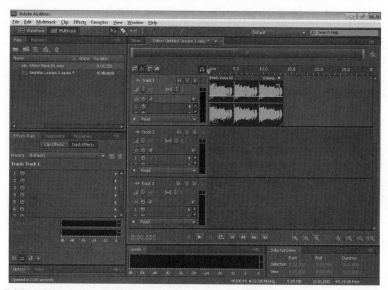

**Figure 5.25** Adobe Audition Multitrack view, where the sound is set to loop three times simply by dragging the right edge of the sound clip to the right.

## 5.6 SHARING YOUR DIGITAL AUDIO

Digital audio may be created solely for music production. However, in digital media production, digital audio is often combined with other media, for example, in video and multimedia presentation. If the audio will be shared on the Web, it can be embedded on a Web page or played in a window external to the browser window. The download time of the audio file is an important consideration.

## 5.6.1 Video

If your audio is intended to import into a video editor, you will need to check the audio file format that is supported by your video editing software. Most video editing programs support .wav, .aif, and .mp3. Adobe Audition also lets you import video using the Multitrack view. As an audio editing program, Adobe Audition does not have the video editing capability you would find in a video editing program. However, being able to import the video into the audio editing program provides you the convenience of synchronizing video and audio without having to switch back and forth between editing programs.

## 5.6.2 Multimedia Authoring

Multimedia authoring programs often support a variety of audio file formats. For example, the types of audio files you can import in Adobe Flash include .wav, .aif, .au, .mp3, and audio-only QuickTime.

## 5.6.3 For the Web

To use audio on the Web, you can embed it on a Web page or simply link to an audio file. Embedding an audio allows autoplay, whereas using a link will require the user to click on the link to download the file and play it in a player window external to the Web page.

To embed an audio on a Web page, you can use HTML5's audio tag to embed HTML5 audio or use the object tag to embed non-HTML5 audio. At the time of writing, the supported HTML5 audio formats are MP3, AAC (MP4), Ogg Vorbis, and WAV. The HTML5 audio is played by the Web browser's built-in player, instead of an external audio player. The code to add an HTML5 audio on a Web page can be as simple as this:

```
<audio src="media/demo.oga" controls></audio>
```

For embedding non-HTML5 audio, how the audio will be played is determined by the viewer's browser plug-in and the audio player that the viewer has on the computer.

Fast download is a crucial criterion for any medium intended for use on the Web. Thus, audio files intended for the Web should be kept as small as possible in file size or in a format that allows streaming or progressive download. Both streaming and progressive download do not require the whole file to be downloaded before playing. The audio starts playing once there has been enough audio data downloaded. Streaming requires a streaming server in addition to a Web server, but progressive download does not. QuickTime and Flash Video support streaming and progressive download. They can be created as audio-only movies.

Chapter 14 covers an introduction to HTML and shows you how to add links on a Web page.

See Chapter 15 for an introduction on HTML5 audio and how to add HTML5 audio on a Web page.

### Quicktime Audio-Only Movies

QuickTime audio-only movies can be exported using digital video editing programs, such as Adobe Premiere Pro and Apple Final Cut Pro. You will need to check the option to export audio only. QuickTime movies that support progressive downloading are known as Fast-Start movies. One simple way to create a Fast-Start QuickTime is to save the QuickTime movie as a self-contained movie. To do so, you will need the Pro version of QuickTime Player, not the free version. First, open the QuickTime movie with QuickTime Pro. Then, select File > Save As . . . . In the File Save dialog box, select the option "Make movie self-contained." If the option is not active, use a different file name or save the movie in a different folder. You can replace the original QuickTime file with the Fast-Start movie later.

### Including Quicktime Audio-Only Movies in a Web Page

To embed a QuickTime movie, whether an audio-only or one that contains a video track, you can use the `<object>` tag. The `src` parameter or `data` attribute specifies the file path to the QuickTime movie. There are other parameters you can set to control how the embedded QuickTime is played on the Web page:

- The `controller` parameter sets the visibility of the movie controller bar.
- The `loop` parameter sets whether the movie loops playback.
- The `autoplay` parameter sets whether the QuickTime movie automatically starts. If it is set to false, the user would have to click on the play button to start the audio playback.

```
<html>
<head>
<title>Demo - Background Play QT Sound</title>
</head>

<body>
<object classid="clsid:02BF25D5-8C17-4B23-BC80-D3488ABDDC6B"
        codebase="http://www.apple.com/qtactivex/qtplugin.cab"
        width="0" height="0">
  <param name="src" value="ylwong-example.mov"/>
  <param name="controller" value="false"/>
  <param name="autoplay" value="true"/>
  <param name="loop" value="true"/>

  <object type="video/quicktime" data="ylwong-example.mov"
          width="0" height="0">
    <param name="controller" value="false"/>
    <param name="autoplay" value="true"/>
    <param name="loop" value="true"/>
    Download <a href="ylwong-example.mov">movie</a>
  </object>

</object>
</body>
</html>
```

**Figure 5.26** HTML code example 1 for embedding QuickTime.

The example shown in Figure 5.26 demonstrates using a QuickTime audio-only movie as background audio. The display of the controller is set to false and the movie dimensions are set to zero. Thus, there is no visual indication of a QuickTime movie on the Web page and the QuickTime movie has to be set to automatically start playing. The width and height can be set to, say 50 and 16, respectively, to display the controller with three buttons: volume control, play/pause, and options (Figure 5.27a). The width attribute can be set longer to display the audio progress slider (Figure 5.27b).

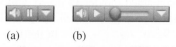

(a)　　　　　(b)

**Figure 5.27** QuickTime controllers set at different widths. (a) Width attribute set to 50 to display only three buttons. (b) Width attribute set to larger than 50, say 100, so the progress slider will appear between the play/pause and options buttons.

To use the example code to add your audio-only QuickTime movie in a Web page, you can copy the code for the <object> elements and change the values (in color) of the parameters and attributes to suit your needs.

> ⏚ **Example Web Pages of Including Audio-only QuickTime** Two Web pages that demonstrate embedding an audio-only QuickTime.

## ABOUT THE EXAMPLE CODE FOR EMBEDDING QuickTime

At the time of writing, the <object> element may not work properly in some browsers. If the browser or its plug-in can interpret the <object> element, then the QuickTime movie will be played. Otherwise, if an alternative content is specified, then the alternative content will be displayed.

In the example code shown in Figure 5.26, the alternative content inserted is a hyperlink to the QuickTime movie file:

Download: `<a href="ylwong-example.mov">movie</a>`

A hyperlink to the file `ylwong-example.mov` will be displayed on the Web page if the browser cannot interpret the <object> element in the code. This will allow the viewer to download the audio. The alternative content is not limited to hyperlinks. An image (such as a static image or a GIF animation) can be inserted as an alternative content.

## 5.6.4 Audio CD

Audio editing programs (such as Adobe Audition) also let you create audio CD projects in which you can specify a title and artist for each track. CD players that support CD text can display such information during playback. These programs also let you designate the length of pauses between tracks, enable or disable copy protection, and add an ISRC (International Standard Burning Software Code) number—a code that is used for commercial distribution. Many CD-burning software programs also let you create audio CDs. However, these programs usually do not have these options.

Audio of audio-CD format must use a 44,100-Hz sampling rate, 16 bits, and stereo. If you are creating audio CDs, you should plan to acquire audio sources that are recorded or generated at least at these settings. If you insert a track with a different sample type in Adobe Audition or a CD recording program, the program automatically will convert the audio to the required settings for you. However, such conversion does not boost the audio quality if you start with a lower sampling rate or bit depth.

## 5.6.5 Podcast

A *podcast* is a collection of files available on a Web server. The files in a podcast are usually audio and video, but they also can be Web pages, text, PDF, images, or any file type. Each file is referred to as an *episode* of the podcast. The Internet addresses of the files are listed in a text file, known as the *feed*.

The feed is posted on a Web server. People can subscribe to a collection by subscribing to its feed, so that whenever new episodes or files become available in the collection, the files will automatically be downloaded to their computers or devices (portable media players such as iPods).

The subscriber's computer or device will need to have a software program that checks the collection periodically for new files and automatically downloads the new items. Such software is called the ***aggregator***. For example, iTunes is a podcast aggregator. The aggregator also is used to subscribe to and play back podcasts.

The files in a podcast can be any file type. These are the same file types that you would find posted on the Web. You do not have to make your audio files or any other media files a podcast in order to deliver them on the Web. The key difference between podcasting and posting the media files on the Web is the automatic mechanism of podcasting. When you post files on the Web, you depend on the audience coming to your site to check new updates and download the files. In podcasting, once the audience has subscribed to your feed, the aggregator will periodically go to your site to check the feed file for updates and automatically download any new items. Of course, you would need to add the information of the new items to the feed text file in addition to posting the new items on the Web.

## How to Podcast Audio[*]

To create a podcast, you will need to have at least two files:

- Your audio content must be saved in a file format that is supported by the aggregator used by your target subscribers. MP3 is the most commonly supported format for podcast aggregators.
- Your podcast feed file must be a text file and an XML file that lists the information of the items in your podcast. A feed file usually has a file extension .rss or .xml. An example of a feed file is shown in the following step-by-step guide.

**Step 1  Create Your Audio Content in MP3**

In this chapter, you have learned how to create digital audio. Almost all digital audio editing programs let you export your audio content to MP3 format:

- Adobe Audition CS5.5: `File > Save As . . .` and choose `MP3 Audio (*.mp3)` for the file format (Figure 5.28a).
- Sony Sound Forge 10: `File > Save As . . .` and choose `MP3 Audio (*.mp3)` for the file type (Figure 5.28b).
- Audacity 1.3 Beta: `File > Export` and choose `MP3 Files` for the file type (Figure 5.28c).
- Sony ACID Pro 7: `File > Render As . . .` and choose `MP3 Audio (*.mp3)` for the file type (Figure 5.28d).

**Step 2  Put Your MP3 Files on a Web Server**

Upload your MP3 files onto a Web server. Note their Internet addresses or URLs.

**Step 3  Create Your Podcast Feed File**

A feed file is a text file that provides links to your MP3 files. You can use any text editor to create a feed file. However, there is a specific format for how the links and other information of the podcast are written in the feed file. There are programs that you can use to generate the feed file. A feed file may look like that in Figure 5.29.

Publishing audio podcasts from your GarageBand project will automatically create a feed file and an MP3 file.

Don't forget that MP3 uses lossy compression. You should save a copy using an uncompressed format or a file format that uses lossless compression, such as Windows PCM WAV or AIFF before exporting the audio as an MP3 file.

For information on other tags for the <channel> element, look up the RSS specifications on the Web.

[*] Useful resources to podcast audio:

Make Your First Podcast:
http://www.podcastingnews.com/articles/How-to-Podcast.html
Understanding RSS News Feeds:
http://www.podcastingnews.com/articles/Understanding_RSS_Feeds.html
Podcasting Software (Publishing):
http://www.podcastingnews.com/topics/Podcasting_Software.html

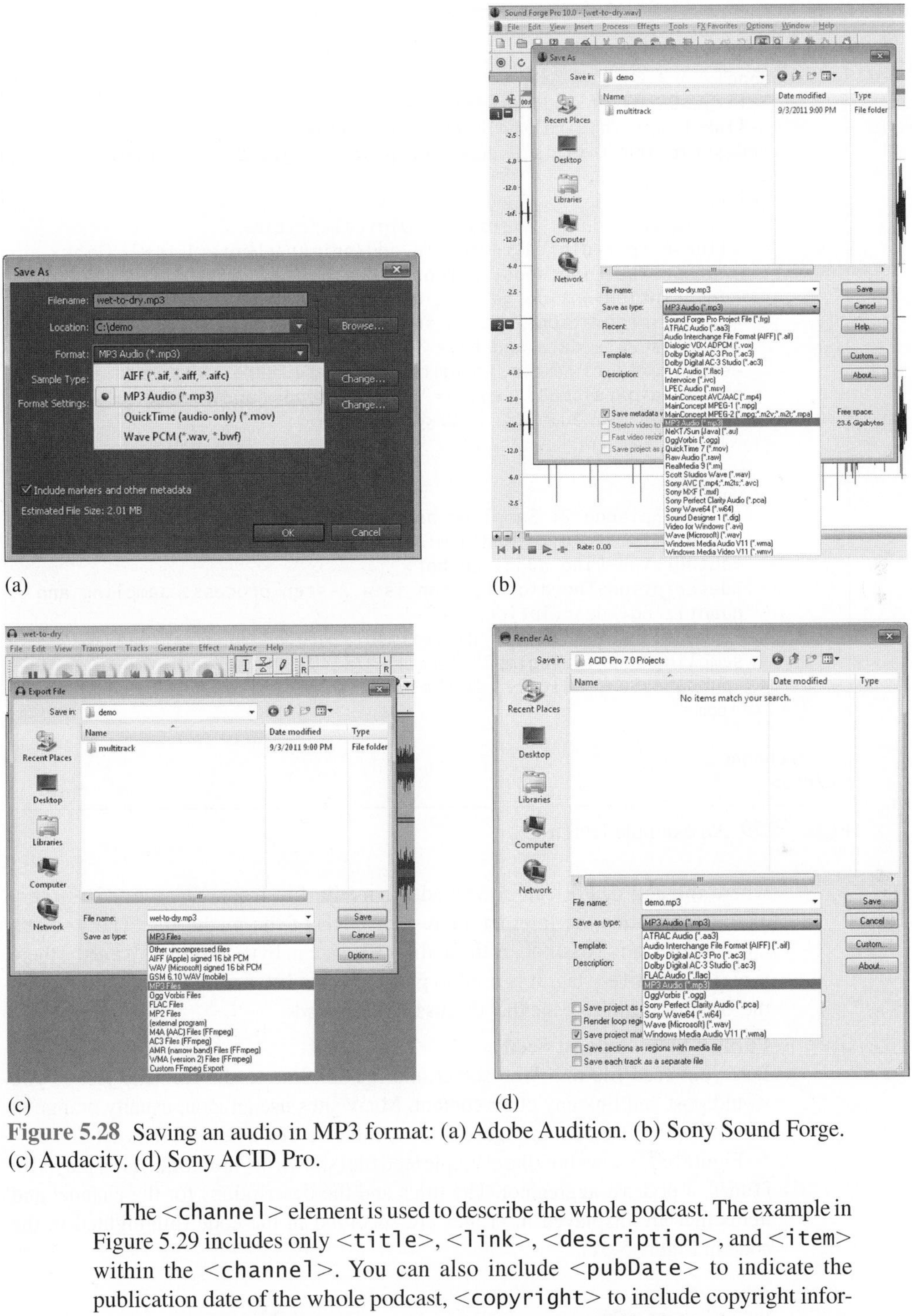

**Figure 5.28** Saving an audio in MP3 format: (a) Adobe Audition. (b) Sony Sound Forge. (c) Audacity. (d) Sony ACID Pro.

The <channel> element is used to describe the whole podcast. The example in Figure 5.29 includes only <title>, <link>, <description>, and <item> within the <channel>. You can also include <pubDate> to indicate the publication date of the whole podcast, <copyright> to include copyright information, and <language> to indicate the language used in the podcast.

The <item> elements are the most important elements in a channel. Each <item> element contains information about each podcast episode, for example,

```
<?xml version="1.0"?>
<rss version="2.0">
   <channel>
       <title>Demos of Podcast</title>
       <link>http://digitalmedia.wfu.edu/</link>
       <description>This is a demo for podcasting.</description>

       <item>
          <title>Episode 1: Analog vs. Digital</title>
          <link>http://digitalmedia.wfu.edu/primer/chapter1.html</link>
          <author>Yue-Ling Wong</author>
          <description>Analog is continuous while digital is discrete.
          Analog information is also infinite. However, computers deal
          with discrete data and have finite capacity. </description>
          <enclosure url="http://digitalmedia.wfu.edu/podcast/media/
          analog-digital.mp3" length="352128" type="audio/mpeg"/>
          <pubDate>Tue, July 24, 2007</pubDate>
       </item>

       <item>
          <title>Episode 2: Sampling and Quantizing</title>
          <link>http://digitalmedia.wfu.edu/primer/chapter1.html</link>
          <author>Yue-Ling Wong</author>
          <description>The digitization is a 2-step process: sampling and
          quantizing</description>
          <enclosure url="http://digitalmedia.wfu.edu/podcast/media/
          sampling-quantizing.mp3" length="73240" type="audio/mpeg"/>
          <pubDate>Sun, July 29, 2007</pubDate>
       </item>

   </channel>
</rss>
```

**Figure 5.29**  An example feed file.

where the aggregator can download the media file from. The `<enclosure>` element specifies the Internet address or URL of the media file. The `length` attribute of `<enclosure>` is the audio's file size in bytes. Within `<item>`, there is also a `<title>` tag. It is used to give the episode a name. The `<link>` gives the URL of the Web page that discusses the episode.

**Step 4  Publish Your Podcast Feed**

Post your feed file to a Web server and make a link to the feed file just as you would post and link any other content. Many sites use an icon, usually orange in color, like those shown in Figure 5.30, to indicate that a news feed is available.

Figure 5.31 shows how the example feed file (shown in Figure 5.29) is displayed in iTunes, a podcast aggregator. The titles and the descriptions for the channel and items that are displayed in iTunes are specified in the code (highlighted in the code in Figure 5.31).

**Figure 5.30**  Icons used on the Web to indicate a news feed is available.

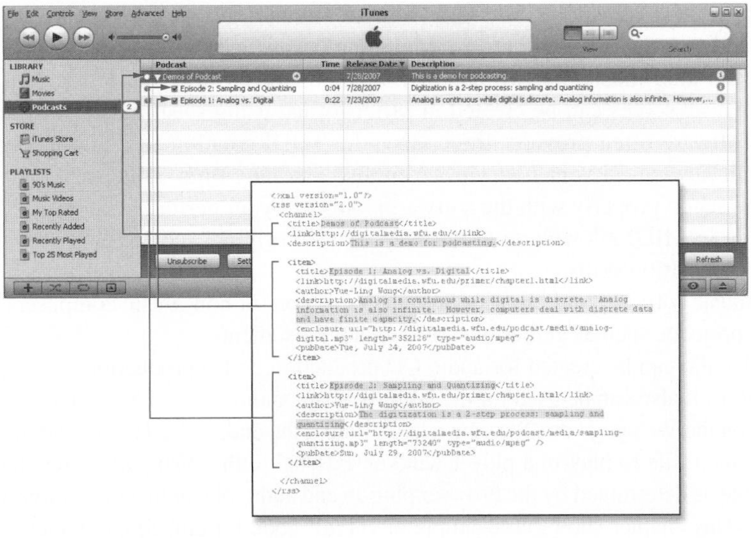

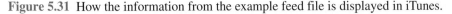

**Figure 5.31** How the information from the example feed file is displayed in iTunes.

## 5.7 SUMMARY

Digital audio can be acquired by two methods: (1) recording sound and directly storing it in digital format and (2) digitizing analog audio media, such as analog audiotapes. To record audio directly into digital format or digitize analog audio, your computer needs to have a sound card. All new computers nowadays come with a sound card installed.

In order to record audio directly, you also need a microphone and a digital audio recording program. Most, if not all, digital audio editing programs are capable of recording audio. Before you start recording, you need to specify the sampling rate, bit depth, and number of channels you want to use. Monitor the sound level meters during recording. Adjust the input volume level so that the meter level stays below the red area, occasionally brushing near the red area without going over it. Going over the red area will cause clipping and distortion of your recording.

To digitize analog audio media, such as cassette tapes, you do not use a microphone but you need to connect the line-out port of the cassette tape deck with the line-in port on your sound card using an audio cable.

The two very basic elements you will find in a digital audio editing program are (1) a waveform display window and (2) the transport controls where you find the play, record, rewind, and fast forward buttons.

In the waveform display, the x-axis represents the time, and the y-axis represents the amplitude value. Many audio editing programs also have a spectral view available. The y-axis in the spectral view represents the audio frequency. The amplitude information is color-coded in the spectral view.

You can reassemble an audio by cutting and pasting the waveform. You can enhance the audio by adjusting the volume of the audio using Amplify, Normalize, or Envelope effects. Some programs have built-in functions for noise reduction to clean up background noise and hiss. Special effects, such as reverb and pitch change, also are available for altering the audio.

Programs such as Adobe Audition, Sony Sound Forge, and Audacity let you mix multiple audio tracks in addition to editing a single waveform.

MIDI and loop music are two common methods for creating music for digital media projects. Music scores can be created in MIDI format using sheet-music software. MIDI creation software often provides three views for MIDI creation and editing: Staff view, Piano Roll view, and Event List view. You also can play on a MIDI keyboard (if connected and set up properly with the software) to record your performance into a MIDI file. Composing in MIDI allows you to create your own original score, but it requires some musical composition skills.

Loop music software and libraries provide a solution for non-music composers to create audio for projects, such as games and product advertisements.

Digital audio can be created for audio CD production, video production, and multimedia presentations. It also can be used for the Web. To share audio on the Web, you can (1) embed the audio on the Web page or (2) create a hyperlink to the audio file. The second method will cause the audio file to play in a player window external to the Web page. How the audio is going to play is determined by the browser plug-in and audio player that the viewer has on the computer. This chapter shows an example of HTML code for embedding QuickTime files. Chapter 15 will show you how to create HTML5 audio files and add them on Web pages.

Podcasting is another way to deliver digital audio on the Web. The key difference between podcasting and posting media files on the Web is the automatic mechanism of podcasting. A podcast is a collection of files available on a Web server. The files in a podcast are usually audio and video, but they can be any file type, such as images and PDF. Each file is referred to as an episode of the podcast. The Internet addresses of the files are listed in a text file, known as the feed. The feed is posted on a Web server. People can subscribe to a collection by subscribing to its feed. The subscriber's computer or device will need to have software that checks the collection periodically for updates and automatically downloads the new items. Such software is called the aggregator. The aggregator also is used to play back podcasts.

## TERMS

## LEARNING AIDS

The following learning aids can be found at the book's companion Web site.

✎ **Setting Recording Controls in Windows 7**
Screen-capture movie that demonstrates how to set the recording device to microphone and adjust the volume in Windows.

◇ **Recording Audio in Adobe Audition**

Screen-capture movie that demonstrates the basic steps of recording audio in Adobe Audition.

◇ **Reassembling Waveforms in Adobe Audition**

Screen-capture movie demonstrating the selecting, cutting, and pasting of audio waveforms in Adobe Audition.

◇ **Applying Noise Reduction in Adobe Audition**

Screen-capture movie demonstrating the application of the Noise Reduction effects to an audio recording in Adobe Audition.

◌ **Audio Manipulation (Lab)**

Practice recording your voice, removing background noise, reassembling the waveform, and applying audio effects.

◇ **Creating and Editing MIDI in Cakewalk SONAR**

Screen-capture movie that demonstrates creating and editing MIDI using Staff, Piano Roll, and Event List views in Cakewalk SONAR.

◇ **Working with Loops in Sony ACID Pro**

Screen-capture movie that demonstrates creating loop music in Sony ACID Pro.

◇ **Working with Loops in Adobe Audition**

Screen-capture movie that demonstrates creating loop music in Adobe Audition.

◌ **Example Web Pages of Including Audio-only QuickTime**

Two Web pages that demonstrate embedding an audio-only QuickTime.

## REVIEW QUESTIONS

When applicable, please choose all correct answers.

1. **True/False:** The optimal meter level for recording is going past the red area of the meter.

2. Which type of microphone is most sensitive to sound coming from the front?

   A. Undirectional
   B. Omnidirectional

3. If you do not know the directional property of a microphone, as a general rule, where do you place the sound source relative to the microphone?

4. Why is it important to monitor the input level meter during recording?

5. The *x*-axis of the waveform view represents the _____.

   A. amplitude value
   B. frequency
   C. time

6. The *y*-axis of the waveform view represents the _____.

   A. amplitude value
   B. frequency
   C. time

7. The *x*-axis of the spectral view represents the _____.

   A. amplitude value
   B. frequency
   C. time

159

8. The *y*-axis of the spectral view represents the _____.

   A. amplitude value
   B. frequency
   C. time

9. The color of the spectral view represents the _____.

   A. amplitude value
   B. frequency
   C. time

10. Which view allows you to inspect the audio frequency distribution over time?

    A. Waveform
    B. Spectral
    C. Multitrack

11. **True/False:** Application of special effects, such as reverb, to a noisy audio should be done before the noise reduction.

12. The fade-in and fade-out effects can be created by applying the _____ effect.

    A. amplify
    B. envelope
    C. noise reduction
    D. normalize
    E. reverb

13. The _____ effect(s) is/are for changing the audio amplitude.

    A. amplify
    B. envelope
    C. noise reduction
    D. normalize
    E. reverb

14. The _____ effect changes the audio amplitude such that the highest is the amplitude you specify.

    A. amplify
    B. envelope
    C. noise reduction
    D. normalize
    E. reverb

15. The _____ effect can create a feeling of being in a big auditorium.

    A. amplify
    B. envelope
    C. noise reduction
    D. normalize
    E. reverb

**16.** The order of performing noise reduction is: _____, _____, _____, _____.

    A. Select the segment of the audio you want to apply noise reduction to.

    B. Select a segment that contains pure noise.

    C. Have the program perform a statistical analysis of the noise to generate a profile.

    D. Have the program reduce the noise of the selected segment based on the noise profile.

**17.** _____ deals with musical notations, staff, and musical instrument assignments.

    A. MIDI

    B. Loop music

**18.** What is the disadvantage of MIDI compared to composing music with loop music?

**19.** Name several uses of digital audio.

**20.** In which of the following uses of audio is a smaller file size generally a more crucial consideration?

    A. Video

    B. Multimedia authoring

    C. Playback on the Web

    D. Music CD

    E. Podcast

**21.** In which of the following uses of audio is the audio quality generally a more crucial consideration?

    A. Video

    B. Multimedia authoring

    C. Playback on the Web

    D. Music CD

    E. Podcast

**22.** What is the advantage of using a streaming format or progressive download for audio playback on the Web?

**23.** The HTML tag that you can use to place a QuickTime movie on a Web page is _____.

    A. `<object>`

    B. `<qt>`

    C. `<rpm>`

    D. `<mov>`

    E. `<src>`

**24.** Which of the following parameters needs to be set to `true` so that a QuickTime embedded in a Web page will start playing automatically?

    A. `autoplay`

    B. `controller`

    C. `loop`

    D. `src`

**25.** Which of the following properties of QuickTime audio-only movies can be set in the HTML code?

A. Visibility of the controller bar
B. Width and height of the controller bar
C. Automatically start playing
D. Looping the audio

## EXPLORING THE APPLICATIONS

1. Explore the workspace of your audio editing program.
   * Locate the transport control.
   * Locate the recording level meter.
   * Find out if your program has spectral view.
   * Find out if your program supports multitrack audio mixing.

2. Explore the audio editing functionalities of your audio editing program by locating the commands for:
   * Resampling the audio, altering bit depth, and changing the number of channels
   * Amplify
   * Normalize
   * Reverb
   * Noise Reduction
   * Using an Envelope graph
   * Creating fade-in and fade-out
   * Saving the final audio as MP3 and WAV files

3. Practice:
   (i)    Recording your voice
   (ii)   Reassembling the waveform of your recording
   (iii)  Applying Noise Reduction to clean up your recording
   (iv)   Normalizing your waveform to a satisfactory amplitude
   (v)    Applying effects such as reverb, fade-in, and fade-out
   (vi)   Exporting your recording to audio-only QuickTime and MP3
   (vii)  Adding your audio on a Web page

# Fundamentals of Digital Video

# 6

## KEY CONCEPTS

- High-definition and standard-definition digital video
- Interlaced and progressive scan
- Overscan and safe zones
- Frame rate
- Frame size and frame aspect ratio
- Pixel aspect ratio
- Counting frames with timecode
- Data rate
- Video compression methods
- MPEG
- GOP, I-frame, P-frame, and B-frame
- Streaming video and progressive download

## GENERAL LEARNING OBJECTIVES

In this chapter, you will learn

- The common terms in digital video.
- The common terms for DTV.
- The file formats of high-definition and standard-definition digital video.
- The relationship among frame size, frame aspect ratio, and pixel aspect ratio.
- How pixel aspect ratio affects the appearance of the video picture.
- How to read video timecodes.
- The difference between true streaming and progressive download.
- What GOP, I-frame, P-frame, B-frame, and the *M* and *N* parameters mean.
- How motion compensation and motion vector in MPEG compression work.
- The different implications of data rate and file size.
- How to determine the suitable video data rate for a playback target.
- The general strategies for video file size optimization.

# 6.1 THE NATURE OF MOTION AND BROADCAST VIDEO

In the natural world, we perceive motion as a continuous flow of events. It is a combination of visual, auditory, and temporal experience. Video cameras have long been available to capture motion on analog media, such as film, VHS tapes, and Hi-8 tapes.

Conceptually, motion is captured as a sequence of pictures at a constant time interval. Each picture is called a *frame*. How fast the pictures are captured or how fast the frames are played back is determined by the *frame rate*, which is measured in *frames per second (fps)*.

There are broadcast standards for digital video's resolution, color spaces, and frame rate to adhere to. The digital video standards have been influenced by the existing analog television broadcast standards. In order to understand the rationale behind digital video standards, it is necessary to learn about analog television broadcast standards.

## 6.1.1 Broadcast Standards

There are three sets of broadcast standards for analog color televisions. These standards pertain to the technical details of how color television pictures are encoded and transmitted as broadcast signals. Each standard is also characterized by its specific frame rate and the number of scan lines in each frame. These important attributes are translated into digital video standards. The number of lines in each frame in the analog broadcast standard is translated to the pixel height of a frame in digital video.

*NTSC* was named after the U.S. National Television Systems Committee, which designated this standard. It is used in North America, Japan, Taiwan, and parts of the Caribbean and South America. *PAL* stands for Phase Alternating Line, which refers to the way the signals are encoded. It is used in Australia, New Zealand, and most of Western Europe and the Asian countries. *SECAM* stands for Séquentiel Couleur avec Mémoire, which translates as sequential color with memory. It is used in France, the former Soviet Union, and Eastern Europe. The standards adopted in Africa and parts of Asia are mostly influenced by their colonial histories.

The implications of the scan lines in a frame will be discussed in Section 6.1.3.

Not all digital video formats have to conform to broadcast standards. Some digital video formats are intended mainly for computer playback—not for television. For example, QuickTime movies do not have to conform to a standard resolution or frame rate. On the other hand, videos intended for DVD playback need to conform to DVD-video standards, which are based on broadcast standards.

## 6.1.2 Frame Rate

Table 6.1 lists the frame rate of different systems. The frame rate for NTSC was originally 30 fps for black-and-white television broadcast. In order to accommodate additional color information for color pictures in the signal, the frame rate was lowered to 29.97 fps.

| TABLE 6.1 | **Frame Rates of Different Video Types** |
|---|---|
| **Video Type** | **Frame Rate (frames per second or fps)** |
| NTSC | 29.97 |
| PAL | 25 |
| SECAM | 25 |
| Motion-picture film | 24 |

## 6.1.3 Interlaced and Progressive Scan

A picture displayed on a television or a computer display is made up of horizontal lines. These lines are traced across the screen one line at a time. For example, a standard-definition NTSC frame contains 525 lines, of which about 480 are for the picture. A standard-definition PAL or SECAM frame contains 625 lines, of which about 576 are for the picture.

There are two ways to display a frame: by displaying the lines from top to bottom in one pass or two passes. Displaying all lines in one pass is called *progressive scan*. For the two-pass method, the set of the lines in the same pass (i.e., the set of even lines or odd lines) is called a *field*. The field containing the topmost scan line (i.e., the first scan line) is called the *upper field*, and the other

> ⍾ **Video Display: Interlaced Scan versus Progressive Scan** An interactive animation illustrates two-pass scanning in interlaced scan and one-pass scanning in progressive scan.

🖱 **Upper Field and Lower Field** An interactive demo shows the upper field and the lower field of a video frame.

◇ **Fast-Action Digital Video Showing the Interlace Artifact** A video clip of Figure 6.1 shows the comb-like interlace artifact.

🖱 **Video Recording: Interlaced Mode versus Progressive Mode** An interactive animation illustrates how the interlace artifact may be produced in fast-action videos.

field is the ***lower field***. This display method of using two alternating fields is called ***interlaced scan***. The first pass traces the one set of lines and the second pass traces the other set to fill in the alternating gaps left by the first pass. For example, for NTSC, the first pass traces the even-numbered lines and the second pass traces the odd-numbered lines.

For video shot in the interlaced mode, because the two fields in a frame are captured at a slightly different moment in time, discontinuities will become apparent for fast-moving objects. Such discontinuities appear as comb-like artifacts, such as in the areas of the soccer ball and the kicker's foot shown in Figure 6.1. The lower field of the frame is shown in Figure 6.1c and the upper field in Figure 6.1e. The interlace artifact usually is not apparent in normal playback. It is, however, discernible in slow motion or freeze frame.

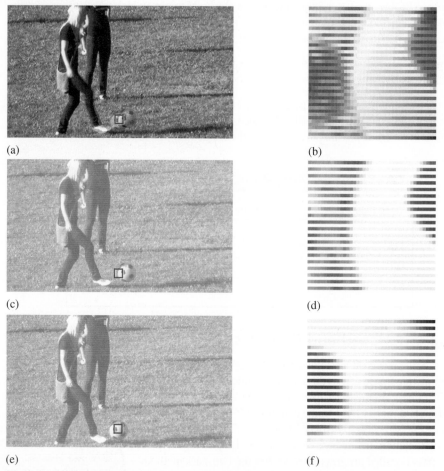

(a)             (b)

(c)             (d)

(e)             (f)

**Figure 6.1** (a) A digital video frame showing comb-like artifact caused by fast action and camera panning. (b) Close-up of the small outlined area in (a). (c) The upper field of the video frame. (d) Close-up of the small outlined area in (c). (e) The lower field of the video frame. (f) Close-up of the small outlined area in (e). 🖥 This image can be found on the insert.

## DEINTERLACE

The interlace artifact can be removed by discarding one field and filling in the gaps by duplicating or interpolating the other field (Figure 6.2). Either method will degrade the image quality.

During normal playback, the interlace artifact is not discernible. Deinterlacing is normally not necessary. However, if you need to capture a freeze frame and the interlace artifact is discernible, you may need to deinterlace the image.

(a)

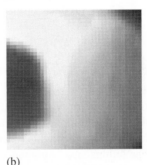

(b)

**Figure 6.2** (a) The video frame deinterlaced by eliminating the upper field and interpolating the lower field to fill in the gaps. (b) Close-up of the small outlined area. This image can be found on the insert.

## 6.1.4 Overscan and Safe Zones

When a video is displayed on a television set, the edge areas of the picture may not be displayed within the viewing area. The area that is outside of the screen is called the *overscan*. The signals are not "lost." For example, if you record a digital television program and play it back on a computer, you will see the whole image. If you watch a DVD movie on a computer, you can see a whole frame. However, if the same DVD movie is played on a television set, the content at the edges of the frame may not be seen on the screen due to the overscan.

As a consequence of overscan, if your target audience will be watching your video on consumer television sets, you should not place the important content too close to the edges when framing your shots. But how close is "too close"? There is no one exact number to fit all televisions, because the amount of overscanning is not consistent across consumer television sets.

There are two common guides that can help you frame your shots: the safe action area and the safe title area. The *safe action area* is where the significant action takes place. The *safe title area* is where you should place critical text titles and critical content. The safe title area is visible on the majority of television sets. In general, the safe action area occupies the center 90% of the frame size and the safe title area 80% (Figure 6.3). This means that the safe action area leaves approximately a 5% border all around the frame and the safe title area leaves about a 10% border around. For the frame shown in Figure 6.3, there is a person on the right edge of the frame walking to the left side of the frame. How much this person will show up within the viewing area on a television set depends on the television set.

If your video is created for viewing on computers, such as for Web playback, the entire frame will be displayed and the overscan will not apply.

**Figure 6.3** (a) Outlines of the safe action area. (b) Outlines of the safe title area.

## 6.1.5 Color Format

RGB is a common color model used for still digital images, but for video, the luminance-chrominance color models are used (for example, *YUV* and *YIQ* color models). These color models divide color into one *luminance* (brightness) component (Y) and two *chrominance* (color or hue) components (U and V in YUV, or I and Q in YIQ).

The reason we introduce the analog broadcast's color models in this chapter is because the YUV color models are also used in the standards for digital video.

The luminance-chrominance color model was invented at the same time as color television for adding color signals to the television broadcast. By using this color model, the same signal could be used for both black-and-white and color television sets: the black-and-white television uses only the luminance (Y) signal, whereas the color set uses both the luminance and chrominance signals.

YUV was originally the color model for analog television broadcasts of the PAL system. YIQ is the model adopted by the National Television System Committee (NTSC) in the United States.

In addition, another luminance-chrominance model called $YC_bC_r$, which is closely related to YUV, is used in MPEG compression. MPEG compression is used in DVD videos and high-definition video formats. MPEG compression will be discussed later in this chapter.

### RELATIONSHIPS BETWEEN RGB AND YUV/YIQ

The CS Module discusses the conversion between color spaces in detail. But to show you that the Y, U, and V, and Y, I, and Q, can be derived from RGB values, here are the equations:

$$Y = 0.299R + 0.587G + 0.114B$$
$$U = 0.492(B - Y) = 0.147R - 0.289G + 0.436B$$
$$V = 0.877(R - Y) = 0.615R - 0.515G - 0.100B$$

$$Y = 0.299R + 0.587G + 0.114B$$
$$I = 0.596R - 0.275G - 0.321B$$
$$Q = 0.212R - 0.523G + 0.311B$$

When you edit digital video, you do not need to explicitly set the color space to YUV or YIQ. If you create digital images for use in video, they can be kept in RGB format. The digital video editing program will convert the images to the correct color format.

# 6.2 SAMPLING AND QUANTIZATION OF MOTION

Each frame in a video is an image. Conceptually, in digital video, these images are digitized in a way similar to digital images by sampling and quantization. The image for each frame is sampled into a grid of discrete samples—the sampling process. Each sample becomes a pixel. The digital video frame size is still measured in pixels, as with digital still images. Each pixel is assigned a color value from a finite list of colors—the quantization process. The finite list of colors is within the video's color space.

In addition to the image frame, the sampling process also occurs in the temporal dimension of video. The sampling rate of the temporal dimension is the frame rate of the video. The higher the frame rate, the more accurate the motion that is sampled. However, for the same video duration, a higher frame rate also means more frames, which results in a larger file size.

*See Chapter 1 for the general concepts of sampling and quantization and Chapter 2 for sampling and quantization in the digital image.*

# 6.3 MEASURING FRAME SIZE AND RESOLUTION OF DIGITAL VIDEO

Because digital videos are basically a sequence of digital images, many aspects of digital images discussed in Chapters 2 and 3 can be applied to a video frame. For example, in digital video, the *frame size* is referred to as **resolution** and is measured in pixel dimensions.

However, unlike digital images, pixel per inch (ppi) is not really applicable in digital video. As discussed in Chapters 2 and 3, the ppi value matters *only* when the image is printed; ppi is meaningless for images intended for the Web or onscreen display. You never find the ppi attribute in digital video. The implication of this is that if you are creating a digital image to use in a digital video, you should set the image size based on the pixel dimension only; the ppi setting does not matter.

Another attribute used to describe the video frame size is its aspect ratio. As you will see in the following sections, a frame aspect ratio is not simply the ratio of its pixel width to its pixel height. This is because of an attribute called the pixel aspect ratio.

## 6.3.1 Frame Size

The *video frame size* (also referred to as resolution) is measured in the pixel dimensions of a frame—its width by its height, expressed in number of pixels. For example:

- For the **HDV** format—one of the high-definition video formats—there are two frame sizes at the time of this writing: 1,440 × 1,080 pixels and 1,280 × 720 pixels.
- For the **DVCPRO HD** format—another high-definition video format—there are three frame sizes at the time of this writing: 1,280 × 1,080 pixels, 1,440 × 1,080 pixels, and 960 × 720 pixels.
- For the NTSC standard-definition DV format, the frame size is 720 × 480 pixels. The frame size for a PAL standard DV frame is 720 × 576 pixels.

## 6.3.2 Frame Aspect Ratio

The *frame aspect ratio* is the ratio of its *viewing* width to height; it is not equivalent to the ratio of the frame's pixel width to height. For example, the frame aspect ratio for

*The terms DV and HDV may appear to be simple abbreviations for digital video and high-definition digital video, respectively. However, DV format and HDV format refer to specific video standards. In this chapter, the terms DV and HDV refer to those specific standards, not shorthands for digital video and high-definition digital video.*

high-definition digital video and high-definition TV (HDTV) is 16:9. For the standard-definition video, the frame aspect ratio for the standard format is 4:3, and the wide-screen format is 16:9 (Figure 6.4). Note that the grid in Figure 6.4 is used as a visual aid only to help you easily tell the width-to-height ratio. The grid cells are *not* representing the image pixels and the number of cells is *by no means* the number of pixels.

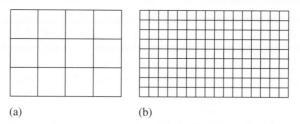

(a)                                 (b)

**Figure 6.4** (a) A frame using an aspect ratio of 4:3. (b) A frame using an aspect ratio of 16:9.

### 6.3.3 Pixel Aspect Ratio

One of the supported frame sizes of HDV format is 1,280 × 720 pixels. The width-to-height ratio is 16:9, which matches the frame aspect ratio of high-definition video. The other frame size of HDV format is 1,440 × 1,080 pixels. Its width-to-height ratio does not match 16:9; it is 12:9. What is missing here?

> The frame size and frame aspect ratio of different high-definition video formats are listed in Table 6.4.

Unlike digital image editing, in which images use square pixels by default, some video formats use nonsquare pixels to make up the frame. The shape of the pixel can be described by an attribute called ***pixel aspect ratio***. It is the ratio of a pixel's width to its height. For a square pixel, its pixel aspect ratio is equal to 1. A pixel aspect ratio of less than 1 depicts a tall pixel, whereas a pixel aspect ratio of greater than 1 depicts a wide pixel.

The pixel aspect ratio for HDV 720p is 1.0, and for HDV 1080i and 1080p is 1.333. Let's see if this makes sense for the HDV frame size and its frame aspect ratio.

- For HDV 720p that has a frame size of 1,280 × 720, its pixel aspect ratio = 1.0, because

$$\text{width} : \text{height} = 1{,}280 \times \text{pixel aspect ratio} : 720$$
$$= 1{,}280 \times 1.0 : 720 = 1{,}280 : 720 = 16{:}9$$

- For HDV 1080i and 1080p that has a frame size of 1,440 × 1,080, its pixel aspect ratio = 1.333 because

$$\text{width} : \text{height} = 1{,}440 \times \text{pixel aspect ratio} : 1{,}080$$
$$= 1{,}440 \times 1.333 : 1{,}080 = 1{,}920 \times 1{,}080 = 16{:}9$$

Similarly, for standard-definition DV format, the pixel aspect ratio for the wide-screen format (16:9) is 1.2, whereas the pixel aspect ratio of the standard format (4:3) is 0.9.

A video should be displayed on a system with the matching pixel aspect ratio; otherwise the image will be distorted. Figure 6.5 illustrates the effects of various pixel aspect ratios displayed on systems with different pixel aspect ratios. Figure 6.5a, d, and g show how video frames of pixel aspect ratios of 1.0, 0.9, and 1.2, respectively, are supposed to look when displayed correctly on a system with the pixel aspect ratio that matches

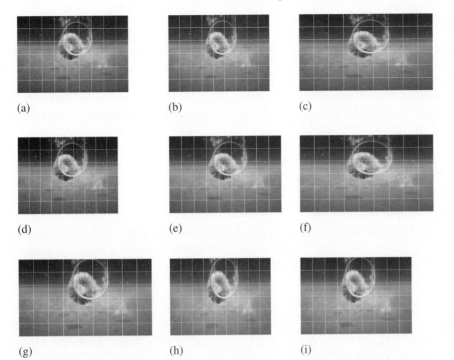

(a)                    (b)                    (c)

(d)                    (e)                    (f)

(g)                    (h)                    (i)

**Figure 6.5** The images in the first column show how they look when displayed with the correct pixel aspect ratio. The other six images demonstrate how they are distorted when displayed with an incorrect pixel aspect ratio. (a) A frame of pixel aspect ratio 1.0 displayed correctly. (b) A frame of pixel aspect ratio 1.0 displayed incorrectly with a pixel aspect ratio of 0.9; the ring is elongated vertically. (c) A frame of pixel aspect ratio 1.0 displayed incorrectly with a pixel aspect ratio of 1.2; the ring looks squashed. (d) A frame of pixel aspect ratio 0.9 displayed correctly. (e) A frame of pixel aspect ratio 0.9 displayed incorrectly with a pixel aspect ratio of 1.0; the ring looks slightly wider than it should. (f) A frame of pixel aspect ratio 0.9 displayed incorrectly with a pixel aspect ratio of 1.2; the ring looks squashed. (g) A frame of pixel aspect ratio 1.2 displayed correctly. (h) A frame of pixel aspect ratio 1.2 displayed incorrectly with a pixel aspect ratio of 0.9; the ring is elongated vertically. (i) A frame of pixel aspect ratio 1.2 displayed incorrectly with a pixel aspect ratio of 1.0; the ring is elongated vertically.

the frame's pixel aspect ratio. Figure 6.5b, c, e, f, h, and i show the distorted frames displayed on systems with a pixel aspect ratio different from the frame's intended pixel aspect ratio.

In short, a frame displayed on a system with a pixel aspect ratio larger than the frame's will stretch the image horizontally, whereas a frame displayed on a system with a smaller pixel aspect ratio will stretch the image vertically. The larger the difference between the frame's pixel aspect ratio and the system's, the greater the distortion.

> **Pixel Aspect Ratio** An interactive demo shows you the effect of an incorrect pixel aspect ratio on an image.

SMPTE, founded in 1916, is an organization to develop standards in the motion picture industry. Its Web site is http://www.smpte.org.

# 6.4 COUNTING TIME IN DIGITAL VIDEO

Video editing requires precise synchronization and hence precise measurement of time. The smallest timing unit in video is a frame, which is usually only a fraction of a second. Therefore, our usual measurement of time in hours, minutes, and seconds is not precise enough for video. *Timecode* is used to number frames. *SMPTE* (Society of Motion Pictures and Television Engineers) video timecode, the most common timecode for digital video, numbers frames in hours, minutes, seconds, and frames. For example, 00:02:32:07 refers to the frame at 2 minutes, 32 seconds, and 7 frames.

There are two types of timecodes: drop frame and non-drop frame. For example, the following indicates video time at 0 hours, 2 minutes, 51 seconds, and 20 frames.

| | |
|---|---|
| Drop-frame timecode | 00;02;51;20 |
| Non-drop-frame timecode | 00:02:51:20 |

Notice that the drop-frame timecode uses semicolons, whereas the non-drop-frame timecode uses colons. This is how you can tell which timecode a system is using. The drop-frame timecode is preferable for the NTSC system.

## WHAT IS THE DIFFERENCE BETWEEN DROP-FRAME AND NON-DROP-FRAME TIMECODES? WHY ARE THERE TWO TIMECODE FORMATS? HOW DO YOU CHOOSE WHICH ONE TO USE? DOES USING DROP-FRAME TIMECODE RESULT IN DELETING FRAMES FROM THE VIDEO?

To help you understand the need for two different timecodes, let's look at an analogous situation in our daily life—the purpose of leap years.

The time it takes for the Earth to orbit the Sun is about 365.242199 days, according to the Encyclopedia Britannica. Because it is not an exact number of days, we need leap years.

How does this work? A year is designated as 365 days because the number 365.242199 is closer to 365 than 366. However, this causes an inevitable slight shift of days—about a 0.24 day each year, or about 24 days for every 100 years. Without leap years, the seasons would shift. By adding one extra day to every fourth year, we get (356 × 3 + 366) days for four years, that is, an average of 365.25 days per year. This offsets the shift very closely.

Why do we need to offset the shift? It is because we want to keep the seasons at the same time of the year every year. But do we skip or delete time from our lives using leap years? No, of course not. We have the same amount of time no matter whether we have leap years or not; it is just a different way of counting days.

A similar situation arises with the NTSC-standard timebase. The NTSC-standard timebase is 29.97, not exactly 30 frames per second (fps). This fractional discrepancy will accumulate to make a significant difference between the actual frame duration and the time duration. Using the drop-frame timecode eliminates this error.

**TABLE 6.2** **Examples of How the Drop-Frame and Non-Drop-Frame Timecodes Count Frames, Where the Length in Minutes Is Calculated by Dividing the Number of Frames by the Frame Rate**

| Number of Frames | Length (minutes) for 29.97 fps | Length (minutes) for 30 fps | Drop-Frame Timecode | Non-Drop-Frame Timecode |
|---|---|---|---|---|
| 1799 | 1.0004 | 0.9994 | 00;00;59;29 | 00:00:59:29 |
| 1800 | 1.001 | 1 | 00;01;00;02 | 00:01:00:00 |
| 17981 | 9.999 | 9.989 | 00:09:59:29 | 00:09:59:11 |
| 17982 | 10 | 9.990 | 00;10;00;00 | 00:09:59:12 |

When you use a drop-frame timecode, the program renumbers the first two frames of every minute except for every 10th minute. To demonstrate what this means, Table 6.2 shows the comparison of the two timecode formats with the length of video calculated based on different frame rates. For example, the drop-frame timecode increments from 00;00;59;29 to 00;01;00;02 in stepping one frame from the 1,799th frame to the 1,800th. The timecode skips 00;01;00;00 and 00;01;00;01—*renumbers two frames*—but *no* frame is actually discarded or dropped. On the other hand, the non-drop-frame timecode increments from 00;00;59;29 to 00;01;00;00.

For video of 29.97 fps, the 1,800th frame is actually a little longer than 1 minute; it is about 1.001 minutes (1,800/29.97). As you see, the drop-frame timecode 00;01;00;02 represents the duration of the 29.97-fps video more accurately than the non-drop-frame timecode 00:01:00:00.

However, the drop-frame timecode increments from 00;09;59;29 to 00;10;00;00 in stepping one frame from the 17,981st frame to the 17,982nd. The timecode now does not renumber any frame because it is the 10th minute—the first 10th. For the 29.97-fps video, the drop-frame timecode represents exactly the length of the video.

The discrepancy between the drop-frame and non-drop-frame timecodes seems very small. However, the discrepancy grows as the frame number progresses. If you have a separate audio created for the video, the discrepancy in video length will cause problems in synchronizing the separate audio track with the video.

In working with digital video editing programs, you need to choose a timecode format—drop frame or non-drop frame—for your project. However, you do not need to compute the timecode. The explanation provided in this section on how drop-frame timecode is computed is intended to help you understand the rationale to use the drop-frame timecode for the NTSC video and how it counts frames to maintain the time accuracy. It also helps you understand why some timecodes, such as 00;01;00;00 and 00;01;00;01, are skipped—not an abnormality. No frame is discarded in the process.

## DROP-FRAME TIMECODE: WHY RENUMBER THE FIRST TWO FRAMES OF EVERY MINUTE? AND WHY SKIP THE RENUMBERING EVERY 10TH MINUTE?

It sounds complicated at first, but let's do a calculation to demonstrate the rationale behind it, so it does not seem complicated anymore.

### Question

1. Why renumber the first two frames of every minute?

Let's first find out the number of frames in a video of exactly 1 minute.

- If the timebase for counting frames is 30 fps:

$$30 \text{ fps} \times 60 \text{ seconds} = 1,800 \text{ frames}$$

- If the timebase for counting frames is 29.97 fps:

$$29.97 \text{ fps} \times 60 \text{ seconds} = 1,798.2 \text{ frames}$$

For a 1-minute video clip, the frame difference between the 30 fps and 29.97 fps is:

$$1,800 - 1,798.2 = 1.8 \text{ frames, or } \textit{approximately two frames}$$

Now you see why the first *two frames* of every minute need to be renumbered in the drop-frame timecode for NTSC-standard timebase.

### Question

2. Why does such renumbering skip every 10th minute?

At exactly 10 minutes, for 30 fps, it is the 18,000th frame. It is denoted as 10:00:00 in non-drop-frame timecode.

But if counted for 29.97 fps, the 18,000th frame is a little over 10 minutes—it is 10 minutes and 18 frames (18,000 frames/29.97 fps).

In the first 9 minutes, drop-frame timecode has already renumbered 18 frames (2 frames each minute) to offset the shift; 18 frames are the offset necessary for 10 minutes. Therefore, when it comes to the 10th minute, it should not renumber another two frames; otherwise, it will overcompensate.

## 6.5 DIGITAL VIDEO STANDARDS

### 6.5.1 Standard Definition

The term *DV* is often used as an abbreviation for *digital video*. However, **DV compression** or DV format refers to specific types of compression. For example, **DV25** is the most common DV compression for **standard-definition digital video**.

DV25 is used by many digital video camcorders. These camcorders compress the video directly inside the camcorder. The video you get on tapes is already compressed into DV format. Table 6.3 lists the specifications for the DV25 format.

DV25 compresses the video at a fixed data rate of 25 megabits per second (Mbps) for the visual component of the video—hence the 25 in its name. This means the video takes up 3.125 MB of storage space per second. The total data rate for video, audio, and other control information is about 3.6 MB per second. The color space and color sampling method for NTSC is YUV 4:1:1. For NTSC, the frame size of the video is 720 × 480 pixels, and the frame rate is 29.97 fps.

**TABLE 6.3    Part of the Specifications of DV25 Format**

| Pixel Dimensions | | 720 × 480 (NTSC) | |
|---|---|---|---|
| Frame Aspect Ratio | | 4:3 | 16:9 |
| Pixel Aspect Ratio | | 0.9 | 1.2 |
| Data Rate | Total (video + audio + control information): | 3.6 megabytes per second (MB/s), i.e., about 4.6 minutes of video per gigabyte of storage space | |
| | Video data only: | 25 megabits per second (Mbps); compressed at a fixed rate of 5:1 | |
| Color Sampling Method | | YUV 4:1:1 | |
| Audio Setting | Sampling rate and bit depth: | Two options:<br>• 48 kHz, 16 bit<br>• 32 kHz, 12 bit | |

## WHAT DOES YUV 4:1:1 MEAN?

While RGB is a common color model used in digital photographs or any still digital images, the common color model used in digital video is a luminance-chrominance model, such as YUV, to represent the color of each pixel. The Y component is the luminance (brightness). The U and V components are the chrominance (color or hue).

The human eye is more sensitive to changes of luminance than it is to chrominance changes. Digital video systems exploit this phenomenon to reduce the storage of information by using fewer bits to storing the chrominance components. In other words, some chrominance data will be discarded. This method is called *chroma subsampling* or color subsampling.

There are several subsampling formats, depending on the ratio of the chrominance information to be discarded. The format is designated with three numbers separated by colons, for example, 4:2:2, to represent the ratio of the Y-component to the two chrominance components, Y:U:V.

The full-color information for each pixel contains one sample each of Y, U, and V. Thus, there are a total of three samples per pixel related to color information.

### 4:4:4

The designation *4:4:4* means for each group of four pixels, four samples of the Y-component and four samples each of the two chrominance components will be stored—that is, a total of 12 samples for each group of four pixels. In other words, there is no saving in storage (no compression), that is, no subsampling.

### 4:2:2

The *4:2:2* subsampling method means that for every four pixels, it will use:

- 4 samples of Y
- 2 samples of U
- 2 samples of V

The need for using fewer bits to store the color information is much higher for digital videos than still digital images because a video file contains many frames resulting in a much larger file than a still image. Using the RGB model for digital videos would not have allowed us to take advantages of the human perception to reduce the file size.

The total of samples used for every four pixels is now reduced from 12 to 8. This means a one-third reduction in storage requirements.

This subsampling method is used in Digital Betacam video format.

### 4:2:0

The *4:2:0* subsampling method means that for every four pixels, it will use:

- 4 samples of Y
- 2 samples of either U or V

The total of samples used for every four pixels is now reduced from 12 to 6. This results in a 50% reduction in storage requirements.

The selection of U and V are alternated by scan lines. In one scan line, the samples from the U are used. In the next scan line, the samples from the V are used.

This subsampling format is used in HDV, MPEG-1, DVD MPEG-2, and PAL DV.

### 4:1:1

The *4:1:1* subsampling method means that for every four pixels, it will use:

- 4 samples of Y
- 1 sample of U
- 1 sample of V

The total of samples used for every four pixels is now reduced from 12 to 6. This means a 50% reduction in storage requirements.

This subsampling method is used in NTSC DV. The DV format is used in the miniDV digital video camcorder.

## 6.5.2 High Definition

Table 6.4 lists several common high-definition video formats. For example, the HDV format supports three picture formats: *720p*, *1080i*, and *1080p*. The number designates the pixel height of the frame size, and the letters "p" and "i" specify the video's scan type—progressive and interlaced, respectively. For the HDV format, the pixel dimensions for the 720p are 1,280 × 720 pixels and for the 1080i and 1080p are 1,440 × 1,080 pixels.

You may recognize these video format names because they are often displayed on the video cameras (Figure 6.6).

Although Table 6.4 seems to be a mere collection of independent factual information, commonalities among these specifications exist. For example:

- The frame aspect ratio is 16:9.
- The picture formats are 1,080 and 720; each can be either interlace or progressive.
- For the 1080 format, the supported frame sizes are 1,440 × 1,080 (with pixel aspect ratio of 1.333—wide pixel) and 1,920 × 1,080 (with pixels aspect ratio of 1.0—square pixel).
- For the 720 format, the supported frame sizes are 960 × 720 (with pixel aspect ratio of 1.333—wide pixel) and 1,280 × 720 (with pixels aspect ratio of 1.0—square pixel).
- The color sampling method is either 4:2:0 or 4:2:2.

The main differences between these formats are the video and audio compression, which combined, in turn, influence the data rate.

**TABLE 6.4    Several High-Definition Video Formats**

| Format | Frame Dimensions | Aspect Ratio | Frame Rate (fps) | Picture Format | Color Sampling Method | Data Rate | Video Compression | Audio Setting |
|---|---|---|---|---|---|---|---|---|
| HDV | • 1,440 × 1,080 (displayed at 1,920 × 1,080) • 1,280 × 720 | 16:9 | • NTSC: 29.97, 59.94 • PAL: 25, 50 • Film: 23.98 | 1080i 1080p 720p | 4:2:0 | 2.5–14 MB/sec. depending on codec | MPEG-2: • Constant bit rate (CBR) • Uses I-, P-, and B-frames • GOP N = 15 | • Sampling rate: 48 kHz • Bit depth: 16 • Encoded using MPEG-1 Layer 2 format with a data rate of 384 kbps |
| DVCPRO HD | • 1,280 × 1,080 (displayed at 1,920 × 1,080) • 1,440 × 1,080 (displayed at 1,920 × 1,080) • 960 × 720 (displayed at 1,280 × 720) | 16:9 | • NTSC: 29.97, 59.94 • PAL: 25, 50 | 1080i 720p | 4:2:2 | 115 Mbps (i.e., 14.4 MB/sec.) | • Uses a variation of DV and DVPRO 50 codecs • Compression ratio = 8.6:1 | • Sampling rate: 48 kHz • Bit depth: 16 |
| AVCHD | • 1,920 × 1,080 • 1,440 × 1,080 (displayed at 1,920 × 1,080) • 1,280 × 720 | 16:9 | • NTSC: 29.97 • PAL: 25 • Film: 23.98 | 1080i 1080p 720p | 4:2:0 | Average bit rate is 5–24 Mbps, depending on the camcorder brand and the quality setting on the camcorder | • Uses Advanced Video Coding (AVC) compression, or H.264 (also known as MPEG-4 part 10) • Uses I-, P-, and B-frames • Uses variable bit rate (VBR) | 5.1-channel surround sound with Dolby Digital (AC-3) up to 7.1-channel surround sound (uncompressed) |
| AVC-Intra | • 1,920 × 1,080 • 1,440 × 1,080 (displayed at 1,920 × 1,080) • 1,280 × 720 • 960 × 720 (displayed at 1,280 × 720) | | • NTSC: 29.97 • PAL: 25 • Film: 23.98 | | 4:2:0 4:2:2 | • 50 Mbps: For 1,440 × 1,080 and 960 × 720, and color sample ratio of 4:2:0 • 100 Mbps: For 1,920 × 1,080 and 1,280 × 720, and color sample ratio of 4:2:2 | • Uses Advanced Video Coding (AVC) compression, or H.264 (also known as MPEG-4 part 10) • I-frame-only compression | 4-channel uncompressed |

(a)  (b)

(c)

**Figure 6.6** High-definition video cameras of different video formats: (a) HDV, (b) AVCHD, and (c) DVCPRO HD.

One of the key differences between high-definition and standard-definition video is their frame size (resolution). To give you an idea of how the frame sizes of high-definition video differ from those of standard-definition video, Figure 6.8 shows a comparison of the frame sizes. Note that the pixel dimensions of a frame may be different from its viewing size because some high-definition digital video standards (for example, HDV 1080i and 1080p) and standard-definition DV use non-square pixels for displaying the frame.

## HIGH-DEFINITION VIDEO PICTURE FORMAT NOTATION

When describing the high-definition video picture format, it is often written in a form such as 1080/60i or 720/30p. Figure 6.7 explains the notation.

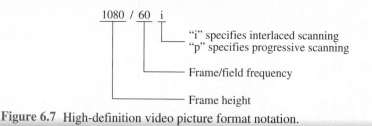

**Figure 6.7** High-definition video picture format notation.

To give you a feel of the relative frame sizes of different digital video formats and how the different frame sizes may affect the details of the image, Figure 6.9 shows a comparison of the viewing frame sizes. Figure 6.9a is a frame from an 1080/60i video. Its pixel

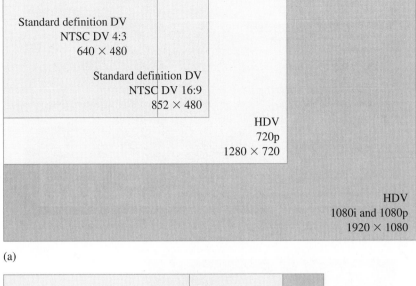

(a)

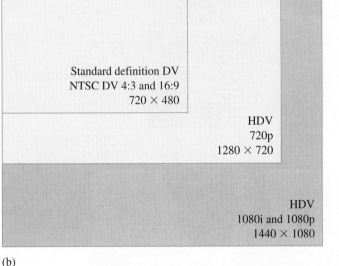

(b)

**Figure 6.8** Comparison of frame sizes of standard-definition and high-definition digital video: (a) Comparison by the viewing frame sizes. (b) Comparison by the pixel dimensions.

dimensions are 1,440 × 1,080. The figure shown is scaled based on its pixel aspect ratio to make the frame conform to the frame aspect ratio of 16:9. Figures 6.9b through 6.9d are scaled to show you how the frame would have looked if it was shot at the resolution for 720p, standard-definition DV 16:9, and standard-definition DV 4:3 format.

At the time of writing, in addition to high-definition camcorders that shoot video in one of the formats listed in Table 6.4, there are also digital SLR cameras that can take high-definition video at 1080p (in full 1,920 × 1,080 pixels) and 720p (in full 1,280 × 720 pixels) in addition to still pictures.

(a)

(b)

(c)                                          (d)

**Figure 6.9** Frame size comparison: (a) A frame from a 1080i video. (b) The same frame in 720p format. (c) The same frame in standard-definition DV wide-screen (16:9) format. (d) The same frame in standard-definition DV standard 4:3 format.

## 6.5.3 Digital Television (DTV)

For more information about ATSC and its standard development, visit its Web site at http://www.atsc.org.

The signals of digital television (DTV) are broadcast over the air or transmitted digitally by a cable or satellite system. In order for the consumer to watch DTV, a decoder is needed to receive and use the signal, which is in digital form, to directly drive the digital TV set.

At the time of this writing, in the United States, ***Advanced Television Systems Committee, Inc. (ATSC)***—an international nonprofit organization that develops voluntary standards

| TABLE 6.5 | The 18 ATSC Formats for DTV | | |
|---|---|---|---|
| | **Frame Size** | **Display Aspect Ratio** | **Frame Rate and Scan Mode** |
| SDTV | 704 × 480 | 16:9 | 24p |
| | | | 30p |
| | | | 60i |
| | | | 60p |
| | | 4:3 | 24p |
| | | | 30p |
| | | | 60i |
| | | | 60p |
| | 640 × 480 | 4:3 | 24p |
| | | | 30p |
| | | | 60i |
| | | | 60p |
| HDTV | 1,920 × 1,080 | 16:9 | 24p |
| | | | 30p |
| | | | 60i |
| | 1,280 × 720 | | 24p |
| | | | 30p |
| | | | 60p |

for DTV—has developed a total of 18 DTV formats: 12 formats for *standard-definition television (SDTV)* and 6 for *high-definition television (HDTV)*.

Table 6.5 lists the 18 formats. Again, the letter "p" or "i" next to the frame rate designates the scan mode: "p" for progressive and "i" for interlaced. The frame rate for the progressive scan refers to frames per second. The number for the interlaced scan is actually in fields per second—for example, 60i refers to 30 frames per second, because each interlaced frame consists of two fields. HDTV uses MPEG-2 format and has a higher resolution than both the traditional analog TV and SDTV. The frame aspect ratio of all six HDTV formats is 16:9.

The Federal Communications Commission (FCC) mandated that all television stations be capable of broadcasting digital television (DTV) by February 17, 2009. In order for consumers to watch DTV, there are several equipment requirements on different parties, for example:

For more information, visit http://www.dtv.gov/consumercorner.html.

- TV stations need production and transmission equipment for DTV programs.
- Consumers need equipment for reception of the DTV signals.

## 6.6 FILE TYPES OF DIGITAL VIDEO

Many digital video editing programs let you choose the video format in which you want to export your video file. The common file types are listed in Table 6.6. The file types often already dictate the available compression method.

Generally, the intended use of your video file determines its file format. Here are several considerations:

- **The file size and data rate limits.**
  - If your video is intended for use on the Web, then you may want to consider a file format that offers high compression or a streaming video file format.
  - If your video is intended for CD-ROM or DVD-DOM playback, you will need to consider a data rate that can be handled by your target audience's computers.
  - If your video is intended to be DVD-video, then you need to export it into DVD MPEG-2 that fits on a DVD disc.
- The *intended* **audience of your video file.**
  - If your video will be played on multiple platforms, then the file format should be cross-platform. The cross-platform formats (see Table 6.6) include Apple QuickTime, MPEG, Flash Video, and RealVideo.
  - If your video is intended for the Web playback, you may want to consider exporting your video into HTML5 video formats. At the time of writing, there are three HTML5 video formats: MP4 (.mp4, .m4v), Ogg Theora (.ogg and .ogv), and WebM (.webm).
  - What equipment is your target audience going to use to watch your video?
    - If they are playing it on mobile devices, then you may want to consider using HTML5 video for the Web playback.
    - If they are playing it on a set-top DVD player, then you need to make a DVD-video.
    - If they are playing it on computers, then what kind of computers are they using— older or newer? This dictates the data rate for your video.
- **Files that are intended to be** *source files* **for future editing.**

You may want to choose a file format that is uncompressed (provided that the frame size is small, the video duration is extremely short, say less than 30 seconds, and

*HTML5 video and audio are covered in Chapter 15.*

**TABLE 6.6    Common Video File Types for Windows and Mac OS**

| File Type | Acronym For | Originally Created By | File Information and Codecs | Platforms |
|-----------|-------------|----------------------|----------------------------|-----------|
| .mov | QuickTime movie | Apple | • Not just for video, but there is also audio-only QuickTime<br>• Also supports MIDI<br>• Files can be streamed with QuickTime Streaming Server<br>• "Fast Start" technology also allows users to play the video as it is being downloaded<br>• Common codecs include H.264, Sorenson Video, Animation, and PlanarRGB | Apple QuickTime player, which is available for Mac and Windows |
| .avi | Audio Video Interleave | Intel | Common codecs include Microsoft RLE and Intel Indeo Video | Primarily used on Windows but Apple QuickTime player can play AVI files |
| .rm | RealVideo or RealMedia | Real Systems | • Supports very high degree of compression<br>• Allows you to choose the compression level in terms of network connection speed<br>• Files can be streamed with RealServer | • Cross-platform<br>• Requires Real player |

*(Continued)*

**TABLE 6.6** *Continued*

| File Type | Acronym For | Originally Created By | File Information and Codecs | Platforms |
|---|---|---|---|---|
| .wmv | Windows Media | Microsoft | | Primarily used with Windows Media Player |
| .divx | | DivX, Inc | • Uses DivX codec, which is based on MPEG-4<br>• Popular format for movies because of the high image quality and small file size<br>• AVI is a common container file format, i.e., a video using DivX codec may have the file extension .avi | • May require downloading DivX codec (available for Mac OS and Windows) for playback and creation of DivX videos because not all computers have the codec pre-installed<br>• Windows Media Player v11.0 comes with DivX codec |
| .mpg<br>.mpeg | MPEG | Motion Picture Experts Group | • DVD-compliant MPEG-2 is used for DVD-video<br>• Blu-ray compliant MPEG-2 is one of the supported Blu-ray formats | Cross-platform |
| .flv | Flash Video | Adobe | • Supports progressive download from a Web server<br>• Can be streamed if the file is hosted on Adobe Flash Media Server<br>Video codecs include:<br>• Sorenson Spark<br>• On2 VP6: This also supports alpha channel, which means the video can have transparency | • Cross-platform<br>• Requires Adobe Media Player to play<br>• Can be embedded in Flash SWF files<br>• A popular video format used by Web sites, such as YouTube |
| .f4v | Flash Video | Adobe | • Builds on MPEG-4 Part 12[1]<br>• Supports H.264/ACC-based content | • A newer Flash Video format than .flv<br>• Cross-platform<br>• Requires Adobe Media Player to play<br>• Can be embedded in Flash SWF files |
| .mp4 | MPEG-4 | Moving Pictures Experts Group | • Video codec: H.264<br>• Audio codec: AAC<br>• One of the HTML5 video formats | Plays in Web browsers that support the MP4 format of HTML5 video; at the time of writing, it is supported by Safari and Internet Explorer (IE) |
| .ogg or .ogv | | Xiph.Org Foundation | • Video codec: Theora<br>• Audio codec: Vorbis<br>• One of the HTML5 video formats<br>• Compared to the other two HTML5 video formats, it has lower quality for the same file size | Plays in Web browsers that support the Ogg Theora format of HTML5 video; at the time of writing, it is supported by Firefox, Chrome, and Opera |
| .webm | | An open source video format from Google | • Video codec: VP8<br>• Audio codec: Vorbis<br>• One of the HTML5 video formats | Plays in Web browsers that support the Ogg Theora format of HTML5 video; at the time of writing, it is supported by Firefox, Chrome, and Opera |

[1]http://www.adobe.com/devnet/f4v.html.

you have enough disk storage) or allows lossless compression. This is not a common option because an uncompressed video or even a video using lossless compression will require a large amount of storage space.

- Most video compression methods are lossy but some allow you to specify the quality of the compressed video. You may want to set a high quality level when exporting videos that are intended to be used as source files for future editing.

## 6.7 DIGITAL VIDEO FILE SIZE AND OPTIMIZATION

Chapter 2 shows that the file size of an uncompressed high-resolution image can be very large. For example, the file size of an uncompressed 3,000-pixel × 2,000-pixel, 24-bit image is 18,000,000 bytes, or about 17 MB.

For digital video, the frame size is not as large. For example, the frame size for the HDV 1080i and 1080p is 1,440 × 1,080 pixels. However, video is comprised of a sequence of images (24 to 30 frames per second), which quickly increases the file size. For example, a 1-minute video at a frame rate of 30 fps comprises 1,800 frames! Even if each frame takes up only 1 MB, 1,800 frames will equal almost 2 GB of data!

Let's look at the size of a video with the following properties:

- 1,440-pixel × 1,080-pixel frame size
- 24-bit color
- 30 fps
- 1-second length
- Audio: stereo (two channels)
- Audio: 48,000-Hz sampling rate and 16 bit

The *uncompressed* file size can be computed as follows:

**For the video:**
Total pixels in each frame:

$$1,440 \times 1,080 \text{ pixels} = 1,555,200 \text{ pixels/frame}$$

File size in bits for each frame:

$$1,555,200 \text{ pixels/frame} \times 24 \text{ bits/pixel} = 37,324,800 \text{ bits/frame}$$

File size in bits for 1-second video:

$$37,324,800 \text{ bits/frame} \times 30 \text{ frames/second} \times 1 \text{ second} = 1,119,744,000 \text{ bits}$$

File size in bytes:

$$1,119,744,000 \text{ bits} / (8 \text{ bits/byte}) = 139,968,000 \text{ bytes} \cong \textbf{133 MB}$$

**For the audio:**
File size of an uncompressed audio file:

Sampling rate × length of the audio × bit depth × number of channels

$$= 48,000 \text{ samples/second} \times 1 \text{ second} \times 16 \text{ bits/sample} \times 2$$
$$= 1,5 36000 \text{ bits}$$
$$= 1,5 36000 \text{ bits} / (8 \text{ bits/byte})$$
$$= 192,000 \text{ bytes}$$
$$\cong \textbf{188 KB}$$

Thus, a 1-second uncompressed video would require 133 MB + 188 KB (video + audio) of storage space, which is about 133 MB!

## 6.7.1 Data Rate

The file size is one of the considerations in deciding video export options for your final video—a larger file requires more storage space. But there is another important factor: its data rate, which is related to the smoothness of the video playback. The ***data rate***, also referred to as bit rate because it is reported in bits per second, refers to the amount of video data to be processed per second. The average data rate of a video is calculated by dividing the file size by the total length or duration of the video in seconds. If the data rate of a video is too high for the computer to handle, its playback will be choppy. This may become less of a concern because computers nowadays are fast enough to handle typical videos. However, for a video on the Web delivered by streaming or pseudostreaming, if its data rate is too high for the viewer's network connection, the video will have to pause frequently to wait for the data.

Streaming and pseudostreaming allow a Web video to start playing while it is being downloaded. See Section 6.10.

### VIDEO FILE SIZE VERSUS DATA RATE

Video file size and data rate are closely related, but they do not have the same implications. File size pertains to the *total* amount of the data. A large file size requires more disk space and longer transfer time.

Data rate refers to the amount of data to be processed *per second*. Hence, a very long video, even with a low data rate, can have a large file size. Data rate affects the smoothness of the video playback. If the data rate is too high for a computer to handle, the data will not be processed fast enough for continuous playback. The playback will be choppy.

### HOW DO I DETERMINE IF THE DATA RATE OF MY VIDEO CAN BE HANDLED BY THE AUDIENCE'S DEVICES?

The properties of a video, such as data rate, file size, and frame size, can be looked up in the QuickTime Player by selecting `Window > Show Movie Inspector`. The `Movie Inspector` shown in Figure 6.10a shows that the file size (data size) of the QuickTime movie example is 98.94 MB, and its average data rate is 31.77 mbits/sec (mbps or megabits per second). But where does the 31.77 mbits/sec come from? Here is how the average data rate is calculated:

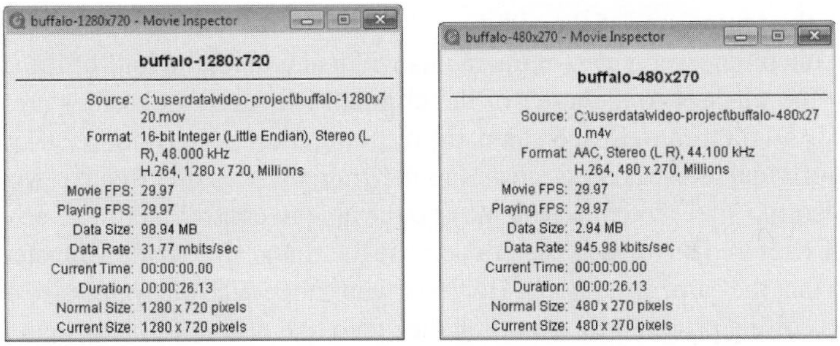

(a)                    (b)

**Figure 6.10** QuickTime Player's Movie Inspector showing the data size and data rate of two QuickTime movies with different frame sizes and compression options.

The movie's data size (i.e., file size) is 98.94 MB. The data rate is reported in mbits/sec. Let's first convert the data size from MB into mbits. Recall from Chapter 1 that 1MB = 1,024 KB, 1 KB = 1,024 bytes, and 1 byte = 8 bits. Thus, the number of bits for 98.94 MB is: 98.94 MB × 1,024 KB/MB × 1,024 bytes/KB × 8 bits/byte = 829,968,875 bits For data rate calculation, 1 mbits = 1,000 kbits and 1 kbit = 1,000 bits. Thus, 829,968,875 bits = 829,968,875 bits / (1,000 bits/kbit) / (1,000 kbits/mbits) = 829.97 mbits The movie's duration is 26.13 seconds. Thus, the data rate is: 829.97 mbits / 26.13 seconds = 31.8 mbits/sec

At the time of writing, the speed of the typical residential broadband connection is in the range of 3–20 mbits/sec. The average download speed of the 4G wrieless connection is in the range of 2 – 6 mbits/sec for laptop modems and 1 – 2 mbits/sec for smartphones.[2] The data rate of the example movie is much higher than these ranges. It will have to pause frequently during playback to wait for data while it is being downloaded.

Figure 6.10b shows the movie information of the same movie but with a smaller frame size (480 × 270 vs. 1,280 × 720 of the original) and different compression options. The data rate is now 945.98 kbits/sec (or 0.946 mbits/sec). For a typical residential broadband or 4G wireless connection, this video should play without having to pause to wait for data while it is still being downloaded. Its data rate also falls within the range of mobile 3G connection speeds (about 1 mbits/sec), and thus it also can play smoothly while being downloaded on 3G mobile devices.

Because video is comprised of a sequence of images and audio, the strategies for reducing the file size of digital images and audio are also applicable for digital video.

Recall that, as discussed in Chapter 2, the strategies for reducing image file sizes are: reducing the pixel dimensions, lowering the bit depth, and compressing the file. Similarly, the strategies for reducing audio file size, as discussed in Chapter 4, are: reducing the audio sampling rate, reducing the audio bit depth, compressing the file, and reducing the number of channels.

There is an additional type of video file compression that is different from those of image file compression. This type of compression method exploits the temporal nature of video. The general concepts of video file compression will be discussed in the next section.

Let's first look at how the general strategies for reducing image file size can be applied to reduce the video data rate. Reducing the video file size can be achieved by reducing the data rate and/or reducing the length of the video. The following discussion on file size optimization assumes that the length of the video is fixed. In this situation, reducing file size also means reducing the average data rate.

- **Lower the frame size of the video.**

  For an uncompressed video, reducing its width and height to half of the original will reduce the file size to a quarter of the original. However, video files are often compressed and for a compressed video, the resulting file size may not be strictly a quarter of the original. Nevertheless, lowering the frame size is an effective way to reduce the video file size. Note that you may not be able to control the frame size of a video footage captured by a video camera because the frame size is often dictated by the file format that the camera supports. However, you can reduce the frame size of a video in a video editing program by exporting the video to a different file format.

---

[2] Mark Sullivan. "4G Wireless Speed Tests: Which Is Really the Fastest? AT&T, Sprint, T-Mobile, and Verizon: PCWorld's exclusive performance tests reveal which 4G network delivers the fastest data speeds." *PCWorld.* March 13, 2011. URL: http://www.pcworld.com/printable/article/id,221931/printable.html

- **Lower the frame rate of the video.**

  Reducing the frame rate of a video means lowering the number of frames per second. Thus, the total number of frames in the video is decreased resulting in a smaller file size. In general, the frame rate is proportional to the file size. That is, reducing the frame rate to half will reduce the file size to half of the original. The digital video footage captured by a video camera often has a specific file format, which dictates the frame rate. However, in the video editing program, you can export your final video to a different file format using a lower frame rate.

  Lowering the frame rate affects the smoothness of fast-action content more than it affects talking-head-type videos. To lower the frame rate of a video that is originally shot at 30 fps, you can start at 15 fps and lower the frame rate as much as possible without making the video too choppy. Sometimes, the talking-head-type videos may work fine at a frame rate of as low as 8 or 10 fps.

- **For QuickTime movies, choose a video compressor that supports higher compression.**

  Sorenson Video 3 and H.264 for QuickTime usually give good compression with optimal picture quality. QuickTime Animation and PlanarRGB compressors are good for computer-generated animation, but the resulting file is less compressed.

- **Lower the picture quality of the video.**

  Some compressors let you set the picture quality. The lower the picture quality, the lower the data rate. Some, such as Sorenson (Figure 6.11), also let you set a limit on data rate. Lowering the data rate sacrifices the video quality. You will need to experiment with the settings and judge whether the resulting quality meets the intended use of the final video.

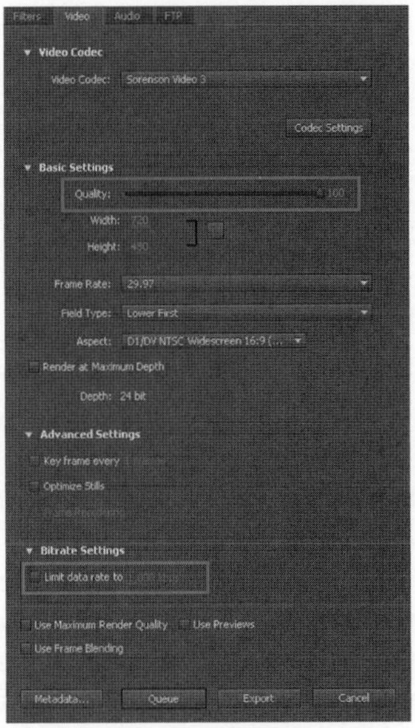

**Figure 6.11** Adobe Premiere Pro CS5.5's Export Movie dialog box with a Sorenson Video 3 compressor chosen.

For example, two QuickTime movies may be compressed with the same compressor, H.264, but one has the picture quality set to 100% and the other is set to 70%. The file size of the 70% quality movie may be about half that of the 100% one, but there is not much perceivable image degradation.

- **Lower the color depth, if appropriate.**
  This is a least-used strategy because:
  - Most digital video standards (DV, HDV, DVD) have specifications of color space.
  - Live videos usually need 24-bit color to look good. They may not work well with 8-bit color.
  - Some compressors support 24-bit color only.

  However, reducing color depth may work well for some computer-generated graphics or presentations that contain less than 256 colors. A compressor that supports 8-bit color is QuickTime Graphics.

- **Lower the sampling rate, bit depth, and number of channels of the audio.**
  This is another seldom-used strategy because:
  - Lowering the quality of the audio generally has much less impact on the file size than lowering the image quality, frame size, and frame rate of the video. For example, in the previous file size calculation, we see that the audio takes up less than 200 KB per second. The video portion for an HDV 1080i or 1080p takes up 25 Mbps (megabits per second) (Table 6.4), or about 3 MB per second, which is about 15 times the rate of the audio portion. This means that even if you eliminate the whole audio, only 1/16th of the file size would be saved.
  - Many digital video standards (such as DV, HDV, DVD, Blu-ray) have specifications for the audio sampling rate and bit depth to conform to.

    If you really need to reduce the file size as much as possible (even by lowering the quality of the audio), here are some general rules. The settings for a CD-quality audio are: 44,100-Hz sampling rate, 16 bit, stereo (two channels). If the content of the audio is speech, then a 22,050-Hz sampling rate should be acceptable. If the target audience will be playing the video with low-end speakers, then changing the audio to mono (i.e., reducing the number of channels to one) may be acceptable.

## 6.8 GENERAL CONCEPTS OF VIDEO FILE COMPRESSION METHODS

A compressed file must be decompressed before it can be used in normal applications. Think of compressing a file like packing a suitcase.

- Packing your clothes neatly in a suitcase makes it more compact to transport, but it takes time to pack.
- The clothes will need to be unpacked or even ironed before you wear them.
- How the clothes are unpacked often depends on how they were originally packed.

Similarly, it takes time to compress a video file. In addition, a compressed video file must be decompressed before it is played. Compression and decompression always go together as a pair. The term *codec* comes from abridging *co*mpressor/*dec*ompressor.

The general idea behind the file compression method is to represent the same content by using less data. Some methods involve discarding original data (lossy compression), whereas others preserve the original data (lossless compression).

Many codecs adopt more than one type of method. In general, you do not encounter the name of these compression methods directly in video editing programs. Instead, you are provided with a list of available codecs from which to choose when you export the final video sequence. The following description of the common compression strategies intends to help you make an educated decision in choosing a codec by understanding what the different types of compression methods do to the file and correlating them to the common codec names.

## 6.8.1 Spatial Compression

The general goal of *spatial compression* is to compact *individual frames*. This means that the pixel information of each frame is compressed independently from the content of other frames.

Some digital image compression algorithms, such as run-length encoding (RLE) and JPEG compression, are used. Codecs that use spatial compression and RLE are QuickTime Animation, QuickTime PlanarRGB, and Microsoft RLE. RLE works well for video with large areas of solid colors, such as most cartoon animation.

## 6.8.2 Temporal Compression

In a typical video sequence, the changes from frame to frame are often very small. *Temporal compression* exploits the repetitious nature of the image content *over time* and the possibility of predicting one frame from the other.

Instead of describing the pixel information of *every* frame, temporal compression only does so in *selected* frames. These frames generally are referred to as *keyframes*. For all other frames, only the *difference* from the previous keyframes is described. If the change between the current frame and the previous keyframe is small, the file size requirement for storing the difference will be smaller than storing the whole frame.

Temporal compression works well for video that contains continuous motion (i.e., the changes from frame to frame are small.) Videos with frequent flickering and scene changes may not be compressed well. Many codecs use temporal compression; for example, Sorenson Video and H.264 for QuickTime.

## 6.8.3 Lossless and Lossy Compression

*Lossless compression* preserves the original data. One of the strategies to do so is to exploit the pattern and repetition of the data, such as with the run-length encoding (RLE) method. Examples of lossless codecs are QuickTime Animation and PlanarRGB—set at the maximum quality setting.

*Lossy compression* discards or alters some of the original data. The discarded data cannot be recovered and thus the video quality will be lowered. However, the algorithms often take human perception into account when deciding which data will be discarded, so the video will maintain its perceptual quality as much as possible.

Usually, lossy compression results in a much smaller file size than lossless compression. In addition, lowering the quality setting for the lossy compressor lowers the data rate by discarding more original data.

### RUN-LENGTH ENCODING (RLE)

Recall from the discussion in Chapter 2 that RLE compacts a file by replacing a sequence of the same repeated value by one instance of the value followed by the number of times it is repeated. For example, imagine that the color blue is represented in 8 bits as 00001010. If there is a section of sky in a digital image where blue is repeated for 100 pixels, then without any compression, this section would require 800 bits. With RLE, we could encode this section as one instance of blue—00001010—followed by the number 100 in binary (1100100). Instead of 800 bits, we've now used 16 bits—16 digits for 00001010 and 1100100.

### 6.8.4 Symmetrical and Asymmetrical Compression

A *symmetrical codec* requires about the same amount of time and processing to compress as to decompress a video. In contrast, the amount of time and the complexity required to compress and decompress are significantly different in *asymmetrical codecs.*

Fast decompression is preferable for video, because the playback will require less wait time. In fact, many codecs fall into the asymmetrical category because it takes much longer to compress a video than to decompress.

The implication of this type of compression pertains to your time management during production. You may choose a fast compression during a time crunch or a fast preview of the work-in-progress video sequence. When you are ready to export the final video, you will need to plan for a much longer time for compression that uses a more efficient codec. For example, the QuickTime Animation codec compresses faster than Sorenson Video. But the video file using the QuickTime Animation codec is generally a lot larger than a file using the Sorenson Video codec.

## 6.9  MPEG COMPRESSION

*MPEG* stands for *Moving Pictures Experts Group*. This committee derives standards for encoding video. The MPEG file format allows high compression. There are several variations of MPEG: MPEG-1, MPEG-2, and MPEG-4.

### WHAT HAPPENED TO MPEG-3?

Do not confuse MPEG-3 with MP3. MP3 uses the MPEG-1 audio layer-3 encoding format. MPEG-3 does *not* mean the MP3 audio format.

MPEG-3 was intended as an extension of MPEG-2 to accommodate the standard for HDTV (high-definition television). However, the HDTV specification was then merged into the MPEG-2 standard and the task for deriving the MPEG-3 standard was ended.

### 6.9.1 MPEG-1

*MPEG-1* provides video quality comparable to VHS tapes and supports frame sizes up to $352 \times 240$ pixels. It is also the file format for VideoCD (VCD), which was popular before DVDs became more widespread. Before MPEG-4, it was used for video intended for the Web and CD-ROM playback.

### 6.9.2 MPEG-2

*MPEG-2* supports the DVD-video, Blu-ray, HDTV, and high-definition video standards. Without going into the details of the specifications of the standard, what this means to digital video production is:

- If your final video is intended for DVD-video, you will need to export the final video into DVD MPEG-2 format. There are different variants of MPEG-2, but only the ones that conform to the DVD specifications can be used for DVD-video.

Most digital video editing programs provide template settings for DVD export, so you do not need to memorize all of the specification details in order to export a correct MPEG-2 for DVD-video.

- If your final video is intended for Blu-ray format, you will need to export the final video into Blu-ray's MPEG-2 format.

This section intends to introduce a very basic and general explanation of MPEG compression, so you will understand the key parameters that you see in digital video editing programs when exporting your video to DVD MPEG format.

A detailed description of the MPEG standards and MPEG compression algorithms is presented in the CS Module.

## How Compression Works

In a typical video sequence, neighboring frames often have a great deal of similarity. This means that there is ***temporal redundancy***. MPEG compression exploits the temporal redundancy by looking for motion differences from one frame to the next in order to reduce file size. The technique it uses is called ***motion compensation***. The basic idea of the steps used in motion compensation is as follows:

1. An image from the video is read as a reference frame, and then the next image is read.
2. The image of this current or target frame is compared one block of pixels at a time with the reference image. There are two possibilities:

   - If the pixels of the two blocks at the same location in the frame are identical, then there will be no need to encode the pixel information of the current block. An instruction will be included to tell the decoder to use the block from the reference image. This will save more storage size than encoding the whole block.
   - If the two blocks are not identical, then it will search the reference image at different locations for a match. A match may or may not be found.
     - If no match is found, then it will encode that block fully. In this case, there is no saving in file size.
     - However, if a match is found, then the data of the block from the reference image plus the displacement information of the block will be encoded. The displacement information of the current block is called a ***motion vector***. It has a two-dimensional value, normally represented by a horizontal component and a vertical component. It tells the decoder exactly where in the reference image to get the data of the pixel block.

The example in Figure 6.12a represents a reference image and Figure 6.12b its subsequent frame. In comparing Figure 6.12b with Figure 6.12a, some pixel blocks in Figure 6.12b can be found in Figure 6.12a; for example, the blocks highlighted in blue in Figure 6.12f. However, some pixel blocks, such as those highlighted in yellow, cannot be found in Figure 6.12a.

Figures 6.13a and 6.13b show frames 1 and 2 of the previous example. The shaded block with the blue outline in frame 2 (Figure 6.13b) has a match in the reference frame (frame 1). The motion vector, depicted by a blue line connecting the two blocks in Figure 6.13c, provides the displacement information of the pixel block.

The example in Figure 6.12 is a very simple situation where all of the objects in the scene are flat and static. In a typical video, the movement of the subjects is much more complex. The subjects move and rotate in three dimensions, and the movement is not limited to a flat plane parallel to the camera. In addition, the lighting condition may change and the same subject may look differently in the next frame. Identical matches are rarely obtained. Instead, the closest matches are usually what the encoder will find.

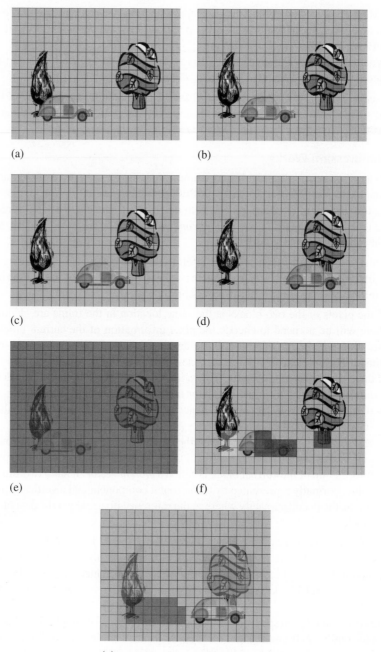

(a)

(b)

(c)

(d)

(e)

(f)

(g)

**Figure 6.12** (a) through (d) The first four frames of a video: (a) Frame 1, being the reference frame or the I-frame. (b) Frame 2, being a B-frame. (c) Frame 3, being a B-frame. (d) Frame 4, being a P-frame. (e) through (g) Areas highlighted in red are original pixel information and areas highlighted in blue are from the previous I-frame. Areas highlighted in cyan are from the previous I-frame at the same location, and those highlighted in yellow are from the next P-frame.  This image can be found on the insert.

*Note:* Not all the blocks are labeled for their encoding method; only some are highlighted to illustrate the points.

(a)                                    (b)

(c)

**Figure 6.13** (a) Frame 1 of the example in Figure 6.12, where the block outlined in blue matches the shaded block outlined in blue in (b). (b) Frame 2 of the same example, where the shaded block with the blue outline is the block under motion search. (c) The location difference is depicted by a blue line—the motion vector.

The color difference between the closest match from the reference frame and the actual pixel block of the current frame will be calculated. If the bits required to store the difference are fewer than encoding the actual pixel block, then the difference and the motion vector will be encoded. Otherwise, the actual pixel block will be encoded.

How does the encoder determine whether it is a match? The basic idea is to measure the differences (color value, pixel by pixel) between the block in the reference frame and the block in the current frame. The one with the minimum difference will be the closest match.

### Group of Pictures (GOP)

Recall that motion compensation is performed by comparing a frame with a reference frame. But how are reference frames chosen? To answer this question, we first need to introduce an important concept in MPEG-1 and MPEG-2: the *group of pictures (GOP)*, which defines the grouping structure of different frame types.

There are three frame types in terms of the information used for encoding the frame: I-frames, P-frames, and B-frames. A GOP structure in an MPEG movie contains one I-frame. It also often consists of a combination of multiple P- and B-frames. A typical MPEG consists of a repeating GOP structure.

*I-frames* stands for *intraframes*. An I-frame is encoded using only the information within that frame. It is called *intracoding*. In other words, I-frames use spatial compression but no temporal compression.

The encoding of an I-frame is very similar to JPEG compression. Artifacts similar to the artifacts in JPEG images can be seen in MPEG videos (Figure 6.14).

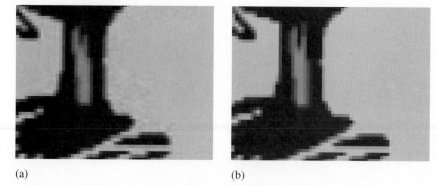

(a)                                        (b)

**Figure 6.14** (a) MPEG artifact, discernible at the intersect area of dark and light colors. (b) The original image before MPEG compression. 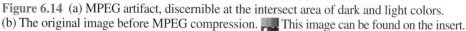 This image can be found on the insert.

A GOP starts with an I-frame; there is only one I-frame in a GOP. The number of frames, including the I-frame, in a GOP is specified by the parameter $N$ of the GOP. The value of $N$ for DVD-compliant MPEG-2 is 15. HDV also supports $N = 15$. Because the I-frame is encoded using spatial compression without temporal compression, it is the least-compressed frame type among the three types of frames.

*P-frames* stands for *predicted frames*. A P-frame is encoded by using the previous I- or P-frame as the reference frame. It is possible that a pixel block in a P-frame will use intra-coding when a match to the reference is not found or when the intracoding will use fewer bits than using the match.

*B-frames* are the frames between the I- and P-frame, the P- and P-frame, and the P- and next GOP's I-frame. B-frames stands for *bidirectional frames*, which means a B-frame is encoded by using the previous and subsequent I- and/or P-frame as the reference frames.

The parameter $M$ of the GOP specifies the number of these frames between the non-B-frames plus one. For DVD-compliant MPEG-2, the $N$ and $M$ parameters for the GOP are 15 and 3, respectively. In other words, the frames in a GOP are structured as

$$\text{I B B P B B P B B P B B P B B}$$

In this GOP, the first two B-frames are encoded using the previous I-frame and the subsequent P-frame as the reference frames.

The example in Figure 6.12 is based on this GOP structure. This means that:

- Frame 1 in the example in Figure 6.12a is the I-frame. The whole frame is intracoded (Figure 6.12e).
- Frame 4 (Figure 6.12d) is the first P-frame in the GOP.
- Frames 2 (Figure 6.12b) and 3 (Figure 6.12c) are B-frames.

Some blocks in frame 4 are intracoded (highlighted in red in the color insert of Figure 6.12g). Some blocks (highlighted in blue in the color insert of Figure 6.12f) in frame 2 (a B-frame) use the I-frame (frame 1) as the reference frame. However, part of a tree trunk in frame 2 is only available in the subsequent P-frame (frame 4), and those blocks (highlighted in yellow) use frame 4 as the reference frame for the tree trunk's pixel information.

You may encounter the $N$ and $M$ settings for the GOP when you export your video to MPEG-2. Some video editing programs hide the GOP settings from you. Some, such as Adobe Premiere Pro, let you check out or even change the $N$ and $M$ settings of the GOP when you export an MPEG-2 (Figure 6.15).

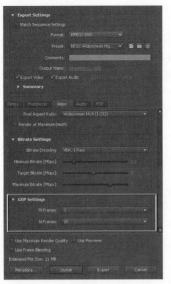

**Figure 6.15** Adobe Premiere Pro CS5.5's DVD MPEG-2 Movie Export window with the red rectangle highlighting the GOP's *M* and *N* parameters.

## Consequences of Configurations of GOP Structure

There are at least two consequences of using GOP structure in video; one pertains to the file size and the other to the video editing.

**For file size, consider the following:**
- An MPEG-2 movie consists of a repeating GOP structure.
- Each GOP contains one I-frame.
- I-frames are the least compressed among the three types of frames, and thus take up more storage space.

What this means to the MPEG-2 file size is that the shorter the GOP (i.e., lower value of *N*), the more I-frames a video will have. This, in turn, means that the overall file size is larger with a smaller value of *N*.

**For video editing, consider the following:**
- The information for a P-frame *depends* on the information of its previous I-frame.
- A B-frame *depends* on the information of its previous and subsequent I- or P-frames.

Because of this dependency, frame-accurate editing for MPEG-2 is more complex than in non-GOP types of videos such as standard-definition DV that uses the DV25 format. Editing MPEG-2 has been difficult because any alteration made on the frame sequence requires decompression and recompression (lossy, and could be slow). However, digital video editing application programs now are designed to allow MPEG editing to work seamlessly.

## 6.9.3 MPEG-4

*MPEG-4* is the newer standard in the MPEG family. It differs from MPEG-1 and MPEG-2 in the coding approach and the range of the target data rate. The new coding approach uses *media objects*. For example, if the car and the two trees from the scene in Figure 6.12 are each a media object, then even if the car is blocking part of a tree trunk in one scene, as in Figure 6.12a, the tree trunk information is still available. This approach allows better motion prediction. As you see in Figure 6.16d, it is easier to locate an exact match for the pixel block for the back of the car than with traditional frame-based coding (Figure 6.16e) in MPEG-1 and MPEG-2. The object-based coding also supports content-based manipulation of the scene and thus user interaction with the media objects.

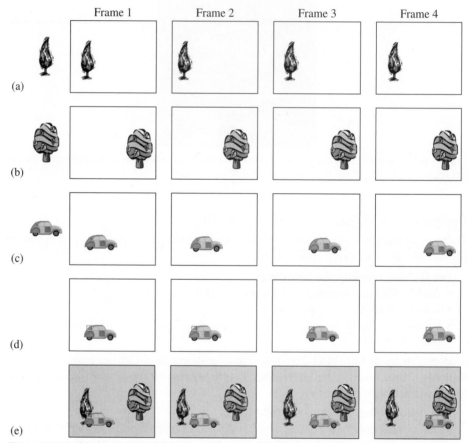

**Figure 6.16** (a) through (c) The rows illustrate the concepts of how elements would be treated as media objects. (d) Same as row (c) but with an outline of a pixel block at the back of the car. (e) A whole frame in traditional frame-based coding; a pixel block at the back of the car is outlined.

Each object in a scene, however, does not have to be separated into a media object in order to produce an MPEG-4 video. A conventional frame-based video—from a digital camcorder—can be converted to MPEG-4 format. In this case, the whole frame, as a rectangular bitmap image, is treated as an object—a degenerated case.

The data rate of the MPEG-4 standard covers a wide range. The low end of the range targets the mobile applications, such as cell phones, that MPEG-1 and MPEG-2 standards do not support. The high end supports the video quality for high-definition television

(HDTV). MPEG-4 is also a video file format supported by HTML5 and many handheld and portable game devices, such as Sony Playstation Portable (PSP).

# 6.10 STREAMING VIDEO AND PROGRESSIVE DOWNLOAD

There are two modes of video playback (i.e., two ways of playing videos):

1. **Play from the local storage of the user's device.**
   In this mode of playback, an entire clip needs to be already in the local storage of the user's device before it can be played. The file can be on a hard drive, a USB drive, or an optical disc (such as CD, DVD, and Blu-ray). If the video needs to be obtained from a Web site or any remote network site, then the entire file needs to be downloaded before it can start playing. All video file types support this mode of playback.

2. **Play over a network (typically the Internet).**
   In this mode, the video will be displayed while it is being downloaded. The video file does not have to be downloaded in its entirety before it can be played. Streaming video and progressive download fall into this mode of video playback. Examples of this mode of video playback include Amazon Instant Video, YouTube videos, and Netflix's online subscription.

The common file formats of *streaming video* on the Web are: Adobe Flash Video, Streaming QuickTime, Real Networks' RealVideo, and Windows Media Video (WMV). Streaming video files can also be played from disc. However, in order to stream the video over the Internet, it requires a streaming server, which is a computer running the appropriate streaming server program. For example, streaming Flash videos requires Adobe Flash Media Server, QuickTime requires Apple QuickTime Streaming Server, RealVideo requires RealNetworks Helix Server, and WMV requires Windows Server.

One of the key advantages of streaming is allowing encoding of multiple copies of the same video in different data rates. The streaming server chooses the appropriate one based on the speed of the viewer's connection to minimize disruption of the video playback. For example, Figure 6.17 shows some choices of different target connection speeds that you can add to a RealVideo file. This technology used by RealVideo and RealAudio is called *SureStream*.

Streaming does not guarantee continuous playback; it still takes time for the data stream to arrive. If the network connection is too slow, there still may be wait time every few frames or longer. When this happens, you usually see a message about "buffering . . ." in your media player.

Unlike other modes of video playback, a true streaming video is never stored on the user's device. If you want to watch the video again, the video will be streamed again.

An alternative method of streaming is *progressive download* or *pseudostreaming*. For example, MP4 and FLV videos can be played back using a mechanism called HTTP Pseudostreaming. This mechanism has been used by YouTube Web site. QuickTime's Fast-Start feature allows playback as soon as enough of the data stream has arrived.

Progressive download does not require a streaming server. The file is transferred to the local storage of the user's device as with non-progressive download. The file usually remains on the user's device after playback, for example, in the Web browser's cache if the video is played in the Web browser. Therefore, after the entire video has been played once, it can be played again from the Web browser's cache on the user's device without having to wait for download again.

A simple way to convert a Quick-Time movie into a Fast-Start movie is to save the Quick-Time movie as a self-contained movie in Quick-Time Pro, a professional version of QuickTime player.

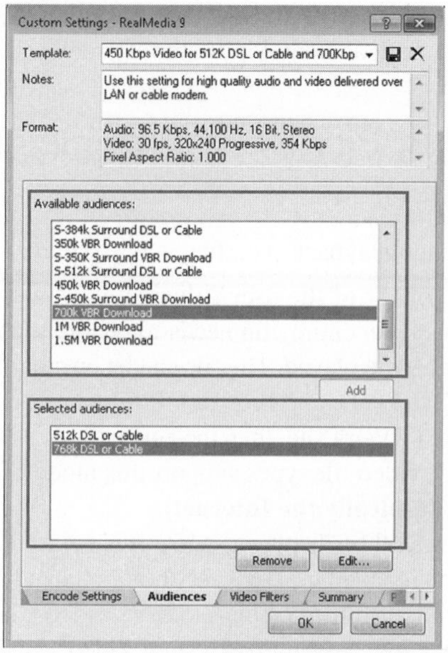

**Figure 6.17** A dialog box showing a list of target connection speeds you can choose from when exporting a video to RealVideo format using Sony Vegas Pro 11.

## 6.11 SUMMARY

Video captures our temporal experience of sights and sounds. Conceptually, video captures motion as a sequence of pictures at a constant time interval. Each picture is called a frame. The frame size also is referred to as resolution of the video. It is measured in the pixel dimensions of a frame—its width by its height, expressed in number of pixels. How fast the pictures are captured or how fast the frames are played back is determined by the frame rate, which is measured in frames per second (fps).

The concepts of sampling and quantization applied to still images also apply to the visual component of the video, and those applied to the digital audio also apply to the auditory component.

In many situations, the available choices in digital video settings, such as frame size and frame rate, are influenced by digital video standards, which, in turn, are influenced by the analog television broadcast standards. There are three sets of broadcast standards for analog color televisions: NTSC, PAL, and SECAM. They differ in frame sizes, frame rates, and color spaces.

For an NTSC standard-definition DV frame, the frame size is 720 × 480 pixels. The frame size for a PAL standard DV frame is 720 × 576 pixels. For high-definition digital video, the HDV format, for example, has two frame sizes: 1,280 × 720 pixels and 1,440 × 1,080 pixels.

The frame aspect ratio is the ratio of its width-to-height dimensions. For example, the frame aspect ratio for the standard-format NTSC DV is 4:3, whereas the wide-screen format is 16:9. The frame aspect ratio for high-definition digital video and high-definition television (HDTV) is 16:9.

Some video formats use non-square pixels to make up the frame. The shape of the pixel can be described by an attribute called pixel aspect ratio. For a square pixel, its pixel aspect ratio is equal to 1. A pixel aspect ratio of less than 1 depicts a tall pixel, whereas a pixel aspect ratio of greater than 1 depicts a wide pixel. A video should be displayed on a system with the matching pixel aspect ratio; otherwise, the image will be distorted.

Timecode is used to number frames in a video. The two common formats of timecode used in digital video are drop frame and non-drop frame. No frame is dropped or lost in either timecode. The drop-frame timecode is preferable for the NTSC system to maintain the time accuracy.

Computers display the picture by displaying lines from top to bottom in one pass—progressive scan. Analog television standards for NTSC, PAL, and SECAM display the picture in two passes. For NTSC, the first pass traces the even-numbered lines, and the second pass traces the odd-numbered lines to fill in the alternating gaps left by the first pass. The set of the lines in the same pass (i.e., the set of even lines or odd lines) is called a field. This display method of using two alternating fields is called interlaced scan.

Digital television (DTV) refers to television signals that are broadcast or transmitted digitally. At the time of this writing, in the United States, there are 18 DTV formats developed by the Advanced Television Systems Committee, Inc. (ATSC). The 18 formats include 12 formats for standard-definition television (SDTV) and 6 for high-definition television (HDTV). There are two frame aspect ratios for the SDTV format—4:3 and 16:9—whereas the frame aspect ratio of all six HDTV formats is 16:9. HDTV has higher resolution than the traditional analog TV and SDTV. It uses the MPEG-2 format.

The data rate refers to the amount of video data to be processed per second. The average data rate of a video is calculated by dividing the file size by the total length of the video in seconds. It provides a measure for predicting the smoothness of the video playback on devices. If a video's data rate is too high for a playback device to handle, the playback of the video will be choppy. Lowering the video data rate can be achieved by reducing the video file size. The general strategies to reduce video file size include: (1) lowering the frame size of the video, (2) lowering the frame rate of the video, and (3) using a compressor that allows higher compression.

MPEG stands for Moving Pictures Experts Group. It is a file format that allows high compression. There are several variations of MPEG: MPEG-1, MPEG-2, and MPEG-4. MPEG-1 supports the VideoCD format. MPEG-2 supports the DVD-video, Blu-ray, high-definition video, and HDTV standards. MPEG-4 is the newer standard of the MPEG family. It differs from MPEG-1 and MPEG-2 in the coding approach and the range of target data rate. MPEG-4's low-end range of data rate targets the mobile applications, such as cell phones, that MPEG-1 and MPEG-2 standards do not support. The high-end supports the video quality for HDTV and high-definition video.

There are two modes of video playback: play from the local storage of the user's device and play over a network. When playing from the user's device, an entire clip needs to be already on the device before it can be played. In playing over the network, the video will be displayed as the data stream arrives. In other words, a video file does not have to be downloaded in its entirety before it can be played. Streaming video and progressive download or pseudostreaming fall into this mode of video playback. True streaming requires a streaming server but progressive download does not.

## TERMS

## LEARNING AIDS

The following learning aids can be found at the book's companion Web site.

### Video display: Interlaced Scan versus Progressive Scan

An interactive animation that illustrates two-pass scanning in interlaced scan and one-pass scanning in progressive scan.

### Upper Field and Lower Field

An interactive demo shows the upper field and the lower field of a video frame.

### Fast-Action Digital Video Showing the Interlace Artifact

A soccer practice video clip of Figure 6.1 shows the comb-like interlace artifact.

### Video Recording: Interlaced Mode versus Progressive Mode

An interactive animation that illustrates how the interlace artifact may be produced in fast-action videos.

### Pixel Aspect Ratio

An interactive demo shows you the effect of an incorrect pixel aspect ratio on an image.

# REVIEW QUESTIONS

When applicable, please choose all correct answers.

1. Which of the following is the television broadcast standard for the United States and Japan?

   A. NTSC
   B. PAL
   C. SECAM

2. Which of the following is the television broadcast standard for most of the Asian countries?

   A. NTSC
   B. PAL
   C. SECAM

3. Which of the following is the most common color model for video?

   A. RGB
   B. HSV
   C. CIE XYZ
   D. luminance-chrominance

4. In the YUV color model, the Y-component is _____, the U-component is _____, and the V-component is _____.

   A. luminance; luminance; chrominance
   B. luminance; chrominance; luminance
   C. luminance; chrominance; chrominance
   D. chrominance; chrominance; luminance
   E. chrominance; luminance; luminance

5. The frame rate for the NTSC system is _____ fps.

   A. 24
   B. 25
   C. 28.9
   D. 29.97
   E. 30

6. The frame rate for the PAL system is _____ fps.

   A. 24
   B. 25
   C. 28.9
   D. 29.97
   E. 30

7. The frame rate for motion-picture film is _____ fps.

   A. 24
   B. 25
   C. 28.9
   D. 29.97
   E. 30

8. Interlaced scan displays the frame by scanning the lines of a frame _____.

   A. in one pass from top to bottom
   B. in two passes: even-numbered lines in one pass and odd-numbered lines in the second

9. Progressive scan displays the frame by scanning the lines of a frame _____.

   A. in one pass from top to bottom
   B. in two passes: even-numbered lines in one pass and odd-numbered lines in the second

10. The comb-like artifact in a digital video, as shown in Figure 6.18, occurs in the _____ video.

Figure 6.18  A digital video frame showing comb-like artifacts.

   A. interlaced
   B. progressive
   C. both A and B

11. **True/False:** There is no sampling and quantization involved in capturing motion in digital video.

12. The frame size of a video refers to the video's _____.

   A. aspect ratio
   B. pixel aspect ratio
   C. resolution
   D. ppi

13. **True/False:** The pixel per inch (ppi) is an important attribute for video resolution and should be set correctly when working with digital video in video editing programs.

14. Pixel aspect ratio means _____.

   A. the ratio of a frame's width (in pixels) to its height (in pixels)
   B. the ratio of a frame's height (in pixels) to its width (in pixels)
   C. the ratio of a pixel's width to its height
   D. the ratio of a pixel's height to its width

15. The pixel aspect ratio of a wide-screen-format, standard-definition video is _____.

   A. 4:3
   B. 16:9
   C. 1.0
   D. 0.9
   E. 1.2

16. The pixel aspect ratio of a standard-format, standard-definition video is _____.

   A. 4:3
   B. 16:9
   C. 1.0
   D. 0.9
   E. 1.2

17. The frame aspect ratio of a wide-screen-format, standard-definition video is _____.

   A. 4:3
   B. 16:9
   C. 1.0
   D. 0.9
   E. 1.2

18. The frame aspect ratio of a standard-format, standard-definition video is _____.

   A. 4:3
   B. 16:9
   C. 1.0
   D. 0.9
   E. 1.2

19. The frame aspect ratio of a high-definition video is _____.

   A. 4:3
   B. 16:9
   C. 1.0
   D. 0.9
   E. 1.2

20. If a frame with a pixel aspect ratio of 1.2 is displayed on a device using a pixel aspect ratio of 1.0, the image will be _____.

   A. stretched horizontally
   B. stretched vertically
   C. cropped at the left and right edges
   D. cropped at the top and bottom
   E. displayed correctly

21. **True/False:** The timecode representing the 35th frame is either 00:00:00:35 or 00;00;00;35.

22. **True/False:** The drop-frame timecode drops or discards frames to preserve the time accuracy of a video.

23. Which of the following is the drop-frame timecode format?

    A. 00:00:00:00
    B. 00;00;00;00
    C. 00,00,00,00
    D. 00.00.00.00

24. Which timecode format is preferable for the NTSC system?

    A. Drop frame
    B. Non-drop frame

25. Chroma subsampling reduces the storage of pixel information by assigning fewer bits to store the _____ components.

    A. RGB
    B. luminance
    C. chrominance

26. The format of chroma subsampling is designated with three numbers separated by colons (for example, 4:2:2) to represent _____.

    A. the ratio of red:green:blue
    B. the ratio of the luminance to the two chrominance components
    C. the ratio of the number of three different types of pixels
    D. hours:minutes:seconds
    E. the ratio of the number of three different types of frames in a GOP

27. **True/False:** The signals of digital television are broadcast or transmitted digitally.

28. **True/False:** The frame aspect ratio of all six HDTV formats is 16:9.

29. HDTV is in _____ format.

    A. MPEG-1
    B. MPEG-2
    C. MPEG-3
    D. MPEG-4
    E. QuickTime
    F. AVI

30. The frame size for NTSC standard-definition DV is _____ pixels, and _____ pixels for the PAL system.

    A. 720 × 480; 720 × 480
    B. 720 × 576; 720 × 576
    C. 720 × 480; 720 × 576
    D. 720 × 576; 720 × 480

31. The numbers 720 and 1080 in the high-definition video picture format notations such as 720/30p and 1080/60i designate the _____.

    A. data rate of the video
    B. width (in pixels) of the frame size
    C. height (in pixels) of the frame size
    D. ppi of the video
    E. none of the above; they are model numbers of different companies

32. The letters "p" and "i" in the high-definition video picture format notations such as 720/30p and 1080/60i stand for _____ and _____, respectively.

    A. pixels; inches
    B. professional; intermediate
    C. progressive; interlaced
    D. pixels per inch; inches per pixel

33. **True/False:** A very long video, even with low data rate, can have a large file size.

34. Suppose you are on broadband connection with a speed of 6 Mbps. For a 1-minute video file with a file size of 20 MB, its playback through pseudostreaming on the Web very likely will be _____.

    A. smooth
    B. choppy

35. Suppose you are on broadband connection with a speed of 6 Mbps. For a 5-second video file with a file size of 20 MB, its playback through pseudostreaming on the Web very likely will be _____.

    A. smooth
    B. choppy

36. Suppose your target audience uses a broadband connection with a speed of 6 Mbps. What is the maximum file size for your 30-second video to have a smooth playback using pseudostreaming on the Web? Show your calculations.

37. Which of the following provides a measure for predicting the smoothness of video playback? If the value of that property is too high for the playback device to handle, the playback of the video will be choppy.

    A. file size
    B. frame size
    C. frame rate
    D. frame aspect ratio
    E. pixel aspect ratio
    F. data rate

38. Name several strategies to reduce the file size of a video.

**39.** What does the term *codec* stand for?

**40.** _____ compression refers to the type of compression method that aims at compacting individual frames.

A. Asymmetric
B. Lossless
C. Lossy
D. Spatial
E. Temporal

**41.** _____ compression refers to the type of compression method that exploits the similarity of the subsequent frame content.

A. Asymmetric
B. Lossless
C. Lossy
D. Spatial
E. Temporal

**42.** _____ compression refers to the type of compression method that preserves the original data.

A. Asymmetric
B. Lossless
C. Lossy
D. Spatial
E. Temporal

**43.** _____ compression refers to the type of compression method that discards or alters some of the original data.

A. Asymmetric
B. Lossless
C. Lossy
D. Spatial
E. Temporal

**44.** _____ compression refers to the type of compression method in which the amount of time and the complexity required to compress and decompress are significantly different.

A. Asymmetric
B. Lossless
C. Lossy
D. Spatial
E. Temporal

**45.** Which of the following compression methods achieves higher compression for videos without much motion difference, such as for talking heads?

A. Spatial compression
B. Temporal compression
C. Lossless compression
D. Asymmetric compression

46. Which of the following types of video can be compressed the most with temporal compression?

   A. Fast action
   B. Slow, continuous motion

47. Which of the following compression methods works best with large areas of solid color, such as in a cartoon animation?

   A. QuickTime Animation
   B. MPEG-1
   C. MPEG-2

48. **True/False:** The MP3 audio is an MPEG-3.

49. Which of the following support the DVD-video, high-definition video, and HDTV standards?

   A. MPEG-1
   B. MPEG-2
   C. MPEG-3
   D. MPEG-4

50. Which of the following also targets mobile applications, such as cell phones?

   A. MPEG-1
   B. MPEG-2
   C. MPEG-3
   D. MPEG-4

51. **True/False:** A typical MPEG-2 consists of a repeating GOP structure.

52. Motion compensation is a key technique in _____ compression.

   A. asymmetric
   B. lossless
   C. lossy
   D. spatial
   E. temporal

53. The _____ is encoded using only the information within that frame.

   A. B-frame
   B. I-frame
   C. P-frame

54. The _____ is encoded using only the previous I- or P-frame as the reference frame.

   A. B-frame
   B. I-frame
   C. P-frame

55. The _____ is encoded using the previous and subsequent I- and/or P-frames as the reference frames.

   A. B-frame
   B. I-frame
   C. P-frame

**56.** The _____ is the least compressed.

    A. B-frame
    B. I-frame
    C. P-frame
    D. none of the above; all are compressed at the same level

**57.** The $M$ parameter of the GOP refers to _____.

    A. the number of B-frames in a GOP
    B. the number of I-frames in a GOP
    C. the number of P-frames in a GOP
    D. the total number of frames in a GOP
    E. one plus the number of frames between the non-B-frames

**58.** The $N$ parameter of the GOP refers to _____.

    A. the number of B-frames in a GOP
    B. the number of I-frames in a GOP
    C. the number of P-frames in a GOP
    D. the total number of frames in a GOP
    E. one plus the number of frames between the non-B-frames

**59.** **True/False:** There is only one I-frame in a GOP structure.

**60.** **True/False:** There is only one I-frame in an MPEG video.

**61.** Explain why, in general, the longer GOP structure allows more file size compression. (*Hint*: Consider the number of I-frames in a GOP structure and the different levels of compression for different frame types.)

**62.** **True/False:** Progressive download requires a streaming server.

**63.** **True/False:** True streaming requires a streaming server.

**64.** **True/False:** Progressive download and pseudostreaming allow the video to start playing as soon as enough of the video data has arrived.

**65.** **True/False:** For streaming video, the file usually remains on the user's device after playback, for example, in the Web browser's cache.

**66.** **True/False:** In progressive download, the file usually remains on the user's device after playback, for example, in the Web browser's cache.

**67.** "After the entire video has been played once in a Web browser, it can be replayed without having to wait for download again."
Which of the following modes of video playback match(es) this description?

    A. True streaming
    B. Progressive download or pseudo-streaming
    C. None of the above

# Digital Video: Post-Production

## TABLE OF CONTENTS

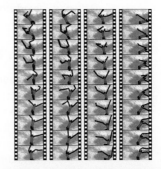

## KEY CONCEPTS

- Asset list, preview, timeline, effects and transitions panels in digital video editing programs
- Nonlinear editing, keying, superimpose
- Menus, submenus, motion menus, multi-angle in DVD authoring

## GENERAL LEARNING OBJECTIVES

In this chapter, you will learn

- The steps for acquiring digital video.
- The common workspace and workflow in digital video editing programs.
- The common workspace and workflow in DVD authoring programs.
- The basic and common digital video editing tools and techniques.
- The export options for sharing digital video.

# 7.1 ACQUIRING DIGITAL VIDEOS

In digital imaging, there are two ways to acquire digital images—by taking digital photos with a digital camera or by scanning an analog print. The latter method is digitizing analog pictures. Similarly, digital video can be acquired by shooting digital video footage using a digital video camera or by digitizing a video shot in analog media. All the new video footage is now shot in digital format. However, there still may be a need for digitizing older analog footage when you need to incorporate the older or historical footage into your digital video project.

Digital video programs share common basic workflow techniques for video capturing and editing. This chapter intends to give you an overview of the basic steps of capturing digital video. Adobe Premiere Pro will be used for examples, but the basic ideas of the workflow can be generalized to other digital video editing programs.

## 7.1.1 Analog Sources

Videotapes, such as VHS and Hi-8, and motion-picture films are analog media. Digitizing converts them into a form that a computer can store and process. For hardware requirements in the digitizing process, you need an appropriate video capture card on your computer to digitize the analog video. You will also need an analog video device, such as an analog video camera or tape deck, to output the analog video signal to the capture card. In addition to hardware, digitizing videos requires video capture programs. Many capture cards are bundled with such programs. Most of these programs also have video editing capability.

## 7.1.2  Digital Video

Videos shot with a digital video camera are already captured in a digital format. They can be captured onto a hard drive if shot on tapes. Many camcorders can record digital video directly to a hard drive, memory card, or DVD disc. Table 7.1 lists the transfer methods for different types of camera storage media.

| TABLE 7.I | Methods of Transferring Digital Video from Video Cameras to Computers | |
|---|---|
| **Storage Media** | **Method of Transferring Digital Video to Computer** |
| Hard disk | Connect the hard disk to a computer. |
| Flash memory | Take the memory card out of the camera and insert into the card slot on a computer. |
| Internal memory | This type of camera often supports USB, which allows you to plug the camera into a computer. |
| MiniDV tape | The video needs to be captured onto a computer through the FireWire port. |
| Optical disc | Take the disc to a computer with an optical disc drive. |

## FIREWIRE

*IEEE 1394* is a standard for high-speed data transfer between computers and peripheral devices. *FireWire* is Apple's trademarked name for its implementation of this standard. It is also known as *i.Link* (Sony's name).

FireWire lets you easily connect different pieces of equipment and transfer data quickly between them. It also features simple cabling and hot-pluggable ability, which means that you can connect the device to the computer without having to turn off the computer first.

At the time of writing, there are three common types of FireWire connectors in dealing with digital video: 4-pin, 6-pin, and 9-pin connectors (Figures 7.1 and 7.2).

- 4-pin connector (FireWire 400): May be found on digital video cameras (Figures 7.2a), laptop computers, and desktop computers
- 6-pin connector (FireWire 400): Found on most FireWire cards for desktop computers (Figure 7.2b)
- 9-pin connector (FireWire 800): Found on Apple MacBook Pro (Figure 7.2c)

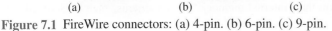

Figure 7.1  FireWire connectors: (a) 4-pin. (b) 6-pin. (c) 9-pin.

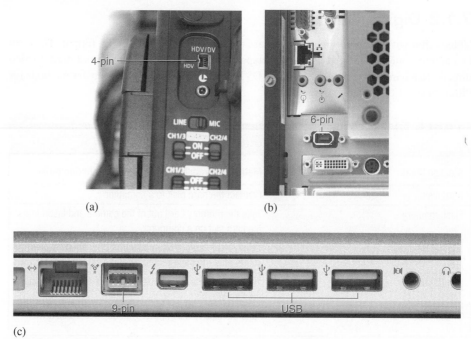

(a)  (b)

(c)

**Figure 7.2** FireWire connectors on devices: (a) A 4-pin FireWire HDV IN/OUT port on a HDV camera. (b) A 6-pin FireWire port on a desktop computer. (c) 9-pin FireWire ports and USB ports on an Apple MacBook Pro.

## 7.2 DIGITAL VIDEO CAMERAS

This section discusses several factors you may want to consider when choosing a video camera for your digital video projects.

### 7.2.1 Video File Format and Storage Media

Table 6.4 lists the common high-definition video formats. Different video formats support certain picture formats and use different video and audio compression methods. The picture format—1080 versus 720—influences the frame size. The compression method as well as the color sampling method affect the video quality and file size. Given the same storage space, the file size dictates the duration of the footage that can be recorded. The video file format in which the digital video camera records often is related to the camera's recording medium. The recording medium can be looked up in the camcorder's specifications. Currently, the five types of camcorder media are hard disk, Flash memory, internal memory, tapes, and optical discs (which include DVD, miniDVD, and Blu-ray). Most tape-type digital cameras record video to *miniDV* tapes (Figure 7.3). The video shot on a tape will need to go through the capturing process through FireWire ports to be transferred to a computer for editing. Videos shot on a hard disk and memory cards can be transferred directly to a computer similar to transferring any files from an external storage. Some cameras store the video on their internal memory. These cameras, such as Sony Bloggie (Figure 7.4), usually support transfer of the video through USB.

Figure 7.3  A miniDV tape.

Figure 7.4  A Sony Bloggie with a flip-out USB.

## DISTINGUISHING BETWEEN DV AND DVD

In some publications, the term *DV* may be used as a general abbreviation for *digital video*. However, it is noteworthy that there is a specific video format called *DV format*. DV is not an abbreviation for general digital video in this context. Videos in DV format conform to certain specifications, such as frame size, color subsampling method, and data rate. For example, MiniDV camcorders record video in DV format. To avoid confusion, this book does not abbreviate digital video as DV and only uses the term DV format to refer to the video format.

*DVD* stands for *digital versatile disc*. DVD does not necessarily mean videos; there is DVD-audio too. Generally, DVD-type camcorders record videos in MPEG-2 format on DVD-R or DVD-RW discs.

## 7.2.2 Resolution

The frame size is dictated by the picture formats that the video camera supports. Table 6.4 lists the common high-definition video formats and their supported frame sizes. The picture formats 1080i and 1080p *display* a frame of $1{,}920 \times 1{,}080$ pixels, although the frame size of some of the video formats is only 1,440 × 1,080 pixels, in which case the pixel aspect ratio is 1.333, as shown in Section 6.3.3. The picture formats 720i and 720p *display* a frame of 1,280 × 720 pixels, although the frame size of some of the video formats is only 960 × 720, in which case the pixel aspect ratio is also 1.333. In addition to video cameras, some digital SLR cameras can take high-definition video at 1080p (in full 1,920 × 1,080 pixels) and 720p (in full 1,280 × 720 pixels) in addition to still pictures.

### 7.2.3 Stereoscopic 3-D

The stereoscopic 3-D camera has two lenses (Figure 7.5), each of which shoots a video, simulating human binocular vision. When these two videos play back such that your right eye sees the video shot by the right lens and your left eye sees the video shot by the left lens, you see the 3-D effect. Most stereoscopic cameras have an LCD screen on which you can watch your 3-D movies without 3-D glasses. You can also watch your 3-D movies on a 3-D TV or a non-3-D TV, on which the 2-D version of the movies will be played. YouTube also supports playing back 3-D videos in an anaglyph format, such as red/cyan. Stereoscopic 3-D editing mode is also available in some video editing programs, such as Sony Vegas 10 (Figure 7.6).

Figure 7.5  A stereoscopic 3-D camera has two side-by-side lenses.

## GENERAL PRACTICES IN CREATING STEREOSCOPIC 3-D VIDEO

For best results of stereoscopic 3-D effects, some practices (such as composition, camera movement, and video transitions) for producing stereoscopic 3-D videos may be different from those for the traditional 2-D videos. Here are some general tips:

- Composition: For the main object that is supposed to appear in front of the screen, try to include the whole object in the frame if possible. If an object is cropped off, its 3-D effect breaks at the edge of the frame where it is cropped causing contradictions of the object's 3-D effect.
- Shooting: Avoid fast movement of the main object, fast camera movement, zooming, and camera rotation. For panning, cut the speed of panning in at least half of the speed you would pan in 2-D.
- Video transition: Avoid using video transitions besides straight-cut. A transition that crosses two video clips mixes the 3-D effect from two different clips. This would cause the viewer's eyes to strain.

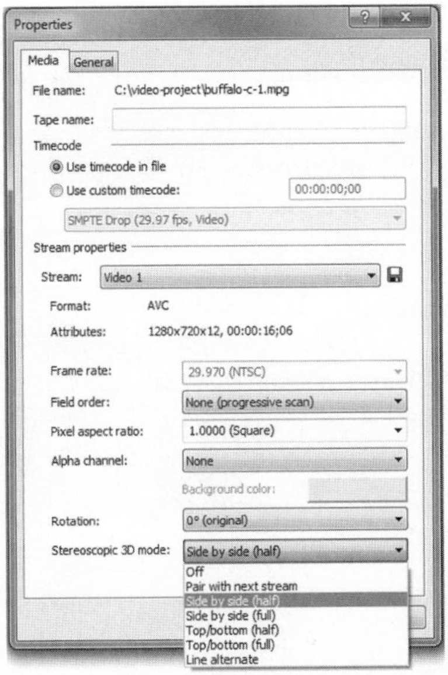

**Figure 7.6**  Sony Vegas 10 supports several stereoscopic 3-D modes.

# 7.3 BASIC WORKSPACE ELEMENTS IN DIGITAL VIDEO EDITING PROGRAMS

Examples of professional digital video editing programs are Adobe Premiere Pro, Apple Final Cut Pro, Sony Vegas, and Avid. There are some basic workspace elements that many of these programs share, which usually are divided into four main areas:

1. *Asset list* manages the imported source materials for the video project. They include the captured or digitized video footage, audio, still images, titles, and vector graphics. The source materials imported are not embedded in the video project file itself; instead, the source files are linked. This means that if you move the source files to another folder or delete the source files later, you will be prompted to locate these linked source files the next time you open the video project.
2. *Preview window* lets you preview your entire video project. Adobe Premiere also has a Dual View Monitor window that you can use to view, edit, and trim the individual source clip.
3. The *Timeline panel* is where you can arrange your source clips in sequence. It usually has video tracks and audio tracks.
4. *Effects* and *transitions* can be found in a separate panel or menu item. Effects include video and audio effects. Many of the video effects work very similarly to the image filters that you may find in image editing programs. Examples of video effects include altering the color balance, desaturating, resizing, clipping, blurring, sharpening, distorting, and stylizing the video clip. Transitions are to make one clip gradually change to the next. The most commonly used video transition is cross dissolve. Other transition types include 3-D motion, page peel, slide, wipe, zoom, and stretch.

Figures 7.7 through 7.9 show screenshots of the workspaces of Adobe Premiere Pro, Apple Final Cut Pro, and Sony Vegas 10, respectively.

At the time of writing, YouTube.com has an online video editor that offers the basic video editing functionalities, such as trim, rotate, and color adjust.

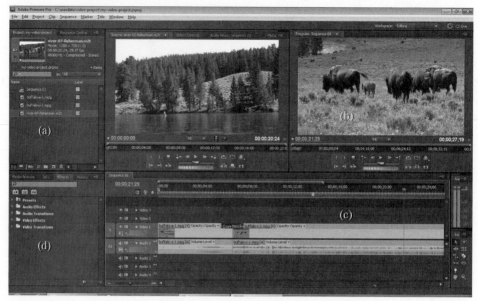

**Figure 7.7** An Adobe Premiere Pro CS5.5 workspace: (a) Asset list. (b) Preview windows. (c) Timeline. (d) Effects and transitions.

**Figure 7.8** An Apple Final Cut Pro X workspace: (a) Asset list. (b) Preview windows. (c) Timeline. (d) Transitions.

**Figure 7.9** A Sony Vegas 10 workspace: (a) Asset list. (b) Preview window. (c) Timeline. (d) Effects and transitions can be accessed in a different tab.

## 7.4 BASIC STEPS OF DIGITAL VIDEO EDITING

After you have collected the raw materials, you will need to import them into a project in a digital video program. Then, you edit the footage, trim away the parts that you don't need, and apply audio, transitions, visual effects, and audio effects.

The basic steps of creating a final digital video are:

**Step 1** **Import the source materials in the video project as assets.**

In most video editing programs, you can import source files (such as video footage, still images, titles, and audio) by selecing `File > Import . . .` These imported files are usually linked—they are not embedded in the project. Therefore, you will need to keep the files stored on the hard drive or an external storage device if you are going to work on the video project later.

**Step 2** **Trim the source clips and arrange the assets on the timeline.**

When you shoot video footage, you should always shoot more than you will actually use in the video project; it is natural that this will happen anyway. If you capture the video from tapes, you capture at least a few seconds before and after the actual segment you want to use. When you use the footage for your video project, you will need to edit out the unnecessary parts.

There are several ways to trim video footage. For example, many video editing programs let you set **In and Out points** for a source clip. The In and Out points define the beginning and end of the segment you want to use. The segments before the In point and after the Out point will not be used on the timeline. Setting In and Out points is not a destructive method for trimming clips—the segments outside of the In/Out range are not really deleted from the original source clip. You can always include them later, if needed, by adjusting the edit points.

Another way to trim a clip is by splitting. Using Premiere, you can split a clip with a Razor tool into multiple segments that then can be arranged on the timeline independently. This tool is nondestructive because it is not physically splitting the source clip *file* into multiple files. The original file is still intact. Only the *copy*—like an alias—of that clip on the timeline is split. If you drag the source clip file

✏ **Trimming a Clip by Setting In and Out Points, and Applying a Video Transition to Video Clips** Screen-capture movies demonstrate the basic steps of setting In and Out points for video clips, and applying a video transition, in two digital video editing application programs: Adobe Premiere Pro and Apple Final Cut Pro.

Nonlinear editing (NLE): With NLE, the video can be assembled in any order, and changes can be made anywhere in the sequence at any time. In linear editing, a video must be assembled from the beginning, and the shots are laid down in the story order. An analogy for NLE versus linear editing in video is the word processor versus the typewriter in publishing.

from the asset list onto the timeline again, the clip will still have the original length.

When you alter the length of a clip that has adjacent clips on the timeline, it will cause one of the following changes in terms of the duration of the entire video sequence:

- The duration of the entire video sequence is changed to accommodate the length change of a clip.
- The duration of the entire video is maintained by altering the length or the In/Out points of the adjacent clips.

There are several useful editing tools available in video editing programs to deal with such situations in *nonlinear editing: ripple edit, rolling edit, slip edit,* and *slide edit.* With these tools, you can edit the length of a clip or its In/Out points on the timeline without having to manually adjust the location of the adjacent clips on the timeline.

For example, suppose you have three video clips sequenced on the timeline, like the one illustrated in Figure 7.10a. For illustrative purposes, symbols (#, $, %, ^, &), letters (C - J), and numbers (1 - 9) in the frames are used to represent the content of the frames in these clips. Now suppose you want to lengthen the middle clip (the blue clip in Figure 7.10a) by two frames, you can use ripple edit to lengthen the middle clip. The subsequent clip (shown in black) will be pushed to the right. Without using the ripple edit tool, you would have to move the black clip to the right to leave room for the blue clip to extend its length. Then, after you extended the duration of the blue clip, you would have to move the black clip back to the end of the blue clip.

Rolling edit maintains the duration of the entire video sequence. For example, Figure 7.10c shows the resulting sequence in which the middle clip (blue color) in Figure 7.10a is lengthened at the end by two frames using rolling edit. The adjacent

(a)

(b)

(c)

(d)

(e)

**Figure 7.10** Illustration of the effect of four nonlinear video editing tools. (a) A video sequence consisting of three video clips (indicated by different colors) placed side by side on a timeline. (b) After ripple edit. (c) After rolling edit. (d) After slip edit. (e) After slide edit.

clip (black) is shortened by two frames at the beginning to maintain the duration of the entire video sequence. Using slip edit (Figure 7.10d), the middle clip's In and Out points are altered. There is no duration change on any of the clips. The duration of the entire video sequence remains the same. It looks similar to the sequence (Figure 7.10a) before the slip edit but note the frame content of the blue clip after the edit is 1, 2, 3, and 4 whereas it was 4, 5, 6, and 7 before the edit. The slip edit shifts the content of the blue clip to the left by three frames. With slide edit, the middle clip can slide to the left or right cutting into the timing of one of its adjacent clips while extending the timing of the other adjacent clip. The duration and content of the middle clip remain the same. The duration of the entire video sequence also remains the same. Figure 7.10e shows the result of a slide edit on the middle blue clip. The Out point of the previous clip (gray) and the In point of the subsequence clip (black) are both moved by two frames earlier.

For simple video sequences, these editing tools may never be used. However, they are indispensable timesavers when editing complex sequences of clips.

**Step 3**  **Apply transitions, video effects, and audio effects, if needed.**

Two of the most commonly used transitions are straight cut and dissolve. *Straight-cut* transitions can be achieved by arranging the two clips next to each other—there is not really a "transition effect" applied to these clips. There are several types of dissolve. In general, the *cross dissolve* transition gives the smoothest fade between two clips.

Many video editing programs come with a variety of video effects. The most common effects include transformation (e.g., resizing and cropping) and image adjustment (e.g., tonal and color adjustment).

Video clips can be *superimposed* on top of each other by placing them on different video tracks, similar to layering images in digital image editing programs. Adjusting the opacity of the top clip allows the clip underneath to show through. For example, Figure 7.11a shows a frame from a video that is placed on track 2, and Figure 7.11b shows a frame from track 1. Figure 7.11c shows the result when the video on track 2 is applied with 60% opacity. Figure 7.11d shows a split-screen effect by repositioning the video track 2 to the left. By resizing the video on track 2 in addition to repositioning, it can create a picture-in-picture effect (Figure 7.11e).

Opacity adjustment for a video on a track applies to the entire frame. However, *keying* allows you to designate transparent areas by color. Many digital video editing programs come with common keys, such as Blue Screen and Green Screen. The *Blue Screen and Green Screen Keys* can be used to key out blue and green screens, respectively, when creating composites. The *Color Key* lets you select a color to be keyed out. For example, with the same video examples shown in Figure 7.11a and Figure 7.11b,

⌁ **Nonlinear Editing Techniques in Digital Video** An interactive tutorial demonstrates the characteristics of ripple edit, rolling edit, slip edit, and slide edit.

Video effects and transitions should be used judiciously, and selected as carefully as your source materials. Transitions add temporal changes or "motion" that is not part of the source footage. Video effects integrate extra visual elements into the video. Indiscriminate use of video effects and transitions can lower the artistic value and dilute the story or statement of the final video.

⊘ **Straight-cut versus Cross Dissolve Transitions** A short video clip shows examples of two different transitions: straight cut and cross dissolve.

⊘ **Applying a Video Effect to Video Clips and Animating the Effect by Keyframing** Screen-capture movies demonstrate the basic steps of applying a Gaussian blur video effect to a clip and keyframing the effect in two digital video editing application programs: Adobe Premiere Pro and Apple Final Cut Pro.

⊘ **Color-Keying Video Clips** Screen-capture movies demonstrate the basic steps of color-keying a video clip using two digital video editing application programs: Adobe Premiere Pro and Apple Final Cut Pro.

(a)

(b)

(c)

(d)

(e)

**Figure 7.11** Examples of superimposing two video tracks. (a) A frame from the video placed on track 2. (b) A frame from the video placed on track 1. (c) Resulting frame when the video on track 2 is applied with 60% opacity. (d) Resulting frame when the video on track 2 is repositioned to the left to create a split-screen effect. (e) Resulting frame when the video on track 2 is repositioned and resized to create a picture-in-picture effect.

**Figure 7.12** Example of Color Key effect.

Figure 7.12 shows the result of applying Color Key to the video on track 2. The color is keyed black, matching the limbs of the dancing windsock figure. The transparent areas now follow the movement of the limbs as long as the limbs are within the keyed color range.

Although audio effects can be added to an audio separately in audio editing programs, video editing programs may come with audio effects that let you apply audio effects without having to switch to a separate audio program. The common audio editing functionalities include trimming the audio, volume adjustments, audio fade-in/out, and panning. More advanced audio effects may include reverb, envelop, and even an audio mixer that lets you create an audio mix with multiple audio tracks.

## 7.5 EXPORTING AND SHARING YOUR FINAL VIDEO

After you have finished assembling your video project, you can export the final video to a different file format. The choice of file format depends on how you want to distribute your final video to your audience. The Web and the optical discs are the common choices of delivery media.

### 7.5.1 The Web

At the time of writing, YouTube is one of the most popular video-sharing Web sites. It supports Adobe Flash Video and HTML5 video. Registered users can upload videos of a variety of video formats to the site. The uploaded video is then encoded into Flash Video (FLV) and HTML5 video formats.

If you are embedding video on your own Web page, the choices of video format include HTML5 video, Flash Video (F4V and FLV), MP4, QuickTime movies, Windows Media, and RealVideo. Many digital video programs let you export your video to QuickTime, Flash Video, and Windows Media formats. In Adobe Premiere Pro CS5.5, you can export your video by choosing `File > Export > Media . . .`, where you can choose from various formats, such as QuickTime, Adobe Flash Video (F4V and FLV), MP4, and Windows Media. For RealVideo, you can use the free software Real Producer Basic from Real Systems to convert your video.

Chapter 15 provides an introduction to HTML5 video and shows example code for adding HTML5 video and FLV on a Web page.

## QUICKTIME PROGRESSIVE DOWNLOAD

QuickTime supports progressive download of movies, known as Fast-Start movies. The Fast-Start QuickTime movie starts playing before the entire file has been downloaded on the viewer's local storage. The experience seems like streaming, but Fast-Start is not video streaming.

One simple way to create a Fast-Start QuickTime is to save the QuickTime movie as a self-contained movie. To do so, you will need the Pro version of the QuickTime player, not the free version. First, open the QuickTime movie with QuickTime Pro. Then, select File > Save As. . . . In the File Save dialog box, select the option "Make movie self-contained" (Figure 7.13). If the option is not active, you may need to give a different file name or save the movie in a different folder. You can replace the original QuickTime with the Fast-Start movie.

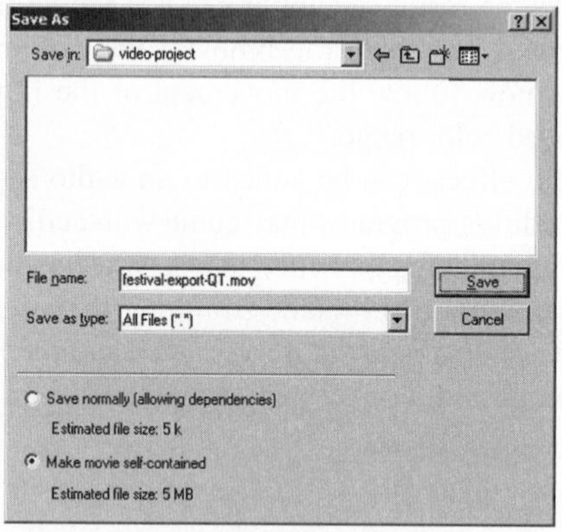

**Figure 7.13** QuickTime Pro File Save dialog box.

> ✐ **Export Video to QuickTime Movie**
> Screen-capture movies demonstrate the basic steps of exporting videos to QuickTime movies in two digital video editing application programs: Adobe Premiere Pro and Apple Final Cut Pro.

## 7.5.2 Optical Disc: Blu-ray and DVD

Blu-ray videos and DVD-videos can be played back on set-top players or on computers that have a optical disc drive and software player.

Generally, there are two ways to create a Blu-ray or DVD-video disc.

Method 1    Export your final video as a Blu-ray- or DVD-compliant file and then author a Blu-ray or DVD project using a DVD authoring program.

In Adobe Premiere Pro CS5.5, you can export your video to a Blu-ray-compliant H.264 and MPEG-2 and DVD-compliant MPEG-2 file by choosing File > Export > Media. . . (Figure 7.14).

Recall that, as discussed in Chapter 6, an MPEG consists of a repeating GOP (group of pictures) structure. The $N$ parameter specifies the length of a GOP, and the $M$ parameter specifies the number of the B-frames between the non-B-frames plus one. Now, you see these $N$ and $M$ parameters in the MPEG-2 export settings (Figure 7.15).

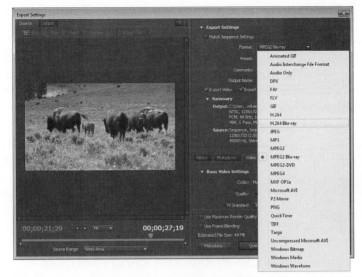

**Figure 7.14** Exporting Blu-ray-compliant H.264 and MPEG-2 file in Adobe Premiere Pro.

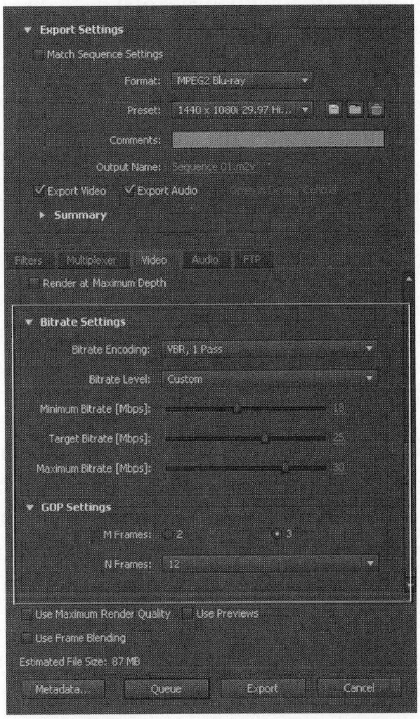

**Figure 7.15** Exporting Blu-ray MPEG-2 using a preset in Adobe Premiere Pro CS5.5.

There is also a Bitrate Settings section (Figure 7.15). The bitrate, or bit rate, is the data rate. Recall that, as discussed in Chapter 6, data rate affects the video file size and quality. A video with higher picture quality often requires a higher data rate. A higher data rate increases file size. The preset shown in Figure 7.15

sets the target bitrate to 25 Mbps (megabits per seconds), or approximately 3.1 MB/s. This means that for a single-layer Blu-ray disc (25 GB), it can fit about 2 hours of the video.

You can import the file into a DVD authoring program, such as Adobe Encore and Sony DVD Architect Pro. You can add menus and multiple videos on a video disc. The general steps to authoring a Blu-ray and DVD-video disc will be discussed in the next section.

**Method 2**  Export your final video directly to disc.

Some digital video editing programs let you export your final video directly to disc. This way, you do not need to export your video to MPEG-2 or H.264 as an intermediate step. The result is a simple single-movie disc without any menu navigation. The video will start playing when the disc is inserted into the disc player.

> 🎞 **Export Video to Blu-ray MPEG-2**
> Screen-capture movies demonstrate the basic steps of exporting videos to Blu-ray MPEG-2 in Adobe Premiere Pro.

### 7.5.3  Optical Disc: CD-R/RW and DVD+/-R/RW

For videos intended for CD-R/RW or DVD+/-R/RW playback, the common options for the file format include QuickTime and MP4. The data rate of your video should be no higher than the data rate of your target audience's playback device. Otherwise, your video may skip frames and become choppy. Modern drives can handle most video, and thus the drive speed becomes less of a concern unless your target audience will be using older computers. For example, the data rate of a 48x-speed CD-ROM drive is about 59 mbits/sec. Both examples shown in Figure 6.10—with data rate of 31.77 and 0.946 mbits/sec—are expected to play smoothly on this drive. The data rate of a 20x-speed CD-ROM drive is about 24 mbits/sec. The playback of the video with the data rate of 31.77 mbits/sec will be choppy on this drive.

Recall that the average data rate is equal to the file size divided by the duration of the video. Thus, if the duration of a video is kept the same, reducing file size can reduce the data rate. In addition, you can reduce the video file size by reducing its frame size and frame rate, and by lowering picture quality in the compressor settings. Here are some suggested steps to determine export settings for your video:

**Step 1**  **Start with the desired frame size, frame rate, and compressor.**
Of course, the frame size and frame rate should not exceed those of the original video. If you do not know which compressor you want to use, start with H.264 or Sorenson Video 3. They are commonly used codecs and give satisfactory compression without much visible degradation in image quality.

**Step 2**  **Export your video.**
After you have exported your video (or a short test segment of your video if your video is very long and thus taking a long time to compress), look up its file size and calculate the data rate.

If the data rate is higher than your target audience's device can handle, then try reducing the frame size, lowering the frame rate, or lowering the picture quality. The nature of your video dictates which strategy you should try first. For example, for a fast-action video, reducing frame rate may be the last option. If your video contains many fine details that you do not want to lose, then reducing frame size is not the best option.

Step 3 **Always test your final production on computer equipment that is as close to the target audience's as possible.**

These suggested steps also can be applied to creating videos intended for the Web. The data limit will be determined by the network connection speed of your target audience instead of the speed of their computer equipment.

## 7.5.4 Tapes and Other Media

When you export your video to tapes, you can record the final video directly onto miniDV tapes. Exporting the final sequence onto miniDV tapes was usually for backup or archival purposes because tapes were less expensive than disk drives. However, tapes are seldom used for storage nowadays because the cost of disk drives is much lower now and many video cameras do not use tapes. You can also export a selected frame of your final video into a still image, or export your final video (in entirety or a segment) into a sequence of still images. You can also extract the audio track of your video by exporting the audio track into an audio file.

# 7.6 CREATING A DVD-VIDEO DISC

This section discusses menu structures and the general steps to create a DVD-video disc. The information presented in this section also applies to creating a Blu-ray video disc.

## 7.6.1 Menu Structures and Navigation Hierarchy

A DVD-video can be as simple as a single-movie DVD that will automatically start playing after the disc is inserted in the player. It also can have a menu system.

### Menus

A *menu* is made up of a background and *buttons*. A background can be a still image or a video. A button can be just text, a still image, or a video clip (with or without text overlaid on it). A menu that contains a video clip as either a background or button is called a *motion menu*.

### Buttons

A button can be linked to a video or another menu. That is, when the button is clicked, whatever is linked to it—a video or a menu—will be displayed. As a user-friendly design, each button should be set up to have some kind of highlight when it is selected. This is especially critical if the intended viewing environment is set-top players. Without such visual feedback, set-top viewers will not know which button is the currently selected choice when they are scrolling among the buttons on screen using their remote control.

### Submenus

A menu structure contains a main menu that can then branch out to other *submenus*. Each submenu can have a button to let the viewer return to the main menu and/or move one level up. It also can have a button that leads to another submenu.

If the items for a menu do not fit on one screen, they can be divided into multiple "pages." Each of these pages is created as a menu, with buttons to let the viewer step through all of the pages.

A flowchart or storyboard type of approach may be used to lay out and visualize the menu hierarchy and the associated content materials of each menu. It also helps to make sure that no content or menu is left orphaned. An orphaned file or menu is one that is included on the disc but not linked or accessible from any other menus. Content that is not linked or used in any menu does not need to be included on the disc. However, having orphaned content may mean that something originally planned is missing from the navigation design. The navigation design needs to be reexamined to make sure all of the necessary contents are properly incorporated and linked.

Although DVD remote controls have options for the viewer to return to the title menu or root menu directly, it is a good practice to include buttons on a submenu to let the viewer return to the main menu and navigate from one menu to the other directly without having to return to the main menu.

The navigation hierarchy and menu structure should be ready before you start authoring a DVD. It would be best to also have all the contents (such as the graphics for the background and buttons) for the menu ready. If the graphics are not finalized, then at least create placeholders with matching pixel dimensions.

Whether your DVD has a menu or not, you can add chapter points in a video. **Chapter points** are like built-in bookmarks of the video. They allow the viewer to quickly jump to a particular location in the video at any time without having to rewind or fast forward.

## 7.6.2 Authoring a DVD Project

There are many off-the-shelf DVD authoring programs available. Some examples include Adobe Encore CS5.1 (Figure 7.16), Sony DVD Architect Pro 5 (Figure 7.17), Corel DVD MovieFactory Pro, and Apple iDVD. Different programs have different workspaces and different workflows to follow. However, there are some basic elements in the workspace and in the workflow that many of these programs share. This section intends to give you a general idea of how to work with these DVD authoring programs.

**Figure 7.16** An Adobe Encore CS5.1 workspace with four basic panels: (a) Project window. (b) Monitor. (c) Timeline. (d) Library.

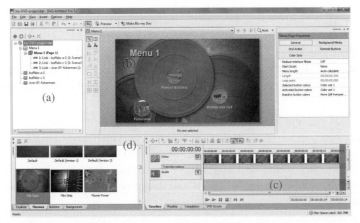

**Figure 7.17** A Sony DVD Architect Pro 5.2 workspace. (a) The Project Overview Window shows a hierarchical view of the menus and titles. (b) The Workspace Window displays the current menu or title. (c) Timeline. (d) Library.

The common elements you find in the workspace of these programs are:

(a) *Asset list* manages the imported source materials for your DVD project. The types of assets include videos, audio, menus, and still images.

(b) *Preview window* lets you preview your video and menus It simulates playback of your DVD.

(c) *Timeline* or *Track* lets you add audio tracks and chapter points. Some programs, such as Sony DVD Architect Pro 5, support *multiple angles* (Figure 7.18). You can add multiple video tracks on a timeline. The different videos could be shot at different angles of a scene. They can also contain independent content. During playback of a multi-angle DVD, the user can press the Angle button on the remote control to switch between video tracks.

(d) *Library* and *Templates* contain preset menus, buttons, and background images to use for building your DVD menus.

**Figure 7.18** A Sony DVD Architect Pro 5.2 workspace showing two video tracks on the timeline for creating multiple angles.

Described next are the general steps for authoring a DVD project with these programs.

**Step 1 Set project settings.**

When you start a DVD authoring project, you need to specify your target audience—for example, Blu-ray (high definition) or DVD (standard definition) and television standard (NTSC or PAL) (Figure 7.19a). For Blu-ray, you will also need to choose the frame size (Figure 7.19b).

**Step 2 Import content as assets.**

You then import the content materials, such as video, audio, images, menus, and buttons, to be included on the disc. Many DVD authoring programs have a pre-set library of menus and buttons to choose from, but also allow you to import custom-created images as buttons and background for the menu. Custom menus can be built by defining the background image (or video, if it is a motion menu) and adding buttons on the menu. Note that these imported media are all externally linked; they are not embedded within the DVD project. This means that you need to keep those media files available when you edit the DVD project.

**Step 3 Build navigation structure—link menus and videos.**

Before designing the navigation structure, let's consider what kind of built-in navigation is already available on a DVD player so that your menu design does not replicate these functionalities. The generic menu built into a DVD player lets the viewer pause or resume playback, move forward or backward frame by frame, return to the title menu or root menu, and switch between camera angles. Without any additional menu structure for a DVD, a simple DVD that contains only video and audio can still allow the viewer to access any point of a DVD title at any time using a remote control. However, a menu structure allows customized user interface and access to special features of your DVD project. For example, you can provide submenus for bonus videos and chapter selections with thumbnails.

Menu creation may be done in a menu editor window or on the "stage" area. Some programs have a separate menu editor window for menu creation, whereas others may have a stage area onto which you can directly drag and drop the background image and the buttons. Then, you need to link each button to a video,

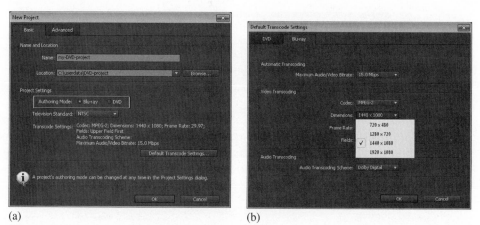

(a)                                                                 (b)

**Figure 7.19** Project settings of Adobe Encore CS5.1. (a) Choices of two authoring modes. (b) Choices of frame dimensions for Blu-ray authoring.

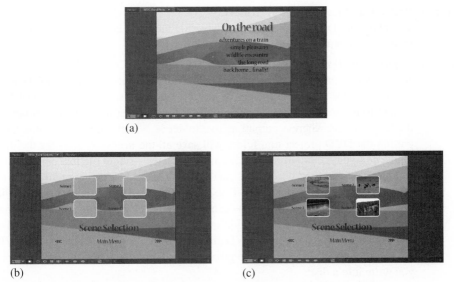

**Figure 7.20** A menu and submenu created in Adobe Encore CS5.1 using a menu template. (a) A main menu set as the first play. (b) A submenu template with four button placeholders. (c) The buttons on the submenu are linked to videos and showing the thumbnails of the linked videos.

audio, or another menu. Many programs allow you to simply drag a video from the Asset list onto the menu. This will automatically create a button that is linked to that video with a thumbnail image of the video. You may also add text on the menu as titles or descriptions for the buttons.

Most programs come with preset menu templates that include placeholders of buttons. For example, Figure 7.20a and Figure 7.20b show a menu and a submenu created from a template in Adobe Encore CS5.1. You can simply drag and drop a video from the asset list onto a placeholder button and the button will automatically link to that video. In addition, a thumbnail image of the video will be displayed on the button (Figure 7.20c). By default, the first frame of the video is used as the thumbnail image for the button. However, many programs allow you to designate a different frame as the thumbnail. If you have more than one menu in a DVD project, you will need to designate one as the first play. The menu designated as the first play will be the first to come up on screen when the DVD is played.

When you export your video into an MPEG-2 DVD-compliant file using your video editing program, you may have the *multiplex* option. If the multiplex option is off, it means your video and audio will be exported into two separate files: an MPEG-2 file for the video (a file with a file extension of .m2v, .mpg, or .mpeg) and an audio file (.wav file). If you turn on the multiplex option, then both video and audio will be combined in one file. If the video and audio are separated into two files, you will need to import both video and audio files into your DVD project. You then add the audio onto the audio track of the timeline.

Some programs support multiple audio tracks, which can be used for multiple languages. Some even support multiple video tracks for multiple-angle video production. Most programs also let you define chapters by adding chapter points on the timeline.

Step 4   **Preview and test play your project.**

Test play your DVD project thoroughly within the DVD authoring program using its Preview feature.

Step 5   **Export your DVD project and make a DVD disc.**

Many DVD authoring programs give you these options of outputting a DVD project: to a folder, as a disc image, or directly onto a disc. Outputting the DVD project to a disc requires a DVD-writer on the computer at the time you output the DVD project whereas outputting to a folder or as a disc image does not. Outputting the DVD project to a folder will save all the necessary files for the disc on the computer. Outputting to a disc image creates a single file that contains the complete contents and necessary structure for the disc. You can burn the folder or disc image onto a DVD disc later. Thus, outputting the DVD to a folder or as a dic image offers an advantage that you can author a DVD project on a computer that does not have a DVD-writer. In addition, you can write the DVD project to a disc later if you do not have a blank DVD disc on hand at the time you output the DVD project. Outputting to a folder also gives you a chance to test play the DVD before you write it to a disc.

## VIDEO_TS AND AUDIO_TS FOLDERS ON A DVD DISC

The information regarding VIDEO_TS and AUDIO_TS folders applies to DVD discs but not Blu-ray discs. A DVD disc may contain two folders: VIDEO_TS and AUDIO_TS. The AUDIO_TS folder is for the audio DVD. For the video DVD, all of the files should be in the VIDEO_TS folder. The AUDIO_TS is empty if it is included on the disc. To make a DVD-video disc, burn the VIDEO_TS folder onto a DVD disc. It is recommended to also include an empty AUDIO_TS folder because older set-top DVD players may not play a DVD disc without an AUDIO_TS folder. Some DVD authoring programs, such as Adobe Encore CS5.1, may not create an AUDIO_TS folder. You can simply create an empty AUDIO_TS folder and burn it to the disc with the VIDEO_TS folder.

The VIDEO_TS and the AUDIO_TS folders have to be written to the disc in its root (i.e., topmost) directory. Do not place them in a subfolder on the disc, or the player will not automatically start playing the video on the disc.

## 7.7 SUMMARY

Digital videos can be acquired by shooting digital video footage using a digital video camera or by digitizing the video from an analog source, such as VHS and Hi-8 tapes.

The video file format that the digital video camera records in is often related to the camera's recording medium. Currently, the most common types of camcorder media are hard drives, Flash memory, internal memory, tapes, and optical discs. Most tape-type digital camcorders (standard-definition DV and HDV formats) record video to miniDV tapes. The video shot on a tape will need to go through the capturing process through FireWire ports to be transferred to a computer for editing. Videos shot on a hard disk and memory cards can be transferred directly to a computer similar to transferring any files from an external storage. Some cameras store the video on their internal memory. These cameras usually support transfer of the video through USB.

Examples of digital video editing programs are Adobe Premiere Pro, Apple Final Cut Pro, Sony Vegas, and Avid. The basic workspace elements that many of these programs share are:

- Asset list
- Preview window
- Timeline
- Effects and transitions

The basic steps of creating a final digital video are:

1. Import the source materials in the video project as assets.
2. Trim the source clips and arrange the assets on the timeline.
3. Apply transitions, video effects, and audio effects, if needed.
4. Export and share your final video.

After you have finished assembling your video project, you can export the final video to a different file format. The choice of file formats depends on how you want to distribute your final video to your audience. The Web and the optical discs are the common choices of delivery media.

**The Web**
- HTML5 video can be playback using the Web browser's built-in player. The HTML5 video formats and the steps to create them are discussed in Chapter 15.
- For YouTube, registered users can upload videos of a variety of video formats to the site. The uploaded videos are then encoded into Flash Video (FLV) and HTML5 video formats.
- Fast-start QuickTime allows progressive download.
- Flash Video (FLV) and MPEG-4 can be used for HTTP pseudostreaming.
- QuickTime, Flash Video, Windows Media, and RealVideo also support streaming on the Web.

**Optical Discs**
- For DVD-video or Blu-ray discs, export the video directly to disc. You can also export your video as a DVD-compliant MPEG-2, Blu-ray-compliant MPEG2, or Blu-ray-compliant H.264 and author a DVD project using a DVD authoring program. Using a DVD authoring program allows you to create menus and submenus.
- For CD or DVD, export your videos to QuickTime or MPEG-4.

For videos intended for CD-R/RW or DVD+/-R/RW playback, the data rate of your video should be no higher than the data rate of your target audience's playback device. Otherwise, your video may skip frames and become choppy.

Here are some suggested steps to determine export settings for CD-R/RW or DVD+/-R/RW playback:

1. Start with the desired frame size, frame rate, and compressor.
2. Export your video. Look up its file size and calculate the data rate.
   If the data rate is higher than your target audience's device can handle, then try reducing the frame size, lowering the frame rate, or lowering the picture quality. The nature of your video dictates which strategy you should try first.
3. Finally, always test your final production on computer equipment that is as close to the target audience's as possible.

These suggested steps also can be applied to creating videos intended for the Web. The data limit will be determined by the network connection speed of your target audience.

Blu-ray videos and DVD-videos can be played back on set-top players or on computers that have the disc drive and player.

Generally, there are two ways to create a DVD-video or Blu-ray disc:

- Method 1: Export your final video as a Blu-ray- or DVD-compliant MPEG-2 file and then author a Blu-ray or DVD project using a DVD authoring program.
- Method 2: Export your final video directly to disc.

The general steps in authoring a DVD project are:

1. Set project settings (disc type, television standard, and frame dimensions.)
2. Import content as assets.
3. Build navigation structure by linking menus and videos.
4. Preview and test play your project.
5. Export your DVD project and make a DVD disc.

## TERMS

| | | |
|---|---|---|
| Asset list  215 | In and Out points  217 | slide edit  218 |
| Blue Screen and | keying  219 | slip edit  218 |
|   Green Screen Keys  219 | Library  227 | Straight cut  219 |
| button  225 | menu  225 | submenus  225 |
| Chapter points  226 | miniDV  212 | superimposed  219 |
| Color Key  219 | motion menu  225 | Templates  227 |
| cross dissolve  219 | multiple angles  227 | Timeline panel  215 |
| Effects  215 | nonlinear editing  218 | Track  227 |
| FireWire  211 | Preview window  215 | transitions  215 |
| i.Link  211 | ripple edit  218 | |
| IEEE 1394  211 | rolling edit  218 | |

## LEARNING AIDS

The following learning aids can be found at the book's companion Web site.

**Trimming a Clip by Setting In and Out Points, and Applying a Video Transition to Video Clips**

Screen-capture movies demonstrate the basic steps of setting In and Out points for video clips, and applying a video transition, in two digital video editing application programs: Adobe Premiere Pro and Apple Final Cut Pro.

**Nonlinear Editing Techniques in Digital Video**

An interactive tutorial demonstrates the characteristics of ripple edit, rolling edit, slip edit, and slide edit.

**Straight-cut versus Cross Dissolve Transitions**

A short video clip shows examples of two different transitions: straight cut and cross dissolve.

### ✎ Applying a Video Effect to Video Clips and Animating the Effect by Keyframing

Screen-capture movies demonstrate the basic steps of applying a Gaussian blur video effect to a clip and keyframing the effect in two digital video editing application programs: Adobe Premiere Pro and Apple Final Cut Pro.

### ✎ Color-Keying Video Clips

Screen-capture movies demonstrate the basic steps of color-keying a video clip using two digital video editing application programs: Adobe Premiere Pro and Apple Final Cut Pro.

### ✎ Export Video to DVD MPEG-2

Screen-capture movies demonstrate the basic steps of exporting videos to DVD MPEG-2 in Adobe Premiere Pro.

### ✎ Export Video to QuickTime Movie

Screen-capture movies demonstrate the basic steps of exporting videos to QuickTime movies in two digital video editing application programs: Adobe Premiere Pro and Apple Final Cut Pro.

## REVIEW QUESTIONS

When applicable, please choose all correct answers.

1. **True/False:** The only way to acquire digital video footage is to shoot video directly in digital format.

2. Which of the following is the best way to capture digital videos?
   A. Capture at least a few seconds of extra footage at the beginning and end of the clip segment than you expect you will need.
   B. Capture at least a few seconds of extra footage at the beginning of the clip segment than you expect you will need, but no extra seconds at the end of the clip.
   C. Capture at least a few seconds of extra footage at the end of the clip segment than you expect you will need, but no extra seconds at the beginning of the clip.
   D. Capture only the clip segment you expect you will need, with no extra seconds at the beginning or end of the clip.

3. In most digital video editing programs, the imported source footage and images to be used in a video project are listed in the _____.
   A. asset list panel
   B. effects and transitions panel
   C. preview panel
   D. timeline panel

4. In most digital video editing programs, the _____ has video and audio tracks, and this is where you can arrange and compose your source clips in sequence.
   A. asset list panel
   B. effects and transitions panel
   C. preview panel
   D. timeline panel

**5.** The figure shows a video sequence consisting of three video clips placed side by side on a timeline. Which nonlinear editing tool lets you lengthen the middle clip (blue color) while pushing the adjacent clip down? The second figure shows the resulting video sequence.

A. Ripple edit
B. Rolling edit
C. Slip edit
D. Slide edit

**6.** The figure shows a video sequence consisting of three video clips placed side by side on a timeline. Which nonlinear editing tool lets you lengthen the middle clip (blue color) while maintaining the duration of the entire video sequence by pushing the In point of the adjacent clip? The second figure shows the resulting video sequence.

A. Ripple edit
B. Rolling edit
C. Slip edit
D. Slide edit

**7.** Export the final video to _____ if it is intended for DVD playback.

A. QuickTime
B. Flash Video
C. MPEG-1
D. MPEG-2 (DVD compliant)
E. Streaming video

**8.** Name three video file types that are suitable for Web playback.

**9.** **True/False:** A DVD-video project must have a menu structure.

**10.** One of the good practices for DVD submenu design is including certain buttons to help in navigation. What are the functions of these buttons?

**11.** A video DVD disc contains a folder called _____ that contains all the necessary files. The disc may also contain an empty folder called _____ that is used for audio DVD discs.

## EXPLORING THE APPLICATIONS

**1.** Find the following information about your **video editing program** from its user manual or online Help menu.

- Workspace:
  - Identify these panels: Asset list, Timeline, Preview, and Effects and transitions
- Capturing videos:
  - Learn how to capture digital video

- Editing source clips:
  - Methods of trimming source clips:
    - Does the program let you set In and Out points? If so, how?
    - What are the other methods of trimming clips? Write down the instructions and the characteristic features for each method.
  - Learn how to change the speed and duration of a clip
- Learn how to create titles
- Composing video sequences:
  - Find out the available transitions, and how to apply them
  - Find out the available video effects, and how to apply them to the clip—for example, resizing and cropping a clip or applying tonal and color adjustments to a clip
  - Locate the ripple edit, rolling edit, slip edit, and slide edit tools, if available
  - Learn how to set the transparency of a clip
  - Learn how to superimpose one clip over another
  - Learn how to adjust the volume of an audio on the timeline
  - Learn how to create a simple fade-in and fade-out of an audio
  - Find out the available audio effects, and how to apply them to the audio
- Exporting video:
  - Learn how to export your final video
  - Find out the supported export video format

2. Find the following information about your **DVD authoring program** from its user manual or online Help menu.

- Workspace:
  - Identify these panels: Asset list, Timeline, Preview, and Media Library
- Starting a new project:
  - Find out how to start a new project and set the proper project settings, such as NTSC or PAL, DVD or Blu-ray, frame size, and aspect ratio
- Media:
  - Find out the file types of video, audio, and images supported by the program
  - Find out how to add a media file to your project
- Learn how to create a simple single-movie DVD project (i.e., without a menu)
- Learn how to set the single movie or a menu to loop
- Creating menu:
  - Learn how to create a menu from a preset template, if available
  - Learn how to create a menu from a blank menu
  - Learn how to add text and graphics for the menu
  - Learn how to link the text and graphics of a menu to a video or another menu
- Learn how to preview or test play your DVD project within the program
- Exporting your DVD project:
  - Learn how to output a DVD project to a folder on a computer
  - Learn how to output a DVD project as a disc image and then burn the disc image to a DVD disc
  - Learn how to output a DVD project directly onto a DVD disc
  - Learn how to burn the DVD folder or disc image onto a DVD disc

# Interactive Multimedia Authoring with Flash: Animation

# 8

## KEY CONCEPTS

- Multimedia authoring
- Frame-by-frame, tweened, and scripted animation
- Tweening
- Tools, Stage, Timeline, Property inspector, and Library panels in Flash workspace
- Symbols and shapes
- Publishing a Flash project

## GENERAL LEARNING OBJECTIVES

In this chapter, you will learn

- The basic workspace and terminology of Flash to get you started on animation and ActionScript.
- The symbols and shapes in Flash.
- The difference between the Merge Drawing and the Object Drawing models.
- How to create animation with Flash.
- How to adjust the playback speed of an animation.
- Frame-by-frame, tweening, and scripted animation.
- When it is best to use the different types of animation.
- The different types of tweens: Motion, Classic, and Shape.
- How to create tweened animation using motion path and motion guide in Flash.
- How to create mask and animated mask in Flash.
- How to publish a Flash project as a projector and SWF, and for iOS and Android devices.

## 8.1 WHAT IS MULTIMEDIA AUTHORING?

*Multimedia authoring* is the process of creating a multimedia production. It involves assembling or sequencing different media elements, adding interactivity, and then packaging the production for distribution to *end users*. The end users are the target audience who will be viewing your final production.

Business presentations, advertising kiosks, games, and educational products are just a few examples of multimedia productions. These multimedia projects can be delivered to end users over the Internet (played in a Web browser or as a download) or as a stand-alone app or executable program suitable for distribution through app stores for mobile devices or CD-ROM and DVD-ROM for personal computers.

Multimedia authoring programs allow you to combine text, images/graphics, audio, video, and animation into an interactive presentation. Many programs also have their own scripting language that lets you add interactivity to your production. Adobe Flash and Director are examples of commercial multimedia authoring programs. Flash's scripting language is called *ActionScript*, and Director's scripting language is called Lingo. You also can develop a multimedia production by programming in languages that are not specific for multimedia authoring, for example, Java, Objective C (for MacOS and iOS), C++, Visual Basic, JavaScript, and HTML5.

This book's multimedia authoring chapters cover the basics of Flash animation and basic to advanced topices of ActionScript programming. ActionScript shares the same basic programming terms and concepts of other programming languages. Hence, you will be able to apply the fundamentals you learn in these chapters to other programming projects.

## 8.2 THE MULTIMEDIA PRODUCTION PROCESS

Multimedia authoring refers to the *assembly* of media elements. The actual creation of the necessary media elements is a separate process. Digital images, video, and audio can be created with programs that are specialized for producing and editing these media.

For example, if you want to use video clips in your multimedia project, you can shoot digital videos, transfer the video to a computer with a video editing program (such as Adobe Premiere Pro), and then edit the video by adding transitions, adjusting durations, adding voice or music to the audio tracks, performing color correction, and adding special effects. Finally, you export the video into a format, such as QuickTime, Flash Video, or a series of images, that you can import into your multimedia authoring program.

In the authoring process, you may specify when your video will show up and how the video should interact with other media elements on the screen when the multimedia production plays. For example, you may specify that your video will play only when the user clicks on a button or wins the game.

This section discusses the general steps of creating an interactive multimedia production to give you a big picture of the multimedia authoring process. The details of working with Flash are covered later in this chapter.

**Step 1**   **Collect the media elements.**

Media elements include text, bitmapped images, vector graphics, digital videos, digital audio, and animation. These elements usually are created outside of the multimedia authoring program, using programs that are specific to the media type.

Flash is a vector-graphics-based multimedia authoring program. It has simple tools for creating and modifying vector graphics to be used in a Flash file. You can also import other types of media files to use.

The following are some of the common file formats supported by Flash:

Bitmap images: Photoshop (PSD), PNG, TIFF, BMP, GIF, JPEG

Vector graphics: Flash Movie (SWF), Adobe Illustrator (AI)

Digital Videos: QuickTime (MOV), AVI, Flash Video (FLV, F4V), MPEG-4, MPEG-2

Digital Audio: WAV, MP3, AIFF, AU

**Step 2**   **Assemble the media elements.**

In Flash, you can create vector graphics using the pencil and brush tools. You can also import various types of media elements. These elements can be arranged on a timeline to control the order and timing of their appearance.

**Step 3**   **Add interactivity.**

Interactivity, such as mouse and keyboard interaction, can be added, for example, by programming in ActionScript in a Flash project.

A multimedia production created in Flash or Director is often referred to as a movie. It does not mean being in the form of a video or film.

**Step 4** **Package the movie for distribution to the end users.**

The two most common forms of distributing multimedia productions are stand-alone apps or executables and movies that play back in a Web browser. Publishing your multimedia project in either of these two formats allows others to view your finished project without the authoring environment. For example, they do not need to have a copy of Flash installed in order to view your Flash movies.

- The Web version of Flash movies is an SWF file. SWF has a smaller size than the stand-alone executable and is designed for the Web. It is playable on Windows, Macintosh, and Linux computers, as long as the Flash player or the browser plug-in is installed.

  To create a version of your Flash movie playable through a Web browser, you need to publish the movie as an SWF file. The file format for the published movie can be selected in the Publish Settings dialog box (File > Publish Settings . . .). In the Publish Settings dialog box (Figure 8.1), you can check to select the format(s) of the movie(s) to be published. SWF and HTML with embedded SWF are the default selection.

**Figure 8.1** Flash's Publish Settings dialog box.

Details about creating an iOS certificate, provisioning profiles, and app IDs can be found at the Apple Developer Web site at http://developer.apple.com/.

Detailed instructions for publishing Flash projects for iOS and Android devices can be found in the Flash Help menu and at the Adobe Web site at http://www.adobe.com/.

- A stand-alone executable does not require a plug-in to play. Stand-alone executables usually are created for distribution on CD-ROM or DVD-ROM. The file size for an executable is larger than that of a Web version, and you need to create separate executables for different operating systems. To create a stand-alone executable in Flash, you publish your movie as a *projector*.

## 8.2.1 Developing for iOS and Android Using Flash

Adobe Flash Professional CS5.5 also lets you publish your ActionScript 3 project to run as an app on iOS and Android devices (Figure 8.2). The publish settings for iOS devices can be set by choosing File > AIR for iOS Settings . . . (Figure 8.3). To publish for iOS devices, you would need to provide an iOS certificate, provisioning profile, and app ID (Figure 8.3b), which require membership in the Apple iOS Developer program. When you click the Publish button, an .ipa file will be generated. The .ipa file can be copied to iTunes on your computer as an app and then synced to your iOS devices.

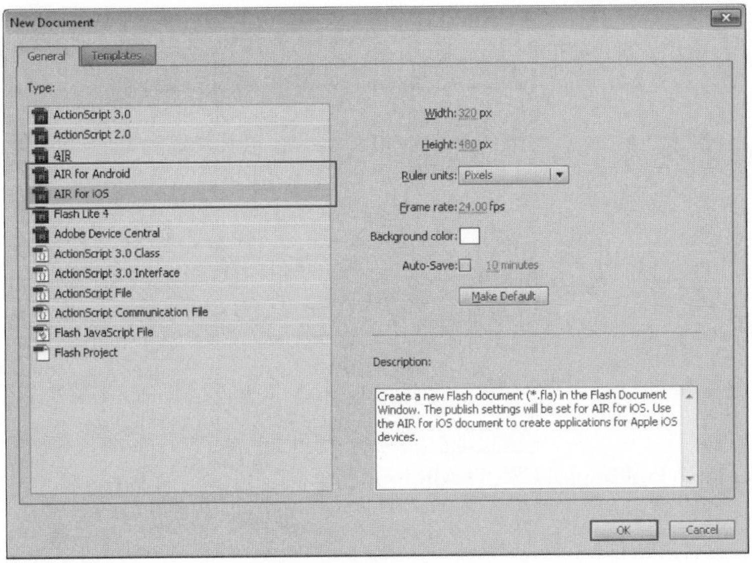

**Figure 8.2** Flash Professional CS5.5's New Document dialog box.

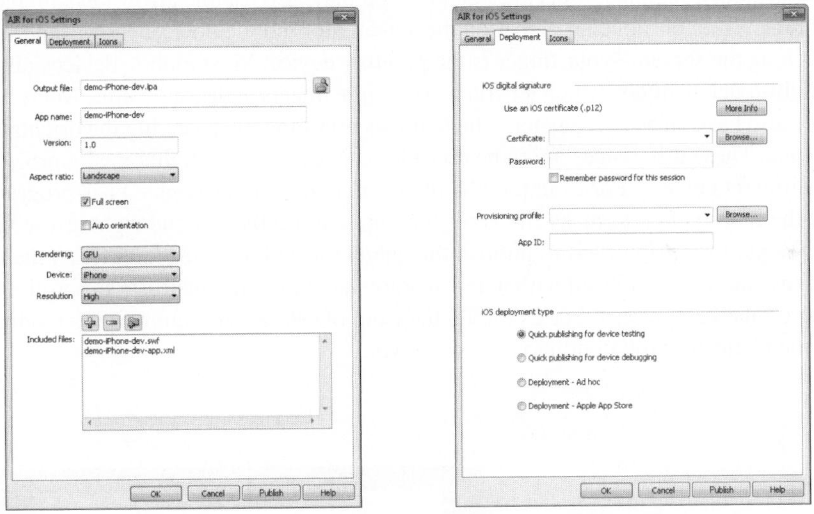

(a)                                          (b)

**Figure 8.3** Flash Professional CS5.5's AIR for iOS Settings: (a) General tab. (b) Deployment tab.

Similarly, the publish settings for Android devices can be accessed by choosing File > AIR for Android Settings. You will also need to provide a certificate, which can be created by choosing the Create . . . button in the Deployment tab (Figure 8.4). By checking the options in the section After publishing, you can test your app right on your Android device connected to your computer after the app has been created.

Although Flash supports project development for different devices (desktop and laptop computers and mobile devices), the different ways that you can interact with different types

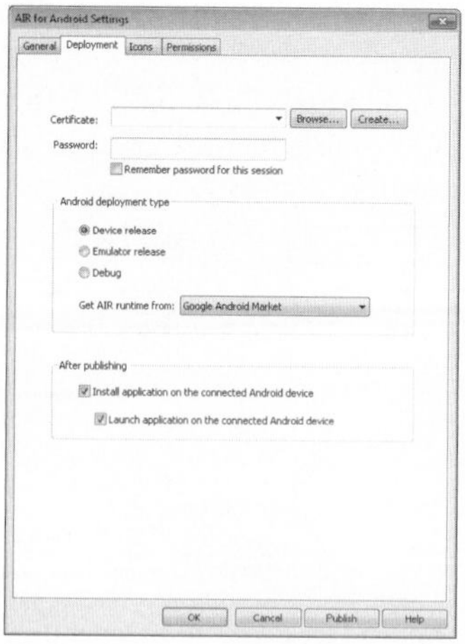

**Figure 8.4** Flash Professional CS5.5's AIR for Android Settings.

of devices influence the user interaction design of your project. In general, you use the mouse and the keyboard to provide input to computers. The mouse cursor is your pointing device. In some programs, especially games, you may also use the arrow keys on the keyboard to navigate or move an object on the screen. For mobile devices, however, you rely on touching the screen—your finger is the pointing device. Most mobile devices also support multi-touch features, which let you use multiple fingers at the same time. Many mobile devices also have an accelerometer, which allows user input by changing the orientation of the device. These differences are to be considered in developing digital media projects for these different devices. For example, the platform game lab in Chapter 11 is programmed to use the mouse click to make the hero jump up and use the left and right arrow keys to scroll the platform. However, to publish this game for iOS or Android devices, the use of arrow keys has to be replaced with a new feature that allows the platform to scroll without relying on the key presses. For example, the example shown in Figure 8.5 is modified to make the platform scroll continuously on it own.

(a) (b)

**Figure 8.5** The side-scrolling platform game lab example from Chapter 11 is modified to publish as an app on (a) iPhone 4 and (b) Android.

# 8.3 ANIMATION

Conceptually, animation is very much like video. It is a sequence of images that creates the illusion of movement when played rapidly in succession. Many multimedia projects make use of animation, and many multimedia authoring programs, such as Flash and Director, allow you to create animation. These programs are frame based. This means that you can sequence the animation content visually on a timeline as a sequence of frames.

There are several different ways to create animations with these programs: frame by frame, tweening, and scripting. These methods are not exclusive of each other in a project; they are often used in combination in creating an animation sequence.

## 8.3.1 Frame-by-Frame Animation

*Frame-by-frame* animation involves explicitly placing or creating different visual content for each frame. Each frame is a *keyframe*, which is a frame that explicitly specifies the content.

For example, Figure 8.6 shows a character running sequence. Figure 8.7a shows a simple nine-frame animation of a bird flying. The visual content of all nine frames is explicitly placed. Figure 8.7b shows an example of a tweened animation, which is discussed next.

**Figure 8.6** An example of frame-by-frame animation.

|  | (a)<br>Frame-by-frame | (b)<br>Tweening |
|---|---|---|
| Timeline → | | |
| Frame ↓ | | |
| 1 | | |
| 2 | | |
| 3 | | |
| 4 | | |
| 5 | | |
| 6 | | |
| 7 | | |
| 8 | | |
| 9 | | |

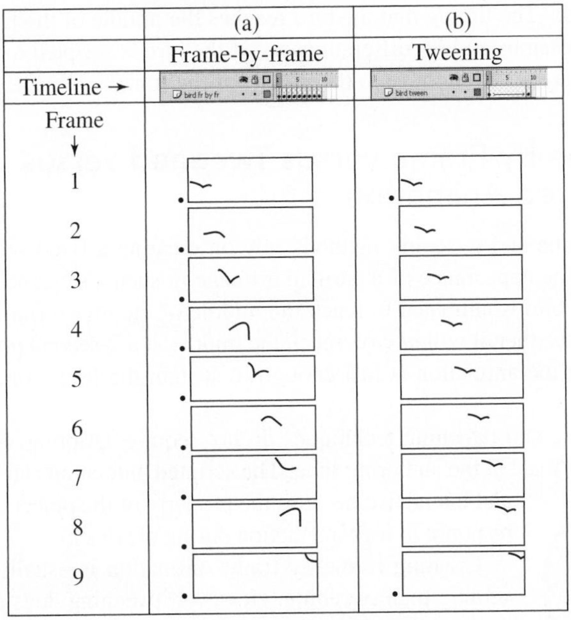

**Figure 8.7** Frame-by-frame method versus tweening, showing the • next to the image frame to indicate that the image is created manually. (a) Frame-by-frame method. (b) Tweening.

### 8.3.2 Tweened Animation

*Tweening* also requires keyframes. You need two keyframes for any tweened segment: one at the beginning and the other at the end. Frames that are between keyframes are called *in-between frames*. The content in these in-between frames is filled in by interpolating the values of the object's properties in the two keyframes. What this means is that you do not manually draw or paste the bird into these in-between frames in the example shown in Figure 8.7b.

Suppose you want to animate a bird moving across the screen from left to right in nine frames. In the first keyframe (frame 1), place the bird on the left side of the screen, and in the last keyframe (frame 9), place it on the right side of the screen (Figure 8.7b). The content in frames 2 through 8 (the in-between frames) is filled in automatically. By default, the positions of the bird in these in-between frames are distributed linearly between the bird's positions in the two keyframes.

In this simple example, the property of the bird that changes in each keyframe is its position. In addition to position, other common properties that can be animated by tweening in animation programs include rotation, size, color, and opacity. The shape of an object also can be tweened in Flash. This type of tweening is called shape tween, which will be discussed in Section 8.6.3 along with other types of tweening in Flash.

### 8.3.3 Scripted Animation

You will learn how to create scripted animation in Chapter 10.

Scripted animation does not rely on a sequence of frames on the timeline. The animation can be scripted to respond to the user's interaction. In the previous example of the flying bird animation, the bird can be scripted to follow the mouse cursor, to start flying after the user has clicked on a button, or to follow a path controlled by gravity and how the user shoots it out. In such cases, the bird is not always at the middle of the frame at the same number of seconds. The timing that the bird reaches the middle of the frame varies in different playback sessions and for different users. If the bird is scripted to follow the mouse cursor, the bird may not even move to the middle of the frame.

### 8.3.4 Frame-by-Frame versus Tweened versus Scripted Animation

The frame-by-frame and tweening methods rely on creating a fixed sequence of images on the timeline. The appearance of a particular image in such a sequence is deterministic. For example, if a bird is animated to reach the middle of the image frame 2 seconds after the animation starts, then it will *always* reach the middle at a 2-second point, assuming the computer playing the animation is fast enough to sustain the frame rate specified in the animation.

Frame-by-frame and tweening techniques do not require scripting. However, the animated sequence is fixed at the authoring time. The scripted animation can be more dynamic and interactive because the property of the object can be changed in response to user interaction during playback.

Creating frame-by-frame animation is usually more time consuming than tweening. However, tweening does not always create the sophisticated effect that you might want. In addition, because the in-between frames are computed, it results in smooth motion. Such smoothness sometimes may give a mechanical feeling to the

⌐ **Frame-by-Frame, Tweening, and Scripted Animation** A side-by-side comparison of frame-by-frame, tweening, and scripted animation using the flying bird example shown in Figure 8.7.

animation. On the other hand, frame-by-frame animation, in which each frame often is drawn manually, can add an organic touch to the animation, such as in the simple flying bird example in Figure 8.7a.

### 8.3.5 Frame Rate and Frame Size

*Frame size* refers to the width and height dimensions of the animation. For digital video, the dimensions are in pixels. In Flash and Director, the size of a frame is the stage dimension of the movie, also in pixels.

*Frame rate* specifies the playback speed of the animation. It is in frames per second (fps). As with video, a low frame rate may make the animation choppy. Too high of a frame rate may also cause choppiness if the computer playing the animation is not fast enough to process and display the frames. Multimedia authoring programs, such as Flash and Director, allow you to set the frame rate for your animation project. The frame rate setting in these programs usually defines the *maximum* rate. This means that the program will not exceed the frame rate you specify in your animation project, but it does not guarantee that your animation will be kept at that frame rate. Slower computers may not be able to keep up with a high frame rate. In addition, the playback of a Flash animation containing complex vector graphics (such as those made up of a large number of anchor points) will not be able to keep up with the frame rate that is acceptable for average projects.

The default frame rate of a Flash file is 24 fps; 30 fps is also an acceptable rate for most computers.

## 8.4 ADJUSTING THE SPEED OF ANIMATION PLAYBACK

Sometimes you may find that the speed of the motion in your animation is a little too fast or too slow. It may seem that the fix is simply a matter of changing the frame rate. However, when you adjust the speed of the animation, you will also need to take into consideration of preserving the smoothness of the motion. For a frame-based animation, both its frame rate and the number of frames in the animation affect the speed of the motion. Here are some guidelines for adjusting the speed of the motion in an animation:

- To speed up the motion: Reduce the number of frames or increase the frame rate (preferred).
- To slow down the motion: Add more frames (preferred) or reduce the frame rate.

Whether you want to slow down or speed up the motion, the basic guideline is to do so without eliminating frames. Eliminating frames in an animation sequence means eliminating the content that makes up the motion. This reduces the continuity of the motion and may break up the motion—causing noticeable jerkiness. However, avoiding elimination of frames is only a guideline and there are certainly exceptions.

### 8.4.1 Slowing Down Motion by Adding More Frames

Suppose that after you have created a tweened animation, you feel that the motion seems a little too fast. A good way to slow down the motion is to add more frames between keyframes instead of lowering the frame rate. An exception to this is when your frame rate is already too high—for example, higher than 30 frames per second.

The example shown in Figure 8.8 demonstrates the different effects of adding more frames versus lowering the frame rate. The original sequence (Column A) contains five frames and its frame rate is 20 fps. This means the animation sequence finishes in 0.4 seconds.

| | (a) | (b) | (c) |
|---|---|---|---|
| | Original sequence that you want to slow down | Approach #1 (preferred):<br><br>Keep the same frame rate<br><br>Increase the number of frames between keyframes to stretch out the animation | Approach #2 (not recommended):<br><br>Lower the frame rate<br><br>Keep the number of frames the same |
| Timeline → | | | |
| Frame rate → | 20 fps | 20 fps | 5 fps |
| Time (sec.) ↓ | | | |
| 0 | | | |
| 0.05 | | | |
| 0.1 | | | |
| 0.15 | | | |
| 0.2 | | | |
| 0.25 | | | |
| 0.3 | | | |
| 0.35 | | | |
| 0.4 | | | |
| 0.45 | | | |
| 0.5 | | | |
| 0.55 | | | |

**Figure 8.8** Different approaches to slowing down an animation illustrated by showing the frame of an animation at each time interval.

| | | | |
|---|---|---|---|
| 0.6 | | | |
| 0.65 | | | |
| 0.7 | | | |
| 0.75 | | | |
| 0.8 | | | |
| 0.85 | | | |
| 0.9 | | | |
| 0.95 | | | |

**Figure 8.8** (*continued*)

Column B and Column C show two different approaches to slow down the animation. Approach #1 shown in Column B maintains the frame rate but slows down the animation by increasing the number of frames, allowing the motion to stretch over a longer period of time. The animation now finishes in 1 second.

Approach #2 shown in Column C slows down the animation by lowering the frame rate. The animation still finishes in 1 second. However, as you see, using Approach #1, the motion of the ball in the resulting animation changes every 0.05 seconds while it updates every 0.2 seconds using Approach #2. Therefore, Approach #1 gives a smoother motion than Approach #2.

> Adjusting the Speed of an Animation: Frame Rate versus Number of Frames A side-by-side comparison of the original sequence and two approaches shown in Figure 8.8.

### 8.4.2 Speeding up Motion

If you want to speed up a frame-based animation, in most situations you may consider increasing the frame rate. The exception for this guideline is when the frame rate is already too high for the target audience's computer to play. In this case, you can try reducing the number of frames in the animation sequence. In addtion, if only part of the animation needs to speed up the motion while the speed for the rest of the animation looks good, you may want to eliminate frames in the part that needs speeding up.

## 8.5 FLASH CS5.5 WORKSPACE

The Flash workspace or authoring environment has a variety of panels. This section gives you an overview of the most essential workspace elements: Tools, Stage, Timeline, Property Inspector, and Library (Figure 8.9). You are encouraged to explore the workspace on your own and use Help menu to look up more information.

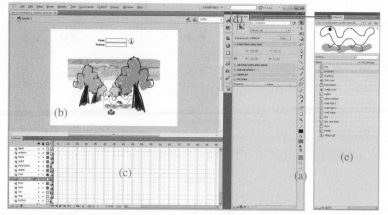

**Figure 8.9** Workspace of Flash CS5.5. (a) Tools panel. (b) Stage. (c) Timeline.
(d) Property Inspector. (e) Library panel.

## 8.5.1 Tools Panel

By default, the Tools panel (Figure 8.9a) is located on the far right. It contains tools to select, draw, scale, and modify the content used in the Flash project.

## 8.5.2 Stage

The Stage (Figure 8.9b) is the area where a Flash movie plays. By default, it is a rectangle in the center of the window. Its color is defined by the background color of the project (Modify > Document . . .) and is white by default. The outside of the stage rectangle is marked in gray color. Any object placed outside of the stage will not be visible by the user when the movie is played in the Flash player, even though it is visible at the authoring time.

## 8.5.3 Timeline

The Timeline panel (Figure 8.9c) is made of a series of frames in a row and a stack of layers. Flash is a frame-based authoring program. The media contents are organized on a timeline (Figure 8.9c) over time in frames and layers. The content on a layer will cover the one beneath it.

The appearance of a frame indicates whether it is a keyframe, a regular frame, or an empty frame.

- A solid black circle in a frame indicates it is a keyframe with content on the Stage.
- A circle means it is an empty keyframe.
- A shaded frame without any circle is a regular frame that contains the same content as the previous keyframe in the same layer.
- A frame with a rectangle is also a regular frame, but it is the end frame of a frame sequence.

## 8.5.4 Property Inspector

By default, the Property Inspector (Figure 8.9d) is located at the right of the window. It displays the information and properties to be edited for the object that is currently selected on the Stage.

When you select *a frame in the Timeline panel*, the Property Inspector displays the *frame property*. If the frame selected is a keyframe, then this is where you can assign a frame label to that frame.

If *an object on the Stage* is selected, then you can alter the *object's properties*, such as its *x* and *y* position and width and height, by entering numbers. If you click on the Stage without selecting any object, then the document properties, such as its frame rate, stage size, and stage color, are displayed and can be altered.

## BEWARE OF WHAT IS SELECTED

Selecting a frame is different from selecting objects on the Stage. To select a frame, you click on the frame in the Timeline panel. This also will cause all of the objects in that frame to be selected. Because a frame is selected, the Property Inspector shows the properties of that frame only—for example, the frame label name. Although objects are selected on the Stage, the properties of the selected objects, such as x, y, width, height and color effects, are not shown in the Property Inspector. If you mean to select an object in a frame to apply a color effect or change its width and height, then make sure you select the object by clicking on it on the Stage—not by clicking on the frame in the Timeline panel.

### 8.5.5 Library Panel

The Library panel (Figure 8.9e) stores symbols, imported bitmaps, and sounds to be used in the project. Symbols are explained in the next section.

## 8.6 FLASH: ESSENTIAL TERMINOLOGY

The visual items used on the Stage in a Flash file can be categorized in two types: shapes and symbols. They have different properties, purposes, and requirements.

### 8.6.1 Shape

A *shape* is made up of strokes and/or fills.

- *Strokes* are lines that are created with the Pencil, Pen, and Ink Bottle tools (Figure 8.10a through c). A stroke's properties, such as width, color, and style of the line, can be modified in the Property Inspector.
- A *fill* is an area of filled content. It can be created by using the Paint Bucket and Brush tools (Figure 8.10d and e).

There are two drawing models for creating shapes: Object Drawing and Merge Drawing. When you select the Pencil, Brush, Pen, Line, or Rectangle tool, you have an option called Object Drawing (Figure 8.10f). You turn on the Object Drawing option to use Object Drawing, and turn it off to return to Merge Drawing.

The *Merge Drawing model* is the default drawing model. The shapes that overlap are merged. In the *Object Drawing model*, the shapes you create are self-contained objects. The drawing objects differ from the shapes drawn in the Merge Drawing model in two ways:

- When you click to select a drawing object on the Stage, you select the whole shape. You see a box around the drawing object. For example, Figure 8.11 show two head

The section on vector graphics programs in Chapter 3 discusses how to create strokes and fills. The techniques of working with anchor points and handles to create and edit paths also apply to Flash.

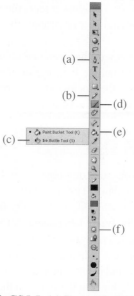

**Figure 8.10** Tools panel of Flash CS5.5. (a) Pen tool. (b) Pencil tool. (c) Ink Bottle tool. (d) Brush tool. (e) Paint Bucket tool. (f) Object Drawing.

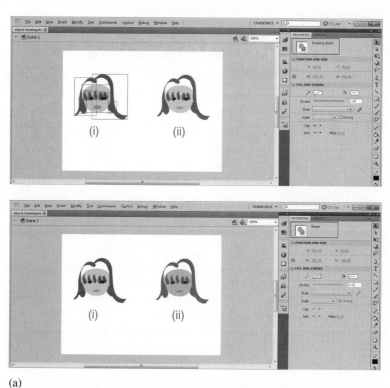

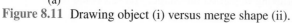

(a)

**Figure 8.11** Drawing object (i) versus merge shape (ii).

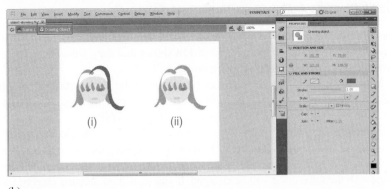

(b)

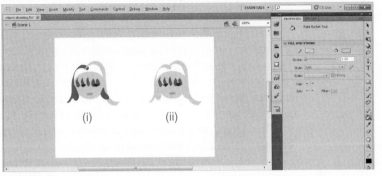

(c)

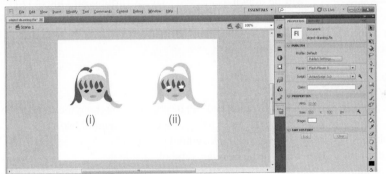

(d)

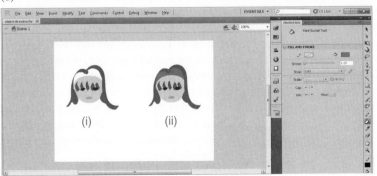

(e)

**Figure 8.11** (*continued*)

drawings: (i) the one on the left is made up of drawing objects; (ii) the one on the right is made up of regular shapes. Figure 8.11a shows that they are selected. Each brush stroke in (i) is an individual drawing object.

You cannot select part of the fill or a segment of the stroke, for example, by using the Lasso tool. Instead, you can double-click on the drawing object to edit its shapes, the same way you would edit regular shapes (Figure 8.11b).

- The overlapped drawing objects do not alter one another. For example, you can change the color of a drawing object (Figure 8.11c[i]) without altering the other objects that it overlaps with. If you fill the same part of the shape, Figure 8.11c[ii], the color in the contiguous shape with the same color will be changed. If you reposition drawing objects, such as the two eyes (Figure 8.11d[i]), the previously overlapping hair (also a drawing object) is not altered. On the other hand, holes are created in the shapes on the right (Figure 8.11d[ii]).

Depending on how you want to create your content, Object Drawing mode may or may not suit your needs. An empty enclosed space created in a merged shape can be filled easily. For example, the empty space can be filled with a green color in Figure 8.11e(ii) using the Paint Bucket tool. However, to make the same area filled with a color in the one made up of drawing objects (Figure 8.11e[i]), you would need to create another shape or drawing object of that color.

> ✎ **Creating Shapes in Flash** A screen-capture movie shows how to create a simple shape using the Pencil, Pen, Ink, and Paint Bucket tools.

> ✎ **Modifying Shapes in Flash** A screen-capture movie shows how to modify a shape.

If you find that you have unintentionally drawn drawing objects on the Stage, select the Pencil, Brush, Pen, Line, or Rectangle tool and make sure Object Drawing is turned off, so that the new shapes will be drawn as merged shapes. Turning off Object Drawing does not convert the existing objects on the Stage to merged shapes. The existing objects still remain, but you can convert them into shapes by selecting the objects and choosing `Modify > Break Apart`.

### 8.6.2 Symbol

**Symbols** are stored in the Library panel and can be reused throughout the project. To create a symbol, you can either: (1) convert an existing shape into a symbol (`Modify > Convert to Symbol . . .`) or (2) create a blank symbol (`Insert > New Symbol . . .`) and then start creating shapes and/or place other symbols inside it.

New symbols are automatically added to the Library panel. To place a symbol on the Stage, you can drag the symbol from the Library panel onto the Stage.

When you select a symbol that is placed on the Stage, a rectangular bounding box appears around the symbol (regardless of the symbol's shape), such as shown around the puppy on the left in Figure 8.12. If you want to edit the shape of the symbol, you will need change to the editing mode of the symbol by double-clicking on the symbol's instance on the Stage or the symbol itself in the Library. You can tell a symbol from a shape on the Stage by looking at the Property Inspector. In Figure 8.12, the puppy selected on the left is a copy of a symbol. The blue rectangular box around it (Figure 8.12a) indicates that the selection is a copy of the symbol. The puppy selected on the right (Figure 8.12b) is a merged shape, as indicated by patterned dots.

There are three types of symbols: graphic, button, and movie clip. The characteristics and purposes of each type are described briefly here:

1. *Graphic*
   - Purposes: To be used as static graphics. Graphic symbols can be placed in other graphic, button, and movie clip symbols in addition to the main timeline.

Chapter 10 explains how to assign actions to a moveclip instance on the Stage and Chapter 11 shows you how to program a movie clip instance to respond to mouse and keyboard interaction.

Movie clips versus buttons: Because movie clips can offer more possibilities in interactivity, all of the ActionScript examples in this book use movie clips instead of buttons. However, the ActionScript code in most of the examples also works for buttons.

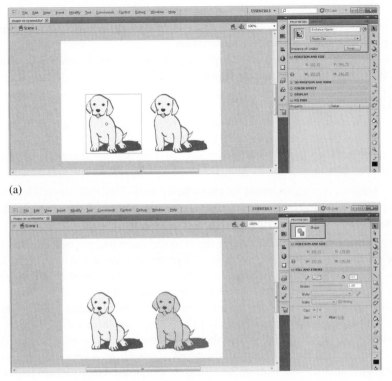

(a)

(b)

**Figure 8.12** Symbol and shapes: (a) The puppy on the left being selected is from a symbol. (b) The puppy on the right being selected is a shape.

- A graphic symbol can contain shapes and other graphic symbols.
- Interactive controls and sounds do not work in a graphic symbol's timeline.

2. **Button**
   - Purposes: To be used as an interactive button in the movie to respond to mouse clicks and rollovers. Button symbols can be placed in movie clip symbols in addition to the main timeline.
   - There are only four special-purpose frames in a button symbol. They correspond to the various states of the button: up, over, down, and hit. *Hit* is to define the hot spot of the button if you only want a certain area of the button to respond to the mouse click. You can add different graphic symbols, movie clips, or just shapes to define the appearance of the different button states.
   - A button symbol can contain shapes, copies of graphic symbols and movie clips, and sounds.
   - You can use ActionScript to control a button that is placed on the timeline.

3. **Movie Clip**
   - Purposes: To be used as a reusable piece of animation because a movie clip has its own timeline that plays independently from the main movie's timeline. You can think of movie clips as mini-Flash movies that can be used inside a main movie. If you think of movie clips and the main movie as flipbooks, then some flipbooks (movie clips) can be placed on any page (frame) of a main flipbook (main movie).

Adding interactivity is one of the main purposes for using movie clips in interactive projects and games because they can be controlled using ActionScript in response to mouse and keyboard interaction.

- A movie clip can contain shapes and copies of other symbols (graphics, buttons, and other movie clips), ActionScript, and sounds.
- You also can use movie clips inside the timeline of a button symbol to create animated buttons.
- If you use movie clips in your movie, you need to select `Control > Test Movie` to preview them, not just `Control > Play`.
- The animation of a movie clip will start playing automatically unless you use an ActionScript to stop it at its first frame.

Using symbols is not a technical requirement for basic Flash animation. Depending on the complexity of a project, some projects may be completed without using symbols, but using only shapes. However, symbols offer at least two advantages:

1. Reusability: Using a symbol multiple times on the Stage will not increase the Flash file size. On the other hand, if you duplicate a shape on the Stage, it will increase the file size.
2. The symbol stored in the Library is a master copy of all the copies used on the Stage. The copies used on the Stage are called the *instances* of that symbol. Changes made to the content of the master copy will be reflected automatically in all of its copies used on the Stage. For example, as shown in Figure 8.13, there are three movie clip instances of the puppy symbol on the Stage. Each instance can be resized independently. By changing the one master copy of the puppy symbol in the Library panel to a Dalmatian puppy, all three instances of the puppy symbol on the Stage become Dalmatians.

(a)

(b)

**Figure 8.13** A symbol and its instances: (a) Three instances (copies) of the movie clip symbol named puppy are placed on the Stage. (b) When the master copy of the symbol puppy, which is stored in the Library panel, is modified to a Dalmatian puppy, all of the instances placed on the Stage are updated automatically.

In situations where the authoring process starts before the visual content of the symbols are ready, symbols with temporary content can be used while waiting for the actual content. Once the final designs of the symbols are ready, each symbol will need to be updated only once in the Library panel. All of the instances used on the Stage will reflect the new content automatically.

> ✧ **Creating Symbols in Flash** A screen-capture movie shows how to create (1) a new symbol and (2) a symbol by converting from a shape.

> 🖰 **Practice Drawing (Lab)** Practice Flash drawing and painting tools, and create movie clip symbols. Create two files:
>
> 1. X-ray (Figure 8.14)
> 2. hairstyles (Figure 8.15)
>
> The X-ray file will be used to create tweened animation in a lab later in this chapter. The hairstyles file will be used in a lab in Chapter 10 where you will learn how to add interactivity to allow the user to change the hairstyle on the character's head by clicking on one of the hairstyle choices.
>
>
>
> (a)                                    (b)
>
> **Figure 8.14** File #1: Create two symbols and put each on a separate layer.
>
>
>
> **Figure 8.15** File #2: Create seven symbols: a character's head (without hair), five hairstyles, and one hairstyle to put on the character's head.

### 8.6.3 Tweening

Tweening is an effective way to create movement and changes in visual contents over time. It requires two keyframes for each tweened sequence or tween span. To create a keyframe, use one of the following methods:

- Select a frame, select `Insert > Timeline > Keyframe`.
- Right-click (Windows) or Control-click (Macintosh) a frame in the Timeline panel, and select `Insert Keyframe`.

*Classic tween is called Motion tween in Flash CS3 and earlier versions.*

There are two types of tweening in Flash: motion and shape. The key differences between them are listed in Table 8.1. *Shape tweens* can create the animation of a shape morphing into another. For tweening motion, there are two different types of tweens: *Motion tweens* and *Classic tweens*.

A Motion tween begins with a keyframe and contains one or more property keyframes. A *property keyframe* belongs to a tween span. A *tween span* refers to a group of frames in which an object on the Stage changes its properties over time. You can specify the property value, such as position, scale, rotation, and skew, for a property keyframe. Unlike a regular keyframe, a property keyframe cannot be assigned with a frame label and script. Figure 8.16 shows an example of creating a motion tweened animation that has two property keyframes in addition to the keyframe at the beginning of the tween span. In each of these keyframes, the position, scale, and rotation of the leaf symbol instance are altered. The in-between frames are filled in automatically by interpolating the position, scale, and rotation of the contents in the two immediate keyframes.

| **TABLE 8.1** | **Comparison between Motion Tween and Shape Tween** |
|---|---|
| **Motion and Classic Tween** | **Shape Tween** |
| Works with **symbols** only. | Works with **shapes** only. |
| Not for creating morphing animation. | Can be used to create a **shape morphing** animation. |
| No more than one copy of a symbol is allowed in a frame that is going to be motion tweened. | Technically, more than one shape can be placed in a frame that is going to be shape tweened. However, if you want more control over which shape to morph to which destination shape, you should separate the shape onto separate layers, which is almost always the case when you create a shape tween. |
| The movement can be tweened to follow a path that is drawn as a stroke. | Does not work with the motion path. |
| The frames of the tween sequence are colored in **blue** (Motion tweens) or **purple** (Classic tweens) on the timeline (Figure 8.16 and Figure 8.18). | The frames of the shape tween sequence are colored in **green** on the timeline (Figure 8.19). |

*Motion path will be explained in Section 8.6.4.*

⬦ Creating Motion Tween in Flash
A screen-capture movie shows how to create a Motion tween animation.

If you apply Motion tween to a keyframe that contains shapes, Flash will prompt you to convert the shapes into a symbol. If the keyframe contains multiple symbols or a mix of shapes and symbols in the same layer, Flash will prompt you to combine them into one symbol. If they are not intended to be combined but animated independently, you should place them in different layers.

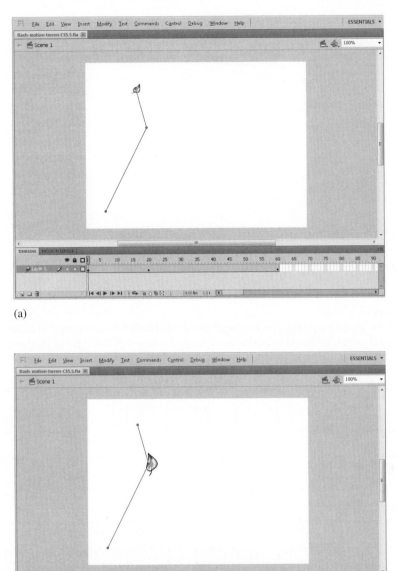

(a)

(b)

**Figure 8.16**  A motion tweened animation. (a) Keyframe at frame 1. (b) A second keyframe at frame 20, where the position, scale, and rotation of the symbol instance are changed. (*continued*)

Figure 8.17 shows the results of this animation sequence in approximately every other frame. The same animation also can be created using Classic tweens. Classic tweens use regular keyframes. Figure 8.18 shows the timeline of the same animation using Classic tweens. With Classic tweens, the color and opacity of the symbol instance also can be

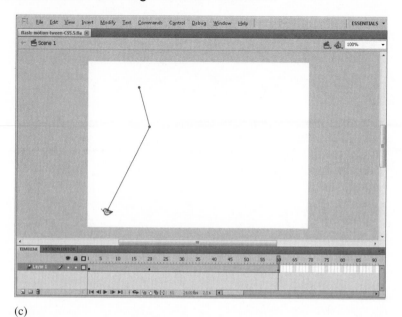

(c)

**Figure 8.16** (*continued*) (c) The last keyframe of this animation sequence at frame 60, with more changes made to the position, scale, and rotation of the symbol instance.

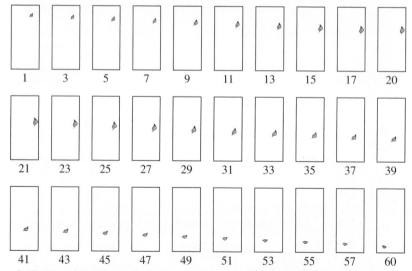

**Figure 8.17** The example motion tweened animation (Figure 8.16) is shown in approximately every other frame with the corresponding frame number.

> ✎ **Creating Classic Tween in Flash**
> A screen-capture movie shows how to create a Classic tween animation.

animated. If you apply Classic tween to a keyframe containing shapes or multiple symbol instances, the tween will not work and a dashed line (instead of a solid-line arrow) will be displayed in the tween span on the timeline.

Figure 8.19 shows an example of creating a three-keyframe shape tweened animation. In each of the three keyframes, the shape and color are altered. The first keyframe contains a shape of the

**Figure 8.18** The timeline of a Classic tween example.

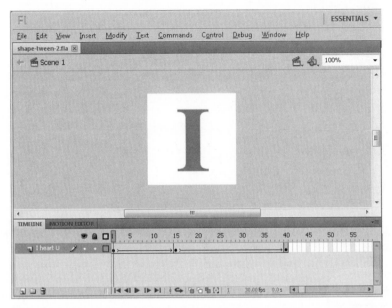

(a)

(b)

**Figure 8.19** A shape tweened animation. (a) Keyframe at frame 1. (b) In the second keyframe (frame 15), the shape and color are altered. ▄▄ This image can be found on the insert. (*continued*)

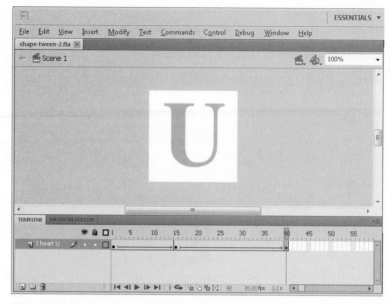

(c)

**Figure 8.19** (*continued*) (c) In the last keyframe of this animation sequence (frame 40), the shape and color are further altered. ▄▄ This image can be found on the insert.

> ⬦ **Creating Shape Tween in Flash**
> A screen-capture movie shows how to create a Shape tween animation.

letter "I" in blue; the second keyframe contains a heart shape in pink; the third keyframe contains a shape of the letter "U" in green. Shape tween is applied to the first keyframe of each segment. The in-between frames then are filled in automatically with shapes and colors that interpolate the shapes in the two immediate keyframes.

Figure 8.20 shows the results of this animation sequence in every other frame. This example demonstrates the shape tweening of the shape and color. Position, scale, rotation,

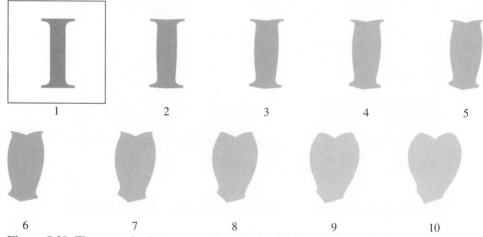

**Figure 8.20** The example shape tweened animation is shown in every frame with the corresponding frame number, where frames 1, 15, and 40 are the keyframes where the shapes are explicitly specified. ▄▄ This image can be found on the insert.

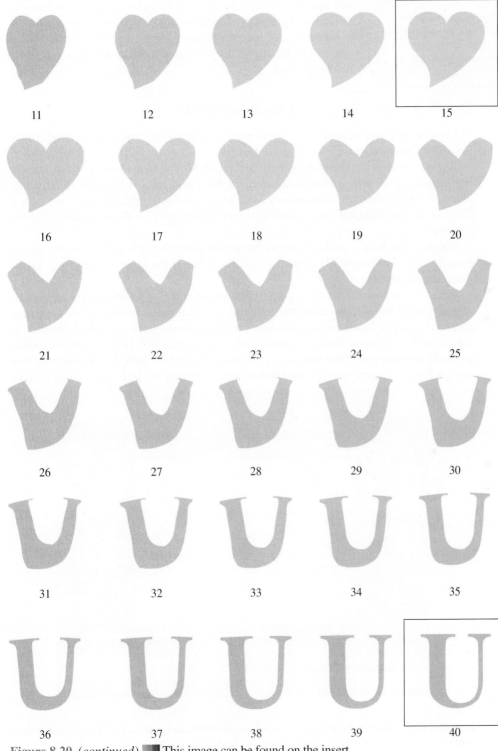

**Figure 8.20** (*continued*) This image can be found on the insert.

and opacity of the shape also can be tweened in a shape tweened sequence. If you apply Shape tween to a keyframe containing symbol instances, the tween will not work and a dashed line (instead of a solid-line arrow) will be displayed in the shape tween sequence on the timeline.

> ⌐ **Creating an Animation in Flash— Tweening (Lab)** A lab practice exercise to: (1) practice creating shapes and symbols and (2) create an animation using Shape, Classic, and Motion tweens.

## 8.6.4 Motion Path and Motion Guide

The ***motion path*** (for Motion tweens) and ***motion guide*** (for Classic tweens) allow you to animate a symbol instance following a stroke that you draw.

A motion path is automatically generated for each Motion tween span. For example, the line connecting the leaf symbol instances in the three keyframes in Figure 8.16 is the motion path that is generated automatically when Motion tween is applied to these keyframes. You can use the Selection and Subselection tools to edit the path the way you would edit a stroke.

You can also draw a stroke to use as the motion path. To apply a stroke as the motion path for a Motion tween: (1) Copy the stroke; (2) Select the Motion tween span on the timeline and paste the stroke.

For a Classic tween, the path is placed on a special layer for the motion guide. In order for the symbol instance to follow the path, the symbol instance in each of the keyframes needs to be snapped onto the path. For demonstration purposes, the example in Figure 8.21 uses only two keyframes. However, more than two keyframes can be used with the motion guide. In each keyframe, the leaf is snapped to one end of the path. If you use more than two keyframes, you can snap the middle keyframes to where the leaf should be on the path

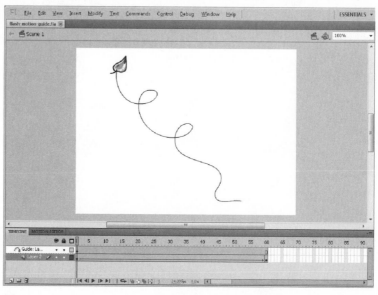

(a)

**Figure 8.21** A motion guide animation where the black line across the stage is the path used as a motion guide on the layer above the leaf layer on the timeline. (a) Keyframe at frame 1: The leaf symbol instance is snapped at the beginning of the path. (*continued*)

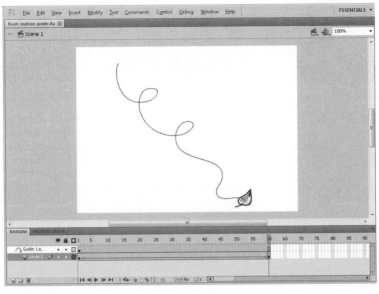

(b)

**Figure 8.21** (*continued*) (b) A second keyframe at frame 60: The leaf symbol instance is snapped at the end of the path.

at those keyframes. In addition, the leaf at the beginning and ending keyframes can be snapped to the middle of the path; it does not have to be snapped at either end of the path.

The sequence of this motion guide animation is shown in every other frame with the corresponding frame number in Figure 8.22. Frames 1 and 60 are the keyframes where the leaf object is snapped to the two ends of the path. The rotation of the leaf in all of the in-between frames is interpolated while following the motion guide. The motion guide,

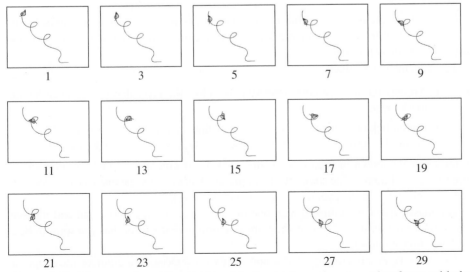

**Figure 8.22** The example motion guide animation is shown in every other frame with the corresponding frame number. (*continued*)

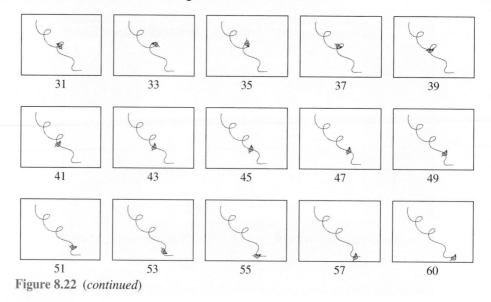

**Figure 8.22** (*continued*)

**Creating Classic Tween Using Motion Guide in Flash** A screen-capture movie shows how to create a motion guide for a Classic tween.

whether it is made hidden in Flash or not, will not appear in the published movie. You do not need to worry about making the guide invisible on the timeline. This example duplicates the path onto a regular layer so that the path shows up in the animation to give you a visual reference of the motion of the leaf object. You do not need to do that.

### 8.6.5 Mask

A *mask* defines areas to *reveal* the maskee layer. The *maskee layer* is the layer being masked. Think of the content in the mask layer as creating a hole that lets the underlying maskee layer show through.

To create the mask effect:

**Step 1** Arrange the maskee layer immediately below the layer that you want to be the mask layer.

**Step 2** Right-click on the mask layer on the timeline, and select Mask. You will see that the maskee layer is indented (Figure 8.23a). It is now linked to the mask layer.

In the example shown in Figure 8.23, the mask layer contains a black circular shape (Figure 8.23b). Figure 8.23c shows the resulting mask effect after the mask layer is locked. You can unlock the mask layer at any time to edit the mask.

The mask layer can be linked with one or more maskee layers. You can add maskee layers to an existing mask layer by dragging and dropping the layer that you want to be a maskee onto the mask layer.

The mask layer can contain shapes and symbol instances. The color of the shape or symbol instance does not matter; the color of the mask will not show up anywhere in the resulting mask effect and will not affect the color of the maskee.

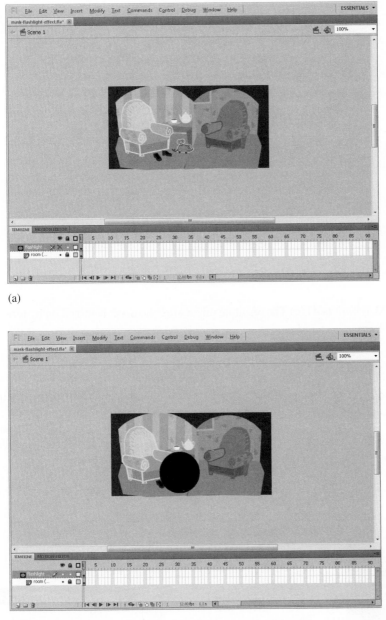

(a)

(b)

**Figure 8.23** Mask in Flash. (a) The visual content on a maskee layer, which is the layer being masked. (b) The black circle is the content on the mask layer in this example. (*continued*)

The shapes or symbol instances in the mask layer can be animated to create interesting effects. In this example, the black circular shape could have been animated to move across the stage using tweening. This will create a spotlight effect that searches for a mouse and reveals only a small part of the room. Masks can be used creatively in combination with tweening to create interesting animation. Let's look at two examples.

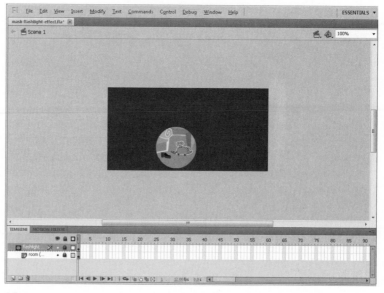

(c)

**Figure 8.23** (*continued*) (c) The resulting effect after the mask is turned on by locking the mask layer.

> ✐ **Animating a Mask in Flash** A screen-capture movie shows how to create the x-ray animation example by motion tweening the mask.

### Mask Animation Example 1: X-ray Effect

In this example, a skeleton created on a black rectangle (Figure 8.24a) serves as the maskee. The rectangle (Figure 8.24b) that represents the scanner bar is the mask. Figure 8.24c shows the resulting mask effect.

If a man graphic (Figure 8.25a) is placed in a layer beneath the mask effect (Figure 8.25b) and aligned with the skeleton position, it will create an illusion that the scanner bar is letting you see through the man (Figure 8.25c).

Note that the man graphic in this example is not a mask or a maskee. It is not part of the mask effect at all. It is on a regular layer. The mask effect works without the man graphic.

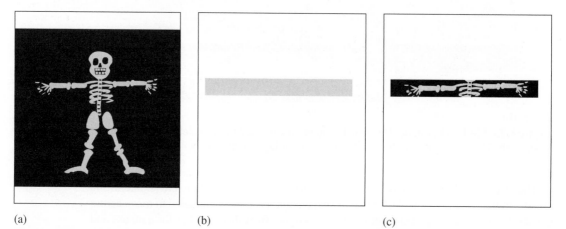

(a)  (b)  (c)

**Figure 8.24** (a) The skeleton is the maskee. (b) A rectangular bar representing a scanner bar used as the mask. (c) The resulting mask effect.

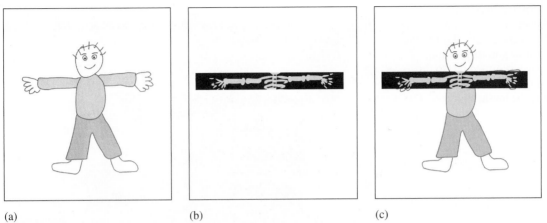

(a)  (b)  (c)

**Figure 8.25** (a) Graphic of a man. (b) Resulting mask effect of the scanner bar masking the skeleton. (c) The mask effect overlays on top of the man graphic, giving an illusion that the man is being x-rayed.

However, with the man graphic placed beneath the mask effect, it creates the desired illusion and gives more meaning to the animation.

## Mask Example 2: Beaming Up and Down

In this example, an animated mask is used to animate the appearance and disappearance of an alien from a spaceship (Figure 8.26).

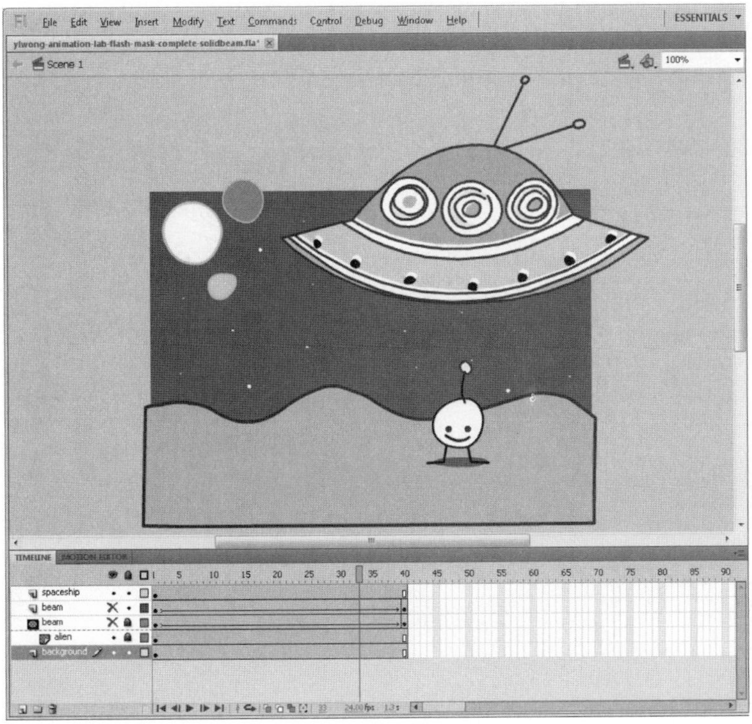

> **Animating a Mask in Flash: X-ray Effect (Lab)** A lab exercise to: (1) create a mask and (2) animate a mask for an interesting X-ray effect.

**Figure 8.26** An animated mask used in conjunction with non-mask animation to create interesting effects. (a) A spaceship and an alien stay static throughout this beaming sequence. (*continued*)

(a)

**Figure 8.26** (*continued*) (b) The rectangle below the spaceship is the mask. The mask is turned off in the figure to show you its position. (c) The mask is turned on, so the alien is showing through the area defined by the mask.

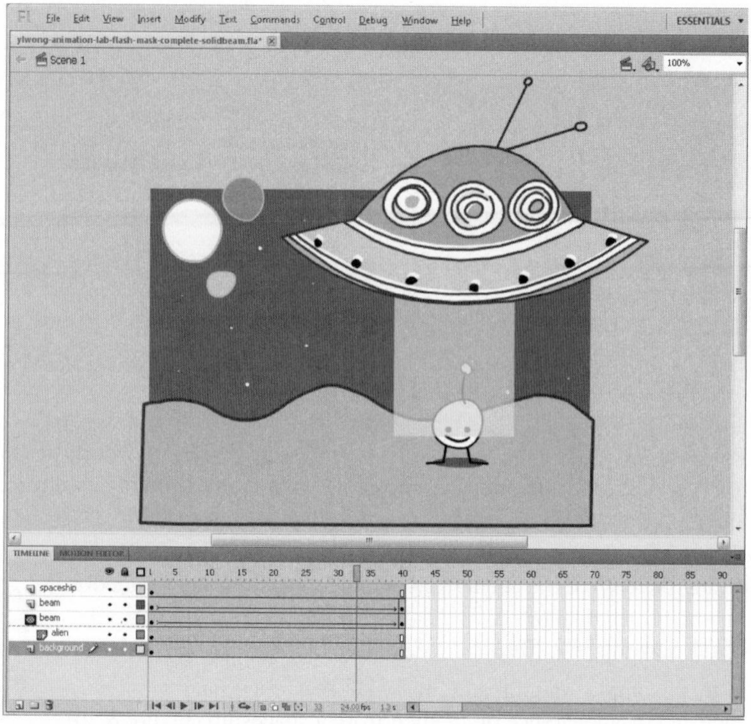

(b)

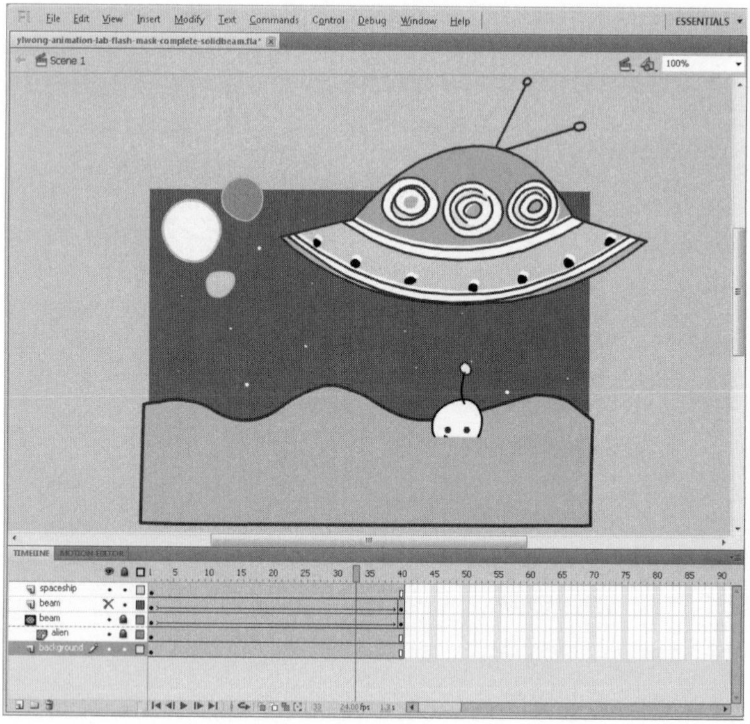

(c)

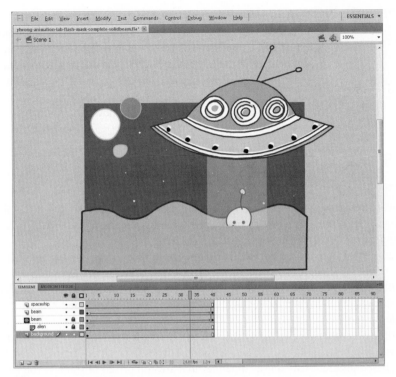

(d)

(e)

**Figure 8.26** (*continued*) (d) A layer (regular, non-masking, and non-masked) that contains a rectangle filled with a semitransparent color is placed on top of the mask layer. (e) The overlaying beam is filled with a gradient instead of a solid color.

To add the light beam, a tweened animation of a light beam on a separate layer is overlaid on the mask effect and synchronized with the mask's animation to create an illusion that the alien is being beaming up and down. Instead of a solid color, the overlaying beam can be filled with a gradient of varying opacities to make it look more like a beam of light (Figure 8.26e).

⌐ Animating a Mask in Flash: Beaming Up and Down (Lab) A lab exercise to: (1) create a mask, (2) animate a mask, and (3) create another layer for the light beam that is visible and synchronizes the motion of the mask.

It is noteworthy that the opacity of the graphics used for the mask does not affect the mask effect at all. The resulting mask effect will be the same as that shown in Figure 8.26c regardless of the opacity of the mask graphic. The soft-edged light beam shown in Figure 8.26e is not because of the opacity of the mask but is produced by overlaying a soft-edged light beam (placed on a regular, non-mask layer) on the masked area shown in Figure 8.26c.

## 8.7 SUMMARY

### Multimedia Authoring

Multimedia authoring is the process of creating a multimedia production. It involves assembling or sequencing different media elements, adding interactivity, and then packaging the production for distribution to end users.

The two most common forms of distributing multimedia productions are stand-alone apps or executables and movies that play back in a Web browser. Publishing in any of these two formats allows others to view your finished project without the authoring environment. Flash lets you publish your movie as a stand-alone executable, called projector, and an SWF file for the Web.

Multimedia authoring programs such as Flash support animation creation and have their own scripting languages. Flash's scripting language is called ActionScript. Flash is a frame-based program which uses timelines that are comprised of frames. You can create frame-based animations using frame-by-frame and tweening techniques. With scripting support, you also can create animation using scripts. Scripting lets you incorporate interactivity and nonlinear playback in your multimedia project.

### Flash's Workspace

This chapter gives you an overview of Flash's workspace, and introduces you the Tools panel, Stage, Timeline panel, Property Inspector, and Library panel.

### Shapes and Symbols

The visual items used on the Stage in a Flash file can be categorized as two types: shapes and symbols. They have different properties, purposes, and requirements.

- A shape is made up of strokes and/or fills.
- A symbol can contain shapes and other symbols. Symbols are stored in the Library panel and can be reused throughout the project. To place a symbol on the Stage, you can drag the symbol from the Library panel onto the Stage.

There are three types of symbols: graphic, button, and movie clip. Graphic symbols are mainly used for static graphics. It can contain shapes and other graphic symbol instances They can be placed inside another graphic, button, or movie clip symbol. Buttons can contain shapes, movie clip instances, and sounds. Buttons can be controlled using ActionScript in response to mouse clicks and rollovers. A button's timeline only has four special-purpose frames, each corresponds to a mouse action on the button: up, over, down, and hit. Unlike a button, each movie clip has a full timeline for frame-based animation. Movie clips can contain shapes, instances of any of the three types of symbols, ActionScript, and sounds. Instances of movie clips can be controlled using ActionScript in response to mouse and keyboard interaction. Adding interactivity is one of the main purposes for using movie clips in interactive projects and games.

## Tweening

Tweening is an effective way to create movement and visual changes over time. There are two types of tweening in Flash: motion tween and shape tween. Shape tweens create the animation of a shape morphing into another. For tweening motion, there are two different types of tweens: Motion tweens and Classic tweens. A Motion tween begins with a keyframe and contains one or more property keyframes. A property keyframe belongs to a tween span. You can specify the property value, such as position, scale, rotation, and skew, for a property keyframe. The in-between frames are filled in automatically by interpolating the properties of the content in the two immediate keyframes. Classic tweens work similarly to Motion tweens but use regular keyframes and allow tweening of a symbol instance's color effect and opacity.

## Motion Path and Motion Guide

The motion path (for Motion tweens) and motion guide (for Classic tweens) allow you to animate a symbol instance following a path that you draw. A motion path is automatically generated for each Motion tween span. You can use the Selection and Subselection tools to edit the path the way you would edit a stroke. You also can draw a stroke to use as the motion path. The path for controlling the motion of a Classic tween is placed on a motion guide layer. In order for the symbol instance to follow the path, the symbol instance in each keyframe in the tween span needs to be snapped onto the path.

## Mask

A mask defines areas to reveal the maskee layer(s). The maskee layer is the layer being masked. The mask layer can be linked with one or more maskee layers. The shapes or symbol instances in the mask layer can be animated to create interesting effects, such as a moving spotlight effect.

## TERMS

# LEARNING AIDS

The following learning aids can be found at the book's companion Web site.

## Frame-by-Frame, Tweening, and Scripted Animation
A side-by-side comparison of frame-by-frame, tweening, and scripted animation using the flying bird example shown in Figure 8.7.

## Adjusting the Speed of an Animation: Frame Rate versus Number of Frames
A side-by-side comparison of the original sequence and two approaches shown in Figure 8.8.

## Creating Shapes in Flash
A screen-capture movie shows how to create a simple shape using the Pencil, Pen, Ink, and Paint Bucket tools.

## Modifying Shapes in Flash
A screen-capture movie shows how to modify a shape.

## Creating Symbols in Flash
A screen-capture movie shows how to create (1) a new symbol and (2) a symbol by converting from a shape.

## Practice Drawing (Lab)
Practice Flash drawing and painting tools, and create movie clip symbols. Create two files:

1. X-ray (Figure 8.14)
2. hairstyles (Figure 8.15)

The X-ray file will be used to create tweened animation in a lab later in this chapter. The hairstyles file will be used in a lab in Chapter 10, where you will learn how to add interactivity to allow the user to change the hairstyle on the character's head by clicking on one of the hairstyle choices.

## Creating Motion Tween in Flash
A screen-capture movie shows how to create a Motion tween animation.

## Creating Classic Tween in Flash
A screen-capture movie shows how to create a Classic tween animation.

## Creating Shape Tween in Flash
A screen-capture movie shows how to create a Shape tween animation.

## Creating an Animation in Flash—Tweening (Lab)
A lab practice exercise to: (1) practice creating shapes and symbols and (2) create an animation using Shape, Classic, and Motion tweens.

## Creating Classic Tween Using Motion Guide in Flash
A screen-capture movie shows how to use a motion guide for a Classic tween.

## Animating a Mask in Flash
A screen-capture movie shows how to create the X-ray animation example by motion tweening the mask.

## Animating a Mask in Flash: X-ray Effect (Lab)
A lab exercise to: (1) create a mask and (2) animate a mask for an interesting X-ray effect.

## Animating a Mask in Flash: Beaming Up and Down (Lab)
A lab exercise to: (1) create a mask, (2) animate a mask, and (3) create another layer for the light beam that is visible and synchronizes the motion of the mask.

## REVIEW QUESTIONS

When applicable, please choose all correct answers.

1. To publish a Flash movie intended for the *Web*, you should publish your Flash movie as a _____.

   A. .swf
   B. projector
   C. .fla

2. To publish a Flash movie intended as a *stand-alone executable*, you should publish your Flash movie as a _____.

   A. .swf
   B. projector
   C. .fla

3. Which of the following animation techniques is more dynamic, allowing the animation to respond to user interaction?

   A. Frame by frame
   B. Tweening
   C. Animation by scripting

4. Which of the following animation techniques does *not* require you to explicitly create visual content in every frame?

   A. Frame by frame
   B. Tweening
   C. Animation by scripting

5. In a tweened animation, the content in the in-between frames is _____.

   A. drawn by the animator
   B. randomly selected by the computer from a sequence of images
   C. selected by the computer from a sequence of images in the order specified by the animator
   D. interpolated by the computer based on the two immediate keyframes

6. Which of the following panels is made up of a stack of layers with frames across?

   A. Tools
   B. Stage
   C. Timeline
   D. Property Inspector
   E. Library

7. In which of the following panels can you create keyframes?

   A. Tools
   B. Stage
   C. Timeline
   D. Property Inspector
   E. Library

8. Which of the following panels contains tools that you can use to draw vector graphics?

   A. Tools
   B. Stage
   C. Timeline panel
   D. Property Inspector
   E. Library

9. Which of the following panels displays the properties of the selected item?

   A. Tools
   B. Stage
   C. Timeline panel
   D. Property Inspector
   E. Library

10. **True/False:** If a graphic is in the gray area that is outside of the stage, the graphic will still show up when the movie plays.

11. How do you change the background color, stage size, and frame rate?

12. Based on the timeline shown in Figure 8.27, which frames do not have any content on the stage?

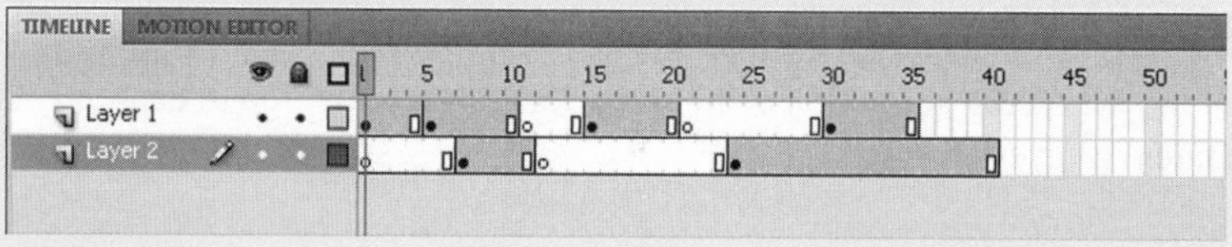

**Figure 8.27**

13. Based on the timeline shown in Figure 8.27, which frames have content from both Layer 1 and Layer 2 on the stage?

14. If you have an outline of a shape and want to fill its inside with a color, you use the _____ tool.

   A. paint bucket
   B. ink bottle

15. If you have a fill of a shape and want to create an outline around it, you use the _____ tool.

   A. paint bucket
   B. ink bottle

16. What are stored in the Library panel?

   A. symbols
   B. shapes
   C. both A and B

17. What are the three types of symbols in Flash?

18. If you use movie clips in your Flash movie, what is the menu item you should select in order to preview your movie properly?

   A. Control > Play
   B. Control > Test Movie

19. A _____ can contain instances of other graphic symbols.

    A. graphic symbol
    B. button symbol
    C. movie clip symbol

20. A _____ can contain instances of other graphic, button, and movie clip symbols.

    A. graphic symbol
    B. button symbol
    C. movie clip symbol

21. A graphic symbol can contain _____.

    A. shapes
    B. instances of graphic symbols
    C. instances of button symbols
    D. instances of movie clip symbols
    E. ActionScript
    F. sounds

22. A button symbol can contain _____.

    A. shapes
    B. instances of graphic symbols
    C. instances of button symbols
    D. instances of movie clip symbols
    E. ActionScript
    F. sounds

23. A movie clip symbol can contain _____.

    A. shapes
    B. instances of graphic symbols
    C. instances of button symbols
    D. instances of movie clip symbols
    E. ActionScript
    F. sounds

24. Scripts and sound work in a _____.

    A. graphic symbol
    B. button symbol
    C. movie clip symbol

25. In order to use script to control the behaviors of an instance of a symbol on the Stage, the symbol type has to be a _____.

    A. graphic symbol
    B. button symbol
    C. movie clip symbol
    D. any of the above

26. A symbol placed on the Stage is called a(n) _____ of that symbol.

   A. keyframe
   B. shape
   C. symbol
   D. instance
   E. tween

27. When you make changes to a _____, the changes will be reflected in all of its copies used on the Stage.

   A. shape
   B. symbol

28. When you click on an object on the Stage, how can you tell it is a symbol?

   A. Individual fills or strokes are being selected.
   B. A blue bounding box appears around the object.
   C. The Property Inspector shows its symbol type and symbol name.

29. Which type of tweening can be used to animate *symbol instances*?

   A. Classic tween
   B. Motion tween
   C. Shape tween

30. Which type of tweening can be used to animate *shapes*?

   A. Classic tween
   B. Motion tween
   C. Shape tween

31. You can animate the movement a symbol instance or shape by tweening its position. Name three other properties of a symbol instance or shape that you can animate using tweening.

32. What is the color of a *Motion tween* span in the Timeline panel?

   A. Purple
   B. Blue
   C. Green

33. What is the color of a *Shape tween* span in the Timeline panel?

   A. Purple
   B. Blue
   C. Green

34. **True/False:** Multiple symbol instances can be used in the same layer in a Motion tween span.

35. **True/False:** Multiple symbol instances can be used in the same layer in a Classic tween span.

36. If a Classic or Shape tween span has problems, a _____ will appear in the tween span in the Timeline panel.

   A. solid-line arrow
   B. dash line

**37.** If a tween sequence is not working, how would you go about troubleshooting? Tips: List the possible causes for a tween sequence not working.

**38.** Motion guides can be used in _____.

A. Classic tweens
B. Motion tweens
C. Shape tweens

**39.** **True/False:** The color and width of the path in the motion guide do not matter.

**40.** **True/False:** In order to hide the path in the motion guide during playback of the animation, you have to make the path invisible.

**41.** Which of the following is correct about masks?

A. The mask item *conceals* the area of linked layers that lie beneath it. The rest of the mask layer reveals everything else on these linked layers.
B. The mask item acts as a window that *reveals* the area of linked layers that lie beneath it. The rest of the mask layer conceals everything else on these linked layers.

**42.** In the Timeline panel, the _____ layer should be immediately above its _____ layer.

A. mask; maskee
B. maskee; mask

**43.** The resulting mask effect can be seen on the stage by locking the _____ layer.

A. mask
B. maskee

# Interactive Multimedia Authoring with Flash: ActionScript—Part 1

## TABLE OF CONTENTS

Courtesy of Cory Bullock

# 9

## KEY CONCEPTS

- Programming languages versus scripting languages
- Programming fundamentals: syntax, keywords, data types, variables, constants, statements, operators, expressions, control structures, functions, procedures, and parameters

## GENERAL LEARNING OBJECTIVES

In this chapter, you will learn

- The computer programming basics that multimedia authoring languages share.
- The basics for programming in ActionScript.

## 9.1 PROGRAMMING LANGUAGES VERSUS SCRIPTING LANGUAGES

A *programming language* specifies the rules for writing instructions that can be followed by a computer. There is a programming language that communicates with a computer through 0s and 1s. It is called *machine language*. Other programming languages that look more like natural language are called *high-level languages*. They are easier for humans to read and write, but they require more translation behind the scenes to make the instructions understandable by the computer. C++ and Java are examples of high-level programming languages.

*Scripting languages* are examples of very-high-level programming languages. Compared to full-fledged programming languages such as C++ and Java, scripting languages do not have a complex array of features that give the programmer control over the details of memory allocation and program execution efficiency. The advantage of scripting languages, however, is that they are easier for nonprogrammers to learn because they use keywords and syntax that look more like natural language, and they still provide enough features for the programmer to be creative in putting together a complex interactive project.

Multimedia authoring programs such as Adobe Flash and Director have their own scripting languages. Flash's scripting language is called ActionScript and Director's is called Lingo. ActionScript and Lingo let you add interactivity to your multimedia projects. The user can interact with your program through mouse clicks or key presses on the keyboard. What the movie does in response to such interaction is determined by your script.

Movie: As noted in Chapter 8, a multimedia production created in Flash or Director is often referred to as a movie. It does not mean video or film.

## 9.2 PROGRAMMING AND SCRIPTING FUNDAMENTALS—PART A

Sample ActionScript and Flash projects are widely available on the Web and in books. You may be able to use them in your project "as is." However, if these sample scripts do not do exactly what you have in mind, you will need to compromise your ideas in order to use them. With the knowledge of basic programming concepts and techniques, you will be able to read and modify the sample scripts to suit your need. You can also write your own scripts from scratch.

ActionScript shares the programming concepts and constructs that are common to all high-level programming languages—for example, variables, functions, conditions, loops, mouse events, and keyboard events. Learning how to program with ActionScript helps you learn other programming languages, and vice versa.

This section will first go over definitions of terms that are common to computer programming languages. These basic terms are interconnected. You may find that the further elaboration of a term may involve other terms that have not been introduced but will be covered later in the section. You may want to read through this section once and then come back and review to get a thorough understanding of these basic terms.

## 9.2.1 Syntax

The *syntax* of a programming or scripting language prescribes the ways in which statements must be written in order for them to be understood by the computer. The syntax of a programming language is like the rules of grammar and punctuation in human language, but the difference is that these rules must be followed *precisely* in computer programming.

Syntax defines things such as whether a statement must end in some kind of punctuation, what characters can be used in names, and what operator symbols are used for operations such as addition and subtraction.

Here are two of the rules of ActionScript 3.0:

- Case-sensitivity: Most programming languages are case-sensitive, and this includes ActionScript. This means that when you use the language's keywords and commands, or any custom-defined variables, their cases have to match exactly how they are originally defined.

   Keywords and variables will be explained later in this section. For now, to give you an idea of the case-sensitivity, a variable name `score` is different from `Score`.
- Each statement ends with a semicolon (`;`). This is optional if a single line of code contains only one statement. However, because many programming languages require ending each statement with a semicolon, all the ActionScript examples in this text follow this rule.

## 9.2.2 Data Types

The value assigned to a variable could be one of many different types, such as integers, individual characters from the alphabet, and strings of text. The type of the value is called its *data type*.

Many programming languages require that you explicitly declare the data type of a variable when the variable is first created. This is called *strict data typing*. Earlier versions of ActionScript (1.0 and 2.0) are *loosely typed* languages. This means that you do not have to specify the data type of a variable when you declare it, and data types are converted automatically as needed during script execution. The current ActionScript 3.0 is strictly typed.

Table 9.1 lists the data types used in the ActionScript 3.0 examples in this book. You will be able to find more information about these data types and other data types in Flash Help.

**TABLE 9.1   A List of Data Types Used in the ActionScript Examples in This Book**

| Data Type | Description |
|---|---|
| int | Stands for ***integers***, which means whole numbers. |
| | Many values stored in programs are whole numbers that may be positive or negative, for example, scores in a game. In some situations a value can be a floating-point number, but you want to store it as a whole number. For example, in keeping time in seconds, it is possible to keep the time as 5.2 seconds. However, depending on the situation, you may only want to keep the time as a whole number—for example, simply round 5.2 seconds to 5 seconds. In this case, you would need to declare the variable that keeps the time as int, or better yet, uint (see below) if it will only have non-negative values. |
| | There is a limit on how large an integer can be stored. (Recall that, as discussed in Chapter 1, computers deal with finite data.) For introductory-level examples and projects, you seldom exceed this limit. However, if you are interested in knowing the limit of an integer in ActionScript, an int variable is stored as a 32-bit integer and the valid integers that can be stored range from $-2,147,483,648$ $(-2^{31})$ to $2,147,483,647$ $(2^{31} - 1)$, inclusive. |
| uint | Stands for ***unsigned integers***, which means non-negative integers. |
| | Like int, an uint variable is also stored as a 32-bit integer but non-negative only. This means that the valid integers that can be stored range from 0 to $4,294,967,295$ $(2^{32} - 1)$, inclusive. Thus, it can accept larger positive numbers than int with the same memory (32 bits for each variable)—an advantage over int for variables that will never have negative values. For introductory-level examples and projects, in which the value of a variable seldom exceeds the limit of an int, using int or uint for a variable will not make noticeable differences. |
| | Examples where values stored in programs are non-negative whole numbers are number of people, number of collected items, number of bullets fired in a game, and number of lives. |
| Number | This can be an integer, unsigned integer, and floating-point number. You can think of a floating-point number as a number with a decimal point, for example, 1.1, 20.849 and 0.2157. |
| | Like int and uint, the Number data type also has a limit but the limit is larger than most projects actually need. The Number data type uses 53 bits to store integers. Thus, the range of integer values it can store ranges from $9,007,199,254,740,992$ $(-2^{53})$ to $9,007,199,254,740,992$ $(2^{53})$. |
| | Recall the eye signal analogy discussed in Chapter 1—the more bits you use to represent information, the more distinct numbers of values you can represent. Now you see why the Number data type (53 bits) has a wider range than int and uint (32 bits). |
| | Although the Number data type accepts integers, int and uint variables operate faster and more efficiently than Number. Thus, for better efficiency, you should use the Number data type only for (1) floating-point numbers or (2) integer values larger than the 32-bit int and uint types can store. |
| String | Simply speaking, the String data type represents a sequence of characters. |
| | The values are enclosed within quotation marks—for example, "This is a text string.". |
| | An empty text string is written as "". |
| | Note: The default value for a variable declared with the String data type that has not been initialized is null. The value null is not the same as the empty string (""). |
| Boolean | The Boolean data type has only two possible values: true and false. |
| | The default value of a Boolean variable that has not been initialized is false. |

## WHAT HAPPENS WHEN THE VALUE OF AN int OR uint IS OUTSIDE THE RANGE?

As noted in Table 9.1, in ActionScript, the valid integers that can be stored in an int variable range from $-2,147,483,648$ ($-2^{31}$) to $2,147,483,647$ ($2^{31} - 1$), inclusive. Say, if you try to store the value $2,147,483,648$ (larger than the maximum of the range by 1) in an int variable, the value will get "wrapped around" to the negative end of the range and become $-2,147,483,648$. Similarly, if you try to store the value $-2,147,483,649$ (less than the minimum of the range by 1) in an int variable, the value will get "wrapped around" to the positive end of the range and become $2,147,483,647$.

Valid integers that can be stored in an uint variable range from 0 to $4,294,967,295$ ($2^{32} - 1$), inclusive. If you try to store the value $4,294,967,296$ (larger than the maximum of the range by 1) in an uint variable, the value will get "wrapped around" to the other end and become 0. If you try to store the value $-1$ (less than the minimum of the range by 1) in an uint variable, you will get a warning about trying to store a negative value in an uint variable and the value will get "wrapped around" to the other end to become $4,294,967,295$.

> Initializing a variable means giving the variable a starting value.

## 9.2.3 Variables

*Variables* are elements used to store values in your program. The value of a variable can be updated and retrieved when the program is running. There are three properties associated with a variable: name, value, and data type.

- **Variable name:** Data is stored in memory as bits (recall the discussion in Chapter 1). A variable name lets you refer to the data's memory location by name.
- **Value:** The value of a variable is the actual data stored.
- **Data type:** Data type specifies the type of data stored.

To use a variable, you need to first declare it—give the variable a name. To declare a variable in ActionScript 3.0, you use the var statement with the variable name. Append the variable name with a colon (:), followed by the variable's data type.

The general syntax to declare a variable in ActionScript 3.0 is like this:

```
var variableName:dataType;
```

For example, the following statement declares a variable called highScore. It is an integer (int).

```
var highScore:int;
```

You can also assign a value to the variable at the declaration, like this:

```
var highScore:int = 0;
```

### Variable Naming

All languages have rules about what constitutes a legal name for a variable. Here is a list of ActionScript rules, which also apply to many programming languages. Variable names

- must contain only letters, numbers, and underscore (_) characters.
- cannot begin with a number.
- can include the dollar sign ($) in ActionScript, even as the first character of the name.
- must not contain spaces.

The general naming convention is that when variable names consist of more than one word, they are written in *camel case*, for example, `sheepCount` and `highScore`. This means

- the variable name starts with a lowercase letter, and
- an uppercase letter is used for starting every new word.

This is the most common practice and is used in all the ActionScript examples in this book.

Another common naming convention is to use all lowercase letters and separate each word with an underscore (_) like this: `sheep_count` and `high_score`.

---

### ? Self-Test Exercise: Variable Names

Which of the following variable names are valid?

1. myScore
2. my_score
3. my score
4. my-score
5. my4score
6. 4score

#### Answers to Self-Test Questions

1. valid
2. valid
3. invalid; no space is allowed
4. invalid; no dash is allowed
5. valid
6. invalid; cannot start with a number

---

### Giving a Value to a Variable

Giving a value to a variable is called *assigning a value* to a variable. The statement that assigns a value to a variable is called an *assignment statement*. Finding out the current value of a variable is called *accessing the variable*.

---

### VARIABLES VERSUS STRING LITERALS

`score` (without quotation marks) and `"score"` in the code have different meanings.

`score` (without the quotation marks) is a variable name. A variable has a value. The value of a variable `score` can be an integer or a text string, depending on its data type.

If `score` has a value of 3, then the expression `score + 9` gives you a value of 12.

A text string is enclosed within quotation marks, for example, `"score"`. `"score"` is a string literal, and it is a value by itself.

In ActionScript, the expression `"score" + 9` gives you a concatenated text string `"score9"`.

**? Self-Test Exercise: Variables versus String Literals**

**Suppose the value of the variable `score` is equal to 3.**

1. An expression `score + score` gives a _____ (text string or number?) equal to _____.
2. An expression score + "score" gives a _____ (text string or number?) equal to _____.
3. An expression "score" + "score" gives a _____ (text string or number?) equal to _____.
4. An expression `score + ""` gives a _____ (text string or number?) equal to _____.

**Answers to Self-Test Questions**

1. number, 6
2. text string, "3score"
3. text string, "scorescore"
4. text string, "3"

## 9.2.4 Statements

*Statements* are instructions that can be executed. Statements can be used to:

- give values to variables—assignment statements, which will be explained in the next subsection.
- cause things to happen only under certain conditions—for example, `if` statements, which will be explained later in the Control Structure section.
- cause instructions to repeat—for example, for-loop, which will also be explained later in the Control Structure section.

## 9.2.5 Assignment Statements

As noted, an assignment statement assigns a value to a variable. In most languages, you use the = operator to assign a value to a variable. For example, the statement:

```
score = 0;
```

is used to assign a value of 0 to a variable named `score`.

One or more variables may be used on the right-hand side of the = operator. For example:

```
newBalance = sales + tax;
```

This statement adds the values of the variables `sales` and `tax`. The sum is then assigned to the variable `newBalance`. Suppose the variable `sales` has a value of 110 and `tax` has a value of 7.7 before this statement is executed. Then after it is executed, `newBalance` has a value of 117.7.

It is possible for a variable to appear on both the left- and right-hand sides of an assignment statement. For example:

```
score = score + 1;
```

This statement increments the value of the variable `score` by 1. Suppose the variable `score` has a value of 10 before this statement is executed. Then after it is executed, it has a value of 11.

It is noteworthy that the operator = in an assignment statement does not have the same meaning as the equal sign in a mathematical equation. In an assignment statement, the value on the right-hand side of the = operator is assigned to the variable on the left-hand side of the = operator. The direction of the assignment matters. It is always the value on the right-hand side being assigned to the variable on the left-hand side of the = operator. Thus, it is always a single variable on the left-hand side. To show you the significance of the direction of the assignment and the difference between the = operator and the equal sign in mathematical equations, let's revisit the previous examples of assignment statements.

- In mathematics, the equation `score` = 0 is the same as 0 = `score` whereas writing 0 = `score` in your code will cause an error message.
- Similarly, writing `sales` + `tax` = `newBalance` in your code will cause an error message whereas in mathematics, writing the equation `sales` + `tax` = `newBalance` is same as writing `newBalance` = `sales` + `tax`.
- Writing `score` + 1 = `score` in your code will cause an error message. In mathematics, the equation `score` = `score` + 1 is the same as `score` + 1 = `score`, but it does not make sense because `score` does not have a solution to satisfy the equation. On the other hand, in programming, `score` = `score` + 1 is a valid assignment statement syntactically. The value of `score` may be, say, 10 and it will be changed to 11 after the assignment statement `score` = `score` + 1 is executed.

There are more assignment operators in addition to the = operator. They will be discussed in the next section.

## 9.2.6 Operators

*Operators* are symbols that cause a new value to be calculated from one or more other values (operands). This section introduces five common types of operators.

### Arithmetic Operators: +, −, *, /, %

An arithmetic operator takes two other values (or operands) and performs an arithmetic calculation to give a new value.

For example, the + (addition) operator is used to add two or more values together to produce a new value—2 + 3 gives a value of 5.

Other common operators are − (subtraction), * (multiplication), / (division), and % (modulo). All of these five operators, +, −, *, /, and %, are available in ActionScript.

The modulo (%) operator gives the remainder in a division, as in these examples:

- 20 % 2 gives 0, because the remainder of 20 divided by 2 is 0.
- 20 % 11 gives 9 because the remainder of 20 divided by 11 is 9

The modulo operator is useful in determining whether the value of a variable is even or odd by dividing the variable by 2. The value is an even number if the remainder is 0; it is an odd number if the remainder is 1.

Another example use of modulo is converting number of seconds into minutes and seconds. Some computer games use a timer to time the player's progress. In ActionScript, the timer counts time in milliseconds. However, the timer displayed in a game is often in minutes and seconds. Let's step through an example of converting milliseconds into minutes and seconds and then construct the statements for the conversion. Suppose the time is 437900 milliseconds. To convert it into seconds, you divide 437900 by 1000 to get

437.9 seconds. To find out how many minutes, you divide 437.9 seconds by 60 seconds/minute to get the quotient 7. The remainder is the number of seconds. This is where the modulo is used. Suppose the variables msecs, minutes, and secs have been declared as int and will store the number of milliseconds, calculated number of minutes and seconds respectively. Thus, the statements for calculating minutes and seconds from milliseconds are:

```
secs = msecs / 1000;
minutes = secs / 60;
secs = secs % 60;
```

Note that the data types for these variables in the example are all int, the values are truncated (not rounded) to integers. For example, if the variable msecs has a value of 437900, the variable secs will have a value of 437 after the first statement.

## Assignment Operators: =, +=, −=, *=, /=, %=

You have seen the usage of the = operator in assignment statements. This section will show you more assignment operators (Table 9.2) that let you write some types of assignment statements in shorthand forms.

**TABLE 9.2   Assignment Operators**

|  | Equivalent Statements |
|---|---|
| score += 3; | score = score + 3; |
| score −= 3; | score = score − 3; |
| score *= 3; | score = score * 3; |
| score /= 3; | score = score / 3; |
| score %= 3; | score = score % 3; |

For example, the statement,

```
score = score + 1;
```

can be written using the *addition assignment operator* (+=) operator as:

```
score += 1;
```

Similarly,

```
score = score − 1;
```

is equivalent to:

```
score −= 1;
```

using the *subtraction assignment operator* (−=). += and −= are useful because increment and decrement are very common operations in a program.

There are also the *multiplication assignment operator* (*=), *division assignment operator* (/=), and *modulo assignment operator* (%=).

## Postfix Operators: ++, −−

The *postfix operators* (++ and −−) take only one operand and either increase or decrease its value by one. Table 9.3 shows the usage of these operators and the equivalent statements.

**TABLE 9.3** **Equivalent Statements for Postfix Operators**

|  | Equivalent Statements |
|---|---|
| score++; | score = score + 1; |
| score−−; | score = score − 1; |

## Comparison Operators: >, >=, <, <=, ==, !=

A *comparison operator* (>, >=, <, <=, ==, !=) takes two values (or operands) and performs a comparison to give one of the two possible values: true or false. For example, the operands in the expression 2 > 3 are 2 and 3. The comparison, 2 greater than 3, gives a value of false.

Table 9.4 shows a list of the comparison operators with a brief description for each.

**TABLE 9.4** **A List of the Comparison Operators**

| Comparison Operator | Description |
|---|---|
| > | greater than |
| >= | greater than or equal to |
| < | less than |
| <= | less than or equal to |
| == | equal to |
| != | not equal to |

Suppose the current value of a variable score is 15.

- The expression score > 10 gives true.
- The expression score >= 10 gives true.
- The expression score > 15 gives false.
- The expression score >= 15 gives true.
- The expression score == 15 gives true.

Note that the equal to (==) operator for comparison has two equal signs. It is different from the assignment operator (=).

- The == operator performs a comparison on two operands and gives a value of true or false. The values of the two operands are not altered after the comparison operation.
- The = operator assigns the value on the right-hand side of the = operator to the variable on the left-hand side of the = operator. The value of the operand on the left of the = operator is changed to the value of the operand on the right of the = operator.

Table 9.5 demonstrates the differences by comparing player == 1 and player = 1.

It is important to understand (and remember) the difference between the == and = operators. To see the significance of the difference, let's look at an example. In a tic-tac-toe game, two players take turns. Suppose you use a variable named player to keep track of the player's turn. Each time after a player marks a cell on the game board, you

**TABLE 9.5   Differences between Two Operators: Comparison for Equality (==) and Assignment (=)**

| | `player == 1` | `player = 1` |
|---|---|---|
| **Type of operation being performed** | Comparison for equality<br><br>It is like getting an answer to the question: Is `player` equal to 1? And you would expect an answer of Yes or No. | Assignment<br><br>It is an action to be carried out: Assign a value to `player`. You would not expect an answer of Yes or No after the action has been carried out. |
| **Results from the operation** | The expression `player == 1` will give one of the two possible values: `true` or `false`.<br><br>If the value of the variable `player` is 1, then the expression `player == 1` gives the value `true`. Otherwise, it will give the value `false`.<br><br>The value of the variable `player` is not changed after the comparison. | The value of the variable player becomes 1. |

check the value of `player`. If `player` is equal to 1, the value of `player` is switched to 2 and it becomes player 2's turn to mark a cell. Otherwise, the value of `player` is switched to 1 and player 1 is allowed to mark a cell. If you mistakenly use `player = 1` instead of `player == 1` to check whose turn it is, the variable `player` will always be assigned with 1 regardless of the current value of `player`. And checking the expression player = 1 will always give the value true if player is not zero. This means that your program will always switch to player 2. Then it always becomes player 2's turn and player 1's will never be allowed to mark a cell.

## Logical Operators: &&, ||, !

The three commonly used logical operators are:

&&   logical AND
||   logical OR
!   logical NOT

*Logical operators* operate on two Boolean values to give a new Boolean value. This may sound complicated, but you have been using these types of operators in daily life, for example:

> If it rains *and* you have to go out, bring an umbrella.

With an "and" in this `if` statement, both conditions have to be true in order to carry out the instruction. You bring an umbrella only when both of these conditions are true. If it rains but you are not going out, you would not bring an umbrella. If you have to go out but it is not raining, you would not bring an umbrella, either.

However, if you say:

> If it rains *or* you have to go out, bring an umbrella.

Then you bring an umbrella whenever it rains regardless of whether you are going out or not. You also bring an umbrella whenever you are going out whether it is raining or not.

The logical operators are often used in conditional statements. It will make more sense when you see examples in the section of if statements later in this chapter.

### 9.2.7 Constants

*Constants* are elements whose values do not change in a program. You can think of constants as "read-only variables." A numeric value is a constant. For example, the number 0 itself is a constant. Aside from numeric constants, many languages have predefined constants in the form of words, such as the constants true and false in ActionScript. Constants like this generally have the obvious meaning.

ActionScript 3.0 also has predefined constants such as Keyboard.UP, Keyboard.DOWN, Keyboard.LEFT, Keyboard.RIGHT and Keyboard.SPACE to represent the *keycodes* (a number associated with each key on the keyboard) for the up, down, left, and right arrow keys, and space bar, respectively. You can use these constants by calling these defined names, saving you time from looking up the numeric keycode values.

You can also declare constants in ActionScript 3.0. To declare a constant in Action-Script 3.0, you use the const statement with the constant's name. Append the constant name with a colon (:), followed by its data type.

The general syntax to declare a variable in ActionScript 3.0 is like this:

```
const constantName:dataType = value;
```

For example, the following statement declares a constant called PENALTY that has a value of 50. It is an unsigned (non-negative) integer (uint).

```
const PENALTY:uint = 50;
```

#### Constant Naming

As with variables, spaces are not allowed in a constant's name. The common naming convention for constants is to use

- all uppercase letters, and
- underscore (_) to separate the words, if the name consists of more than one word.

For example:

```
GRAVITY
MAX_SHEEP
```

This book uses this naming convention for constants in all ActionScript examples.

### CONSTANTS VERSUS VARIABLES

If, instead of declaring a constant for an element that does not change its value in a program, you declare it as a variable, the program generally would run the same from the user's perspective. However, for compiled languages, such as ActionScript and C++, using constants can make the code run faster than using variables. For introductory-level examples and projects, however, the speed-up generally is indiscernible. Nevertheless, it is a good learning experience to adopt the practice of using constants like in large real-world projects.

With compile languages, the code you entered is converted to a set of machine-specific instructions before being saved as an executable file.

## 9.2.8 Keywords

In general, *keywords* refer to reserved words that have a special meaning in a programming language. These words are not to be used for any other purpose, such as variable or function names, because they are predefined with special meanings in the language. For example, the word `if` is a keyword in most programming languages. Giving a variable the name `if` will result in an error message.

The following list is a small set of keywords in ActionScript. You will see these keywords in the examples throughout the multimedia authoring chapters of this book.

```
break
case
const
default
else
false
for
function
if
null
return
switch
this
true
var
void
while
```

## 9.2.9 Expressions

An *expression* is any part of a statement that produces a value. Example expressions and the values produced by these expressions are shown in Table 9.6.

| TABLE 9.6 | Example Expressions and the Values That the Expressions Produce |
|---|---|
| **Expression** | **Value That the Expression Produces** |
| `2 + 2` | 4 |
| `(a + b + c)/3` | the sum of the values of the three variables, a, b, and c, divided by 3 |
| `a > b` | `true` or `false`, depending on whether the value of the variable a is greater than the value of b |

⌨ **Syntax Review and Code-Writing Exercise for Part 1 Materials** A worksheet for reviewing the syntax by writing general syntax and example code; the completed worksheet can be used as a quick reference for programming labs and for studying for tests and exams.

### ? Self-Test Exercise: Identify Programming Constructs

Before moving on to Part B of programming fundamentals, let's stop for a self-test exercise to review the materials you have learned so far.

### About This Exercise

The purposes of this exercise are:

(1) to let you look at the complete code of a program to get an idea of how the programming elements you have learned so far are placed together in a program, and

(2) to serve as a self-test by identifying the programming elements you have learned.

Figure 9.1 shows the complete code in ActionScript 3.0 for a simple shoot-them-up game. You are *not* expected to understand the code now. Most of the concepts and programming constructs used in the code have not been covered yet. So don't worry about understanding the complete code for now. All you need to do in this self-test is to identify the programming constructs you have learned so far, such as variables, constants, expressions, and operators. Think of this self-test exercise as a *Where's Waldo?* game.

```
1   const PENALTY:int = 50;
2   const MISSILE_SPEED:int = 7;
3   const SPACESHIP_SPEED:int = 5;
4
5   var isFired:Boolean = false;
6   var isHit:Boolean = false;
7   var missed:int = 0;
8
9   reset();
10
11  addEventListener(Event.ENTER_FRAME, OnGameLoop);
12  stage.addEventListener(KeyboardEvent.KEY_DOWN, onKeyControl);
13
14  function OnGameLoop(evt:Event):void
15  {
16     spaceship_mc.x += SPACESHIP_SPEED;
17
18     if (isFired == true)
19     {
20        missile_mc.y -= MISSILE_SPEED;
21     }
22
23     if (spaceship_mc.hitTestPoint(missile_mc.x, missile_mc.y, true) &&
       isHit == false)
24     {
25        isHit = true;
26        missed--;
27        spaceship_mc.gotoAndPlay("explosion");
28     }
29
30     if (spaceship_mc.x > stage.stageWidth + 100 || missile_mc.y < -50
       || spaceship_mc.currentFrame == spaceship_mc.totalFrames)
```

**Figure 9.1** A complete code for a simple shoot-them-up game shown in Figure 9.2. (*continued*)

```
31    {
32        reset();
33    }
34  }
35
36  function onKeyControl(evt:KeyboardEvent):void
37  {
38    if (isFired == false)
39    {
40        if (evt.keyCode == Keyboard.RIGHT)
41        {
42            missile_mc.x += MISSILE_SPEED;
43        }
44        else if (evt.keyCode == Keyboard.LEFT)
45        {
46            missile_mc.x -= MISSILE_SPEED;
47        }
48        else if (evt.keyCode == Keyboard.SPACE)
49        {
50            isFired = true;
51        }
52    }
53  }
54
55  function reset():void
56  {
57        if (isHit == false)
58        {
59            missed++;
60        }
61
62        isHit = false;
63        isFired = false;
64        spaceship_mc.x = -100;
65        spaceship_mc.y = missed * PENALTY;
66        spaceship_mc.gotoAndStop(1);
67        missile_mc.y = stage.stageHeight - 20;
68  }
```

**Figure 9.1** (*continued*)

To do this self-test, you do not need to know the logic behind the code. However, knowing how the game plays may help you understand the roles of some of the variables and constants in this program. Following is a description of how the game works. The Flash file can be downloaded from the book's Web site.

Figure 9.2 shows two screen shots of how this game works. When the game starts, a spaceship moves horizontally from left to right. The blue circle at the bottom of the screen is the missile (Figure 9.2a). The user can use the left and right arrow keys on the keyboard to move the missile horizontally. Pressing the space bar will fire the missile, which will travel up. If the missile hits the spaceship, you will see an explosion animation (Figure 9.2b). Then, the spaceship will start again from the left of the screen, but higher. On the other hand, if the missile misses the spaceship, the spaceship will start again from the left and move down 50 pixels closer to the missile—this is a penalty.

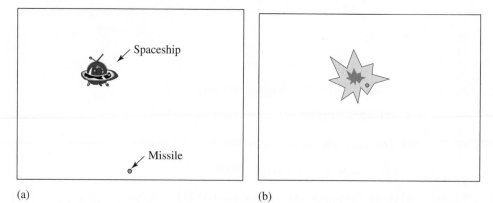

(a)                                    (b)

**Figure 9.2** How the game works: (a) A spaceship is moving across the screen from left to right. The user can control the horizontal position of the missile by using the left and right arrow keys. (b) Pressing the space bar will fire the missile. If it hits the spaceship, an explosion animation will play.

Questions

1. **Identify variables**

   There are three custom-defined variables defined in the code (Figure 9.1).
   (a) What are the names of these variables?
   (b) Where are they declared? Give the line number for each.
   (c) What is the data type of each variable?
   (d) What is the initial value assigned to each variable at declaration?
   (e) Where are these variables accessed or modified in the code? Give the line numbers for all the occurrences.

2. **Identify custom-defined constants**

   There are three custom-defined constants defined in the code (Figure 9.1).
   (a) What are the names of these constants?
   (b) Where are they declared? Give the line number for each.
   (c) What is the data type of each constant?
   (d) What is the value assigned to each constant?

3. **Identify ActionScript predefined constants**

   There are at least five predefined constants used in the code (Figure 9.1).
   (a) What are the names of these constants?
   (b) Where are they used? Give the line number for each.

4. **Identify assignment operators**

   Circle in the code all the occurrences of the following operators. Mark "none" for those that are not used in the code at all.
   (a) addition assignment ($+=$)
   (b) subtraction assignment ($-=$)
   (c) multiplication assignment ($*=$)
   (d) division assignment ($/=$)
   (e) postfix increment ($++$)
   (f) postfix decrement ($--$)

5. **Read expressions**

   If the value of the variable `missed` is equal to 3, then the resulting value from the expression `missed` * PENALTY (line 65) will be _____.

Answers to Self-Test Questions

1. **Variables**
   (a) `isFired`, `isHit`, and `missed`
   (b) `isFired`: line 5;      `isHit`: line 6;    `missed`: line 7
   (c) `isFired`: Boolean;   `isHit`: Boolean; `missed`: int
   (d) `isFired`: false;      `isHit`: false;    `missed`: 0
   (e) `isFired`: lines 18, 38, 50, 63
       `isHit`: lines 23, 25, 57, 62
       `missed`: lines 26, 59, 65

2. **Custom-defined constants**
   (a) `PENALTY`, `MISSILE_SPEED`, `SPACESHIP_SPEED`
   (b) `PENALTY`: line 1;  `MISSILE_SPEED`: line 2; `SPACESHIP_SPEED`: line 3
   (c) `PENALTY`: uint;   `MISSILE_SPEED`: uint;  `SPACESHIP_SPEED`: uint
   (d) `PENALTY`: 50;     `MISSILE_SPEED`: 7;     `SPACESHIP_SPEED`: 5

3. **Predefined constants**
   (a) `Event.ENTER_FRAME`, `KeyboardEvent.KEY_DOWN`, `Keyboard.RIGHT`,
       `Keyboard.LEFT`, `Keyboard.SPACE`, `true`, `false`
   (b) `Event.ENTER_FRAME`: `line 11`
       `KeyboardEvent.KEY_DOWN`: `line 12`
       `Keyboard.RIGHT`:line 40
       `Keyboard.LEFT`: line 44
       `Keyboard.SPACE`: line 48
       `true`: lines 18, 23, 25, 50
       `false`: lines 5, 6, 23, 38, 57, 62, 63

4. **Assignment operators**
   (a) +=: lines 16, 42
   (b) −=: lines 20, 46
   (c) *=: none
   (d) /=: none
   (e) ++: line 59
   (f) −−: line 26

5. 150, because PENALTY is equal to 50 (line 1) and missed is equal to 3.

# 9.3 PROGRAMMING AND SCRIPTING FUNDAMENTALS—PART B

## 9.3.1 Control Structures

A program is written as a sequence of statements as instructions. The program executes the instructions sequentially—one instruction after the other, in the order in which they appear in the code. However, using *control structures*, you can write statements that cause your program to execute instructions nonsequentially. For example:

- **Loop:** A set of statements is executed repeatedly until a certain condition is reached. The statements that let you execute instructions repeatedly—loops—will be introduced in Chapter 11.
- **Conditional:** A set of statements is executed only if some conditions are met. There are two types of statements that let you define conditions under which a set of instructions will be executed: `if` *statements* and `switch` *statements*.

### if **Statement**

The general syntax of an `if` statement is as follows:

```
if (logical expression(s))
{
   statement(s)
}
```

Here is an example of `if` statement in ActionScript:

```
if (score > 60)
{
   grade = "pass";
}
```

This `if` statement checks to see whether the value of a variable `score` is greater than 60. The expression `score > 60` is a logical expression, which will give a value of `true` or `false`. If the condition is satisfied—that is, the expression `score > 60` is evaluated to be true—then the value of another variable named `grade` will be set to `"pass"`.

If there is only one statement to be executed, the curly braces are optional. Thus, the example above can also be written like this:

```
if (score > 60)
   grade = "pass";
```

or like this, on a single line:

```
if (score > 60) grade = "pass";
```

### if...else **Statement**

In the simple `if` statement just presented, there is not a specified statement to be executed when `score` is not greater than 60. To specify an alternative set of instructions for the condition being false, you can use an `if...else` statement.

The general syntax of an `if...else` statement is like this:

```
if (logical expression(s))
{
   statement(s)
}
else
{
   statement(s)
}
```

Here is an example of an `if...else` statement:

```
if (score > 60)
{
   grade = "pass";
}
else
{
   grade = "fail";
}
```

## if...else if **Statement**

The if...else if statements let you test for more than one condition.

Here is an example of an if...else if statement:

```
if (score > 90)
{
   grade = "A";
}
else if (score > 80)
{
   grade = "B";
}
else if (score > 70)
{
   grade = "C";
}
else if (score > 60)
{
   grade = "D";
}
else
{
   grade = "F";
}
```

In a group of if...else if statements, the conditions are checked one at a time sequentially. Once a condition is found to be true, the statement(s) for that condition will be executed and the rest of the conditions in the if...else if statements group will not be checked. For example, suppose score has a value of 85. Let's see what value the variable grade will have after executing this group of if...else if statements. The first condition, score > 90, will be checked first. If you imagine substituting score with 85 in the expression, the expression becomes 85 > 90, which is false. Then the second condition, score > 80, will be checked next. Again, if you imagine substituting score with 85 in the expression, the expression becomes 85 > 80, which is true. The statement, grade = "B", will be executed and the rest of the conditions in the if...else if statements group will not be checked. Thus, when score is 85, the variable grade will have a value of "B".

Because the checking will stop once the a condition in a group of if...else if statements is found to be true, the order of the if...else if statements in the group sometimes matters. To see what this means, let's rewrite the previous example by switching the orders of these two conditions: score > 90 and score > 60.

```
if (score > 60)
{
   grade = "D";
}
else if (score > 80)
{
   grade = "B";
}
```

```
else if (score > 70)
{
    grade = "C";
}
else if (score > 90)
{
    grade = "A";
}
else
{
    grade = "F";
}
```

Now, let's see what value the variable grade will have with score equal to 85. Again, the first condition will be checked first. Here the first condition is score > 60, which is true. The statement, grade = "D", will be executed and none of the rest of the conditions in the if...else if statements group will be checked. As a result, the variable grade will have a value of "D". In fact, using this if...else if statements group, you will always get a "D" for grade whenever score is greater than 60. If score is less than or equal to 60, grade will be "F". If this group of if...else if statements was used to assign student grades, nobody would get a grade higher than D!

## ? Self-Test Exercise: if Statements versus if...else if Statements

### Question

Suppose the variables a and b are both greater than 0. What are the resulting values of s from the following two code segments?

| | |
|---|---|
| `s = 0;`<br>`if (a > 0) s++;`<br>`if (b > 0) s++;` | `s = 0;`<br>`if (a > 0) s++;`<br>`else if (b > 0) s++;` |

### Answer to Self-Test Question

For the code on the left, s will be equal to 2 because s will be increased by one twice. Unlike a group of if...else if statements, the individual if statements are independent of each other. The condition in the second if statement will be checked regardless of the result of the first if statement.

For the code on the right, s is equal to 1.

## ? Self-Test Exercise: if...else if Statements and Comparison Operators

### Question

In which of the following if...else if statements does the order of the tests matter?

```
if (score == 1) x = n;          | if (score <= 1) x = n;
else if (score == 2) x = n*n;   | else if (score <= 2) x = n*n;
else if (score == 3) x = n*n*n; | else if (score <= 3) x = n*n*n;
else x = -1;                    | else x = -1;
```

### Answer to Self-Test Question

For the code on the left, the order does not matter. For the code on the right, the order matters.

In the first case, for each logical expression in the `if...else if` statement, there is only one value for the variable `score` to make the expression give a true value. In the second case, for each logical expression in the `if...else if` statement, there is a range of values for the variable `score` to make the expression give a true value. Note that there is some overlap among these three ranges, `score <= 1`, `score <= 2`, and `score <= 3`. All values that are `<= 1` also satisfy the other two conditions. The values that are `<= 2` all satisfy the condition `score <= 3`. The order of the tests matters in determining which statement should be executed.

Suppose `score` is equal to 1; the statements that will be executed are colored in the following table.

```
if (score == 1) x = n;          | if (score <= 1) x = n;
else if (score == 2) x = n*n;   | else if (score <= 2) x = n*n;
else if (score == 3) x = n*n*n; | else if (score <= 3) x = n*n*n;
else x = -1;                    | else x = -1;
```

```
if (score == 3) x = n*n*n;      | if (score <= 3) x = n*n*n;
else if (score == 2) x = n*n;   | else if (score <= 2) x = n*n;
else if (score == 1) x = n;     | else if (score <= 1) x = n;
else x = -1;                    | else x = -1;
```

### Nested if statements

`if` statements can be placed inside another `if` statement to create different combinations of conditions for different sets of instructions.

```
Example 1:
if (age < 40)
{
    if (weight < 150)
    {
        group = 2;
    }
    else
    {
        group = 3;
    }
}
```

```
Example 2:
if (age < 40)
{
    if (weight < 150)
    {
        group = 2;
    }
}
else
{
    group = 3;
}
```

Be aware of the placement of the closing curly braces. Note that the nested `if` statements in Example 1 and Example 2 have different meanings. In Example 1, the statement, group = 3, is executed when age is less than 40 and weight is greater than or equal to 150. In Example 2, the statement, group = 3, is executed whenever age is greater than or equal to 40 regardless of the value of weight. Table 9.7 shows the results from these two examples with different values of age and weight.

**TABLE 9.7   Different Results Are Generated from Two Different Nested if Statements**

| Age | Weight | Statement Executed in Example 1 | Statement Executed in Example 2 |
|---|---|---|---|
| 38 | 145 | group = 2 | group = 2 |
| 38 | 157 | group = 3 | none; group is not changed |
| 46 | 145 | none; group is not changed | group = 3 |
| 46 | 157 | none; group is not changed | group = 3 |

### switch Statement

switch statements may be used as an alternative to if...else if...else statements in cases that a single expression or variable is compared against several values. For example, let's consider the following if...else if...else statements:

```
if (score == 100)
{
   bonus = 10;
}
else if (score == 200)
{
   bonus = 20;
}
else if (score == 300)
{
   bonus = 30;
}
else
{
   bonus = 0;
}
```

The single variable score is compared against 100, 200, and 300. They can be implemented using a switch statement as follows:

```
switch (score)
{
   case 100:
      bonus = 10;
      break;
```

```
   case 200:
      bonus = 20;
      break;
   case 300:
      bonus = 30;
      break;
   default:
      bonus = 0;
      break;
}
```

Note that the keywords `case`, `break`, and `default` are also used in `switch` statements. The general syntax of a `switch` statement is as follows:

```
switch (expression)
{
   case value1:
      statement(s)
      break;
   case value2:
      statement(s)
      break;
   . . .
   default:
      statement(s)
      break;
}
```

Here is what happens during execution of a `switch` statement. The expression is first evaluated. In the example, the variable `score` is checked for its value. Then, starting from the case value from top down, it looks for a match. Once a match is found, the statements of the matched case are executed until a `break` statement or the end of the `switch` statement is encountered. In our example, suppose `score` has a value of 200. It will be checked against the case value 100 first. Because this is not a match, it is then checked against the next case value, which is 200. This is a match. The statement `bonus = 20` is executed. The subsequent statement is `break` and thus the `switch` statement now ends.

It is noteworthy that the `break` statement is crucial in terminating the execution for the matched case. If the `break` statement is missing, execution will fall through to the next case and so on until a `break` or the end of the `switch` is reached. If the `break` in the second case, which checks against 200, in our score example was removed, execution would continue and the statement `bonus = 30` would be executed before it reaches a `break` under `case 300`. The resulting value of `bonus` would be 30, not 20.

The fall-through without a `break` is not a fault of the `switch` statement. Rather, fall-through can be used as the logical OR. Let's look at the following example of `if . . . else if . . . else` statements.

```
if (month == 1 || month == 3 || month == 5 || month == 7 ||
month == 8 || month == 10 || month == 12)
{
   numDays = 31;
}
```

```
else if (month == 4 || month == 6 || month == 9 || month == 11)
{
    numDays = 30;
}
else if (month == 2)
{
    numDays = 28;
}
else
{
    numDays = 0;
}
```

These if...else if...else statements can be implemented using a switch statement as follows:

```
switch (month)
{
    case 1:
    case 3:
    case 5:
    case 7:
    case 8:
    case 10:
    case 12:
        numDays = 31;
        break;
    case 4:
    case 6:
    case 9:
    case 11:
        numDays = 30;
        break;
    case 2:
        numDays = 28;
        break;
    default:
        bonus = 0;
        break;
}
```

The advantage of switch statements over if...else if...else statements is that its code is more concise and thus offers better code readability. However, switch statements can be applied only in limited circumstances—it only compares using equality and against one single expression or variable.

### Logical Operators in *if* Statements

Recall that there are three common logical operators: logical AND (&&), logical OR (||), and logical NOT (!). Table 9.8 shows the general syntax of each, with descriptions of the new Boolean values generated.

**TABLE 9.8    General Syntax for the Logical Operators and the New Boolean Values Generated**

| General Syntax | New Boolean Value Generated |
|---|---|
| `logicalExpression1 &&`<br>`logicalExpression2` | `true`: *only when both* logicalExpression1 and logicalExpression2 are `true`<br>`false`: *when either* logicalExpression1 or logicalExpression2 is `false` |
| `logicalExpression1 ||`<br>`logicalExpression2` | `true`: *when either* logicalExpression1 or logicalExpression2 is `true`<br>`false`: *only when both* logicalExpression1 and logicalExpression2 are `false` |
| `!logicalExpression1` | `true`: when logicalExpression1 is `false`<br>`false`: when logicalExpression1 is `true` |

Let's look at some examples.

```
Example 1:
if (age < 40 && weight < 150)
{
   group = 2;
}
else
{
   group = 3;
}
```

```
Example 2:
if (age < 40 || weight < 150)
{
   group = 2;
}
else
{
   group = 3;
}
```

Table 9.9 shows the new Boolean values generated from the logical operators in different scenarios. The new Boolean value determines which set of statements will be executed.

**TABLE 9.9    Different Results Are Generated from `if` Statements Using Different Logical Operators**

| Age | Weight | Boolean Value for `age < 40 && weight < 150` | Statement Executed in Example 1 | Boolean Value for `age < 40 || weight < 150` | Statement Executed in Example 2 |
|---|---|---|---|---|---|
| 38 | 145 | true | group = 2 | true | group = 2 |
| 38 | 157 | false | group = 3 | true | group = 2 |
| 46 | 145 | false | group = 3 | true | group = 2 |
| 46 | 157 | false | group = 3 | false | group = 3 |

## ? Self-Test Exercise: if...else if Statements and Comparison Operators

| (a) | (b) |
|---|---|
| ```
i = 1;
n = 2;
if (choice == 1 &&
positive == true)
{
    i = n;
}
else if (positive == false)
{
    i = n * n;
}
else if (choice == 3)
{
    i = n * n * n;
}
else
{
    i = 0;
}
``` | ```
i = 1;
n = 2;
if (choice == 1)
{
    if (positive == true)
        i = n;
    else
        i = -n;
}
else
{
    if (positive == true)
        i = n * n;
    else
        i = -n * n;
}
``` |

### Question

Predict the value of i for each of the scenarios.

|  |  | What is the value of i after executing the code shown in (a)? | What is the value of i after executing the code shown in (b)? |
|---|---|---|---|
| **(i)** | choice = 1<br>positive = true | | |
| **(ii)** | choice = 2<br>positive = true | | |
| **(iii)** | choice = 3<br>positive = true | | |
| **(iv)** | choice = 1<br>positive = false | | |
| **(v)** | choice = 2<br>positive = false | | |
| **(vi)** | choice = 3<br>positive = false | | |

### Answers to Self-Test Questions

For code segment (**a**): (i) 2    (ii) 0    (iii) 8    (iv) 4    (v) 4    (vi) 4
For code segment (**b**): (i) 2    (ii) 4    (iii) 4    (iv) −2    (v) −4    (vi) −4

## 9.3.2 Functions and Procedures

A *function* is a block of program instructions (also called *code*) that forms a discrete unit with a name. This discrete unit is the function's definition. The instructions in a *function definition* are not executed immediately when the program runs. They will be executed only when the function is called or invoked.

To define a function in ActionScript, you use the keyword `function`. The general syntax for defining a function looks like this:

```
function functionName():dataType
{
    statement(s)
}
```

For example:

```
function startGame():void
{
    score = 0;
    health = 100;
}
```

A *function call* invokes the function and is simply a statement with the function name followed by a pair of parentheses, which looks like this:

```
startGame();
```

When a statement containing a function call is executed, the program jumps to the block of code that constitutes the function's definition and then executes its block of code. When it is finished with the function block, it returns to execute the statement after the one in which the function call has occurred.

### Returning a Value

Before going into further explanation of functions versus procedures, let's look at an analogy. Suppose you work as a manager in a company and you need a signature from your supervisor on a contract. So you send your assistant to take the contract to your supervisor to sign. When your assistant takes the contract to your supervisor, he may need to go to a different floor, talk to your supervisor's secretary, and so forth. However, you only need to give him a simple "command" to get the contract signed. You did not need to go through with your assistant all these details of how to get to your supervisor's office because your assistant can look up the detailed directions that are kept elsewhere. Your simple "command" is like the function call. The set of the exact steps to get to your supervisor's office and get the signature is like the block of code defined in the function.

Once the supervisor has signed the contract, the task is complete. However, you can either have your assistant bring the signed contract back to you or leave the contract with your supervisor. Whether your assistant brings back the signed contract or not, the contract is signed—a task has been performed.

The assistant bringing back the signed contract is analogous to what we called returning a value in a function. A function *returns a value* to the calling statement. In this analogy, the returned value is the signed contract that the assistant brings back. The calling statement is your "command" sending your assistant to get the signature.

If the assistant does not need to bring back the signed contract, the contract is still signed. The supervisor may continue on to whatever he is supposed to do with the contract.

The assistant getting the job done without bringing something back for you is analogous to a *procedure* in the terminology of most programming languages.

### How to Write Procedure and Function Definitions in ActionScript

Procedures are closely related to functions. In common usage, a ***procedure*** is exactly like a function except it does not return a value. A procedure still does some useful activities, such as sorting a list of numbers, displaying values on the screen, or checking collision between two game sprites. In the previous analogy, the activity is to get the supervisor's signature.

Although the terms *function* and *procedure* are sometimes used interchangeably, some programming languages reserve the word *function* specifically for procedures that return a value. In ActionScript, functions and procedures are all referred to as functions. The keyword `function` is used to define functions and procedures. Here, definitions of function and procedure will be referred to as function definitions.

The data type of the return value has to be specified in the function definition. If the function does not return a value, then its data type is `void`.

Here is an example of a function definition in ActionScript that returns a value:

```
function calcTax():Number
{
    var tax:Number = sales * taxRate;
    return tax;
}
```

The previous code defines a function name `calcTax`. The function name is followed by a pair of parentheses. The block of code is enclosed within the curly braces `{}`. The last statement is a `return` statement. It returns the value of the variable `tax`.

Here is an example of a function definition in ActionScript that does not return a value:

```
function startGame():void
{
    score = 0;
    health = 100;
}
```

The previous code defines a function (or a procedure) named `startGame`. This function simply sets two variables to some values: `score` to zero and `health` to 100. It performs activities, but does not return any value.

### How to Call a Function That Does Not Return a Value

The calling statements for a procedure and a function are different. To call a procedure—a function that does not return a value—in ActionScript, you simply use the name of the function followed by a pair of parentheses. For example, the following statement calls the procedure `startGame`:

```
startGame();
```

### How to Call a Function That Returns a Value

What about a function that returns a value? Where would the returned value go? The function call may be used on the right-hand side of an assignment statement. For example, `calcTax()` in the following statement causes the `calcTax()` function to be executed to calculate the tax and returns the calculated value.

```
newBalance = sales + calcTax();
```

Suppose the values of the variables `sales` and `taxRate` in the function definition for `calcTax()` are 120 and 0.07 respectively. Then the returned value of `calcTax()` is 8.4. Imagine that `calcTax()` in the statement `newBalance = sales + calcTax()` "melts away" into its returned value, 8.4. Thus, the value assigned to the variable `newBalance` is 120 + 8.4 = 128.4.

Now, what happens to the statement `newBalance = sales + calcTax()` if `calcTax()` does not return a value?

```
function calcTax():void
{
    var tax:Number = sales * taxRate;
}
```

In this case, the value assigned to the variable `newBalance` will be 120 + undefined, which results in NaN, which stands for *Not a Number*.

The function call may also be used in a logical expression. For example, the following statement causes the `calcTax()` function to be executed—calculating the tax and returning the calculated value. Then the returned value is used to compare to the value 100 in the `if` statement.

```
if (calcTax() > 100)
{
    discount = 10;
}
```

Most programming languages have predefined functions and procedures. This means that the function definitions for these functions and procedures are already built into the language and you can call these functions and procedures in your code without having to write these function definitions yourself. You just need to know what predefined functions exist and how to use them. For example, `trace()` is a built-in function in ActionScript. It will display a specified message in the Output panel.

`trace()` statements are useful in troubleshooting your code and will be explained in Chapter 10.

## 9.3.3 Parameters and Arguments

A function (and procedure too) can have **parameters** so that it receives values when it is called, and these values can be used in the function (and procedure). Values that are passed into functions or procedures are called **arguments**.

The general syntax for defining a function that takes arguments look like this:

```
function functionName(parameter1:dataType1, parameter2:
dataType2, . . .):dataType
{
    statement(s)
}
```

In the function definition, the parameters are listed inside the parentheses that follow the function name. The data type of each parameter has to be specified. The parameter name is followed by a colon (:) and then its data type. Parameters are like variables but they are available only within the function that defines them.

For example, the function `calcTotal()`, shown next, has two parameters named `sales` and `taxrate`. The data types for these two parameters are `int` and `Number`, respectively. What this function does is that it adds the values passed into these two parameters, and assigns the sum to the variable named `total`.

```
function calcTotal(sales:int, taxrate:Number):void
{
        total = sales * (1 + taxrate);
}
```

This function would be called with a statement like this:

```
calcTotal(120, 0.07);
```

Parameters versus arguments: Arguments are the actual values that are passed into the function. In the current example, the arguments are the values 120 and 0.07. The two parameters of the function `calcTotal()` are `sales` and `taxrate`. However, the terms *parameter* and *argument* are often used interchangeably.

The two arguments that are passed into the function call are: 120 and 0.07. When the function is executed as a result of this function call:

- the parameter `sales` gets the value 120 and `taxrate` gets the value 0.07;
- the two values are used in the statement `total = sales * (1 + taxrate)` and `total` gets the sum of 128.4.

Parameters can also be used in functions that return a value. For example,

```
function calcTotal(sales:int, taxrate:Number):Number
{
    var total:Number;
    total = sales * (1 + taxrate);
    return total;
}
```

This function may be called with a statement like this:

```
newBalance = calcTotal(120, 0.07);
```

## 9.3.4 Comments

*Comments* allow you to provide descriptive notes for your codes. In ActionScript, there are two ways to signify the comments:

- `//` for a single-line comment, and
- `/*` and `*/` for a multiline comment.

Two forward slashes `//` signify that the text following the two slashes until the end of the line is a comment and will not be checked for syntax or executed. For example:

```
function calculateScore()            // to increment the score by 1
{
        score = score + 1;
}
```

and

```
function calculateScore()
{
    // This function is to increment the
    // score by 1.
    score = score + 1;
}
```

*The indentation in the script, including the comments, is not a syntactical requirement, but the indentation makes the code easier to read.*

To make multiline comments in a block, use /* at the beginning and */ at the end of the comments. For example:

```
function calculateScore()
{
    /* This function is to increment the
    score by 1. */
    score = score + 1;
}
```

The /* and */ do not have to be on the same lines as the descriptive notes. The previous example can also be written like this:

```
function calculateScore()
{
    /*
    This function is to increment the
    score by 1.
    */
}
```

## ? Self-Test Exercise: Identify if Statements, Function Definitions, Function Calls, and Parameters

Let's revisit the example code from the previous Self-Test Exercise. This time, you are asked to identify if statements, function definitions, function calls, and parameters.

### Questions

1. **Identify function definitions and function calls**
   There are three custom-defined functions in the code (Figure 9.3).
   (a) What are the names of these functions?
   (b) Where are they defined? Give the line numbers for each.
   (c) For each function, what is the data type of the returned value?
   (d) Which functions take argument(s)? How many argument(s) do they take?
   (e) Where are these functions called? Give the line numbers.

2. **Identify function calls of predefined functions**
   There are some function calls to predefined functions (Figure 9.3). You can tell by the parentheses. (Recall that a function call uses the name of the function followed by a pair of parentheses. If the function takes arguments, then you will also see arguments within the parentheses.)
   (a) What are the names of these functions? Give the line number for each of these function calls.
   (b) Which functions take argument(s)? How many argument(s) do they take?

```
1    const PENALTY:int = 50;
2    const MISSILE_SPEED:int = 7;
3    const SPACESHIP_SPEED:int = 5;
4
5    var isFired:Boolean = false;
6    var isHit:Boolean = false;
7    var missed:int = 0;
8
9    reset();
10
11   addEventListener(Event.ENTER_FRAME, onGameLoop);
12   stage.addEventListener(KeyboardEvent.KEY_DOWN, onKeyControl);
13
14   function onGameLoop(evt:Event):void
15   {
16       spaceship_mc.x += SPACESHIP_SPEED;
17
18       if (isFired == true)
19       {
20           missile_mc.y -= MISSILE_SPEED;
21       }
22
23       if (spaceship_mc.hitTestPoint(missile_mc.x, missile_mc.y, true) &&
         isHit == false)
24       {
25           isHit = true;
26           missed--;
27           spaceship_mc.gotoAndPlay("explosion");
28       }
29
30       if (mc_spaceship.x > stage.stageWidth + 100 || missile_ mc.y < -50 ||
         spaceship_mc.currentFrame == spaceship_mc.totalFrames
31       {
32           reset();
33       }
34   }
35
36   function onKeyControl(evt:KeyboardEvent):void
37   {
38       if (isFired == false)
39       {
40           if (evt.keyCode == Keyboard.RIGHT)
41           {
42               missile_mc.x += MISSILE_SPEED;
43           }
44           else if (evt.keyCode == Keyboard.LEFT)
45           {
46               missile_mc.x -= MISSILE_SPEED;
47           }
48           else if (evt.keyCode == Keyboard.SPACE)
49           {
50               isFired = true;
51           }
52       }
53   }
54
```

**Figure 9.3** The complete code for the simple shoot-them-up game from the previous Self-Test Exercise. (*continued*)

```
55  function reset():void
56  {
57     if (isHit == false)
58     {
59        missed++;
60     }
61
62     isHit = false;
63     isFired = false;
64     spaceship_mc.x = -100;
65     spaceship_mc.y = missed * PENALTY;
66     spaceship_mc.gotoAndStop(1);
67     missile_mc.y = stage.stageHeight - 20;
68  }
```

**Figure 9.3** (*continued*)

3. **Identify if statements**

   Give the line numbers where if statements (including if . . . else and if . . . else if) are used.

4. **Identify logical operators**

   Circle in the code all the occurrences of the following operators. Mark "none" for those that are not used in the code at all.

   (a) logical AND (&&)

   (b) logical OR (| |)

   (c) logical NOT (! !)

## Answers to Self-Test Questions

1. function definitions and function calls
   (a) onGameLoop, onKeyControl, and reset
   (b) onGameLoop: lines 14–34; onKeyControl: lines 36–53; reset: lines 55–68
   (c) onGameLoop: void; onKeyControl: void; reset: void
   (d) onGameLoop: 1 argument; onKeyControl: 1 argument
   (e) reset: lines 9 and 32

2. Function calls to predefined functions
   (a) addEventListener: lines 11 and 12
       hitTestPoint: line 23
       gotoAndPlay: line 27
       gotoAndStop: line 66
   (b) addEventListener: 2 arguments
       hitTestPoint: 3 arguments
       gotoAndPlay: 1 argument
       gotoAndStop: 1 argument

3. **if statements**

   if statements: lines 18–21, 23–28, 30–33, 38–52, 57–60

   if . . . else if statements: lines 40–51

4. **Logical operators**
   (a) &&: line 23
   (b) ||: 2 occurrences in line 30
   (c) !: none

> ⚙ **Flash File Used in the Self-Test Exercise** You can download the Flash file that is used in the Self-Test Exercise. Run it to see how it works. Here are some experiments you can try in the code:
>
> - Change the values of the variables and constants.
> - Rewrite some of the assignment statements that use the + = or - = operator to use the = operator.

> ⚙ **Syntax Review and Code-Writing Exercise for Part 2 Materials** A worksheet for reviewing the syntax by writing general syntax and example code; the completed worksheet can be used as a quick reference for programming labs and for studying for tests and exams.

## 9.4 SUMMARY

Adobe Flash is a multimedia authoring program that supports animation creation and has its scripting language. The scripting language for Flash is called ActionScript. Scripting lets you incorporate interactivity and nonlinear playback into your multimedia project.

ActionScript shares many programming concepts and constructs that are common to all high-level programming languages—for example, variables, functions, conditions, loops, mouse events, and keyboard events. This chapter gives an overview of these concepts, terms, and ActionScript syntax to prepare you to start scripting in ActionScript 3.0 in the subsequent chapters.

*Syntax:* The syntax of a programming or scripting language prescribes the ways in which statements must be written in order for them to be understood by the computer. For example, ActionScript is case-sensitive and each statement ends with a semicolon.

*Data Types:* The type of a value is called its data type. This chapter introduces several basic data types that are commonly used in introductory-level ActionScript. They are: `int` (integer), `uint` (unsigned integer), `Number`, `String` (text string), and `Boolean` (true or false).

*Variables:* Variables are elements used to store values that are used in your program. Their values can be updated and retrieved when the program is running. There are three properties associated with a variable: name, value, and data type. To use a variable, you need to first declare it. The general syntax to declare a variable in ActionScript 3.0 is as follows:

```
var variableName:dataType;
```

*Statements:* Statements are instructions that can be executed.

*Assignment Statements:* An assignment statement assigns a value to a variable. In most languages, you use the = operator to assign a value to a variable. For example, the statement:

```
score = 0;
```

*Operators:* Operators are symbols that cause a new value to be calculated from one or more values (operands). This text introduces five common types of operators:

- Arithmetic operators: +, −, *, /, %
- Assignment operators: =, +=, −=, *=, /=, %=
- Postfix operators: ++, −−
- Comparison operators: >, >=, <, <=, ==, !=
- Logical operators: &&, ||, !

***Constants:*** Constants are elements in a program whose values do not change. You can think of constants as "read-only variables." ActionScript 3.0 also has predefined constants such as `Keyboard.UP`, `Keyboard.DOWN`, `Keyboard.LEFT`, `Keyboard.RIGHT`, and `Keyboard.SPACE` to represent the keycode values (a number associated with each key on the keyboard) for the up, down, left, and right arrow keys, and space bar, respectively. You can also declare constants in ActionScript 3.0. The general syntax to declare a variable in ActionScript 3.0 is like this:

```
const constantName:dataType = value;
```

***Keywords:*** In general, keywords refer to reserved words that have a special meaning in a programming language. You are not allowed to use these words for any other purpose, such as variable or function names, because they are predefined with special meanings in the language. For example, the word `if` is a keyword in most programming languages. You are not allowed to give a variable the name `if`; it will result in an error message.

***Expressions:*** An expression is any part of a statement that produces a value, for example:

```
2 + 2, (a + b + c) /3, a > b
```

***if statements***: The general syntax of an `if` statement is as follows:

```
if (logical expression(s))
{
    statement(s)
}
```

The general syntax of an `if...else` statement is as follows:

```
if (logical expression(s))
{
    statement(s)
}
else
{
    statement(s)
}
```

The general syntax of an `if...else if` statement is as follows:

```
if (logical expression(s))
{
    statement(s)
}
else if (logical expression(s))
{
    statement(s)
}
```

***Functions and Procedures:*** A function is a block of program instructions (also called code) that forms a discrete unit with a name. This discrete unit is the function's definition. The instructions in a function definition are not executed immediately when the program runs. They will be executed only when the function is called or invoked. A procedure is exactly like a function except that it does not return a value.

In ActionScript, this type of construct is referred to as a function whether the function returns a value or not.

To define a function in ActionScript 3.0, you use the keyword `function`. The following shows the general syntax for defining a function:

```
function functionName():dataType
{
      statement(s)
}
```

*Parameters and Arguments:* A function or procedure can be defined to have parameters so that it receives values to use in the function when the function is called. Values that are passed into functions or procedures are called arguments. The terms *parameter* and *argument* are often used interchangeably.

The general syntax for defining a function that takes arguments is as follows:

```
function functionName(parameter1:dataType1, parameter2:
dataType2, . . .):dataType
{
      statement(s)
}
```

*Comments:* Comments allow you to provide descriptive notes for your codes. For ActionScript, two forward slashes // signify that the text following the two slashes until the end of the line is a comment that will not be executed. To make multiline comments in a block, use /* at the beginning and */ at the end of the comments.

## TERMS

## LEARNING AIDS

The following learning aids can be found at the book's companion Web site.

### ⌐ Flash File Used in the Self-Test Exercise

You can download the Flash file that is used in the Self-Test Exercise. Run it to see how it works. Here are some experiments you can try in the code:

- Change the values of the variables and constants.
- Rewrite some of the assignment statements that use the += or −= operator to use the = operator.

### ⌐ Syntax Review and Code-Writing Exercise for Part 1 Materials

A worksheet for reviewing the syntax by writing general syntax and example code; the completed worksheet can be used as a quick reference for programming labs and studying for tests and exams.

### ⌐ Syntax Review and Code-Writing Exercise for Part 2 Materials

A worksheet for reviewing the syntax by writing general syntax and example code; the completed worksheet can be used as a quick reference for programming labs and studying for tests and exams.

## REVIEW QUESTIONS

When applicable, please choose all correct answers.

**Programming Fundamentals**

1. **True/False:** If it is strict data typing, a programming language requires that you explicitly declare the data type of a variable when the variable is first created.

2. The type of the value is called a(n) _____.

   A. variable
   B. function or procedure
   C. argument
   D. statement
   E. data type

3. _____ are used to store values, which can be updated and retrieved when the program is running.

   A. Variables
   B. Functions and procedures
   C. Arguments
   D. Statements
   E. Data types

4. A(n) _____ contains a block of program instructions, which form a discrete unit with a name.

   A. variable
   B. function or procedure
   C. argument
   D. statement
   E. data type

**5.** Values passed into functions or procedures are called _____.

    A. variables

    B. arguments

    C. statements

    D. data types

**6.** _____ can be used to make the program execute nonsequentially.

    A. `if` statements

    B. Loops

**7. True/False:** A function definition is executed automatically when the program runs.

**8. True/False:** A function is executed only when it is called within the program.

**9.** A difference between a function and a procedure is that a _____ returns a value to the calling statement.

    A. function

    B. procedure

**10. True/False:** Another difference between a function and a procedure is that one takes parameters, whereas the other does not.

**11.** `sum = addTogether(2,5);`

By looking at the previous statement, you can tell that `addTogether()` _____.

    A. definitely returns a value

    B. does not return a value

    C. takes arguments

    D. does not take arguments

    E. It is not possible to tell whether or not it returns a value.

    F. It is not possible to tell whether or not it takes arguments.

**12.** `sum = addTogether();`

By looking at the previous statement, you can tell that `addTogether()` _____.

    A. definitely returns a value

    B. does not return a value

    C. takes arguments

    D. does not take arguments

    E. It is not possible to tell whether or not it returns a value.

    F. It is not possible to tell whether or not it takes arguments.

**13.** `addTogether(2,5);`

By looking at the previous statement, you can tell that `addTogether()`_____.

    A. definitely returns a value

    B. may not return a value

    C. takes arguments

    D. does not take arguments

    E. It is not possible to tell whether or not it returns a value.

    F. It is not possible to tell whether or not it takes arguments.

**14.** `addTogether();`

By looking at the previous statement, you can tell that `addTogether()`_____.

A. definitely returns a value
B. may not return a value
C. takes arguments
D. does not take arguments
E. It is not possible to tell whether or not it returns a value.
F. It is not possible to tell whether or not it takes arguments.

## ActionScript

**15.** ActionScript is a _____ language.

A. strictly typed
B. loosely typed

**16.** The statement in ActionScript ends with a _____.

A. colon (`:`)
B. semicolon (`;`)
C. closing parenthesis (`)`)
D. closing curly brace (`}`)

**17.** **True/False:** ActionScript syntax is case-sensitive.

**18.** Which of the following is a valid variable name in ActionScript?

A. 3_high_score
B. high score
C. high_score
D. high-score

**19.** To declare a variable, you use the keyword _____.

**20.** To declare a constant, you use the keyword _____.

**21.** To define a function, you use the keyword _____.

**22.** Write an `if` statement to do the following. (Assume the variables have been declared. You do not need to declare the variables. Simply construct an `if` statement.) Hint: You will need to use comparison operators and a logical operator.

**If both variables a and b are greater than 0, then increment the value of the variable c by 1.**

**23.** Write an `if` statement to do the following. (Assume the variables have been declared. You do not need to declare the variables. Simply construct an `if` statement.) Hint: You will need to use comparison operators and a logical operator.

**If either variable a or b is equal to 0, then increment the value of the variable c by 1.**

# Interactive Multimedia Authoring with Flash: ActionScript—Part 2

## TABLE OF CONTENTS

Courtesy of Emma Edgar

Courtesy of Enna Edgar

CHAPTER

# 10

## KEY CONCEPTS
- Movie clips and nested movie clips
- Syntax errors and logical errors in scripts

## GENERAL LEARNING OBJECTIVES
In this chapter, you will learn
- How to program in ActionScript.
- The difference between syntax errors and logical errors.
- How to read and fix syntax errors in ActionScript in Flash IDE.

## 10.1 ActionScript: ESSENTIAL TERMINOLOGY AND BASIC CONCEPTS

The basic programming concepts introduced in the previous chapters apply to Action-Script and other programming languages. However, when it comes to programming in Flash's authoring environment, there are elements—such as symbols, the Stage, and timelines—that are specific to Flash and ActionScript. To prepare you for programming in ActionScript in the next chapter, this chapter will discuss these specific aspects of ActionScript.

The movie clip symbol is particularly useful when you want to add interactivity to control animated objects whose animation is timeline-based. For example, the spaceship and missile in the self-test exercises in Chapter 9 are movie clip symbols. The spaceship movie clip symbol contains an animated sequence of the explosion on its timeline. It is programmed to play the animation when the missile hits the spaceship.

To be able to control these movie clip objects on the Stage, you need to know how to refer to them in your script. This section will discuss how to refer to movie clip objects on the Stage by names—instance names, not their symbol names that appear in the Library.

### 10.1.1 Movie Clips: Instances and Naming

Movie clip symbols and other symbols are stored in the Library panel. When you drag a movie clip from the Library onto the Stage, an instance of that movie clip symbol is created. An *instance* means a copy or an occurrence of the original movie clip symbol.

A movie clip can be used multiple times in a Flash movie, even in the same frame. The appearance and behaviors of a movie clip instance placed on the Stage can be controlled by ActionScript. Such an instance needs to be assigned with a name so that you can refer to the instance by its instance name in your code. Within the same frame on a timeline, each instance—whether it is from the same symbol or not—that will be controlled by script must have a unique name. The same name may be used again in a different frame.

It is important to remember that it is the movie clip's instance name—not the movie clip's symbol name that appears in the Library—that you should use in the code to refer to the object on the Stage.

To assign a name to an instance, select the movie clip instance on the Stage, and enter a name in the Property Inspector (Figure 10.1[iii]). Note that in Figure 10.1[i], the name of the movie clip symbol, as listed in the Library, is `character` and the two instances are named `tommy_mc` and `joe_mc`, as shown in the Property Inspector. Note that the sizes of these two instances can be altered independently. Other properties of an instance, such as position, rotation, color, and alpha, can also be adjusted independently. Thus, you can, for example, program to move `tommy_mc` on the Stage, rotate, change size, change color, and change opacity without affecting `joe_mc`.

Movie clip instance naming convention used throughout this chapter: The movie clip instance names in all the examples end with _mc. This is not a technical requirement in ActionScript. However, it improves the code readability—identifying that the name refers to a movie clip instance. In addition, a code hint listing the available properties and methods will appear when you put a dot after the instance name ending with _mc.

## 10.1.2 Movie Clips: Each Has Its Own Timeline

Each movie clip has its own timeline and it is different from the main timeline of a scene—another key point to remember. The significant aspects of having multiple timelines in a Flash movie are that:

- There can be more than one frame with the same frame number, say Frame 2.
- Hence, you need to be specific about which timeline when sending a playhead to another frame using ActionScript.

(a)

(b)

**Figure 10.1** Two instances of the same movie clip symbol, named `character`: (a) `tommy_mc` and (b) `joe_mc`. The symbol name of the master copy is shown in the Library (i) and in the Property Inspector (ii). The instance name is assigned in the Property Inspector (iii).

When you refer to a certain frame in the code, make sure you specify which timeline. Referring to the timeline of a particular movie clip will need a little more explanation because movie clips can be nested—a movie clip can be placed inside another movie clip. The next subsection will discuss this in detail.

## 10.1.3 Nesting Movie Clips and Dot Syntax

Added to the complication of the existence of multiple timelines in the same project—one for each movie clip—are the ***nesting movie clips***. A movie clip can contain instances of other symbols—graphics, buttons, and movie clips. Therefore, one movie clip instance can be placed inside another movie clip; that is, one timeline containing an animation can be placed inside another timeline.

Although it may seem confusing at first, this is a very useful feature and commonly used in projects. With more than one timeline, how do you specify in ActionScript which timeline's animation should be played? The answer is to use a target path to specify the "address" of the instance (or the timeline that the instance is in) you want to target. A ***target path*** is constructed using ***dot syntax*** by stringing together the instance names using periods (.) according to their hierarchical relationship.

Let's return to the example shown in Figure 10.1. Suppose:

- In the movie clip `character`, there is an instance of another movie clip as the head. This head is assigned with an instance name `head_mc`.
- Inside this head movie clip symbol, you place other movie clip instances: `hair_mc`, `eyeL_mc`, `eyeR_mc`, and `mouth_mc` (Figure 10.2).
- The timeline of the mouth movie clip contains a mouth moving animation.

**Figure 10.2** The movie clip symbol named `head with eyes and mouth` contains an instance of the movie clip symbol name `mouth`; this instance's name is `mouth_mc`, and it is on the timeline of the movie clip symbol `head with eyes and mouth`, not the main timeline.

Now, suppose you want to let the user click on the character instance `tommy_mc` to start the talking animation. You need to be able to specify the mouth timeline to start playing the animation. The target path for the mouth instance is:

`tommy_mc.head_mc.mouth_mc`

and the statement to make the mouth to start playing animation is:

`tommy_mc.head_mc.mouth_mc.play();`

The ActionScript function `play()` causes the playhead on the timeline—the one specified by the path—to start. The timeline that the above path refers to is the `mouth_mc` that is inside `head_mc`, which in turn is inside `tommy_mc`.

Let's look at another organization of the mouth. Now, suppose the `mouth_mc` is placed on the main timeline instead of the `head_mc`'s. Visually, it is not different from the previous example, but the target path for the mouth instance now is:

`mouth_mc`

and the statement to make the mouth start playing animation is:

`mouth_mc.play();`

Dots can be used for more than constructing paths to a movie clip instance. Dots can be used to:

- denote the target path to a timeline;
- invoke a method for a specific movie clip instance (i.e., tell the object to do something, such as `play()` in the example above);
- denote the property of a movie clip, such as position and size.

The previous examples demonstrate the first two usages of dots. You will see more examples for the third usage in the section on controlling objects in Chapter 11. For example, the lines of codes to change the size of the mouth to 60% are:

```
tommy_mc.head_mc.mouth_mc.scaleX = 0.6;
tommy_mc.head_mc.mouth_mc.scaleY = 0.6;
```

## 10.2 WHERE DO SCRIPTS GO?

The script should be added to a keyframe. The code is entered in the Actions panel.

### 10.2.1 Keyframe

The script is placed in a frame on the timeline. The frame has to be a keyframe. If the frame you want to place a script in is not a keyframe, you will need to convert it into a keyframe first. The script will be executed when the playhead reaches that frame. In the examples throughout Chapters 10 and 11, the script will be placed in the first frame only.

### 10.2.2 Actions Panel

You can create or edit ActionScript code in the Actions panel (Figure 10.3a). To open the Actions panel, choose `Window` > `Actions`, or press the F9 key. Before you do so, you

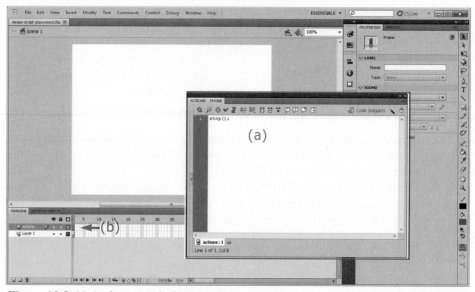

**Figure 10.3** (a) Actions panel. (b) A keyframe that has a script; the "a" displayed in the frame (Figure 10.4) indicates that the frame has a script.

**Figure 10.4** A keyframe that has a script shows an "a" on top of the circle.

need to select the frame first. If you are creating a new script, select a keyframe and then open the Actions panel. To edit an existing script, select the keyframe that has the script and open the Actions panel. The keyframe that has a script will show an "a" above the circle (Figure 10.3b and Figure 10.4). You can tell whether or not a frame has a script simply by looking at the timeline.

## 10.2.3 "actions" Layer

Although ActionScript can be placed in any keyframe in any layer, it is a best practice to create a layer dedicated to holding the script. By doing so, the ActionScript keyframes will not interfere with the keyframes that are created for visual or audio content, and the placement of the keyframes for frame scripts is independent of the animation keyframes.

It is a common practice to name the layer that is dedicated to hold the script "actions" or "action." This layer is arranged as the topmost layer, or the second topmost layer if there is a topmost layer for the frame label. All the ActionScript examples in this book follow this convention.

# 10.3 SCRIPT ERRORS

Do not feel frustrated when your first programs do not run properly or even at all. Even when writing an essay, there are often errors, such as spelling and grammatical mistakes. Even if you have had your essay go through a spelling and grammar checker, your reader or proofreader may still find some parts of the essay difficult to understand. Then you will need to analyze the essay's logic and flow, and make adjustments. These errors are experienced by writers of all levels.

Scripting errors are experienced by scripters of all skill levels, too. The errors in a computer program are often referred to as *bugs* and the process of finding and fixing them is referred to as *debugging*. There are tools and techniques to help you fix the errors. But first, let's look at two main types of errors: syntactical errors and logical errors.

## 10.3.1 Syntactical Errors

*Syntactical errors* are analogous to the spelling and grammatical errors in essay writing. When you test or export a movie, Flash's *compiler* analyzes the code syntactically. If there are no syntactical errors, then the compiler converts the code into the machine language (in 0s and 1s) that the computer's processor understands. The Compiler Errors panel will display a list of the syntactical errors found in your script. It tells you the location of the error by giving you the scene name, layer name, frame number, and line number.

You can also check syntax by clicking the Check Syntax button (Figure 10.5) in the Actions panel.

The code shown in Figure 10.6 is missing a closing parenthesis. The Output panel lists two errors. This tells you the location of the source: Scene 1, Layer "action," Frame 1, Line 32. Both errors are related to the same typo: missing closing parenthesis in Line 32. Once you have fixed the closing parenthesis, both errors will go away.

This simple example demonstrates that:

- One syntax error can lead to more than one reported error.
- The error description may not (and often is not sufficient to) pinpoint the exact problem. However, it leads you to the "area" where the faulty code is.

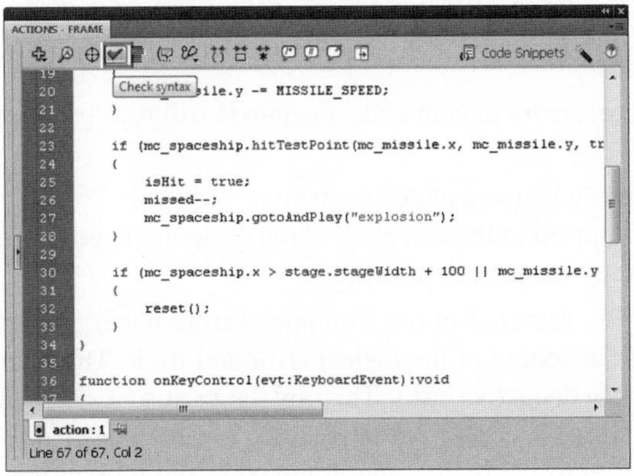

Figure 10.5 The Actions panel with the Check Syntax button highlighted.

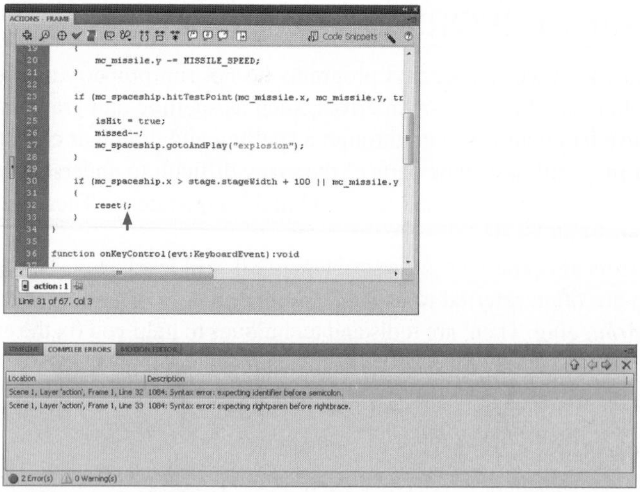

**Figure 10.6** A closing parenthesis is missing in Line 32; the Compiler Errors panel (bottom window) lists two errors.

A strategy to locate and fix syntax errors is:

1. Fix the errors one at a time from the first one on the error list.
   Look at the first error on the list and note the line number. Read the explanation of the error. Return to your code and examine the code on the reported line number. If you do not find any error on that line, then based on the description of the error, try to identify the actual location and the cause of the error.
2. Every time you have made one change in the code, test the movie *immediately*. See if the error has been fixed. Fixing one error may clear up more than one problem. If you do not fix the correct error, then more errors or different errors may come up. Revert the most recent change in the code if it leads to more errors.
   *Do not wait* until you have made multiple changes before testing the movie again. If you do and there are still errors or even more errors, it will be difficult to determine which of your changes actually fix the errors, and which changes cause new errors.

## 10.3.2 Logical Errors

When there are *logical errors* in your code, the movie still runs but does not work properly. For example:

- Nothing happens when you click on a button.
- Objects do not appear at the correct position or do not appear at all.
- The problem may seem random at times.

There are no errors reported in the Compiler Errors panel. It may take some logical deduction to locate the source of the logical error and fix it. There are two tools that can help you perform these deductive tasks. They are the `trace()` statement and the debugger. We will look at `trace()` here. The debugger is a very powerful debugging tool. For example, it allows you to pause at a line in the code and look at the value of a variable. A hands-on exploration of the debugger is available as a learning aid of this chapter.

## 10.3.3 `trace()` Statement

The **trace()** function lets you display a specified message or the result of a specified expression in the Output panel. The message can be a string or the value of a variable used in the movie. It is a very useful function to help you debug your program and trace the progress of your program by displaying messages in the Output panel while testing your Flash movie.

To determine where to put a `trace()` statement, you need to first identify some possible sources of an error:

- If it is a variable or movie clip property, then trace it at various places in the code where the variable or the property get changed. See if its value is changing as expected.
- If it is a code segment, such as a `for` loop or `if` statement, then trace a fixed text message and see if the code segment is actually executed as expected.

Here are some examples of how you may use `trace()` to help you track down the errors.

- If you are not sure whether a function is executed when you click on a button, you can put a `trace()` statement as the first statement inside the function definition. The expression to be traced out can be just a simple string, for example:

```
trace("OK");
```

If the function is executed, the word "OK" will appear in the Output panel.

- Similarly, if you are not sure whether an `if` statement is executed correctly, you can put a `trace()` statement as the first statement inside the statement block. For an `if . . . else` or `if . . . else if` statement, you may need to put a `trace()` statement in each of the statement block, like this:

```
if (score > 90)
{
    trace(90);
    grade = "A";
}
else if (score > 80)
{
    trace(80);
    grade = "B";
}
else if (score > 70)
{
    trace(70);
    grade = "C";
}
else if (score > 60)
{
    trace(60);
    grade = "D";
}
else
{
    trace("less than 60");
    grade = "F";
}
```

In this particular example of an `if . . . else if` statement, all the conditions use the variable `score`. Thus, if the message traced is different from what you expect, it may mean that there are errors in the value of the `score`. In this case, you should try adding a `trace()` statement like this:

```
trace(score);
```

right before the `if` statement.

- You can trace a variable, as just shown. Here is an example. Suppose you have a variable called `score` to keep track of the player's score in a shoot-them-up game, and the value of `score` is supposed to be incremented by one every time a missile hits a spaceship. However, you see that the score shown on the screen is not incrementing correctly. You can output the value of `score` by placing the following statement in the code right *before* and *after* the statement that increments the score:

```
trace("before: " + score);
score++;
trace("after: " + score);
```

Notice that in these `trace()` statements, we are not simply tracing the value of the variable `score`. We also add a short text string to label the message, so that we can distinguish the two `score` values at different times: before and after the increment. An example output is shown in Figure 10.7a. Figure 10.7b shows the same example without adding the string `"before: "` and `"after: "` to label the score. As you see, the output is much easier to read with the added text to label the score (Figure 10.7a).

Note that the text strings `"before: "` and `"after: "` are enclosed within quotation marks. The value of the variable `score` is appended to the string using the operator +.

You will learn more about the syntax for the movie clip's properties, such as position and size, in Chapter 11.

- You can trace a property of a movie clip instance. For example, if a movie clip instance named `ball_mc` is not moving across the Stage properly, then you can place the `trace()` statement as shown next:

```
trace(ball_mc.x);
```

at several places in the code to help you see how the *x*-coordinate of `ball_mc` changes.

(a)

(b)

**Figure 10.7** An example of tracing the value of a variable. (a) Tracing the value of the variable with text added. (b) Same trace with no text added.

# 10.3.4 Lists of Common Errors

The following is a list of some common errors in writing code. Knowing the common errors will help you avoid and identify them in ActionScript programming.

- Missing or mismatching closing curly braces or parentheses: Every open curly brace must have a matching closing brace, and the same for parentheses.
- Misspelling of variable and function names: Don't forget that ActionScript is case-sensitive. Be aware of the plural forms of the names. `numFlower` is different from `numFlowers`. If you find it difficult to remember which names use the plural form, then you may want to make all names singular.
- Missing quotation marks for text strings: Recall that `"score"` is a literal string—a text string—which is a value itself, but `score` is a variable name that has a value.
- Forgetting to declare and initialize a variable before using it
- Using the = operator (assignment operator) instead of the == operator (the comparison for equality) in an `if` statement

> **Practice Using Compiler Errors Panel and `trace()` Statement for Debugging (Lab)**
> Objectives of this lab:
>
> - Get acquainted with the Flash ActionScript authoring environment.
> - Use `trace()` to output custom messages.
> - Distinguish variables and literal strings.
> - Learn to read syntax error reports.
> - Locate and fix syntax errors.
> - Identify pairing curly braces and parentheses.

> **Exploring the Debugger (Lab)** Objectives of this lab:
>
> - Get acquainted with the interface of ActionScript debugger in Flash.
> - Add and remove break points.
> - Trace the code using step over, step in, step out, and continue.
> - Learn to look at values of variables.
> - Locate and fix logical errors.

# 10.4 SUMMARY

**Movie Clip Symbols vs. Instances:** Movie clip symbols and other symbols are stored in the Library panel. When you drag a movie clip from the Library onto the Stage, an instance of that movie clip symbol is created. An instance means a copy or an occurrence of the original symbol. In the code, to refer to the object on the Stage, you use the movie clip's instance name, not the movie clip's symbol name that appears in the Library.

**Dot Syntax:** Dots can be used to: (1) denote the target path to a timeline; (2) invoke a method for a specific movie clip instance (for example, tell the object to do something, such as `tommy_mc.head_mc.mouth_mc.play()`); and (3) denote the property of a movie clip, such as position and size—for example, `tommy_mc.head_mc.mouth_mc.scaleX = 0.6`.

**Where Do Scripts Go?** The script is placed in a keyframe on the timeline. To create or edit the code, select the keyframe and open the Actions panel (`Window` > `Actions` or press the F9 key). Although the script can be placed on any layer, it is a common convention to dedicate the topmost layer to hold the script (or the second topmost if there is a topmost layer for the frame labels), and to name this layer "actions."

**Script Errors:** There are two main types of script errors: syntactical errors and logical errors. Syntactical errors are often detected by the compiler when you test or export your movie. The errors are listed in the Compiler Errors panel, giving you information that helps you locate and fix the errors. You can also click the Check Syntax button in the Actions panel to check the syntax.

Logical errors are not detected by the compiler. You may notice that the movie simply does not work properly. It may take some logical deduction to locate the source of the logical error and fix it. There are two tools that can help you to perform these deductive tasks. They are the `trace()` statement and the debugger. `trace()` lets you display a specified message in the Output panel. This chapter discusses how you may use `trace()` statements to help you debug, for example, by tracing the variable in question, the property of a movie clip instance that is not behaving as expected, or a simple text message inside a function or `if` statement that is in question.

## TERMS

| | | |
|---|---|---|
| bugs 325 | instance 320 | target path 322 |
| compiler 325 | logical errors 326 | `trace()` 327 |
| debugging 325 | nesting movie clips 322 | |
| dot syntax 322 | syntactical errors 325 | |

## LEARNING AIDS

The following learning aids can be found at the book's companion Web site.

🖰 **Practice Using Compiler Errors Panel and `trace()` Statement for Debugging (Lab)** Objectives of this lab:

- Get acquainted with the Flash ActionScript authoring environment.
- Use `trace()` to output custom messages.
- Distinguish variables and literal strings.
- Learn to read syntax error reports.
- Locate and fix syntax errors.
- Identify pairing curly braces and parentheses.

🖰 **Exploring the Debugger (Lab)** Objectives of this lab:

- Get acquainted with the interface of ActionScript debugger in Flash.
- Add and remove break points.
- Trace the code using step over, step in, step out, and continue.
- Learn to look at values of variables.
- Locate and fix logical errors.

## REVIEW QUESTIONS

When applicable, please choose all correct answers.

1. It is the _____ that you use in the code to refer to the object on the Stage.

   A. movie clip's instance name
   B. movie clip's symbol name that appears in the Library
   C. Flash movie's file name

2. Fill in the blanks with `tommy_mc` or `head_mc`:
   You use a statement like this,

   ```
   tommy_mc.head_mc.scaleX = 0.6;
   ```

   when the movie clip instance _____ is nested inside _____, and you want to set the `scaleX` of _____ to 0.6.

3. You can create or edit ActionScript code in the Actions panel. How do you open the Actions panel?

4. _____ errors are displayed in the Compiler Errors panel when you test or export a Flash movie.

   A. Syntactical
   B. Logical

5. The ActionScript function _____ can be used to show a specified message or the result of a specified expression in the Output panel. This is a very useful tool to debug.

   A. `alert()`
   B. `trace()`
   C. `output()`
   D. `out()`
   E. `print()`

6. An ActionScript is placed on _____.

   A. a keyframe on the timeline
   B. a movie clip instance
   C. the Stage

# Interactive Multimedia Authoring with Flash: ActionScript—Part 3

## KEY CONCEPTS
- Mouse and keyboard events and event handling
- Frame events and event handling
- Controlling objects' appearance and behaviors with Flash ActionScript

## GENERAL LEARNING OBJECTIVES
In this chapter, you will learn
- To program in ActionScript 3.0 to control an object's appearance and behaviors.
- To create animation using ActionScript 3.0.
- To program in ActionScript 3.0 to let the user control an object's appearance and behaviors using the mouse and keyboard.

# 11.1 ADDING INTERACTIVITY

Multimedia projects and especially computer games are visually oriented and often highly interactive. In general, computer users interact with computer programs using a mouse and a keyboard. Thus, the most common types of interactivity in a multimedia project respond to mouse clicks, mouse movement, and keystrokes initiated by the user. Actions such as animation and sound effects happen in response to the user's mouse activity and keystrokes.

An *event* is something that happens while a program is running and interrupts the program's flow. Mouse clicks, mouse movements, and keystrokes are the most common events that can be initiated by the user. These events can be used to signal that an animation or sound should be played, a different image should be shown, or a line of text should be displayed. Events like these make it possible for the user to provide input and feedback to the program, exert some control over what happens, and become directly engaged in the activity onscreen. Hence, the key characteristic of programming in an interactive multimedia authoring environment is that it is event driven.

*Event handling* refers to specifying the actions in response to events. In this chapter, we will discuss event handling for mouse and keyboard events in ActionScript 3.0.

Before you write any code for event handling, you need to identify three elements:

- The event: How is it going to trigger the response? For example, it may be a mouse click or pressing a certain key on the keyboard.
- The event target: The *event target* is the object to which the event is going to happen. For example, it may be a button, a game sprite, or anywhere in the window of your program.
- The response: This is the action in response to the event. For example, it may be the playback of an animation with sound effects or a game sprite jumping up.

The main idea to add interactivity to your multimedia project is simply to associate responding actions with the event and the event target. To do so in ActionScript 3.0, you need to understand the concepts of event listeners and event handlers.

# 11.2 CONCEPTS OF EVENT LISTENERS AND EVENT HANDLERS

An *event listener* is an object that listens for events, such as mouse and keyboard events. An *event handler* refers to a function that will be executed when the event occurs.

The term object refers to objects in object-oriented programming. Object-oriented programming is introduced in Chapters 12 and 13.

A subscriber–publisher metaphor can be useful to explain how to program to deal with events and the event listener in ActionScript 3.0. As you may know, many online stores let you subscribe to their newsletters. They email all the subscribers their newsletters whenever a newsletter is published. You will receive a copy of their newsletter if you are subscribed to their newsletters. In this metaphor, you are the listener. The event is the publication of the newsletter.

Let's stretch this subscription scenario a little in order to explain how to program with events in ActionScript 3.0. Suppose these online stores have various sales events: Summer sales, Christmas sales, Closeout sales, Back-to-School sales, and so forth. In addition, you can choose to track whether an individual product is on sale during the sales event. Up to this point, it should be quite clear that in this metaphor: (1) these sales events are analogous to the events—mouse and keyboard events; (2) you are a listener to those sales events; (3) the individual product you want to keep an eye on is the event target.

But what is the event handler in this metaphor? Well, what are you going to do when your desired product is on sale during these sales events? How you respond to this information is the event handler function. Suppose your response is to go buy it online. If we were using ActionScript event listener syntax to describe your subscription to the Christmas sales event newsletter to track if your favorite smartPhone was on sale, this is how we would say it:

```
smartPhone.addEventListener(ChristmasSalesEvent, goBuyItOnline);
```

*addEventListener()* is an ActionScript method. `ChristmasSalesEvent` is certainly not a valid event in ActionScript. Later, you will see the valid events available in ActionScript. For now, let's keep on interpreting the statement based on our sales event metaphor. `addEventListener()` is a method of `smartPhone`, and it associates the `goBuyItOnline` function with the `ChristmasSalesEvent`.

There are several points from this metaphor we want to make regarding writing event listener code in ActionScript:

- Each store has various sales events, but you can subscribe to listen to each event separately.
  Likewise, if you want to let the user click on a movie clip instance named `balloon_mc`, to play an animation of popping the balloon, you write it like this, assuming you have the event handler function named `popIt()` defined in the code:

```
balloon_mc.addEventListener(MouseEvent.MOUSE_UP, popIt);
```

## ABOUT OBJECT

In Object-Oriented Programming (OOP), an object has properties and behaviors. The properties are variables or constants that represent the object's qualities or attributes. The behaviors are functions that define what the object can do.

In ActionScript, an event listener is an object. Event listener is not the only object used in ActionScript. You deal with objects all the time in writing code in ActionScript, but you may not notice it. Movie clip instances are objects, too. They have properties, such as position and size. They have functions that define what they can do—for example, `gotoAndStop()`. The properties and functions of movie clips will be discussed later in the chapter.

You also can associate another event with a different or same function. Suppose you want to play a sound when the user places the mouse cursor over the `balloon_mc`. You can add the following statement, assuming you have the event handler function named `playASound()` defined in the code:

```
balloon_mc.addEventListener(MouseEvent.MOUSE_OVER, playASound);
```

- A store may have a Christmas sales event, but the sales may not apply to the smartPhone. Similarly, in a Flash movie, the user may click on somewhere on the Stage. This triggers a mouse up event. However, if the mouse up does not occur on the event target, the specified event handler function will not be performed.

## 11.3 WRITING EVENT LISTENER CODE IN ActionScript 3.0

When you write event listener code, you need to write two things:

1. An event handler function: It is a function definition that specifies the actions to be carried out in response to the event. Here is the general syntax for this function definition:

```
function handlerFunctionName(eventObject:EventType):void
{
        statement(s)
}
```

The elements in italics are placeholders that you will need to fill in for your case. This is a function definition, but with two requirements: it does not return a value and it requires a parameter of an event type.
- *eventObject* is a parameter. You can give any name as long as it is a valid parameter name. In the examples throughout this text, we will name it `evt` to stand for "event." However, `evt` is not a syntactical requirement. Any valid parameter name will work.
- *EventType*: You will need to use the correct name available in ActionScript for the intended event's type. There are many different event types available in ActionScript. The mouse and keyboard event types are *MouseEvent* and *KeyboardEvent*, respectively.
2. A statement to call the `addEventListener()` method: You need to use the `addEventListener()` method to associate the event target with the event handler function, so that when the event takes place on the event target, the function's actions are performed. Here is the general syntax:

```
eventTarget.addEventListener(EventType.EVENT_NAME,
handlerFunctionName);
```

The usage of `addEventListener()` has been explained in the `balloon_mc` example.
- *eventTarget*: This is the object on which the event takes place.
- *EventType*: For a mouse event, the EventType should be `MouseEvent`. For a keyboard event, it should be `KeyboardEvent`.

- *EVENT_NAME*: There are different event names available for different event types. For example, MOUSE_UP is one of the event names for MouseEvent, and KEY_UP is one of the event names for KeyboardEvent. You will see a list of event names for MouseEvent and KeyboardEvent in the next section.
- *handlerFunctionName*: This is the name of the function that you have defined, in the first step, to respond to the event.

In summary, the basic structure of writing event listener code is:

```
eventTarget.addEventListener(EventType.EVENT_NAME,
handlerFunctionName);
function handlerFunctionName(eventObject:EventType):void
{
        statement(s)
}
```

## WRITE EVENT LISTENER CODE

### Activity/Exercise

The objective of this activity is to practice the two-step process for writing event listener code.

### Instructions

### Part I—Preparing the file

1. Create a new Flash file (ActionScript 3.0).
2. Create a movie clip, and put it on the Stage. Name this movie clip instance balloon_mc.
3. Create a new layer as the top layer. Name the layer "actions." The script will be placed in this top layer in Part II.

### Part II—Write code

1. Select the first frame of the "actions" layer. Open the Actions panel (Window > Actions, or hit the F9 key).
2. Write the code as shown in Figure 11.1a. Note that we have
   (i) a function definition, and
   (ii) a statement to call the addEventListener() method.
   Also note that the function defined here is to handle a mouse up event. Thus, the event type used in the function's parameter and in the addEventListener() is MouseEvent.
3. Test your movie (Control > Test Movie, or press Ctrl–Enter).

Now, if you click on the balloon, you will see the message "You have clicked on the balloon." displayed in the Output panel (Figure 11.1b).

Let's summarize what is going on here. The balloon_mc is the event target. By using addEventListener() like that in the code, balloon_mc is set to respond to the mouse up event by executing the function clickBalloonHandler().

In this simple example, there is only one trace() statement in the clickBalloon-Handler() function. It simply traces out the message "You have clicked on the balloon." The balloon is not programmed to do anything visually.

This is a very simple example. It is intended to give you a feel of how the event target, event type, event name, and handler function all work together in the code. Later in the chapter, you will see more examples and learn how to incorporate more complex and interesting interactivity by using this same basic structure.

```
balloon_mc.addEventListener(MouseEvent.MOUSE_UP, clickBalloonHandler);
function clickBalloonHandler(evt:MouseEvent):void
{
    trace("You have clicked on the balloon.");
}
```

(a)

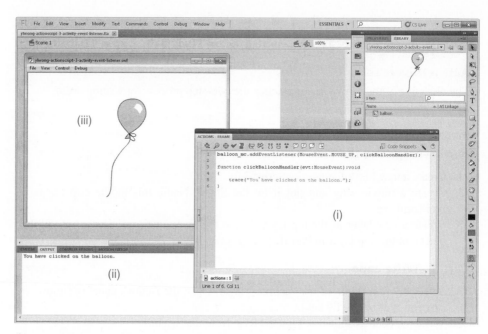

(b)

**Figure 11.1** (a) Completed code for the Activity/Exercise. (b) (i) The code in the Actions panel. (ii) The message is displayed in the Output panel upon clicking on the balloon (iii).

 **ActionScript Example: Event Listener**
The completed Flash file for the Activity/Exercise on writing event listener code.

In the discussion of this two-step process for writing event listener code, we discuss the handler function definition before the addEventListener() step. However, in the code shown in the previous Activity/Exercise, the addEventListener() statement goes before the handler function definition. It is noteworthy that the order of these two in the code does not matter for the event listener code to work. However, it is the convention of this text to place all the function definitions at the end and the function calls at the top.

# 11.4 MOUSE EVENTS

The way a user uses a mouse to interact with a program is basically clicking or moving the mouse cursor. To interact with an object onscreen with a mouse, the user can click on the object or move the mouse cursor over it.

Clicking actually involves two physical activities, each triggering a different mouse event: (1) mouse down: pressing the mouse button; and (2) mouse up: releasing the mouse button.

Recall the general syntax for the `addEventListener()` function:

```
eventTarget.addEventListener(EventType.EVENT_NAME,
handlerFunctionName);
```

Table 11.1 lists the different mouse events available in ActionScript. It shows each `EventType.EVENT_NAME` (the name of the event to pass in the function `addEventListerner()`) in two forms—as an ActionScript constant and as a string.

**TABLE 11.1    Mouse Events in ActionScript 3.0**

| EventType.EVENT_NAME | | Description |
|---|---|---|
| **As Event Constant** | **As String** | |
| MouseEvent.MOUSE_DOWN | "mouseDown" | when the mouse button is pressed down on the event target |
| MouseEvent.MOUSE_UP | "mouseUp" | when the mouse button is released on the event target. Note: The object on which the mouse button is released can be different from the one on which the mouse button is pressed—this is different from CLICK (see below) |
| MouseEvent.CLICK | "click" | when the mouse button is pressed *and* released on the same object |
| MouseEvent.DOUBLE_CLICK | "doubleClick" | when the user double-clicks on the event target |
| MouseEvent.MOUSE_MOVE | "mouseMove" | when the mouse cursor is being moved and is on the event target |
| MouseEvent.MOUSE_OUT | "mouseOut" | when the mouse cursor is moved off the event target |
| MouseEvent.MOUSE_OVER | "mouseOver" | when the mouse cursor is over the event target—does not require pressing the mouse button on it |
| MouseEvent.MOUSE_WHEEL | "mouseWheel" | when the mouse wheel is spun over the event target |

The example code shown in Figure 11.1a passes in the event name using the constant, `MouseEvent.MOUSE_UP`. Let's look at the code again:

```
balloon_mc.addEventListener(MouseEvent.MOUSE_UP,
clickBalloonHandler);
function clickBalloonHandler(evt:MouseEvent):void
{
    trace("You have clicked on the balloon.");
}
```

The code can also be written using the string, `"mouseUp"`, like this:

```
balloon_mc.addEventListener("mouseUp", clickBalloonHandler);
function clickBalloonHandler(evt:MouseEvent):void
{
    trace("You have clicked on the balloon.");
}
```

The first method using the ActionScript constant is the recommended method and the one this book uses. If you mistype the constant name, you will get an error message to point you to the typo when you test your movie. However, if you mistype the string, you will not get error messages; your event handler is simply not being called. This may cost you hours of trying to figure out why it is not working.

## 11.5 KEYBOARD EVENTS

A common way for a user to interact with the computer via the keyboard is by entering words in a text field on the screen, as when filling out a form. However, keyboard interaction does not only mean text input. This is especially true for interactive multimedia projects and games. For example, a user may move a game sprite on the screen by pressing a key. In programming games, you often want to allow the arrow keys to be used to control the direction of an object's movement. You may also want to allow the use of the space bar, CTRL-key, or other keys on the keyboard to control certain properties and behaviors of an object.

Like the mouse click, hitting a key also involves two activities, and each causes a separate key event: (1) key down: pressing the key down; and (2) key up: releasing the key. Table 11.2 lists the different keyboard events available in ActionScript. It is worth emphasizing that the constants `KeyboardEvent.KEY_DOWN` and `KeyboardEvent.KEY_UP` do *not* mean the DOWN and UP arrow keys; instead, they refer to the state of the key when the intended action should be executed.

| TABLE 11.2 | Keyboard Events in ActionScript 3.0 | |
|---|---|---|
| **EventType.EVENT_NAME** | | **Description** |
| **Event Constant** | **String** | |
| `KeyboardEvent.KEY_DOWN` | `"keyDown"` | when a key is pressed |
| `KeyboardEvent.KEY_UP` | `"keyUp"` | when a key is released |

Figure 11.2 shows a simple example demonstrating a script to make a movie clip instance named `balloon_mc` move 5 pixels to the left every time the user presses the LEFT arrow key, 5 pixels to the right when the RIGHT arrow key is pressed, 7 pixels up when the UP arrow key is pressed, and 7 pixels down when the DOWN arrow key is pressed.

Key control is not limited to arrow keys. Each key on the keyboard has a key code—like an ID number—associated with it. For example, the key code for the LEFT arrow key is 37,

```
stage.addEventListener (evt:keyboardEvent): void
function keyDownHandler (evt:keyboardEvent): void
{
    if (evt.keyCode == keyboard.LEFT)
    {
        balloon_mc.x -= 5;
    }
    else if (evt.keycode == Keyboard.RIGHT)
    {
        balloon_mc.x += 5;
    }
    else if (evt.keycode == Keyboard.UP)
    {
        balloon_mc.y -= 7;
    }
    else if (evt.keycode == Keyboard.DOWN)
    {
        balloon_mc.y += 7;
    }
}
```

A switch statement also can be used in place of the if...else if statements.

**Figure 11.2** An example of keyboard event listener code.

RIGHT arrow key 39, UP arrow key 38, and DOWN arrow key 40. The key codes for the letters "A" to "Z" are 65 to 90. The key codes for the numbers "0" to "9" are 48 to 57. These codes are based on ASCII codes, not specific to Flash ActionScript.

In fact, Keyboard.LEFT is a predefined constant in ActionScript (recall the description of constants in the programming fundamentals section in Chapter 9). It is defined as 37, which is the key code for the LEFT arrow key. If you replace Keyboard.LEFT with 37, the preceding code can be written as shown:

```
stage.addEventListener(KeyboardEvent.KEY_DOWN, keyDownHandler);

function keyDownHandler(evt:KeyboardEvent):void
{
    if (evt.keyCode == 37)
    {
        balloon_mc.x -= 5;
    }
    if (evt.keyCode == Keyboard.RIGHT)
    {
        balloon_mc.x += 5;
    }
    else if (evt.keyCode == Keyboard.UP)
    {
        balloon_mc.y -= 7;
    }
    else if (evt.keyCode == Keyboard.DOWN)
    {
        balloon_mc.y += 7;
    }
}
```

The code can also be rewritten to use the "A", "D", W", and "S" keys to replace the use of the LEFT, RIGHT, UP, and DOWN arrow keys, respectively:

```
stage.addEventListener(KeyboardEvent.KEY_DOWN, keyDownHandler);

function keyDownHandler(evt:KeyboardEvent):void
{
      if (evt.keyCode == 65) // the 'a' key
      {
            balloon_mc.x -= 5;
      }
      else if (evt.keyCode == 68) //the 'd' key
      {
            balloon_mc.x += 5;
      }
      else if (evt.keyCode == 87) //the 'w' key
      {
            balloon_mc.y += 5;
      }
      else if (evt.keyCode == 83) //the 's' key
      {
            balloon_mc.y += 5;
      }
}
```

Do not forget to use the `if . . . else if` statements to check the key codes in the keyboard event handler function. Any statements outside of such `if . . . else if` statements in the keyboard event handler function will be executed upon pressing *any* key. For example, the following event listener code will make a movie clip instance named `balloon_mc` move 5 pixels to the left every time the user presses any key on the keyboard.

```
stage.addEventListener(KeyboardEvent.KEY_DOWN,
keyDownHandler);

function keyDownHandler(evt:KeyboardEvent):void
{
      balloon_mc.x -= 5;
}
```

> **ActionScript Example: Keyboard Event Listener Code**
>
> 1. Flash file: Demonstrates the code for moving a movie clip instance left when the LEFT arrow key is pressed, right when the RIGHT arrow key is pressed, up when the UP arrow key is pressed, and down when the DOWN arrow key is pressed.
> 2. Flash file: Control an object using other keys besides the arrow keys.

## 11.6 FRAME EVENTS FOR ANIMATION

In addition to the mouse and keyboard events, there are frame events in ActionScript. Frame events are specific to frame-based authoring programs such as Flash. Unlike mouse and keyboard events, a frame event does not directly respond to user interaction. However, the `enterFrame` event is useful for creating scripted animation. The `enterFrame` event is triggered repeatedly at the frame rate of the movie. The statements in the `enterFrame` event handler function are executed constantly at the frame rate.

Like writing code for mouse and keyboard events, you need to call the function addEventListener() when writing code for a frame event. Recall the general syntax for the addEventListener() function:

```
eventTarget.addEventListener(EventType.EVENT_NAME,
handlerFunctionName);
```

The type for the enterFrame event is: "enterFrame", or Event.ENTER_FRAME. The event type is Event. The event target is stage.

In the frame event handler function, if you, for example, specify a statement like this:

```
balloon_mc.x += 5;
```

then balloon_mc will be moving to the right 5 pixels at a time, at the frame rate.

Suppose there is a movie clip instance called balloon_mc on the Stage. The following code makes the movie clip instance balloon_mc move 5 pixels to the right and 10 pixels up, at the frame rate.

```
stage.addEventListener(Event.ENTER_FRAME, frameEventHandler);

function frameEventHandler(evt:Event):void
{
    balloon_mc.x += 5;
    balloon_mc.y -= 10;
}
```

> ⌁ **ActionScript Example: Frame Event Listener Code:** A Flash file demonstrates using Event.ENTER_FRAME in a scripted animation to move a square to the left.

## ABOUT THE enterFrame EVENT

Flash movies update the screen according to the frame rate. This means that you will see all the changes specified in the frame event handler function at once, at the frame rate. To show you the significance of what it means, let's look at an example.

In the previous example, you will see balloon_mc move 5 pixels to the right and 10 pixels down *all at once* at the frame rate. If the frameEventHandler function is modified to look like this,

```
function frameEventHandler(evt:Event):void
{
    balloon_mc.x += 5;
    balloon_mc.y -= 10;
    balloon_mc.x += 5;
    balloon_mc.y -= 10;
    balloon_mc.x += 5;
    balloon_mc.y -= 10;
}
```

you will see balloon_mc move 15 pixels to the right and 30 pixels up *all at once* at the frame rate. In contrast to a common misconception about how frame event works, balloon_mc in this example is not moving stepwise 5 pixels to the right and then 10 pixels up.

## 11.6.1 Adding Gravity in Games

As you have learned from the `enterFrame` event listener example, the following code makes the movie clip instance `cannonBall_mc` move 2 pixels down at the frame rate.

```
stage.addEventListener(Event.ENTER_FRAME, frameEventHandler);
function frameEventHandler(evt:Event):void
{
    cannonBall_mc.y += 2;
}
```

In real life, however, a cannon ball falls faster and faster under gravity. The gravity effect can be approximated by increasing the falling velocity of the cannon ball at the frame rate. So let's add a variable, say vy, to store the velocity of the cannon ball. Let's also add a constant, say GRAVITY, to store the value by which the velocity is increased at the frame rate. The previous frame event listener code can be rewritten as follows:

```
var vy:Number = 2;
const GRAVITY:Number = 0.7;

stage.addEventListener(Event.ENTER_FRAME, frameEventHandler);
function frameEventHandler(evt:Event):void
{
    cannonBall_mc.y += vy;
    vy += GRAVITY;
}
```

Let's see why this new code will make the cannon ball fall faster and faster. The first time `frameEventHandler()` is executed, vy is 2 and the cannon ball moves down by 2 pixels. Then vy is increased to 2.7 (because of the statement vy += GRAVITY). So the second time `frameEventHandler()` is executed, vy is 2.7 and the cannon ball moves down by 2.7 pixels. Then vy is increased to 3.4. Similarly, the third time `frameEventHandler()` is executed, vy is 3.4 and the cannon ball moves down by 3.4 pixels and then vy is increased to 4.1, and so forth. Thus, the cannon ball moves in a bigger step each time at the frame rate.

In this example, the velocity vy starts with 2. This gives the cannon ball an initial velocity of going down because the vertical coordinate of the Stage increases as it goes down (Section 11.7.1). On the other hand, initializing vy with a negative value will give the cannon ball an initial velocity of going up. This is as if the cannon ball is shot upwards. The more negative the initial velocity, the harder the cannon ball appears to be shot upwards.

The cannon ball in this example falls straight down faster and faster. What if you want the cannon ball to also move horizontally creating the projectile effect of shooting across the screen as shown in Figure 11.3? You can simply add a statement in the event handler function to change the x coordinate of the cannon ball. The horizontal movement of the cannon ball is not affected by the gravity.

The approach of simulating gravity presented here is only an approximation. The equations and discussion for computing physically based projectiles can be found in college physics textbooks. A brief discussion on these equations also can be found on this book's Web site.

> **Adding Gravity (Lab):** Modify the code example provided in the section on gravity to program a cannon ball shooting across the screen. The lab can be extended to be a projectile game, in which the player can use the mouse and keyboard to control the velocities and direction of the cannon to shoot at a target.

> **Physically Based Projectiles:** A Web page explains the physics equations for projectiles.

**Figure 11.3** A cannon ball projectile that is shot across the screen with gravity effect.

## 11.7 CONTROLLING OBJECTS ON STAGE

Controlling objects using script is the fundamental and most common building block for interactive multimedia projects. The common types of tasks in controlling onscreen objects are:

- controlling and monitoring an object's:
  - position,
  - size, and
  - rotation.
- making objects disappear.
- changing the visual content of an object.
- making an object draggable.

Table 11.3 lists the ActionScript syntax that can be used for these tasks, along with brief descriptions and example usages.

To help you see the underlying concept and the very basic structure of the code required for the task, each example used in the following subsections focuses only on a single task at a time. The resulting interactivity in one example itself may seem uninteresting. However, these techniques can be extended and combined to build a complex project.

It is noteworthy that there is always more than one way to get the same results. The code that the examples in this section are demonstrating represents only one possible way—one that the author feels is the most straightforward and clear for beginners in general to learn. The code may not be the most efficient or robust way that a proficient ActionScript programmer would choose. Learning to optimize codes is an important topic, but is not the focus of this introduction to ActionScript.

Most of the examples for this section are provided as complete Flash files, available at this book's Web site. You are encouraged to download the example files, study how the ActionScript is constructed and where it is placed, test run them, and experiment by modifying the code.

### 11.7.1 Controlling and Monitoring an Object's Screen Position: *x* and *y*

In order to program an object's screen position, there are at least two things you need to know: (1) how the coordinate on the Stage is measured, and (2) the ActionScript syntax for getting or setting an object's position on the Stage. As shown in Table 11.3, the ActionScript coordinates for a movie clip instance's position are x and y. Now let's look at the coordinates of the Stage (Figure 11.4).

The Stage dimension is measured in pixels. The position of each pixel can be referenced with an (*x*, *y*) coordinate. The coordinate (0, 0) refers to the pixel at the upper-left corner of the Stage. The *x*-coordinate increases from left to right, and the *y*-coordinate increases

**TABLE 11.3  A List of Commonly Used Properties of Movie Clips and Buttons Available in ActionScript 3.0**

| Category | ActionScript 3.0 | Description | Example |
|---|---|---|---|
| position | x<br>y | x-coordinate, in pixels<br>y-coordinate, in pixels | balloon_mc.x = 300;<br>balloon_mc.y = 300; |
| size | scaleX | Horizontal scale;<br>1.0 means 100% | balloon_mc.scaleX = 0.5;<br>This halves the original width of balloon_mc. |
|  | scaleY | Vertical scale;<br>1.0 means 100% | balloon_mc.scaleY = 3;<br>This triples the original height of balloon_mc. |
|  | width | Horizontal dimension, in pixels | balloon_mc.width = 110;<br>This sets the width of balloon_mc to 110 pixels. |
|  | height | Vertical dimension, in pixels | balloon_mc.height = 260;<br>This sets the height of balloon_mc to 260 pixels. |
| orientation | rotation | Rotation angle, in degrees, from the object's original orientation. Positive values represent clockwise; negative values represent counter-clockwise. | balloon_mc.rotation = 30;<br>This rotates balloon_mc to 30° clockwise. |
| visibility | alpha | Transparency is from is 0 to 1—0 is fully transparent, and 1 is fully opaque.<br>The object is still enabled, that is, can be clickable, even when its alpha is set to 0. | balloon_mc.alpha = 0.5;<br>This sets the transparency of balloon_mc to 50%. |
|  | visible | True or false to specify whether or not the object is visible.<br>When set to false, the object is disabled, that is, it cannot be clicked. | balloon_mc.visible = false;<br>This sets balloon_mc to be invisible. It also disables balloon_mc. |

Note that the y-coordinate of the Stage increases in the direction *opposite* to the y-axis in the Cartesian coordinate system you see in mathematics textbooks.

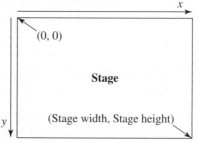

**Figure 11.4** The Stage coordinates in Flash.

from top to bottom. Hence, the coordinates for the lower-right corner are (stage width, stage height). In ActionScript, they are stage.stageWidth and stage.stageHeight.

All the coordinates within the Stage area are positive, but the coordinates of an object can be negative. A negative x-coordinate is outside the left edge of the Stage, and negative y-coordinate is outside the top edge of the Stage.

The object to be controlled should be either a movie clip instance or a button instance. There is another type of objects, Sprite objects, that you can control using script. This text will focus only on movie clips and buttons. Either one will need to have an instance name.

Suppose you want to place a movie clip instance named `balloon_mc` at (300, 100); the ActionScript code looks like this:

```
balloon_mc.x = 300;
balloon_mc.y = 100;
```

To reposition the balloon upon a mouse click, you will need to add the event handling code for a mouse click. Recall that you need to identify the event target, the type of event, and the actions in response to the event.

- Event target: It is `balloon_mc` for this example, because `balloon_mc` is the object to be clicked on.
- Type of event: It is a mouse event. For a mouse click, we can choose CLICK or MOUSE_UP. There are slight differences between CLICK and MOUSE_UP, which are described in Table 11.1. Let's choose MOUSE_UP here.
- The actions in response to the event: These would be the code to relocate the `balloon_mc`.

Now that we have identified these three elements, we are ready to write the event listener code. Recall that in writing event listener code, you need to (1) define an event handler function, and (2) call `addEventListener()`. This is how the code looks:

```
balloon_mc.addEventListener(MouseEvent.MOUSE_
UP, clickBalloonHandler);
function clickBalloonHandler(evt:MouseEvent)
:void
{
    balloon_mc.x = 300;
    balloon_mc.y = 100;
}
```

> ⊕ **ActionScript Example: Controlling and Monitoring an Object's Screen Position**
>
> 1. Flash file: Demonstrates the code for placing a balloon movie clip instance at (300, 100) upon a mouse click on it.
> 2. Web page: Discussion for variations.

> ⊕ **Interactive X-Ray Scanner (Lab)** Let's revisit the x-ray mask example (Figure 11.5) from Chapter 8. The animation of the mask in this example is a tweened animation. Now, you can program to make the scanner bar follow your mouse. The code involves a mouse move event listener, **mouseY**, and the scanner bar's **y** property.

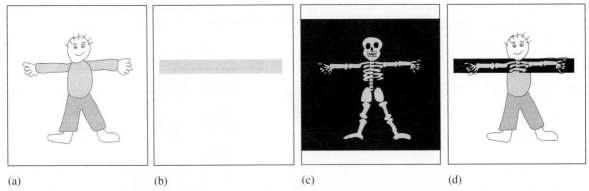

(a)                 (b)                 (c)                 (d)

**Figure 11.5** The movie clips used in the x-ray mask example in Chapter 8: (a) A graphic of a man, placed at the layer below the mask and maskee. (b) A rectangular bar representing a scanner bar; it is the mask. (c) The skeleton is the maskee, that is, the object being masked.

### 11.7.2 Making Objects Disappear: x, y, alpha, and visible

All of the preceding situations deal with objects currently on the screen. However, there are occasions when you want to make an object disappear, for example, a missile disappearing after hitting a target enemy. Here are three ways you can do so:

1. Move the movie clip instance to outside of the Stage—for example, to a large negative *x*- and/or *y*-coordinate. If the object will appear again soon on the Stage later and it is not constantly being animated off the Stage, this can be a good trick to make the object disappear.

2. Set the visibility property of a movie clip instance: `visible` controls the visibility of a movie clip instance. For example, the following code sets the movie clip called `balloon_mc` to be invisible:

   ```
   balloon_mc.visible = false;
   ```

3. If the movie clip instance is generated dynamically using `addChild()` (Section 11.10.4), it can be removed using `removeChild()`.

The first two methods are simpler than the third and they work for movie clip instances that are dynamically generated or manually placed on the Stage. If a movie clip instance is going to disappear only temporarily and will be reappear soon, then these two simple methods may work well. However, if a movie clip instance is supposed to disappear for the rest of the running time of the project, then the third method would be a better choice because a movie clip instance—even it is moved off the Stage or set to be invisible—still uses computing resources, such as memory and computation time to process it.

### 11.7.3 Changing the Visual Content of an Object

In an interactive multimedia program, the visual content of an object can often be changed in response to certain events. For example, a balloon pops when the user clicks on it. Another example: the user may change the hairstyle of a character by clicking on one of the hairstyle selections (Figure 11.6).

One simple way to accomplish this in Flash is to make use of the movie clip's timeline and ActionScript's predefined methods to control the playhead on the timeline. The underlying idea is that different visual content possibilities are placed on the movie clip's timeline, each frame containing one possible visual content. To display a particular content, you send the playhead to the frame that contains the content.

**Figure 11.6** The user can change the character's hairstyle by clicking on one of the hairstyles on the right.

We are not using the timeline for animation here, but for holding a series of possible visual content choices—for example, a different hairstyle on each frame.

For example, you can create a movie clip in which the first frame contains the balloon and the second frame contains the popped balloon. The first frame has a stop() statement as the frame script to pause the playhead at the balloon image. When the user clicks on it, the playhead is sent to Frame 2, where the popped balloon is.

Suppose the balloon movie clip instance is named balloon_mc and is placed on the first frame of the main timeline; here is the ActionScript:

```
balloon_mc.addEventListener(MouseEvent.MOUSE_UP,
clickBalloonHandler);
function clickBalloonHandler(evt:MouseEvent)
:void
{
    balloon_mc.gotoAndStop(2);
}
```

> **ActionScript Example: Changing the Visual Content of an Object** A Flash file demonstrates the code for popping a balloon upon a mouse click on it.

gotoAndStop() is one of ActionScript's predefined functions for controlling the movie clip playback. Other useful functions for controlling playback include stop(), play(), and gotoAndPlay().

### stop()

*stop()* pauses the playhead; that is, an animation on the timeline stops playing.

Suppose you have a movie clip that contains two frames: Frame 1 shows a balloon and Frame 2 shows a popped balloon. If you simply place this movie clip on the Stage, this two-frame animation will play continuously. You will see flickering between the balloon and the popped balloon.

Suppose you name this movie clip instance balloon_mc. You can pause the playback by placing the following code on the first keyframe on the main timeline:

balloon_mc.stop();

Alternatively, you may add a simple line of stop(); in the first frame of the balloon movie clip.

### play()

If the animation on the timeline has been paused, you can start the playback again by using *play()*, for example,

balloon_mc.play();

### gotoAndStop()

Calling *gotoAndStop()* sends the playhead to pause at the frame that is specified as an argument. In the following example, a value of 2 is passed. It will send the playhead in balloon_mc to Frame 2 and pause.

balloon_mc.gotoAndStop(2);

You can also pass in the name of the frame label. For example, if the frame label of Frame 2 of the balloon movie clip is "pop," then the code can also be written like this:

balloon_mc.gotoAndStop("pop");

To assign a frame label to a frame, the frame has to be a keyframe. Select the keyframe, and enter the name in the Property Inspector (Figure 11.7a). A frame having a frame label shows a red flag symbol (Figure 11.7b).

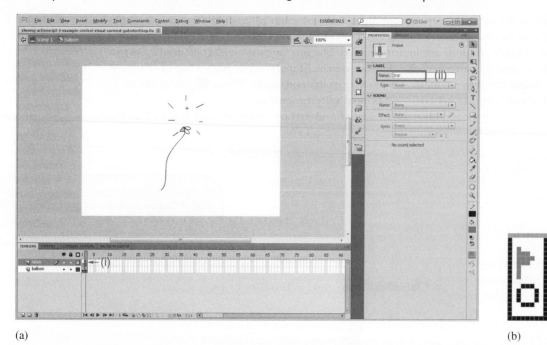

(b)

**Figure 11.7** Frame label. (a) Giving a frame label to a frame: (i) select the keyframe, and (ii) enter the label in the Property Inspector. (b) A red flag symbol in a frame indicates the presence of a frame label.

Using frame labels has advantages over frame numbers. If later the visual content in a frame gets moved to a different frame, you will not need to change your ActionScript code as long as you keep the same label with the frames. Using frame labels can also improve code readability because frame labels are more descriptive than frame numbers.

Note that frame labels are case-sensitive. That is, the cases of a frame label used in the code have to be the same as how it is assigned in the Property Inspector.

> ⏏ **Hairstyle Customization (Lab)** The hairstyle on a character changes to the one on which the user clicks (Figure 11.6). This lab lets you practice programming: (1) for a mouse up event, and (2) for controlling the playhead using `gotoAndStop()` to change the visual content of a movie clip. Feel free to design your hairstyles and the character's head.

### gotoAndPlay()

*gotoAndPlay()* is very similar to `gotoAndStop()`. Like `gotoAndStop()`, calling `gotoAndPlay()` sends the playhead to the frame that is specified as an argument. However, it will then start playing from that frame instead of pausing. For example,

```
balloon_mc.gotoAndPlay(2);
```

or

```
balloon_mc.gotoAndPlay("pop");
```

## 11.7.4 Making an Object Draggable: startDrag() and stopDrag()

The ActionScript method for making a movie clip instance draggable is:

```
startDrag()
```

To use *startDrag()*, you need to use the dot notation to specify which movie clip instance becomes draggable. Don't forget to define the trigger too, that is, when the movie clip instance becomes draggable.

Suppose you have a movie clip instance named `racket_mc` that you want to be draggable when the user holds the mouse button on it. In this case, pressing the mouse button (mouse down event) is the trigger. The code looks like this:

```
racket_mc.addEventListener(MouseEvent.MOUSE_UP,
stopDragRacketHandler);
racket_mc.addEventListener(MouseEvent.MOUSE_DOWN,
dragRacketHandler);
function dragRacketHandler(evt:MouseEvent):void
{
    racket_mc.startDrag();
}
function stopDragRacketHandler(evt:MouseEvent):void
{
    racket_mc.stopDrag();
}
```

Note that this script also includes the mouse up event to stop the dragging by calling *stopDrag()*, so that when the user releases the mouse button, the `racket_mc` will stop following the mouse. If you do not include the `stopDrag()` code for the mouse up, then once the `racket_mc` is clicked, it will always follow the mouse even after the user has released the mouse button.

> ⬦ **ActionScript Example: Making an Object Draggable** A Flash file demonstrates the code for clicking to drag a movie clip instance on the Stage.

## 11.8 MONITORING THE MOUSE POSITION

Interactivity often involves interaction with an object on the Stage—for example, clicking on an object or placing the mouse cursor over an object. However, sometimes you may want to track the mouse position. For example, you may want to

- place a tool tip at where the user clicks.
- let the user use the mouse to draw freehand lines.
- let the user use the mouse's position to control the direction of scrolling of a visual content, such as a big image or a long list of items.

The ActionScript keywords for mouse position are *mouseX* and *mouseY*.

Suppose you have a movie clip instance called `balloon_mc`. To make `balloon_mc` move to the mouse cursor wherever the mouse clicks (more specifically, when mouse up), the code looks like this:

```
stage.addEventListener(MouseEvent.MOUSE_UP,
clickBalloonHandler);

function clickBalloonHandler(evt:MouseEvent):
void
{
        balloon_mc.x = mouseX;
        balloon_mc.y = mouseY;
}
```

> ⬦ **ActionScript Example: Tracking the Mouse Position** A Flash file demonstrates the code for placing a balloon at where the user clicks on the Stage.

Note that the event target now is the Stage, `stage`, because we want to detect the mouse up anywhere on the Stage, not just on `balloon_mc`.

> ⚪ **A Ball-and-Paddle Game (Lab): Part 1 of 3** You may know about a video game called Pong. In the game, on one side of the screen, there is a thin vertical rectangle representing a paddle. There is a small square block representing a ball. The player controls the vertical position of the paddle to hit the flying ball.
>
> How the finished game of this lab is supposed to do:
>
> You can use the mouse to control the vertical location of a paddle (Figure 11.8). A ball, starting at a random vertical position, flies horizontally toward the paddle. If the paddle catches the ball, the ball bounces back. Main ideas and techniques to be applied in Part 1 of this lab:
>
> 1. Use the mouseMove event to make the paddle follow the mouse cursor whenever the cursor moves.
> 2. Use the vertical location of the mouse (mouseY) to control the vertical position of the paddle.
> 3. Use the enterFrame event and the x property of the ball to animate the ball to move across the screen.
>
> Note: Parts 2 and 3 of this lab can be found later in this chapter, where additional concepts and knowledge in ActionScript syntax are introduced.

**Figure 11.8** In this Ball-and-Paddle Game lab, the rectangular paddle on the left follows the vertical position of the mouse cursor.

## 11.9 DETECTING COLLISION BETWEEN TWO OBJECTS

Collision detection—detecting whether two objects overlap—is a common technique used for drag-and-drop activities and in games, especially shoot-them-up games. There are two pre-defined methods in ActionScript for collision detection: hitTestObject() and hitTestPoint().

Both methods will give a value of **true** or **false**. If overlap occurs, the method will return **true**; otherwise, it will return **false**. These methods are used in combination with **if** statements.

### 11.9.1 hitTestObject()

The general syntax for *hitTestObject()* is as follows:

*objectA*.hitTestObject(*objectB*);

You use this to check whether two movie clip instances, **objectA** and **objectB**, overlap. For example, the following code checks whether the two movie clip instances, named `paddle_mc` and `ball_mc`, overlap. If they do, then the value of the variable named `score` will be incremented by one.

```
if (paddle_mc.hitTestObject(ball_mc))
{
        score += 1;
}
```

`objectA` and `objectB` are interchangeable. The following code works the same as the preceding one.

```
if (ball_mc.hitTestObject(paddle_mc))
{
        score += 1;
}
```

The bounding box of the movie clip instance is used in this collision test. A **bounding box** is the rectangular area that encloses an object (Figure 11.9).

It works well with rectangular objects, but not with nonrectangular objects. For example, the two circles shown in Figure 11.10 would be found to intersect based on their bounding boxes, although their actual pixel contents do not overlap.

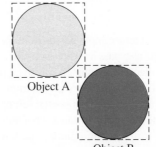

Object A

Object B

**Figure 11.10** `objectA.hitTestObject(objectB)` would return true because their bounding boxes intersect.

— Bounding box of the object

— Actual content of the object

**Figure 11.9** Bounding box of an object versus the object's actual content.

# 11.9.2 hitTestPoint()

The general syntax for *hitTestPoint()* is as follows:

```
objectA.hitTestPoint(x-coordinate,
y-coordinate, trueOrFalse);
```

You can use `hitTestPoint()` to check whether a point at (x-coordinate, y-coordinate) intersects with the movie clip instance, objectA. The third parameter takes a value of `true` or `false`. Here is how you determine which one you want to use:

- If set to `true`, the hit test will check against the *actual pixel content* of objectA.
- If set to `false`, the hit test will check against the *bounding box* of objectA.

⌖ **A Ball-and-Paddle Game (Lab): Part 2 of 3** Building on Part 1 of this lab, you will apply the following new concepts and techniques:

1. Apply collision detection (`hitTestObject()`) to determine if the paddle hits the ball.
2. Use a variable to control the direction of the ball—toward the paddle or bounced away from the paddle.

Note: Part 3 of this lab can be found later in this chapter, where additional concepts and Action-Script syntax are introduced.

**TABLE 11.4    A Comparison of Collision Test Results in Different Scenarios**

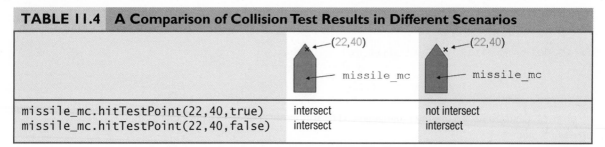

| | | |
|---|---|---|
| `missile_mc.hitTestPoint(22,40,true)` | intersect | not intersect |
| `missile_mc.hitTestPoint(22,40,false)` | intersect | intersect |

Table 11.4 shows the collision test result in different scenarios. As shown in the last column, the third argument makes a difference in the collision test result when the point is outside of the object's actual pixel content but still within the object's bounding box.

For example, the following code checks whether a point at the coordinate (22, 40) intersects with the actual pixel content of a movie clip instance named `missile_mc`. If it does, then the value of the variable named `score` will be incremented by one.

```
if (missile_mc.hitTestPoint(22,40,true))
{
        score += 1;
}
```

This example passes in numeric values for the point's *x*- and *y*-coordinates. However, you can also pass in expressions for a point's coordinates. Passing in the coordinates of a movie clip instance is a common way to perform collision detection. By doing so, you check the coordinates of the movie clip's registration point against another movie clip instance. Of course, do not forget the third parameter, setting whether you want to check against the actual pixel content or the movie clip instance's bounding box. To show you what this means, let's look at an example.

Suppose in a game, you have a squirrel jumping from tree to tree (Figure 11.11). You want to check whether the squirrel lands on a tree. The setup for this Flash file is like this:

- Trees: The trees are in one movie clip. Figure 11.10 shows its bounding box in dashed lines. Its instance name is `tree_mc`.
- Squirrel: The registration point of the squirrel is set at its foot (Figure 11.12). Its instance name is `squirrel_mc`.

**Figure 11.11** In a platform game, checking whether the squirrel is landing on a tree[*] can be performed using `hitTestPoint()`.

---

[*]Courtesy of Kevin Crace, who created these graphics in his platform game lab assignment.

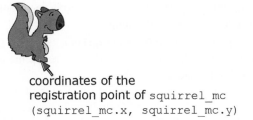

coordinates of the
registration point of `squirrel_mc`
(`squirrel_mc.x`, `squirrel_mc.y`)

**Figure 11.12** The registration point of the squirrel movie clip is placed at the bottom at its foot. The x and y properties of its instance `squirrel_mc` refer to its registration point's *x*- and *y*-coordinates of on the Stage.

To detect if the squirrel lands on a tree, we need to check the squirrel's coordinates against the actual pixel content of `tree_mc`. Thus, the third argument to pass in `hitTestPoint()` should be `true`. The first two arguments should be `squirrel_mc.x` and `squirrel_mc.y`.

The `if` statement using `hitTestPoint()` looks like this:

> 🖱 **ActionScript Example: Detecting Collision of Objects**
> 1. A Flash file: If a missile hits a spaceship, the spaceship plays the explosion animation.
> 2. Web page: Discussion for variations.

```
if (tree_mc.hitTestPoint(squirrel_mc.x,
squirrel_mc.y,true))
{
    // stop falling down

}
```

Table 11.5 shows the collision detection results using different hit test strategies for the scenario shown in Figure 11.11, in which `tree_mc.hitTestPoint(squirrel_mc.x, squirrel_mc.y,true)` gives the correct result regarding whether the squirrel has landed on a tree. The other two do not.

| TABLE 11.5 | The Collision Detection Results for Different Hit Test Strategies |
|---|---|
| **Different Hit Test Strategies** | **Collision Test Result** |
| `tree_mc.hitTestPoint(squirrel_mc.x, squirrel_mc.y,true)` | not intersect |
| `tree_mc.hitTestPoint(squirrel_mc.x, squirrel_mc.y,false)` | intersect |
| `tree_mc.hitTestObject(squirrel_mc)` | Intersect |

## USING EXPRESSIONS FOR A POINT'S COORDINATES IN `hitTestPoint()`

As noted and demonstrated in the previous squirrel platform game example, passing in the coordinates of a movie clip instance is a common way to perform collision detection. However, you also can pass in expressions for a point's coordinates in `hitTestPoint()`. Let's look at some examples.

- **Example 1:** `tree_mc.hitTestPoint(squirrel_mc.x, squirrel_mc.y + 10, true)` would check the point that is 10 pixels below the squirrel's registration point against the pixel content of the tree.

- **Example 2:** Now suppose the registration point of `squirrel_mc` is at its center. Then `tree_mc.hitTestPoint(squirrel_mc.x, squirrel_mc.y + squirrel_mc.height * 0.5, true)` would check the point at the bottom (and horizontal center) of the squirrel against the pixel content of the tree.

- **Example 3:** Suppose in a 2-D maze game in which the player controls a little critter (`critter_mc`) to navigate out of a maze (`maze_mc`). The critter cannot pass through the maze walls. Suppose the registration point of `critter_mc` is at its center. If you simply use `maze_mc.hitTestPoint(critter_mc.x, critter_mc.y, true)` to perform collision detection between the critter and the maze to prevent the critter from going in the maze walls, the critter can go through the wall up to its registration point. There are four cases you will need to perform a collision detection of the critter against the maze:

  - **Case 1:** When the critter tries to move up (say, when the player presses the up arrow key), use `maze_mc.hitTestPoint(critter_mc.x, critter_mc.y - critter_mc.height * 0.5, true)` to check the top of the critter against the maze's pixel content.

  - **Case 2:** When the critter tries to move down (say, when the player presses the down arrow key), use `maze_mc.hitTestPoint(critter_mc.x, critter_mc.y + critter_mc.height * 0.5, true)` to check the bottom of the critter against the maze's pixel content.

  - **Case 3:** When the critter tries to move to the left (say, when the player presses the left arrow key), use `maze_mc.hitTestPoint(critter_mc.x - critter_mc.width * 0.5, critter_mc.y, true)` to check the left of the critter against the maze's pixel content.

  - **Case 4:** When the critter tries to move to the right (say, when the player presses the right arrow key), use `maze_mc.hitTestPoint(critter_mc.x + critter_mc.width * 0.5, critter_mc.y, true)` to check the right of the critter against the maze's pixel content.

---

**A Side-Scrolling Platform Game (Lab)** Here is how the completed game works: You can control a "hero" to run forward or backward on a platform using the LEFT or RIGHT arrow keys to scroll the "platform." There are "treasures," such as a spinning coin and a mysterious box. Mouse up on the Stage makes the hero jump to collect the treasures. The treasure disappears when the hero touches it. Figure 11.13 shows examples of the completed lab with a variety of heroes, platforms, and treasures.

Main Ideas and Techniques:

1. Use keyboard and mouse events.
2. Use an enterFrame event to animate the hero jumping.
3. Move the platform movie clip instances using the x property.
4. Apply collision detection (`hitTestObject()`) to determine if the hero is in contact with the treasure.
5. Apply collision detection (`hitTestPoint()`) to determine if the hero has landed on the platform.

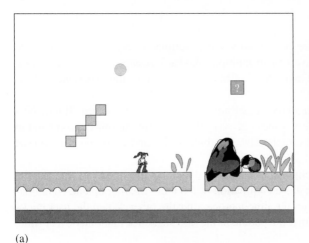

(a)

(b)

(c)

**Figure 11.13** Examples of the completed platform game lab. (a) A traditional platform game: the hero, a humanoid character; the platform, rectangular ground; the treasures, coin and mystery box. (b) A nontraditional platform game[†]: the hero, a squirrel; the platform, trees; the treasures, coin and mystery box. (c) Another nontraditional platform game[‡]: the hero, a fish; the platform, water; the treasures, coin and sand dollar.

# 11.10 OTHER USEFUL FUNCTIONS AND CONSTRUCTS FOR INTERACTIVE MULTIMEDIA AUTHORING

There are common tasks in programming games, for example, randomization, working with a list of items, and dynamically placing movie clip instances on the Stage. This section discusses some useful functions and keywords that you can use to accomplish these tasks.

---

[†] Courtesy of Kevin Crace.
[‡] Courtesy of Gretchen Edwards.

## 11.10.1 Randomize

Randomization is useful for adding nonlinearity and variations to an interactive project to provide unique experiences for users or in multiple playback sessions for the same user. Adding randomness to the "what and when" of the game can make the experience a little unpredictable and add surprises.

Suppose when a user clicks on a box, something will come out of the box. It may be a little monotonous if the same object comes out every time or different objects come out in the same order every time—for example, always a bubble the first time you click on the box, and always a bird the second time you click.

Suppose there are two movie clip instances on the stage: one is named hat_mc and the other magic_mc. magic_mc contains an animation of a bubble floating up and an animation of a bird flying—sequenced on the timeline one after the other. When the user clicks on the hat, magic_mc will play either the bubble or the bird sequence randomly every time. Here is how the script may look:

```
hat_mc.addEventListener(MouseEvent.MOUSE_UP, magicHandler);

function magicHandler(evt:MouseEvent):void
{
    var r:Number = Math.random();
    if (r < 0.5)
    {
        magic_mc.gotoAndPlay("bubble");
    }
    else
    {
        magic_mc.gotoAndPlay("bird");
    }
}
```

> ✋ **ActionScript Example: Math. random(): Magic Hat Example** A Flash file of the magic hat example demonstrates the use of **Math.random()**. Upon clicking on a hat, one of the two animations (floating bubbles and flying bird) will be selected randomly to play.

This script stores the random number in a variable r. An if statement is used to determine if r is less than 0.5. If r is less than 0.5, magic_mc plays the bubble animation; otherwise, it plays the bird animation. Why 0.5? Well, this example makes the chance of playing bubble or bird about 50–50. If you want to make the bubble have a higher chance than the bird to appear, then you will need to increase the value 0.5 in the condition. In addition, it is not necessary to use less than in the if-condition statement. Using r > 0.5 instead of r < 0.5 should give about the same result in this example.

In the Ball-and-Paddle Game lab exercise, you can randomize the vertical position of the ball every time it is reset to start over, so that the ball will fly out from the right at a random vertical position. You can also randomize its direction and speed by randomizing its vertical or horizontal increment.

In addition to randomizing the *what,* timing is another element that can be randomized. For example, the timing of two birds starting to fly across the screen can be randomized to create a different combination of bird flying scenes every time the project is played.

In ActionScript, *Math.random()* generates a random number $>= 0$ and $< 1$. Although Math.random() can only give you a random number of between 0 and 1, you can use it in an expression to generate a number within any range. Here is the general idea of the formula:

```
Math.random() * (max. of the range - min. of the range)
+ min. of the range
```

Let's look at some examples:

- If you want to generate a random number between −10 and 30, then the expression is as shown:

```
Math.random() * (30 - (-10)) + (-10)
```

or

```
Math.random() * 40 - 10
```

Let's plug in some numbers to check if this expression will give a number within 10 and 30.

- If `Math.random()` generates a zero, then you will have:

```
0 * 40 - 10 = -10
```

Yes, this is the minimum end of the range from which you want to generate a random number.

- If `Math.random()` generates 0.9999 . . . , then you will have:

```
0.9999 . . . * 40 - 10 = 29.9999 . . .
```

This is the maximum end of the range.

- If you want to generate a random number between −11 and 11, then the expression is as follows:

```
Math.random() * (11 - (-11)) + (-11)
```

or

```
Math.random() * 22 - 11
```

---

**?  Self-Test Exercise: Generate a Random Number within a Specified Range**

Write expressions that can generate a random number from the ranges specified below.

1. >= −20 and < 20
2. >= 0 and < 20
3. >=12 and < 20
4. >= 1 and < 6

Answers to Self-Test Questions

1. `Math.random() * 40 - 20`
2. `Math.random() * 20`
3. `Math.random() * 8 + 12`
4. `Math.random() * 5 + 1`

> ⏚ **A Ball-and-Paddle Game (Lab): Part 3 of 3** Building on Part 2 of this lab, you will apply the following concepts and techniques:
>
> 1. Use `Math.random()` to randomize the vertical position of the ball every time it is reset to start over on the right.
> 2. Construct expressions to make the ball move and bounce at an angle.

## 11.10.2 Array

You can use an *array* to store a list of items, for example, a repertoire of words that may be used in a hangman word game. Each item in an array is *indexed*, that is, numbered according to its order in the array. The index of the first item is 0, the second item is 1, and so forth. The index of the last item in an array is equal to the number of items in the array minus one.

### Creating an Array

Like creating a variable, you need to use the keyword `var` to declare an array. The array name is followed by `:Array`. There are several ways to create an array. Here are two examples:

- **Method 1:** Create an empty array and populate the array later.
  For example, to create an array called `fruit`:

  ```
  var fruit:Array = new Array();
  ```

- **Method 2:** Populate the array when it is created.
  For example, to create an array called `fruit` that contains a list of text items: "apple," "orange," "grape," "pear":

  ```
  var fruit:Array = new Array("apple", "orange", "grape", "pear");
  ```

Note that in the first method, we show you how to create an empty array, but have not shown you how to populate the array after it is created. Regardless of how an array is originally created, you can always add or update items in the array. The following subsections show you how to do so.

### Accessing an Item in an Array

To access an item in an array, you can refer to its index number by using `[]`. For example, if you want to get the first item of this array `fruit` and store it in a variable named `a`, the statement looks like this:

```
a = fruit[0];
```

### Adding Items to an Array

If you want to add more items to the end of the array after it is created, you can use *push()*. For example, the following code will add "peach" to the end of the array `fruit`:

```
fruit.push("peach");
```

The array `fruit` will become ["apple", "orange", "grape", "pear", "peach"].

You can also add an item by index. For example, the following gives the same result as the push example above:

```
fruit[4] = "peach";
```

You also can use *unshift().* to add a new item to the beginning of an array. For example, suppose the array `fruit` is ["apple", "orange", "grape", "pear"]. The following code will add "peach" to the beginning of the array `fruit`:

```
fruit.unshift("peach");
```

The array `fruit` will become ["peach", "apple", "orange", "grape", "pear"].

If you want to add items in the middle of an array, you can use *splice().* To use `splice()` to add items to an array, you need to pass in at least three arguments. The first parameter is the starting index and the second parameter is the number of items to be deleted, which should be zero for adding items. The third parameters and on are items to be added to the array. For example, suppose the array `fruit` is ["apple", "orange", "grape", "pear"]. The following code will add "peach" at the index 2 of the array `fruit`:

```
fruit.splice(2, 0, "peach");
```

The array `fruit` will become [ "apple", "orange", "peach", "grape", "pear"].

### Removing Items from an Array

If you want to remove the last item from the array, you can use *pop().* For example, suppose the array `fruit` is ["apple", "orange", "grape", "pear"]. The following code will remove "pear" from the array `fruit`:

```
fruit.pop();
```

The array `fruit` will become ["apple", "orange", "grape"].

You also can use *shift()* to remove the first item from an array. For example, suppose the array `fruit` is ["apple", "orange", "grape", "pear"]. The following code will remove "apple" from the array `fruit`:

```
fruit.shift();
```

The array `fruit` will become ["orange", "grape", "pear"].

In addition to adding items, the method `splice()` also can be used to remove any items from an array, in which case you only need to pass in two arguments. For example, the following statement removes one item from the array `fruit` starting from index 2.

```
fruit.splice(2, 1);
```

The following statement removes three items from the array `fruit` starting from index 1.

```
fruit.splice(1, 3);
```

### Replacing Items in an Array

To replace an item of an array, use an assignment statement and set the item by referring to its index number using []. For example, suppose the array `fruit` is ["apple", "orange", "grape", "pear"]. The following assignment statement will replace the third item (index 2) with "peach":

```
fruit[2] = "peach";
```

The array `fruit` will become ["apple", "orange", "peach", "pear"].

Although the examples shown here add only one item at a time, more than one items can be added to an array using push(), unshift(), and splice(). Look up these methods in Flash ActionScipt Help menu for more information.

### Application of Arrays

Arrays are useful in storing information as a list of data or objects, for example, a list of treasures the player has collected in a game, a list of card names in a card game, or a list of words available in a word-guessing game.

The types of items that an array can store in ActionScript are not limited to text or numbers. You can also use arrays to store a list of movie clip instances. When used in combination with loop (which will be discussed in the next subsection), an array can be looped through to perform a set of instructions on the items of the array. For example, in the Star Catcher Game lab exercise (Figure 11.14) at the end of this chapter, the star movie clip instances are stored in an array. A set of instructions, such as rotating the star and checking collision detection with the wizard, is looped through every element in the array at the frame rate, so that each star movie clip instance is performing the rotation and checking if it hits the wizard.

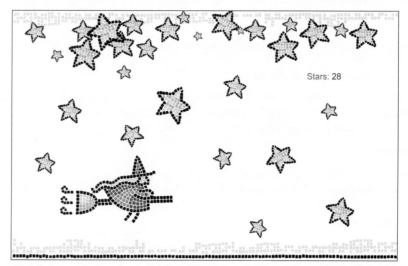

**Figure 11.14** A screenshot from the completed Star Catcher Game lab exercise. The stars are stored as movie clip instances in an array.

## 11.10.3 Loop

Instructions that execute repeatedly are called *loops*. Loops let you repeat a block of statements while a specified condition is satisfied. There are five types of loops in ActionScript: for loop, for each . . . in loop, for . . . in loop, while loop, and do . . . while loop. Each type of loop behaves somewhat differently and is useful for different purposes. In some situations, any of these types can be used, but some types may require fewer codes than the others. The for loop is the most common type of loop. In this chapter, only the for loop is introduced and used in the examples that require loops.

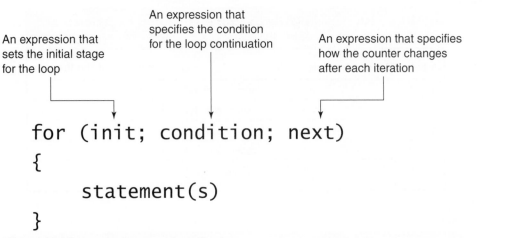

An expression that sets the initial stage for the loop

An expression that specifies the condition for the loop continuation

An expression that specifies how the counter changes after each iteration

```
for (init; condition; next)
{
      statement(s)
}
```

**Figure 11.15** A general syntax for a for loop.

In a for loop, a block of statements is looped a predefined number of times. The general syntax and explanation for a for loop is shown in Figure 11.15.

An example for loop in ActionScript looks like this:

```
var i:int;
for (i = 1; i < 5; i++)
{
    sum = sum + i;
}
```

This code shows an example of a for loop. The curly braces ({}) are used to enclose the block of statements to be executed by the for statement.

The variable i in this example serves as a counter to control how many times the statements inside the loop is executed. The parentheses after the keyword for contain three parts:

- init: This specifies the start value of a counter.
  In this example, the loop starts with a counter of one, as specified in the first part, i = 1, in the parentheses.
- condition: This specifies the condition that allows the continuation of the loop.
  In this example, this is i < 5, which specifies that the loop will continue as long as i is less than five.
- next: This defines how the counter changes after each iteration.
  In the example, this is i++, which means that the counter i increases by one after each iteration.

**Iteration:** Each pass of execution within a loop is called an iteration.

Thus, the for loop example will loop a total of four times, starting with i = 1 to i = 4. Table 11.6 explains this for loop iteration by iteration. As you see, when i become five, it breaks the condition of i < 5, and ends the loop. Suppose the variable sum is zero before the loop, then at the end of the loop, the value of sum will equal $(1 + 2 + 3 + 4)$, that is, 10.

**TABLE 11.6  Tracing the Example for Loop Iteration by Iteration**

| i Before This Iteration | Is i < 5? | | i at the End of This Iteration |
|---|---|---|---|
| i = 1 | yes | sum = sum + 1 | i = 2 |
| i = 2 | yes | sum = sum + 2 | i = 3 |
| i = 3 | yes | sum = sum + 3 | i = 4 |
| i = 4 | yes | sum = sum + 4 | i = 5 |
| i = 5 | no | | |

## <= VERSUS <

It is worth noting that rewriting the continuation condition i < 5 as i <= 4 in the previous for loop example would give the same result—it will iterate from i = 1 to i = 4. However, i < 5 is preferred because <= requires two operations (< and ==) to compare the values whereas < only requires one operation. Thus using i < 5 is more efficient than i <= 4. Whenever possible, using the operators < and > are preferred to <= and >= respectively.

## ? Self-Test Exercise: for Loop

How many iterations does each of the following loops execute?

```
1. for (i = 1; i <= 10; i++)
2. for (i = 0; i < 10; i++)
3. for (i = 0; i <= 10; i++)
4. for (i = 0; i <= 9; i++)
5. for (i = 10; i > 0; i--)
6. for (i = 0; i < 10; i = i + 2)
7. for (i = 0; i <= 10; i = i + 2)
```

Answers to Self-Test Questions

1. 10 (i = 1, 2, 3, 4, 5, 6, 7, 8, 9, 10)
2. 10 (i = 0, 1, 2, 3, 4, 5, 6, 7, 8, 9)
3. 11 (i = 0, 1, 2, 3, 4, 5, 6, 7, 8, 9, 10)
4. 10 (i = 0, 1, 2, 3, 4, 5, 6, 7, 8, 9)
5. 10 (i = 10, 9, 8, 7, 6, 5, 4, 3, 2, 1)
6. 5 (i = 0, 2, 4, 6, 8)
7. 6 (i = 0, 2, 4, 6, 8, 10)

This simple `for` loop example intends to show you how a `for` loop works. Using the `for` loop to calculate a sum is by no means an interesting application. The `for` loop can be used in the visual environment, not just for simple number crunching.

For example, in Flash, the `for` loop can be used to automatically place a large amount of graphics on the Stage. To do so, you will also need to call other ActionScript functions in the loop to specify the graphic. The next section, Generate Movie Clip Instances Dynamically, shows you how to generate multiple movie clip instances without having to manually place them on the Stage.

### Use with Arrays

The `for` loop is often used with arrays to perform a series of statements on each item in the array. The counter in the `for` loop in such cases is used to refer to the index of the item in the array. Recall that the index of the first item in an array is 0. Thus the initial condition of a `for` loop that loops through all the items in an array starts the counter variable with 0. Recall that the index of the last item in an array is the total number of items in the array minus one. Thus the loop's continuation condition is that the counter variable is less than the total number of items in the array. The following code uses a `for` loop to perform a linear search on an array called `fruit` to see whether the word "grape" is in the array:

```
var fruit:Array = new Array ("apple", "orange", "grape", "pear");
var found:int = −1;
var i:int;
for (i = 0; i < fruit.length; i++)
{
    if (fruit[i] == "grape")
    {
        found = i;
        break;
    }
}
```

`fruit.length` refers to the number of items in the array, `fruit`. The example code loops from the first item (index 0) of the array `fruit` to see if the item is "grape." If "grape" is found, then the variable `found` is assigned with the value of `i` and the loop will be terminated (`break`). If the word "grape" is not in the array, then the value of `found` will remain −1.

## LOOPS VERSUS ANIMATION "LOOPS"

The loops just discussed are different from *animation* loops. Let's look at an example.

Suppose you want to animate an object, say move 10 times to the right, 5 pixels each time. The loops just discussed are not the right tool. If you write a `for` loop to loop an object moving to the right 5 pixels for 10 times, all you will see is the very final result where the object has been moved 50 pixels to the right in one step.

If you want to loop a scripted animation, use the ENTER_FRAME event listener or Timer event listener.

> **Timer Event Listener:** This learning aid provides an introduction to the Timer event listener and example code of using Timer events. It also includes a lab exercise to program a hare-and-tortoise race using timers.

If you want to loop a nonscripted animation—such as a tweened animation—that is sequenced on a timeline, you can simply add a `gotoAndPlay()` at the end frame of the animation sequence and specify the beginning frame number or label of the sequence inside the parentheses. For example, if a tweened animation starts at Frame 10, whose frame label is "walk," and ends at Frame 120, then you add a script at Frame 120. The frame script contains one statement:

```
gotoAndPlay("walk");
```

Design time refers to the time when you are authoring your project in Flash. Run time refers to the time when your project is playing.

## 11.10.4 Generate Movie Clip Instances Dynamically

So far, in the examples shown, movie clip instances are manually placed on the Stage at design time. The manual placement of movie clip instances on the Stage has its limitations. For example,

- It will be a lot more work if you need many more movie clip instances on the Stage, such as bullets for a shoot-them-up game and the stars in our Star Catcher Game lab exercise. It would be tedious to manually place, say, 50 stars in our Star Catcher Game and give each an instance name.
- The number of movie clip instances available at run time—when the movie plays—is limited by the number of the instances you place on the Stage at design time. Suppose you want to place a graphic of an ink blob at the mouse cursor whenever the user clicks. It would not be possible to tell how many such ink blob movie clip instances you would need to place on the Stage during design time.

This section shows you how to use ActionScript to add movie clip instances on the Stage. You will need to first set the *Linkage* for the movie clip symbol that you want to be able to add to the Stage using script. Assigning a Class name to the Linkage of a movie clip symbol lets you refer to the symbol by that name in the code, so that you can create new instances of that movie clip on the Stage using code.

There are two ways you can set the Linkage of movie clip symbols:

- **Method 1:** Set Linkage when you first create the movie clip symbol.
  1. In the Create New Symbol dialog box (Figure 11.16), in the Linkage section, check the check box labeled "Export for ActionScript."
  2. Enter a name for the Class.
     - Remember the name you give for the Class. It is what you will use in your script.
     - The Class name is not the name of the movie clip symbol. The Class name and the movie clip name are different things. You do not need to make the Class name and the movie clip name the same.
     - The Class name must start with an alphabet and may contain alphabets, numbers, and underscores only.
     - It is a best practice to use an uppercase letter for the first letter, although it is not a technical requirement.
  3. Check the check box "Export to first frame" if it is not checked yet.
  4. The Base class should have been filled in automatically for you after you check the check box `Export for ActionScript`. For the purposes of the exercises in this book, keep it as is and do not change it.

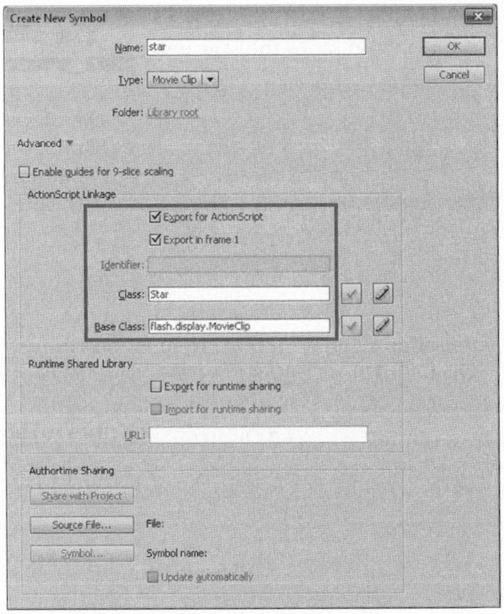

**Figure 11.16** Setting Linkage for a movie clip symbol.

- **Method 2:** Set Linkage after the movie clip symbol has been created.
  1. In the Library panel, right-click on the movie clip symbol, and select `Properties`....
  2. Follow steps 2–4 of Method 1.

To write code to add the movie clip symbol on the Stage, you can use the following basic structure:

```
var instanceName:ClassName = new ClassName();
addChild(instanceName);
```

The instance is created as a variable, as you can tell by the keyword `var`. The `instanceName` is the name you assign to the movie clip instance you want to create on the Stage. This is the movie clip instance name you would have entered in the Property Inspector if you were putting it on the Stage manually. The `ClassName` is the Class name you have given to the movie clip symbol as its Linkage properties (Figure 11.16). The `addChild()` statement lets you add the instance onto the Stage.

For example, suppose the class name of a movie clip symbol is assigned as `Star`. The script to add an instance of this movie clip symbol on the Stage would look like this:

```
var star_mc:Star = new Star();
addChild(star_mc);
```

The instance `star_mc` will be placed at the coordinates (0, 0) on the Stage—the upper-left corner of the Stage—unless you specify its position. Recall that a movie clip instance's position is defined by its x and y properties. To place a star instance on the Stage at (100, 200) using script, the script would look like this:

```
var star_mc:Star = new Star();
star_mc.x = 100;
star_mc.y = 200;
addChild(star_mc);
```

If you do not remember the class name that you have given to a movie clip, you can repeat this step to look it up any time.

This example places only one star instance on the Stage. To place multiple star instances, you can use a `for` loop and store the star instances in an array, like this:

```
var i:uint = 0;
var arrStars:Array = new Array();
for (i = 0; i < 10; i++)
{
    var star_mc:Star = new Star();
    arrStars.push(star_mc);
    addChild(arrStars[i]);
}
```

The `for` loop generates 10 star instances and stores them in an array named `arrStars`. Instead of assigning an instance name to each instance, all the star instances are then referred to in the code through the `arrStars` array and their index numbers. The 10 star instances can be referred to using `arrStars[0]`, `arrStars[1]`, . . . , `arrStars[9]`.

---

**A Star Catcher Game (Lab)** In this lab exercise, stars are falling from the top of the Stage and the player controls the wizard at the lower half of the screen to catch the stars (Figure 11.14). Of course, feel free to create your own falling object and catcher object graphics.

You will be able to practice many of the important programming concepts and ActionScript code writing techniques you have learned in this and previous chapters. You will write code for: `mouseMove` event, frame event, controlling a movie clip instance's properties, generating random numbers, `for` loop, arrays, variable declarations, assignment statements, `if` statements, function definitions, function calls, and collision detection. You will also be able to practice generating the star instances on the Stage dynamically by setting Class Name in the Linkage and using `addChild()`. This game is simple to play, but it is not trivial to program.

---

## 11.11 USING ACTIONSCRIPT TO PLAY SOUND

The sound file that you want to play in your Flash movie may be imported into the Library. However, it does not have to be imported into the Library in order for your movie to use it. There two ways to play sound in your Flash movies using ActionScript depending on whether the sound file is imported in the Library or not.

- **Method 1:** To import a sound file into the Library, select `File > Import to Library . . .` and choose the sound file. The supported sound file formats include WAV, MP3, AIFF, and AU. Before writing script to play the sound, you will need to set the Linkage properties for the sound first. To do so, in the Library panel, right-click on the imported sound and choose Properties . . . In the ActionScript tab, you will see the ActionScript Linkage similar to that is shown in Figure 11.16. Check the option "Export for ActionScript." The Base Class field will be filled in as: flash.media.Sound. Enter a name in the Class Name field, using the same naming rules that are noted in Section 11.10.4. Remember the class name because you will use it in your script.

  To write code to play the sound, you can use the following basic structure:

```
var instanceName:ClassName = new ClassName();
instanceName.play();
```

The first statement is similar to that generates movie clip instances dynamically (Section 11.10.4). The `ClassName` is the class name you have given to the imported sound as its Linkage properties. The `play()` statement makes the sound play.

For example, suppose the class name for the imported sound is assigned as LaserSound. The script to play the sound would look like this:

```
var fireSnd:LaserSound = new LaserSound();
fireSnd.play();
```

If you test play your Flash movie with these two statements, the sound will play immediately when the Flash movie starts. The play() statement does not have to be right after the variable declaration statement. If you want to play the laser sound only when the user clicks on a laser movie clip instance, then the play() statement should be placed in the mouse event handler function for the laser.

- **Method 2:** With this method, the sound file is not imported into the Flash file but will be loaded using ActionScript. Because the sound file is not imported into the Library, there is no setting the Linkage properties as described in Method 1. However, it takes two extra statements to load the sound. In addition, the supported sound file format is MP3 only. Here is how the basic structure of the code looks like:

```
var instanceName:Sound = new Sound();
var urlreq:URLRequest = new URLRequest("filename");

instanceName.load(urlreq);
instanceName.play();
```

Suppose the filename of your laser sound is laser.mp3 and it is stored in the same folder as your Flash file. The script to load and play this sound would look like this:

```
var fireSnd:Sound = new Sound();
var urlreq:URLRequest = new URLRequest("laser.mp3");

fireSnd.load(urlreq);
fireSnd.play();
```

Each of these two methods has its pros and cons, which are summarized in Table 11.7.

The volume and panning of a sound also can be controlled using ActionScript. For more information, look up SoundChannel and SoundTransform in the Flash Help menu for ActionScript.

**TABLE 11.7   Comparison between the Two Methods of Using ActionScript to Play a Sound**

| Method 1: Importing the Sound to the Library | Method 2: Do Not Import the Sound but Load it Using ActionScript |
|---|---|
| Need to assign a class name to the imported sound in the Linkage properties. | No need to assign a class name to the sound. |
| Requires only two statements to set up and play a sound. | Requires at least four statements to set up and play a sound. |
| Because the sound is imported into the Flash file, the sound will increase the file size of the Flash file and its published movie. | Using a sound file this way does not increase the file size of the Flash file and its published movie. |
| When you play the published movie, you do not need to keep the sound file with the published movie. When you transfer or back up the Flash file to another device, you do not have to transfer the sound file with it. | The sound file is loaded during the movie plays. Thus, in order for the sound to play in the published movie, the sound file has to be kept in the appropriate folder—the way how the file is referred to in URLRequest(). When you transfer or back up the Flash file to another device, you will need to also transfer the sound file with it. |

## 11.12 SUMMARY

In interactive multimedia projects, you often need to program to make the appearance and behaviors of objects respond to the user's interaction with the computer. The common ways of a user interacting with a computer program are through mouse clicks, mouse movement, and keystrokes. To program mouse and keyboard interaction, you will need to learn to write event listener code.

**Events, Event Listener, Event Handling:** An event is something that happens while a program is running and interrupts the program's flow. Mouse clicks, mouse movements, and keystrokes are the most common events that can be initiated by the user. Event handling refers to specifying the actions in response to events. An event listener is an object that listens for events, such as mouse and keyboard events. An event handler is a function that will be executed when the event occurs.

The basic structure for writing event listener code is:

```
eventTarget.addEventListener(EventType.EVENT_NAME,
handlerFunctionName);
function handlerFunctionName(eventObject:EventType):void
{
    statement(s)
}
```

An example code for a mouse up event:

```
balloon_mc.addEventListener(MouseEvent.MOUSE_UP,
clickBalloonHandler);
function clickBalloonHandler(evt:MouseEvent):void
{
    balloon_mc.x += 5;
}
```

An example code for a keyboard event:

```
stage.addEventListener(KeyboardEvent.KEY_DOWN, keyDownHandler);
function keyDownHandler(evt:KeyboardEvent):void
{
    if (evt.keyCode == Keyboard.LEFT)
    {
        balloon_mc.x -= 5;
    }
    else if (evt.keyCode == Keyboard.RIGHT)
    {
        balloon_mc.x += 5;
    }
}
```

An example code for an ENTER_FRAME event:

```
stage.addEventListener(Event.ENTER_FRAME, frameEventHandler);
function frameEventHandler(evt:Event):void
{
    balloon_mc.x += 5;
}
```

The statements in the enterFrame event handler function are executed constantly at the frame rate. The enterFrame event is useful for creating scripted animation.

**Controlling Objects on Stage:** The commonly used properties of movie clip instances that you can use to control them on the Stage include: x, y, scaleX, scaleY, width, height, rotation, alpha, visible.

Controlling movie clip playback can be used to change its visual content. The idea behind this is that the different visual content options of a movie clip are placed on the movie clip's timeline, each frame containing one possible visual content. To display a particular content, you send the playhead to the frame that contains the content. The commonly used methods for movie clip playback introduced in this chapter are: stop(), play(), gotoAndStop(), and gotoAndPlay().

**Monitoring the Mouse Position:** To track the mouse position, you can use mouseX and mouseY.

**Detecting Collision Between Two Objects:** The two methods in ActionScript for collision detection are: hitTestObject() and hitTestPoint(). hitTestObject() can be used to check whether the bounding boxes of two movie clip instances overlap whereas hitTestPoint() offers two options to check whether a point is within a movie clip instance: within its actual pixel content or bounding box.

**Randomize:** Math.random() generates a random number >=0 and < 1. It can be used to generate a random number within any range by constructing an expression with it. Here is a general formula for the expression:

```
Math.random() * (max. of the range - min. of the range)
+ min. of the range
```

**Array:** An array is used to store a list of items. Each item has an index number. The first item in the array has an index of 0. The index of the last item in an array is equal to the number of items in the array minus one.

This chapter introduces two ways to create an array:

- Create an empty array and populate the array later. For example, to create an array called fruit:

```
var fruit:Array = new Array();
```

- Populate the array when it is created. For example, to create an array called fruit that contains a list of text items: "apple," "orange," "grape," "pear":

```
var fruit:Array = new Array("apple", "orange", "grape", "pear");
```

To access an item in an array, you can refer to its index number by using [], for example:

```
a = fruit[0];
```

You can add an item to the end of an array using push(), for example:

```
fruit.push("peach");
```

You can also add an item by index, for example:

```
fruit[4] = "peach";
```

To add an item to the beginning of an array, use unshift(), for example:

```
fruit.unshift("peach");
```

To remove the last item of an array, use pop(), for example:

```
fruit.pop();
```

To remove the first item of an array, use shift(), for example:

```
fruit.shift();
```

To replace an item of an array, use an assignment statement and set the item by referring to its index number using [], for example:

```
fruit[2] = "peach";
```

**Loops:** Loops let you repeat a block of statements while a specified condition is satisfied. This chapter introduces the for loop. The general syntax for a for loop is:

```
for (init; condition; next)
{
    statement(s)
}
```

**Generate Movie Clip Instances Dynamically:** Here are the basic steps to add movie clip instances on the Stage dynamically using script:

1. Set a Class name for your movie clip symbol's Linkage properties.
2. To add an instance of the movie clip symbol to the Stage, you can follow this basic structure:

```
var instanceName:ClassName = new ClassName();
addChild(instanceName);
```

The instance will be placed at the coordinates (0, 0) on the Stage if you do not specify its x and y properties. So don't forget to specify the position of a movie clip instance that is placed on the Stage using addChild().

To place multiple star instances, you can use a for loop and store the movie clip instances in an array. For example:

```
var i:uint = 0;
var arrStars:Array = new Array();
for (i = 0; i < 10; i++)
{
    var star_mc:Star = new Star();
    arrStars.push(star_mc);
    addChild(arrStars[i]);
}
```

## TERMS

## LEARNING AIDS

The following learning aids can be found at the book's companion Web site.

⌐ **ActionScript Example: Event Listener**

The completed Flash file for the Activity/Exercise on writing event listener code.

⌐ **ActionScript Example: Keyboard Event Listener Code**

1. Flash file: Demonstrates the code for moving a movie clip instance left when the LEFT arrow key is pressed, right when the RIGHT arrow key is pressed, up when the UP arrow key is pressed, and down when the DOWN arrow key is pressed.

2. Flash file: Control an object using other keys besides the arrow keys.

⌐ **ActionScript Example: Frame Event Listener Code**

A Flash file demonstrates using Event.ENTER_FRAME in a scripted animation to move a square to the left.

⌐ **Physically Based Projectiles**

A Web page explains the physics equations for projectiles.

⌐ **Adding Gravity (Lab)**

Modify the code example provided in the section on gravity to program a cannon ball shooting across the screen. The lab can be extended to be a projectile game, in which the player can use mouse and keyboard to control the velocities and direction of the cannon to shoot at a target.

⌐ **ActionScript Example: Controlling and Monitoring an Object's Screen Position**

1. Flash file: Demonstrates the code for placing a balloon movie clip at (300, 100) upon a mouse click on it.

2. Web page: Discussion for variations.

⌐ **Interactive X-Ray Scanner (Lab)**

Let's revisit the X-ray mask example (Figure 11.5) from Chapter 8. The animation of the mask in this example is a tweened animation. Now, you can program to make the scanner bar follow your mouse. The code involves a mouse move event listener, mouseY, and the scanner bar's y property.

### ActionScript Example: Changing the Visual Content of an Object

A Flash file demonstrates the code for popping a balloon upon a mouse click on it.

### Hairstyle Customization (Lab)

The hairstyle on a character changes to the one on which the user clicks (Figure 11.6). This lab lets you practice programming: (1) for a mouse up event, and (2) for controlling the playhead using `gotoAndStop()` to change the visual content of a movie clip. Feel free to design your hairstyles and the character's head.

### ActionScript Example: Making an Object Draggable

A Flash file demonstrates the code for clicking to drag a movie clip instance on the Stage.

### ActionScript Example: Tracking the Mouse Position

A Flash file demonstrates the code for placing a balloon at where the user clicks on the Stage.

### A Ball-and-Paddle Game (Lab): Part 1 of 3

You may know about a video game called Pong. In the game, on one side of the screen, there is a thin vertical rectangle representing a paddle. There is a small square block representing a ball. The player controls the vertical position of the paddle to hit the flying ball.

How the finished game of this lab is supposed to do:
You can use the mouse to control the vertical location of a paddle (Figure 11.8). A ball, starting at a random vertical position, flies horizontally toward the paddle. If the paddle catches the ball, the ball bounces back.

Main ideas and techniques to be applied in Part 1 of this lab:

1. Use the `mouseMove` event to make the paddle follow the mouse cursor whenever the cursor moves.
2. Use the vertical location of the mouse (`mouseY`) to control the vertical position of the paddle.
3. Use the `enterFrame` event and the x property of the ball to animate the ball to move across the screen.

### A Ball-and-Paddle Game (Lab): Part 2 of 3

Building on Part 1 of this lab, you will apply the following new concepts and techniques:

1. Apply collision detection (`hitTestObject()`) to determine if the paddle hits the ball.
2. Use a variable to control the direction of the ball—toward the paddle or bounced away from the paddle.

### ActionScript Example: Detecting Collision of Objects

1. A Flash file: If a missile hits a spaceship, the spaceship plays the explosion animation.
2. Web page: Discussion for variations.

### A Side-Scrolling Platform Game (Lab)

Here is how the completed game works:
You can control a "hero" to run forward or backward on a platform using the LEFT or RIGHT arrow keys to scroll the "platform." There are "treasures," such as a spinning coin and a mysterious box. Mouse up on the Stage makes the hero jump to collect the treasures. The treasure disappears when the hero touches it. Figure 11.13 shows examples of the completed lab with a variety of heroes, platforms, and treasures.

Main Ideas and Techniques:

1. Use keyboard and mouse events.
2. Use an enterFrame event to animate the hero jumping.

3. Move the platform movie clip instances using the x property.
4. Apply collision detection (`hitTestObject()`) to determine if the hero is in contact with the treasure.
5. Apply collision detection (`hitTestPoint()`) to determine if the hero has landed on the platform.

### ActionScript Example: `Math.random()`: Magic Hat Example

A Flash file of the magic hat example demonstrates the use of `Math.random()`. Upon clicking on a hat, one of the two animations (floating bubbles and flying bird) will be selected randomly to play.

### A Ball-and-Paddle Game (Lab): Part 3 of 3

Building on Part 2 of this lab, you will apply the following concepts and techniques:

1. Use `Math.random()` to randomize the vertical position of the ball every time it is reset to start over on the right.
2. Construct expressions to make the ball move and bounce at an angle.

### Timer Event Listener

This learning aid provides an introduction to the Timer event listener and example code of using Timer events. It also includes a lab exercise to program a hare-and-tortoise race using timers.

### A Star Catcher Game (Lab)

In this lab exercise, stars are falling from the top of the Stage and the player controls the wizard at the lower half of the screen to catch the stars (Figure 11.14). Of course, feel free to create your own falling object and catcher object graphics.

You will be able to practice many of the programming concepts and ActionScript code writing techniques you have learned in this and previous chapters. You will write code for: `mouseMove` event, frame event, controlling a movie clip instance's properties, generating random numbers, `for` loops, arrays, variable declarations, assignment statements, `if` statements, function definitions, function calls, and collision detection. You will also be able to practice generating the star instances on the Stage dynamically by setting Class Name in the Linkage and using `addChild()`. This game is simple to play, but it is not trivial to program.

## REVIEW QUESTIONS

When applicable, please choose all correct answers.

1. The properties for a movie clip instance's *x*- and *y*-coordinates are _____ and _____.

2. The property that you can use to specify the angle of rotation of a movie clip instance is _____. The unit of the angle is in _____. (Choices: degrees or radian)

3. The property that you can use to specify the transparency of a movie clip instance is _____. The value of this property ranges from _____ to _____; _____ is fully transparent and _____ is fully opaque.

4. The property that you can use to specify the visibility of a movie clip instance is _____. The value of this property can only be _____ or _____.

**5.** If you want to resize a movie clip instance relative to its original size—say 200%—you should use the properties _____.

A. x and y
B. scaleX and scaleY
C. width and height

**6.** If you want to resize a movie clip instance to a specified pixel dimension—say 200 pixels—you should use the properties _____.

A. x and y
B. scaleX and scaleY
C. width and height

**7.** The properties for the mouse position are _____.

A. x and y
B. xmouse and ymouse
C. xMouse and yMouse
D. mousex and mousey
E. mouseX and mouseY

**8.** The method to make an instance draggable is _____.

A. drag()
B. dragStart()
C. startDrag()
D. beginDrag()

**9.** Which of the following methods can be used to perform collision detection?

A. hitTest()
B. hitTestObject()
C. hitTestPoint()
D. There is no predefined method in ActionScript to do collision detection.

**10.** Which of the following methods can be used to perform collision detection between two objects based on their bounding boxes?

A. hitTest()
B. hitTestObject()
C. hitTestPoint()
D. There is no predefined method in ActionScript to do collision detection.

**11.** Which of the following methods can be used to perform collision detection between a point and a movie clip instance?

A. hitTest()
B. hitTestObject()
C. hitTestPoint()
D. There is no predefined method in ActionScript to do collision detection.

**12.** Which of the following statements generates a random number $>= 2$ and $< 10$.

    A. `Math.random()`

    B. `Math.random(2, 10)`

    C. `Math.random() * 10 + 2`

    D. `Math.random() * 2 + 10`

    E. `Math.random() * 8 + 2`

    F. `Math.random() * 2 + 8`

**13.** Suppose an array `fruit` is `["apple", "orange", "grape", "peach"]`; `fruit[0]` is _____.

    A. "apple"

    B. "orange"

    C. "grape"

    D. "peach"

    E. None of the above. There is no fruit[0]. You will get an error trying to access fruit[0].

**14.** Suppose an array `fruit` is `["apple", "orange", "grape", "peach"]`; `fruit[1]` is _____.

    A. "apple"

    B. "orange"

    C. "grape"

    D. "peach"

    E. None of the above. There is no `fruit[1]`. You will get an error trying to access `fruit[1]`.

**15.** Suppose an array `fruit` is `["apple", "orange", "grape", "peach"]`; `fruit[4]` is _____.

    A. "apple"

    B. "orange"

    C. "grape"

    D. "peach"

    E. None of the above. There is no `fruit[4]`. You will get an error trying to access `fruit[4]`.

**16.** Suppose an array `reptiles` is `["snake", "turtle", "lizard"]`;

To add "crocodile" to the end of the array, use the statement _____.

    A. `reptiles.push("crocodile");`

    B. `reptiles.push();`

    C. `reptiles.pop("crocodile");`

    D. `reptiles.pop();`

    E. `reptiles.unshift("crocodile");`

    F. `reptiles.unshift();`

    G. `reptiles.shift("crocodile");`

    H. `reptiles.shift();`

**17.** Suppose an array `reptiles` is `["snake", "turtle", "lizard"];`

To add "crocodile" to the beginning of the array, use the statement _____.

A. `reptiles.push("crocodile");`
B. `reptiles.push();`
C. `reptiles.pop("crocodile");`
D. `reptiles.pop();`
E. `reptiles.unshift("crocodile");`
F. `reptiles.unshift();`
G. `reptiles.shift("crocodile");`
H. `reptiles.shift();`

**18.** Suppose an array `reptiles` is `["snake", "turtle", "lizard"];`

To add "crocodile" between the second and third items (i.e., between "turtle" and "lizard"), use the statement:

`reptiles.splice(_____,_____,_____);`

**19.** Suppose an array `reptiles` is `["snake", "turtle", "lizard", "crocodile"];`

To remove the last item from the array, use the statement _____.

A. `reptiles.push("crocodile");`
B. `reptiles.push();`
C. `reptiles.pop("crocodile");`
D. `reptiles.pop();`
E. `reptiles.unshift("crocodile");`
F. `reptiles.unshift();`
G. `reptiles.shift("crocodile");`
H. `reptiles.shift();`

**20.** Suppose an array `reptiles` is `["crocodile", "snake", "turtle", "lizard"];`

To remove the first item from the array, use the statement _____.

A. `reptiles.push("crocodile");`
B. `reptiles.push();`
C. `reptiles.pop("crocodile");`
D. `reptiles.pop();`
E. `reptiles.unshift("crocodile");`
F. `reptiles.unshift();`
G. `reptiles.shift("crocodile");`
H. `reptiles.shift();`

**21.** Suppose an array `reptiles` is `["snake", "turtle", "crocodile", "lizard"];`

To remove the third item, which is "crocodile", use the statement:

`reptiles.splice(_____,_____);`

**22.** Suppose an array `reptiles` is `["crocodile", "snake", "turtle", "lizard"];`

To replace the second item with "chameleon", use the statement _____.

A. `reptiles[1] = "chameleon";`
B. `reptiles[2] = "chameleon";`
C. `reptiles[3] = "chameleon";`
D. `"chameleon" = reptiles[1];`
E. `"chameleon" = reptiles[2];`
F. `"chameleon" = reptiles[3];`

23. How many times does each of the following loops execute? Assume that `i` is not changed in the loop body.

```
 i. for (i = -10; i <= 10; i++)
 ii. for (i = 10; i >= 0; i++)
iii. for (i = -10; i <= 10; i = i + 3)
 iv. for (i = -10; i <= 10; i = i + 2)
```

24. What will be displayed in the Output panel when the following code is executed? Feel free to try out the code in Flash.

```
var s:int = 1;
var n:int;
for (n = 1; n < 5; n++)
{
    s = s + n;
    trace(s);
}
```

25. Complete the code below. Suppose upon mouse up on a movie clip instance `balloon_mc`, it will move 5 pixels to the right.

```
balloon_mc._____(_____._____,_____);
function clickBalloonHandler(evt:_____):void
{
    balloon_mc._____ += 5;
}
```

26. Complete the code below. Suppose a movie clip instance `kite_mc`, it will move up 5 pixels every time the user presses the UP arrow key and 5 pixels down when the user presses the DOWN arrow key.

```
_____.addEventListener(_____._____,_____);
function keydownHandler(evt:_____):void
{
    if (evt.keyCode == _____._____)
    {
        kite_mc._____ -= 5;
    }
    if (evt.keyCode == _____._____)
    {
        kite_mc._____ += 5;
    }
}
```

**27.** Complete the code below. Suppose a movie clip instance `bird_mc` moves up 4 pixels and to the right 7 pixels constantly at frame rate.

```
_____.addEventListener(_____._____,_____);
function onGameLoop(evt:_____):void
{
    bird_mc._____ += _____;
    bird_mc._____ -= _____;
}
```

**28.** To generate a movie clip instance dynamically, you need to:

i. Assign a _____ to the Linkage of the movie clip symbol.

ii. Create the instance as a variable:
    var *instanceName*:*ClassName* = _____ _____;

iii. Use the following statement to add the instance onto the Stage:
    _____(instanceName);

# OOP Basics with Flash ActionScript 3.0

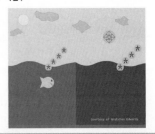

Courtesy of Gretchen Edwards

# 12

## KEY CONCEPTS

- Classes and objects
- Properties and methods
- Object-oriented programming (OOP)
- Constructor
- Static properties and methods

## GENERAL LEARNING OBJECTIVES

In this chapter, you will learn

- The concepts of classes and objects.
- How to depict classes using class diagrams.
- How to implement classes and create objects in ActionScript.
- How to assign a visual representation to objects in ActionScript.
- How to use arrays and `for` loops for multiple objects.
- What static properties and methods are, and when they are needed.
- How to add an event listener in a class file.

# 12.1 CONCEPTS OF OBJECTS

You encounter objects all the time in everyday life—cars, houses, lamps, shoes, scooters, and puppies. When you tell your friends about your new shoes, you probably would talk about their color, type (such as sneaker, sandal, or boots), size, brand, price, and even their special features (such as lighting up and having skate wheels for roller skating). When you tell your friends about your pet, you probably would talk about its type (such as a dog, a cat, or a goldfish), its name, its color, its age, and what it does. The quality or attributes such as color, size, kind, and name are the object's *properties*, and what it can do are its *behaviors*. Every object can be described in terms of properties and behaviors.

In computer games, you encounter objects all the time too. For example, in a shoot-them-up game, each spaceship may have a different location, size, speed, type of weapon, type of shield, and health points. Each laser gun may have a different value of remaining power and a different value of damage it can cause. The spaceship may fly up and down, turn left and right, and fire. The laser gun may turn left and right and also fire. The location, size, speed, type of weapon, type of shield, and health points are the properties of the spaceship object. The laser gun's properties are the remaining power and the damage it can cause. The behaviors of the spaceship object include flying up and down, turning left and right, and fire. The behaviors of the laser gun include turning left and right, and fire. In a monster game in which there are different types of monsters, each monster may have a different height, weight, strength, and speed. The monsters can run, swim, fly, and turn invisible. The height, weight, strength, and speed are the properties of the monsters, and their behaviors are running, swimming, flying, and turning invisible.

Let's revisit the Ball-and-Paddle Game lab and the Side-Scrolling Platform Game lab from Chapter 11. Suppose there are multiple balls in the ball-and-paddle game in which each ball may have a different location, size, speed, and points. These are the properties of the ball object. Each ball can bounce off the paddle and the top and bottom edge of the Stage. When it goes off the left or right side of the Stage, it restarts at the right edge of the Stage. These are the ball's behaviors.

In the side-scrolling platform game, suppose there are multiple spinning coins and each coin may have a different location and reward points. These are the properties of the coin object. Each coin disappears and is repositioned upon colliding with the hero. This is a behavior of the coin object.

## 12.2  CONCEPTS OF CLASSES

Before defining what classes are, let's start with an analogy of building a house. To build a house, you may have an architect to draft a blueprint and a builder to actually build the house using the blueprint. In this analogy, the house is an object and the blueprint is a class. Like the house blueprint, a class is only a description for the object; it is not something that can act on its own. The object is something you can actually act on. For example, you can move into a house but you cannot move into a blueprint. In addition, you can use the same blueprint to build multiple houses. Similarly, you can generate multiple objects from a class. Objects are also referred to as *instances* of a class or *class instances*. Creating an object from a class is referred to as *instantiating* a class.

Conceptually, a *class* is a self-contained description of a set of properties and behaviors. Its object possesses these properties and behaviors. From the code-centric view, a class contains a set of variables and functions. The behaviors are implemented as functions and the properties are defined as variables in the class. The functions defined in a class are called *methods*. Unlike the functions defined outside the class definition, only the objects of the class can use these functions. The variables defined in the class are also called *member variables*, and only the objects of the class can use these variables.

## 12.3  OBJECT-ORIENTED PROGRAMMING (OOP)

*Object-oriented programming (OOP)* provides a way of thinking to break down a particular problem or programming project into a collection of classes and objects, which are used as the building blocks in software application development. This is different from the approach introduced in Chapter 11, in which a program is written as a sequence of instructions or statements, telling the computer step by step what to do. It is called *procedural programming*.

To understand the difference between procedural programming and object-oriented programming, let's revisit our ball-and-paddle game. For the sake of simplicity and without loss of generality, let's consider a highly simplified version of this lab in which the ball is only moving horizontally without the collision detection with the paddle. Figure 12.1 shows how the code may look. A variable named vx is used as the velocity of the ball in the horizontal direction. The onPlayGame() function, an enterFrame event handler function, is executed at frame rate. This function contains instructions for two main tasks:

1. Move the ball horizontally by the amount of vx.

```
ball_mc.x += vx;
```

Does the term *instance* sound familiar? Recall the term *movie clip instance* in the previous chapter. Actually, MovieClip is a pre-defined class in ActionScript. When you put a copy of the movie clip symbol on the Stage, you create an instance of the MovieClip class— you instantiate the MovieClip class. The MovieClip instance is an object. You may not have realized it, but you have been using classes and objects the whole time.

```
var vx:int = -5;

stage.addEventListener(MouseEvent.MOUSE_MOVE, onMovePaddle);
stage.addEventListener(Event.ENTER_FRAME, onPlayGame);

function onMovePaddle(evt:MouseEvent):void
{
   paddle_mc.y = mouseY;
}

function onPlayGame(evt:Event):void
{
   ball_mc.x += vx;

   if (ball_mc.x < 0 || ball_mc.x > stage.stageWidth)
   {
     ball_mc.x = stage.stageWidth;
     vx = -5;
   }
}
```

**Figure 12.1**  A simplified version of the ball-and-paddle game code.

2. Check if the ball is outside the left or right edge of the Stage. If it is, then reposition the ball at the right edge of the Stage and reset the vx to −5, which will make the ball move to the left when the ball's x is incremented by vx.

```
if (ball_mc.x < 0 || ball_mc.x > stage.stageWidth)
{
    ball_mc.x = stage.stageWidth;
    vx = -5;
}
```

Now suppose you want to make a multi-ball game. To add a second ball to the game, you would first add a second movie clip instance of the ball on the Stage. Suppose you name it ball2_mc. Because the two balls move at a different random speed, a new variable named vx2 is created for the second ball. Figure 12.2 shows the revised code for the new two-ball game. Basically, you copy and paste some of the statements and change the ball_mc to ball2_mc and vx to vx2 in the second copy. Similarly, Figure 12.3 shows the code for the new three-ball game. What about having more balls? The code duplication becomes a big problem.

As you see, the procedural programming is fine for small projects, for example, your ball-and-paddle game with a single ball. However, when you start to add more game sprites, code duplication becomes a problem. With object-oriented programming, Figure 12.4 shows how the onPlayGame() function may look for the three-ball game. It is much simpler and easier to read. You may wonder what exactly move() is and where all the code that makes the ball move and the if statement that checks whether the ball is outside the Stage goes. Does move() magically make the ball do all these? The following sections will answer these questions.

With the object-oriented thinking, the balls in your game are objects. Each ball object has a different velocity. Each can move horizontally at its own velocity and check if it is outside the Stage. Each ball object can be thought of as an instance of a class that has a property of horizontal velocity. This class also has behaviors: moving horizontally and checking whether its object is outside the Stage. Recall that behaviors are implemented as

Code duplication is an undesirable practice. For example, if you want to make changes to your code that involves duplicated code segments, you will have to look through your code to make the exact changes for all the duplicates. It is inefficient and error-prone.

```
var vx:int = -5;
var vx2:int = -5;

stage.addEventListener(MouseEvent.MOUSE_MOVE, onMovePaddle);
stage.addEventListener(Event.ENTER_FRAME, onPlayGame);

function onMovePaddle(evt:MouseEvent):void
{
    paddle_mc.y = mouseY;
}

function onPlayGame(evt:Event):void
{
    ball_mc.x += vx;
    ball2_mc.x += vx;

    if (ball_mc.x < 0 || ball_mc.x > stage.stageWidth)
    {
        ball_mc.x = stage.stageWidth;
        vx = -5;
    }

    if (ball2_mc.x < 0 || ball2_mc.x > stage.stageWidth)
    {
        ball2_mc.x = stage.stageWidth;
        vx2 = -5;
    }
}
```

**Figure 12.2** Revised ball-and-paddle game code for two balls.

methods, which are functions defined in a class. In this case, move() is a method that encases the statements for moving the ball itself and checks whether the ball itself is outside the Stage. In the next two sections, you will learn how to create a class for the ball. Then you will learn how to instantiate the class to create the ball objects and make all ball objects move using the simple code shown in Figure 12.4.

## 12.4 CREATING CLASSES IN ActionScript

This section provides a step-by-step instruction on creating a ball class in ActionScript 3.0 for our ball-and-paddle game example discussed in the previous section. These are general steps that apply to creation of any classes in ActionScript 3.0. As you will see, the class file is built up in complexity step by step. However, the order after Step 2 is not a technical requirement. For example, adding methods (Step 4) before adding properties (Step 3) will not give you an error. Like writing an essay, a class file usually goes through several iterations of editing. The properties and methods may be added, deleted, and modified during the development.

**Step 1  Start a blank class file.**
To create a new class file, select File > New . . . and choose ActionScript File (not Flash file or ActionScript 3.0). Save the file with a file extension of .as. The filename has to match the class name exactly in both spelling and cases. For the ball-and-paddle game example, let's save the file as Ball.as.

If you are using Flash Professional CS5, you can also choose ActionScript 3.0 Class, which will automatically fill in the basic code structure described in Step 2.

```
var vx:int = -5;
var vx2:int = -5;
var vx3:int = -5;

stage.addEventListener(MouseEvent.MOUSE_MOVE, onMovePaddle);
stage.addEventListener(Event.ENTER_FRAME, onPlayGame);

function onMovePaddle(evt:MouseEvent):void
{
    paddle_mc.y = mouseY;
}

function onPlayGame(evt:Event):void
{
    ball_mc.x += vx;
    ball2_mc.x += vx;
    ball3_mc.x += vx;

    if (ball_mc.x < 0 || ball_mc.x > stage.stageWidth)
    {
        ball_mc.x = stage.stageWidth;
        vx = -5;
    }

    if (ball2_mc.x < 0 || ball2_mc.x > stage.stageWidth)
    {
        ball2_mc.x = stage.stageWidth;
        vx2 = -5;
    }
    if (ball3_mc.x < 0 || ball3_mc.x > stage.stageWidth)
    {
        ball2_mc.x = stage.stageWidth;
        vx2 = -5;
    }
}
```

**Figure 12.3** Revised ball-and-paddle game code for three balls.

```
function onPlayGame(evt:Event):void
{
    ball.move();
    ball2.move();
    ball3.move();
}
```

**Figure 12.4** Revised onPlayGame() when object-oriented programming is used.

Naming convention of the class name: The class name is usually a singular word and starts with an uppercase letter. If it contains more than one word, use camel case naming convention or use the underscore to separate the words.

### Step 2  Fill in the basic structure of a class file.

Figure 12.5 shows the general structure of a class file. You should replace the className with the name of the class you are creating. This will create an empty class. Don't forget that the class name and the filename (without the .as part) have to be the same—the cases must match too. For the Ball class in the ball-and-paddle game example, let's replace the className with Ball (Figure 12.6).

```
package
{
    public class ClassName
    {
        public function ClassName()
        {
        }
    }
}
```

**Figure 12.5** General structure of a class file in ActionScript 3.0.

Pay attention to the pairing of the curly braces. Misplacing any of these curly braces will cause errors when you try to test your game that uses the class file. To help you see the relationships of these curly braces, Figure 12.7 color-codes and boldfaces the pairing of the curly braces along with the units that the curly braces are associated with.

```
package
{
    public class Ball
    {
        public function Ball()
        {
        }
    }
}
```

**Figure 12.6** `Ball.as` file: An empty `Ball` class.

Note that there is a function with the same name as the class name. This is a special function called *constructor*. A constructor is invoked at the creation of the object. The constructor by default returns the object. Because the constructor of a class is executed when an object is created, the code that initializes the object should be placed in the constructor. Initialization of an object may include giving each property, such as speed, a starting value and invoking methods that perform certain tasks, such as placing an object at a starting location. Like any functions, the constructor can also have parameters. The parameters are often used for initializing the properties. This allows you to pass in arguments to the constructor to initialize the object. This may not make sense right now, but it will after you have seen examples in the section on instantiating a class.

Syntactically, the constructor should not specify a return type. Note that unlike other function definitions, the constructor does not have `:void` or any `:dataType` after `function Ball()`. Also note that there is a special word `public` at the beginning of the line `function Ball()`. The keyword `public` is an access specifier, which will be explained in the section on access specifiers in Chapter 13. There are other access specifiers, but the constructor has to be `public`, except in certain special cases that are beyond the scope of this text.

At this point, you have an empty `Ball` class but syntactically it is a working one. What this means is that if you now skip to the section on instantiating a class, you can

If you do not define a constructor method in your class, the compiler will automatically create an empty constructor for you.

instantiate this empty class to create a `Ball` object, no problem. However, an object from an empty class will not do anything. In order for the `Ball` object to perform as expected in our ball-and-paddle game, the rest of the following steps are necessary.

**Step 3  Define properties.**

Properties are defined as variables in the class. The declarations of these variables are placed inside the `public class Ball` block and before the constructor. Figure 12.7 shows that the property `vx` is defined in the `Ball` class. If there are multiple properties, multiple declarations can be added similarly.

```
package
{
    public class Ball
    {
        public var vx:int;

        public function Ball()
        {
        }
    }
}
```

**Figure 12.7** `Ball.as` file: A property `vx` is added to the `Ball` class.

Here we keep the same variable name, `vx`, as the one used in the lab using the procedural programming approach. This is to help you see the connection between the procedural version and the OOP version of the code, but it is not a technical requirement. You do not have to have a version of your game using procedural programming in order to develop an OOP version.

Before moving on to the next step, let's initialize the `vx` property in the constructor so that each `Ball` instance will have a starting value for `vx`. Otherwise, it gets a default value of zero, which will not make the `Ball` objects move at all. The `vx` is initialized to −5 (Figure 12.8) so that after Step 4, the `Ball` object can move to the left 5 pixels at a time. With the current code, each `Ball` object will start with the same velocity of −5. In Section 12.4.1, you will see how to rewrite the code slightly to allow each `Ball` object to move at a different velocity.

```
package
{
    public class Ball
    {
        public var vx:int;

        public function Ball()
        {
            vx = -5;
        }
    }
}
```

**Figure 12.8** `Ball.as` file: The property `vx` is initialized to −5 in the constructor.

**Step 4  Add methods (i.e., function definitions in the class).**

The syntax for writing methods is the same as that for writing any functions, except that the method definition has to start with one of the access specifier keywords, such as `public`. There are other access specifier keywords that can be used. They will be explained in the section on access specifiers in Chapter 13. For now, let's stick with `public`.

Methods implement the behaviors of the object. Behaviors are what the object can do. For the Ball object, it can move horizontally and check whether it is outside the Stage. Let's define a method named move() to encase the statements that perform these tasks. The statements in the method move() (Figure 12.9) are basically the same as the version using procedural programming (Figure 12.1). The main difference is the replacement of ball_mc with the keyword this. The keyword this refers to the object itself. In the procedural programming version of the code, ball_mc refers to a particular movie clip instance on the Stage. However, recall that a class is only a description; you have not had any object yet. In a class file, you use the keyword this to refer to the object that will be created. In Figure 12.9, the keyword this is also added to use with the property vx.

The usage of the keyword this is optional in ActionScript. For example, just x would work the same as this.x. The code examples in this text always use the keyword this.

```
package
{
    public class Ball
    {
        public var vx:int;

        public function Ball()
        {
            this.vx = -5;
        }

        public function move():void
        {
            this.x += this.vx;
            if (this.x < 0 || this.x > stage.stageWidth)
            {
                this.x = stage.stageWidth;
                this.vx = -5;
            }
        }
    }
}
```

**Figure 12.9** Ball.as file: A method move() is added.

**Step 5** **Add the keywords extends MovieClip and an import statement if the class instances will use a movie clip symbol as their visual representation.**

In order for the Ball object to use a movie clip as a visual representation, you will need to add the keywords extends MovieClip in the class file. You will also need an import statement in order to use the keyword MovieClip in the class file. Figure 12.10 shows the code with the keywords and the import statement. The keyword extends is related to inheritance, which will be introduced in the next chapter.

If the class file does not have any reference to the Stage, the class file would be completed at this point. However, the Ball class file contains reference to the Stage. The next step shows you how to use an import statement so that the Stage is recognized in the class file.

**Step 6** **Add an import statement if there are any references to the Stage.**

In order for the keyword stage to be recognized in the class file, an additional import statement is added to the class file (Figure 12.11).

```
package
{
    import flash.display.MovieClip;

    public class Ball extends MovieClip
    {
        public var vx:int;

        public function Ball()
        {
            this.vx = -5;
        }

        public function move():void
        {
            this.x += this.vx;

            if (this.x < 0 || this.x > stage.stageWidth)
            {
                this.x = stage.stageWidth;
                this.vx = -5;
            }
        }
    }
}
```

**Figure 12.10** `Ball.as` file: The keywords `extends MovieClip` and the `import` statement are added to allow the `Ball` object to use a movie clip as its visual representation.

```
package
{
    import flash.display.MovieClip;
    import flash.display.Stage;

    public class Ball extends MovieClip
    {
        public var vx:int;

        public function Ball()
        {
            this.vx = -5;
        }

        public function move():void
        {
            this.x += this.vx;

            if (this.x < 0 || this.x > stage.stageWidth)
            {
                this.x = stage.stageWidth;
                this.vx = -5;
            }
        }
    }
}
```

**Figure 12.11** `Ball.as` file: An `import` statement is added to allow the use of the keyword `stage` in the class file.

## 12.4.1 Improving the Game

In the `Ball` class, the `vx` property is set to −5 in the constructor. This makes every `Ball` object start with the same velocity of −5. To add variety and unpredictability, you can assign a random number to the `vx` in the constructor. In addition, you can randomize it again when the ball restarts at the right edge of the Stage after moving outside of the Stage. The code shown in Figure 12.12 randomizes the value of `vx` between −2 and −12. Each `Ball` object's `vx` will get a random number independent of each other. This demonstrates an important concept in OOP that each object maintains its own set of values for the properties.

Section 11.10.1 explains how to construct an expression for generating a random number within a range.

In many situations, you want to assign specific values rather than random values to the object's properties at the object's creation. You will then need to use parameters in the constructor. Section 12.7 will explain the use of parameters in the constructor.

```
package
{
    import flash.display.MovieClip;
    import flash.display.Stage;

    public class Ball extends MovieClip
    {
        public var vx:int;

        public function Ball()
        {
            this.vx = -(Math.random() * 10 + 2);
        }

        public function move():void
        {
            this.x += this.vx;

            if (this.x < 0 || this.x > stage.stageWidth)
            {
                this.x = stage.stageWidth;
                this.vx = -(Math.random() * 10 + 2);
            }
        }
    }
}
```

**Figure 12.12** `Ball.as` file: The `vx` of a `Ball` object is randomized when it is first created and also every time it restarts at the right edge of the Stage after going outside of the Stage.

## TURNING A NUMBER INTO AN INT

`Math.random()` generates a random number in the range of $>= 0$ and $< 1$. It is a decimal fraction. Further mathematical operations on the number will still be a number with a decimal fraction. If you want to preserve such numeric value, assign it to a variable of the Number data type. However, if you assign it to a variable of the int data type (integer), the number will be truncated (not rounded) into an integer—the decimal fraction is removed. For example, 0.4 and 0.6 will become 0; −2.1 and −2.8 will become −2, and 12.99999 will still become 12.

Note that in Figure 12.12, the expression (Math.random() * 10 + 2) gives a number with decimal fraction. However, the data type of vx is int. Thus, the statement this.vx = −(Math.random() * 10 + 2) will truncate the random number into an integer. If assigned to a variable of int data type, the minimum value generated from the expression (Math.random() * 10 + 2) is 2 and the maximum is 11, not 12.

It is true that if you declare vx or every variable as a Number, then you will never need to worry about any potential problems caused by truncation of the value. However, it is worth noting that on computers, mathematical operations are more efficient (faster) for integers than for values of the Number data type. In our ball-and-paddle game, the game will work basically the same with or without having a decimal fraction in vx. Thus we opt for efficiency by choosing the int data type.

When you are working with an integer variable, be careful not to increment it with a decimal fraction. For example, the following statement increments the variable score by 0.5:

```
score += 0.5;
```

If the date type of score is Number, it will increment by 0.5, no problem. However, if the date type of score is int, score will stay the same and never be incremented even if the statement is executed multiple times.

## 12.5  INSTANTIATING A CLASS TO CREATE OBJECTS

Now that you have a Ball class file, let's see how to use it to create Ball objects. An object is created as a variable. The syntax to declare a variable for the object is same as that for declaring any variables:

```
var objectName:ClassName = new ClassName();
```

The objectName is the variable name for the object. The instantiation statement is added in the code the same way as you would add any variable declaration statements. For example, the following statement instantiates the Ball class to create a Ball object with a variable name ball2.

Don't forget that a variable must be declared before it is used in the code.

```
var ball2:Ball = new Ball();
```

It can be placed in a script where the Ball object will be used, for example, in a Flash file (the file with the .fla file extension) or in another class, but not the Ball class file (Ball.as). The next section will discuss the setup in a Flash file so that the Ball objects will show up on the Stage. It will also show the full code of the script for the Flash file.

## 12.6  ADDING VISUAL REPRESENTATION OF OBJECTS

Game objects often have a visual representation, for example, a movie clip representing the object on the Stage. To assign a movie clip symbol as a visual representation of instances of a class, there are three things to set up:

1. In the class file (.as), add the keywords extends MovieClip and an import statement. See Step 5 in Section 12.4.
2. In the Flash file (.fla) in which the objects will be created, set the linkage for the movie clip symbol that you want to assign as the visual representation of the class instances.

Enter the exact name of the class in the Class Name field of the linkage section shown in Figure 11.15. See Section 11.10.4 for the detailed instruction and a screenshot.

3. In the script that is in the Flash file (.fla), add an addChild() statement after the instantiation statement. This will add the object on the Stage. Again, see Section 11.10.4 for the detailed instruction.

Figure 12.13 shows how the revised script in the Flash file for our ball-and-paddle game may look. Comparing to the code listed in Figure 12.3, it is simpler and more readable—you get a clearer big picture of what the game does. For this simple example, it may seem that the work required—write the Ball class file and set up the Flash file to assign a movie clip symbol as a visual representation for the class instances—is more than simply copying and pasting the code over and over as shown in Figure 12.3. However, real-world projects are much more complex than this simple example. Using object-oriented programming will reduce code duplication and make the code more readable. In addition, objects are self-contained. That is, each object has its own set of values for the properties. For example, each Ball object has its own vx and you do not add extra vx variables every time you add a ball to the game.

```
var ball:Ball = new Ball();
var ball2:Ball = new Ball();
var ball3:Ball = new Ball();

addChild(ball);
addChild(ball2);
addChild(ball3);

stage.addEventListener(MouseEvent.MOUSE_MOVE, onMovePaddle);
stage.addEventListener(Event.ENTER_FRAME, onPlayGame);

function onMovePaddle(evt:MouseEvent):void
{
    paddle_mc.y = mouseY;
}

function onPlayGame(evt:Event):void
{
    ball.move();
    ball2.move();
    ball3.move();
}
```

**Figure 12.13** Revised code of the ball-and-paddle game using the Ball class.

You can make an object do the things defined in a method by using the dot syntax like this:

*objectName.methodName();*

The statement ball.move() is to invoke the move() method, which is defined in the Ball class, on the object named ball. This makes the object ball do the things defined in the move() method, which include moving the object horizontally and checking if it is outside of the Stage. Similarly, the objects ball2 and ball3 are also invoked with move() in this example.

It is important to keep in mind that methods of a class are available to its instances only. For example, the move() method is only available to the Ball objects. If you try to call the move() function as colored in blue in Figure 12.14, you will get an error.

```
var ball:Ball = new Ball();
var ball2:Ball = new Ball();
var ball3:Ball = new Ball();

addChild(ball);
addChild(ball2);
addChild(ball3);

stage.addEventListener(MouseEvent.MOUSE_MOVE, onMovePaddle);
stage.addEventListener(Event.ENTER_FRAME, onPlayGame);

function onMovePaddle(evt:MouseEvent):void
{
    paddle_mc.y = mouseY;
}

function onPlayGame(evt:Event):void
{
    ball.move();
    ball2.move();
    ball3.move();
    move();
}
```

**Figure 12.14** Making a function call to a non-existent function move() will give an error.

```
var ball:Ball = new Ball();
var ball2:Ball = new Ball();
var ball3:Ball = new Ball();

addChild(ball);
addChild(ball2);
addChild(ball3);

stage.addEventListener(MouseEvent.MOUSE_MOVE, onMovePaddle);
stage.addEventListener(Event.ENTER_FRAME, onPlayGame);

function onMovePaddle(evt:MouseEvent):void
{
    paddle_mc.y = mouseY;
}

function onPlayGame(evt:Event):void
{
    ball.move();
    ball2.move();
    ball3.move();
    move();
}

function move():void
{
    trace("Hello there! Move it!");
}
```

**Figure 12.15** Making a function call to a function move() that is defined in the Flash file but has the same name as the move() method in the Ball class.

Now let's look at a different scenario. The code shown in Figure 12.15 also has a function call to move() but does not give an error. The function call move() (colored in blue) invokes the function move() (colored in gray), which will trace out the message "Hello there! Move it!". This move() function has absolutely no relationships with the move() method defined in the Ball class. If you are new to object-oriented programming, to avoid confusion it is advisable not to name a function in the Flash file using an existing method name that you have defined in a class. For example, the code in Figure 12.16 renames the function to moveIt() and does the same things as the code in Figure 12.15 but is less confusing to beginners.

```
var ball:Ball = new Ball();
var ball2:Ball = new Ball();
var ball3:Ball = new Ball();

addChild(ball);
addChild(ball2);
addChild(ball3);

stage.addEventListener(MouseEvent.MOUSE_MOVE, onMovePaddle);
stage.addEventListener(Event.ENTER_FRAME, onPlayGame);

function onMovePaddle(evt:MouseEvent):void
{
    paddle_mc.y = mouseY;
}

function onPlayGame(evt:Event):void
{
    ball.move();
    ball2.move();
    ball3.move();
    moveIt();
}

function moveIt():void
{
   trace("Hello there! Move it!");
}
```

**Figure 12.16**  Making a function call to a function moveIt() defined in the Flash file.

## 12.7 USING PARAMETERS IN THE CONSTRUCTOR

Like any functions, a constructor can also take parameters. Parameters in constructors are defined and used the same way as any other functions. See Section 9.3.3 for explanations and examples of parameters and arguments. The parameters in constructors are often used for initializing the properties.

In the Ball class example, the property vx is initialized to −5 (Figure 12.11). This makes every Ball object start with the same horizontal velocity of −5. Suppose you want to assign different values to the vx at the creation of each Ball object. You may modify the constructor to take a parameter as shown in Figure 12.17. The changes for using a parameter in the constructor are colored in blue. The code Math.abs(this.vx) in blue is not directly

```
package
{
    import flash.display.MovieClip;
    import flash.display.Stage;

    public class Ball extends MovieClip
    {
        public var vx:int;

        public function Ball(velocityx:int)
        {
            this.vx = velocityx;
        }

        public function move():void
        {
            this.x += this.vx;

            if (this.x < 0 || this.x > stage.stageWidth)
            {
                this.x = stage.stageWidth;
                this.vx = -Math.abs(this.vx);
            }
        }
    }
}
```

**Figure 12.17** The Ball constructor takes one parameter, which is used to set the vx.

Naming a parameter with the corresponding property name is a naming convention, not a syntactical requirement. Having both the parameter and property share the same name often causes confusion to beginners. However, because it is a common convention, this text adopts this convention.

Section 11.10.1 explains how to construct an expression for randomizing a number within a range.

related to the use of the parameter, but a necessary change in the context of the game. `Math.abs(this.vx)` gives an absolute value of vx. The statement:

```
this.vx = -Math.abs(this.vx);
```

ensures vx has a negative value. In the current simplified example, there is no apparent reason for this statement because the vx never changes its value. However, in the completed game, the ball bounces off of the paddle. Its vx changes to positive when it bounces off of the paddle. Thus, it is necessary to ensure that vx has a negative value when it restarts at the right edge of the Stage.

It is a common naming convention for constructor parameters to name the parameters with the corresponding property names that the parameters are used for. Figure 12.18 rewrites the code in Figure 12.17 using this convention. The keyword `this` is now crucial to distinguish the parameter from the property, because both have the same name vx.

With the change in the constructor, the instantiation of the class will also need to pass in an argument. Figure 12.19 shows the updated code for the Flash file; −5, −8, and −3 are passed in as an argument at the creation of ball, ball2, and ball3, respectively. Thus ball, ball2, and ball3 move at the velocity of −5, −8, and −3, respectively.

If you want to assign a random number between −2 and −10 to the vx of each Ball object, you can rewrite the three instantiation statements as follows:

```
var ball:Ball = new Ball( -(Math.random() * 8 + 2) );
var ball2:Ball = new Ball( -(Math.random() * 8 + 2) );
var ball3:Ball = new Ball( -(Math.random() * 8 + 2) );
```

The Ball class constructor may also need an additional parameter. When a Ball object moves, it also needs to check if it hits the paddle. Suppose you have a paddle as a movie

```
package
{
    import flash.display.MovieClip;
    import flash.display.Stage;

    public class Ball extends MovieClip
    {
        public var vx:int;

        public function Ball(vx:int)
        {
            this.vx = vx;
        }

        public function move():void
        {
            this.x += this.vx;

            if (this.x < 0 || this.x > stage.stageWidth)
            {
                this.x = stage.stageWidth;
                this.vx = -Math.abs(this.vx);
            }
        }
    }
}
```

**Figure 12.18** `Ball.as`. The parameter in the constructor uses the same name as the property, vx, that the parameter is used for.

```
var ball:Ball = new Ball(-5);
var ball2:Ball = new Ball(-8);
var ball3:Ball = new Ball(-3);

addChild(ball);
addChild(ball2);
addChild(ball3);

stage.addEventListener(MouseEvent.MOUSE_MOVE, onMovePaddle);
stage.addEventListener(Event.ENTER_FRAME, onPlayGame);

function onMovePaddle(evt:MouseEvent):void
{
    paddle_mc.y = mouseY;
}

function onPlayGame(evt:Event):void
{
    ball.move();
    ball2.move();
    ball3.move();
}
```

**Figure 12.19** In a Flash file (`.fla`) that uses the `Ball` class, now that the `Ball` constructor takes an int parameter, the instantiation of the `Ball` class needs to pass in an integer.

In this example, each `Ball` object keeps its own property of the paddle. However, it is the same paddle movie clip instance for all `Ball` objects. It is not necessary to have each `Ball` object allocate memory to keep a copy of the same paddle movie clip instance. A better way to set the property for the paddle is to use the `static` attribute. The keyword `static` is explained in Section 12.11.

clip instance on the Stage. In order for the `Ball` object to perform collision detection with this paddle, you can add a property in the `Ball` class to store the paddle movie clip instance. In the `Ball` constructor, you add a second parameter so that the paddle movie clip instance on the Stage in a Flash file can be passed to the constructor, which then sets the paddle property. Figure 12.20 shows the new `Ball` class with the paddle property and a constructor that takes a second parameter for the paddle. A `hitTestObject()` condition is also added in the `move()` method to show the use of the paddle property.

```
package
{
    import flash.display.MovieClip;
    import flash.display.Stage;

    public class Ball extends MovieClip
    {
        public var vx:int;
        public var paddle:MovieClip;

        public function Ball(vx:int, paddle:MovieClip)
        {
            this.vx = vx;
            this.paddle = paddle;
        }

        public function move():void
        {
            this.x += this.vx;

            if (this.x < 0 || this.x > stage.stageWidth)
            {
                this.x = stage.stageWidth;
                this.vx = -Math.abs(this.vx);
            }

            if (this.hitTestObject(this.paddle))
            {
                this.vx = Math.abs(this.vx);
            }
        }
    }
}
```

**Figure 12.20** `Ball.as`. The second parameter in the constructor is used to set the property `paddle`.

Now that the `Ball` constructor is expecting two parameters—the first being an integer for the starting speed and the second a movie clip instance for the paddle—the statement to instantiate the `Ball` class looks like this:

```
var ball:Ball = new Ball(-5, paddle_mc);
```

## 12.8 CLASS DIAGRAMS

For the rest of this book, we will often use the ***class diagram*** to depict the structure of one or more classes and the relationships between classes in a Flash ActionScript project. The class diagram is a notation that depicts a class as a rectangle, which in turn is composed of three rectangles stacked on top of one another. The class name appears in the topmost rectangle. The middle rectangle lists the properties of the class and the bottom rectangle list the methods. For example, Figure 12.21 shows a class diagram for the `Ball` class that is listed in Figure 12.18.

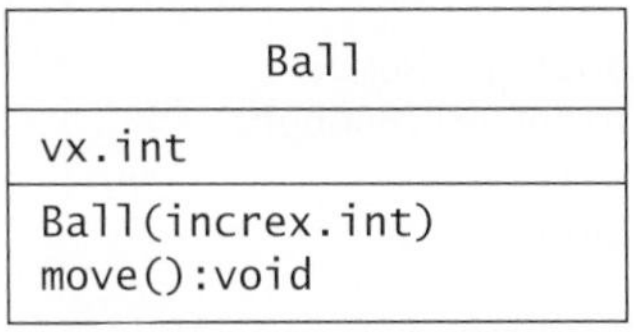

```
                 Ball
    vx.int
    Ball(increx.int)
    move():void
```

**Figure 12.21** Class diagram for the `Ball` class example.

## 12.9 MORE CLASS EXAMPLES

This section provides more examples of writing class definitions and using classes in a Flash file. The examples in this section are to be used as game sprites that have a visual representation. Thus the class files use the keywords `extends MovieClip` and include the `import` statement for MovieClip. However, not all classes need to use a movie clip as a visual representation on the Stage. For these classes, you do not need to add the keywords `extends MovieClip` and the `import` statement for MovieClip.

For the purposes of demonstrating the basic structure of a class file, only a few properties and methods are defined in each example. In addition, the methods in these examples may be left empty or contain only a few simple statements.

### 12.9.1 A Car Class

The class diagram for this `Car` class example is shown in Figure 12.22. Here, a `Car` object has two properties:

- `fuelCapacity`: It is to store the maximum fuel that a `Car` object can hold.
- `remainingFuel`: It is to store the fuel remaining in a `Car` object.

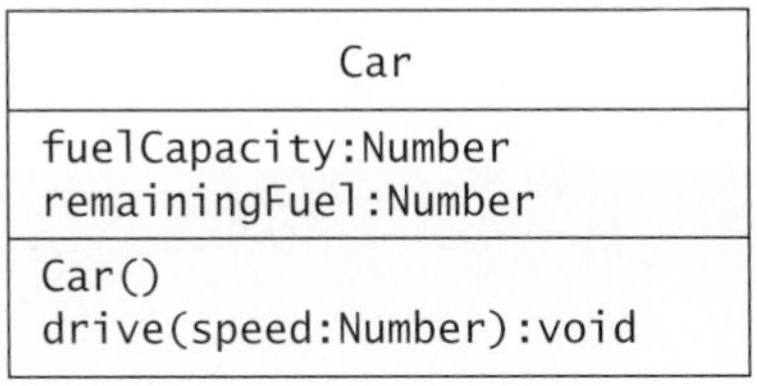

```
                  Car
    fuelCapacity:Number
    remainingFuel:Number
    Car()
    drive(speed:Number):void
```

**Figure 12.22** Class diagram for the `Car` class example.

The code for the `Car` class is listed in Figure 12.23. In the constructor, `fuelCapacity` and `remainingFuel` are set to 15. This means that every `Car` object will start with a full tank of 15 when it is created. The class has only one method: `drive()`. It takes a parameter, `speed`, and moves the `Car` object horizontally by the amount of `speed`. In addition, every time it moves, its `remainingFuel` is decreased by the amount of `speed * 0.01`.

Figure 12.24 shows an example of using the `Car` class in a Flash file. Here a `Car` object named `betty` is created. The object `betty` is invoked with its `drive()` method in an enterFrame event handler function, `onPlayGame()`. A value of 5 is passed in the `drive()` method as an argument. Thus, the object `betty` is moving to the right 5 pixels at a time at frame rate.

```
package
{
    import flash.display.MovieClip;

    public class Car extends MovieClip
    {
        public var fuelCapacity:Number;
        public var remainingFuel:Number;

        public function Car()
        {
            this.fuelCapacity = 15;
            this.remainingFuel = 15;
        }
        public function drive(speed:int):void
        {
            this.x += speed;
            this.remainingFuel -= speed * 0.01;
        }
    }
}
```

**Figure 12.23** `Car.as`

```
var betty:Car = new Car();
addChild(betty);

stage.addEventListener(Event.ENTER_FRAME, onPlayGame);

function onPlayGame(evt:Event):void
{
    betty.drive(5);
}
```

**Figure 12.24** ActionScript in a Flash file (`.fla`) that uses the `Car` class.

### ❓ Self-Test Exercise: Improving the Car Class

#### Questions

Note that in the example shown in Figure 12.24, the `remainingFuel` of the Car object `betty` will eventually become negative.

1. After how many times of invocation of `drive(5)` on `betty` will its `remainingFuel` become negative?
2. Modify the `drive()` method so that the `Car` object will not move when the `remainingFuel` is not enough to move by the amount of `speed`.

#### Answers to Self-Test Questions

1. Full tank is 15. Each invocation of `drive(5)` on `betty` will decrease its `remainingFuel` by 5 * 0.01 = 0.05. Thus, `betty`'s `remainingFuel` will become negative after 15 / 0.05 = 300 times of invocation.

2. ```
public function drive(speed:int):void
   {
       if (this.remainingFuel >= speed * 0.01)
       {
           this.x += speed;
           this.remainingFuel -= speed * 0.01;
       }
   }
```

> ✏️ **A Car Class (Lab): Part 1 of 3** Follow the description in Section 12.9.1 to create a Car class, instantiate a Car object, and place the object on the Stage. When you test the movie, you should see that your car object starts at the upper-left corner of the Stage (assuming that the registration point of your car movie clip is around the center of the car) and moves to the right.

## 12.9.2 A Car Class with a Constructor That Takes One Parameter

The class diagram for this Car class example is shown in Figure 12.25. The class file and an example of using the Car class are shown in Figure 12.26 and Figure 12.27, respectively. This example is basically the same as the previous Car class example, except that its constructor takes a parameter that is used to set the fuel capacity of a Car object. This offers an advantage that you can pass in different values to the constructor to set the fuel capacity for different Car objects. In the previous example, all Car objects have the same fuel capacity of 15 that is hard-coded in the constructor.

| Car |
| --- |
| fuelCapacity:Number<br>remainingFuel:Number |
| Car(fuelCapacity:Number)<br>drive(speed:Number):void |

**Figure 12.25** A class diagram for the Car class example in which the constructor takes a parameter for its fuel capacity.

## 12.9.3 A LaserTurret Class

This example demonstrates a class with a constructor that takes multiple parameters. Two of the parameters are used to set the object's position on the Stage. The example class is called LaserTurret. As shown in its class diagram (Figure 12.28), it has two properties:

- remainingPower: It is to store the remaining power of a LaserTurret object.
- firePower: It is to store the power that is consumed every time a LaserTurret object fires.

In the constructor (as shown in Figure 12.29), these two properties are assigned with the values of the parameters of the same names. The parameters x and y are used to set the object's x and y. Setting the x and y properties in the constructor will place the object at that position when it is created.

If an object's x and y are not assigned with any values when the object is created, it will be placed at (0, 0), which is the upper-left corner of the Stage.
```

```
package
{
    import flash.display.MovieClip;

    public class Car extends MovieClip
    {
        public var fuelCapacity:Number;
        public var remainingFuel:Number;

        public function Car(fuelCapacity:Number)
        {
            this.fuelCapacity = fuelCapacity;
            this.remainingFuel = fuelCapacity;
        }
        public function drive(speed:int):void
        {
            this.x += speed;
            this.remainingFuel -= speed * 0.01;
        }
    }
}
```

**Figure 12.26** `Car.as`

```
var betty:Car = new Car(15);
addChild(betty);

stage.addEventListener(Event.ENTER_FRAME, onPlayGame);

function onPlayGame(evt:Event):void
{
    betty.drive(5);
}
```

**Figure 12.27** ActionScript in a Flash file (`.fla`) that uses the `Car` class.

| LaserTurret |
| --- |
| remainingPower:Number<br>firePower:Number |
| LaserTurret(remainingPower:Number, firePower:Number, x:int, y:int)<br>turn():void<br>fire():void |

**Figure 12.28** Class diagram for the `LaserTurret` class example.

The class has two methods:

- `turn()`: This method rotates the `LaserTurret` object by 10 degrees.
- `fire()`: This method decreases the object's `remainingPower` by the amount of its `firePower`.

Figure 12.30 shows an example of using the `LaserTurret` class in a Flash file. Here two `LaserTurret` objects, myLaser1 and myLaser2, are created. For myLaser1, values 100, 5, 150, and 230 are passed to the constructor. Thus, myLaser1

```
package
{
    import flash.display.MovieClip;

    public class LaserTurret extends MovieClip
    {
        public var remainingPower:Number;
        public var firePower:Number;

        public function LaserTurret(remainingPower:Number,
        firePower:Number, x:int, y:int)
        {
            this.remainingPower = remainingPower;
            this.firePower = firePower;
            this.x = x;
            this.y = y;
        }

        public function turn():void
        {
            this.rotation += 10;
        }

        public function fire():void
        {
            this.remainingPower -= this.firePower;
        }
    }
}
```

**Figure 12.29** `LaserTurret.as`

```
var myLaser1:LaserTurret = new LaserTurret(100, 5, 150, 230);
var myLaser2:LaserTurret = new LaserTurret(100, 8, 90, 310);

addChild(myLaser1);
addChild(myLaser2);

myLaser1.addEventListener(MouseEvent.MOUSE_DOWN, fireLaser1);
myLaser2.addEventListener(MouseEvent.MOUSE_DOWN, fireLaser2);

function fireLaser1(evt:MouseEvent):void
{
   myLaser1.fire();
}

function fireLaser2(evt:MouseEvent):void
{
   myLaser2.fire();
}
```

**Figure 12.30** ActionScript in a Flash file (`.fla`) that uses the `LaserTurret` class.

starts with a remaining power of 100, has a fire power of 5, and is placed at (150, 230) on the Stage when it is created. Similarly, For `myLaser2`, values 100, 8, 90, and 310 are passed to the constructor. Thus, `myLaser2` starts with a remaining power of 100, has a fire power of 8, and is placed at (90, 310) on the Stage when it is created. Both objects have a mouse event listener such that when you click on either of them, it invokes its `fire()` method.

---

### ❓ Exercise: Improving the `Car` Class

#### Questions

1. Modify the `Car` class (Figure 12.26) constructor to take four parameters: one to set its fuel capacity, one to set its remaining fuel, and two to set its x and y.
2. Show an example use (similar to Figure 12.27) of this modified `Car` class—instantiate the class to create an object and invoke the `drive()` method on the object. Suppose the car will be placed at (40, 230) on the Stage when it is created. You can choose any value for the fuel capacity and remaining fuel but they have to be valid values in the context of a car. For example, they have to be non-negative and the remaining fuel is not more than the fuel capacity.
3. Note that with the current code in the constructor, you can pass in the arguments to the constructor such that the remaining fuel is more than fuel capacity. However, a car's remaining fuel should never be more than its fuel capacity. Modify the `Car` class constructor (from Question 1) to enforce that the remaining fuel is not more than the fuel capacity.

#### Answers to Self-Test Questions

1. 
```
public function Car(fuelCapacity:Number, remainingFuel:Number,
x:int, y:int)
{
    this.fuelCapacity = fuelCapacity;
    this.remainingFuel = remainingFuel;
    this.x = x;
    this.y = y;
}
```

2. 
```
var betty:Car = new Car(15, 10, 40, 230);
stage.addEventListener(Event.ENTER_FRAME, onPlayGame);
function onPlayGame(evt:Event):void
{
    betty.drive(5);
}
```

3. 
```
public function Car(fuelCapacity:Number,
remainingFuel:Number, x:int, y:int)
{
    this.fuelCapacity = fuelCapacity;
    if (fuelCapacity < remainingFuel)
    {
        this.remainingFuel = fuelCapacity;
    }
    else
    {
        this.remainingFuel = remainingFuel;
    }
    this.x = x;
    this.y = y;
}
```

The if statement is used to enforce that the remaining fuel is not more than the fuel capacity. For example, if the Car class is instantiated using the following statement that attempts to set the fuel capacity to 15 and remaining fuel to 1,000, the remaining fuel is capped at 15.

```
var betty:Car = new Car(15, 1000, 40, 230);
```

The solution provided here is to cap the remaining fuel at no more than the fuel capacity. This is not the only strategy to enforce that the remaining fuel is not more than the fuel capacity. Depending on how you want to design your Car class, you may raise the fuel capacity to match the value of remaining fuel that is passed into the constructor.

---

**A Car Class (Lab): Part 2 of 3** Improve Part 1 of the Car Class lab using the solutions of the Improving the Car Class exercise. When you test the completed movie, you should see a car start moving to the right from about the left center of the Stage.

## 12.9.4 A LaserTurret Class with Event Listener Code

In the previous LaserTurret example, a mouse event listener is set up for each LaserTurret object so that they can be clicked to fire. If all the LaserTurret objects are clickable, it would be better to add the event listener code in the class so that you do not have to write the event listener code for each LaserTurret object in the Flash file. This example modifies the LaserTurret example from the previous section to include the event listener code in the class file. It has an additional method, which is the mouse event handler function. Figure 12.31 shows its class diagram.

| LaserTurret |
|---|
| remainingPower:Number<br>firePower:Number |
| LaserTurret(remainingPower:Number, firePower:Number, x:int, y:int)<br>handleMouseDown(evt:MouseEvent):void<br>turn():void<br>fire():void |

**Figure 12.31** A class diagram for the LaserTurret class example with mouse event handler.

The class file (Figure 12.32) shows the event listener code. Writing event listener code in a class file is basically the same as writing it in a Flash file. The differences are as follows:

- For the event handler function, a keyword for the access specifier is needed before the keyword function. The access specifier used in this example is public, but this may not be the best choice. Access specifiers will be discussed in Chapter 13 and you will see the other access specifier options.
- The addEventListener() statement is added. In this example, the addEvent-Listener() statement is added in the constructor. This will make the LaserTurret object clickable when it is created. The addEventListener() statement does not have to be placed in the constructor, however. For example, if it is added in the turn() method, then the LaserTurret object will become clickable only after the turn() method is invoked.

```
package
{
    import flash.display.MovieClip;
    import flash.events.MouseEvent;

    public class LaserTurret extends MovieClip
    {
        public var remainingPower:Number;
        public var firePower:Number;

        public function LaserTurret(remainingPower:Number,
        firePower:Number, x:int, y:int)
        {
            this.remainingPower = remainingPower;
            this.firePower = firePower;
            this.x = x;
            this.y = y;
            this.addEventListener(MouseEvent.MOUSE_DOWN,
            handleMouseDown);
        }

        public function handleMouseDown(evt:MouseEvent):void
        {
            fire();
        }

        public function turn():void
        {
            this.rotation += 10;
        }

        public function fire():void
        {
            this.remainingPower -= this.firePower;
        }
    }
}
```

**Figure 12.32** `LaserTurret.as`

- An `import` statement is added so the `MouseEvent` class is available to the `LaserTurret` class; that is, the mouse event listener code is recognized in the `LaserTurret` class.

With this new `LaserTurret` class with the event listener code (Figure 12.32), the event listener code in a Flash file shown in Figure 12.31 can be removed. Figure 12.33 shows the new code that works the same as in the previous `LaserTurret` example.

```
var myLaser1:LaserTurret = new LaserTurret(100, 5, 150, 230);
var myLaser2:LaserTurret = new LaserTurret(100, 8, 90, 310);

addChild(myLaser1);
addChild(myLaser2);
```

**Figure 12.33** ActionScript in a Flash file (`.fla`) that uses the new `LaserTurret` class containing the event listener code.

## 12.10 MULTIPLE OBJECTS USING ARRAYS

Our ball-and-paddle example (Figure 12.13) creates and moves three Ball objects by writing three instantiation statements, three addChild() statements, and three statements to invoke the move() methods on the objects. An array and for loops can be used to make the code more compact. The code in Figure 12.13 can be rewritten using an array and for loops as shown in Figure 12.34. An array arrBalls is created to store the three Ball objects. The first for loop iterates three times. The Ball class is instantiated in each iteration. The new instance is added to the array and placed on the Stage using the addChild() statement. This for loop replaces the three instantiation and three addChild() statements of Figure 12.13. The class instances are not referred to by their instance names. Instead, they are referred to through the array and their indexes. Thus, to invoke a method on all the objects in the array, a for loop is used to loop through the array invoking the method on each object in the array. For example, the three move() statements in onPlayGame() are replaced by a for loop, which loops through the array arrBalls, invoking the method move() on each object in the array.

*Arrays and loops are covered in Section 11.10.4.*

```
var arrBalls:Array = new Array();

for (var i:int = 0; i < 3; i++)
{
    var ball:Ball = new Ball();
    arrBalls.push(ball);
    addChild(arrBalls[i]);
}

stage.addEventListener(MouseEvent.MOUSE_MOVE, onMovePaddle);
stage.addEventListener(Event.ENTER_FRAME, onPlayGame);

function onMovePaddle(evt:MouseEvent):void
{
    paddle_mc.y = mouseY;
}

function onPlayGame(evt:Event):void
{
    for (var i:int = 0; i < arrBalls.length; i++)
    {
        arrBalls[i].move();
    }
}
```

**Figure 12.34** Using an array and for loops for multiple objects.

In the first for loop, it uses the push() method to add the new Ball object to the array. The push() method adds the new item to the end of the array. The other method to add an item to an array is unshift(), which adds the new item to the beginning of the array—the new item becomes the first item in the array and all other items in the array are shifted down by one position. The first for loop in Figure 12.34 can be rewritten using unshift() as follows:

```
for (var i:int = 0; i < 3; i++)
{
    var ball:Ball = new Ball();
    arrBalls.unshift(ball);
    addChild(arrBalls[0]);
}
```

Note that the index of the new item to be added on the Stage is now zero because the new item is always the first item in the array.

> 🖑 A Car Class (Lab): Part 3 of 3  Modify Part 2 of the Car Class lab to use an array and for loops to create 10 moving Car objects. In addition, randomize the starting position of each Car object. When you test the completed movie, you should see 10 cars start moving to the right from random positions within the Stage.

## 12.11 THE KEYWORD static

Let's revisit the LaserTurret example (Figure 12.29 and Figure 12.30) in Section 12.9.3. Each of the two LaserTurret objects, myLaser1 and myLaser2, starts with the remainingPower of 100. The total power you have in the game is 200. The remainingPower of the two LaserTurret objects are independent of each other. You may keep firing myLaser1 until its power runs out while myLaser2 may still have full power of 100 because it has never been fired.

Now suppose you want to have both LaserTurret objects share the ammunition supply. If you fire myLaser1 until there is no power left, myLaser2 will not be able to fire even if it has never been fired. For this situation, the property remainingPower would need to set as a static variable. The ***static*** keyword specifies that a property or method is created *only once per class* instead of in every object of that class. In other words, all the objects instantiated from the same class share the value of the property that is static.

To assign a static attribute to a property or a function, simply add the keyword static before the keywords var or function. Figure 12.35 shows the assignment of the static attribute to the property remainingPower of the LaserTurret. Note that the keyword this should not be used with remainingPower any more.

Now that we have introduced the keyword static, we will introduce two new terms that describe static and non-static members of a class. Non-static methods, that is, methods that are declared without using the keyword static, are called ***instance methods*** because they are attached to an instance of a class. The methods that you have seen in the examples of this chapter so far are instance methods. Static methods are also called ***class methods*** because they are attached to the class as a whole, instead of an instance of a class. Similarly, the non-static property is also called the ***instance property***. All the properties in the examples before this section are instance properties. For example, the remainingPower in the LaserTurret class shown in Figure 12.29 is an instance property. Each LaserTurret object keeps its own value of remainingPower.

The following subsections discuss the rules of using of static properties and methods.

### 12.11.1 In Its Class File: No Keyword this

The parameter name remainingPower in the constructor is changed to power to avoid the confusion.

The statements in an instance method (non-static), on the other hand, can use static properties.

The static methods act at the class level, not the instance level. What this means is that the statements in a static method cannot refer to an instance of the class. When a static member is used within its class file, it should not be used with the keyword this because they are not attached to an individual object. Note that in Figure 12.35, all the usages of remainingPower do not have the keyword this.

There are also restrictions for writing a static method. A static method (class method) cannot have statements that use the keyword this, use non-static properties, or invoke methods that use non-static properties.

```
package
{
    import flash.display.MovieClip;

    public class LaserTurret extends MovieClip
    {
        public static var remainingPower:Number;
        public var firePower:Number;

        public function LaserTurret(power:Number, firePower:Number,
        x:int, y:int)
        {
            this.remainingPower = power;
            this.firePower = firePower;
            this.x = x;
            this.y = y;
        }

        public function turn():void
        {
            this.rotation += 10;
        }

        public function fire():void
        {
            this.remainingPower -= this.firePower;
        }
    }
}
```

**Figure 12.35** `LaserTurret.as` in which the `remainingPower` is a `static` property.

## 12.11.2 Used Outside Its Class Definition: Use with Class Name NOT Object Name

To access a static property or invoke a static method outside its class file definition, you do not need to instantiate the class to create an object because a static member is attached to its class, not the instance of the class.

In addition, you use a static property with its *class name* (NOT an object name) like this:

*ClassName*`.propertyName`

Note that it is not *objectName*`.propertyName`. For example, to set the static property `remainingPower` of the `LaserTurret` to 200 in a Flash file where you are using the `LaserTurret` class, use a statement like this:

`LaserTurret.remainingPower = 200;`

but not:

`myLaser1.remainingPower = 200;`

or

`myLaser2.remainingPower = 200;`

Attempting to set or retrieve a static property using an object name will give an error.

Similarly, to invoke a static method, you use the following syntax:

*ClassName*`.methodName();`

For example, suppose the `LaserTurret` class has a static method named `recharge()`, in which the `remainingPower` is reset to 100 (Figure 12.36). To invoke this `recharge()` method in a Flash file that uses the `LaserTurret` class, the statement would be like this:

`Laser.recharge();`

but not:

`myLaser1.recharge();`

or

`myLaser2.recharge();`

Invoking a static method on an object, such as `myLaser1` and `myLaser2`, will cause an error.

```
package
{
    import flash.display.MovieClip;

    public class LaserTurret extends MovieClip
    {
        public static var remainingPower:Number;
        public var firePower:Number;

        public function LaserTurret(power:Number, firePower:Number,
        x:int, y:int)
        {
            remainingPower = power;
            this.firePower = firePower;
            this.x = x;
            this.y = y;
        }

        public function turn():void
        {
            this.rotation += 10;
        }

        public function fire():void
        {
            remainingPower -= this.firePower;
        }

        public static function recharge():void
        {
            remainingPower = 100;
        }
    }
}
```

**Figure 12.36** `LaserTurret.as` with a static method named `recharge()`.

## ? Self-Test Exercises: Static Property

Questions

1. Suppose the LaserTurret class shown in Figure 12.29 is used.
   Do you get an error if you add the following trace() statements (only one at a time) at the end of the code listed in Figure 12.37 and test the movie? If not, what will be traced out?
   (a) trace(LaserTurret.remainingPower);
   (b) trace(myLaser1.remainingPower);
   (c) trace(myLaser2.remainingPower);

2. Suppose the LaserTurret class shown in Figure 12.35 is used.
   Do you get an error if you add the following trace() statements (only one at a time) at the end of the code listed in Figure 12.37 and test the movie? If not, what will be traced out?
   (a) trace(LaserTurret.remainingPower);
   (b) trace(myLaser1.remainingPower);
   (c) trace(myLaser2.remainingPower);

```
var myLaser1:LaserTurret = new LaserTurret(100, 5, 70, 120);
var myLaser2:LaserTurret = new LaserTurret(100, 8, 50, 200);

myLaser1.fire();
myLaser2.fire();
myLaser1.fire();
myLaser1.fire();
```

**Figure 12.37** The LaserTurret class is instantiated to create two LaserTurret objects, myLaser1 and myLaser2.

Answers to Self-Test Questions

1.
   (a) Error because remainingPower is an instance property; it works with an object, not the class.
   (b) 85 because myLaser1 is fired 3 times, with the fire power of 5 each time—total power of 15 is used. The remainingPower of myLaser1 starts with 100, and thus the remainingPower becomes $100 - 15 = 85$.
   (c) 92 because myLaser2 is fired 1 time, with the fire power of 8. The remaining-Power of myLaser2 starts with 100, and thus the remainingPower becomes $100 - 8 = 92$.

2.
   (a) 77 because myLaser1 is fired 3 times (with the fire power of 5 each time) and myLaser2 is fired 1 time (with the fire power of 8). The total power used $= 3 \times 5 + 8 = 23$. The remainingPower starts with 100, and thus the remaining-Power becomes $100 - 23 = 77$.
   (b) Error because remainingPower is a static property; it works with the class, not a class instance myLaser1.
   (c) Error because remainingPower is a static property; it works with the class, not a class instance myLaser2.

### ❓ Self-Test Exercises: Static Property

Figure 12.38 shows the code of a class file for a class named SoccerPlayer.

```
 1 package
 2 {
 3      public class SoccerPlayer
 4      {
 5           public var score:int;
 6
 7           public function SoccerPlayer()
 8           {
 9                score = 0;
10           }
11           public function getScore():int
12           {
13                return score;
14           }
15           public function goal():void
16           {
17                score++;
18           }
19      }
20 }
```

**Figure 12.38** SoccerPlayer.as file.

### Questions

Suppose, in a Flash file, SoccerPlayer is instantiated to create two objects named smith and johnson. The object smith invokes the goal() method *five times*, and the object johnson invokes the goal() method *three times*.

1. Do you get an error with the following trace() statements? If not, what will be traced out?
   (a) trace(smith.score);
   (b) trace(johnson.score);

2. Do you get an error with the following trace() statement? If not, what will be traced out?
   trace(SoccerPlayer.score);

3. Now, add to the code above to make score a *static* property.

Now that score is changed to a *static* property, you test the same movie again, with the object smith invoking the goal() method *five times*, and the object johnson invoking the goal() method *three times*.

4. Do you get an error with the following trace() statements? If not, what will be traced out?
   (a) trace(smith.score);
   (b) trace(johnson.score);

5. Do you get an error with the following trace() statement? If not, what will be traced out?
   trace(SoccerPlayer.score);

Answers to Self-Test Questions
1. No error.
   (a) 5
   (b) 3
2. Error
3. Line 5 should become: `public static var score:int;`
4. Error for both (a) and (b)
5. 8 because of 5 + 3

# 12.12 DECIDING WHAT NEEDS TO BE `static`

The `static` keyword specifies that a property or method is created *only once per class* instead of in every object from that class. Therefore, static properties are useful in situations where all instances of a class need to share the same data.

## 12.12.1 Static Properties

Set a property to static when you want all the instances of the class to share its value. Let's revisit the `SoccerPlayer` class in the self-test exercise. If the property score is not a static property, each `SoccerPlayer` object will keep its own score. If the score is a static property, then all the `SoccerPlayer` objects will share one score. The score is incremented by one in the `goal()` method. Thus, no matter which `SoccerPlayer` object invokes the `goal()` method, the score will increase by one. You may think of it as a team score. Here are some example scenarios in which static properties are useful.

### Example 1: Shoot-them-up games in which multiple guns share one stock of ammunition

Suppose you have multiple gun objects in a game but all the gun objects share the same stock of ammunition. Whenever a gun fires, the ammunition stock decreases. One gun may use up all the ammunition while other guns may never fire. In this case, the gun class may have a static property for the ammunition.

### Example 2: Our Multi-ball ball-and-paddle game

Let's revisit the ball-and-paddle game. In the `Ball` class, if you add an instance property (i.e., non-static) `score` to keep the score, each ball will keeps its own score. For example, `ball2` may have a score of 4 and at the same time `ball3` may have a score of 7 because `ball2` has hit the paddle 4 times and `ball3` has hit the paddle 7 times in the game. When `ball2` hits the paddle again, its score becomes 5 while `ball3`'s score remains at 7. Normally this is not the scoring system you would expect in this game. Instead, you expect one total score and it adds up whenever a ball hits the paddle. This means that all the `Ball` objects share the same score data. Therefore, the `score` property in the `Ball` class should be a static property.

The `Ball` class shown in Figure 12.20 has a property `paddle` to store the movie clip instance of the paddle on the Stage. However, there is only one paddle in the game. There is no need for every `Ball` object to keep a copy of the paddle. Instead, the paddle is needed only once for the `Ball` class. Thus, `paddle` should be a static property too.

In addition, there is only one textfield for displaying the score in the game. The `Ball` class also needs to have a static property for the textfield for displaying the score. For example, the new `Ball` class (Figure 12.39) contains these three static properties and statements demonstrating the use of these properties.

```
package
{
    import flash.display.MovieClip;
    import flash.display.Stage;

    public class Ball extends MovieClip
    {
        public var vx:int;
        public static var score:int;
        public static var scoreText:Textfield;
        public static var paddle:MovieClip;

        public function Ball()
        {
            this.vx = -(Math.random() * 10 + 2);
            score = 0;
        }

        public function move():void
        {
            this.x += this.vx;

            if (this.x < 0 || this.x > stage.stageWidth)
            {
            this.x = stage.stageWidth;
            this.vx = -(Math.random() * 10 + 2);
            }

            if (this.hitTestObject(paddle))
            {
                this.vx = Math.abs(this.vx);
                score++;
                scoreText.text = score + "";
            }
        }
    }
}
```

**Figure 12.39** `Ball.as` file with three static properties.

The use of this new `Ball` class to create three balls may follow the code shown in Figure 12.13 but with additional statements to set the properties `paddle` and `scoreText`. For example, suppose you have a movie clip instance named `paddle_mc` on the Stage that is used as the paddle and a textfield named `score_txt` on the Stage for displaying the score. Figure 12.40 shows the revised code of Figure 12.13 to include statements to set the static properties.

⌁ **An OOP Multi-ball Ball-and-Paddle Game (Lab): Part 1 of 2** Convert the non-OOP version of the ball-and-paddle game (from Chapter 11) into a three-ball game using OOP.

```
Ball.paddle = paddle_mc;
Ball.scoreText = score_txt;

var ball:Ball = new Ball();
var ball2:Ball = new Ball();
var ball3:Ball = new Ball();

addChild(ball);
addChild(ball2);
addChild(ball3);

stage.addEventListener(MouseEvent.MOUSE_MOVE, onMovePaddle);
stage.addEventListener(Event.ENTER_FRAME, onPlayGame);

function onMovePaddle(evt:MouseEvent):void
{
    paddle_mc.y = mouseY;
}

function onPlayGame(evt:Event):void
{
    ball.move();
    ball2.move();
    ball3.move();
}
```

**Figure 12.40** Revised code of Figure 12.13 for the ball-and-paddle game to include statements to set the static properties of the `Ball` class.

> 🖱 **An OOP Multi-ball Ball-and-Paddle Game (Lab): Part 2 of 2**  Modify Part 1 of this lab to use an array and `for` loops to handle the three `Ball` objects.

### Example 3: Keeping the total rewards earned by different characters

Suppose a game has multiple characters with different abilities, such as different speed and power. The player can switch to any one of these characters at any time to complete a mission. During a mission, the character may collect coins and earn points. If you want to keep the total points and the total number of coins, the properties for points and number of coins in the character class will need to be static properties.

### Example 4: Maintaining the number of concurrently alive enemies

Suppose the enemies in a game are spawned one at a time. After the player destroys one enemy object, it will spawn a new enemy object but the total number of enemy objects at any time is maintained at a certain number. Then you may want to add a static property, say `currentAlive`, in the enemy class (Figure 12.41) to keep track of the total number of the concurrently alive enemies. Whenever an enemy object is destroyed, you decrement `currentAlive` by one. When the value of `currentAlive` is lower than the threshold, say 10, a new enemy object is spawned and the `currentAlive` is incremented by one.

### Example 5: Card games

A `Card` class may have the instance properties for the rank and suit because each `Card` object must have its own rank and suit. For the games, such as the memory game, in which no more than two cards are allowed to be face up, you may also need to add static properties to keep track of which cards are currently face up. When the third card is about to be flipped face up, the two face-up cards are flipped face down.

```
package
{
    import flash.display.MovieClip;

    public class Enemy extends MovieClip
    {
        public static var currentAlive:int;

        public function Enemy()
        {
            . . .
        }

        public function setDirection():void
        {
            . . .
        }

        public function moveEnemy():void
        {
            . . .
        }

        public function destroyed():void
        {
            currentAlive--;
        }

        public function spawn():void
        {
            if (currentAlive < 10)
            {
                // Add some statements to spawn a new Enemy object

                currentAlive++;
            }
        }
    }
}
```

**Figure 12.41** Enemy.as file.

Figure 12.42 shows an example Card class. It is not a fully functional class file for a memory game but it intends to demonstrate the use of static properties to keep track of the two cards that are face up. The basic idea is to have two static properties, say firstCard and secondCard, to store the cards that are currently face up. When there is no card facing up, both firstCard and secondCard are set to null. When a card is about to be flipped up, there are three possible cases:

- Case 1: There are already two cards facing up. The condition (firstCard != null && secondCard != null) will be true. In this case, both cards will need to be flipped face down, and firstCard and secondCard are reset to null.
- Case 2: There is no card facing up. The condition (firstCard == null) will be true. In this case, the card that is about to flip up will become the firstCard. Thus, firstCard = this.

- Case 3: There is only one card facing up. The conditions for Cases 1 and 2 would be false. In this case, the card that is about to flip up will become the secondCard. Thus, secondCard = this.

```
package
{
    import flash.display.MovieClip;

    public class Card extends MovieClip
    {
        public var id:int;
        public var facedown:Boolean;
        public static var firstCard:Card;
        public static var secondCard:Card;

        public function Card(id:int, x:int, y:int)
        {
            this.id = id;
            this.x = x;
            this.y = y;
            firstCard = null;
            secondCard = null;
        }

        public function flipCard():void
        {
            if (this.facedown == true)
            {
                if (firstCard != null && secondCard != null)
                {
                    // This is when there are already two cards faceup.
                    // You need to flip both cards facedown.

                    firstCard.facedown = true;
                    secondCard.facedown = true;
                    firstCard = null;
                    secondCard = null;

                    // Also add statements to make both firstCard
                    // and secondCard show facing down

                }
                if (firstCard == null)
                {
                    // This is when there is no card faceup.
                    // The current card will become the firstCard.

                    firstCard = this;
                    this.facedown = false;

                    // Also add statements to make the current card to
                    // show facing up

                }
```

**Figure 12.42** An example Card.as file for memory games. (*continued*)

```
                    else
                    {
                        // This is when there is only one card faceup.
                        // The current card will become the secondCard.

                        secondCard = this;
                        this.facedown = false;

                        // Also add statements to make the current card to
                        // show facing up

                        if (firstCard.id == id)
                        {
                            // This is when the firstCard's id matches with
                            // the current card's id, i.e., got a match!

                            // Add statements to do things when a match is
                            // found

                            firstCard = null;
                            secondCard = null;
                        }
                    }
                }
            }
        }
    }
}
```

**Figure 12.42** (*continued*)

In this Card class example, instead of using rank and suit, a property named id is used because in a memory game, a card is normally characterized by its graphic design instead of rank and suit. The property id is used to label the design of the card with an integer number.

⌐ **An OOP Side-Scrolling Platform Game (Lab): Part 1 of 2** Convert the non-OOP version of the side-scrolling platform game (from Chapter 11) into an OOP version. When you test the completed movie, it should play exactly the same as the non-OOP version of the game from the player's perspective. However, from the code-centric view, the coin is an object instantiated from a new Coin class.

⌐ **An OOP Side-Scrolling Platform Game (Lab): Part 2 of 2** Modify Part 1 of this lab to use an array and for loops to handle multiple coins. When you test the completed movie, you should see more than one coin in the game. All the coins behave the same; that is, they scroll with the platform, disappear when colliding with the hero, and reappear over and over.

⌐ **An OOP Side-Scrolling Platform Game (Lab): A List of Extra Challenges** This provides a list of extra features that will make the game more fun to play and are feasible to implement. You are encouraged to pick and choose one or more challenges from the list to implement.

## 12.12.2 Static Methods

Set a method to static when the method is not supposed to attach to an instance but has to act at the class level. Static methods are common in utility classes. For example, ActionScript's Math class contains methods for performing basic numeric operations such as converting a number to an absolute number, and elementary exponential, logarithm, square root, and trigonometric functions. These methods can be invoked without instantiation of the class. For example, recall the use of Math.random() to generate a random number. The random() method is a static method in ActionScript's Math class. You use the class name, Math, with it.

In some situations, you may want to set a method to static when it is to update static properties. For example, the recharge() method in the LaserTurret example (Figure 12.36) updates the static property remainingPower. Whenever you want to recharge, instead of invoking the recharge() method on any particular instance, you invoke the method like this: LaserTurret.recharge().

# 12.13 NOTATION FOR STATIC PROPERTIES AND METHODS IN CLASS DIAGRAMS

The static properties and methods are underlined in the class diagrams. For example, the class diagram shown in Figure 12.43 depicts the LaserTurret class (Figure 12.36).

| LaserTurret |
| --- |
| <u>remainingPower:Number</u><br>firePower:Number |
| LaserTurret(remainingPower:Number, firePower:Number, x:int, y:int)<br>turn():void<br>fire():void<br><u>recharge():void</u> |

**Figure 12.43** A class diagram for the LaserTurret class example that contains a static property remainingPower and a static method recharge().

# 12.14 USING EVENT LISTENER CODE IN CLASS FILES

The LaserTurret class example in Section 12.9.4 demonstrates the use of event listener code for the mouse event. Similarly, other types of event listener code, such as ENTER_FRAME and the keyboard event, can be used in a class file.

### Frame Event Listener Code

Let's revisit the Car example shown in Figure 12.24, in which a frame event listener code is set up to invoke the drive() method on betty. Suppose every Car object needs to be invoked with the drive() method at frame rate. You could write the frame event listener code for each of the objects individually. You may also move the event listener code in the Car class so that you do not have to write the frame event listener code for each of the objects individually.

The Car class shown in Figure 12.44 includes a frame event listener code. An event handler function named handleEnterFrame() is added to the class. For the purpose of this example, the function contains only one statement that invokes the drive() method. The addEventListener() statement is added in the constructor. This will make the Car object start executing the statements defined in handleEnterFrame() when it is created. Note that the statement import flash.events.Event; is needed so that the Action-Script class Event is available to the Car class.

```
package
{
    import flash.display.MovieClip;
    import flash.events.Event;

    public class Car extends MovieClip
    {
        public var fuelCapacity:Number;
        public var remainingFuel:Number;

        public function Car(x:int, y:int)
        {
            this.fuelCapacity = 15;
            this.remainingFuel = 15;
            this.x = x;
            this.y = y;
            this.addEventListener(Event.ENTER_FRAME, handleEnterFrame);
        }

        public function handleEnterFrame(evt:Event):void
        {
            drive(5);
        }

        public function drive(speed:int):void
        {
            this.x += speed;
            this.remainingFuel -= speed * 0.01;
        }
    }
}
```

Figure 12.44 Car.as with ENTER_FRAME event listener code.

With this revised Car class, the code shown in Figure 12.24 can be rewritten as the code shown in Figure 12.45. Here a Car object named betty is created. There is no need to write the frame event listener code here. The object betty will automatically start driving to the right 5 pixels at a time just like the code shown in Figure 12.24 would do using the Car class shown in Figure 12.23.

```
var betty:Car = new Car(40, 230);
addChild(betty);
```

Figure 12.45 ActionScript in a Flash file (.fla) that uses the Car class.

## Keyboard Event Listener Code

Let's continue with the Car example. Suppose you want to be able to control the driving direction of betty the Car object by pressing the LEFT and RIGHT arrow keys. You could add the keyboard event listener code in a Flash file as shown in Figure 12.46. In order to allow changing the Car object's speed outside the class definition, the Car class is modified to include a property speed and a method setSpeed() (Figure 12.47).

```
var betty:Car = new Car(40, 230);
addChild(betty);

stage.addEventListener(KeyboardEvent.KEY_DOWN, handleKeyDown);

function handleKeyDown(evt:KeyboardEvent):void
{
    if (evt.keyCode == Keyboard.RIGHT)
    {
        betty.setSpeed(5);
    }
    else if (evt.keyCode == Keyboard.LEFT)
    {
        betty.setSpeed(-5);
    }
}
```

**Figure 12.46** ActionScript in a Flash file (.fla) with keyboard event listener code.

You may also move the keyboard event listener code to the Car class. Then all Car objects will respond to the LEFT and RIGHT arrow keys the same way without having to write event listener code for each of them. For example, the Car class shown in Figure 12.48 modifies Figure 12.47 to include keyboard event listener code. Writing keyboard event listener code in the class is similar to writing the frame and mouse event listener code but it takes an additional step. The reason for the extra step is that the keyboard event listener is added to the Stage but the Stage is not available until the object has been created and added to the Stage. This means that adding the following addEventListener() statement in the constructor will cause an error:

```
stage.addEventListener(KeyboardEvent.KEY_DOWN, handleKeyDown);
```

One solution is to use the ADD_TO_STAGE event listener (Figure 12.48) such that the addEventListener() statement for the keyboard event will be executed only after the object is added to the Stage. Note that the import statements for KeyboardEvent and Keyboard classes are needed so that they are available to the Car class.

This Car class can be used the same way as shown in Figure 12.45. With the code shown in Figure 12.45, a Car object named betty is created. The drive() method is invoked at frame rate and it increments the x of the object by the amount of speed. The object betty will not move at first because its speed is set to zero in the constructor. However, when the RIGHT arrow key is pressed, its speed is set to 5 and it moves to the right 5 pixels at a time at frame rate. Similarly, it moves to the left when the LEFT arrow key is pressed.

```
package
{
    import flash.display.MovieClip;
    import flash.events.Event;

    public class Car extends MovieClip
    {
        public var fuelCapacity:Number;
        public var remainingFuel:Number;
        public var speed:int;

        public function Car(x:int, y:int)
        {
            this.fuelCapacity = 15;
            this.remainingFuel = 15;
            this.speed = 0;
            this.x = x;
            this.y = y;
            this.addEventListener(Event.ENTER_FRAME, handleEnterFrame);
        }

        public function handleEnterFrame(evt:Event):void
        {
            drive(this.speed);
        }
        public function drive(speed:int):void
        {
            this.x += speed;
            this.remainingFuel -= speed * 0.01;
        }

        public function setSpeed(speed:int):void
        {
            this.speed = speed;
        }
    }
}
```

**Figure 12.47** Car.as of Figure 12.44 is modified by adding a property `speed` and a method `setSpeed()`.

Figure 12.49 shows the code using an array and a `for` loop to generate 10 Car objects using this new Car class (Figure 12.48). Note that there is no extra keyboard event listener code in Figure 12.49 but the driving direction of all 10 Car objects responds to the LEFT and RIGHT arrow keys.

> ✍ **Using Frame and Keyboard Event Listener Code in Car Class (Lab)** Using the Car class shown in Figure 12.48, instantiate a Car object (Figure 12.45), and place the object on the Stage. When you test the movie, you should see your Car object stay at the left center of the Stage. When you press the RIGHT arrow key, the car moves to the right. When you press the LEFT arrow key, the car moves to the left. Then improve the class so that the Car object will return to the other side of the Stage after it goes off the edge of the Stage.

```
package
{
    import flash.display.MovieClip;
    import flash.events.KeyboardEvent;
    import flash.events.Event;
    import flash.ui.Keyboard;

    public class Car extends MovieClip
    {
        public var fuelCapacity:Number;
        public var remainingFuel:Number;
        public var speed:int;
        public function Car(x:int, y:int)
        {
            this.fuelCapacity = 15;
            this.remainingFuel = 15;
            this.speed = 0;
            this.x = x;
            this.y = y;
            this.addEventListener(Event.ENTER_FRAME, handleEnterFrame);
            this.addEventListener(Event.ADDED_TO_STAGE,
            handleAddedToStage);
        }

        public function handleAddedToStage(evt:Event):void
        {
            stage.addEventListener(KeyboardEvent.KEY_DOWN,
            handleKeyDown);
        }

        public function handleKeyDown(evt:KeyboardEvent):void
        {
            if (evt.keyCode == Keyboard.RIGHT)
            {
                this.speed = 5;
            }
            else if (evt.keyCode == Keyboard.LEFT)
            {
                this.speed = -5;
            }
        }

        public function handleEnterFrame(evt:Event):void
        {
            drive();
        }

        public function drive():void
        {
            this.x += this.speed;
            this.remainingFuel -= this.speed * 0.01;
        }
    }
}
```

**Figure 12.48** Car.as with ENTER_FRAME and keyboard event listener code.

```
var arrCars:Array = new Array();

for (var i:int = 0; i < 10; i++)
{
    var car:Car = new Car(40, Math.random()*stage.stageHeight);
    arrCars.push(car);
    addChild(arrCars[i]);
}
```

**Figure 12.49** ActionScript in a Flash file (.fla) generates 10 Car objects using the new Car class that includes keyboard event listener code.

---

### ❓ Self-Test Exercise: Improving the Car Class

Question

Note that in the example shown in Figure 12.48, the remainingFuel of the Car object will increase when its speed is negative. This means that its remainingFuel will increase when it drives to the left. What a way to regenerate fuel! However, this is not how it normally works, even in games.

Modify the code in Figure 12.48 so that the remainingFuel will always decrease regardless of its driving direction.

Answer to Self-Test Question

Convert the value of speed into an absolute number in the second statement in the drive() method: `this.remainingFuel -= Math.abs(this.speed) * 0.01;`

## 12.15 SUMMARY

Object-oriented programming (OOP) provides a way of thinking to break down a particular problem into a collection of classes and objects, which are used as the building blocks in software application development. Every object can be described in terms of properties and behaviors. Objects are created by instantiating a class. A class is a self-contained description of a set of properties and behaviors. Objects are also referred to as instances of a class or class instances. From the code-centric view, the behaviors are implemented as functions and the properties are defined as variables in the class. The functions defined in a class are called methods. Unlike the functions defined outside the class definition, only the objects of the class can use these functions. The variables defined in the class are also called member variables, and only the objects of the class can use these variables.

The following are the basic steps to create a class in ActionScript 3.0:

**Step 1** Start a blank class file (.as): File > New . . . and choose ActionScript File.
**Step 2** Fill in the basic structure of the class file.
**Step 3** Define properties.
**Step 4** Add methods.
**Step 5** Add the keywords extends MovieClip and an import statement if the class instances will have a visual representation using a movie clip symbol.
**Step 6** Add an import statement if there are any references to the Stage.

In the class file, there is a function with the same name as the class name. This is a special function called constructor. The constructor is invoked at the creation of a class instance. Because the constructor of a class is executed when an object is created, the code that initializes the object usually is placed in the constructor.

To create an object, declare it as a variable using the general syntax like this:

```
var objectName:ClassName = new ClassName();
```

To give a visual representation to an object, there are three things to set up:

1. In the class file (.as), add the keywords extends MovieClip and an import statement.
2. In the Flash file (.fla) in which the objects will be created, set the linkage using the name of the class for the movie clip symbol that you want to assign as the visual representation of the class instances.
3. In the script in a Flash file (.fla) that uses the class, add an addChild() statement after the instantiation statement to add the object on the Stage.

To generate multiple objects, an array and for loops can be used to make the code more compact. The array is used to store the objects and the for loop iterates multiple times; each time to create a new class instance, add the new instance to the array, and use an addChild() statement to place the new instance on the Stage. The class instances are not referred to by their instance names. Instead, they are referred to through the array and their indexes. Thus, to invoke a method on all of the objects in the array, a second for loop is used to loop through the array invoking the method on each object in the array.

A class diagram is a notation that depicts a class as a rectangle, which in turn is composed of three rectangles stacked on top of one another. The class name appears in the topmost rectangle. The middle rectangle lists the properties of the class, and the bottom rectangle list the methods. The class diagram can be used to depict the structure of one or more classes and the relationships between classes.

The properties and methods may be assigned with an attribute static. The static keyword specifies that a property or method is created *only once per class* instead of in every object instantiated from that class. Static properties are useful when all the objects instantiated from the same class share the value of the properties. Static methods are useful when they are intended to act at the class level—they can be invoked without having to instantiate an object first. In a class diagram, the static properties and methods are underlined.

To use a static property or method outside its class definition, use it with its class name, not an object name, like these examples:

```
ClassName.propertyName
ClassName.methodName()
```

A class file can also have event listener code. For example:

- If every object from the class is clickable, you may add mouse event listener code in the class file. Then you do not have to write the mouse event listener code for each individual object.
- If every object will perform certain tasks at frame rate, you may add frame event listener code in the class file so that you do not have to write the frame event listener code for each individual object.
- If every object will respond to the same key presses, you may add keyboard event listener code in the class file so that you do not have to add the keyboard event listener code for each individual object.

## TERMS

behaviors 382
class 383
class diagram 398
class instances 383
class methods 408
constructor 387

instance methods 408
instance property 408
instances 383
instantiating 383
member variables 383
methods 383

object-oriented
  programming (OOP) 383
procedural
  programming 383
properties 382
static 408

## LEARNING AIDS

### ⌐ A Car Class (Lab): Part 1 of 3

Follow the description in Section 12.9.1 to create a Car class, instantiate a Car object, and place the object on the Stage. When you test the movie, you should see that your Car object starts at the upper-left corner of the Stage (assuming that the registration point of your car movie clip is around the center of the car) and moves to the right.

### ⌐ A Car Class (Lab): Part 2 of 3

Improve Part 1 of the Car Class lab using the solutions of the Improving the Car Class exercise. When you test the completed movie, you should see a car start moving to the right from about the left center of the Stage.

### ⌐ A Car Class (Lab): Part 3 of 3

Modify Part 2 of the Car Class lab to use an array and for loops to create 10 moving Car objects. In addition, randomize the starting position of each Car object. When you test the completed movie, you should see 10 cars start moving to the right from random positions within the Stage.

### ⌐ An OOP Multi-ball Ball-and-Paddle Game (Lab): Part 1 of 2

Convert the non-OOP version of the ball-and-paddle game (from Chapter 11) into a three-ball game using OOP.

### ⌐ An OOP Multi-ball Ball-and-Paddle Game (Lab): Part 2 of 2

Modify Part 1 of this lab to use an array and for loops to handle the three Ball objects.

### ⌐ An OOP Side-Scrolling Platform Game (Lab): Part 1 of 2

Convert the non-OOP version of the side-scrolling platform game (from Chapter 11) into an OOP version. When you test the completed movie, it should play exactly the same as the non-OOP version of the game from the player's perspective. However, from the code-centric view, the coin is an object instantiated from a new Coin class.

### ⌐ An OOP Side-Scrolling Platform Game (Lab): Part 2 of 2

Modify Part 1 of this lab to use an array and for loops to handle multiple coins. When you test the completed movie, you should see more than one coin in the game. All the coins behave the same; that is, they scroll with the platform, disappear when colliding with the hero, and reappear over and over.

### ⌐ An OOP Side-Scrolling Platform Game (Lab): A List of Extra Challenges

This provides a list of extra features that will make the game more fun to play and are feasible to implement. You are encouraged to pick and choose one or more challenges from the list to implement.

## Using Frame and Keyboard Event Listener Code in Car Class (Lab)

Using the `Car` class shown in Figure 12.48, instantiate a `Car` object (Figure 12.45), and place the object on the Stage. When you test the movie, you should see your `Car` object stay at the left center of the Stage. When you press the RIGHT arrow key, the car moves to the right. When you press the LEFT arrow key, the car moves to the left. Then improve the class so that the `Car` object will return to the other side of the Stage after it goes off the edge of the Stage.

## REVIEW QUESTIONS

When applicable, please choose all correct answers.

1. In the analogy of building a house, _____ is like a blueprint and _____ is like the actual house built from the blueprint.

    A. a class; an object            B. an object; a class

2. _____ is an instance of _____.

    A. A class; an object            B. An object; a class

3. In OOP, what are the two aspects you use to describe an object?

    A. Class                   B. Instance
    C. Properties           D. Behaviors
    E. Static

4. In a class file, the _____ are defined as variables.

    A. class                  B. instance
    C. properties          D. behaviors
    E. static

5. In a class file, the _____ are defined as methods.

    A. class                  B. instance
    C. properties          D. behaviors
    E. static

6. The general steps to create a class in ActionScript are:

    Step 1: Start a blank class file (`.as`): `File > New . . .` and choose _____.
    Step 2: Fill in _____.
    Step 3: Add properties by declaring _____.
    Step 4: Implement behaviors by adding _____.
    Step 5: Add the keywords _____ _____ and an _____ statement if the class
               instances will have a visual representation using a _____ symbol.
    Step 6: Add an _____ statement if there are any references to the Stage.

7. In any class file, it must have at least one function, which has the same name as the class. This special function is called a _____.

    A. constructor
    B. static method
    C. class method
    D. instance method

8. Fill in the blanks using these words: `ClassName ClassName() objectName var new`

The general syntax to instantiate a class to create an object in ActionScript is:

_____ _____:_____ = _____ _____;

9. What is the general syntax to invoke an instance method on an object?

A. `ClassName.method()`
B. `ObjectName.method()`

10. What is the general syntax to invoke a static method?

A. `ClassName.method()`
B. `ObjectName.method()`

11. By looking at a class diagram, how do you tell a property or method is static?

12. The three things you need to do to assign a movie clip to a class instance as its visual representation and make it appear on the Stage are:

1. In the class file (`.as`), add the keywords _____ _____ and an _____ statement.

2. In the Flash file (`.fla`), set the _____ for the movie clip symbol that you want to assign as the visual representation of the class instance. Specifically, enter the _____ in the Class Name field of the linkage section.

3. In the script that is in the Flash file (`.fla`), add an _____ statement after the instantiation statement to place the object on the Stage.

13. Figure 12.50 shows a `Car` class that has not been set up for a visual representation of its objects. Add code to the `Car` class so that its objects have a visual representation as a movie clip.

```
package
{

    public class Car
    {
        public var fuelCapacity:Number;
        public var remainingFuel:Number;

        public function Car()
        {
            this.fuelCapacity = 15;
            this.remainingFuel = 15;
        }
        public function drive(speed:int):void
        {
            this.x += speed;
            this.remainingFuel -= speed * 0.01;
        }
    }
}
```

**Figure 12.50** `Car.as`

# Inheritance and Polymorphism

Courtesy of Robert Hay

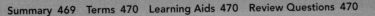

## KEY CONCEPTS

- Inheritance
- Superclass, parent class, subclass, child class, derived class
- Polymorphism
- Overriding methods
- Access specifiers
- Setters and getters

## GENERAL LEARNING OBJECTIVES

In this chapter, you will learn

- The concepts of inheritance.
- The concepts of polymorphism.
- How to implement inheritance in ActionScript.
- How to depict inheritance in class diagrams.
- The differences between the different access specifiers.
- How to implement polymorphism in ActionScript.
- The motivation for using inheritance, polymorphism, and access specifiers.
- How to identify the need for inheritance and polymorphism.

# 13.1 START WITH A SCENARIO

Let's start this chapter with a scenario that builds on our LaserTurret example (Figure 13.1) from Chapter 12. Suppose you want to add a new type of laser turret, say Rechargeable LaserTurret, that can recharge. In addition to all of the basic functionalities the LaserTurret can do, the new RechargeableLaserTurret can also recharge the remaining power to 100. The RechargeableLaserTurret class may simply copy all of the properties and functionalities from the LaserTurret class and adds a recharge() method. Figure 13.2 shows how the class diagram for this new laser turret may look and Figure 13.3 lists the code for the RechargeableLaserTurret class. However, the RechargeableLaserTurret class contains a duplicate of the LaserTurret class code.

| LaserTurret |
| --- |
| remainingPower:Number<br>firePower:Number |
| LaserTurret(remainingPower:Number, firePower:Number, x:int, y:int)<br>turn():void<br>fire():void |

**Figure 13.1** Class diagram for the LaserTurret class example.

| RechargeableLaserTurret |
|---|
| remainingPower:Number<br>firePower:Number |
| RechargeableLaserTurret(remainingPower:Number, firePower:Number, x:int, y:int)<br>turn():void<br>fire():void<br>recharge():void |

**Figure 13.2** Class diagram for the `RechargeableLaserTurret` class without using inheritance.

```
package
{
    public class RechargeableLaserTurret
    {
        public var remainingPower:Number;
        public var firePower:Number;

        public function RechargeableLaserTurret(remainingPower:Number,
        firePower:Number, x:int, y:int)
        {
            this.remainingPower = remainingPower;
            this.firePower = firePower;
            this.x = x;
            this.y = y;
        }

        public function turn():void
        {
            this.rotation += 10;
        }

        public function fire():void
        {
            this.remainingPower -= this.firePower;
        }

        public function recharge():void
        {
            this.remainingPower = 100;
        }
    }
}
```

**Figure 13.3** `RechargeableLaserTurret.as` without using inheritance. The colored code highlights the changes compared to `LaserTurret.as`.

What if later you decide to add additional properties and methods to the `LaserTurret` class or modify the code in the `turn()` and `fire()` functions? You would then also need to duplicate the exact same changes over to the `RechargeableLaserTurret` class. Duplicating code is an error-prone and inefficient practice for writing and maintaining your code. Inheritance provides a better solution to this problem.

## 13.2 INHERITANCE

This section will introduce a concept called ***inheritance***, which allows creating new classes by extending or enhancing the functionalities of an existing class without having to rewrite those existing functionalities. When new classes are created this way, we say that they ***inherit*** the functionalities from the existing class. These new classes and the existing class establish a class hierarchy with an inheritance relationship.

### 13.2.1 Class Hierarchy

Figure 13.4 illustrates the concept of a class hierarchy. The first (or the topmost) class in the hierarchy is called the ***base class***. In this example, the Life class is the base class. The next classes below a class are its ***subclasses***. They are also called ***derived classes*** or ***child classes***. They inherit from the previous class. Each subsequent class down the hierarchy inherits from the previous one. The class from which a subclass inherits is its ***superclass*** or ***parent class***. In the hierarchy shown in Figure 13.4, all of the classes, except the Life class, are subclasses of some classes. For example, the Whale class is a subclass of the Mammal class, which in turn is a subclass of the Animal class. The eight classes at the bottom of the hierarchy do not have subclasses. All classes except these eight classes are superclasses of some classes. For example, the Mammal class is the superclass of the Whale and Dog classes. The Animal class is the superclass of the Mammal class. The animal class is the grandparent, also called ***ancestor***, of the Whale and Dog classes.

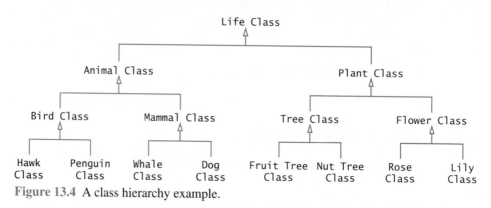

**Figure 13.4** A class hierarchy example.

The subclass encompasses (inherits) all of the properties and methods defined in its parent class. The subclass also can have extra properties and methods that are not defined in its parent class. These extras are specific to the subclass. For example, the Whale objects have all of the properties and functionalities defined in the Mammal class. A Whale object can do all of the things that a Mammal object can do. In this sense, the Whale object *is a* Mammal object. However, the reverse is not true. A Mammal object does not have all of the properties and functions defined in the Whale class. For example, a Whale object may have a breaching function, which is not defined in the Mammal class.

This special *is-a* relationship is not only specific to Mammal and Whale classes in this example but it also exists between any subclass and its parent class. Every object of a subclass is also an object of its parent class, but *not* vice versa. Suppose class S is a subclass of class P (parent class). Then, we say an S object *is a* P object. It means that an S object has all of the properties that a P object has and an S object can do all of the things that a P object can do.

A game may have different types of characters, for example, heroes, villains, helper characters who assist the player to accomplish certain tasks, and other neutral characters who do not help or obstruct the player. All of these characters may share some common properties and behaviors. For example, all of them may be able to walk, talk, and avoid walking into a tree. However, they also possess different characteristics and abilities. For example, only the hero can cast spells and only the helper can heal the hero. You may need at least four classes of characters: Hero, Villain, Helper, and Neutral. You may also need a Character class that contains all of the properties and behaviors that are shared across the different types of characters. Each type of character is a subclass of the Character class (Figure 13.5). In other words, each of these subclasses inherits all of the properties and methods defined in the Character class plus additional properties and methods that are specific to the subclass itself.

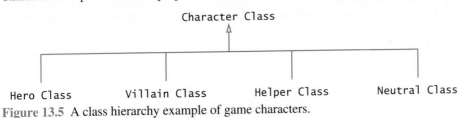

Figure 13.5 A class hierarchy example of game characters.

## 13.2.2 Notation in Class Diagrams

The class inheritance relationship is denoted using a vertical arrow (a vertical line with a triangle) pointing from the subclass to the parent class (Figure 13.6). Only the properties and methods that are specific to the subclass are included in the subclass's rectangles. All of the properties and methods of the parent class are inherited by the subclass and should not be included in the subclass's rectangles.

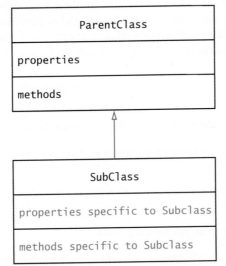

Figure 13.6 Class diagram showing the inheritance relationship.

Let's return to the RecharageableLaserTurret example (Figure 13.2 and Figure 13.3) discussed in Section 13.1. Because RechargeableLaserTurret can do everything that LaserTurret can do and has all of the properties that LaserTurret has, RechargeableLaserTurret can be a subclass of LaserTurret. Now the

RechargeableLaserTurret class needs to define *only* the properties and methods that are specific to it. In this example, the only additional item RechargeableLaserTurret needed to define is the recharge() method. The class diagram is depicted in Figure 13.7. Inheritance is also said to be a form of code reuse—the subclass is reusing the code already defined in its parent class. Code reuse removes the code duplication presented in Figure 13.2 and Figure 13.3.

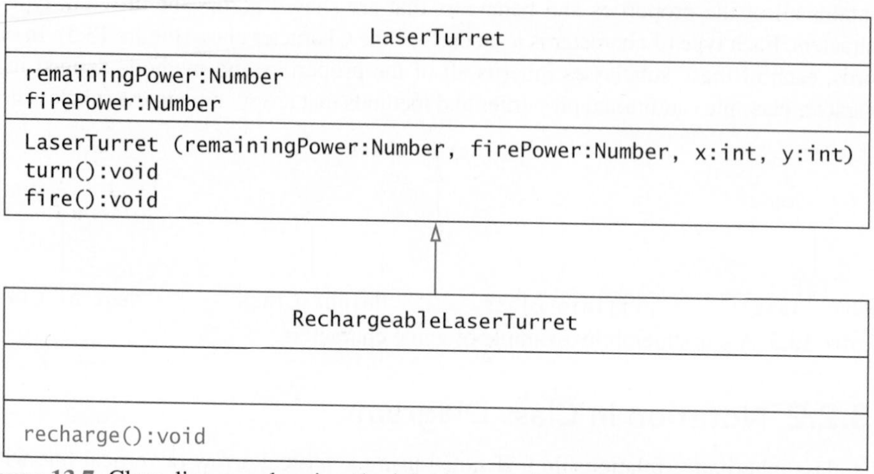

**Figure 13.7** Class diagram showing the inheritance relationship between the classes: LaserTurret (parent class) and RechargeableLaserTurret (subclass).

From the code-centric standpoint, there are keywords for setting up the inheritance relationship in ActionScript. The next section explains these keywords and their usages. These keywords are colored in the code for the RechargeableLaserTurret class (Figure 13.8) that sets up an inheritance relationship with the LaserTurret class. As you see, the code is substantially simplified compared to that without inheritance (Figure 13.3).

```
package
{
    public class RechargeableLaserTurret extends LaserTurret
    {
        public function RechargeableLaserTurret(remainingPower:Number,
        firePower:Number, x:int, y:int)
        {
            super(remainingPower, firePower, x, y);
        }

        public function recharge():void
        {
            this.remainingPower = 100;
        }
    }
}
```

**Figure 13.8** RechargeableLaserTurret.as defined as a subclass of LaserTurret. Keywords specific to inheritance are colored.

# 13.3 CODING INHERITANCE IN ActionScript

To indicate the inheritance relationship between two classes, in the subclass file you use the keyword extends after the subclass name in the line that starts with public class. The keyword is followed by the name of the parent class. For example, the keyword extends followed by LaserTurret in the RechargeableLaser class (Figure 13.8) makes it a subclass of LaserTurret.

The keyword extends can only be used once in a class; it cannot be stringed together to have multiple parents.

## 13.3.1 The Keyword super

The keyword super is used in a subclass to refer to the parent class. There are two usages of super: super() and super.*method*(). The first one is used in the subclass's constructor to invoke its parent class's constructor. The second one is used in the subclass for invoking a method defined in its parent class. In the RechargeableLaser example (Figure 13.8), super is used in the constructor.

### Usage 1: super() in the Subclass's Constructor

Before explaining the usage of super(), let's first explain the process behind instantiation of a subclass. This will help make sense of the requirement for using the super() statement in a subclass's constructor.

When a subclass is instantiated, it has to first invoke its parent class's constructor before executing any statements in its constructor. This can be done by having a super() statement in the subclass's constructor. If there is no super() statement in the subclass's constructor, the Flash ActionScript compiler will automatically include the super() statement before the first statement in the constructor body.

If the constructor of the parent class takes parameters, correct parameters must be passed in super() to be passed along to the parent class's constructor. For the RechargeableLaser example (Figure 13.8), the constructor of the parent class LaserTurret (Figure 13.1) takes four parameters in this order: remainingPower, firePower, x, and y. The first two have the Number data type and the last two have the int data type. The super() statement in the constructor of RechargeableLaserTurret has to pass in four parameters with matching data types in the same order. The super() statement in the constructor of RechargeableLaserTurret is written as follows:

```
super(remainingPower, firePower, x, y);
```

It passes the four parameters of its constructor along to LaserTurret's constructor.

Because the parameter names in both constructors are the same, there may be a misconception that these parameters are automatically related. They are not related simply by giving them the same names and they do not need to have the same names. To clarify this potential misconception, Figure 13.9 rewrites RechargeableLasetTurret using arbitrary parameter names, a, b, c, and d. This works the same as Figure 13.8. The statement super(a, b, c, d) will pass the first parameter of RechargeableLaserTurret, which is a, as the first parameter to the LaserTurret constructor. It will be used to set the remainingPower in LaserTurret's conctructor. Similarly, the second parameter of RechargeableLaserTurret, which is b, is passed as the second parameter to the LaserTurret constructor, and so forth for the third and the fourth parameters. Naming parameters arbitrarily is not a good practice, however. The purpose of using arbitrary names for parameters in Figure 13.9 is to demonstrate that the parameter naming in

```
package
{
    public class RechargeableLaserTurret extends LaserTurret
    {
        public function RechargeableLaserTurret(a:Number, b:Number,
        c:int, d:int)
        {
            super(a, b, c, d);
        }

        public function recharge():void
        {
            this.remainingPower = 100;
        }
    }
}
```

**Figure 13.9** RechargeableLaserTurret.as using arbitrary names for the constructor parameters.

the parent class and subclass's constructor are not the key that makes the super() statement work. The key is to pass the parameters with the matching data types in the order that matches the parameters of the parent class's constructor.

If the subclass's constructor has the same set of parameters as that of its parent class's constructor, the super() statement can be omitted. For example, Figure 13.10 will work the same as Figure 13.8. Note that having the same set of parameters does not mean having the same parameter names. The technical requirement is simply that the data types must match. Thus, Figure 13.11 also will work the same as Figure 13.8. However, Figure 13.12 will not work without a super() statement because the order of the parameter data types does not match the order of those for the LaserTurret's constructor. Figure 13.12 will work if the following super() statement is added in the constructor:

```
super(remainingPower, firePower, x, y);
```

```
package
{
    public class RechargeableLaserTurret extends LaserTurret
    {
        public function RechargeableLaserTurret(remainingPower:Number,
        firePower:Number, x:int, y:int)
        {
            super(remainingPower, firePower, x, y);
        }

        public function recharge():void
        {
            this.remainingPower = 100;
        }
    }
}
```

**Figure 13.10** RechargeableLaserTurret.as works without a super() statement in its constructor.

```
package
{
    public class RechargeableLaserTurret extends LaserTurret
    {
        public function RechargeableLaserTurret(a:Number, b:Number,
        c:int, d:int)
        {
            super(a, b, c, d);
        }

        public function recharge():void
        {
            this.remainingPower = 100;
        }
    }
}
```

**Figure 13.11** RechargeableLaserTurret.as works without a super() statement in its constructor.

```
package
{
    public class RechargeableLaserTurret extends LaserTurret
    {
        public function RechargeableLaserTurret(x:int, y:int,
        remainingPower:Number, firePower:Number)
        {

        }

        public function recharge():void
        {
            this.remainingPower = 100;
        }
    }
}
```

**Figure 13.12** RechargeableLaserTurret.as will not work without a super() statement in its constructor because in terms of the data types, the order of the parameters of the constructor does not match the order of the parameters of LaserTurret's constructor.

Although the *technical* requirement is simply that the data types must match, you have to make sure the usage of the parameters matches up. For example, syntactically Figure 13.12 would not cause errors if the following super() statement was added in the constructor:

```
super(firePower, remainingPower, x, y);
```

However, whatever is passed as the fourth parameter (firePower) in RechargeableLaserTurret's constructor would be passed to LaserTurret's constructor as the first parameter, which then would be used to set the remainingPower of the object. This would be incorrect and a mismatch in terms of the context of the game.

The code listed in Figure 13.13 shows another example of the RechargeableLaserTurret class. Its constructor does not take any parameters but has a super() statement,

```
package
{
    public class RechargeableLaserTurret extends LaserTurret
    {
        public function RechargeableLaserTurret()
        {
            super(80, 6, 120, 260);
        }

        public function recharge():void
        {
            this.remainingPower = 100;
        }
    }
}
```

**Figure 13.13** RechargeableLaserTurret.as that always generates a RechargeableLaserTurret object that starts with a remaining power of 80, a firing power of 6, and a position at (120, 260).

super(80, 6, 120, 260). This will always generate a RechargeableLaserTurret object that starts with a remaining power of 80, a firing power of 6, and at a position of (120, 260). Figure 13.14 shows the instantiation of this RechargeableLaserTurret class to create two RechargeableLaserTurret objects: upgradedLaser1 and upgradedLaser2. There is no parameter passing in the constructor. Both start with a remaining power of 80, a firing power of 6, and at the position (120, 260).

```
var upgradedLaser1:RechargeableLaserTurret = new RechargeableLaserTurret();
var upgradedLaser2:RechargeableLaserTurret = new RechargeableLaserTurret();
```

**Figure 13.14** Instantiation of the RechargeableLaserTurret class (Figure 13.13) to generate two objects: upgradedLaser1 and upgradedLaser2.

In the context of the laser turret game, you would probably want to be able to pass in the values to set the remaining power, firing power, and starting position of the rechargeable laser at its creation. The code listed in Figure 13.8 allows you to pass in different values to specify these values for the RechargeableLaserTurret object at its creation. With the class definition shown in Figure 13.8, the two RechargeableLaserTurret objects generated from the code listed in Figure 13.15 now have different starting remaining power, firing power, and positions. The upgradedLaser1 starts with a remaining power of 90, a firing power of 10, and a position at (120, 260), whereas the upgradedLaser2 starts with a remaining power of 75, a firing power of 4, and a position at (210, 190).

```
var upgradedLaser1:RechargeableLaserTurret = new RechargeableLaserTurret(90, 10, 120, 260);
var upgradedLaser2:RechargeableLaserTurret = new RechargeableLaserTurret(75, 4, 210, 190);
```

**Figure 13.15** Instantiation of the RechargeableLaserTurret class (Figure 13.8).

## Usage 2: `super.method()`

The general syntax `super.method()` is used when the subclass needs to invoke a method that is defined in its parent class. For example, suppose when a RechargeableLaserTurret object recharges, it first performs the `turn()` method that is defined in the LaserTurret class before charging up the power to 100. Figure 13.16 shows the revised code for the RechargeableLaserTurret class based on Figure 13.8.

The keyword `super` is used only in a subclass file to refer to its parent class. The keyword `super` is not used outside of a subclass file.

```
package
{
    public class RechargeableLaserTurret extends LaserTurret
    {
        public function RechargeableLaserTurret(remainingPower:Number,
        firePower:Number, x:int, y:int)
        {
            super(remainingPower, firePower, x, y);
        }

        public function recharge():void
        {
            super.turn();
            this.remainingPower = 100;
        }
    }
}
```

**Figure 13.16** RechargeableLaserTurret.as in which the `recharge()` method calls its parent class's `turn()` method before filling up the power to 100.

If `super()` and `super.method()` are needed in the constructor body, be sure to call `super()` first. Otherwise, the `super.method()` will not behave as expected. Let's return to the RechargeableLaserTurret class shown in Figure 13.8, and suppose the rechargeable laser will fire once when it is created. Thus, the `fire()` method should be called in the constructor body, as shown in Figure 13.17. Note the order of the `super()` and `super.fire()` statements.

```
package
{
    public class RechargeableLaserTurret extends LaserTurret
    {
        public function RechargeableLaserTurret(remainingPower:Number,
        firePower:Number, x:int, y:int)
        {
            super(remainingPower, firePower, x, y);
            super.fire();
        }

        public function recharge():void
        {
            this.remainingPower = 100;
        }
    }
}
```

**Figure 13.17** RechargeableLaserTurret.as. The constructor has both `super()` and `super.fire()` statements.

### 13.3.2 Accessing a Subclass's Members

A subclass inherits all of the properties and methods from its parent class. Thus, an object can be invoked with the methods defined in its class and its parent class. For example, let's revisit the `LaserTurret` and `RechargeableLaserTurret` example (Figure 13.7). Figure 13.18 shows instantiation of each of these two classes. The `LaserTurret` object `genericLaser` is then invoked with the `turn()` and `fire()` methods. The `RechargeableLaserTurret` object `upgradedLaser` is then invoked with the `turn()`, `fire()`, and `recharge()` methods. Note that you will get an error if you invoke `recharge()` on `genericLaser` because `recharge()` is only available to `RechargeableLaserTurret` objects, but not objects of its parent class.

```
var genericLaser:LaserTurret = new LaserTurret(100, 5, 120, 230);
var upgradedLaser:RechargeableLaserTurret = new
RechargeableLaserTurret(90, 15, 190, 350);

genericLaser.turn();
genericLaser.fire();

upgradedLaser.turn();
upgradedLaser.fire();
upgradedLaser.recharge();
```

**Figure 13.18** Invoking methods on objects of a subclass and its parent class.

## 13.4 INHERITANCE EXAMPLES

In a fully implemented class, all properties are used. Any properties that are unused should be removed from the class.

So far the `RechargeableLaserTurret` and `LaserTurret` classes have been used as the example to explain the inheritance concept and coding. This section provides more examples to demonstrate the thought process of organizing classes into an inheritance hierarchy. For each example, class diagrams will be used to depict the classes before and after the inheritance hierarchy. The examples are not intended to be comprehensive implementation for a game. For the purposes of demonstrating the thought process in organizing the class hierarchy, only a few properties and methods are defined in these examples. Some properties, such as `fuelCapacity`, may even be unused in any of the methods. The body of the methods in the example may be left empty or contain only a few simple statements. The code for the class files and for using the class files will be provided for the first example (Section 13.4.1). The rest of the examples are discussed using class diagrams only.

### 13.4.1 Parent Class: Car Subclass: `TimeVehicle`

Let's revisit the `Car` class (Figure 13.19) from Chapter 12. Suppose you want to add a different class of car to your game. The new class, say `TimeVehicle`, has all of the properties and functionalities of the existing `Car` class (highlighted in color in Figure 13.20) but it also can time travel.

The `Car` and `TimeVehicle` classes share some common properties and methods. All of the common properties and methods can be organized in a parent class. Because the

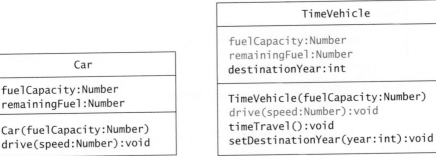

Figure 13.20 Class diagram of a new class TimeVehicle.

**Figure 13.19** Class diagram of the Car example from Chapter 12.

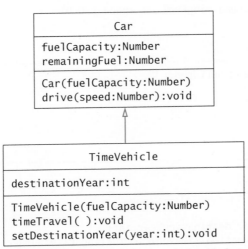

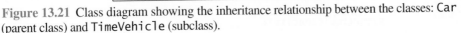

**Figure 13.21** Class diagram showing the inheritance relationship between the classes: Car (parent class) and TimeVehicle (subclass).

Car class contains all of the common properties and methods, it can be the parent class and TimeVehicle becomes its subclass (Figure 13.21).

Figure 13.22 shows the class file for the Car class. It remains the same as before it becomes a parent class of TimeVehicle. The class file for TimeVehicle is shown in Figure 13.23. The words extends Car make the class a subclass of Car. As a subclass of Car, TimeVehicle does not need to include the definition of the method drive() and the declarations of fuelCapacity and remainingFuel properties; they are already available to TimeVehicle. The only property declared in TimeVehicle is destinationYear, which is specific to TimeVehicle. The methods defined in TimeVehicle are timeTravel() and setDestinationYear(), which are specific to TimeVehicle.

```
package
{
    import flash.display.MovieClip;

    public class Car extends MovieClip
    {
        public var fuelCapacity:Number;
        public var remainingFuel:Number;

        public function Car(fuelCapacity:Number)
        {
            this.fuelCapacity = fuelCapacity;
            this.remainingFuel = fuelCapacity;
        }
        public function drive(speed:int):void
        {
            this.x += speed;
            this.remainingFuel -= speed * 0.01;
        }
    }
}
```

Figure 13.22 Car.as from Chapter 12.

```
package
{
    public class TimeVehicle extends Car
    {
        public var destinationYear:int;
        public function TimeVehicle(fuelCapacity:Number)
        {
            super(fuelCapacity);
        }

        public function timeTravel():void
        {

        }

        public function setDestinationYear(year:int):void
        {
            destinationYear = year;
        }
    }
}
```

Figure 13.23 TimeVehicle.as.

> **?** **Self-Test Exercise: Accessing Members of Subclass versus Parent Class**

The Car and TimeVehicle classes are instantiated to create two objects named betty and pete respectively as follows:

```
var betty:Car = new Car(100);
var pete:TimeVehicle = new TimeVehicle(120);
```

Questions

Which of the following statements do not give an error?

1. betty.drive(5);
2. betty.timeTravel();
3. betty.setDestinationYear(2056);
4. betty.remainingFuel = 30;
5. betty.destinationYear = 2056;
6. pete.drive(5);
7. pete.timeTravel();
8. pete.setDestinationYear(2056);
9. pete.remainingFuel = 30;
10. pete.destinationYear = 2056;

Answers to Self-Test Questions

1. No error because betty is a Car object and the drive() method is defined in the Car class.
2. Error because betty is a Car object and timeTravel() is not defined in the Car class.
3. Error because betty is a Car object and setDestinationYear() is not defined in the Car class.
4. No error because betty is a Car object and remainingFuel is defined in the Car class.
5. Error because betty is a Car object and destinationYear is not defined in the Car class.
6. No error because pete is an object of TimeVehicle, which inherits the drive() method from the Car class.
7. No error because pete is an object of TimeVehicle and timeTravel() is defined in the TimeVehicle class.
8. No error because pete is an object of TimeVehicle and setDestinationYear() is defined in the TimeVehicle class.
9. No error because pete is an object of TimeVehicle, which inherits remainingFuel from the Car class.
10. No error because pete is an object of TimeVehicle and destinationYear is defined in the TimeVehicle class.

## 13.4.2 Parent Class: Item Subclasses: Coin and Bee

This example revisits Chapter 12's OOP Side-Scrolling Platform Game Lab, in which a Coin class will be created. As shown in the class diagram in Figure 13.24, the Coin class has a static property of hero and these methods:

- checkTouchedByHero(): This method checks if the Coin object is touched by the hero. If it is, then the Coin object disappears by being relocated off the Stage.

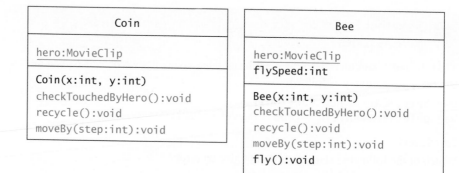

Figure 13.24 Class diagram of two classes: Coin and Bee.

- recycle(): This method repositions the Coin object to get on the Stage again when it is scrolled beyond a certain threshold outside of the Stage.
- moveBy(): This method moves the Coin object horizontally by the amount of the input parameter step. This method allows scrolling the Coin object with the platform.

Now suppose you want to add a new type of object, a bee, that can also fly. The class diagram for a Bee class is shown in Figure 13.24. Because Coin contains all of the common properties and methods, it could be the parent class for Bee (Figure 13.25). However, conceptually it does not seem right to think of Bee as a subclass of Coin. An alternative class hierarchy, as shown in Figure 13.26, is to create a new parent class with a general name, say, Item, that contains all of the common properties and methods of Coin and Bee. This approach has an advantage of allowing future changes in Coin that Bee should not have. For example, you may want the Coin object but not the Bee object to change color. With the class hierarchy shown in Figure 13.26, a method for changing color could be added to the Coin class without affecting the Bee class. On the other hand, with the class hierarchy shown in Figure 13.25, the method added to Coin for changing color would be also available to Bee.

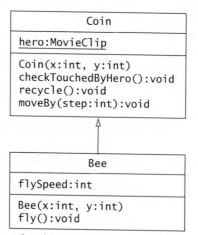

Figure 13.25 Class diagram showing a possible class hierarchy between the classes: Coin (parent class) and Bee (subclass).

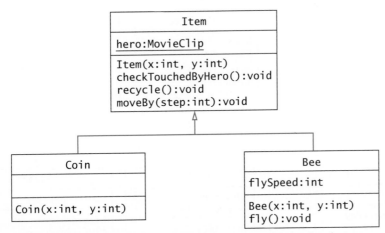

**Figure 13.26** Class diagram showing a possible class hierarchy for the classes: Item (parent class), Coin (subclass), and Bee (subclass).

⚙ **An OOP Side-Scrolling Platform Game with Inheritance (Lab)** Add a flying bee to the OOP Side-Scrolling Platform Game Lab (from Chapter 12) by implementing the Bee class that is shown in Figure 13.26, instantiating the class, and invoking methods on the Bee object.

## 13.4.3 Parent Class: Character Subclasses: Hero, Villain, and Wizard

In this example, we will look at three classes, Hero, Villain, and Wizard, that share some common properties and methods but no one class contains all of the common properties and methods. In addition, some are shared among all three classes and some between two classes. The common properties and methods shared among all three classes are highlighted in color in the class diagram in Figure 13.27.

| Hero |
|---|
| keys:Array<br>magicPower:int<br>weapons:Array<br>shield:int<br>health:int |
| Hero()<br>walk():void<br>jump():void<br>heal():void<br>heroAttack():void<br>useMagic(power:int):void<br>updateHealth():void |

| Villain |
|---|
| spells:Array<br>weapons:Array<br>health:int |
| Villain()<br>villainAttack():void<br>walk():void<br>jump():void<br>castSpell():void<br>updateHealth():void |

| Wizard |
|---|
| magicPower:int<br>health:int |
| Wizard()<br>walk():void<br>jump():void<br>fly():void<br>useMagic(power:int):void<br>updateHealth():void |

**Figure 13.27** Class diagram of three classes: Hero, Villain, and Wizard.

A new class, say, Character (Figure 13.28), that contains all of the properties and methods that are shared among all three classes may be created as the parent class for Hero, Villain, and Wizard.

You may also further subclass Hero and Wizard under a new class, say, GoodGuy (Figure 13.29), which contains all of the common properties and methods shared by Hero and Wizard.

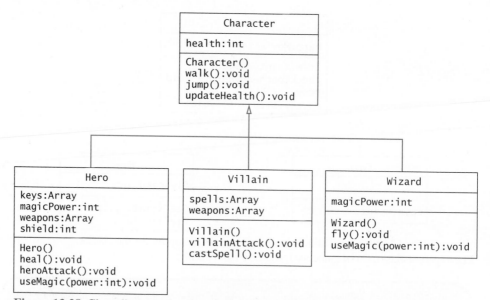

**Figure 13.28** Class diagram showing the inheritance relationship between the classes: Character (parent class), Hero (subclass), Villain (subclass), and Wizard (subclass).

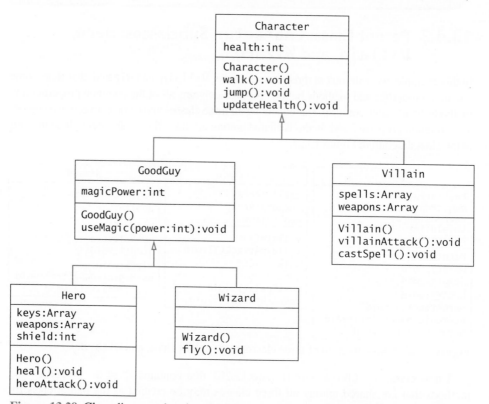

**Figure 13.29** Class diagram showing the inheritance relationship between the classes: Character (parent class of GoodGuy and Villain), GoodGuy (subclass of Character and parent class of Hero and Wizard), Villain (subclass of Character), Hero (subclass of GoodGuy), and Wizard (subclass of GoodGuy).

**? Self-Test Exercise: Accessing Members of Subclass versus Parent Class**

This exercise is based on the class hierarchy shown in Figure 13.29. Each of the five classes is instantiated to create an object as follows:

```
var noName:Character = new Character();
var genericGoodGuy:GoodGuy = new GoodGuy();
var bigBoss:Villain = new Villain();
var peter:Hero = new Hero();
var harry:Wizard = new Wizard();
```

List the properties and methods that are available to each object.

Answers

| Object | Properties | Methods |
|---|---|---|
| noName | health | walk() <br> jump() <br> updateHealth() |
| genericGoodGuy | health <br> magicPower | walk() <br> jump() <br> updateHealth() <br><br> useMagic(power:int) |
| bigBoss | health <br> spells <br> weapons | walk() <br> jump() <br> updateHealth() <br><br> villainAttack() <br> castSpell() |
| peter | health <br> magicPower <br> keys <br> weapons <br> shield | walk() <br> jump() <br> updateHealth() <br><br> useMagic(power:int) <br> heal() <br> heroAttack() |
| harry | health <br> magicPower | walk() <br> jump() <br> updateHealth() <br><br> useMagic(power:int) <br> fly() |

# 13.5 THE KEYWORDS extends MovieClip

Now that we have introduced the concept of inheritance and the keyword extends, let's revisit the use of the keywords extends MovieClip to give an object a visual representation using a movie clip (Section 12.6 and Step 5 in Section 12.4). The keywords extends

MovieClip make the class a subclass of MovieClip, which is a built-in class of Action-Script. The MovieClip class has properties, such as x, y, width, height, rotation, and alpha, and methods, such as gotoAndStop(), gotoAndPlay(), stop(), and play(). Making a class a subclass of MovieClip allows the class to use all of the properties and methods available to MovieClip.

If a class's parent class is a subclass of MovieClip, then it also inherits MovieClip's properties and methods. For example, in our RechargeableLaserTurret example, if LaserTurret is a subclass of MovieClip, then all of the MovieClip's properties and methods are also available to its subclass RechargeableLaserTurret.

## 13.6 ACCESS SPECIFIERS: public, protected, AND private

So far you have seen the use of public specifier for the members of a class. There are actually four specifiers in ActionScript 3.0: public, protected, private, and internal. They are used to specify the scope of a class member, that is, whether a class member is visible, or can be accessed, in other program units outside of the class. This text will cover public, protected, and private.

Table 13.1 compares the scope of these three specifiers. *Public* properties and methods can be accessible inside and outside of the class. They are accessible by the class's subclasses, other classes, and in a Flash file. *Protected* properties and methods are accessible within the class and its subclasses. They are not accessible from a Flash file or other classes that are not the class's subclasses. *Private* has the most restrictive scope among the three. Private properties and methods are accessible only within the class that defines them.

The constructor has to be public in order for the class to be instantiated.

Let's revisit the LaserTurret and RechargeableLaserTurret classes (Figure 13.7 and Figure 13.8) and use the property remainingPower to demonstrate the different scope of public, protected, and private. Figure 13.30 through Figure 13.32 set remainingPower to public, protected, and private respectively. The code shown in

| TABLE 13.1 | Comparison of the Scope of public, protected, and private Access Specifiers | | |
|---|---|---|---|
| | Accessible within the class in which the member is defined | Accessible within the subclass of the class in which the member is defined | Accessible outside of the class in which the member is defined, for example, in a Flash file or a different class that is not its subclass |
| | | Example: Figure 13.33 | Example: Figure 13.34 |
| public Example: Figure 13.30 | ✔ | ✔ | ✔ |
| protected Example: Figure 13.31 | ✔ | ✔ | ✘ |
| private Example: Figure 13.32 | ✔ | ✘ | ✘ |

**Example 1: remainingPower as a public property**

```
package
{
    import flash.display.MovieClip;

    public class LaserTurret extends MovieClip
    {
        public var remainingPower:Number;
        public var firePower:Number;

        public function LaserTurret(remainingPower:Number,
        firePower:Number, x:int, y:int)
        {
            this.remainingPower = remainingPower;
            this.firePower = firePower;
            this.x = x;
            this.y = y;
        }

        public function turn():void
        {
            this.rotation += 10;
        }

        public function fire():void
        {
            this.remainingPower -= this.firePower;
        }
    }
}
```

**Figure 13.30** LaserTurret.as with remainingPower being a public property.

**Example 2: remainingPower as a protected property**

```
package
{
    import flash.display.MovieClip;

    public class LaserTurret extends MovieClip
    {
        protected var remainingPower:Number;
        public var firePower:Number;

        public function LaserTurret(remainingPower:Number,
        firePower:Number, x:int, y:int)
        {
            this.remainingPower = remainingPower;
            this.firePower = firePower;
            this.x = x;
            this.y = y;
        }
```

**Figure 13.31** LaserTurret.as with remainingPower being a protected property. *(continued)*

```
        public function turn():void
        {
            this.rotation += 10;
        }

        public function fire():void
        {
            this.remainingPower -= this.firePower;
        }
    }
}
```

Figure 13.31 *(continued)*

## Example 3: remainingPower as a private property

```
package
{
    import flash.display.MovieClip;

    public class LaserTurret extends MovieClip
    {
        private var remainingPower:Number;
        public var firePower:Number;

        public function LaserTurret(remainingPower:Number,
        firePower:Number, x:int, y:int)
        {
            this.remainingPower = remainingPower;
            this.firePower = firePower;
            this.x = x;
            this.y = y;
        }

        public function turn():void
        {
            this.rotation += 10;
        }

        public function fire():void
        {
            this.remainingPower -= this.firePower;
        }
    }
}
```

Figure 13.32 LaserTurret.as with remainingPower being a private property.

Figure 13.33 accesses remainingPower in the subclass LaserTurret. This works fine when remainingPower is either public or protected. However, you will get an error if remainingPower is private. The code shown in Figure 13.34 accesses remainingPower in a Flash file. This works fine only when remainingPower is public. You will get an error if remainingPower is either protected or private.

```
package
{
    public class RechargeableLaserTurret extends LaserTurret
    {
        public function RechargeableLaserTurret(remainingPower:Number,
        firePower:Number, x:int, y:int)
        {
            super(remainingPower, firePower, x, y);
        }

        public function recharge():void
        {
            this.remainingPower = 100;
        }
    }
}
```

**Figure 13.33** `RechargeableLaserTurret.as`: The property `remainingPower` is being accessed in the `recharge()` method.

```
var upgradedLaser:RechargeableLaserTurret = new
RechargeableLaserTurret(90, 15, 190, 350);

upgradedLaser.remainingPower = 100;
```

**Figure 13.34** In a Flash file (`.fla`): The `RechargeableLaserTurret` object `upgradedLaser` tries to access the property `remainingPower`.

```
package
{
    public class Bird
    {
        protected var species:String;

        public function Bird(species:String)
        {
            this.species = species;
        }

        private function huntForFood():void
        {
            trace("Bird::huntForFood()");
        }

        public function feed():void
        {
            trace("Bird::feed()");
        }
    }
}
```

**Figure 13.35** `Bird.as`.

```
package
{
    public class Goose extends Bird
    {
        private var Regional:Boolean;

        public function Goose(species:String, regional:Boolean)
        {
            super(species);
            this.regional = regional;
        }

        public function fly():void
        {
            trace("Goose::fly()");
        }
    }
}
```

Figure 13.36 Goose.as.

```
package
{
    public class Penguin extends Bird
    {
        public var temperateZone:Boolean;

        public function Penguin(species:String, temperateZone:Boolean)
        {
            super(species);
            this.temperateZone = temperateZone;
        }

        public function swim():void
        {
            trace("Penguin::swim()");
        }
    }
}
```

Figure 13.37 Penguin.as.

```
var tweet:Bird = new Bird("unknown");
var grandmaGoose:Goose = new Goose("Snow Goose", true);
var dancingFeet:Penguin = new Penguin("Emperor", false);
```

Figure 13.38 In a Flash file (.fla): Instantiation of the Bird, Goose, and Penguin classes to create three objects.

## ❓ Self-Test Exercise: Access Specifiers

This exercise is based on the classes shown in Figure 13.35 through Figure 13.38.

### Questions

Which of the following will give an error? Explain why or why not.

1. In `Bird.as`, the `feed()` method has the following statement.
   `this.huntForFood();`
2. In `Goose.as`, the `fly()` method has the following statement.
   `super.huntForFood();`
3. In `Penguin.as`, the `swim()` method has the following statement.
   `super.huntForFood();`
4. In `Bird.as`, the `feed()` method has the following statement.
   `trace(this.species);`
5. In `Goose.as`, the `fly()` method has the following statement.
   `trace(this.species);`
6. In `Penguin.as`, the `swim()` method has the following statement.
   `trace(this.species);`
7. The code shown in Figure 13.38 has the following statement added at the end.
   `tweet.huntForFood();`
8. The code shown in Figure 13.38 has the following statement added at the end.
   `tweet.feed();`
9. The code shown in Figure 13.38 has the following statement added at the end.
   `grandmaGoose.huntForFood();`
10. The code shown in Figure 13.38 has the following statement added at the end.
    `grandmaGoose.feed();`
11. The code shown in Figure 13.38 has the following statement added at the end.
    `grandmaGoose.fly();`
12. The code shown in Figure 13.38 has the following statement added at the end.
    `dancingFeet.huntForFood();`
13. The code shown in Figure 13.38 has the following statement added at the end.
    `dancingFeet.feed();`
14. The code shown in Figure 13.38 has the following statement added at the end.
    `dancingFeet.swim();`
15. The code shown in Figure 13.38 has the following statement added at the end.
    `tweet.species = "finch";`
16. The code shown in Figure 13.38 has the following statement added at the end.
    `grandmaGoose.species = "finch";`
17. The code shown in Figure 13.38 has the following statement added at the end.
    `dancingFeet.species = "finch";`
18. The code shown in Figure 13.38 has the following statement added at the end.
    `grandmaGoose.regional = false;`
19. The code shown in Figure 13.38 has the following statement added at the end.
    `dancingFeet.temperateZone = false;`

### Answers to Self-Test Questions

1. No error because the `huntForFood()` method is defined in the `Bird` class and thus it is accessible within the `Bird` class.
2. Error because `huntForFood()` is a private method defined in the `Bird` class and thus it is not accessible outside of the `Bird` class, such as in its subclass.

3. Same as the answer for Question 2.

4. No error because `species` is a property defined in the `Bird` class.

5. No error because `species` is a protected property defined in the `Bird` class and thus it is accessible in `Goose`, a subclass of `Bird`.

6. No error because `species` is a protected property defined in the `Bird` class and thus it is accessible in `Penguin`, a subclass of `Bird`.

7. Error because `huntForFood()` is a private method of `Bird` and thus it is not accessible outside of the `Bird` class, such as in a Flash file.

8. No error because `feed()` is a public method of `Bird` and thus it is accessible outside of the `Bird` class, such as in a Flash file.

9. Error because `huntForFood()` is a private method of `Bird` and thus it is not accessible outside of the `Bird` class, such as in a Flash file. (Note: `Goose` does inherit `huntForFood()` but the method is not accessible outside of `Bird`.)

10. No error because `Goose` inherits the `feed()` method from `Bird` and `feed()` is a public method.

11. No error because `fly()` is a public method of `Goose` and thus it is accessible outside of the `Goose` class, such as in a Flash file.

12. Error because `huntForFood()` is a private method of `Bird` and thus it is not accessible outside of the `Bird` class, such as in a Flash file. (Note: `Penguin` does inherit `huntForFood()` but the method is not accessible outside of `Bird`.)

13. No error because `Penguin` inherits the `feed()` method from `Bird` and `feed()` is a public method.

14. No error because `swim()` is a public method of `Penguin` and thus it is accessible outside of the `Penguin` class, such as in a Flash file.

15. Error because `species` is a protected property of `Bird` and thus it is not accessible outside of the `Bird` class or its subclasses, such as in a Flash file.

16. Same answer as that of Question 15. (Note: `Goose` does inherit the property `species` but the property is not accessible outside of `Bird` or its subclasses.)

17. Same answer as that of Question 15. (Note: `Penguin` does inherit the property `species` but the property is not accessible outside of `Bird` or its subclasses.)

18. Error because `regional` is a private property of `Goose` and thus it is not accessible outside of `Goose`, such as in a Flash file.

19. No error because `temperateZone` is a public property of `Penguin` and thus it is accessible outside of `Penguin`, such as in a Flash file.

## 13.6.1 Notation for Access Specifiers in Class Diagrams

A symbol of +, #, or − is placed to the left side of the member in a class diagram to denote the public, protected, or private specifier, respectively. For example, the class diagram shown in Figure 13.39 depicts the classes `Bird` (Figure 13.35), `Goose` (Figure 13.36), and `Penguin` (Figure 13.37).

## 13.6.2 Motivation

The access specifiers provide a mechanism to control the visibility, or access, of class members outside of the class. For programming assignments in an introductory programming course, in which you are the one who writes the classes and uses the classes, the

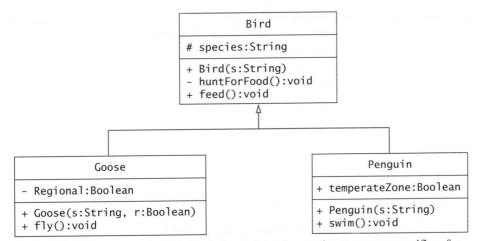

**Figure 13.39** Class diagram with symbols, +, #, and −, to denote access specifiers for the class members.

benefit of such access control may not be obvious. It may seem unnecessary to go through such trouble of assigning the protected and private specifiers only to restrict the freedom accessing the class members and to open the possibilities for errors.

Recall that in the house building analogy, a class file is like a house blueprint and a class instance is like the actual house built from the blueprint. Now let's extend the analogy one step further. In the building process, architects draft the blueprint and builders build houses based on the blueprints. The builders do not have to know the internal design decisions that the architect has made for the blueprint. In the software development process, software developers are like the architects and programmers are like the builders. The software developers design classes and programmers use the classes to create objects to use in their software projects. The programmers who use the class should be shielded from the internal design decisions and implementation details that the software developer has made for the class. To understand the benefit better, let's consider some scenarios that will open the possibility of bugs when the properties are made public.

## Scenario 1: Changing `remainingPower` of `LaserTurret` Outside of Class

If the `remainingPower` of `LaserTurret` is set to public, the `remainingPower` of any `LaserTurret` object may be set to any high value outside of the class. This would make any `LaserTurret` object rechargeable too and rechargeable to any arbitrarily high value. However, the `LaserTurret` object is not supposed to be rechargeable. The distinction between the `LaserTurret` and `RechargeableLaserTurret` classes becomes blurred. In addition, suppose the class also contains methods to display a power bar onscreen to show the percentage of the power remaining. Setting the `remainingPower` to a negative value or an arbitrarily large value would blow off the power bar. For example, as shown in Figure 13.40, the `remainingPower` of the `genericLaser` is set to 100,000. Syntactically, it is allowed because `remainingPower` is a public property; you will not get an ActionScript

```
var genericLaser:LaserTurret = new LaserTurret(100, 5, 120, 230);
genericLaser.remainingPower = 100000;
```

**Figure 13.40** The value of `remainingPower` of the `LaserTurret` object is set to 100,000.

error. However, from the game design point of view, it is not desirable. Without imposing any restrictions on remainingPower, you can only rely on the programmers who use these classes to always assign a valid value to remainingPower.

If the remaining power of a LaserTurret object is not allowed to change except during firing, then remainingPower should be set to private. If it is allowed to change, then still set the remainingPower to protected or private but add a new method to allow setting the remainingPower. For example, as shown in Figure 13.41, the new method,

```
package
{
    import flash.display.MovieClip;

    public class LaserTurret extends MovieClip
    {
        private var remainingPower:Number;
        public var firePower:Number;

        public function LaserTurret(remainingPower:Number,
        firePower:Number, x:int, y:int)
        {
            this.remainingPower = remainingPower;
            this.firePower = firePower;
            this.x = x;
            this.y = y;
        }

        public function turn():void
        {
            this.rotation += 10;
        }

        public function fire():void
        {
            this.remainingPower -= this.firePower;
        }

        public function setRemainingPower(power:Number):void
        {
            if (power < 0)
            {
                this.remainingPower = 0;
            }
            else if (power > 100)
            {
                this.remainingPower = 100;
            }
            else
            {
                this.remainingPower = power;
            }
        }
    }
}
```

**Figure 13.41** LaserTurret.as with private remainingPower and a method for setting remainingPower.

setRemainingPower(), also contains an if statement to impose a limit on the new value for remainingPower to be within 0 and 100. Changing the value of remainingPower now has to go through the method setRemainingPower() instead of directly setting the value of remainingPower. Because remainingPower is now a private property, directly changing the value of remainingPower outside of the class, such as using the second statement in Figure 13.40, will cause a complier error.

Figure 13.40 may be rewritten as shown in Figure 13.42. Now even if a value of 100,000 is passed into the setRemainingPower() method, the remaining power of genericLaser is capped at 100.

```
var genericLaser:LaserTurret = new LaserTurret(100, 5, 120, 230);
genericLaser.setRemainingPower(100000);
```

**Figure 13.42** Set remainingPower of the LaserTurret object by invoking the setRemainingPower() method.

The if statement in setRemainingPower() to limit the new power value between 0 and 100 can be replaced by the following statement:
this.remainingPower = Math.min(100, Math.max(0, power));

## Scenario 2: Keeping Count of Number of Recharge of RechargeableLaserTurret

Suppose RechargeableLaserTurret has a property bonusPoints. Every 10 bonus points earned will allow one recharge. So, every time recharge() is invoked, it has to take off 10 bonus points in addition to filling up the remaining power. Figure 13.43 shows the revised RechargeableLaserTurret class. For the sake of simplicity, the methods that handle earning of bonus points are omitted.

> Math.min (a, b) returns the least value of the two values a and b. Math. max(a, b) returns the higher value of a and b.

```
package
{
    public class RechargeableLaserTurret extends LaserTurret
    {
        private var bonusPoints:int;

        public function RechargeableLaserTurret(remainingPower:Number,
        firePower:Number, x:int, y:int)
        {
            super(remainingPower, firePower, x, y);
            bonusPoints = 0;
        }

        public function recharge():void
        {
            if (this.bonusPoints >= 10)
            {
                this.bonusPoints -= 10;
                this.remainingPower = 100;
            }
        }
    }
}
```

**Figure 13.43** RechargeableLaserTurret.as with a private property bonusPoints and revised recharge() method to enforce the bonus point system for recharging.

To enforce the bonus point system for recharging, remainingPower of LaserTurret has to be set to private. Otherwise, remainingPower may be set outside of the class similar to Figure 13.40 bypassing the bonus point system for recharging. The property bonusPoints also has to be private. Otherwise, even with remainingPower being private, bonusPoints may be set outside of the class, as shown in Figure 13.44, bypassing the earning of bonus points.

```
var upgradedLaser:RechargeableLaserTurret = new
RechargeableLaserTurret(100, 5, 120, 230);
upgradedLaser.bonusPoints = 1000;    // undesirable
```

**Figure 13.44** The value of bonusPoints is set to 1,000 without having the upgradedLaser to earn it.

## 13.6.3 Setters and Getters

It is a good and common practice to set all of the properties to private. For properties that are allowed to be accessed directly outside of the class, use methods to set or get their values. A *get method*, also called an *accessor* function or *getter*, allows you to query a class property without changing it. A *set method*, also called a *mutator* function or *setter*, allows you to change the value of a class property. The naming convention for these functions is that the function name starts with the word *set* or *get* followed by the property name, for example, setRemainingPower() and getRemainingPower(). Figure 13.41 shows an example of adding a method setRemainingPower() to allow setting remainingPower a new value. It uses if statements to restrict the range of the value for remainingPower. However, depending on the class design, the body of these methods may be as simple as one statement, as shown in Figure 13.45.

To directly set and get the value of remainingPower outside of the LaserTurret class, such as in a Flash file, you use the method setRemainingPower() and getRemainingPower(), as shown in Figure 13.46.

The set and get methods do not have to go in a pair. Depending on the class design, a property may have only a set method without a get method, and vice versa. Any property that is not allowed to be accessed directly outside of the class at all should not have a set or get method.

## SET AND GET IN ActionScript

ActionScript 3.0 also provides a mechanism to allow the setter and getter to share the same name, which is an advantage because you do not have to keep two different method names—one for the set method and one for the get. For example, Figure 13.47 renames the property remainingPower to _remainingPower, and names the new setter and getter remainingPower(). The use of these setter and getter methods is shown in Figure 13.48. Note that the statements to set and get the remaining power look as if remainingPower is a public property. However, because the set and get methods are used, additional statements such as the if statements in the set method may be used to enforce the validity of the new value.

```
package
{
    import flash.display.MovieClip;

    public class LaserTurret extends MovieClip
    {
        private var remainingPower:Number;
        public var firePower:Number;

        public function LaserTurret(remainingPower:Number,
        firePower:Number, x:int, y:int)
        {
            this.remainingPower = remainingPower;
            this.firePower = firePower;
            this.x = x;
            this.y = y;
        }

        public function turn():void
        {
            this.rotation += 10;
        }

        public function fire():void
        {
            this.remainingPower -= this.firePower;
        }

        public function setRemainingPower(power:Number):void
        {
            this.remainingPower = power;
        }

        public function getRemainingPower():Number
        {
            return this.remainingPower;
        }
    }
}
```

**Figure 13.45** LaserTurret.as with a set and a get method for the private property remainingPower.

```
var genericLaser:LaserTurret = new LaserTurret(100, 5, 120, 230);
var currentPower:Number;

genericLaser.setRemainingPower(100000);
currentPower = getRemainingPower();
```

**Figure 13.46** Set and get remainingPower of the LaserTurret object by invoking the setRemainingPower() and getRemainingPower() methods, respectively.

```
package
{
    import flash.display.MovieClip;

    public class LaserTurret extends MovieClip
    {
        private var _remainingPower:Number;
        public var firePower:Number;

        public function LaserTurret(remainingPower:Number,
        firePower:Number, x:int, y:int)
        {
            this._remainingPower = remainingPower;
            this.firePower = firePower;
            this.x = x;
            this.y = y;
        }

        public function turn():void
        {
            this.rotation += 10;
        }

        public function fire():void
        {
            this._remainingPower -= this.firePower;
        }

        public function set remainingPower(power:Number):void
        {
            if (power < 0)
            {
                this._remainingPower = 0;
            }
            else if (power > 100)
            {
                this._remainingPower = 100;
            }
            else
            {
                this._remainingPower = power;
            }
        }

        public function get remainingPower():Number
        {
            return this._remainingPower;
        }
    }
}
```

**Figure 13.47** LaserTurret.as with a setter and a getter for the private property _remainingPower.

```
var genericLaser:LaserTurret = new LaserTurret(100, 5, 120, 230);
var currentPower:Number;

genericLaser.remainingPower = 100000;
currentPower = genericLaser.remainingPower;
```

**Figure 13.48** The statements to set and get the remaining power look as if remainingPower is a public property but they invoke the set and get methods, respectively.

## 13.7 POLYMORPHISM

*Polymorphism* is another key concept in object-oriented programming. It refers to the ability to use a single method name for a method that behaves differently with objects instantiated from different classes. From the code-centric standpoint, making an inherited method behave differently for different objects can be accomplished by redefining the method. Recall that a subclass inherits all of the properties and methods from its parent class. The inherited properties and methods are available to the subclass objects without having to redefine them in the subclass. However, when you want these methods to perform tasks different from those defined in the parent class, they should be redefined in the subclass.

### 13.7.1 An Example: Violinist, Pianist, and TrumpetPlayer

To better understand what redefinition of methods means and why it is necessary, let's look at an example. Suppose you have three classes (Figure 13.49): Violinist, Pianist, and TrumpetPlayer. They share some common properties: payPerHour and instrument. However, because they play different instruments, they have different methods for playing an instrument. The Violinist class has a method called playViolin(), the Pianist class has playPiano(), and the TrumpetPlayer class has playTrumpet().

| Violinist |
| --- |
| payPerHour:Number<br>instrument:String |
| Violinist()<br>playViolin():void |

| Pianist |
| --- |
| payPerHour:Number<br>instrument:String |
| Pianist()<br>playPiano():void |

| TrumpetPlayer |
| --- |
| payPerHour:Number<br>instrument:String |
| TrumpetPlayer()<br>playTrumpet():void |

**Figure 13.49** Class diagram for three individual classes: Violinist, Pianist, and TrumpetPlayer.

The similarities among these three classes suggest an inheritance relationship. A new class Musician that contains the shared properties of the three classes is created to be a parent class. The three classes then can be the subclasses of Musician (Figure 13.50).

Now suppose you have 10 violinists, 2 pianists, and 12 trumpet players in your game. In a Flash file, you may create three arrays—one to store the 10 Violinist objects, one to store the 2 Pianist objects, and one to store the 12 TrumpetPlayer objects. The code shown in Figure 13.51 sets up these three arrays.

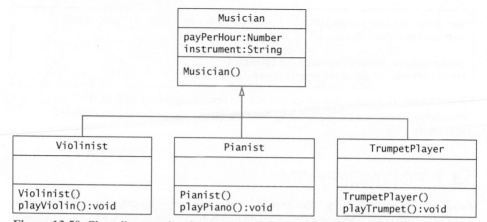

**Figure 13.50** Class diagram showing the inheritance relationship between the classes: Musician (parent class), Violinist (subclass), Pianist (subclass), and TrumpetPlayer (subclass)

```
var i:int = 0;
var arrayViolinist:Array = new Array();
var arrayPianist:Array = new Array();
var arrayTrumpetPlayer:Array = new Array();

for (i = 0; i < 10; i++)
{
    arrayViolinist.unshift( new Violinist() );
    stage.addChild(arrayViolinist[0]);
}

for (i = 0; i < 2; i++)
{
    arrayPianist.unshift( new Pianist() );
    stage.addChild(arrayPianist[0]);
}

for (i = 0; i < 12; i++)
{
    arrayTrumpetPlayer.unshift( new TrumpetPlayer() );
    stage.addChild(arrayTrumpetPlayer[0]);
}
```

**Figure 13.51** In a Flash file (.fla): The Violinist, Pianist, and TrumpetPlayer classes are instantiated and the instances are added to three arrays.

Suppose these different musicians will be playing their instruments continuously during the game. The frame event listener code is added (Figure 13.52). The function playOrchestra() will be executed at frame rate. In the playOrchestra(), it loops through each of the three musician arrays to invoke the specific instrument-playing

```
var i:int = 0;

var arrayViolinist:Array = new Array();
var arrayPianist:Array = new Array();
var arrayTrumpetPlayer:Array = new Array();

stage.addEventListener(Event.ENTER_FRAME, playOrchestra);

for (i = 0; i < 10; i++)
{
    arrayViolinist.unshift( new Violinist() );
    stage.addChild(arrayViolinist[0]);
}

for (i = 0; i < 2; i++)
{
    arrayPianist.unshift( new Pianist() );
    stage.addChild(arrayPianist[0]);
}

for (i = 0; i < 12; i++)
{
    arrayTrumpetPlayer.unshift( new TrumpetPlayer() );
    stage.addChild(arrayTrumpetPlayer[0]);
}

function playOrchestra(evt:Event):void
{
    var i:int;
    for (i = 0; i < arrayViolinist.length; i++)
    {
        arrayViolinist[i].playViolin();
    }

    for (i = 0; i < arrayPianist.length; i++)
    {
        arrayPianist[i].playPiano();
    }

    for (i = 0; i < arrayViolinist.length; i++)
    {
        arrayTrumpetPlayer[i].playTrumpet();
    }
}
```

**Figure 13.52** In a Flash file (.fla): Using the Violinist, Pianist, and TrumpetPlayer classes.

method on each musician object. Think of it as if telling the musicians, "Violinists, play your violins. Pianists, play your pianos. Trumpet players, play your trumpets." What if you have 10 different musicians? Then you would have to set up 10 arrays and 10 for loops in the playOrchestra(). Wouldn't it be nice to have the code equivalent to simply give one general instruction to the musicians, "Everyone, play your instrument," and

If `playInstrument()` does not reappear in the subclass, it means that the subclass uses the exact definition of the `Musician`'s `playInstrument()`.

everyone will play their own instruments even if they play different instruments? This is how the redefining methods can simplify the coding. The next section shows you how to simplify the code by redefining the method that plays an instrument. Now, let's see how to set up the classes so that one method name can be used for playing different instruments for different objects.

The methods `playViolin()`, `playPiano()`, and `playTrumpet()` do different things, but if you generalize them, they all play an instrument. Let's define a new method called `playInstrument()` in `Musician`. Then in each subclass, `playInstrument()` is redefined to play the instrument specific to the subclass. For example, in the `Violinist` class, you include a definition of the method `playInstrument()`. Inside `playInstrument()`, put in the same statements that were in the `playViolin()` method. Similarly, inside the `Pianist`'s `playInstrument()`, put in the same statements that were in `playPiano()`. Inside the `TrumpetPlayer`'s `playInstrument()`, put in the same statements that were in `playTrumpet()`. The revised class diagram is shown in Figure 13.53. Note that `playInstrument()` reappears in each of the subclasses, depicting that it is redefined in the subclass.

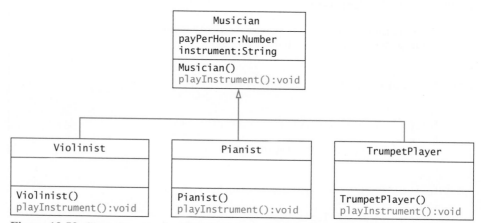

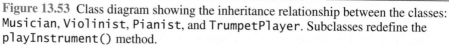

**Figure 13.53** Class diagram showing the inheritance relationship between the classes: `Musician`, `Violinist`, `Pianist`, and `TrumpetPlayer`. Subclasses redefine the `playInstrument()` method.

In ActionScript, to redefine a method in a subclass, you use the keyword `override`. The use of this keyword is discussed in the subsection on `override`. Here let's focus on identifying the need for method redefinition by examining the class diagrams, and not worry about the syntax and coding for method redefinition. The section on the keyword `override` will show you how to redefine methods.

Let's now look at how the redefinition of the `playInstrument()` method simplifies the code in the musician example. Because all three subclasses have a method called `playInstrument()`, you now can store all of the different musicians in one array and you only need one `for` loop in `playOrchestra()` to invoke the method `playInstrument()` on each musician (Figure 13.54). When a `Violinist` object is invoked with `playInstrument()`, the statements defined in `Violinist`'s `playInstrument()`—to play

```
var i:int = 0;

var arrayMusicians:Array = new Array();

stage.addEventListener(Event.ENTER_FRAME, playOrchestra);

for (i = 0; i < 10; i++)
{
    arrayMusicians.unshift( new Violinist() );
    stage.addChild(arrayMusicians[0]);
}

for (i = 0; i < 2; i++)
{
    arrayMusicians.unshift( new Pianist() );
    stage.addChild(arrayMusicians[0]);
}

for (i = 0; i < 12; i++)
{
    arrayMusicians.unshift( new TrumpetPlayer() );
    stage.addChild(arrayMusicians[0]);
}

function playOrchestra(evt:Event):void
{
    for (var i:int = 0; i < arrayMusicians.length; i++)
    {
        arrayMusicians[i].playInstrument();
    }
}
```

**Figure 13.54** In a Flash file (.fla): Placing the Violinist, Pianist, and TrumpetPlayer objects in a single array and invoking these objects with playInstrument().

violin—will be executed. When a Pianist object is invoked with playInstrument(), the statements in Pianist's playInstrument()—to play piano—will be executed. When a TrumpetPlayer object is invoked with playInstrument(), the statements in TrumpetPlayer's playInstrument()—to play trumpet—will be executed. As you see, a single method name, playInstrument() in this example, is used for a method that behaves differently with objects instantiated from different classes.

## 13.7.2 The Keyword override

To redefine an inherited method, simply add the keyword override before the keyword function. For example, Figure 13.55 shows the use of override to redefine the method playInstrument().

```
package
{
    public class Violinist extends Musician
    {
        public var magicPower:int;
        public function Violinist()
        {

        }

        public override function playInstrument():void
        {
            // Here you can put in statements for a violinist object
            // playing violin
        }
    }
}
```

**Figure 13.55** `Violinist.as`: Use of the keyword `override` to redefine `playInstrument()`.

## 13.8 IDENTIFYING INHERITANCE AND POLYMORPHISM

This section will walk through the thought process of identifying inheritance and polymorphism in two examples.

### 13.8.1 Example: `Hero` and `Villain`

Figure 13.56 shows a class diagram of two independent classes, `Hero` and `Villain`. Assume that the methods with the same names have the exact same statements. These classes share several properties and methods. They could be better organized using inheritance to reduce code duplication.

| Hero |
|---|
| keys:int<br>money:int<br>magic:Array<br>weapon:Array<br>health:int |
| Hero()<br>walk():void<br>heal():void<br>heroAttack():void<br>useMagic():void<br>calcHealth():void |

| Villain |
|---|
| spell:Array<br>weapon:Array<br>health:int |
| Villain()<br>villainAttack():void<br>walk():void<br>fly():void<br>castSpell():void<br>calcHealth():void |

**Figure 13.56** Class diagram for two individual classes: `Hero` and `Villain`. The members that both classes share are highlighted in color.

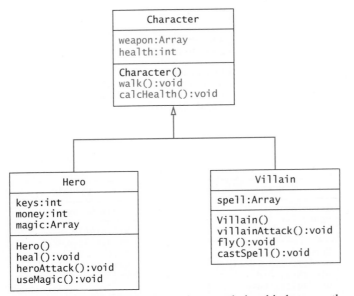

**Figure 13.57** Class diagram showing the inheritance relationship between the classes: Character (parent class), Hero (subclass), and Villain (subclass).

The common properties and methods are first identified. Because neither Hero nor Villain contains all of the common properties and methods, a new class, say, Character, that contains the common properties and methods is created. Hero and Villain can then be the subclasses of Character. Figure 13.57 shows the new class diagram depicting the class hierarchy of these classes.

Now both the Hero and Villain objects can perform attack but they attack differently. The current design is that the Hero and Villain each has its own different method to perform attack: the Hero class has heroAttack() and the Villain class has villainAttack(). The methods heroAttack() and villainAttack() contain different statements. The Hero object would invoke heroAttack() to attack, and the Villain object would invoke villainAttack() to attack. However, polymorphism can be applied to improve the class design. A new method called attack() can be added to Character. Hero, and Villain can then redefine attack() (Figure 13.58) so that a single attack() method name is used for the attack behavior that performs different actions with objects instantiated from different classes. In Hero's attack(), it contains the statements that perform the original heroAttack(). Similarly, in Villain's attack(), it contains the statements that perform the original villainAttack().

## 13.8.2 Example: Coin, Bee, and Cloud for the Side-Scrolling Platform Game Lab

This example continues with the OOP side-scrolling platform game example (Section 13.4.2) by adding a new feature: a cloud that floats slowly but does not interact with the hero; it does nothing when touched by the hero. A new class Cloud is created. It is very similar to Bee and thus we will also make it a subclass of Item. However, in doing

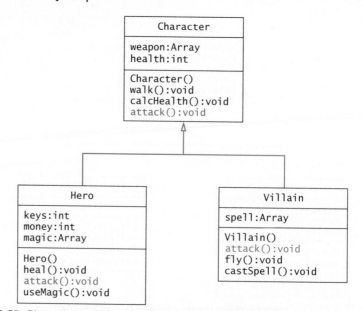

**Figure 13.58** Class diagram showing the inheritance relationship between the classes: Character, Hero, and Villain. Subclasses redefine the attack() method.

so, Cloud also inherits the method checkTouchedByHero(), which checks collision with the hero and is relocated if touched by the hero. To satisfy the requirement that the Cloud object will not interact with the hero, checkTouchedByHero() could be redefined in Cloud (Figure 13.59) but with an empty body.

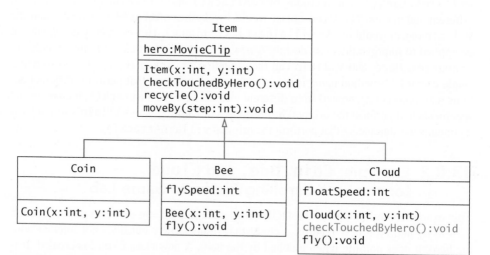

**Figure 13.59** Class diagram showing the inheritance relationship between the classes: Item, Coin, Bee, and Cloud. Cloud redefines the checkTouchedByHero() method.

🖱 **An OOP Side-Scrolling Platform Game with Inheritance and Polymorphism (Lab)** Add a `Cloud` object to the OOP Side-Scrolling Platform Game Lab (from Section 13.4.2) by implementing the class design shown in Figure 13.59.

## 13.9 SUMMARY

Inheritance refers to creating new classes by extending or enhancing the functionalities of an existing class without having to rewrite the existing functionalities. The classes forming the inheritance relationship establish a class hierarchy. The topmost class in the hierarchy is called the base class. The next classes below a class are its subclasses. They are also called derived classes or child classes. Each subsequent class down the hierarchy inherits from the previous one. The class from which a subclass inherits is its superclass or parent class. The subclass encompasses (inherits) all of the properties and methods defined in its parent class. The subclass can also have extra properties and methods that are not defined in its parent class. There exists an is-a relationship between any subclass and its parent class. Every object of a subclass is also an object of its parent class, but NOT vice versa.

From the code-centric standpoint, the keyword `extends` is used to establish the inheritance between two classes in ActionScript. The keyword `super` is used in a subclass to refer to the parent class. There are two usages of `super`: `super()` and `super.method()`. The first one is used in the subclass's constructor to invoke its parent class's constructor. The second one is used in the subclass for invoking a method defined in its parent class.

This chapter covers three access specifiers: `public`, `protected`, and `private`. They specify different scopes for class members. They provide a mechanism to control the visibility, or access, of class members outside of the class. Public has the least restrictive scope. Public properties and methods can be accessed inside and outside the class; they are accessible by the class's subclasses, other classes, and in a Flash file. Protected properties and methods are accessible within the class and its subclasses. They are not accessible from a Flash file or other classes that are not the class's subclasses. Private has the most restrictive scope among the three. Private properties and methods are accessible only within the class that defines them.

It is a good and common practice to set all of the properties to private. For properties that are allowed to be accessed directly outside of the class, use public methods to set or get their values. A get method, also called an accessor function or getter, allows you to query a class property without changing it. A set method, also called a mutator function or setter, allows you to change the value for a class property.

Polymorphism refers to the ability to use a single method name for a method that behaves differently with objects instantiated from different classes. From the code-centric standpoint, this can be accomplished by having a subclass to redefine an inherited method to perform tasks different from what are defined in its parent class. To redefine an inherited method, add the keyword `override` before the keyword `function`.

In the class diagram, the class inheritance relationship is denoted using a vertical arrow (a vertical line with a triangle) pointing from the subclass to the parent class. Only the properties and methods that are specific to the subclass are included in the subclass's rectangles. If a subclass redefines an inherited method, then the method also appears in the subclass's rectangle. The access specifiers `public`, `protected`, and `private` are depicted using the symbols $+$, $\#$, and $-$, respectively.

## TERMS

accessor 458  
ancestor 432  
base class 432  
child classes 432  
derived classes 432  
get method 458  
getter 458  

inherit 432  
inheritance 432  
is-a 432  
mutator 458  
parent class 432  
polymorphism 461  
private 448  

protected 448  
public 448  
set method 458  
setter 458  
subclasses 432  
superclass 432  

## LEARNING AIDS

The following learning aids can be found at the book's companion Web site.

🔗 **An OOP Side-Scrolling Platform Game with Inheritance (Lab)**
Add a flying Bee object to the OOP Side-Scrolling Platform Game Lab (from Chapter 12) by implementing the class design shown in Figure 13.26.

🔗 **An OOP Side-Scrolling Platform Game with Inheritance and Polymorphism (Lab)**
Add a Cloud object to the OOP Side-Scrolling Platform Game Lab (from Section 13.4.2) by implementing the class design shown in Figure 13.59.

## REVIEW QUESTIONS

When applicable, please choose all correct answers.

1. In the class hierarchy shown in Figure 13.4, Penguin is a _____ of Bird and Bird is a _____ of Penguin.

   A. subclass; parent class
   B. parent class; subclass

2. Based on the class hierarchy shown in Figure 13.4, a Flower object is a _____ object.

   A. Lily
   B. Rose
   C. Plant
   D. Tree

3. This question is based on the class hierarchy shown in Figure 13.4. Add code to the following code to indicate the inheritance relationship between the Plant and Tree classes.

```
package
{
    public class Tree
    {
        public function Tree()
        {
        }
    }
}
```

4. True/False: When you instantiate an object from a subclass, only the subclass's constructor will be invoked.

5. When you instantiate an object from a subclass, which constructor will be invoked first?

   A. Parent class's
   B. Subclass's

6. Objects instantiated from a subclass can access the _____ properties and methods of the parent class.

   A. public
   B. protected
   C. private

7. True/False: Subclasses do not inherit the private properties and methods of the parent class.

8. Suppose you have a `Burger` class. It has a property named `numCheese`. In order to change the value of the `numCheese` property of the `Burger` object, you may use the following in a Flash file:

```
var krabbyPatty:Burger = new Burger();
krabbyPatty.numCheese = 0;
```

   The `numCheese` is a _____ property in the `Burger` class, or the `Burger` class has a setter and getter for `numCheese`.

   A. public
   B. protected
   C. private

9. It is a good practice to set the properties of a class to _____.

   A. public
   B. protected
   C. private

10. What is the best practice to access properties of a class?

    A. Set the properties to public.
    B. Set the properties to private and use setters and getters.

11. Inheritance refers to _____.

    A. the ability to use a single method name for a method that behaves differently with objects instantiated from different classes
    B. creating new classes by extending or enhancing the functionalities of an existing class without having to rewrite the existing functionalities

12. From the code-centric standpoint, inheritance can be implemented by _____.

    A. redefining inherited methods
    B. using the keyword `extends` in ActionScript

13. Polymorphism refers to _____.

   A. the ability to use a single method name for a method that behaves differently with objects instantiated from different classes
   B. creating new classes by extending or enhancing the functionalities of an existing class without having to rewrite the existing functionalities

14. From the code-centric standpoint, polymorphism can be implemented by _____.

   A. redefining inherited methods
   B. using the keyword `extends` in ActionScript

15. The ActionScript keyword used for redefining an inherited method in a subclass is _____.

   A. public
   B. protected
   C. private
   D. extends
   E. override
   F. redefine

# Introduction to HTML

KEY CONCEPTS
- HTML documents
- XHTML
- Tags and attributes
- Nested tags
- Links
- Relative and absolute paths

GENERAL LEARNING OBJECTIVES

In this chapter, you will learn

- The basic structure for an HTML document.
- How to use the HTML tags: <p>, <br>, <h1>-<h6>, <b>, <i>, <strong>, <em>, <a>, <img>, and tags for tables.
- How to construct absolute and relative file paths.
- How to construct and read document-relative file paths in creating links and embedding images on a Web page.

## 14.1 WEB PAGES, HTML, AND WEB BROWSERS

In general, the term *Web pages* refers to documents that are written in a language called HTML. *HTML* stands for *Hypertext Markup Language*. An HTML file is a text file. The text file consists of plain text (i.e., the text itself does not have any formatting), so there is no boldface or italics. The tabs and line breaks in the text file do not appear when the document is viewed on a Web browser. However, the text can be marked with special markup codes called *tags*. These markup tags tell the Web browser how to display the page. For example, you will need to add a tag to create a line break on a Web page. Think of the HTML code as the written *instructions* of how the page should look. A *Web browser* is an application that can interpret these instructions and display the document in the format and layout according to the markup tags.

You can create an HTML document using a text editor, such as Notepad in Windows or TextEdit in Mac OS. You also can create an HTML document using a Web page editor, such as Adobe Dreamweaver. No matter which way an HTML document is created or edited, it is still a text file. For instance, if you create a Web page in Dreamweaver, you still can open it with Notepad, and vice versa. The difference between editing an HTML document with a text editor and a Web page editor is that you see only HTML code in a text editor. A Web page editor lets you see both the code and how the page may be displayed in a Web browser while you are editing the page. It also allows you to edit the page visually without having to manually add markup tags.

Before introducing the basics of writing HTML documents, let's first explain some common terms for working with the Web as a medium.

## URL

*URL* stands for *Uniform Resource Locator*. This is the standard for specifying the address of Web pages and other resources on the World Wide Web. URLs for Web pages have a similar structure that is made up of segments representing standard information. Let's look at the following example to see how an URL is structured.

`http://digitalmedia.wfu.edu/project/index.html`

- **Beginning segment:** `http://`
  This means that the page is located on a Web server. *http* stands for *Hypertext Transfer Protocol*. It refers to the sets of rules that govern the information transfer between the Web server and your computer (referred to as a Web client) that is requesting to view the page.
- **Next segment:** `digitalmedia.wfu.edu`
  This is the domain name of the Web server.
- **Rest of the address:** `/project/index.html`
  This is the file path of the document `index.html`. The file path is the location information of the page on the Web server. In this example, the file name of the page is `index.html`. It is located in a folder called `project`.

## XHTML

*XHTML* stands for *Extensible Hypertext Markup Language*. It is intended to be a replacement for HTML. It has stricter rules for writing HTML and is almost identical to the HTML 4.01 standard. There are different rules for HTML and XHTML, but most of the tags are the same. The stricter rules enforced in XHTML also are supported—but may not be enforced—in HTML. If you have working experience with HTML, you may have been following these rules all along. These rules will be discussed in Section 14.2.3, where you will learn how to construct a basic HTML document from scratch.

Unless specified, the term *HTML*, such as in HTML documents and HTML tags, used in this text refers to both HTML and XHTML in general.

## Cascading Style Sheets (CSS)

*Style sheets* allow you to define styles to display HTML elements. Multiple style definitions can be combined or cascaded into one—thus the term *cascading style sheets*. Like HTML documents, style sheet files are text files. The styles defined in the files follow specific rules and syntax. CSS is widely used for Web page design and layout.

## JavaScript and Dynamic HTML (DHTML)

*JavaScript* is a scripting language for Web pages. It can be used to add interactivity, generate content on the Web page based on the viewer's choice, validate online forms before submission, and create and track cookies.

*Dynamic HTML (DHTML)* itself is not a programming language but a combination of HTML, CSS, and JavaScript. JavaScript can make a Web page more dynamic. When combined with CSS, JavaScript can be used to control properties such as text styles, color, visibility, and positioning of HTML elements dynamically.

## HTML5

HTML5 is the newest standard of HTML. At the time of writing, its specifications are still a work in progress. The new features of HTML5 include:

- video and audio tags.
- content-specific tags, such as footer, header, nav, article, section, figure, summary, and aside.

Chapter 15 covers an introduction to HTML5 and HTML5 video and audio.

- tags for form elements
- canvas element that allows drawing graphics and displaying images dynamically using JavaScript
- allowing storage and retrieval of data on the user's device using JavaScript

## 14.2 BASIC ANATOMY OF AN HTML DOCUMENT

This section explains the basic structure of a HTML document.

### 14.2.1 Tags and Attributes

HTML documents are written as text files that do not have formatting. The line breaks in the text file, the font, and the font size used in the text editor to create the text file are ignored when the file is displayed in the Web browser. The formatting or presentation of the text is specified using special markup code (called *tags*). These markup tags tell the Web browser how to format the text when displaying it.

Each HTML tag is surrounded by two angle brackets: < and >. For example, the paragraph tag is <p>. Each tag comes in pairs, for example, <p> and </p>. The first tag, <p>, is the *start tag*. The second tag, </p>, is the *end tag* or *closing tag*. To mark up a block of text as a paragraph, you put the text between the <p> and </p> tags, like this:

```
<p> This is a paragraph.</p>
```

The text placed between the start and end tags is the *element content*. In this example the element content of this <p> tag is: This is a paragraph. The whole element begins with the start tag and ends with the closing tag. You will learn some common tags and examples of their use later in the chapter.

There are some tags that do not have element content. Examples of these tags are the line break <br> and the image tag <img>. For these tags, you either can add a closing tag (such as </br> and </img>) or end the tag with /> (for example, <br />). Section 14.3 will introduce the usage of some commonly used HTML tags, including these two.

#### Attributes

A tag may have attributes. *Attributes* of a tag specify properties of the element that is marked up by the tag. For example, the id attribute assigns a name to the element. The following shows the HTML code where an id attribute is added to a <p> tag.

```
<p id="introduction">This is a paragraph.</p>
```

In this example, an id attribute is added inside the <p> tag and assigned with a value of "introduction". id is a useful attribute. You can use JavaScript to refer to the element by its id to control its properties, such as the position and the element content.

There are several rules for adding attributes in XHTML:

- Attributes are added inside the start tag.
- Attributes come in as name-value pairs. The name and the value are separated by an equal sign. In the previous example, the attribute name is id, and its value is "introduction".
- The value must be enclosed with quotation marks.
- The attribute names are lowercase.

## 14.2.2 A Bare-Bones Structure of an HTML Document

The very basic, bare-bones structure of an HTML document looks like this:

```
<html>
<head>
<title>This is a title.</title>
</head>
<body>
This is the content of the Web page.
</body>
</html>
```

### <html> Tag

The first tag in an HTML document is <html>. This tag tells your browser that this is the start of an HTML document. Its end tag </html> is the last tag of the document. This tag tells your browser that this is the end of the HTML document.

### <head> Tag

The text placed between the <head> and </head> is the header information. The header information is not displayed in the browser window. Things that may be placed in the header section include the title element (See the <title> tag below), the function definitions of the JavaScript, links to the source of external JavaScript, and links to external style sheets.

### <title> Tag

The text between the <title> tag and </title> tag is the title of your document. The title is displayed on the Window bar of your browser window. In addition, when people bookmark your Web page, this title text is used as the default title stored in their browser's bookmark list.

### <body> Tag

The content between the <body> tags is the content of the Web page that will be displayed in the browser.

### Nested Tags

Markup elements can be nested in another element (i.e., placed within another element's content). For example, the header and body elements are nested inside the <html>, and the <title> is nested inside the <head> (Figure 14.1). Also notice the placement of the end tags in this example. This is similar to how parentheses are paired in a mathematical equation.

```
<html>
  <head>
    <title>This is a title.</title>
  </head>
  <body>
  This is the content of the Web page.
  </body>
</html>
```

Figure 14.1 Pairing of markup tags in an HTML document.

## 14.2.3 XHTML

An XHTML document has the same basic structure as an HTML document, plus it has a DOCTYPE declaration.

### DOCTYPE Declaration

**DOCTYPE** stands for *document type*. The DOCTYPE declaration uses the <!DOCTYPE> tag. The declaration is placed in the very first line in an HTML document, before the <html> tag. The declaration tells the browser which HTML or XHTML specification the document uses, so that the browser will display the page correctly using the appropriate specification. If the code used in the HTML document does not match the DOCTYPE declared, then some of the elements may not be displayed as expected.

The XHTML 1.0 specifies three document types:[*] Strict, Transitional, and Frameset.

- Strict
  The DOCTYPE declaration for the Strict document type is
  ```
  <!DOCTYPE html PUBLIC "-//W3C//DTD XHTML 1.0 Strict//EN"
  "http://www.w3.org/TR/xhtml1/DTD/xhtml1-strict.dtd">
  ```
- Transitional
  The DOCTYPE declaration for the Transitional document type is
  ```
  <!DOCTYPE html PUBLIC "-//W3C//DTD XHTML 1.0 Transitional//EN"
  "http://www.w3.org/TR/xhtml1/DTD/xhtml1-transitional.dtd">
  ```
  This is currently the most common type of DOCTYPE used in Web pages. The Transitional document type allows some leniency for tags and attributes that are going to be deprecated and replaced by CSS.
- Frameset
  The DOCTYPE declaration for the Frameset document type is
  ```
  <!DOCTYPE html PUBLIC "-//W3C//DTD XHTML 1.0 Frameset//EN"
  "http://www.w3.org/TR/xhtml1/DTD/xhtml1-frameset.dtd">
  ```
  The Frameset document type should be used with documents that are framesets. Frames are not preferable for Web page design and are the least used DOCTYPE for new Web pages.

### Basic Document Structure of an XHTML Document

The basic HTML document example that is shown in Figure 14.1 can be rewritten into an XHTML document using the Transitional document type like this:

```
<!DOCTYPE html PUBLIC "-//W3C//DTD XHTML 1.0 Transitional//EN"
"http://www.w3.org/TR/xhtml1/DTD/xhtml1-transitional.dtd">
<html xmlns="http://www.w3.org/1999/xhtml">
<head>
<title>This is a title.</title>
</head>
<body>
This is the content of the Web page.
</body>
</html>
```

---

[*] http://www.w3.org/TR/xhtml1/.

Except for the code added at the beginning of the document, the basic document structure is the same as that of the HTML document shown in Figure 14.1.

### Differences between the Rules for XHTML and HTML

Here are several main differences between XHTML and HTML coding:

- XHTML elements must always be closed or paired.

   For example, the paragraph <p> tag must have a closing tag </p>. For empty elements, such as <br> or <img> tags, you either can add a closing tag (such as </br> and </img>) or end the tag with /> (for example, <br />).
- XHTML tags and attributes must be in lowercase.
- XHTML elements must be properly nested within each other.

   Figure 14.2 shows the proper and improper nesting of the <p> and <div> tags.

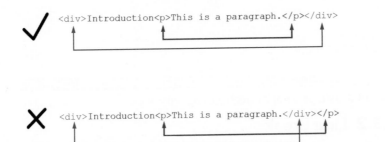

**Figure 14.2**  (a) The <div> and <p> tags are properly nested (b) The <div> and <p> tags are not properly nested.

- An XHTML document must have one root element (i.e., the topmost element).

   The <html> is the root element of an XHTML document. Elements can have subelements or child elements. Subelements must be in pairs and correctly nested within their parent element. The HTML element must designate the XHTML namespace, like this:

```
<html xmlns="http://www.w3.org/1999/xhtml">
```

xmlns is the namespace attribute. The value used here is an URL. Although this Web address carries information about the definitions of the XHTML tags, it is not used by the browser to look up information. Its purpose is to give the namespace a unique name.

   When a namespace is defined like this in the start tag of an element, all of its child elements also are associated with the same namespace. Here, the namespace is defined in <html>, which is the root element of the document. Thus, all of the tags in the document are associated with the same namespace.
- There must be a DOCTYPE declaration in the document prior to the root element.

## 14.3  COMMON HTML TAGS

This section introduces some common HTML tags.

## 14.3.1 Paragraph

The <***p***> tag is used to define paragraphs. For example,

```
<p>This is the first paragraph.</p>
<p>This is the second paragraph.</p>
```

Figure 14.3 shows how the two paragraphs in this example are displayed in a Web browser. By default, a blank line is automatically inserted before and after a paragraph. Two contiguous paragraphs are separated by one blank line.

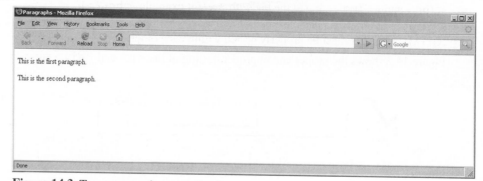

**Figure 14.3** Two paragraphs created using <p> tags.

## 14.3.2 Line Break

The <***br***> tag is used to create a line break—to force a new line without starting a new paragraph. Unlike the <p> tag, <br> will not insert a blank line by default. The new line created using the <br> tag keeps the single-line spacing with the rest of the paragraph.

<br> does not have any element content. To conform to the rule of a closing tag, a closing tag </br> can be added like this: <br></br>. However, it commonly is written as: <br />.

Here is an example code using <br />.

```
<p>This is the first paragraph.<br />This is a new line of the
same paragraph.</p>
<p>This is the second paragraph.</p>
```

Figure 14.4 shows how this example is displayed in a Web browser. The second line "This is a new line of the same paragraph." is forced to a new line using the <br /> tag. Note that this line has single-line spacing with the same paragraph.

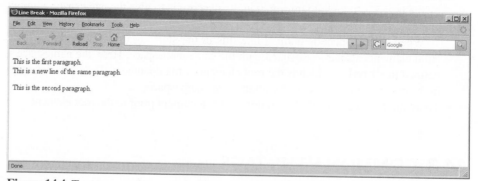

**Figure 14.4** Two paragraphs created using <p> tags. The first paragraph uses a <br /> tag to insert a line break.

### 14.3.3 Headings

There are several heading tags: `<h1>` through `<h6>`. The number in the heading tag indicates the heading level. For example:

```
<h1>This is a heading 1</h1>
<h2>This is a heading 2</h2>
<h3>This is a heading 3</h3>
<h4>This is a heading 4</h4>
<h5>This is a heading 5</h5>
<h6>This is a heading 6</h6>
```

By default, `<h1>` has the largest text and `<h6>` the smallest. Figure 14.5 shows how these headings are displayed in a Web browser. Note that by default, a blank line is inserted before and after a heading.

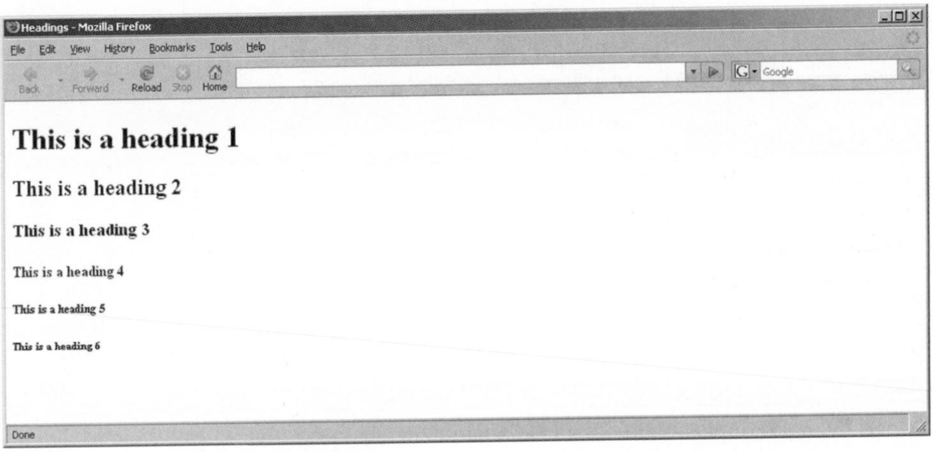

**Figure 14.5** Examples of headings.

### 14.3.4 Bold and Italics

The `<b>` or `<strong>` tag can be used to indicate boldfaced text, and the `<i>` or `<em>` tag to indicate italicized text. For example:

`<b>` and `<i>` were widely used before CSS was available. Some existing Web pages may still contain these tags.

```
<p>This is normal text.</p>
<p>
<b>This text is bold. </b>
<i>This text is italic.</i>
</p>
<p>
<b><i>This text is bold and italic.</i></b>
</p>
<p>
<i><b>This text is also bold and italic.</b></i>
</p>
```

Using <strong> and <em> tags, the previous code can be rewritten as:

```
<p>This is normal text.</p>
<p>
<strong>This text is bold.</strong>
<em>This text is italic.</em>
</p>
<p>
<strong><em>This text is bold and italic.</em></strong>
</p>
<p>
<em><strong>This text is also bold and italic.</strong></em>
</p>
```

Figure 14.6 shows how the text looks in a browser. Note that you can nest both <strong> (or <b>) and <em> (or <i>) tags to make text bold and italic. To conform to the XHTML standard, the closing tags need to be placed in the correct order. Think of how the parentheses are closed in mathematical equations.

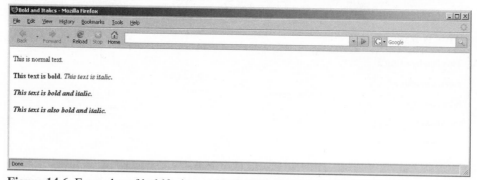

**Figure 14.6** Examples of boldfacing and italicizing text.

The two lines of code here produce the same effect. The <strong> and <em> tags are closed properly in both cases.

```
<strong><em>This text is bold and italic.</em></strong>
<em><strong>This text is bold and italic.</strong></em>
```

The tags in the following statements are not properly closed. These codes may not give errors with current Web browsers and the text may even be displayed correctly as bold and italic. However, future Web browsers may not have such leniency.

```
<p><strong><em>This text is bold and italic.</strong></em></p>
<p><em><strong>This text is also bold and italic.
</em></strong></p>
```

It is worth noting that using these tags to format individual text is not recommended. Instead, you should use cascading style sheets to define text formatting as styles based on the semantics of the element, and then apply the style to the HTML element.

## 14.3.5  List

An HTML list displays a list of items marked with bullets, numbers, or even images. There are two types of lists: ordered lists and unordered lists. They are categorized by how the items are marked. Items in an **ordered list** are marked with auto numbers. An **unordered list** marks items with bullets or images.

The tag for the ordered list is *<ol>*, and the tag for the unordered list is *<ul>*. Each item in the list (regardless of which type) is marked up using the tag *<li>*. For example:

Ordered List:

```
<ol>
    <li>Item A</li>
    <li>Item B</li>
    <li>Item C</li>
</ol>
```

Unordered List:

```
<ul>
    <li>Item A</li>
    <li>Item B</li>
    <li>Item C</li>
</ul>
```

Figure 14.7 shows how these ordered and unordered lists are displayed in the Web browser.

(a)

(b)

**Figure 14.7**
(a) The items in an ordered list are automatically marked with numbers. (b) The items in an unordered list are marked with bullets.

### 14.3.6 Link

The *anchor tag* (denoted by <*a*>) is used to create a link to another document. The attribute href is used to specify the address of the document to be linked to. The general syntax to create a link is

```
<a href="url or a file path">Text to be displayed as a clickable
link</a>
```

Do not confuse the text content with the value (i.e., the actual URL) for the href attribute. The actual URL is not displayed on the Web page in the browser.

The following example creates a link to http://www.google.com/. With this code, the Web browser will display the text Google Web Site as a clickable link. The URL specified for the href attribute http://www.google.com/, however, is not displayed on the Web page.

```
<a href="http://www.google.com/">Google Web Site</a>
```

🖱 **HTML: Basic HTML Document Structure, Paragraphs, Line Breaks, Lists, Links, Heading, Bold and Italic Text (LAB)** Hand-code two HTML documents using basic HTML document structure.

The document to be linked is not limited to an HTML document but can be any file, such as an image, a digital video, an audio, a Microsoft Word document, a PowerPoint file, or an Adobe Acrobat document. If the linked file cannot be opened within the Web browser, the browser will prompt you to download and save the file.

### 14.3.7 Image

The <*img*> tag lets you insert an image on a Web page. The attribute src (which stands for *source*) is used to specify the location where the image is stored. The general syntax for the <img> tag is:

```
<img src="url or a file path" />
```

The <img> tag does not have any element content. To conform to the rule of a closing tag, a slash is added before the closing angle bracket. Alternatively, an end tag </img> can be added like this:

```
<img src="url or a file path"></img>
```

Adding a slash before the closing angle bracket is most commonly used. The following example adds an image to the Web page. The image is called logo.jpg and it is stored in the same folder as the HTML document on which the image is being inserted.

```
<img src="logo.jpg" />
```

Note that unlike inserting an image in a Microsoft Word document, you are not copying and pasting an image directly into the HTML document. The image is not part of the document itself but remains an external file. This means that when you save an HTML document, the image is *not* saved within the HTML file. The src attribute tells the browser where to find the image. Thus, the image file has to exist in the location as specified in the src attribute when the Web browser loads the HTML document. Otherwise, the image will not show up and become what we call a broken image.

## 14.3.8 Table

The basic tags for constructing a table are <**table**>, <**tr**>, and <**td**>. Each table definition begins with a <table> tag. A table is divided into rows, designated with the <tr> tag. The letters tr stand for *table row*. The <tr> tags are placed between the <table> and </table> tag.

Each row is divided into data cells using the <td> tag. The letters td stand for *table data*. The <td> tags are placed between the <tr> and </tr> tags. The content intended to appear in a table cell has to be placed between <td> and </td>. If the content is placed within a table element but outside of <td>, how it is displayed in a browser will be unpredictable.

The following example defines a table of two rows and two columns. The text content "This is OK." will be displayed inside the table cells, because they are enclosed within <td> and </td>. However, the text "This line is not OK!!" that is placed outside of <td> will not be displayed inside a table cell.

```
<table>
    This line is not OK!!
    <tr>
        This line is not OK!!
        <td>This is OK.</td>
        This line is not OK!!
        <td>This is OK.</td>
    </tr>
    This line is not OK!!
    <tr>
        <td>This is OK.</td>
        <td>This is OK.</td>
    </tr>
</table>
```

A table cell can contain other HTML elements, such as text, images, lists, forms, and other tables. Note that a table is constructed row by row. Each row is divided into cells. You may think of the cells as columns for each row. Figure 14.8a shows an example HTML code using these tags to construct a table of three rows and two columns. Figure 14.8b shows how this table is displayed on a Web browser.

This simple example shows a bare-bones table. Without a table border, it may be hard to tell that it is a table. Figure 14.9 shows the same table as that in Figure 14.8, except that a border is added by specifying the border attribute for the <table> tag.

---

🖑 **HTML: Images and Tables (LAB)**  Hand-code three HTML documents:
- One HTML document contains a table with image thumbnails. Clicking on the image thumbnail will go to the page containing the full image.
- Two HTML documents: Each contains the full image of the thumbnail.

```
<!DOCTYPE html PUBLIC "-//W3C//DTD XHTML 1.0 Transitional//EN"
    "http://www.w3.org/TR/xhtml1/DTD/xhtml1-transitional.dtd">
<html xmlns="http://www.w3.org/1999/xhtml">
<head>
<meta http-equiv="Content-Type" content="text/html;
charset=utf-8 /">
<title>Table Example</title>
</head>
<body>
<table>
    <tr>
        <td>row 1, column 1</td>
        <td>row 1, column 2</td>
    </tr>
    <tr>
        <td>row 2, column 1</td>
        <td>row 2, column 2</td>
    </tr>
    <tr>
        <td>row 3, column 1</td>
        <td>row 3, column 2</td>
    </tr>
</table>
</body>
</html>
```

(a)

(b)

**Figure 14.8** (a) Full HTML code for a Web page that contains a table without specifying a border, with the tags for constructing the table given in color. (b) How the table looks in a Web browser.

🖰 **Dreamweaver Workspace Overview** An overview of the workspace and most commonly used panels in Adobe Dreamweaver.

🖰 **Web Authoring Using Adobe Dreamweaver (LAB)** Get acquainted with Adobe Dreamweaver. Set up a Web site in Dreamweaver. Create and edit Web pages using the visual editor.

```
<!DOCTYPE html PUBLIC "-//W3C//DTD XHTML 1.0 Transitional//EN"
    "http://www.w3.org/TR/xhtml1/DTD/xhtml1-transitional.dtd">
    <html xmlns="http://www.w3.org/1999/xhtml">
    <head>
    <meta http-equiv="Content-Type" content="text/html;
    charset=utf-8 /">
    <title>Table Example</title>
    </head>
    <body>
    <table border="1">
        <tr>
            <td>row 1, column 1</td>
            <td>row 1, column 2</td>
        </tr>
        <tr>
            <td>row 2, column 1</td>
            <td>row 2, column 2</td>
        </tr>
        <tr>
            <td>row 3, column 1</td>
            <td>row 3, column 2</td>
        </tr>
    </table>
    </body>
    </html>
```

(a)

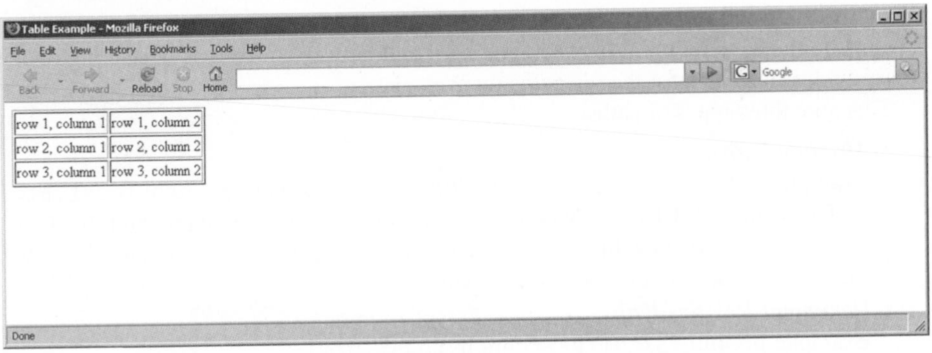

(b)

**Figure 14.9** (a) Full HTML code for a Web page that contains a table with a border.
(b) How the table looks in a Web browser.

## 14.4 UNDERSTANDING FILE PATHS

HTML documents, images, sounds, and videos are stored as files on a computer. *Folders* (also called directories) are used to organize files. When you open a folder, you may see other folders and/or files inside the folder. When you open a file, you will see the content of the file. To view the content of a file correctly, you will need to open the file using the right application program—for example, Notepad (Windows) and TextEdit (Mac OS) for plain text files, and Adobe Photoshop for digital images.

## 14.4.1 File Paths

A *file path* refers to the location of a file on a computer, like an address to a house. When you address an envelope, you follow a certain order—for example, the name of the person, the street, the city, and then the state or country. Similarly, to write a file path, you write the folder names in the order of the folder hierarchical structure—start from the outermost folder to the inner folders. A file path to a file ends with the filename.

The folder names are separated by a delimiter, which is a forward slash (/) or backslash (\). Forward slashes (/) are used most commonly for file paths in HTML documents.

## 14.4.2 Types of File Paths for Web Pages

Suppose someone asks you for directions to see a particular painting in an art exhibition. If the art exhibition is out of town, you probably will give the person a full address, specifying the building, city, and state where the exhibition takes place. On the other hand, if the exhibition is right inside the building you are located at—but on a different floor—then you will give the person directions for how to get to the other floor from where you are standing. The full address with the city and state is also a valid direction, but you would not choose to give such direction in this situation. If you are in the room where the painting is, you may just point to the painting and tell the person that it is right there. You would not even mention the floor and room. You give different types of directions depending on the situation. It is the same for the file paths for Web pages.

There are three types of paths:

- *Absolute Paths.*
  Example: `http://www.mysite.com/products/coffee/french-roast.html`
  This is the full URL to a Web page or any media. It is like giving the full address for an out-of-town art exhibition. If you are linking to a page that is on a different Web site, you will need to use the absolute path.
- *Document-Relative Paths.*
  Example: `products/coffee/french-roast.html`
  This is the most common type of file path in Web authoring. It is like giving directions to get to another floor in the art exhibition scenario or pointing at the painting if you are in the same room of the painting. The direction you give is *relative* to where the person is standing. The direction is only valid for that specific location where the person is. The same direction becomes invalid if the person asks in another building or a different floor of the same building. The example path shown here is relative to where this `french-roast.html` is being requested. You will see examples on constructing document-relative paths in the next subsection.
- *Site Root-Relative Paths.*
  Example: `/products/coffee/french-roast.html`
  A site root-relative path always starts with a forward slash (/). It means starting from the root folder of the site. A *root folder* is the outermost folder of the site structure.

## 14.4.3 Rules for Creating Links Using Document-Relative Paths

Suppose you have a site with a folder structures shown in Figure 14.10. Figure 14.10 shows two different graphical representations of the folder structure of a site called my-site. The graphical representations help you create a mental model for the relationships of the folders and files in the site.

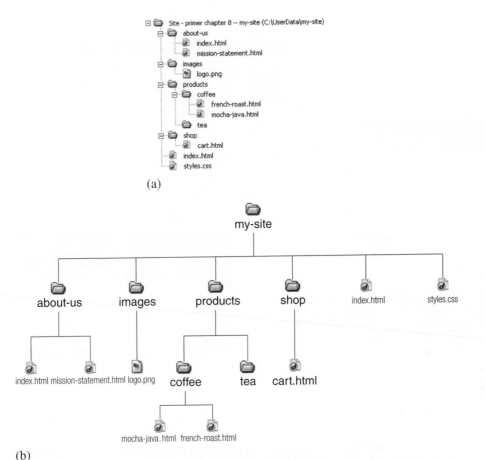

(a)

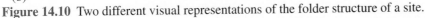

(b)

**Figure 14.10** Two different visual representations of the folder structure of a site.

In this example, the root folder for the site is called my-site. Inside the my-site folder, there are four folders (about-us, images, products, and shop) and two files (index.html and styles.css). Inside each of these four folders are other folders and files. Figure 14.11 shows how it looks when you navigate this folder structure on your computer. When you double-click on a folder, you see the folder(s) and file(s) stored there.

To construct a document-relative path, you need to know the relative location between the target page (the page being linked *to*) and the source page (the page containing the link or the page being linked *from*) in the site structure.

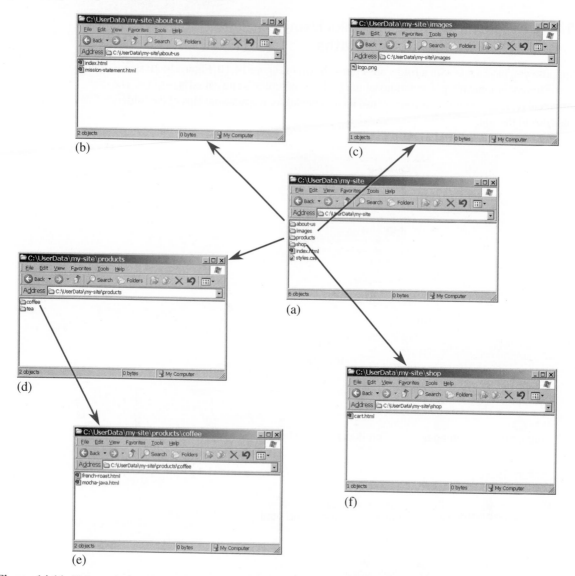

**Figure 14.11** Using windows to navigate the folder structure. (a) A window showing the content of a folder. (b) Opening the folder about-us in (a). (c) Opening the folder images in (a). (d) Opening the folder products in (a). (e) Opening the folder coffee in (d). (f) Opening the folder shop in (a).

### Rule #1

To link to another file that is in the same folder as the current document, simply use the filename as the path. For example, to add a link in mocha-java.html to link to french-roast.html (Figure 14.12), the file path is simply the filename french-roast.html.

Returning to the art exhibition scenario, this is like when the person asking for directions is in the same room as where the painting is. You can simply point to the painting. You do not need any extra information regarding navigation to another building, floor, or room.

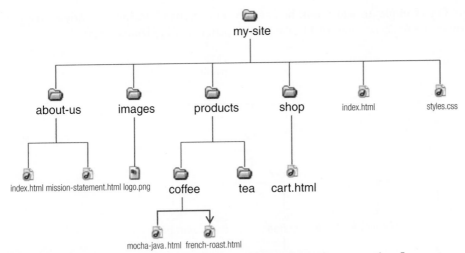

**Figure 14.12** Navigating from `mocha-java.html` to `french-roast.html`.

## Rule #2

To link to a file that is in a subfolder of the current document's folder, use the subfolder name followed by a forward slash (/) and then the filename. Each forward slash (/) represents moving down one level in the folder.

For example, to add a link in `index.html` (in `my-site` folder) to link to `french-roast.html` (Figure 14.13), the relative path is `products/coffee/french-roast.html`.

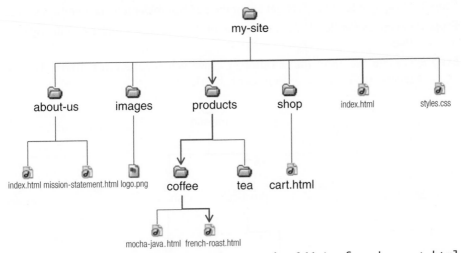

**Figure 14.13** Navigating from `index.html` (in `my-site` folder) to `french-roast.html`.

## Rule #3

To link to a file that is outside of the current document's folder, start the path with `../` (where `../` means going up one level in the folder hierarchy), followed by the folder name, a forward slash (/), and then the filename. Multiple `../` can be appended for going up multiple levels in the folder hierarchy.

For example, to add a link in `french-roast.html` to link to `index.html` (in `my-site` folder) (Figure 14.14), the relative path is `../../index.html`.

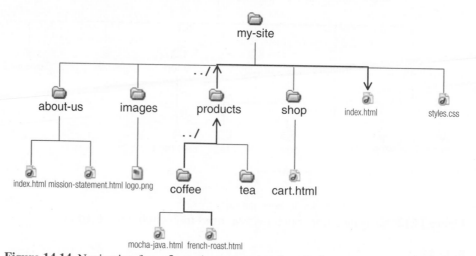

**Figure 14.14** Navigating from `french-roast.html` to `index.html` (in `my-site` folder). `../` is used to indicate going up one level in the folder hierarchy.

To construct the file path that links from `french-roast.html` to `cart.html` (in the `shop` folder) (Figure 14.15), imagine you have the `coffee` folder open. You see the `french-roast.html` file. From there, to see `cart.html`, you need to follow the following steps.

**Step 1** Go up one level (`../`) to get out of the `coffee` folder into the `products` folder.

**Step 2** Go up another level (`../`) to get out of the `products` folder into the `my-site` folder.

**Step 3** Go into the `shop` folder (`shop/`). Now, you see the `cart.html`. Thus, the relative path is `../../shop/cart.html`.

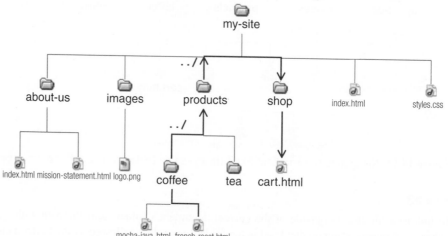

**Figure 14.15** Navigating from `french-roast.html` to `cart.html` (in `shop` folder). `../` used to indicate going up one level in the folder hierarchy.

## 14.4.4 Why Is It Important to Understand File Paths for Web Page Creation?

It is essential to understand the file paths in order to create valid links and embed images. File paths are used in the HTML document for the hyperlinked files, such as HTML documents, images, and videos. A path serves as a direction or address to retrieve the linked files. Incorrect paths lead to broken images or broken links on Web pages.

Web page editing programs let you insert images and links using a graphical interface, and they automatically construct relative paths for you. You seldom need to figure out file paths. If you rename or move files and folders around in your site, those file paths inserted in your HTML document prior to the change will no longer be valid and will need to be updated. Web site management programs (such as Adobe Dreamweaver) can automatically update the file paths for renamed and moved files if you rename or move the files within the program. However, if you do not use the program to rename or move the files of your site, the links will not be updated automatically. You may use the program to check for broken links and fix them. Nevertheless, being able to read and construct the file paths helps troubleshoot broken links without having to rely on a program; in some situations, you do not have access to such a program.

## 14.5 SUMMARY

The term *Web pages* refers to documents that are written in a language called HTML. HTML stands for Hypertext Markup Language. An HTML file is a text file. The text formatting, tabs, and line breaks in the text file do not appear when the document is viewed on a Web browser. However, the text can be marked with markup tags that tell the Web browser how to display the page. A Web browser is an application that can display the HTML document in the correct format and layout according to the markup tags. An HTML document can be created using a text editor, such as Notepad in Windows or TextEdit in Mac OS. It also can be created using a Web page editor, such as Adobe Dreamweaver.

XHTML stands for Extensible Hypertext Markup Language. It is intended to be a replacement for HTML. It is almost identical to the HTML 4.01 standard but has stricter rules for writing HTML.

Style sheets allow you to define styles to display HTML elements. Multiple style definitions can be combined or cascaded into one—thus the term *cascading style sheets*.

JavaScript is a scripting language for Web pages. It can be used to generate the Web page content in response to the user's interaction. Dynamic HTML (DHTML) is a combination of HTML, CSS, and JavaScript. When combined with CSS, JavaScript can be used to control properties such as text styles, color, visibility, and positioning of HTML elements dynamically.

URL stands for Uniform Resource Locator. This is the standard for specifying the address of Web pages and other resources on the World Wide Web.

Markup tags come in pairs, for example, <p> and </p>. The first tag, <p>, is the start tag. The second tag, </p>, is the end tag or closing tag. Tags may have attributes. Attributes of a tag specify the properties of the element.

The very basic, bare-bones structure of an HTML document looks like this:

```
<html>
<head>
<title>This is a title.</title>
</head>
<body>
This is the content of the Web page.
</body>
</html>
```

An XHTML document has the same basic structure as an HTML document, plus it has a DOCTYPE declaration.

Common tags are introduced in the chapter. These include: `<p>`, `<br>`, `<h1>`–`<h6>`, `<b>`, `<i>`, `<strong>`, `<em>`, `<a>`, `<img>`, and tags for tables.

A file path refers to the location of a file on a computer. There are three types of paths used in an HTML document:

- Absolute Paths: This is the full URL to a Web page or any media, for example: `http://www.mysite.com/products/coffee/french-roast.html`.
- Document-Relative Paths: The path is relative to where a file is being requested, for example, `products/coffee/french-roast.html`.
- Site Root-Relative Paths: A site root-relative path always starts with a forward slash (/), for example: `/products/coffee/french-roast.html`. A path starting with a forward slash means starting from the root folder of the site. A root folder is the outermost folder of the site structure.

## TERMS

## LEARNING AIDS

The following learning aids can be found at the book's companion Web site.

🖰 **HTML: Basic HTML Document Structure, Paragraphs, Line Breaks, Lists, Links, Heading, Bold and Italics Text (Lab)**
Hand-code two HTML documents using basic HTML document structure.

🖰 **HTML: Images and Tables (Lab)**
Hand-code three HTML documents:

- One HTML document contains a table with image thumbnails. Clicking on the image thumbnail will go to the page containing the full image.
- Two HTML documents: Each contains the full image of the thumbnail.

🖰 **Dreamweaver Workspace Overview**
An overview of the workspace and most commonly used panels in Adobe Dreamweaver.

🖰 **Web Authoring Using Adobe Dreamweaver (Lab)**
Get acquainted with Adobe Dreamweaver. Set up a Web site in Dreamweaver. Create and edit Web pages using the visual editor.

## REVIEW QUESTIONS

When applicable, please select all correct answers.

1. HTML documents are _____.

   A. text files
   B. JPG files
   C. PSD files
   D. MP3 files

2. Dynamic HTML is a combination of _____, _____, and _____.

3. **True/False:** Dynamic HTML is a special programming language by itself.

4. For the URL: `http://www.schoolname.edu/departments/art/index.html`:

   i. The domain name of the Web server is _____.
   ii. This URL is a Web address of a file named _____.
   iii. This file is located in the folder named _____, which is inside another folder named _____.

5. _____ are markup codes in an HTML document that tell the Web browser how to format the text when displaying it.

   A. Attributes                    B. Tags

6. In the HTML code:
   `<p>This is a paragraph.</p>`
   `<p>` is the _____, and `</p>` is the _____. The text "`This is a paragraph.`" is the _____.

   A. element content; start tag; end tag        B. element content; end tag; start tag
   C. start tag; end tag; element content         D. start tag; element content; end tag
   E. end tag; start tag; element content         F. end tag; element content; start tag

7. Fill in the correct start tags and end tags to create a basic HTML document.

```
<_____>
<_____>
<_____>This is the page title.<_____>
<_____>
<_____>
This is the content of the Web page.
<_____>
<_____>
```

8. Describe briefly how XHTML is different from HTML in terms of each of the following:

   i. Tag pairing
   ii. Cases of tags
   iii. Tag nesting
   iv. Root element of a page
   v. DOCTYPE declaration

9. The _____ tag is used to create a line break—to force a new line without starting a new paragraph. By default, the line created using this tag has _____-line spacing.

10. The _____ tag is used to create a heading 1 element.

11. Fill in the blanks for the HTML code below to create a link to your favorite Web site. Use a valid URL.

```
<_____ _____ = "_____">My Favorite Web site<_____>
```

12. Fill in the blanks for the HTML code below to embed an image called logo.jpg on a Web page. Suppose logo.jpg is in the same folder as the HTML document that embeds it.

```
<_____ _____ = "_____" _____>
```

13. Fill in the blanks for the HTML code to create a list as shown.

   1. Preheat oven to 450 degrees.
   2. Heat butter and oil in a large saucepan.
   3. Cook the shrimp for 10 minutes.

```
<_____>
<_____>Preheat oven to 450 degrees.<_____>
<_____>Heat butter and oil in a large saucepan.<_____>
<_____>Cook the shrimp for 10 minutes.<_____>
<_____>
```

14. Fill in the blanks for the HTML code to create a list as shown.

   • Elephants
   • Tigers
   • Frogs

```
<_____>
<_____>Elephants<_____>
<_____>Tigers<_____>
<_____>Frogs<_____>
<_____>
```

**15.** Fill in the blanks for the HTML code to create a table as shown.

| Elephants | Tulips |
|-----------|--------|
| Tigers    | Roses  |

```
<table>
    <tr>
        <td>_____</td>
        <td>_____</td>
    <_____>
    <tr>
        <td>_____</td>
        <td>_____</td>
    <_____>
<_____>
```

**16.** For the site shown in Figure 14.10, to add a link on the page mocha-java.html to link to the Web page french-roast.html, the document-relative file path is _____.

**17.** For the site shown in Figure 14.10, to embed the image logo.png on the homepage index.html (in the my-site folder), the document-relative file path is _____.

**18.** For the site shown in Figure 14.10, to embed the image logo.png on the Web page french-roast.html, the document-relative file path is _____.

# HTML5 Video and Audio

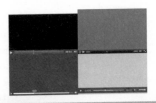

KEY CONCEPTS
- HTML5 versus XHTML
- HTML5 video and audio tags
- HTML5 video and audio formats
- HTML5 video and audio fallback strategies

GENERAL LEARNING OBJECTIVES
In this chapter, you will learn
- The new features in HTML5.
- The differences between HTML5 and XHTML.
- How to use video and audio tags to add video and audio to a Web page.
- How to create fallback for HTML5 video and audio.
- How to create HTML5 video and audio.

## 15.1 INTRODUCTION TO HTML5

There are depre-
cated tags and attri-
butes in the current
working draft
of the HTML5
specifications. The
specifications state
that deprecated ele-
ments are not to be
used but the brows-
ers must continue
to support them.

*HTML5* is the latest revision of HTML. At the time of writing, its specifications are still a work in progress. However, HTML5 allows backward compatibility with previous versions of HTML. In other words, HTML5 is defined in a way that a Web browser supporting it can still continue to support the content developed using the previous versions of HTML.

The new key features of HTML5 include:

- Video and audio tags
- Content-specific tags
- Tags for form elements
- The canvas element
- Storage of user data

### Video and Audio Tags

The new video and audio tags allow simple code for adding video and audio on a Web page. They also allow the video and audio to be played back by the Web browser's built-in player instead of relying on external players and plug-ins. The use of these new video and audio elements is the main focus of this chapter. This chapter also discusses the file formats of the currently supported HTML5 video and audio.

### Content-Specific Tags

The new content-specific tags, such as footer, header, nav, article, section, figure, summary, and aside, provide a standardized system to classify the information on a Web page by semantics. This facilitates computers to process the information by its meaning and thereby potentially help users to find the right information. In addition, information with the same meaning, even from different sources, can become compatible for exchange, comparison, and integration.

### Form Elements

The new form elements include new form controls, such as date pickers, color pickers, numeric steppers, and new input types, such as email, url, and search. They can enhance the user's experience.

### Canvas

The new canvas element allows you to draw graphics and place images dynamically inside it using JavaScript. The visual content inside the canvas area can be scripted to change over time and in response to the user interaction, such as mouse click and key presses. The canvas element together with JavaScript is very useful for animation and game development.

### Storage of User Data

Before HTML5, methods of storing user data, such as pages a visitor has visited and items a shopper added to the shopping cart, were limited to cookies and server-side storage. A cookie has a size limit of only 4 KB. The server-side storage often requires databases and setup of user accounts on a server. The Web storage feature of HTML5 allows storage and retrieval of data on the user machine without user login or servers. In addition, the storage limit is about 5 MB, which is significantly larger than that of cookies.

## 15.1.1  HTML5 versus XHTML

*XHTML* 1.0 is a reformulation of HTML4 in XML 1.0.[1] XHTML has stricter syntax rules than HTML4. Chapter 14 provides an introduction to XHTML and highlights the differences between XHTML and HTML4. Table 15.1 summarizes some major differences between HTML5 and XHTML.

The working draft of the HTML5 differences from HTML4 can be found at http://www.w3.org/TR/html5-diff/.

Although HTML5 is less restrictive and the Web browsers supporting HTML5 also support XHTML, it is a good practice to keep your coding style consistent. It would be good to still follow the lowercase rule, keep the attribute value in quotation marks, and keep the end tags for non-self-closing tags. Figure 15.1 shows an example of a very basic HTML5 document, which uses the new DOCTYPE declaration and character encoding. The <br> and the <img> elements in this example are not self-closing. However, the example still follows the rules of XHTML about cases, end tags, and enclosing attribute values in quotation marks.

Figure 15.2 rewrites the example of Figure 15.1 by arbitrarily changing the tag letters to uppercase, removing some end tags, and removing the quotation marks for the attribute values. It is still a valid HTML5 document but it is less readable than the example shown in Figure 15.1.

A markup validator is available at http://validator.w3.org/ to validate Web documents.

---

[1] XHTML™ 1.0 The Extensible HyperText Markup Language (Second Edition), http://www.w3.org/TR/xhtml1/.

**TABLE 15.1 Major Differences between HTML5 and XHTML**

| | XHTML | HTML5 |
|---|---|---|
| **DOCTYPE declaration** | Three doctypes: Strict, Transitional, and Frameset (see Section 14.2.3)<br>For example:<br>`<!DOCTYPE html PUBLIC "-//W3C// DTD XHTML 1.0 Transitional//EN" "http://www.w3.org/TR/xhtml1/DTD/ xhtml1-transitional.dtd">` | Only one simplified doctype declared like this:<br>`<!DOCTYPE HTML>` |
| **Character encoding** | `<meta http-equiv="Content-Type" content="text/html; charset=utf-8" />` | Simplified as follows:<br>`<meta charset="UTF-8"/>` |
| **Cases for tag and attribute names** | All lowercase | No restriction |
| **Value of an attribute** | Enclosed in quotation marks | Does not have to be in quotation marks |
| **Boolean attribute (has only either true or false)** | The value "true" or "false" has to be written out and enclosed in quotation mark; for example:<br>`<div hidden="true"/>` | No need to write out the value—just the presence of the attribute means it is true; for example:<br>`<div hidden/>` |
| **End tag** | Required for each start tag | Not required; thus, self-closing is not required for those tags without content, such as `<br>` and `<img>` |

```
<!doctype html>
<html lang="en">
<head>
<meta charset="utf-8" />
<title>This is a title of the page</title>
</head>
<body>
<p>This is the content of the Web page.<br>
<img src="images/demo.png" alt="demo">
</p>
</body>
</html>
```

**Figure 15.1** An HTML5 document.

```
<!doctype html>
<HtML lang=en>
<hEAd>
<meta charset=utf-8 />
<TITLe>This is a title of the page</tiTLE>
<boDY>
<P>This is the content of the Web page.<br>
<IMg src=images/demo.png alt=demo>
```

**Figure 15.2** The HTML5 document of Figure 15.1 is rewritten by arbitrarily changing the case of the tag letters, removing some end tags, and removing the quotation marks for the attribute values.

## 15.2 HTML5 VIDEO AND AUDIO

If the media are added to a Web page using HTML5 video and audio tags, they will be played by the Web browser's built-in player. This means that how the video and audio are played depends on the Web browser. For example, each Web browser may support different features of video and audio playback and have its own visual design of the player controller (Figure 15.3). On the other hand, using video such as Flash Video that requires a plug-in, the video can be expected to play with the same interface across different Web browsers.

**Figure 15.3** Screenshots of HTML5 video playback in different browsers. (a) Firefox 3.6. (b) Safari 5. (c) Chrome 13. (d) IE 9.

At the time of writing, the Web browsers that support HTML5 video and audio include Firefox 3.5+, Safari 3+, IE 9+, Chrome, and Opera 10.5+. There are three video formats supported by Web browsers as HTML5 video and four audio formats as HTML5 audio. The video formats are H.264 MPEG-4/AVC, Ogg, and WebM. The four audio formats are WAV, Ogg, MP3, and AAC. Table 15.2 and Table 15.3 list the browser support for these different formats.

To show a video on a Web page using HTML5, the code can be as simple as the following using the *<video>* tag:

```
<video src="media/demo.ogv" controls></video>
```

| TABLE 15.2 | Browser Support for HTML5 Video Formats | | |
|---|---|---|---|
| | **H.264 MPEG-4/AVC** | **Ogg** | **WebM** |
| **Firefox** | | 3.5+ | 4.0+ |
| **Safari** | 3.0+ | | |
| **IE** | 9.0+ | | |
| **Chrome** | Yes but will discontinue support[2] | 5.0+ | 6.0+ |
| **Opera** | | 10.5+ | 10.6+ |

| TABLE 15.3 | Browser Support for HTML5 Audio Formats | | | |
|---|---|---|---|---|
| | **WAV** | **Ogg Vorbis** | **MP3** | **AAC** |
| **Firefox** | X | X | | |
| **Safari** | X | | X | X |
| **IE** | | | X | X |
| **Chrome** | X | X | X | X |
| **Opera** | X | X | | |

Similarly, to add an audio on a Web page using the *<audio>* tag:

```
<audio src="media/demo.oga" controls></audio>
```

The examples code above use two attributes: src and controls.

- src: This is to specify the file path of the media.
- controls: When this attribute is present, the player controller—containing the controls for play and pause—will be displayed with the video.

At the time of writing, not all Web users are using the browsers that support HTML5 video and audio. Figure 15.4 shows adding a line of text in <video> to notify the user whose browser does not support HTML5 video. The text will be displayed when the video tag is not supported by the Web browser. However, an alternative should be provided for these users to still play the video in another format. Section 15.3 discusses several fallback strategies that allow these users to play non-HTML5 video and audio.

```
<video src="media/demo.ogv" controls>
    <p>Your browser does not support HTML5 video.</p>
</video>
```

**Figure 15.4** Adding a text display as fallback.

---

[2] HTML Video Codec Support in Chrome, http://blog.chromium.org/2011/01/html-video-codec-support-in-chrome.html.

## 15.2.1 Setting up a Source List for Fallback Content

Different browsers support different HTML5 video and audio formats and there is not a format that is supported across all browsers. A source list can be set up using the <**source**> tag to provide multiple video or audio sources for different browsers. Figure 15.5 shows the use of <source> tags. It is worth noting that for video, the WebM source (.webm) is listed before the Ogg source (.ogv) so that a browser that supports both Ogg and WebM will play the WebM, which is generally higher quality than Ogg of the same file size.

The MP4 source is listed first because at the time of writing, the browser on iPad seems to only read the first source and MP4 is its only supported HTML5 video format.

```
<video controls>
    <source src="media/demo.mp4" type="video/mp4" />
    <source src="media/demo.webm" type="video/webm" />
    <source src="media/demo.ogv" type="video/ogg" />
    <p>Your browser does not support HTML5 video.</p>
</video>
```

(a)

```
<audio controls>
    <source src="media/demo.m4a" type="audio/mp4" />
    <source src="media/demo.oga" type="audio/ogg" />
    <p>Your browser does not support HTML5 audio.</p>
</audio>
```

(b)

**Figure 15.5** Use of <source> to set up multiple video or audio sources.

## 15.2.2 Preloading

The attribute preload can be added to <video> and <audio> to specify the preload setting of the media. There are three possible values for the preload attributes: none, auto, and metadata.

- none: The Web browser will not start loading the media until the user clicks the play button.
- auto: The Web browser will decide whether the media will be preloaded. For example, on Apple iOS devices, the browser will not preload the media.
- metadata: The Web browser will preload only the metadata of the media, such as duration, frame size, and the first frame of the video. At the time of writing, not all browsers support this attribute. For those that do not support this attribute, metadata is treated as auto.

Examples of using the preload attribute are shown in Figure 15.6 and Figure 15.7. Preloading a video takes up bandwidth, which increases network traffic and, depending on the

```
<video controls preload="auto">
    <source src="media/demo.mp4" type="video/mp4" />
    <source src="media/demo.webm" type="video/webm" />
    <source src="media/demo.ogv" type="video/ogg" />
    <p>Your browser does not support HTML5 video.</p>
</video>
```

**Figure 15.6** An example of using preload attribute, which is set to auto.

```
<audio controls preload="none">
    <source src="media/demo.m4a" type="audio/mp4" />
    <source src="media/demo.oga" type="audio/ogg" />
    <p>Your browser does not support HTML5 audio.</p>
</audio>
```

**Figure 15.7** An example of using `preload` attribute, which is set to `none`.

user's Internet plan, may cost the user extra fees. Thus, if a Web page contains multiple videos, use the `auto` attribute *judiciously*. The attribute may be set to `auto` only for the main video of the page and to `none` for all other videos.

## 15.2.3 Autoplay, Looping, Width, and Height

Table 15.4 lists the information on the `autoplay`, `loop`, `width`, and `height` attributes for `<video>`. An example of using these attributes is shown in Figure 15.8.

| TABLE 15.4 | Information on the `autoplay`, `loop`, `width`, and `height` Attributes for the `<video>` Tag | |
|---|---|---|
| **Attribute** | **Value** | **Description** |
| `autoplay` | None; simply add the attribute | The video or audio automatically starts playing as soon as it has been loaded |
| `loop` | None; simply add the attribute | The video or audio starts over after it has reached the end |
| `width` | Number of pixels | Video only; sets the width of the video player |
| `height` | Number of pixels | Video only; sets the height of the video player |

```
<video controls preload="auto" autoplay loop width="480" height="320">
    <source src="media/demo.mp4" type="video/mp4" />
    <source src="media/demo.webm" type="video/webm" />
    <source src="media/demo.ogv" type="video/ogg" />
    <p>Your browser does not support HTML5 video.</p>
</video>
```

**Figure 15.8** An example of using the `autoplay`, `loop`, `width`, and `height` attributes.

If no `width` and `height` attributes are set for a video, then how the video player looks on the page depends on several factors:

Poster image will be explained in the next subsection.

- If there is a poster image, the video player shows the poster image using its width and height.
- If there is no poster image but preload is enabled, the video player shows the first frame of the video. Thus its size matches that of the actual video.
- If there is no preload and no poster image, the video player appears blank. The size of the video player does not match the actual video frame size until the user clicks to play the video.

If the width and height do not match the frame aspect ratio of the video, the video will be scaled such that its frame aspect ratio is maintained. For example, if the `width` attribute is set too wide, then the video will be scaled such that it fills the player vertically and leave empty space on the left and right sides.

The `width` and `height` attributes are for video only. They do not have any effect on the audio. However, the width of the audio player controller can be adjusted using the CSS (cascading style sheet). The CSS is beyond the scope of this text. Figure 15.9 shows an example of using an inline style to set the width of the audio player to 480 pixels.

The preferred way to use the CSS is to set up an external style sheet instead of using inline styles.

```
<audio controls style="width:480px;">
    <source src="media/demo.m4a" type="audio/mp4" />
    <source src="media/demo.oga" type="audio/ogg" />
    <p>Your browser does not support HTML5 audio.</p>
</audio>
```

**Figure 15.9** An example of using an inline style to set the width of the audio controller.

## 15.2.4 Poster Image

A *poster image* is an image that is shown in place of the video before the video starts. The `poster` attribute (Figure 15.10) can be used to set an image as the poster image for the video. Table 15.5 summarizes the effect of the poster image with and without video preload.

The `poster` attribute does not work on Apple iOS3, which was shipped with the first iPad, iPhone 3 and 3GS, and iPod Touch of the same time frame. If you want your HTML5 video to work for iOS3 users, you may want to avoid using the `poster` attribute.

```
<video controls preload="none" poster="media/demo-poster.png">
    <source src="media/demo.mp4" type="video/mp4" />
    <source src="media/demo.webm" type="video/webm" />
    <source src="media/demo.ogv" type="video/ogg" />
    <p>Your browser does not support HTML5 video.</p>
</video>
```

**Figure 15.10** An example of using the `poster` attribute to set the poster image for a video.

| TABLE 15.5 | Effect of the Poster Image with and without Video Preload | |
|---|---|---|
| | **No preload** | **Has preload** |
| **No poster image** | Blank | Show the first frame of the video |
| **Has poster image** | Show the poster image | Show the poster image |

The poster image for a video is usually an image representative of the video. It is a common practice to choose a frame from the video as its poster image. Most video editing applications let you export a frame from the video as a still image. Apple QuickTime Pro also lets you extract a frame.

## 15.3 FALLBACK STRATEGIES

This section discusses several strategies to provide alternatives for users whose browsers do not support HTML5 video and audio. The basic idea is to add extra HTML code, which is not HTML5 specific, in the <video> element to tell the browser what to display. If the Web browser does not support HTML5 video and audio, it will ignore the HTML5 video and audio tags and use the additional code.

As you will see, the extra code makes the <video> code bulky. However, when the browsers of the majority of users support HTML5, the fallback code will not be needed and the <video> code can be as simple and clean as that shown in Figure 15.5.

### 15.3.1 Flash Video

The first strategy is to add the <object> element to embed an alternative video format that a browser not supporting HTML5 can play. The most common video format for Web playback is Flash video. Figure 15.11 rewrites the code shown in Figure 15.10 by adding code to embed a Flash video. Although the code looks complicated, it is the regular embed code for a Flash video. When you insert a Flash video in Adobe Dreamweaver, the code will be automatically generated for you. The Open Source Media Framework Web site (http://www.osmf.org/configurator/fmp/) also provides Flash media playback setup that can generate the embed code for you.

```
<video controls preload="none" poster="media/demo-poster.png">
    <source src="media/demo.mp4" type="video/mp4" />
    <source src="media/demo.webm" type="video/webm" />
    <source src="media/demo.ogv" type="video/ogg" />
    <object width="480" height="320">
        <param name="movie"
            value="http://fpdownload.adobe.com/strobe/
            FlashMediaPlayback.swf">
        </param>
        <param name="flashvars"
            value="src=media/demo.flv&poster=images/poster-demo.png">
        </param>
        <param name="allowFullScreen" value="true"></param>
        <param name="allowscriptaccess" value="always"></param>
        <embed
            src="http://fpdownload.adobe.com/strobe/FlashMediaPlayback.swf"
            type="application/x-shockwave-flash"
            allowscriptaccess="always"
            allowfullscreen="true"
            width="480" height="320"
            flashvars="src=media/demo.flv&poster=images/poster-demo.png">
        </embed>
    </object>
    <p>Your browser does not support HTML5 video.</p>
</video>
```

**Figure 15.11** Adding <object> code to embed a Flash video as fallback.

## 15.3.2 Links to Download Video

This strategy provides a fallback for devices that do not support Flash video playback by displaying a link for users to download the video. Figure 15.12 shows that the code for video links is added within <video>. The links will be displayed in browsers that do not support HTML5 video. However, the code can be moved to outside of <video> so that the links are displayed for all users.

```
<video controls preload="none" poster="media/demo-poster.png">
    <source src="media/demo.mp4" type="video/mp4" />
    <source src="media/demo.webm" type="video/webm" />
    <source src="media/demo.ogv" type="video/ogg" />
    <object width="480" height="320">
        <param name="movie"
            value="http://fpdownload.adobe.com/strobe/
            FlashMediaPlayback.swf">
        </param>
        <param name="flashvars"
            value="src=media/demo.flv&poster=images/poster-demo.png">
        </param>
        <param name="allowFullScreen" value="true"></param>
        <param name="allowscriptaccess" value="always"></param>
        <embed
            src="http://fpdownload.adobe.com/strobe/FlashMediaPlayback.swf"
            type="application/x-shockwave-flash"
            allowscriptaccess="always"
            allowfullscreen="true"
            width="480" height="320"
            flashvars="src=media/demo.flv&poster=images/poster-demo.png">
        </embed>
    </object>
    <p>Your browser does not support HTML5 video.</p>
    <p>Download Videos:
        <a href="media/demo.mp4">MP4</a>
        <a href="media/demo.webm">WEBM</a>
        <a href="media/demo.ogv">OGG</a>
    </p>
</video>
```

Figure 15.12 Adding video download links in addition to a Flash Video as fallback.

## 15.3.3 Image

This strategy is also a fallback for devices that do not support Flash video playback, but it displays an image in place of the video. It is a fallback for the <object> code for Flash video and thus the changes are made in the <object> element (Figure 15.13). The <embed> element is removed and additional attributes are needed for <object>. An <img> element is added for displaying an image. In the example shown in Figure 15.13, the poster image for the video is used.

> HTML5 Video and Audio (Lab) Create an HTML5 document with video and audio and test the page with different Web browsers. Also add fallback code.

```
<video controls preload="none" poster="media/demo-poster.png">
    <source src="media/demo.mp4" type="video/mp4" />
    <source src="media/demo.webm" type="video/webm" />
    <source src="media/demo.ogv" type="video/ogg" />
    <object width="480" height="320"
        type="application/x-shockwave-flash"
        data="http://fpdownload.adobe.com/strobe/FlashMediaPlayback.swf">
        <param name="movie"
            value="http://fpdownload.adobe.com/strobe/
            FlashMediaPlayback.swf">
        </param>
        <param name="flashvars"
            value="src=media/demo.flv&poster=images/poster-demo.png">
        </param>
        <param name="allowFullScreen" value="true"></param>
        <param name="allowscriptaccess" value="always"></param>
        <img src="media/demo-poster.png" alt="browser does not support
        HTML5 video" />
    </object>
    <p>Your browser does not support HTML5 video.</p>
    <p>Download Videos:
        <a href="media/demo.mp4">MP4</a>
        <a href="media/demo.webm">WEBM</a>
        <a href="media/demo.ogv">OGG</a>
    </p>
</video>
```

**Figure 15.13** Using an image in addition to a Flash Video and download links as fallback.

## 15.4 CREATING HTML5 VIDEO AND AUDIO

At the time of writing, there are several free tools available for converting video and audio into HTML5 video and audio. Table 15.6 lists the information about some of these tools. Figure 15.14 shows a screenshot of Firefogg with settings for WebM export.

> 🖑 **Using MediaCoder** MediaCoder can export all three HTML5 formats but requires some manual settings. Screenshots of MediaCoder showing settings for exporting different HTML5 video formats are provided here.

> 🖑 **Using VLC** Screenshots of VLC showing settings for different HTML5 audio formats are provided here.

**TABLE 15.6    Tools for Converting Video and Audio into HTML5-Supported Formats**

| Application Name | Web Site | Supported OS | Output |
|---|---|---|---|
| MediaCoder | http://www.mediacoderhq.com/ | Windows, Mac OS, Linux | Video: MP4, WebM, Ogg<br>Audio: MP3, Ogg, ACC |
| HandBrake | http://handbrake.fr/ | Windows, Mac OS, Linux | Video: MP4 |
| Firefogg | http://firefogg.org/ | As a Firefox 6+ plug-in | Video: WebM, Ogg |
| VLC | http://www.videolan.org/vlc/ | Windows, Mac OS, Linux | Audio: MP3, AAC, Ogg |

**Figure 15.14** A screenshot of Firefogg with the settings for WebM export.

## 15.5 SUMMARY

HTML5 is the latest revision of HTML. At the time of writing, its specifications are still a work in progress. Its specifications allows backward compatibility with previous versions of HTML. The new features of HTML5 include:

- Video and audio tags
- Content-specific tags
- Tags for form elements
- The canvas element
- Storage of user data

HTML5 has a simplified doctype declaration and character encoding declaration. The syntax rules for HTML5 are looser than those for XHTML. It does not have restrictions on the end tag and cases of tag and attribute names. The value of an attribute does not have to be in quotation marks. In addition, Boolean attributes do not have to write out the value—just the presence of the attribute means it is true.

If the media are inserted on a Web page using HTML5 video and audio tags, the media will be played by the Web browser's built-in player. Each Web browser may support different features of video and audio playback and have its own visual design of the player controller. This is different from using video plug-ins, such as Flash Player, with which the video can be expected to play the same across different Web browsers.

At the time of writing, the Web browsers that support HTML5 video and audio include Firefox 3.5+, Safari 3+, IE 9+, Chrome, and Opera 10.5+. The three video formats supported by the Web browsers as HTML5 video are H.264 MPEG-4/AVC, Ogg, and WebM. The four supported audio formats are WAV, Ogg, MP3, and AAC.

To add a video on a Web page using HTML5, the code can be as simple as the following:

```
<video src="media/demo.ogv" controls></video>
```

The `<video>` and `<audio>` have these attributes: `src`, `controls`, `preload`, `autoplay`, and `loop`. The `<video>` element also has `width`, `height`, and `poster` attributes. No one single video or audio format is supported across all the browsers. However, a source list using `<source>` can be added to the `<video>` element to provide multiple video or audio sources for different browsers.

Several strategies to provide alternatives for users whose browsers do not support HTML5 video and audio are discussed. The basic idea is to add extra HTML code, which is not HTML5 specific, in the <video> element to tell the browser what to display. The fallbacks include playing a non-HTML5 video such as Flash Video, displaying video download links, and displaying an image.

## TERMS

| | | |
|---|---|---|
| <audio> 504 | poster image 507 | <video> 503 |
| HTML5 500 | <source> 505 | XHTML 501 |

## LEARNING AIDS

The following learning aids can be found at the book's companion Web site.

**⌨ HTML5 Video and Audio (Lab)**
Create an HTML5 document with video and audio and test the page with different Web browsers. Also add fallback code.

**⌨ Using MediaCoder**
MediaCoder can export all three HTML5 formats but requires some manual settings. Screenshots of MediaCoder showing settings for exporting different HTML5 video formats are provided here.

**⌨ Using VLC**
Screenshots of VLC showing settings for different HTML5 audio formats are provided here.

## REVIEW QUESTIONS

When applicable, please select all correct answers.

1. What are the new features of HTML5 that are overviewed in this chapter?

2. HTML5 video and audio are played back _____.
   A. by the Web browser's built-in player
   B. using an external player or a plug-in

3. Which of the following is correct about HTML5?
   A. Three doctypes: Strict, Transitional, and Frameset
   B. Only one simplified doctype declared like this: <!DOCTYPE HTML>

4. Which of the following is correct about cases for the tag and attribute names in HTML5?
   A. No restriction on cases
   B. All lowercase
   C. All uppercase
   D. Capitalized

5. Which of the following is correct about the use of quotation marks for the attribute value in HTML5?

   A. No quotation marks are required.
   B. The value has to be enclosed in quotation marks.

6. Which of the following is correct about the use of end tags in HTML5?

   A. Not required
   B. Required

7. Which of the following is correct character encoding declaration in HTML5?

   A. `<meta  http-equiv="Content-Type"  content="text/html; charset=utf-8" />`
   B. `<meta charset="UTF-8" />`

8. To provide multiple video or audio sources for different browsers, _____.

   A. use the `preload` attribute
   B. use the `controls` attribute
   C. use the `autoplay` attribute
   D. use the `loop` attribute
   E. use the `poster` attribute
   F. set up a source list using `<source>` elements

9. To display an image in place of the video before it starts, _____.

   A. use the `preload` attribute
   B. use the `controls` attribute
   C. use the `autoplay` attribute
   D. use the `loop` attribute
   E. use the `poster` attribute
   F. set up a source list using `<source>` elements

10. To display the controller for the video or audio, _____.

    A. use the `preload` attribute
    B. use the `controls` attribute
    C. use the `autoplay` attribute
    D. use the `loop` attribute
    E. use the `poster` attribute
    F. set up a source list using `<source>` tags

11. If there are multiple videos on a page, you should avoid turning on _____ to reduce network traffic.

    A. `preload`
    B. `controls`
    C. `autoplay`
    D. `loop`
    E. `poster`
    F. `<source>`

12. A poster image is an image that is shown in place of the video _____.

    A. before an HTML5 video starts
    B. as a fallback for browsers that do not support HTML5 video

# Credits

# Index